Intelligence

Eighth Edition

Intelligence

From Secrets to Policy

Eighth Edition

Mark M. Lowenthal

FOR INFORMATION:

CQ Press

An Imprint of SAGE Publications, Inc.

2455 Teller Road

Thousand Oaks, California 91320

E-mail: order@sagepub.com

SAGE Publications Ltd.

1 Oliver's Yard

55 City Road

London EC1Y 1SP

United Kingdom

SAGE Publications India Pvt. Ltd.

B 1/I 1 Mohan Cooperative Industrial Area

Mathura Road, New Delhi 110 044

India

SAGE Publications Asia-Pacific Pte. Ltd.

18 Cross Street #10-10/11/12

China Square Central

Singapore 048423

Printed in the United States of America

Library of Congress Cataloging-in-Publication Data

Names: Lowenthal, Mark M., author.

Title: Intelligence : from secrets to policy / Mark M. Lowenthal.

Description: Eighth edition. | Thousand Oaks, California : CQ Press, 2020. | Includes bibliographical references and index.

Identifiers: LCCN 2019027254 | ISBN 9781544325064 (paperback) | ISBN 9781544358376 (epub)

Subjects: LCSH: Intelligence service—United States—Planning. | Intelligence service—United States—Forecasting.

Classification: LCC JK468.I6 L644 2020 | DDC 327.1273—dc23 LC record available at https://lccn.loc.gov/2019027254

This book is printed on acid-free paper.

Acquisitions Editor: Anna Villarruel

Editorial Assistant: Lauren Younker

Production Editor: Jane Martinez

Copy Editor: Amy Marks

Typesetter: C&M Digitals (P) Ltd.

Proofreader: Jeff Bryant

Indexer: Judy Hunt

Cover Designer: Candice Harman

Marketing Manager: Jennifer Jones

19 20 21 22 23 10 9 8 7 6 5 4 3 2 1

CONTENTS

TABLES, FIGURES, AND BOXES

TABLES

FIGURES

BOXES

PREFACE

In years past, when academics who taught courses on intelligence got together, one of the first questions they asked one another was, "What are you using for readings?" They asked because there was no standard text on intelligence. Available books were either general histories that did not suffice as course texts or academic discussions written largely for practitioners and aficionados, not for undergraduate or graduate students. Like many of my colleagues, I had long felt the need for an introductory text. I wrote the first edition of this book in 2000 to fill this gap in intelligence literature.

Intelligence: From Secrets to Policy is not a how-to book: It will not turn readers into competent spies or even better analysts. Rather, it is designed to give readers a firm understanding of the role that intelligence plays in making national security policy and insight into its strengths and weaknesses. The main theme of the book is that intelligence serves and is subservient to policy and that it works best—analytically and operationally—when tied to clearly understood policy goals.

The book has a U.S.-centric bias. I am most familiar with the U.S. intelligence establishment, and it is the largest, richest, and most multifaceted intelligence enterprise in the world. At the same time, readers with interests beyond the United States should derive from this book a better understanding of many basic issues in intelligence collection, analysis, and covert action and of the relationship of intelligence to policy.

This volume begins with a discussion of the definition of intelligence and a brief history and overview of the U.S. intelligence community. The core of the book is organized along the lines of the intelligence process as practiced by most intelligence enterprises: requirements, collection, analysis, dissemination, and policy. Each aspect is discussed in detail in terms of its role, strengths, and problems. The book's structure allows the reader to understand the overall intelligence process and the specific issues encountered in each step of the process. The book examines covert action and counterintelligence in a similar vein. There is a discussion of the role of the policy makers and of the overseers, especially in Congress. Three chapters explore the issues facing U.S. intelligence in terms of both nation-states and transnational issues and the moral and ethical issues that arise in intelligence. The book also covers intelligence reform and foreign intelligence services.

Intelligence has grown primarily out of courses that I have taught for many years: "The Role of Intelligence in U.S. Foreign Policy," at the School of International and Public Affairs, Columbia University from 1994 to 2007; "Intelligence: From Secrets to Policy," at the Zanvyl Krieger School of Arts and Sciences at Johns Hopkins University since 2008; and "Intelligence and National Security" at the Paris Institute of Political Studies (Sciences Po), beginning in 2015. As I tell my students, I provide neither a polemic against intelligence nor an apology for it. This volume takes the view that intelligence is a normal function of government: Sometimes it works well; sometimes it does not. Any intelligence service, including that of the United States, can rightly be the recipient of both praise and criticism. My goal is to raise important issues and to illuminate the debate over them, as well as to provide context for the debate. I leave it to professors and students to come to their own conclusions. As an introduction to the subject of intelligence, the book, I believe, takes the correct approach in not asking readers to agree with the author's views.

As an introductory text, the book is not meant to be the last word on the subject. It is intended instead as a starting point for a serious academic exploration of the issues inherent in intelligence. Each chapter concludes with a list of readings recommended for a deeper examination of relevant issues. Additional bibliographic citations and websites are provided in Appendix 1. Appendix 2 lists some of the most important reviews and proposals for change in the U.S. intelligence community since 1945.

This is the eighth edition of *Intelligence*. The major changes in each edition reflect the changes that have confronted the intelligence community since 2000. The second edition added material about the September 11 attacks and the beginning of the war on terrorists. The third edition covered the investigations into the September 11 attacks, the Iraq weapons of mass destruction (WMD) estimate and its aftermath, and the creation of the director of national intelligence (DNI) position, the most substantial change in U.S. intelligence since 1947. The fourth edition reflected several new areas: implementation of the DNI reforms and their successes and strains; the ongoing legal, operational, and ethical issues raised by the war against terrorists; the growth of such transnational issues as WMD; and the growing politicization of intelligence in the United States, especially through the declassified use of national intelligence estimates (NIEs). In the fifth edition, many of the issues raised by the war against terrorists continued to be at issue as did the management of the overall community and the role of the DNI. At the same time, new issues such as cyberspace were more prominent. The sixth edition reflected an ongoing shift in U.S. intelligence priorities, as policy makers began to deemphasize terrorism to a degree, and the widespread repercussions of the Manning and Snowden leaks. This leaked intelligence remains and should be considered classified, despite the fact that it has been leaked. Therefore, I cannot discuss the details of some of these leaks or comment on their veracity unless there are official comments on the subject. The seventh edition reassessed the still evolving cyberspace issue, including the issue of cyber as a new collection discipline and added new sections offering a brief summary of the major laws governing U.S. intelligence; domestic intelligence collection; a discussion of whistle-blowers, as opposed to leakers; and the growing field of financial intelligence.

In this eighth edition, as has been true in the past, there have been many developments in collection. There is also a shift in the emphasis of U.S. intelligence, away, to some degree, from transnational issues and back to nation-states, particularly China and Russia, as well as the increasingly aggressive espionage activities of these two states. The advent of the Trump administration has created strains between policy makers and the intelligence community that are different from those that are an inherent part of the relationship and have had to be addressed. There has also been much updating in chapter 15, on foreign intelligence, and in the various bibliographies.

Given the dynamic nature of intelligence, any textbook on the subject runs the risk of containing dated information. This may be an even greater problem here, given the fluid and dynamic international situation. This replicates the intelligence analyst's dilemma of needing to produce finished intelligence during changing circumstances. The risk cannot be avoided. However, I am confident that most aspects of intelligence—and certainly the main issues discussed—are more general, more long-standing, and less susceptible to being outdated rapidly than the ever-changing character of intelligence might suggest.

All statements of fact, opinion, or analysis expressed are those of the author and do not reflect the official positions or views of the Office of the DNI or any other U.S. government agency. Nothing in the contents should be construed as asserting or implying U.S. government authentication of information or DNI endorsement of the author's views. This material has been reviewed by the intelligence community to prevent the disclosure of classified information.

Several words of thanks are in order: first, to my wife, Cynthia, and our children—Sarah and Adam—who have supported my part-time academic career despite the missed dinners it means. Cynthia also has been immensely supportive during the entire lengthy revision process. Next, thanks go to three friends and colleagues—the late Sam Halpern, Loch Johnson, and Jennifer Sims—who reviewed early drafts and made substantial improvements. The following scholars also provided extremely helpful comments for this edition: Kimberly A. Urban, Virginia Commonwealth University; Antony Field, California State University, San Bernardino; John W. King, Notre Dame College; Armin Krishnan, East Carolina University; and Richard J. Norton, United States Naval War Academy. Anthony Spadaro and Jim Barnett provided me and many other colleagues with a constant stream of updated articles across the range of intelligence issues. Hayden Peake kept me apprised of new books and articles on foreign intelligence services. Jason Healey provided useful comment and discussion about intelligence and cyberspace. None of these individuals is responsible for any remaining flaws or any of the views expressed. I would also like to thank the reviewers for the previous editions: William Green, California State University at San Bernardino; Patrick Morgan, University of California, Irvine; Donald Snow, University of Alabama; James D. Calder, University of Texas at San Antonio; Robert Pringle, University of Kentucky; L. Larry Boothe, Utah State University; Matthew Donald, Ohio State University; John Syer, California State University, Sacramento; John Comiskey, Monmouth University; Peter Hickman, Arizona State University; Paul M. Johnson, Auburn University; Michael Bogart, University of Maryland University College; Alan More, Notre Dame College; Michael Siler, California State University; Peter Olesen, University of Maryland University College; Loch Johnson, University of Georgia; Gary Kessler, Embry-Riddle Aeronautical University; Greg Moore, Notre Dame College; and James Calder and Glen Schaffer, University of Texas–San Antonio. Moreover, I have been most fortunate to collaborate with the following at CQ Press: Scott Greenan, acquisitions editor; Lauren Younker, editorial assistant; Jane Martinez, production editor; and Amy Marks, my superb copy editor. Working with them has been most enjoyable. Thanks to Space Imaging, Inc., for supplying the series of overhead images of San Diego.

As I have in past editions, I continue to thank all of my colleagues across the intelligence community for all they have taught me and for their dedication to their work. Finally, thanks to all of my students over the years, whose comments and discussions have greatly enriched my courses and this book. Again, I am solely responsible for any shortcomings in this volume.

Mark M. Lowenthal
Reston, Virginia

ACRONYMS

ABI	activity-based intelligence
ABM	antiballistic missile
ACH	alternative competing hypothesis
ADDNI	assistant deputy director of national intelligence
AGI	advanced geospatial intelligence
AI	artificial intelligence
AIDS	acquired immune deficiency syndrome
AIPAC	American Israel Public Affairs Committee
Aman	Agaf ha-Modi'in (Military Intelligence) (Israel)
AOR	area of responsibility
ARC	Analytic Resources Catalog
ASAT	anti-satellite weapon
ASIO	Australian Secret Intelligence Organisation
ASIS	Australian Secret Intelligence Service
BDA	battle damage assessment
BfV	*Bundesamt für Verfassungsschutz* (Federal Office for the Protection of the Constitution) (Germany)
BND	*Bundesnachrichtendienst* (Federal Intelligence Service) (Germany)
BW	biological weapons
CBW	chemical and biological weapons
CCMD	Combatant Command
CCP	Consolidated Cryptologic Program
CDA	congressionally directed action
CEO	chief executive officer
CESG	Communications Electronics Security Group (Britain)
CI	counterintelligence
CIA	Central Intelligence Agency
CIARDS	CIA Retirement and Disability System
CIC	Counterintelligence Center

CIG	Central Intelligence Group
CISEN	Center for Investigation and National Security (Mexico)
CMA	Community Management Account
CMC	Central Military Commission (China)
CNA	computer network attack
CNC	Counternarcotics Center
CNE	computer network exploitation
CNI	National Intelligence Center (Mexico)
CNR	(1) *coordonnateur national du renseignement* (national intelligence coordinator); (2) *conseil national du renseignement* (national intelligence council) (both France)
COI	Coordinator of Information
COIN	counterinsurgency
COMINT	communications intelligence
COO	chief operating officer
COS	chief of station
CRS	Congressional Research Service
CSE	Communications Security Establishment (Canada)
CSIS	Canada's Security Intelligence Service
CSRS	Counter Surveillance Reconnaissance System
CT	counterterrorism
CTC	Counterterrorism Center
CW	chemical weapons
D&D	denial and deception
DARP	Defense Airborne Reconnaissance Program
DBA	dominant battlefield awareness
DC	Deputies Committee (NSC)
DCI	director of central intelligence
DCIA	director of the Central Intelligence Agency
DCP	Defense Cryptologic Program
DCRI	*Direction Centrale du Renseignement Intérieur* (France)
DCS	Defense Clandestine Service
DEA	Drug Enforcement Administration
DGIAP	Defense General Intelligence Applications Program

DGSE	*Direction Générale de la Sécurité Extérieure* (General Directorate for External Security) (France)
DHS	Department of Homeland Security
DI	Directorate of Intelligence
DIA	Defense Intelligence Agency
DICP	Defense Intelligence Counterdrug Program
DIS	Defence Intelligence Staff (Britain)
DISTP	Defense Intelligence Special Technologies Program
DITP	Defense Intelligence Tactical Program
DMZ	demilitarized zone
DNI	director of national intelligence
DO	Directorate of Operations (CIA)
DOD	Department of Defense
DOE	Department of Energy
DPSD	*Directoire de la Protection et de la Sécurité de la Défense* (Directorate for Defense Protection and Security) (France)
DRM	*Directoire du Renseignement Militaire* (Directorate of Military Intelligence) (France)
DS&T	Directorate of Science and Technology (CIA)
DSRP	Defense Space Reconnaissance Program
ELINT	electronic intelligence
EO	electro-optical; executive order
EOD	entry on duty
EU	European Union
ExCom	Executive Committee
FAPSI	*Federalnoe Agenstvo Pravitelstvennoi Svyazi I Informatsii* (Federal Agency for Government Communications and Information) (Russia)
FARC	*Fuerzas Armadas de Colombia* (Colombia)
FBI	Federal Bureau of Investigation
FBIS	Foreign Broadcast Information Service
FIA	Future Imagery Architecture
FININT	financial intelligence
FISA	Foreign Intelligence Surveillance Act
FISC	Foreign Intelligence Surveillance Court

FISINT	foreign instrumentation intelligence
FMV	full motion video
FSB	*Federal'naya Sluzba Besnopasnoti* (Federal Security Service) (Russia)
GAO	Government Accountability Office
GCHQ	Government Communications Headquarters (Britain)
GDIP	General Defense Intelligence Program
GDP	gross domestic product
GEO	geosynchronous orbit
GEOINT	geospatial intelligence
GNP	gross national product
GRU	*Glavnoye Razvedyvatelnoye Upravlenie* (Main Intelligence Administration) (Russia)
GU	*Glavnoye Upravlenie* (Main Administration) (Russia)
HEO	highly elliptical orbit
HPSCI	House Permanent Select Committee on Intelligence
HSI	hyperspectral imagery
HSINT	homeland security intelligence
HSIP	Homeland Security Intelligence Program
HUMINT	human intelligence
I&A	intelligence and analysis
I&W	indications and warnings
IAEA	International Agency for Atomic Energy
IC	intelligence community
IG	inspector general
IMINT	imagery (or photo) intelligence
INF	intermediate nuclear forces
INR	Bureau of Intelligence and Research (Department of State)
INTs	collection disciplines (HUMINT, GEOINT, MASINT, OSINT, SIGINT)
IR	infrared imagery
IRA	Irish Republican Army
IRGC	Iranian Revolutionary Guard Corps
IRTPA	Intelligence Reform and Terrorism Prevention Act
ISC	Intelligence and Security Committee (Britain)

ISID	Inter-Services Intelligence Directorate (Pakistan) (usually called ISI)
ISG	Iraq Survey Group
ISR	intelligence, surveillance, and reconnaissance
IT	information technology
JCS	Joint Chiefs of Staff
JIC	Joint Intelligence Committee (Britain)
JICC	Joint Intelligence Community Council
JIO	Joint Intelligence Organisation (Britain)
JIOC	Joint Intelligence Operations Center
JMIP	Joint Military Intelligence Program
JTAC	Joint Terrorism Analysis Center (Britain)
JTTF	Joint Terrorism Task Force
KGB	*Komitet Gosudarstvennoi Bezopasnosti* (Committee of State Security) (Russia)
KJs	Key Judgments
LEO	low earth orbit
MAD	mutual assured destruction
MASINT	measurement and signatures intelligence
MEO	medium earth orbit
MI5	Security Service (Britain)
MI6	Secret Intelligence Service (Britain)
MIP	Military Intelligence Program
MOIS	Ministry of Intelligence and Security (Iran)
MON	memo of notification
Mossad	*Ha-Mossad Le-Modin Ule Tafkidim Meyuhadim* (Institute for Intelligence and Special Tasks) (Israel)
MSI	multispectral imagery
NAB	National Assessment Bureau (New Zealand)
NATO	North Atlantic Treaty Organization
NCPC	National Counterproliferation Center
NCS	National Clandestine Service
NCSC	National Counterintelligence and Security Center
NCTC	(1) National Counterterrorism Center; (2) National Counter-Terrorism Committee (Australia)

NFIP	National Foreign Intelligence Program
NGA	National Geospatial-Intelligence Agency
NIA	National Intelligence Agency (South Africa)
NIC	National Intelligence Council
NIE	national intelligence estimate
NIM	national intelligence manager
NIMA	National Imagery and Mapping Agency
NIO	national intelligence officer
NIP	National Intelligence Program
NIPF	National Intelligence Priorities Framework
NOC	nonofficial cover
NRO	National Reconnaissance Office
NRP	National Reconnaissance Program
NSA	National Security Agency
NSC	National Security Council
NSL	national security letters
NTM	national technical means
NTRO	National Technical Research Organization (India)
OCO	overseas contingency operations
ODNI	Office of the Director of National Intelligence
OMB	Office of Management and Budget
ONA	Office of National Assessments (Australia)
ORCON	originator controlled
OSD	Office of the Secretary of Defense
OSE	Open Source Enterprise
OSINT	open-source intelligence
OSS	Office of Strategic Services
P&E	processing and exploitation
PC	Principals Committee (NSC)
PCLOB	Privacy and Civil Liberties Oversight Board
PCO	Privy Council Office (Canada)
PDB	President's Daily Brief
PFIAB	President's Foreign Intelligence Advisory Board

PFLP	Popular Front for the Liberation of Palestine
PHIA	professional head of intelligence analysis (Britain)
PHOTINT	photo intelligence
PIAB	President's Intelligence Advisory Board
PIOB	President's Intelligence Oversight Board
PIPs	Presidential Intelligence Priorities
QFR	question for the record
RAW	Research and Analysis Wing (India)
RMA	revolution in military affairs
S&T	science and technology
SAC	(1) special agent in charge (FBI); (2) Strategic Air Command (now called STRATCOM)
SALT	strategic arms limitation talks
SAM	surface-to-air missile
SARS	severe acute respiratory syndrome
SAS	Special Air Service (Britain)
SBS	Special Boat Service (Britain)
SBSS	space-based surveillance satellite
SCIFs	sensitive compartmented information facilities
SDI	Strategic Defense Initiative
SGAC	Senate Governmental Affairs Committee
Shin Bet	*Sherut ha-Bitachon ha-Klali* (General Security Service) (Israel)
SIGINT	signals intelligence
SIS	Secret Intelligence Service (Britain)
SMO	support to military operations
SNIE	special national intelligence estimate
SOCMINT	social media intelligence
SOCOM	Special Operations Command
SPA	special political action
SRA	Systems and Research Analyses
SSCI	Senate Select Committee on Intelligence
START	Strategic Arms Reduction Treaty
STRATCOM	Strategic Forces Command

SVR	*Sluzhba Vneshnei Razvedki* (External Intelligence Service) (Russia)
SWIFT	Society for Worldwide Interbank Financial Telecommunications
TacSat	tactical satellite
TECHINT	technical intelligence
TELINT	telemetry intelligence
TIARA	Tactical Intelligence and Related Activities
TOR	terms of reference
TPEDs	tasking, processing, exploitation, and dissemination
TUAVs	tactical unmanned aerial vehicles
UAVs	unmanned aerial vehicles
UCR	unanimous consent request
UIS	unifying intelligence strategies
UN	United Nations
UNSCOM	United Nations Special Commission
USDI	under secretary of defense for intelligence
VoIP	Voice-over-Internet Protocol
WIRe	Worldwide Intelligence Review
WMD	weapons of mass destruction

CHAPTER ONE

WHAT IS "INTELLIGENCE"?

W hat is **intelligence**? Why is its definition an issue? Virtually every book written on the subject of intelligence begins with a discussion of what "intelligence" means, or at least how the author intends to use the term. This editorial fact reveals much about the field of intelligence. If this were a text on any other government function—defense, housing, transportation, diplomacy, agriculture—there would be little or no confusion about, or need to explain, what was being discussed.

Intelligence is different from other government functions for at least two reasons. First, much of what goes on is secret. Intelligence exists because governments seek to hide some information from other governments, who, in turn, seek to discover hidden information by means that they wish to keep secret. All of this secrecy leads some authors to believe that issues exist about which they cannot write or may not have sufficient knowledge. Thus, they feel the need to describe the limits of their work. Although numerous aspects of intelligence are—and deserve to be—kept secret, this is not an impediment to describing basic roles, processes, functions, and issues.

Second, this same secrecy can be a source of consternation to citizens, especially in a democratic country such as the United States. The U.S. intelligence community is a relatively recent government phenomenon. Since its creation in 1947, the intelligence community has been the subject of much ambivalence. Some Americans are uncomfortable with the concept that intelligence is a secret entity within an ostensibly open government based on checks and balances. Moreover, the intelligence community engages in activities—spying, eavesdropping, covert action—that some people regard as antithetical to what they believe the United States should be as a nation and as a model for other nations. Some citizens have difficulty reconciling American ideals and goals with the realities of intelligence.

To many people, intelligence seems little different from information, except that it is probably secret. However, distinguishing between the two is important. Information is anything that can be known, regardless of how it is discovered. Intelligence refers to information that meets the stated or understood needs of policy makers and has been collected, processed, and narrowed to meet those needs. Intelligence is a subset of the broader category of information. Intelligence and the entire process by which it is identified, obtained, and analyzed responds to the needs of policy makers. All intelligence is information; not all information is intelligence.

WHY HAVE INTELLIGENCE AGENCIES?

The major theme of this book is that intelligence exists solely to support policy makers in myriad ways. Any other activity is either wasteful or illegal. The book's focus is firmly on the relationship between intelligence, in all of its aspects, and policy making. The policy maker is not a passive recipient of intelligence but actively influences all aspects of intelligence. (This concept of the policy maker–intelligence relationship would also be true for business as well as government. The focus in this book is on governments.)

Intelligence agencies exist for at least four major reasons: to avoid strategic surprise; to provide long-term expertise; to support the policy process; and to maintain the secrecy of information, needs, and methods.

To Avoid Strategic Surprise. The foremost goal of any intelligence community must be to keep track of threats, forces, events, and developments that are capable of endangering the nation's existence. This goal may sound grandiose and far-fetched, but several times since the early twentieth century, nations have been subjected to direct military attacks for which they were, at best, inadequately prepared—Russia was surprised by Japan in 1904, both the Soviet Union (by Germany) and the United States (by Japan) in 1941, and Israel (by Egypt and Syria) in 1973. The terrorist attacks of September 11, 2001, on the United States are another example of this pattern, albeit carried out on a much more limited scale. (*See box, "The Terrorist Attacks on September 11, 2001: Another Pearl Harbor?"*)

Strategic surprise should not be confused with tactical surprise, which is of a different magnitude and, as Professor Richard Betts of Columbia University pointed out in his article, "Analysis, War, and Decision: Why Intelligence Failures Are Inevitable," cannot be wholly avoided. To put the difference between the two types of surprise in perspective, suppose, for example, that Mr. Smith and Mr. Jones are business partners. Every Friday, while Mr. Smith is lunching with a client, Mr. Jones helps himself to money from the petty cash. One afternoon Mr. Smith comes back from lunch earlier than expected, catching Mr. Jones red-handed. "I'm surprised!" they exclaim simultaneously. Mr. Jones's surprise is tactical: He knew what he was doing but did not expect to get caught; Mr. Smith's surprise is strategic: He had no idea the embezzlement was happening.

Tactical surprise, when it happens, is not of sufficient magnitude and importance to threaten national existence, although it can be psychologically devastating. To some extent, the 9/11 attacks were tactical surprises. Repetitive tactical surprise, however, suggests some significant intelligence problems.

The advent of missiles with intercontinental ranges, armed with nuclear weapons, put an increased emphasis on intelligence to avoid surprise attack for the United States and the Soviet Union. Today, the use of cyberspace offers possibilities for devastating attacks that could be even more difficult to detect or to deter.

THE TERRORIST ATTACKS ON SEPTEMBER 11, 2001: ANOTHER PEARL HARBOR?

Many people immediately described the September 11, 2001, terrorist attacks on the World Trade Center in New York City and the Pentagon as a "new Pearl Harbor." This is understandable on an emotional level, as both were surprise attacks. However, important differences exist.

First, Pearl Harbor was a strategic surprise. U.S. policy makers expected a move by Japan but not against the United States. The Soviet Union was seen as a possible target, but the greatest expectation and fear was a Japanese attack on European colonies in Southeast Asia that bypassed U.S. possessions, thus allowing Japan to continue to expand its empire without bringing the United States into the war.

The terrorist attacks were more of a tactical surprise. The enmity of Osama bin Laden and his willingness to attack U.S. targets had been amply demonstrated in earlier attacks on the East African embassies and on the USS *Cole*. Throughout the summer of 2001, U.S. intelligence officials had warned of the likelihood of another bin Laden attack. What was not known—or guessed—were the target and the means of attack.

Second, Japan and the Axis powers had the capability to defeat and destroy U.S. power and the U.S. way of life. The terrorists do not pose a threat on the same level.

To Provide Long-Term Expertise. Compared with the permanent bureaucracy, all senior policy makers are transients. The average time in office for a president of the United States is five years. Secretaries of state and defense serve for less time than that, and their senior subordinates—deputy, under, and assistant secretaries—often hold their positions for even shorter periods. Although these individuals often enter their respective offices with an extensive background in their fields, it is virtually impossible for them to be well versed in all of the matters with which they will be dealing. Inevitably, they will have to call upon others whose knowledge and expertise on certain issues are greater. Much knowledge and expertise on national security issues reside in the intelligence community, where the analytical cadre is more stable than the political office holders. (This changed somewhat in the United States after 2001. See chap. 6.) Stability tends to be greater in intelligence agencies, particularly in higher-level positions, than in foreign affairs and defense agencies. Also, intelligence agencies tend to have far fewer political appointees than do the State and Defense Departments. However, these two personnel differences (stability and nonpolitical) have diminished somewhat over the past decade. As will be discussed later, the senior position in U.S. intelligence, the director of national intelligence (DNI), had been extremely volatile, with four DNIs in the first five years (2005–2010). Lt. Gen. James Clapper (USAF, ret.), who was DNI from 2010 to 2017, offered greater continuity by remaining in the position longer than all of his predecessors combined.

To Support the Policy Process. Policy makers have a constant need for tailored (meaning written for their specific needs), timely intelligence that will provide background, context, information, warning, and an assessment of risks, benefits, and likely outcomes. Policy makers also occasionally need alternative means to achieve specific policy ends. Both of these needs are met by the intelligence community.

In the ethos of U.S. intelligence, a strict dividing line exists between intelligence and policy. The two are seen as separate functions. The government is run by the policy makers. Intelligence has a support role and may not cross over into the advocacy of policy choices. Intelligence officers who are dealing with policy makers are expected to maintain professional objectivity and not push specific policies, choices, or outcomes. To do so is seen as threatening the objectivity of the analyses they present. If intelligence officers have a strong preference for a specific policy outcome, their intelligence analysis may display a similar bias. This is what is meant by **politicized intelligence**, one of the strongest expressions of opprobrium that can be leveled in the U.S. intelligence community. This is not to suggest that intelligence officers do not have preferences about policy choices. They do. However, they are trained not to allow these preferences to influence their intelligence analysis. If intelligence officers were allowed to make policy recommendations, they would then have a strong urge to present intelligence that supported the policy they had first recommended. At that point, all objectivity would be lost.

Three important caveats should be added to the distinction between policy and intelligence. First, the idea that intelligence is distinct from policy does not mean that intelligence officers do not care about the outcome and do not influence it. One must differentiate between attempting to influence (that is, inform) the process by providing intelligence, which is acceptable, and trying to manipulate intelligence so that policy makers make a certain choice, which is not acceptable. Second, senior policy makers can and do ask senior intelligence officials for their opinions, which are given. Third, this separation works in only one direction, that of intelligence advice to policy. Nothing prevents policy makers from rejecting intelligence out of hand or offering their own analytic inputs. When doing so, however, policy makers cannot present their alternative views as intelligence per se, in part because they lack the necessary objectivity. There are no hard-and-fast rules here, but there is an unwritten and generally agreed standard. This became an issue in 2002, when Under Secretary of Defense for Policy Douglas Feith created an office that, to many observers, appeared to offer alternative intelligence analyses even though it was in a policy branch. Assuming that policy makers stay within their bounds, they will likely see their offering alternative views as being different from imposing their views on the intelligence product per se. This would also politicize intelligence, which is an accusation policy makers as well as intelligence officials hope to avoid because it calls into question the soundness of their policy and the basis on which they have made decisions. The propriety of a policy maker rejecting intelligence was central to the 2005 debate over the nomination of John Bolton to be U.S. ambassador to the United Nations. Critics charged that Bolton, as under secretary of state, had engaged in this type of action when intelligence did not provide the answers he preferred. (*See box, "Policy Versus Intelligence: The Great Divide."*)

To Maintain the Secrecy of Information, Needs, and Methods. Secrecy does make intelligence unique. That others would keep important information from you, that you need certain types of information and wish to keep your needs secret, and that you have the means to obtain information that you also wish to keep secret are major reasons for having intelligence agencies.

POLICY VERSUS INTELLIGENCE: THE GREAT DIVIDE

One way to envision the distinction between policy and intelligence is to see them as two spheres of government activity that are separated by a semiperme-able membrane. The membrane is semipermeable because policy makers can and do cross over into the intelligence sphere, but intelligence officials cannot cross over into the policy sphere.

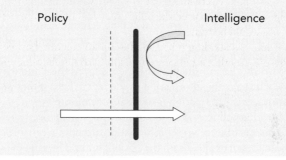

Policy   Intelligence

WHAT IS INTELLIGENCE ABOUT?

The word "intelligence" largely refers to issues related to national security—that is, defense and foreign policy and certain aspects of homeland and internal security, which has been increasingly important since the terrorist attacks of 2001. In U.S. law (the Intelligence Reform and Terrorist Prevention Act, 2004) all intelligence is now defined as **national intelligence**, which has three subsets: foreign, domestic, and homeland security. This specification was written to overcome the past divide between foreign and domestic intelligence, which had come to be seen as an impediment to intelligence sharing, especially on issues like terrorism, which overlaps both areas. It is important to note that practitioners are experiencing some difficulty distinguishing among homeland, internal, and domestic security.

The actions, policies, and capabilities of other nations and of important non-state groups (international organizations, terrorist organizations, and so on) are primary areas of concern. But policy makers and intelligence officers cannot restrict themselves to thinking only about enemies—those powers that are known to be hostile or whose policy goals are in some way inimical. They must also keep track of powers that are neutrals, friends, or even allies who are rivals in certain contexts. For example, the European Union is made up largely of nations that are U.S. allies. However, the United States competes with many of them for global resources and markets, so in that sense they are rivals. This type of relationship with the United States is also true of Japan and South Korea. Furthermore, circumstances may arise in which a country would need to keep track of the actions and intentions of friends. For example, an ally might be pursuing a course that could involve it in conflict with a third party. Should this not be to a country's liking—or should it threaten to involve that country as well—it would be better to know early on what this ally was doing. Adolf Hitler, for example, might have been better served had he known in advance of Japan's plans to attack the U.S. fleet at Pearl Harbor in 1941. He had no interest in seeing the United States become an active combatant and might have argued against a direct attack by Japan (as opposed to a Japanese attack to the south against European colonies but avoiding U.S. territories). In the late twentieth and early twenty-first centuries it has become increasingly important for the United States to keep track of non-state actors—terrorists, narcotics traffickers, freelance proliferators, cyber hackers, and others.

Information is needed about these actors, their intentions, their likely actions, and their capabilities in a variety of areas, including economic, military, and societal. The United States built its intelligence organizations in recognition of the fact that some of the information it would like to have is either inaccessible or being actively denied. In other words, the information is secret as far as the United States is concerned, and those who have the information would like to keep it that way.

The pursuit of secret information is the mainstay of intelligence activity. At the same time, reflecting the political transformation brought about by the end of the cold war, increasing amounts of once secret information are now accessible, especially in states that were satellites of or allied with the Soviet Union. The ratio of open to secret information has shifted dramatically. One former senior intelligence official estimated that during the cold war, 80 percent of the intelligence the U.S. needed was secret, and 20 percent was open, but in the post–cold war world, those ratios had reversed. Still, foreign states and actors harbor secrets that the United States must pursue. And not all of this intelligence is in states that are hostile to the United States in the sense that they are enemies.

Most people tend to think of intelligence in terms of military information—troop movements, weapons capabilities, and plans for surprise attack. This is an important component of intelligence (in line with avoiding surprise attack, the first reason for having intelligence agencies), but it is not the only one. Many different kinds of intelligence (political, economic, social, environmental, health, and cultural) provide important inputs to analysts. Policy makers and intelligence officials must think beyond foreign intelligence. They must consider intelligence activities focused on threats to internal security, such as subversion, espionage, and terrorism.

Other than the internal security threats, domestic intelligence, at least in the United States and kindred democracies, had been treated as a law enforcement issue, although this has become an issue of contention in the United States when it comes to terrorism and the treatment of potential terrorists. However, this nexus between domestic intelligence and law enforcement differentiates the practice of intelligence in Western democracies from that in totalitarian or authoritarian states. The Union of Soviet Socialist Republics' State Security Committee (*Komitet Gosudarstvennoi Bezopasnosti*, or KGB), for example, served a crucial internal secret police function that the Central Intelligence Agency (CIA) does not. Thus, in many respects, the two agencies were not comparable.

"AND YE SHALL KNOW THE TRUTH . . ."

Upon entering the old entrance of the Central Intelligence Agency headquarters, one will find the following inscription on the left-hand marble wall:

And ye shall know the truth, and the truth shall make you free.

John VIII–XXXII

It is a nice sentiment, but it overstates and misrepresents what is going on in that building or any other intelligence agency.

What is intelligence *not* about? Intelligence is not about truth. If something were known to be true—or false—states would not need intelligence agencies to collect the information or analyze it. Truth is such an absolute term that it sets a standard that intelligence rarely would be able to achieve. It is better—and more accurate—to think of intelligence as proximate reality. Intelligence agencies face issues or questions and do their best to arrive at a firm understanding of what is going on. They can rarely be assured that even their best and most considered analysis is true. Their goals are intelligence products that are reliable, unbiased, and honest (that is, free from politicization). These are all laudable goals, yet they are still different from truth. (*See box, "And ye shall know the truth . . ."*)

It is also important to understand that the target of intelligence is secrets and not mysteries. Secrets refers to intelligence that someone, somewhere knows—just not us. The goal is to gain access to that intelligence. Mysteries refers to things that cannot be explained and for which no reliable intelligence likely exists—such as who built Stonehenge.

Is intelligence integral to the policy process? The question may seem rhetorical in a book about intelligence, but it is important to consider. At one level, the answer is yes. Intelligence should and can provide warning about imminent strategic threats, although, as noted, several nations have been subjected to strategic surprise.

Intelligence officials can also play a useful role as seasoned and experienced advisers. The information their agencies gather is also of value given that it might not be available if agencies did not undertake secret collection. Therein lies an irony: Intelligence agencies strive to be more than just collectors of secret information. They emphasize the value that their analysis adds to the secret information, although equally competent analysts can be found in policy agencies. The difference is in the nature of the work and the outcomes for which the two types of analysts are responsible—intelligence versus policy decisions.

At the same time, intelligence suffers from a number of potential weaknesses that tend to undercut its function in the eyes of policy makers. Not all of these weaknesses are present at all times, and sometimes none is present. They still represent potential pitfalls.

First, a certain amount of intelligence analysis may be no more sophisticated than current conventional wisdom on a given issue. Conventional wisdom is usually—and sometimes mistakenly—dismissed out of hand. But policy makers expect more than that, in part justifiably.

Second, analysis can become so dependent on data that it misses important intangibles. For example, a competent analysis of the likelihood that thirteen small and somewhat disunited colonies would be able to break away from British rule in the 1770s would have likely concluded that defeat was inevitable. After all, Britain was the largest industrial power; it already had trained troops stationed in the colonies; colonial opinion was not united (nor was Britain's); and Britain could use the Native Americans as an added force, among other reasons. A straightforward political-military analysis would have missed several factors—the strength of British divisiveness, the possibility of help from royalist France—that turned out to be of tremendous importance.

Third, **mirror imaging**, or assuming that other states or individuals will act just the way a particular country or person does, can undermine analysis. The basis of this problem is fairly understandable. Every day people make innumerable judgments—when driving, walking on a crowded street, or interacting with others at home and at the office—about how other people will react and behave. They assume that their behavior and reactions are based on the golden rule. These judgments stem from societal norms and rules, etiquette, and experience. Analysts too easily extend this commonplace thinking to intelligence issues. However, in intelligence it becomes a trap. For example, no U.S. policy maker in 1941 could conceive of Japan's starting a war with the United States overtly (instead of continuing its advance while bypassing U.S. territories), given the great disparity in the strength of the two nations. In Tokyo, however, that same disparate strength argued compellingly for the necessity of starting war sooner rather than later. The other problem with mirror imaging is that it assumes a certain level of shared rationality. It leaves no room for the irrational actor, an individual or nation whose rationality is based on something different or unfamiliar—for example, suicidal terrorists viewed through the eyes of Western culture.

Fourth, and perhaps most important, policy makers are free to reject or to ignore the intelligence they are offered. They may suffer penalties down the road if their policy has bad outcomes, but policy makers cannot be forced to take heed of intelligence.

Thus, they can dispense with intelligence at will, and intelligence officers cannot press their way (or their products) back into the process in such cases.

This host of weaknesses seems to overpower the positive aspects of intelligence. It certainly suggests and underscores the fragility of intelligence within the policy process. How, then, can it be determined whether intelligence matters? The best way, at least retrospectively, is to ask: Would policy makers have made different choices with or without a given piece of intelligence? If the answer is yes, or even maybe, then the intelligence mattered. The answer to this can still be elusive because much intelligence may not be related to a specific event or decision. Richard Kerr, a former deputy director of central intelligence, reviewed fifty years of CIA analysis across a range of issues and concluded that, despite highs and lows of performance, intelligence helped reduce policy makers' uncertainty and provided them with understanding and with warning on a fairly consistent basis. That should be seen as a valuable service even if one admits that intelligence will not always be correct. (*See box, "Intelligence: A Working Concept."*)

INTELLIGENCE: A WORKING CONCEPT

Intelligence is the process by which specific types of information important to national security are requested, collected, analyzed, and provided to policy makers; the products of that process; the safeguarding of these processes and this information by counterintelligence activities; and the carrying out of operations as requested by lawful authorities.

We return to the question: What is intelligence? Alan Breakspear, a veteran Canadian intelligence officer, defines intelligence as a capability to forecast changes—either positive or negative—in time to do something about them. We often tend to think about intelligence-related events in the negative. Breakspear's addition of "positive" is important and is akin to "opportunity analysis." (See chap. 6.)

In this book, we will think about intelligence in several ways, sometimes simultaneously:

- Intelligence as process: Intelligence can be thought of as the means by which certain types of information are required and requested, collected, analyzed, and disseminated, and as the way in which certain types of covert action are conceived and conducted.

- Intelligence as product: Intelligence can be thought of as the product of these processes—that is, as the analyses and intelligence operations themselves.

- Intelligence as organization: Intelligence can be thought of as the units that carry out its various functions.

KEY TERMS

intelligence 1

mirror imaging 8

national intelligence 5

politicized intelligence 4

FURTHER READINGS

Each of these readings grapples with the definition of intelligence, either by function or by role, in a different way. Some deal with intelligence on its own terms; others attempt to relate it to the larger policy process.

Betts, Richard. "Analysis, War, and Decision: Why Intelligence Failures Are Inevitable." *World Politics* 31 (October 1978). Reprinted in *Power, Strategy, and Security*. Ed. Klaus Knorr. Princeton, N.J.: Princeton University Press, 1983.

Breakspear, Alan. "Intelligence: The Unseen Instrument of Governance." In *Governance and Security as a Unitary Concept*. Eds. Tom Rippon and Graham Kemp. Victoria, British Columbia: Agio, 2012.

Hamilton, Lee. "The Role of Intelligence in the Foreign Policy Process." In *Essays on Strategy and Diplomacy*. Claremont, Calif.: Claremont College, Keck Center for International Strategic Studies, 1987.

Herman, Michael. *Intelligence Power in Peace and War*. New York: Cambridge University Press, 1996.

Heymann, Hans. "Intelligence/Policy Relationships." In *Intelligence: Policy and Process*. Ed. Alfred C. Maurer and others. Boulder, Colo.: Westview Press, 1985.

Hilsman, Roger. *Strategic Intelligence and National Decisions*. Glencoe, Ill.: Free Press, 1958.

Kent, Sherman. *Strategic Intelligence for American Foreign Policy*. Princeton, N.J.: Princeton University Press, 1949.

Kerr, Richard J. "The Track Record: CIA Analysis from 1950 to 2000." In *Analyzing Intelligence*. Eds. Roger Z. George and James B. Bruce. Washington, D.C.: Georgetown University Press, 2008.

Laqueur, Walter. *A World of Secrets: The Uses and Limits of Intelligence*. New York: Basic Books, 1985.

Oleson, Peter C., ed. *AFIO's Guide to the Study of Intelligence*. Falls Church, Va.: Association of Former Intelligence Officers (AFIO), 2016.

Scott, Len, and Peter Jackson. "The Study of Intelligence in Theory and Practice." *Intelligence and National Security* 19 (summer 2004): 139–169.

Shulsky, Abram N., and Gary J. Schmitt. *Silent Warfare: Understanding the World of Intelligence*. 2d rev. ed. Washington, D.C.: Brassey's, 1993.

Shulsky, Abram N., and Jennifer Sims. *What Is Intelligence?* Washington, D.C.: Consortium for the Study of Intelligence, 1992.

Troy, Thomas F. "The 'Correct' Definition of Intelligence." *International Journal of Intelligence and Counterintelligence* 5 (winter 1991–1992): 433–454.

Warner, Michael. "Wanted: A Definition of Intelligence." *Studies in Intelligence* 46 (2002): 15–23.

CHAPTER TWO

THE DEVELOPMENT OF U.S. INTELLIGENCE

Each nation practices intelligence in ways that are specific—if not peculiar—to that nation alone. This is true even among countries that have a common heritage and share a great deal of their intelligence, such as Australia, Britain, Canada, New Zealand, and the United States—the group known as the **Five Eyes**. A better understanding of how and why the United States practices intelligence is important because the U.S. intelligence system remains the largest and most influential in the world—as model, rival, or target. (The practices of several foreign intelligence services are discussed in chap. 15.) Therefore, this chapter discusses the major themes and historical events that shaped the development of U.S. intelligence and helped determine how it continues to function.

The phrase "intelligence community" is used throughout the book as well as in most other discussions of U.S. intelligence. The word "community" is particularly apt in describing U.S. intelligence. The community is made up of agencies and offices whose work is often related and sometimes combined, but they serve different needs or different policy makers and work under various lines of authority and control. The intelligence community grew out of a set of evolving demands and without a master plan. It is highly functional and yet sometimes dysfunctional. One director of central intelligence (DCI), Richard Helms (1966–1973), testified before Congress that, despite all of the criticisms of the structure and functioning of the intelligence community, if one were to create it from scratch, much the same community would likely emerge. Helms's focus was not on the structure of the community but on the services it provides, which are multiple, varied, and supervised by a number of individuals. This approach to intelligence is unique to the United States, although others have copied facets of it. The 2004 legislation that created a director of national intelligence (DNI; see chap. 3) made changes in the superstructure of the intelligence community but not to the essential functions of the various agencies.

MAJOR THEMES

A number of major themes contributed to the development of the U.S. intelligence system.

Liberty and Security. Throughout the history of the United States under the Constitution there has been a constant debate and sometimes tension between two equally desired outcomes: liberty and security. These goals are not in opposition but, at certain times, one value has had to give way to the other. In the John Adams administration (1797–1801), Congress passed legislation, the Alien and Sedition Acts, designed to limit criticism of the government in speech or the press. During the Civil War, Abraham Lincoln (1861–1865) suspended habeas corpus (the requirement to be charged with a crime after arrest) several times (as did Jefferson Davis in the Confederacy). During World War I, Woodrow Wilson (1913–1921) used the Espionage Act to arrest those opposed to certain wartime policies. In the period after that war, Attorney General A. Mitchell Palmer conducted raids and arrest against American left-wing radicals. At the onset of U.S. entry into World War II, Japanese citizens (Nisei) were forced into internment camps. During the early part of the cold war, Sen. Joseph McCarthy, R-WI, held numerous hearings to root out suspected Communist infiltrators in the government, often with little evidence. During the Vietnam War, Presidents Lyndon B. Johnson (1963–1969) and Richard M. Nixon (1969–1974) both used the Federal Bureau of Investigation (FBI) to investigate war and civil rights protestors. Finally, during the campaign against terrorists there have been concerns about National Security Agency (NSA) programs and their breadth and degree of intrusiveness within the United States.

The Novelty of U.S. Intelligence. Of the major powers of the twentieth and twenty-first centuries, the United States has the briefest history of significant intelligence beyond wartime emergencies. The great Chinese military philosopher, Sun Tzu, wrote about the importance of intelligence in the fifth century BCE. British intelligence dates from the reign of Elizabeth I (1558–1603), French intelligence from the tenure of Cardinal Richelieu (1624–1642), and Russian intelligence from the reign of Ivan the Terrible (1533–1584). Even given that the United States did not come into being until 1776, its intelligence experience is brief. The first glimmer of a **national intelligence** enterprise did not appear until 1940. Although permanent and specific naval and military intelligence units date from the late nineteenth century, a broader U.S. national intelligence capability began to arise only with the creation of the Coordinator of Information (COI) in 1941, the predecessor of the World War II–era Office of Strategic Services (OSS).

What explains this 165-year absence of organized U.S. intelligence? For most of its history, the United States did not have strong foreign policy interests beyond its immediate borders. The success of the 1823 Monroe Doctrine (which stated that the United States would resist any European attempt to colonize in the Western Hemisphere), abetted by the acquiescence and tacit support of Britain, the most powerful of the European states, solved the basic security interests of the United States and its broader foreign policy interests. The need for better intelligence became apparent only after the United States achieved the status of a world power and became involved in wide-ranging international issues at the end of the nineteenth century.

Furthermore, the United States faced no threat to its security from its neighbors, from powers outside the Western Hemisphere, or—with the exception of the

Civil War (1861–1865)—from large-scale internal dissent that was inimical to its form of government. This benign environment, so unlike that faced by all European states, undercut any perceived need for national intelligence.

Until the cold war with the Soviet Union commenced in 1945, the United States severely limited expenditures on defense and related activities during peacetime. Intelligence, already underappreciated, fell into this category. Historians have noted, however, that intelligence absorbed a remarkable and anomalous 12 percent of the federal budget under President George Washington. This was the high-water mark of intelligence spending in the federal budget, a percentage that was never approached again. The intelligence request for fiscal year 2020 amounts to $85.75 billion, the highest request for intelligence, which is 1.8% of the total budget request. These data suggest that although there has been a great increase in intelligence spending in terms of dollars since the 9/11 terrorist attacks, intelligence has not increased substantially as a national priority since 2001, going from 1.6 percent of the federal budget during the pre- and post-attack period and increasing slightly thereafter. In other words, intelligence spending has increased as has the rest of the federal budget, but intelligence has increased only barely the share of the federal budget that it consumes, which is a more important indicator than dollar-spending levels.

Intelligence was a novelty in the 1940s. At that time, policy makers in both the executive branch and Congress viewed intelligence as a newcomer to national security. Even within the Army and Navy, intelligence developed relatively late and was far from robust until well into the twentieth century. As a result, intelligence did not have long-established patrons in the government, but it did have many rivals with competing departments, particularly the Army, the Navy, and the FBI, none of which was willing to share its sources of information. Furthermore, intelligence did not have well-established traditions or modes of operation and thus was forced to create these during two periods of extreme pressure: World War II and the cold war.

A Threat-Based Foreign Policy. With the promulgation of the Monroe Doctrine, the United States assumed a vested interest in the international status quo. This interest became more pronounced after the Spanish-American War in 1898. With the acquisition of a small colonial empire, the United States achieved a satisfactory international position—largely self-sufficient and largely unthreatened. However, the twentieth century saw the repeated rise of powers whose foreign policies were direct threats to the status quo: Kaiserine Germany in World War I, the Axis in World War II, and then the Soviet Union during the cold war.

Responding to these threats became the mainstay of U.S. national security policy. The threats also gave focus to much of the operational side of U.S. intelligence, from its initial experience in the OSS during World War II to broader covert actions in the cold war. Intelligence operations were one way in which the United States countered these threats.

The terrorism threat in the late twentieth and early twenty-first centuries fits the same pattern of an opponent who rejects the international status quo and has emerged as an issue for U.S. national security. However, now the enemy is not a nation-state— even when terrorists have the support of nation-states or appear to be quasi-states, as did the Islamic State (ISIL) for a period—which makes it more difficult to deal with the problem. The refusal to accept the status quo could be more central to terrorists than it was to nation-states such as Nazi Germany and the Soviet Union, for whom the international status quo was also anathema. Such countries can, when necessary or convenient, forgo those policies, temporarily accept the status quo, and continue to function. Terrorists, however, cannot accept the status quo without giving up their *raison d'être*.

Being the guarantor of the status quo imposes costs—economic and military—that are usually seen as being offset by the benefits of the status quo. Some observers have questioned whether Donald Trump's administration (2017–) understands and is willing to bear those costs. If not, there will be additional intelligence challenges as the international community adjusts to this changed position of the United States. DNI Dan Coats's 2019 *Worldwide Threat Assessment* suggests that such a process was already underway among some U.S. allies and partners.

The Influence of the Cold War. Historians of intelligence often debate whether the United States would have had a large-scale intelligence capability had there been no cold war. The view here is that the answer is yes. The 1941 Japanese attack on Pearl Harbor, not the cold war, prompted the initial formation of the U.S. intelligence community.

Even so, the prosecution of the cold war became the major defining factor in the development of most basic forms and practices of the U.S. intelligence community. Until the collapse of the Soviet Union in 1991, the cold war was the predominant national security issue, taking up to half of the intelligence budget, according to former DCI Robert M. Gates (1991–1993). Moreover, the fact that the Soviet Union and its allies were essentially closed targets had a major effect on U.S. intelligence, forcing it to resort to a variety of largely remote technical systems to collect needed information from a distance.

The Global Scope of Intelligence Interests. The cold war quickly shifted from a struggle for predominance in postwar Europe to a global struggle in which virtually any nation or region could be a pawn between the two sides, especially as decolonization created many new independent states. Although some areas always remained more important than others, none could be written off entirely. Thus, U.S. intelligence began to collect and analyze information about, and station intelligence personnel in, every region.

A Wittingly Redundant Analytical Structure. Intelligence can be divided into four broad activities: collection, analysis, covert action, and counterintelligence. The United States developed unique entities to handle the various types of collection (imagery, signals, espionage) and covert action; counterintelligence is a function that is found in virtually every intelligence agency. But, for analysis, U.S. policy makers purposely created three agencies whose functions appear to overlap: the Central Intelligence Agency's (CIA) Directorate of Analysis (until 2015, the Directorate of Intelligence, or DI), the State Department's Bureau of Intelligence and Research (INR), and the Defense Intelligence Agency (DIA). Each of these agencies is considered an all-source analytical agency; that is, their analysts have access to the full range of collected intelligence, and they work on virtually the same issues, although with differing degrees of emphasis, reflecting the interests of their primary policy customers.

Two major reasons explain this redundancy, and they are fundamental to how the United States conducts analysis. First, different consumers of intelligence—policy makers—have different intelligence needs. Even when the president, the secretary of state, the secretary of defense, and the chairman of the Joint Chiefs of Staff are working on the same issue, each has different operational responsibilities and concerns. The United States developed analytical centers to serve each policy maker's specific and unique needs. Also, each policy agency wanted to be assured of a stream of intelligence analysis dedicated to its needs.

Second, the United States developed the concept of **competitive analysis**, an idea that is based on the belief that by having analysts in several agencies with different backgrounds and perspectives work on the same issue, parochial views more likely will be countered—if not weeded out—and proximate reality is more likely to be achieved. Competitive analysis should, in theory, be an antidote to **groupthink** and forced consensus, although this is not always the case in practice. For example, during the prewar assessment of Iraq's weapons of mass destruction (WMD) programs, divisions formed among agencies about the nature of some intelligence (such as the possible role of aluminum tubes in a nuclear program) and whether the totality of the intelligence indicated parts of a nuclear program or a more coherent program. But these differences did not appreciably alter the predominant view with respect to the overall potential Iraqi nuclear capability.

As one would expect, competitive analysis entails a certain cost for the intelligence community because it requires having many analysts in several agencies. During the 1990s, as intelligence budgets contracted severely under the pressure of the post–cold war peace dividend and because of a lack of political support in either the executive branch or Congress, much of the capability to conduct competitive analysis was lost. There simply were not enough analysts. According to DCI George J. Tenet (1997–2004), the entire intelligence community lost some 23,000 positions during the 1990s, affecting all activities. One result was a tendency to do less competitive analysis and, instead, to allow agencies to focus on certain issues exclusively, which resulted in a sort of analytical triage.

Consumer-Producer Relations. The distinct line that is drawn between policy and intelligence leads to questions about how intelligence producers and consumers should relate to each other. The issue is the degree of proximity that is desirable.

Two schools of thought have been evident in this debate in the United States. The distance school argued that the intelligence establishment should keep itself separate from the policy makers to avoid the risk of providing intelligence that lacks objectivity and favors or opposes one policy choice over others. Adherents of the distance school also feared that policy makers could interfere with intelligence so as to receive analysis that supported or opposed specific policies. This group believed that too close a relationship increased the risk of politicized intelligence.

The proximate group argued that too great a distance raised the risk that the intelligence community would be less aware of policy makers' needs and therefore produce less useful intelligence. This group maintained that proper training and internal reviews could avoid politicization of intelligence.

By the late 1950s to early 1960s, the proximate school became the preferred model for U.S. intelligence. But the debate was significant in that it underscored the early and persistent fears about intelligence becoming politicized.

In the late 1990s, there were two subtle shifts in the policy-intelligence relationship. The first was a greatly increased emphasis on support to military operations, which some believed gave too much priority to this sector—at a time when threats to national security had seemingly decreased—at the expense of other intelligence consumers. The second was the view among some analysts that they were being torn between operational customers and analytical customers.

The apotheosis of the proximate relationship may have come under President George W. Bush (2001–2009) who, upon taking office, requested that he receive an intelligence briefing six days a week. DCI George Tenet and Porter J. Goss (2004–2006), the last DCI and first DCIA, attended these daily briefings, which was unprecedented for a DCI. This greatly increased degree of proximity at the most senior level led some observers to question its possible effects on the DCI's ability to remain objective about the intelligence being offered. This practice continued under DNIs John Negroponte (2005–2007) and Mike McConnell (2007–2009). President Barack Obama (2009–2017) received a President's Daily Brief (PDB), not necessarily presented to him by the DNI but there was a postbrief meeting that the DNI or his deputy attended. Under Donald Trump, the DNI and the director of the CIA (DCIA) sometimes both attend the briefing. This suggests that a regular president-DNI meeting has become a standard part of the policy-intelligence relationship.

The Relationship Between Analysis and Collection and Covert Action. Parallel to the debate about producer-consumer relations, factions have waged a similar debate about the proper relationship between intelligence analysis, on the one hand, and intelligence collection and covert action, on the other.

The issue has centered largely on the structure of the CIA, which includes both analytical and operational components: the Directorate of Analysis (DA) and the Directorate of Operations (DO). (A similar structure exists in DIA with both analysts and a clandestine service, now called the Defense Clandestine Service, or DCS, but DIA has not usually been the focus of these concerns.) The DO is responsible for both espionage and covert action. Again, distance and proximate schools of thought took form. The distance school argued that analysis and the two operational functions are largely distinct and that housing them together could be risky for the security of human sources and methods and for analysis. Distance adherents raised concerns about the ability of the DI (as it then was) to provide objective analysis when the DO is concurrently running a major covert action. Will covert operators exert pressure, either overt or subliminal, to have analysis support the covert action? As an example of such a conflict of interest, such stresses existed between some analytical components of the intelligence community and supporters of the counterrevolutionaries (contras) who were fighting the Sandinista government in Nicaragua in the 1980s.

Some analysts questioned whether the contras would ever be victorious, which was seen as unsupportive by some advocates of the contras' cause.

The proximate school argued that separating the two functions deprives both analysis and operations of the benefits of a close relationship. Analysts gain a better appreciation of operational goals and realities, which can be factored into their work, as well as a better sense of the value of sources developed in espionage. Operators gain a better appreciation of the analyses they receive, which can be factored into their own planning.

Although critics of the current structure have repeatedly suggested separating analytical and operational components, the proximate school has prevailed. In the mid-1990s, the then-DI and DO entered a partnership that brought together their front offices and various regional offices. This did not entirely improve their working relationship. One of the by-products of the 2002 Iraq WMD national intelligence estimate (NIE) was an effort to give analysts greater insight into DO sources. This was largely a reaction to the agent named CURVE BALL, a human source under German control whose reporting on Iraqi biological weapons proved to be fabricated, unbeknownst to some analysts, who unwittingly continued to use this reporting as part of their supporting intelligence even after the reporting had been recalled. In 2015, DCIA John Brennan (2013–2017) announced a major reorganization of the CIA into a series of regional and topical mission centers that would combine analytic and operational staffs and functions. These mission centers, each headed by an assistant director, have become the loci of all CIA activities, with the DA and DO essentially becoming logistical supports for the mission centers. Thus, the proximate model is still the preferred one, although some observers have raised concerns about this new structure homogenizing the unique cultures and attributes of the DA and the DO.

The Debate Over Covert Action. As discussed in chapter 1, covert action in the United States has always generated some uneasiness among those concerned about its propriety or acceptability as a facet of U.S. policy—secret intervention, perhaps violently, in the affairs of another state. In addition, many debated the propriety of paramilitary operations—the training and equipping of large foreign irregular military units, such as the contras in Nicaragua or the mujahideen in Afghanistan. Other than assassination, paramilitary operations have been among the most controversial aspects of covert action, and they have an uneven record. The vigor of the debate for and against paramilitary operations has varied widely over time. Little discussion occurred before the abortive Bay of Pigs invasion (1961), and afterward there was little discussion until the 1970s, when the Vietnam War fostered a collapse of the bipartisan cold war consensus that had supported an array of measures to counter Soviet expansion. At the same time, a series of revelations about intelligence community misdeeds fostered more skepticism if not opposition to intelligence operations. The debate revived once again during the contras' paramilitary campaign against Nicaragua's government in the mid-1980s. In the aftermath of the terrorist attacks in the United States in 2001, however, broad agreement reemerged on a full range of covert actions—as opposed to a later debate on interrogation techniques and renditions, meaning non-judicial apprehension of terrorists overseas.

Two more recent aspects of this continuing debate over covert action are the use of armed UAVs (unmanned aerial vehicles or drones) to attack terrorists overseas—including U.S. citizens, which has raised questions about propriety and legality, and whether the use of cyberspace as a preemptive or precursor weapon is a military action or a covert action. (Both of these issues are discussed in more detail in chaps. 8 and 12.)

The Continuity of Intelligence Policy. Throughout most of the cold war, no difference existed between Democratic and Republican intelligence policies. The cold war consensus on the need for a continuing policy of containment vis-à-vis the Soviet Union transcended politics until the Vietnam War, when a difference emerged between the two parties that was in many respects more rhetorical than real. For example, both Jimmy Carter (1977–1981) and Ronald Reagan (1981–1989) made intelligence policy an issue in their campaigns for the presidency. Carter, in 1976, lumped together revelations about the CIA and other intelligence agencies' misconduct with Watergate and the Vietnam War; Reagan, in 1980, spoke of restoring the CIA, along with the rest of U.S. national security. Although the ways in which the two presidents supported and used intelligence differed greatly, it would be wrong to suggest that one was anti-intelligence and the other pro-intelligence.

A similar broad continuity of intelligence policy initially emerged over the issue of terrorism. As a candidate, Barack Obama pledged to make a number of changes in U.S. policy toward terrorism and terrorists. Although he took steps to signal a changed direction, such as ordering the eventual closure of the prison at Guantanamo, this proved to be difficult to do. The terrorist detention center remained open as of 2019. The Obama administration also ordered UAV attacks on terrorist targets four times as often as did the George W. Bush administration and continued to authorize programs to gather data from telephones and computer communications. Interestingly, the Obama administration's 2011 counterterrorism strategy noted the continuity between the Bush and Obama administrations in this area. There has been more continuity than change overall, especially as the terrorist threat went from larger attacks to more individual ones. Similarly, the *Worldwide Threat Assessment* presented annually by the DNI has not changed very much from DNI James Clapper to his Trump-appointed successor, Dan Coats (2017–2019).

Heavy Reliance on Technology. Since the creation of the modern intelligence community in the 1940s, the United States has relied heavily on technology as the mainstay of its collection capabilities. A technological response to a problem is not unique to intelligence. It also describes how the United States has waged war, beginning as early as the Civil War in the 1860s. Furthermore, the closed nature of the major intelligence target in the twentieth century—the Soviet Union—required remote technical means to collect information.

The reliance on technology is significant beyond the collection capabilities it engenders because it has had a major effect on the structure of the intelligence community and how it has functioned. Some people maintain that the reliance on technology resulted in an insufficient use of human intelligence collection (espionage). No empirical data are available supporting this view, but this perception has persisted since at least the 1970s. The main argument, which tends to arise when intelligence is perceived as having performed less than optimally, is that human intelligence can collect certain types of information (intentions and plans) that technical collection cannot, although this intelligence can sometimes be obtained via signals intelligence. Little disagreement is heard about the strengths and weaknesses of the various types of collection, but such an assessment does not necessarily support the view that espionage always suffers as compared with technical collection. The persistence of the debate reflects an underlying concern about intelligence collection that has never been adequately addressed—that is, the proper balance (if such balance can be had) between technical and human collection. This debate arose again in the aftermath of the terrorist attacks in 2001. (See chap. 12 for a discussion of the types of intelligence collection required by the war on terrorists.)

Secrecy Versus Openness. The openness that is an inherent part of a representative democratic government clashes with the secrecy required by intelligence operations. No democratic government with a significant intelligence community has spent more time debating and worrying about this conflict than the United States. How open can intelligence be and still be effective? At what point does secrecy pose a threat to democratic values? The issue cannot be settled with finality, but the United States has made an ongoing series of compromises between its values—as a government and as an international leader—and the requirements for some level of intelligence activity as it has continued to explore the boundaries of this issue. In the debates over the use of UAVs and the NSA collection programs, there were frequent calls for more "transparency," which is simply another way of framing this same debate. In October 2015, DNI Clapper released principles for transparency, which he noted were important not only to give more insight into what intelligence does but also to build greater support for intelligence based on this greater insight.

The Role of Oversight. For the first twenty-eight years of its existence, the intelligence community operated with a minimal amount of oversight from Congress. One reason was the cold war consensus. Another was a willingness on the part of Congress to abdicate rigorous oversight. Secrecy was also a factor, which appeared to impose procedural difficulties in handling sensitive issues between the two branches. After 1975, congressional oversight changed suddenly and dramatically, increasing to the point where Congress became a full participant in the intelligence process and a major consumer of intelligence. Since 2002, Congress has also become more of an independent intelligence consumer in its own right, in several cases requesting NIEs on specific topics. Within the larger oversight issue is a second issue: Do the intelligence committees serve well as surrogates for the rest of the Congress, or should this responsibility be shared more broadly?

Managing the Community. The size of U.S. intelligence is a strength, in that it allows for greater breadth and depth across a range of intelligence activities and issues. But the size also poses a challenge when it comes to coordinating the various agencies toward specific goals. From 1947 to 2004, the DCIs (directors of central intelligence) had this responsibility, but they tended to function more as "first among equals" rather than as empowered heads of the community. The DCIs also tended to focus more on their CIA responsibilities, which were the source of most of their bureaucratic clout. The DNI (director of national intelligence) now has this community role, minus the CIA function. A major issue, whether under the DCIs or DNIs, is the fact that all of the intelligence components, with the exception of the CIA, belong to a Cabinet department, diminishing the DNI's ability to give them orders. A succession of staffs have been created to support the DCIs and now the DNIs in their community role, but the effectiveness of these staffs is tied directly to the effectiveness of the DNI. DNI Clapper made "intelligence integration" his major area of emphasis when it came to community management, which can best be described as ongoing efforts to foster unity of purpose and of effort. DNI Coats continued to emphasize intelligence integration in his 2018 mission statement and his 2019 *National Intelligence Strategy*.

MAJOR HISTORICAL DEVELOPMENTS

In addition to the themes that have run through much of the history of the intelligence community, several specific events played pivotal roles in the shaping and functioning of U.S. intelligence.

The Creation of COI and OSS (1941–1942). Until 1941, the United States did not have anything approaching a national intelligence establishment. The important precedents were the COI (Coordinator of Information, 1941) and the OSS (Office of Strategic Services, 1942), both created by President Franklin D. Roosevelt (1933–1945). The COI and then the OSS were headed by William Donovan, who had advocated their creation after two trips to Britain before the United States entered World War II. Donovan was impressed by the more central British government organization and believed that the United States needed to emulate it. Roosevelt gave Donovan much of what he wanted but in such a way as to limit Donovan's authority, especially in his relationship to the military, making OSS part of the newly created Joint Chiefs of Staff in 1942 rather than making it an independent entity.

In addition to being the first steps toward creating a national intelligence capability, the COI and OSS were important for three other reasons. First, both organizations were heavily influenced by British intelligence practices, particularly their emphasis on what is now called covert action—guerrillas, operations with resistance groups behind enemy lines, sabotage, and so on. For Britain this wartime emphasis on operations was the natural result of being one of the few ways the country could strike back at Nazi Germany in Europe until the Allied invasions of Italy and France. These covert actions, which had little effect on the outcome of the war, became the main historical legacy of the OSS.

Second, although OSS operations played only a small role in the Allied victory in World War II, they served as a training ground—both technically and in terms of esprit—for many people who helped establish the postwar intelligence community, particularly the CIA. However, as former DCI Richard Helms, himself an

OSS veteran, points out in his memoirs, most of the OSS veterans had experience in espionage and counterintelligence and not in covert action.

Third, the OSS had a difficult relationship with the U.S. military. The military leadership was suspicious of an intelligence organization operating beyond its control and perhaps competing with organic military intelligence components (that is, military intelligence units subordinated to commanders). The Joint Chiefs of Staff therefore insisted that the OSS become part of its structure, refusing to accept the idea of an independent civilian intelligence organization. Therefore, Donovan and the OSS were made part of the Joint Chiefs structure. Tension between the military and nonmilitary intelligence components has continued, with varying degrees of severity or cooperation. It was evident as recently as 2004, when the Department of Defense (DOD), and its supporters in Congress, successfully resisted efforts to expand the authority of the new director of national intelligence to intelligence agencies within DOD. (See chap. 3 for details.)

Pearl Harbor (1941). Japan's surprise attack in 1941 was a classic intelligence failure. The United States overlooked a variety of indicators; U.S. processes and procedures were deeply flawed, with important pieces of intelligence not being shared across agencies or departments; and mirror imaging blinded U.S. policy makers to the reality of policy decisions in Tokyo. The attack on Pearl Harbor was most important as the guiding purpose of the intelligence community that was established after World War II. The fundamental mission was to prevent a recurrence of a strategic surprise of this magnitude, especially in an age of nuclear-armed missiles.

MAGIC and ULTRA (1941–1945). One of the Allies' major advantages in World War II was their superior signals intelligence, that is, their ability to intercept and decode Axis communications. MAGIC refers to U.S. intercepts of Japanese communications; ULTRA refers to British, and later British-U.S., interceptions of German communications. This wartime experience demonstrated the tremendous importance of this type of intelligence, perhaps the most important type practiced during the war. Also, it helped solidify U.S.-British intelligence cooperation, which continued long after the war. Moreover, in the United States the military, not the OSS, controlled MAGIC and ULTRA. This underscored the friction between the military and the OSS. The military today continues to direct signals intelligence, in NSA. NSA is a DOD agency and is considered a combat support agency, a legal status that gives DOD primacy over intelligence support at certain times. Both the secretary of defense and the DNI have responsibility for NSA.

The National Security Act (1947). The National Security Act gave a legal basis to the intelligence community, as well as to the position of director of central intelligence, and created a CIA under the director. The act signaled the new importance of intelligence in the nascent cold war and also made the intelligence function permanent, a significant change from the previous U.S. practice of reducing the national security apparatus in peacetime. Implicitly, the act made the existence and functioning of the intelligence community a part of the cold war consensus.

Several aspects of the act are worth noting. Although the DCI could be a military officer, the CIA was not placed under military control, nor could a military DCI have command over troops. The CIA was not to have any domestic role or police powers, either. The legislation does not mention any of the activities that came to be most commonly associated with the CIA—espionage, covert action, even analysis. Its stated job, and President Harry S. Truman's (1945–1953) main concern at the time, was to coordinate the intelligence being produced by various agencies.

Finally, the act created an overall structure that included a secretary of defense and the National Security Council (NSC); this structure was remarkably stable for fifty-seven years. Although minor adjustments of roles and functions were made during this period, the 2004 intelligence legislation (see chap. 3 for a fuller discussion of this act) and the establishment of a director of national intelligence brought about the first major revision of the structure created in the 1947 act.

Korea (1950). The unexpected invasion of South Korea by North Korea, which triggered the Korean War, had two major effects on U.S. intelligence. First, the failure to foresee the invasion led DCI Walter Bedell Smith (1950–1953) to make some dramatic changes, including increased emphasis on national intelligence estimates. Second, the Korean War made the cold war global. Having previously been confined to a struggle for dominance in Europe, the cold war spread to Asia and, implicitly, to the rest of the world. This broadened the scope and responsibilities of intelligence.

The Coup in Iran (1953). In 1953, the United States staged a series of popular demonstrations in Iran that overthrew the nationalist government of Premier Mohammad Mossadegh and restored the rule of the shah, who was friendlier to Western interests. The success and ease of this operation made covert action an increasingly attractive tool for U.S. policy makers, especially during the tenure of DCI Allen Dulles (1953–1961) during Dwight D. Eisenhower's administration (1953–1961).

The Guatemala Coup (1954). In 1954, the United States overthrew the leftist government of Guatemalan president Jacobo Arbenz Guzmán because of concern that this government might prove sympathetic to the Soviet Union. The United States provided a clandestine opposition radio station and air support for rebel officers. The Guatemala coup proved that the success in Iran was not unique, thus further elevating the appeal of this type of action for U.S. policy makers.

The Missile Gap (1959–1961). In the late 1950s, concern arose that the apparent Soviet lead in the "race for space," prompted by the launch of the artificial satellite Sputnik in 1957, also indicated a Soviet lead in missile-based strategic weaponry. The main proponents of this argument were Democratic aspirants for the 1960 presidential nomination, including Sens. John F. Kennedy of Massachusetts and Stuart Symington of Missouri. The Eisenhower administration knew, by virtue of the U.S. reconnaissance program, that the accusations about a Soviet lead in strategic missiles were untrue, but the administration did not respond to the charges in an effort to safeguard the sources of the intelligence, especially the fact that U-2 flights were violating Soviet airspace. When Kennedy (1961–1963) took office, his administration learned that the charges were indeed untrue, but the new secretary of defense, Robert S. McNamara (1961–1968), came to believe that intelligence had inflated the Soviet threat to safeguard the defense budget. This was an early example of intelligence becoming a political issue, raised primarily by the party out of power.

The way in which the missile gap is customarily portrayed in intelligence history is incorrect. According to legend, the intelligence community, perhaps for base and selfish motives, overestimated the number of Soviet strategic missiles. But the legend is untrue. The overestimate came largely from political critics of the Eisenhower administration, not the intelligence agencies themselves. Not only did these critics overestimate the number of strategic-range Soviet missiles, but the intelligence community also underestimated the number of medium- and intermediate-range missiles that the Soviets were building to cover their main theater of concern, Europe. McNamara's distrust of what he perceived as self-serving Air Force parochialism moved him to create the Defense Intelligence Agency.

This use of intelligence for political purposes also underscored the problem of secrecy, in that President Eisenhower did not believe he was able to reveal the true state of the strategic missile balance, which he knew. He did not want to be asked how he knew, which might have led to a discussion of the U-2 program, in which manned aircraft equipped with cameras penetrated deep into Soviet territory in violation of international law. U-2 flights over the Soviet Union continued until May 1960, when Francis Gary Powers, on contract with the CIA, was shot down over Sverdlovsk. Powers survived and was put on trial. Eisenhower was initially reluctant to admit responsibility for the overflights, although he eventually did, placing the blame on the Soviet Union for their bellicosity and secrecy. (The Soviet Union knew about the U-2 flights and also knew the true state of the strategic balance, as the size of U.S. forces was not classified.)

The Bay of Pigs (1961). The Eisenhower administration planned an operation in which Cuban exiles trained by the CIA would invade Cuba and force leader Fidel Castro from power. The operation was not launched until Kennedy had assumed the presidency, and he took steps to limit overt U.S. involvement to preserve the fiction that the Bay of Pigs invasion was a Cubans-only exercise. The abysmal failure of the invasion showed the limits of large-scale paramilitary operations in terms of their effectiveness and of the United States's ability to mask its role in them. It was a severe setback for the Kennedy administration and for the CIA, several of whose top leaders—including DCI Allen Dulles—were retired as a result, as were all of the members of the Joint Chiefs of Staff when their terms expired.

The Cuban Missile Crisis (1962). Although now widely interpreted as a success, the confrontation with the Soviet Union over its planned deployment of medium- and intermediate-range missiles in Cuba was initially a failure in terms of intelligence analysis. All analysts, with the notable exception of DCI John McCone (1961–1965), had argued that Soviet premier Nikita Khrushchev would not be so bold or rash as to place missiles in Cuba. Analysts also assumed that no Soviet tactical nuclear missiles were in Cuba and that local Soviet commanders did not have authority to use nuclear weapons without first asking Moscow—both of which turned out to be false, although this was not known until 1992. The missile crisis was a success in that U.S. intelligence discovered the missile sites before they were completed, giving President Kennedy sufficient time to deal with the situation without resorting to force. U.S. intelligence was also able to give Kennedy firm assessments of Soviet strategic and conventional force capabilities, which bolstered his ability to make difficult decisions. It was an excellent example of different types of intelligence collection working together to support one another and to provide tips to other potential collection opportunities. The intelligence community's performance in this instance went a long way toward rehabilitating its reputation after the failure of the Bay of Pigs.

The Vietnam War (1964–1975). The war in Vietnam had three important effects on U.S. intelligence. First, during the war concerns grew that frustrated policy makers were politicizing intelligence to be supportive of policy. The Tet offensive in 1968 is a case in point. U.S. intelligence picked up Viet Cong preparations for a large-scale offensive in South Vietnam. President Johnson had two unpalatable choices. He could prepare the public for the event, but then face being asked how this large-scale enemy attack was possible if the United States was winning the war. Or he could attempt to ride out the attack, confident that it would be defeated. Johnson took the second choice. The Viet Cong were defeated militarily in Tet after some bitter and costly fighting, but the attack and the scale of military operations that the United States undertook to defeat them turned a successful intelligence warning and a military victory into a major political defeat. Many people wrongly assumed that the attack was a surprise.

Second, often-heated debates on the progress of the war took place between military and nonmilitary intelligence analysts. This was seen most sharply in the order of battle debate, which centered on how many enemy units were in the field. Military leaders believed that intelligence analysis (primarily from the CIA) was not accurately reporting the progress being made on the battlefield. The argument on the enemy order of battle centered on CIA analysis that showed more enemy units than the military believed to be operating. Or, to put it conversely, if the United States was making the progress being reported by the military, how could the enemy have so many units in the field? Third, the more long-lasting and most important result of the war was to undercut severely the cold war consensus under which intelligence operated.

The ABM Treaty and SALT I Accord (1972). The Nixon administration negotiated limits on antiballistic missiles (ABMs) and strategic nuclear delivery systems (the land-based and submarine-based missile launchers and aircraft, not the weapons on them) with the Soviet Union. These initial strategic arms control agreements—the ABM treaty and the strategic arms limitation talks (SALT I) accord—explicitly recognized and legitimized the use of **national technical means**, or NTM (that is, a variety of satellites and other technical collectors), by both parties to collect needed intelligence, and they prohibited overt interference with NTM. Furthermore, these agreements created the new issue of **verification**—the ability to ascertain whether treaty obligations were being met. (**Monitoring**, or keeping track of Soviet activities, had been under way since the inception of the intelligence community, even before arms control. Verification consists of policy judgments or evaluations based on monitoring.) U.S. intelligence was central to these activities, with new accusations by arms control advocates and opponents that intelligence was being politicized. Those concerned that the Soviets were cheating held that cheating was either being undetected or ignored. Arms control advocates argued that the Soviets were not cheating or, if they were, the cheating was minimal and therefore inconsequential, regardless of the terms of the agreements, and they maintained that some cheating was preferable to unchecked strategic competition. Either way, the intelligence community found itself to be a fundamental part of the debate.

Intelligence Investigations (1975–1976). In the wake of revelations late in 1974 that the CIA had violated its charter by spying on U.S. citizens, a series of investigations examined the entire intelligence community. A panel chaired by Vice President Nelson A. Rockefeller concluded that violations of law had occurred. Investigations by House and Senate special committees went deeper, discovering a much wider range of abuses.

Coming so soon after the Watergate scandal (which involved political sabotage and criminal cover-ups and culminated in the resignation of President Nixon in 1974) and the loss of the Vietnam War, these intelligence hearings further undermined the public's faith in government institutions, in particular the intelligence community, which had been largely sacrosanct. Since these investigations, intelligence has never regained the latitude it once enjoyed and has had to learn to operate with much more openness and scrutiny. Also, Congress faced the fact of its own lax oversight. Both the Senate and the House created permanent intelligence oversight committees, which have taken on much more vigorous oversight of intelligence and, as mentioned earlier in the chapter, are now major taskers of intelligence themselves.

Iran (1979). In 1979, Ayatollah Ruhollah Khomeini's revolution forced the shah of Iran from his throne and into exile. U.S. intelligence, in part because of policy decisions made by several administrations that severely limited collection in Iran, was largely blind to the growing likelihood of this turn of events. Successive administrations had restricted U.S. contacts with opposition groups lest the shah would be offended. In addition to these limits placed on collection, some intelligence analysts failed to grasp the severity of the threat to the shah once public demonstrations began. The intelligence community took much of the blame for the result despite the restrictions within which it had been working. Some people even saw the shah's fall as the inevitable result of the 1953 coup that had restored him to power.

One ramification of the shah's fall was the closure of two intelligence collection sites in northern Iran that the United States used to monitor Soviet missile tests, thus impairing the ability to monitor the SALT I agreement and the SALT II agreement then under negotiation.

Iran-Contra (1986–1987). The Reagan administration used proceeds from missile sales to Iran (which not only contradicted the administration's own policy of not dealing with terrorists but also violated the law) to sustain the contras in Nicaragua fighting against the pro-Soviet Sandinista government—despite congressional restrictions on such aid. The Iran-contra affair provoked a constitutional crisis and congressional investigations. The affair highlighted a series of problems, including the limits of oversight in both the executive branch and Congress, the ability of executive officials to ignore Congress's intent, and the disaster that can result when two distinct and disparate covert actions become intertwined. The affair also undid much of President Reagan's efforts to rebuild and restore intelligence capabilities.

The Fall of the Soviet Union (1989–1991). Beginning with the collapse of the Soviet satellite empire in 1989 and culminating in the dissolution of the Soviet Union itself in 1991, the United States witnessed the triumph of its long-held policy of containment, first postulated by U.S. diplomat George Kennan in 1946–1947 as a way to deal with the Soviet menace. The collapse was so swift and so stunning that few can be said to have anticipated it.

Critics of the intelligence community argued that the inability to see the Soviet collapse coming was the ultimate intelligence failure, given the centrality of the Soviet Union as an intelligence community issue. Some people even felt that this failure justified radically reducing and altering the intelligence community. Defenders of U.S. intelligence argued that the community had made known much of the inner rot that led to the Soviet collapse.

In the aftermath of the cold war there were several major studies that looked at how U.S. intelligence was organized and how it functioned, with a view to possible changes, although very few major changes resulted until after the 2001 terrorist attacks and Iraq WMD.

This debate has not ended. Significant questions remain not only about U.S. intelligence capabilities but also about intelligence in general and what can reasonably be expected from it. (See chap. 11 for a detailed discussion.)

The Ames (1994) and Hanssen Spy Cases (2001). The arrest and conviction of Aldrich Ames, a CIA employee, on charges of spying for the Soviet Union and for post-Soviet Russia for almost ten years shook U.S. intelligence. Espionage scandals had broken before. For example, in the "year of the spy" (1985), several cases came to light—the Walker family sold Navy communications data to the Soviet Union, Ronald Pelton compromised NSA programs to the Soviet Union, and Larry Wu-tai Chin turned out to be a sleeper agent put in place in the CIA by China.

Ames's unsuspected treachery was, in many respects, more searing. Despite the end of the cold war, Russian espionage against the United States had continued. Ames's career revealed significant shortcomings in CIA personnel practices (he was a marginal officer with a well-known alcohol problem), in CIA counterespionage and counterintelligence, and in CIA-FBI liaison to deal with these issues. The spy scandal also revealed deficiencies in how the executive branch shared information bearing on intelligence matters with Congress.

The arrest in 2001 of FBI agent Robert Hanssen on charges of espionage underscored some of the concerns that first arose in the Ames case and added new ones. Hanssen and Ames apparently began their espionage activities at approximately the same time, but Hanssen went undetected for much longer. It was initially thought that Hanssen's expertise in counterintelligence gave him advantages in escaping detection, but subsequent investigations revealed a great deal of laxness at the FBI that was crucial to Hanssen's activities. Hanssen, like Ames, spied for both the Soviet Union and post-Soviet Russia. Hanssen's espionage also meant that the damage assessment done after Ames was arrested would have to be revised, as both men had access to some of the same information. Finally, the Hanssen case was a severe black eye for the FBI, which had been so critical of the CIA's failure to detect Ames. FBI investigators had focused on a CIA officer, Brian Kelley, insisting incorrectly until very late in the investigation that Kelley was the spy.

In addition to the internal problems that both scandals revealed, the two cases served notice that espionage among the great powers continued despite the end of the cold war. Some people found this offensive, in terms of either Russian or U.S. activity. Others accepted it as an unsurprising and normal state of affairs.

The Terrorist Attacks and the War on Terrorists (2001–). The terrorist attacks in the United States in September 2001 were important for several reasons. First, although al Qaeda leader Osama bin Laden's enmity and capabilities were known, the nature of these specific attacks had not been anticipated. Some critics called for the resignation of DCI George Tenet, but President George W. Bush supported him. Congress, meanwhile, began a broad investigation into the performance of the intelligence community. Second, in the immediate aftermath of the attacks, widespread political support emerged for a range of intelligence actions to combat terrorists, including calls to lift the ban on assassinations and to increase the use of human intelligence. The first major legislative response to the attacks, the USA PATRIOT Act of 2001, allowed greater latitude in some domestic intelligence and law enforcement collection and took steps to improve coordination between these two areas. In 2004, in the aftermath of a second investigation (and also prompted by the failure to find WMD in Iraq that intelligence had assessed were there), legislation was passed to revamp the command structure of the intelligence community. (See chap. 3 for details.) Third, in the first phase of combat operations against terrorists, dramatic new developments took place in intelligence collection capabilities, particularly the use of UAVs and more real-time intelligence support for U.S. combat forces. (See chap. 5 for details.) The war on terrorists also resulted in an expansion of some CIA and NSA authorities. CIA captured suspected terrorists overseas and then **rendered** (delivered) them to a third country for incarceration and interrogation. This activity became controversial as some observers questioned the basis on which people were rendered and the conditions to which they were subjected in these third nations, especially during interrogations. The use of certain techniques became political issues during the 2008 presidential election although, as noted earlier, President Obama's overall policy toward terrorists was not dramatically different from that of President Bush. Under authority of the USA PATRIOT Act, NSA greatly expanded its collection of telephone and Internet data, in most cases the metadata (location of calls, time) but not the contents. This program was leaked in 2013 and also became controversial as critics held that NSA had exceeded its legislative authority and failed to keep Congress informed. (See later in this chapter.)

By 2004, two intensive investigations of U.S. intelligence performance prior to the 2001 terrorist attacks had taken place. Although both resulting reports noted a number of flaws, neither was able to point up the intelligence that could have led to a precise understanding of al Qaeda's plans. The tactical intelligence for such a conclusion (as opposed to strategic intelligence suggesting the nature and depth of al Qaeda's hostility) did not exist.

As the terrorist threat seemed to change in 2009 from large-scale attacks to smaller, individual attempts, new concerns arose about the intelligence community's ability to prevent these threats. Some of these were domestic in origin and appeared to call more on domestic police capabilities than national intelligence capabilities. The May 2011 operation that resulted in the death of bin Laden helped restore confidence in U.S. intelligence. The operation was also a good example of the use of multiple types of intelligence collection (human, signals, imagery), painstaking analysis over many years, and intelligence sharing both within the intelligence community and with the military.

By 2013, the decade-plus war against terrorists had also begun to cause new strains. As noted above (and discussed in more detail in chap. 8), the continued use of UAVs was subject to increased debate for two reasons: the concern that those being targeted were of lesser importance and that the ongoing campaign was turning people against the United States; and the more controversial use of UAVs to target and kill U.S. citizens working with terrorists. The revelation of NSA programs to mine communications data raised concerns among some observers about the balance between security and liberty and also the degree of oversight being conducted on such programs. Over a decade of concentration on counterterrorism and counterinsurgency had some larger effects on the analytic community, especially for the CIA, which some people felt had become too tactical and too militarized. (See chap. 6.)

Finally, the rise of ISIL (also known as ISIS or Daesh) further complicated the terrorism war as ISIL had pretentions to being a state, controlling large amounts of territory and people. It demonstrated, in a series of attacks in November 2015 and March 2016, that it had wide geographic reach as a terrorist organization. However, a U.S.-backed offensive helped roll back ISIL, greatly reducing the territory the terrorists controlled. This led to new concerns, however, including the return of ISIL fighters to their homelands in Europe and elsewhere, where they might conduct terrorist activities.

Intelligence on Iraq (2003–2008). The George W. Bush administration was convinced, as was most of the international community, that Iraqi leader Saddam Hussein harbored weapons of mass destruction, despite his agreement at the end of the 1991 Persian Gulf War to dispose of them and to submit to international inspections. (The fall 2002 debate at the United Nations was over the best way to determine if Iraq held these weapons and how best to get rid of them—not over whether or not Iraq had them.) However, more than two years after the onset of the military conflict, the WMD had not been found. As a result, the two main issues that arose were how the intelligence could come to such an important conclusion that proved to be erroneous and how the intelligence was used by policy makers. Coupled with the conclusions drawn from the two investigations of the 2001 terrorist attacks, intelligence performance in Iraq led to irresistible calls to restructure the intelligence community. The Senate Intelligence Committee found that groupthink was a major problem in the Iraq analysis, along with a failure to examine previously held premises. At the same time, the committee found no evidence that the intelligence had been politicized. The WMD Commission (formally the Commission on the Intelligence Capabilities of the United States Regarding Weapons of Mass Destruction), established by President George W. Bush, came to the same conclusion regarding politicization but was critical about how the intelligence community handled both collection and analysis on Iraq WMD and on other issues.

In addition to intelligence that may have provided a *casus belli* (justification for the acts of war), subsequent intelligence on Iraq continued to be controversial. As Iraq descended into a bloody insurgency, former intelligence officials pointed out prewar estimates that suggested such a possible outcome. In 2007, at the request of Congress, the intelligence community produced an estimate on the likely course of events in Iraq and possible indicators of success or failure. The **key judgments** of this estimate were published in unclassified form, adding additional fuel to the political debate over Iraq.

As terrible as the 2001 terrorist attacks were, the initial Iraq WMD estimate points to much more fundamental questions for U.S. intelligence. The analytical failure in Iraq likely will be a burden for U.S. intelligence for many years to come. Subsequent analyses also seemed to point to increased politicization of intelligence, not by those who wrote it but by those in the executive branch and in Congress seeking to gain political advantage by using unclassified versions of intelligence.

The Iraq analytical controversy continued to serve as a touchstone for future intelligence analyses. In 2007, DNI McConnell released unclassified key judgments of an NIE on Iran's nuclear weapons program, which reversed its earlier (2005) findings and concluded that the weapons aspects of the program had stopped in 2003. This immediately became controversial not only because of the judgments themselves but also as some observers wondered whether this reflected either "lessons learned" from Iraq or some means of compensating for earlier errant estimates, a curious view that betrayed significant misunderstandings of the estimative process. In 2013, the debate over whether to attack Syria for chemical weapons (CW) use again raised issues about the accuracy of current WMD intelligence, given the past problem in Iraq.

Intelligence Reorganization (2004–2005). Three factors contributed to the 2004 passage of legislation reorganizing the intelligence community: (1) reaction to the 2001 terrorist attack; (2) the subsequent 2004 report of the National Commission on Terrorist Attacks upon the United States, more popularly known as the 9/11 Commission; and (3) the absence of Iraq WMD, despite intelligence community estimates that indicated otherwise. Congress replaced the DCI with a DNI who would oversee and coordinate intelligence but who would be divorced from a base in any intelligence agency. This was the first major restructuring of U.S. intelligence since the 1947 act. (See chap. 3 for details.) In March 2005, the WMD Commission issued its report, recommending additional changes in intelligence structure and in the management of analysis and collection.

In 2006, CIA director Porter Goss resigned. By 2007, the first DNI, John Negroponte, had stepped down to return to the State Department after less than two years in the DNI position. Retired vice admiral Mike McConnell replaced Negroponte. McConnell resigned at the end of the George W. Bush administration and was replaced by retired admiral Dennis Blair, the third DNI in less than four years. Blair stepped down in 2010, after a little more than a year in the job. His successor, retired general James Clapper, thus became the fourth DNI in just over five years. Several senior jobs on the DNI's staff proved difficult to fill. Many observers took such staffing problems as evidence that the new structure was not working as smoothly as proponents had hoped. Clapper's six and a half years as DNI offered some stability, but some of the fundamental questions about the nature of the DNI position and its relative authority remain.

The incoming Trump administration, in 2017, appeared to prefer not to appoint a DNI and to return his authorities to the DCIA. However, it was pointed out that this would require legislation, and so a new DNI was named, former senator and ambassador to Germany Dan Coats.

The Manning and Snowden Leaks. In January 2010, then-Pvt. Bradley Manning downloaded some 700,000 documents from classified systems, which he shared with WikiLeaks, a website devoted to publishing classified information. In June 2013, newspapers in the United States and Britain began to publish details of NSA programs to collect metadata from the Internet and telephone lines in the United States and worldwide leaked to them by Edward Snowden, a contract employee working for NSA. Snowden also leaked a great deal of other highly classified intelligence that had nothing to do with those programs. The two leaks were different in content: Manning's material consisted, in part, of many diplomatic cables; Snowden's material concerned ongoing intelligence collection programs. The Snowden leaks are, arguably, the worst leaks in U.S. history in terms of both content and effects. Both leaks engendered controversies. Among these have been the following: how individuals could get access to so much material and remove them from secure areas; the adequacy of U.S. laws to deal with leakers and/or spies; the future of the emphasis in U.S. intelligence on sharing as much intelligence internally as possible; the effects of the leaks on U.S. diplomatic relations and intelligence capabilities; and, in the case of the NSA leaks, whether NSA had overstepped its authorities and the adequacy of both executive and legislative oversight. Manning was found guilty under the Espionage Act and sentenced to thirty-five years in prison. In January 2017, President Obama commuted Manning's sentence to seven years; Manning was released in May 2017. Snowden had been granted temporary asylum in Russia. In January 2014, in a speech addressing the NSA programs that had been revealed, President Obama largely defended these programs, stating that they had been managed lawfully and had not purposely abused their authorities.

There has been a veritable deluge of leaks in the years since Manning and Snowden, raising serious questions about intelligence community security. There has also been an increase in prosecutions for leaks. The Obama administration prosecuted ten people for leaking, which is the most by any administration. Some of these leaks inevitably involved journalists, which in turn raises questions about freedom of the press.

Russian Hacking and the 2016 Election. Press reports in 2016 indicated concern about possible efforts by Russia to influence the pending U.S. presidential election. In January 2017, the intelligence community briefed President-elect Trump and released an assessment coordinated by the CIA, the FBI, and NSA that found that Russian president Vladimir Putin had ordered "an influence campaign" designed to support Trump over Hillary Clinton. The report made no assessment as to the effect of this Russian campaign.

Trump initially disputed the report, seeing it as questioning the legitimacy of his election. However, the issue did not go away and, in fact, became more complex as allegations surfaced about possible collusion between members of the Trump campaign and Russian officials. The Justice Department appointed former FBI director Robert Mueller as special counsel to investigate. Mueller's investigation quickly became the subject of extremely rancorous partisan debate in Congress, especially in the House Intelligence Committee. Mueller's report found no collusion between the Trump campaign and Russia but affirmed Russian interference in the election.

Trump also began his term having made disparaging remarks about U.S. intelligence agencies, marking what has been the most difficult transition of a new administration with the intelligence community. This rift became even more noticeable after Trump's July 2018 Helsinki meeting with Putin, in which Trump accepted Putin's denials of interference rather than intelligence community assessments. Trump tried to clarify his remarks after a political firestorm erupted, but this did not undo the damage. Instead, his equivocation kept the issue alive. In November 2018, Trump publicly dismissed findings by the CIA of the culpability of Saudi crown prince Mohammed bin Sultan in the murder of U.S.-based Saudi journalist Jamal Khashoggi in the Saudi consulate in Istanbul.

One other issue related to the 2016 election and Russia is the question of what the Obama administration did or did not do in light of the intelligence that it had. Obama administration officials have stated that Obama was reluctant to take more forceful overt action as he did not want to be seen as possibly intervening in the election in favor of Clinton.

The Legal Framework of Intelligence. U.S. intelligence operates within a legal framework that has evolved over time. Here are some of the key laws and orders:

- **The Constitution of the United States of America.** The Constitution sets forth the roles and responsibilities of the three branches of government. The key aspects in terms of intelligence are Congress's power to create departments and agencies, its power of the purse, and the basis for congressional oversight; the president's role as commander-in-chief and his obligation to defend the nation; and the judiciary's role in determining the constitutionality of laws and orders. In addition, the Bill of Rights (Amendments I–X) establishes citizens' rights that have to be taken into account in intelligence activities, including freedom of speech and the press (First Amendment); no search and seizure of personal possessions without a specific warrant showing cause (Fourth Amendment); no deprivation of life or liberty without due process of law (Fifth Amendment); and no cruel or unusual punishments (Eighth Amendment).

- **The Espionage Act, 1917.** Enacted to safeguard U.S. military operations and the operation of the draft during World War I, this act has become the main basis for prosecuting leaks of classified material.

- **The National Security Act, 1947.** This act created the modern U.S. national security apparatus—the National Security Council (NSC); a secretary of defense and the Joint Chiefs of Staff (JCS); a director of central intelligence (DCI) under the NSC, responsible for foreign intelligence; and the CIA under the DCI. It also set forth, in vague terms, a CIA charter that included no police or subpoena power but the ability to "perform such other functions" as directed.

- **S. Res. 400, 1976.** This resolution set forth the charter of the Senate Select Committee on Intelligence.

- **Foreign Intelligence Surveillance Act, 1978.** This act created procedures to conduct physical or electronic surveillance for foreign intelligence purposes, typically requiring a warrant, although there are special and limited conditions for warrantless surveillance. It also created the Foreign Intelligence Surveillance Court (FISC) to oversee this process.

- **Intelligence Oversight Act, 1980.** This act made congressional oversight of intelligence explicit. This act requires that Congress be kept "fully and currently informed" about intelligence activities, including "any significant anticipated activity."

- **Classified Intelligence Procedures Act, 1980.** This act limits the ability of defendants in criminal cases who are in possession of classified information to use that as a means of circumventing prosecution, sometimes called "graymail," by allowing judges to hear the material without divulging it to the jury.

- **Intelligence Identities Protection Act, 1982.** This act makes it a federal crime for those with access to classified information or those who systematically seek to identify and expose covert agents to intentionally reveal the identity of a U.S. intelligence agent.

- **USA PATRIOT Act, 2001.** In reaction to the 9/11 attacks, Congress enacted a series of acts to enhance the ability of intelligence to counter terrorism, including enhanced surveillance of both citizens and noncitizens, so-called "roving wiretaps," improved intelligence sharing, and so on. The act was extended and revised several times.

- **Intelligence Reform and Terrorism Prevention Act (IRTPA), 2004.** The first major revision of U.S. intelligence structure since the 1947 act, this act created a director of national intelligence (DNI) as the head of U.S. intelligence, overseeing "national intelligence," which means foreign, domestic, and homeland intelligence. The DNI is separate from any intelligence agency. The head of the CIA is redesignated the director of the CIA (DCIA).

- **USA FREEDOM Act, 2015.** This act revised some of the collection programs created under the USA PATRIOT Act, ending the bulk collection program (Sec. 215). It also provides for the publication (with redactions, if necessary) of significant FISC decisions.

- **Executive Order 12333, 1981; amended 2004 and 2008–United States Intelligence Activities.** First promulgated by President Reagan, EO 12333 sets out the roles and responsibilities of U.S. intelligence writ large and by specific agencies, as well as rules for the conduct of intelligence activities so as to protect civil liberties.

- **Executive Order 13526, 2009–Classified National Security Information.** This is the current executive order regarding the classification, safeguarding, and declassification of national security information.

- **Intelligence Community Directives (ICDs).** The DNI issues directives establishing policies for the intelligence community. These can be found at https://www.dni.gov/index.php/what-we-do/ic-related-menus/ic-related-links/intelligence-community-directives. These include the following:
  - **ICD 107:** Civil Liberties and Privacy
  - **ICD 112:** Congressional Notification
  - **ICD 116:** Intelligence Planning, Programming, Budgeting, and Evaluation System
  - **ICD 120:** IC Whistleblower Protection
  - **ICD 203:** Analytic Standards
  - **ICD 304:** Human Intelligence
  - **ICD 403:** Foreign Disclosure and Release of Classified National Intelligence
  - **ICD 700:** Protection of National Intelligence
  - **ICD 701:** Unauthorized Disclosures of Classified National Security Information
  - **ICD 703:** Protection of Classified National Intelligence, Including SCI

KEY TERMS

competitive analysis 15
Five Eyes 11
groupthink 15
key judgments 29
monitoring 25

national intelligence 12
national technical means 24
render 27
verification 25

FURTHER READINGS

Most histories of U.S. intelligence tend to be CIA-centric, and these suggested readings are no exception. Nonetheless, they still offer some of the best discussions of the themes and events reviewed in this chapter.

Ambrose, Stephen E., with Richard H. Immerman. *Ike's Spies: Eisenhower and the Espionage Establishment.* Garden City, N.Y.: Doubleday, 1981.

Best, Richard A., Jr. "Intelligence and U.S. National Security Policy," *International Journal of Intelligence and Counterintelligence* 28 (fall 2015): 449–467.

Brugioni, Dino A. *Eyeball to Eyeball: The Inside Story of the Cuban Missile Crisis.* Ed. Robert F. McCort. New York: Random House, 1990.

———. *Eyes in the Sky: Eisenhower, the CIA and Cold War Aerial Espionage.* Annapolis, Md.: Naval Institute Press, 2010.

Colby, William E., and Peter Forbath. *Honorable Men: My Life in the CIA.* New York: Simon and Schuster, 1978.

Draper, Theodore. *A Very Thin Line: The Iran-Contra Affair.* New York: Hill and Wang, 1991.

Garthoff, Douglas J. *Directors of Central Intelligence as Leaders of the U.S. Intelligence Community 1946–2005.* Washington, D.C.: Center for the Study of Intelligence, CIA, 2005.

Gates, Robert M. *From the Shadows.* New York: Simon and Schuster, 1996.

Helms, Richard M. *A Look Over My Shoulder: A Life in the Central Intelligence Agency.* New York: Random House, 2003.

Herman, Michael, J. Kenneth McDonald, and Vojtech Mastny. *Did Intelligence Matter in the Cold War?* Oslo: Norwegian Institute for Defence Studies, 2006.

Hersh, Seymour. "Huge CIA Operations Reported in U.S. Against Anti-War Forces, Other Dissidents in Nixon Years." *New York Times*, December 22, 1974, 1.

Houston, Lawrence R. "The CIA's Legislative Base." *International Journal of Intelligence and Counterintelligence* 5 (winter 1991–1992): 411–415.

Jameson, W. George. "Intelligence and the Law: Introduction to the Legal and Policy Framework Governing Intelligence Community Counterterrorism Efforts." In *The Law of Counterterrorism.* Ed. Lynne K. Zusman. Washington, D.C.: American Bar Association Publishing, 2011.

Jeffreys-Jones, Rhodri. *The CIA and American Democracy.* New Haven, Conn.: Yale University Press, 1989.

Lowenthal, Mark M. *U.S. Intelligence: Evolution and Anatomy.* 2d ed. Westport, Conn.: Praeger, 1992.

Montague, Ludwell Lee. *General Walter Bedell Smith as Director of Central Intelligence: October 1950– February 1953.* University Park: Pennsylvania State University Press, 1992.

Moynihan, Daniel Patrick. *Secrecy: The American Experience.* New Haven, Conn.: Yale University Press, 1998.

Persico, Joseph. *Casey: From the OSS to the CIA.* New York: Viking, 1990.

Pillar, Paul. *Intelligence and U.S. Foreign Policy: Iraq, 9/11 and Misguided Reform.* New York: Columbia University Press, 2011.

Powers, Thomas. *The Man Who Kept the Secrets: Richard Helms and the CIA.* New York: Knopf, 1979.

Prados, John. Lost Crusader: *The Secret Wars of CIA Director William Colby.* New York: Oxford University Press, 2003.

Ranelagh, John. *The Rise and Decline of the CIA.* New York: Touchstone, 1987.

Rhodes, Jill D., ed. *National Security Law: Fifty Years of Transformation.* Washington, D.C.: ABA Publishing, 2012.

Tenet, George. *At the Center of the Storm: My Years at the CIA.* New York: HarperCollins, 2007.

Troy, Thomas F. *Donovan and the CIA: A History of the Establishment of the Central Intelligence Agency.* Frederick, Md.: University Publications of America, 1981.

Turner, Michael. "A Distinctive U.S. Intelligence Identity." *International Journal of Intelligence and Counterintelligence* 17 (summer 2004): 42–61.

U.S. Department of Justice. Report on the Investigation Into Russian Interference in the 2016 Presidential Election. Washington, D.C.: Author, March 2019.

U.S. Senate. Select Committee to Study Governmental Operations with Respect to Intelligence Activities [Church Committee]. Final Report. Book IV: Supplementary Detailed Staff Reports on Foreign and Military Intelligence. 94th Cong., 2d sess., 1976. (Also known as the Karalekas report, after its author, Anne Karalekas.)

Warner, Michael. "The Rise of the U.S. Intelligence System, 1917–1977." In *The Oxford Handbook of National Security Intelligence.* Ed. Loch Johnson. Oxford, U.K.: Oxford University Press, 2010.

Wohlstetter, Roberta. *Pearl Harbor: Warning and Decision.* Stanford, Calif.: Stanford University Press, 1962.

Wyden, Peter. *Bay of Pigs: The Untold Story.* New York: Simon and Schuster, 1979.

CHAPTER THREE

THE U.S. INTELLIGENCE COMMUNITY

Although various agencies had been added to the intelligence community over the years, the basic structure had been remarkably stable since its establishment in the National Security Act of 1947. As discussed in the previous chapter, this changed in the aftermath of the September 11, 2001, terrorist attacks. The National Commission on Terrorist Attacks upon the United States, more popularly known as the 9/11 Commission, made a series of recommendations in its 2004 report to restructure the intelligence community. Aided by a savvy public relations effort by the commission, its staff, and some of the September 11 families, many commission recommendations were enacted after a relatively brief debate and intense bargaining among members of Congress and the George W. Bush administration.

The major change made by the Intelligence Reform and Terrorism Prevention Act (IRTPA) of 2004 was the creation of a director of national intelligence (DNI), who supplanted the director of central intelligence (DCI) as the senior intelligence official, head of the intelligence community, and principal intelligence adviser to the president and the National Security Council (NSC). Previously, U.S. practice had divided intelligence into two types: foreign and domestic. The DCI had been responsible for foreign intelligence—or, as it was sometimes called, national foreign intelligence—to distinguish it from the more narrow defense-related intelligence. The IRTPA redefines the term "intelligence." Now there is only national intelligence, which has three subsets: foreign, domestic, and homeland security. Thus, the DNI has broader responsibilities than did the DCI for aspects of domestic intelligence. Much of the impetus behind the act was the concern that agencies did not share intelligence well, especially across the foreign-domestic intelligence divide. Therefore, the DNI is to have access to all intelligence and is responsible for ensuring that it is disseminated as needed across the intelligence community. The DNI's ability to do this has been an area of recurring concern. The DNI also has legal responsibility for the protection of intelligence sources and methods.

Unlike the DCI, the DNI is not directly connected to any intelligence agency but oversees them all. The DNI does this through a large staff, the size of which (approximately 1,700 in 2018, including the staff of the National Counterterrorism Center, or NCTC) has been a source of criticism. Some 40 percent of the Office of the Director of National Intelligence (ODNI) staff are on rotation from other agencies. The head of the Central Intelligence Agency (CIA) is now the director of the CIA, or DCIA. In addition to the DNI's staff, the DNI controls NCTC, the National Counterproliferation Center (NCPC), the National Intelligence Council (NIC), the National Counterintelligence and Security Center (NCSC; see chap. 7 for details), and the Cyber Threat Intelligence Integration Center (CTIIC; discussed later).

In short, the intelligence community entered a new era, with major new offices and relationships. How well various offices work and whether they achieve the desired goals is still not entirely evident. As most people in government realize and as some academics fail to appreciate, personalities matter a great deal. The early years of the DNI were marked by a certain degree of instability, with four DNIs serving between 2005 and 2010. This constant turnover in the top job, as well as the repeated difficulty in filling the principal deputy DNI position, suggested that the DNI had not yet found firm footing in the intelligence community. Some observers believe that the problems encountered in finding suitable candidates for these jobs (including the first DNI nomination) reflected the inherent difficulty of the jobs themselves and the bureaucratic struggles they faced. Lt. Gen. James Clapper (USAF, ret.) became the fourth DNI in 2010 and brought stability to the position, holding the post until early 2017, longer than all of his predecessors combined.

Clapper's nomination as DNI led some in Congress and some observers to raise concerns about the influence of the military in the intelligence community. Two of his three predecessors were retired flag officers (Vice Adm. Mike McConnell, 2007–2009, and Adm. Dennis Blair, 2009–2010), as was the first principal deputy DNI (Gen. Michael Hayden). Although there had also been several DCIs and deputy DCIs who were military officers, they never served simultaneously, nor have the military DNIs and their principal deputies. During the years in which there was a DCI and two deputy DCIs (one for the CIA, one for the intelligence community, 1996–2005), the law stated that only one of the three could be a military officer, meaning active duty or retired within the previous ten years. Clapper overcame Senate concerns and was confirmed. The fifth DNI, Dan Coats (2017–2019), is a former senator and ambassador to Germany.

One of the issues facing any DNI is the continuing disparity between responsibilities for the intelligence community and authority over the various agencies, a problem that existed under the DCI as well. The first DNI, Ambassador John Negroponte (2005–2007), did not test his authority (especially vis-à-vis the secretary of defense) to a great extent. (For a more extensive discussion of the state of intelligence reform, see chap. 14.) Negroponte spent more time giving general direction to the intelligence community, publishing a *National Intelligence Strategy* in October 2005 and other strategic plans. This was understandable, to some degree, given that Negroponte had to get the new organization started and on a firm footing and encountered hostility from both the CIA and the Department of Defense (DOD). By contrast, DNI Blair engaged in a series of disputes, largely with DCIA Leon Panetta (2009–2011), that served to undermine Blair's standing with the Obama administration. The disputes apparently centered on the relationship of the DNI and the Directorate of Operations (DO; at the time, called the National Clandestine Service), the defining component of the CIA. Blair asserted his right to name, on occasion, the chief of station (COS) in certain countries. The COS is the senior U.S. intelligence representative in a given country and in the vast majority of cases is a CIA officer. But the COS is also, technically, the DNI's representative in that country, thus Blair's assertion that he should be allowed, in some cases, to name the COS and perhaps to choose an officer from an agency other than the CIA. Blair also wanted greater oversight with respect to covert actions, which are usually conducted by the DO and are among the most sensitive intelligence activities. This often-acrimonious dispute was eventually settled by National Security Adviser Gen. James Jones, who essentially sided with the CIA, although the DNI was given authority to evaluate the effectiveness of specific covert actions when requested by the White House. But the dispute underscored the problem of the DNI responsibilities versus the position's authority. In September 2012, DNI Clapper signed ICD 402, "DNI Representatives," setting forth the DNI's responsibilities and authorities in this area but acknowledging the CIA's role regarding chiefs of station.

Congress has expressed dissatisfaction with the pace of reform, although its concept of what reform would look like or what the results would be have always been a bit vague. A report from the House Intelligence Committee in July 2006 complained about a "lack of urgency" in intelligence reform. At the same time, efforts by some in Congress to enhance the DNI's authority have run afoul of members protecting the interests of other agencies, particularly DOD. Perhaps more notably, during the Bush-Obama transition, the inspector general of the ODNI published a highly critical review of the management challenges facing the DNI.

The key question is this: How would one know that intelligence reform was working? The answer apparently would be the ability of the DNI to enforce a series of procedural and cultural reforms on the intelligence community that would result in the various agencies working better together and sharing more information. This is a laudable but somewhat vague result, which underscores the problems inherent in judging the pace of intelligence reform. DNI Clapper set his goal as trying to improve the integration of collection and analysis, in addition to the direct support of the president. (DNI Coats has continued this emphasis on integration.) This vision came out clearly in *The National Intelligence Strategy of the United States of America 2014*, which Clapper published in September 2014. This also underscored some of the underlying conceptual weakness in the IRTPA. If the various commissions had been able to identify very specific shortcomings, then a less grandiose response would have sufficed. However, the broader but vaguer findings, many of which had been identified multiple times in years past, led to a more significant but also more amorphous approach. The 2019 *National Intelligence Strategy* continues to emphasize the importance of integration as a goal and an operating principle.

The U.S. intelligence community is generally perceived as being hierarchical and bureaucratic, emphasizing vertical lines of authority. Figure 3.1 offers such a view but also categorizes agencies by intelligence budget sectors: the National Intelligence Program (NIP, formerly the National Foreign Intelligence Program, renamed to recognize the inclusion of homeland security and domestic intelligence) and the Military Intelligence Program (MIP), made up of two former military intelligence budget programs, the Joint Military Intelligence Program (JMIP) and Tactical Intelligence and Related Activities (TIARA).

Figure 3.1 The Intelligence Community: An Organizational View

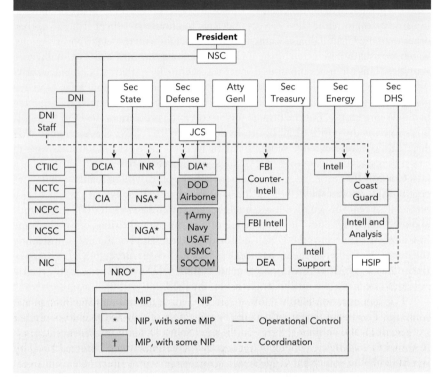

Note: A wiring diagram that shows both hierarchical control and how agencies fall into the budget programs. Note that the secretary of defense controls much more of the intelligence community—75 to 80 percent—on a daily basis than does the DNI. CIA = Central Intelligence Agency; CTIIC = Cyber Threat Intelligence Integration Center; DCIA = director of the CIA; DEA = Drug Enforcement Administration; DHS = Department of Homeland Security; DIA = Defense Intelligence Agency; DNI = director of national intelligence; DOD = Department of Defense; FBI = Federal Bureau of Investigation; HSIP = Homeland Security Intelligence Program; INR = Bureau of Intelligence and Research; JCS = Joint Chiefs of Staff; MIP = Military Intelligence Program; NCPC = National Counterproliferation Center; NCSC = National Counterintelligence and Security Center; NCTC = National Counterterrorism Center; NIC = National Intelligence Council; NIP = National Intelligence Program; NGA = National Geospatial-Intelligence Agency; NRO = National Reconnaissance Office; NSA = National Security Agency; NSC = National Security Council; SOCOM = Special Operations Command; USAF = U.S. Air Force; USMC = U.S. Marine Corps.

The NSC has authority over the director of national intelligence, who in turn oversees, but does not direct, the CIA. The CIA, unlike the Bureau of Intelligence and Research (INR) at the Department of State or the Defense Intelligence Agency (DIA) at DOD, has no cabinet-level patron but reports to the DNI, although the DNI does not have operational control over the CIA, as evidenced by the Blair-Panetta dispute. The CIA's main clients continue to be the president and the NSC. This relationship has both benefits and problems. The CIA has access to the ultimate decision maker, but it can no longer count on this access through its own director given that much of that role now comes under the DNI. The DNI and the new DCIA can be rivals for access to the president. The CIA as a whole can therefore find itself in a weaker position compared with other intelligence agencies. A disparity always existed in that agencies other than the CIA had cabinet-level supporters. However, the DCI had authority across the intelligence community. With this lever gone, the CIA may find itself in a less enviable position on occasion. Signs were evident both before and after passage of the new law that other agencies sought to enlarge the areas in which they worked, usually at the expense of the CIA. The most prominent of these were the Federal Bureau of Investigation (FBI) and DOD. Under President Trump, DCIA Mike Pompeo (2017–2018) had a much greater role than did his predecessors in the Obama administration. The Trump administration had initially decided not to name a DNI and to devolve those duties back to the DCIA—until it was pointed out that this would require legislation.

As noted previously, Porter Goss served as the last DCI (2004–2005) and the first director of the CIA (2005–2006). His tenure proved to be tumultuous, and the press reported numerous stories about friction between the staff that Goss brought with him from Congress and senior CIA officials, many of whom—especially in the DO—ultimately resigned. Goss's short tenure as DCIA indicated that the CIA remained central despite its director's loss of responsibility across the intelligence community. DNI Negroponte found that he could not be effective in his role if the CIA was riven by internal bickering.

The secretary of defense continues to control much more of the intelligence community on a day-to-day basis than does the DNI. The panoply of agencies that are part of DOD—National Security Agency (NSA), Defense Intelligence Agency, National Geospatial-Intelligence Agency (NGA, originally the National Imagery and Mapping Agency, NIMA), airborne reconnaissance programs, the service intelligence units, and the intelligence components in each of the ten unified combatant commands—vastly outnumbers the CIA and the components under the DNI, in terms of both people and dollars. As a rule of thumb, the secretary of defense controls some 75 to 80 percent of the intelligence community. At the same time, the secretary of defense will not have the same level of interest in intelligence as the DNI does. In fact, much of the responsibility for intelligence within DOD is delegated to the under secretary of defense for intelligence (USDI), a position created in 2002.

Control of the intelligence budget was one of the most controversial parts of the debate over the new intelligence structure. Those who advocated less sweeping change had argued that giving the then-DCI **budget execution authority** over the NIP (that is, the ability to determine the actual spending of dollars versus the allocation of money to agencies) would have solved the authority problems across the community as well as significantly increased the leverage of the DCI. However, such a minimalist solution was not politically palatable as it was not seen as sweeping enough. It also was opposed by DOD and its supporters in Congress.

In the debate over the creation of the DNI, DOD and its supporters argued successfully that the department needed to maintain control over the budgets of some national intelligence components: NSA, NGA, and the NRO (National Reconnaissance Office). This devolved into an odd and factually off-base debate about the military chain of command and control of specific reconnaissance assets. The real concern was the ability of military commanders to call on intelligence support when they need it. This has been an area of controversy, as many senior military commanders have increasingly come to treat national intelligence assets as their own.

The DNI develops and determines the NIP, based on the submissions made by the various intelligence agencies. The DNI can provide the agencies with budget guidance. The DNI can transfer or reprogram up to $150 million or no more than 5 percent of any NIP funds for an agency. Certain criteria were set out for such transfers, such as a higher priority or emergent need. Such transfers cannot be used to terminate an acquisition program.

Figure 3.1 is somewhat deficient in that it does not describe the varied functions of the agencies, which are central to their relationships. Several different ways of looking at the U.S. intelligence community are needed to get a better appreciation of what it does and how it works.

ALTERNATIVE WAYS OF LOOKING AT THE INTELLIGENCE COMMUNITY

Before examining further the structure of the intelligence community, it is useful to look at its basic functions.

The intelligence community has, in effect, two broad functional areas: management and execution. Within each of them are many specific tasks. Management covers requirements, resources, collection, and production. Execution covers the development of collection systems, the collection and production of intelligence, the conduct of operations, and the maintenance of the infrastructure support base. In Figure 3.2, a horizontal line divides management and execution, but one function straddles the line: evaluation. Evaluation (assessing how well one is meeting one's goals) is not one of the strongest functions of the intelligence community. Relating intelligence means (resources: budgets, people) to intelligence ends (outcomes: analyses, operations) is a difficult task and is not undertaken with great relish, although improvements were made under DNI Clapper through the Systems and Research Analyses (SRA) office. This is an important task and one that can yield dividends to intelligence managers when done systematically and broadly. All agencies make an effort to evaluate their performance. Before the advent of SRA, the broadest evaluation activity in the intelligence community was carried out within the **National Intelligence Priorities Framework** (NIPF), created under DCI George J. Tenet in 2003 and now part of the DNI's office. The NIPF continues to provide another means by which to assess performance beyond setting priorities.

The flow suggested by Figure 3.2 is idealized, but it shows how the main managerial and execution concerns relate to one another. The flow is circular, going in endless loops. If one were to suggest starting at a particular point, it would be requirements. Without them, little that happens afterward makes sense. Given their proper role, requirements should drive everything else. The NIPF has been the main driver for requirements and remains the highest level of priorities, divided into Presidential Intelligence Priorities (PIPs) and then those of other NSC-level policy makers.

Figure 3.2 Alternative Ways of Looking at the Intelligence Community: A Functional Flow View

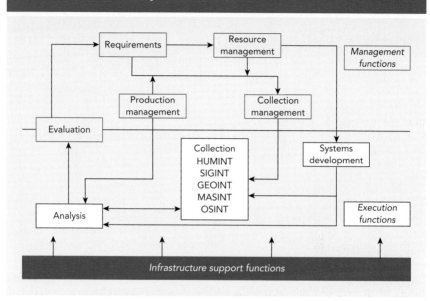

Source: U.S. House Permanent Select Committee on Intelligence, IC21: The Intelligence Community in the 21st Century, 104th Congress, 2d session, 1966.

Note: HUMINT = human intelligence; SIGINT = signals intelligence; GEOINT = geospatial intelligence; MASINT = measurement and signatures intelligence; OSINT = open-source intelligence.

DNI Clapper's emphasis on intelligence integration led to the creation of national intelligence managers (NIMs) who are responsible for unifying intelligence strategies (UIS), both of which are discussed in chapter 6.

The various aspects of collection—systems development and collection itself—occupy much more of the figure than does analysis. This reflects the realities of the intelligence community, whether desirable or not.

THE MANY DIFFERENT INTELLIGENCE COMMUNITIES

Within the broader U.S. intelligence community are many different intelligence communities. (*See box, "The Simplicity of Intelligence."*) Figure 3.3 gives a better sense of what they are by showing what each agency or subagency component does, while preserving the sense of hierarchy. The vertical lines should be viewed as flowing from the topmost organizations through each of the agencies or components below, not subordinating each successive box to the one above it.

Figure 3.3 Alternative Ways of Looking at the Intelligence Community: A Functional View

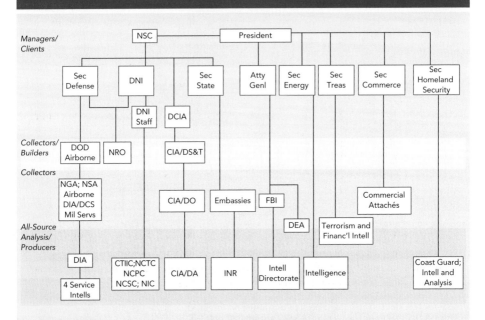

Note: This graphic is somewhat more informative in that it describes functions as well as hierarchy. Note that it is not hierarchical in the sense that, for example, CIA/DO (CIA/Directorate of Operations) controls CIA/DA (CIA Directorate of Analysis). It represents vertical lines of agencies and the various roles they carry out. NGA, NSA, and the military services are listed in collection. Each of them has single-source analysts but not all-source national intelligence analysts as do the agencies listed in analysis/production. This is a question of role and function, not of status. Finally, again note the disparity between the DNI and the secretary of defense. CIA = Central Intelligence Agency; DCIA = director of the CIA; CTIIC = Cyber Threat Intelligence Integration Center; DIA = Defense Intelligence Agency; DCS = Defense Clandestine Service; DA = Directorate of Analysis; DEA = Drug Enforcement Administration; DNI = director of national intelligence; DO = Directorate of Operations; DOD = Department of Defense; DS&T = Directorate of Science and Technology; FBI = Federal Bureau of Investigation; INR = Bureau of Intelligence and Research; NCPC = National Counterproliferation Center; NCSC = National Counterintelligence and Security Center; NCTC = National Counterterrorism Center; NGA = National Geospatial-Intelligence Agency; NIC = National Intelligence Council; NRO = National Reconnaissance Office; NSA = National Security Agency; NSC = National Security Council.

At the top of the hierarchy are the entities that are major intelligence managers, major policy clients, or both. The president is *the* major policy client but is not an intelligence manager. The secretaries of defense, state, treasury, commerce, and energy and the attorney general are clients, and three of them—the secretaries of defense and state and the attorney general—control significant intelligence assets. State has INR; DOD has numerous defense intelligence organizations, which respond to a broad range of needs. The attorney general oversees the FBI and the Drug Enforcement Administration (DEA).

DOD organizations participate in national-level intelligence processes and products, providing indications and warning of impending attack (see chap. 6) and intelligence support for military operations at all levels—from theater (broad regional commands) down to tactical (small units engaged in operations or combat). The Department of Homeland Security (DHS), created in 2002, has two components that are part of the intelligence community, the Coast Guard, which has its own intelligence unit, and the Office of Intelligence and Analysis. The attorney general has control over the FBI and now has an assistant attorney general for national security in the Justice Department who oversees intelligence policy, counterintelligence, and counterespionage. Some see this as a move that could lead to an entity like Britain's MI5 (the British Security Service, see chap. 15), which would constitute a major change for the United States, a country that has always kept domestic and foreign intelligence separate. The FBI now has a National Security Branch, under an executive assistant director. The new branch combines the intelligence, counterintelligence, and counterterrorism elements of the FBI and adds an office focusing on weapons of mass destruction (WMD). The Department of Energy has a small intelligence office devoted to its specific concerns and to coordinate the intelligence activities of the various national laboratories; and the Department of Commerce controls the commercial attachés, who are assigned to embassies and serve an overt intelligence function. The DCIA is manager of the CIA. The Department of Treasury has an Office of Terrorism and Financial Intelligence, which is increasingly important in stopping illicit international financial transactions that support terrorism, crime, and narcotics.

THE SIMPLICITY OF INTELLIGENCE

In the baseball movie *Bull Durham*, a manager tries to explain to his hapless players the simplicity of the game they are supposed to be playing: "You throw the ball; you hit the ball; you catch the ball."

Intelligence has a similar deceptive simplicity: You ask a question; you collect information; you answer the question.

In both cases, many devils are in the details.

The IRTPA also created a Joint Intelligence Community Council (JICC) to assist the DNI. Under DNI McConnell, the JICC was bypassed in favor of the Executive Committee (EXCOM) that he created, although the JICC still meets semiannually. The EXCOM consists of the DNI and the heads of the intelligence components, plus senior policy makers, usually at the under secretary level, with the stated goal of bringing together policy customers and senior intelligence officers at the highest level to ensure that the intelligence community is providing the support that is needed. Interestingly, a similar EXCOM existed during the tenure of DCI Robert M. Gates (1991–1993); Gates became secretary of defense, replacing Donald Rumsfeld, in December 2006. There is also a DEXCOM, or Deputies Executive Committee.

At the next level down are the builders of technical collection systems. The main one is the NRO, which is responsible for the design, building (via contractors), and launching (via the Air Force or the National Aeronautics and Space Administration) of satellite collection systems. DOD also has an airborne reconnaissance responsibility for air-breathing systems such as airplanes and unmanned aerial vehicles (UAVs) or drones, which are of increasing importance on the battlefield for tactical collection and, in the Afghanistan campaign and the war on terrorists, for air attack as well. Finally, the CIA Directorate of Science and Technology (DS&T) has a role in some technical collection programs.

Several offices are responsible for the collection (including processing and exploitation) of intelligence. Within DOD are NSA, which collects signals intelligence (SIGINT), the interception of various types of communications; NGA, which processes and exploits what was known as imagery intelligence (IMINT)—that is, photos—and is now known as geospatial intelligence (GEOINT); DOD airborne systems; and the Defense Attaché System (overt HUMINT) and the Defense Clandestine Service (DCS) of DIA (clandestine HUMINT). The CIA is responsible for espionage (HUMINT) collection via the Directorate of Operations (DO). (Types of intelligence are discussed in detail in chap. 5.) The State Department collects for itself and for others via its array of embassies and Foreign Service officers, although its activities most often are not "tasked intelligence"—that is, they are not usually undertaken in response to a specific requirement, as are the others. The Commerce Department collects via the commercial attachés. The FBI collects counterintelligence information through its National Security Branch and has legal attachés posted in many U.S. embassies overseas. The DNI has authority to manage and task collection.

The most important of the producers of finished intelligence are the three agencies responsible for producing all-source intelligence: CIA's Directorate of Analysis (DA), which is the largest producer of all-source intelligence; DIA's Directorate of Intelligence (DI); and State's INR. As noted, CIA/DA analysts are now housed in mission centers alongside DO officers. Within DOD, the four service intelligence offices also produce finished intelligence. The FBI has a relatively new Intelligence Directorate, which is also codified in the 2004 legislation. This created something of a culture clash within the FBI, which has always thought of itself as primarily a law enforcement agency. The FBI has been adjusting to the presence of intelligence analysts in the Intelligence Directorate who do not have any role as sworn agents; the bureau must therefore create ways to manage them, create meaningful career paths for them, and integrate them into the FBI, all of which has been difficult to date. DHS has the under secretary for intelligence and analysis; Energy has its intelligence and counterintelligence office. The DNI controls the National Intelligence Council, which is made up of the national intelligence officers (NIOs) and is responsible for national intelligence estimates (NIEs) and some other analyses. The DNI also has responsibility for the National Counterterrorism Center (NCTC), which produces analysis on all terrorism and counterterrorism issues, except those that are purely domestic; the National Counterproliferation Center (NCPC); and the Cyber Threat Intelligence Integration Center (CTIIC). The NCPC coordinates strategic planning for WMD proliferation intelligence, identifies gaps or shortfalls in this area, and comes up with solutions for these gaps. Thus, the NCPC does not produce intelligence per se. Again, the DNI has authority to manage and task analysis. CTIIC was established in 2015 at the behest of the Obama White House and despite some pushback from the intelligence community. CTIIC is envisioned as the integrator of all-source intelligence related to foreign cyber threats and cyber incidents affecting national security.

The IRTPA focuses much more on the analytic process. The DNI has three specific charges. First, the DNI is to create a process to ensure the use of alternative analysis as appropriate. Second, the DNI is to assign an official or office to be responsible for analytic integrity, which includes timeliness, objectivity, and the use of all appropriate sources and proper analytic tradecraft. Third, the DNI is to appoint someone who will oversee and report on the objectivity of analysis and the quality of its associated tradecraft. These mandates reflect the unstated Iraq-related issues that shaped the legislation, not September 11, which was the ostensible basis for the new law. In 2007, the assistant deputy DNI for analytic integrity and standards released a set of standards for evaluating the quality of analysis. (See chap. 6 for details.)

Figure 3.3 does not delineate counterintelligence or counterespionage functions. Each agency has certain internal security responsibilities beyond the NCSC under the DNI. The FBI's National Security Branch coordinates foreign counterintelligence activities in the United States. CIA's DO has its own counterintelligence and counterespionage components. In addition, the director of NSA is also the director of the Central Security Service, with responsibility for safeguarding the communications of the United States from interception. The basic relationships, strengths, and weaknesses noted in Figure 3.1 are still evident, but discerning functions is easier in Figure 3.3.

Below the structure of the various agencies is a substructure of centers, the functions of which are to focus on particularly difficult issues, either across the intelligence community, representing several agencies, or within a single agency. The NCTC, the NCPC, and CTIIC represent the cross-agency type. Within the CIA, there were the Counterintelligence and Counternarcotics Centers (CIC and CNC), as well as its own Counterterrorism Center (CTC). As noted, all issues at the CIA are now handled by mission centers. DIA hosts several issue-specific centers: the National Center for Medical Intelligence, focusing on infectious disease, especially as it relates to deployed forces; the Missile and Space Intelligence Center; the National Media Exploitation Center, which derives intelligence from documents and other media; the Underground Facilities Analysis Center, responsible for finding, characterizing, and assessing underground facilities used by state and non-state adversaries; the Joint Intelligence Task Force/Counterterrorism; and the POW-MIA Analytic Cell. In addition, there are also military service centers: the Marine Corps Intelligence Activity, the National Air and Space Intelligence Center, the National Maritime Intelligence Center, and the National Ground Intelligence Center. This substructure underscores a certain amount of organizational flexibility on the part of U.S. intelligence, but it also raises questions of fragmentation or overlap and increased problems of intelligence sharing and coordination.

INTELLIGENCE COMMUNITY
RELATIONSHIPS THAT MATTER

Bureaucracies love organizational charts, popularly called wiring diagrams. All wiring diagrams, no matter how sophisticated, are deceptive. They portray where agencies or offices sit in relation to one another, but they cannot portray how they interact and which relationships matter and why. Moreover, personalities do matter. However much people like to think of government as a system of laws and institutions, the personalities and relationships of those filling important positions affect agency working relations.

The DNI's Relationships. The relationship between the DNI and the president is crucial for the institutional well-being of the intelligence community. The DNI is the embodiment of the intelligence community, and the president is the ultimate policy consumer. DCI Richard Helms (1966–1973) put it succinctly when he observed that the DCI's authority derived directly from the perception that he had access to the president. The same is now true for the DNI, although the DNI now has more rivals than did the DCI. If the DNI does not have access and is not included in meetings where intelligence should be a contributor, there are several ramifications. For the DNI, the problem is personal and professional; for the intelligence community, the problem is being left out of the process. The role of the DNI thus would be diminished in the perception of others who become aware of the situation. The cases of some past DCIs are instructive. DCI John McCone (1961–1965) enjoyed good access to President Kennedy and, initially, to President Johnson, but Johnson began to exclude McCone when the DCI disagreed with his incremental approach to the Vietnam War. After a short period of frustration, McCone resigned. Similarly, DCI R. James Woolsey (1993–1995), after his resignation, made no secret of the fact that he had little access to President Bill Clinton (1993–2001). Photographs of National Security Council meetings under both George W. Bush and Barack Obama show both the DNI and the DCIA attending. The DNI is the senior intelligence official, but the DCIA controls the largest number of all-source analysts as well as the DO. There are, in effect, two senior intelligence officials attending the NSC with the creation of the DNI.

The Trump NSC was initially structured so that the DNI and chairman of the Joint Chiefs of Staff would attend those NSC meetings "where issues pertaining to their responsibilities and expertise are to be discussed." Although this was a return to the initial formulation under George W. Bush, many observers saw this as downgrading of access, especially as Stephen Bannon, the president's chief strategist, was made a regular NSC attendee. Also, some observers found it difficult to think of an issue where there was not some intelligence aspect that should be discussed. This structure later changed to allow regular NSC attendance by the DNI and the Joint Chiefs chairman. Bannon was fired in August 2017.

How close should the relationship between the DNI and the president be? Some observers worry that, if it is too close, the DNI may lose some of the intelligence objectivity needed to support the policy process. Policy makers must be able to rely on the professionalism of the DNI. Still, if the intelligence community were forced to choose between the two extremes, an overly close relationship would probably be preferable to a very distant one. The relationship that George Tenet (1997–2004) had with George W. Bush was among the closest of any DCI to a president, but it was also controversial. The intelligence provided on the eve of the war with Iraq in 2003 concerning the presence of WMD is seen by some as an indicator of lost objectivity. However, a report issued by the Senate Intelligence Committee that was highly critical of intelligence analysis on Iraq WMD also found that there was no evidence that intelligence had been politicized.

The boundaries between expertise and advocacy or what constitutes partisan behavior remain vague. The DNI, like most senior officials, serves at the pleasure of the president. Beyond the vague requirement in the IRTPA that the DNI have extensive national security experience, there are no professional qualifications given in the law for a candidate to become the DNI. Very few past DCIs were professional intelligence officers (Richard Helms, William Colby, Robert Gates). Some of the others had past intelligence experience (Allen Dulles, William J. Casey). Four of the eight DCIAs or acting DCIAs have had significant intelligence experience: Michael Hayden; Michael Morrell, who was acting DCIA for two long periods; John Brennan; and the latest DCIA, Gina Haspel. All DCIs and now DCIAs are chosen for a variety of political reasons. The same is true of the DNI. If a DNI is uncomfortable with a position taken by the administration or with a position that an administration advocates, the DNI can always resign. But the DNI cannot operate entirely independently of the administration. In July 2018, DNI Coats staked out a strongly different position from President Trump, affirming past intelligence assessments that Russia had interfered in the 2016 election. President Trump also publicly took issue with Coats's testimony based on the 2019 *Worldwide Threat Assessment*, in which he disagreed with certain administration assumptions but did not contradict policy, which would have been out of bounds. DCIs who have found themselves at odds with administration policy ended up being ignored. But if a DNI feels strongly about some proposal, then the DNI is going to do more than explain why it is a good or bad idea. The DNI is likely to advocate for or against a proposal, depending on the issue. This already occurs in certain areas, such as the budget. DNIs do not just present a budget to Congress. They advocate overall amounts and argue for or against specific programs. The fact that the DNI has control over few analytical components (essentially the NIC and the NCTC) means that the DNI, or the DNI staff, has to spend a great deal of time trying to keep track of analytic activities across the sixteen intelligence agencies. It also means that the DNI has a relatively weak institutional base. Several of the heads of intelligence agencies are rivals to the DNI as they will have greater insight into and control over activities that are of concern to policy makers. This was the apparent issue for DNI Blair vis-à-vis the CIA regarding covert action. It also places the DNI in a somewhat anomalous position. The DNI is the senior intelligence adviser to the president but is relying on analysis controlled and produced by other agency heads, especially the CIA, given that the DNI controls so few analysts.

To make the appointment a more professional and less political one, suggestions were made in the past that the DCI, like the director of the FBI, be subject to a fixed term of office. (The FBI director serves for ten years, although President

Obama asked Congress, in 2011, to extend Robert Mueller's term for two years.) Politicization of intelligence appointments was a possibility in the past but did not become a reality until 1977, when incoming president Jimmy Carter asked for the resignation of DCI George H. W. Bush (1976–1977). Bush became the first DCI who was asked to resign because of a change in the party controlling the White House. Prior to that, DCIs had not been asked to resign as part of a presidential transition even when it meant a change of parties controlling the presidency. This partisan turnover then became the practice for DCIs when partisan control of the White House shifted, until President George W. Bush asked DCI Tenet, a Clinton appointee, to stay on in 2001. DNI McConnell resigned at the advent of the Obama administration in 2009 and was succeeded by retired admiral Blair, whose tenure as DNI lasted sixteen months. DNI Clapper resigned at the end of the Obama administration, as did DCIA John Brennan.

Another argument in favor of a fixed term is that it would allow DNIs to serve under presidents who had not appointed them, thus increasing the chances for objectivity. The main argument against it, and one that was voiced by several former DCIs, goes back to the personal nature of the relationship between the DNI and the president. The concern is that, under a fixed DNI term that overlaps the cycle of elections, the president would inherit a DNI not of his or her choosing and with whom there might be no rapport, thus increasing the likelihood that the DNI's access would diminish. Moreover, the DNI and the director of the FBI did not hold comparable positions. The DNI is responsible for the entire intelligence community, whereas the director of the FBI runs an agency within an executive department (Justice). The strained relations between FBI director Louis J. Freeh and both Attorney General Janet Reno and President Clinton during the latter part of the Clinton administration underscore the problems that can arise with a fixed term, as did President Trump's firing of James Comey (2013–2017). The 2004 intelligence act did not set a fixed term for the DNI, who continues to serve at the pleasure of the president. The selection of Ambassador Negroponte as the first DNI also established the precedent that the DNI need not be a professional intelligence officer. As noted, this was also true of the DCI position.

The relationship of the DNI with the CIA remains crucial. The CIA was perceived as having lost status within the intelligence community with the creation of the DNI. However, it has retained several key roles, including all-source analysis, HUMINT, intelligence operations, and foreign liaison. Former DCIs William H. Webster (1987–1991) and Tenet argued that the DNI cannot be effective without control over these activities, but those in favor of the new law were adamant about keeping the DNI separate from any agency. This source of tension arose between DNI Blair and DCIA Panetta, resulting in Blair's resignation after it became clear that he had little support in the administration. Blair and Clapper also faced the issue that Obama's counterterrorism adviser, John Brennan, was a former CIA officer and had much more access to the president on an ongoing basis, thus becoming a potential rival to the DNI. Brennan became the DCIA in 2013 (a position he had been unable to be nominated for in 2009), eliminating the intelligence rivalry in the White House but creating a DCIA with an already established close relationship to the president. This again underscores for the DNI the importance of good relations with the DCIA.

Much attention, indeed, probably too much attention, has focused on the control and presentation of the President's Daily Brief (PDB). Until the George W. Bush administration, the PDB had been delivered by a senior intelligence officer. Bush requested that DCI Tenet, and then each of his successors as DCI or DNI, be present for the brief, which was still delivered by a senior intelligence officer. Under the DCIs, the PDB had been a CIA product, emphasizing that agency's relationship to the president. The PDB is now a DNI product, although the CIA continues to contribute some 75 percent of the content. President Obama received the PDB at the start of each day (save Sunday). After reading the PDB, Obama met with the DNI and his senior national security team to discuss the PDB's contents, implications, and other intelligence community–related issues as raised by the DNI. This was a change in that President Obama read the PDB first and then had the meeting; under President Bush this all happened in one meeting. President Trump initially questioned the need for a daily briefing but now apparently has a regular PDB brief that is an entirely oral presentation. It appears that sometimes the DNI has been the senior intelligence officer present and sometimes it is the DCIA. The PDB itself and the manner of its presentation are changed to meet the preferences and needs of each president.

Similarly, senior CIA officers and analysts have usually provided the intelligence support for the **Principals Committee** (PC) and **Deputies Committee** (DC) of the NSC. The PC is the senior policy coordinating body of the NSC structure, consisting of the assistant to the president for national security affairs, sometimes the vice president, the secretaries of state and defense, the DNI, usually the DCIA as well, and the chairman of the Joint Chiefs of Staff. Other cabinet officials (attorney general, secretaries of homeland security, energy, and so on) attend as necessary. The DC is made up of the deputies of the PC members and has a similar function, working on issues before the PC considers them. This intelligence function is important not only for its role in supporting policy but also for the insights it gives to intelligence officials about the possible courses of policy being considered. Such support requires substantive knowledge of the issues being discussed. The DNI is the intelligence participant at PCs although, as noted, the DCIA also attends PCs. The DNIs now rely primarily on national intelligence officers for analytic support. A great deal of this work involves the coordination of papers and the assembling of briefing books. It is a necessary activity but perhaps not one that should be carried out by the NIC, whose primary job is to provide senior analytic expertise on key issues. Under the DCIs, this role was carried out by support staff in the CIA. Some observers have suggested that, over time, the DNI's reliance on the CIA's DA may create pressure to shift the DA from the CIA to the DNI. This would be a major change, which would mirror the British structure. Given the restructuring of the CIA and the creation of DA-DO mission centers, a shift of the DA seems much less likely.

Much depends on how DNIs choose to define their role. As Judge Richard Posner has pointed out (*Preventing Surprise Attacks: Intelligence Reform in the Wake of 9/11*, 2005), the DNI can function as the chief executive officer (CEO) or chief operating officer (COO) of the intelligence community. The CEO function keeps the DNI at a higher, community level. The COO function gets the DNI more involved in details. The preliminary indicators were that the DNI was being forced into the chief operating function by virtue of such daily demands as the PDB, PCs, and DCs, as well as the fact that policy makers and Congress look to the DNI, as the senior intelligence officer, when there is an intelligence-related issue. This, once again, highlights the disparity between the DNI's responsibilities and authority. DNI Clapper tried to take on more of a CEO function. However, the DNI will always be held responsible for the overall performance of U.S. intelligence no matter which role he or she chooses.

The DNI's relationship with the director of the NCTC is also important. The director of the NCTC has semiautonomous status. This director is appointed by the president, confirmed by the Senate, and serves as the principal adviser to the DNI on analysis and operations related to terrorism and counterterrorism. Given the importance of terrorism as a national security issue, the director of NCTC is likely to enjoy a fair amount of access to senior officials, including the president, thus creating the potential for rivalry with the DNI. The 2004 law is specific in stating that the director of NCTC reports directly to the president on the planning and progress of joint counterterrorism operations.

The secretary of state is the chief foreign policy officer below the president; intelligence under the DNI is widely viewed as an arm of foreign policy. At least two issues are important in the relationship between the secretary of state and the DNI: coordinating proposed intelligence operations with foreign policy goals and using the State Department (that is, the Foreign Service) as cover for clandestine intelligence officers overseas. Inevitably, tension arises between the bureaucracies under these two officials. Using the State Department for cover could prove to be a source of concern between the secretary of state and the DCIA. Few DCIs and secretaries of state have the warm relationship that DCI Allen Dulles (1953–1961) and his brother John Foster Dulles (secretary of state, 1953–1959) enjoyed. At best, the relationship usually has a slight edge; at worst, it is outright competitive.

Overseas, a long tradition of tension has been evident between U.S. ambassadors and their senior intelligence officers, usually called chiefs of station (COSs) and usually CIA officers. The ambassador is in charge of the entire country team—meaning all U.S. personnel assigned to the embassy, regardless of their parent organizations. (Larger country teams may have representatives from State, the CIA, DOD, Justice, Treasury, Commerce, and Agriculture.) But COSs have not always kept the ambassador—whether career Foreign Service or political appointee—apprised of their intelligence activities. Despite repeated efforts to address this problem, it still occurs. In addition, several new issues have arisen. The first is, who does the COS represent? In theory, the COS is now the representative of the DNI. But, given the DCIA's continued responsibility for HUMINT, intelligence operations, and foreign liaison, it is also obvious that the stations are a key component of the DCIA's activities. Moreover, the COSs look to the DCIA for their promotions, evaluations, assignments, and so forth. Thus, they will continue to think of the CIA as their home. Tension between the DNI and the DCIA over control of HUMINT and covert action could make the stations even less willing to share information with ambassadors as yet another way of keeping it from the DNI. These were the sorts of issues that arose between DNI Blair and DCIA Panetta, a dispute the NSC decided in the CIA's favor. ICD 402, cited earlier, states that CIA chiefs of station shall act as DNI representatives and that the DNI can raise with the DCIA the performance of chiefs of station not performing his DNI functions effectively. The DNI can recommend removal, but the DCIA is still in control of his or her chiefs of station.

On a day-to-day basis, the secretary of defense controls more of the intelligence community (NSA, DIA, NGA, and the service intelligence units) than does the DNI (NIC, NCTC, NCPC, NCSC, and CTIIC). The secretary of defense also represents the vast majority of the intelligence client base, because of the broad range of defense intelligence requirements. Moreover, the intelligence budget has been hidden within the defense budget and, in many ways, is beholden to it. (This bureaucratic subterfuge continues, largely at the behest of Congress, even after the 2010 decision of Secretary Gates and DNI Clapper to declassify both the NIP and the MIP for the previous fiscal year. Each current year request is now declassified as well.) Therefore, the relationship between the secretary of defense and the DNI is vital. No matter how collegial the relationship may appear, it is not one of equals. The outcome of the debate over the intelligence budget in the 2004 intelligence act underscores the political clout of the secretary of defense in Congress. It is not clear if the DNI will be stronger or weaker than was the DCI in relationship to the secretary of defense. On the one hand, the DNI lacks the institutional base that the DCI could fall back on—the CIA. On the other hand, the DNI has a large staff and enough authority in law that, if exercised properly, could give the DNI a more equal relationship with DOD. DNI Negroponte faced an aggressive secretary of defense and under secretary of defense for intelligence (Donald Rumsfeld and Stephen Cambone, respectively). Many of their intelligence initiatives appeared to aim at creating separate intelligence capabilities under DOD. The advent of Gates as secretary of defense was a significant change, as he brought his own background as a DCI, when he also faced a formidable secretary of defense, Richard Cheney (1989–1993). Early in his tenure at the Pentagon, Gates signaled that he would scale back some of the previous team's intelligence initiatives. Gates apparently was a prime mover in the selection of Clapper, then serving as USDI, as the next DNI, after Blair resigned. However, basic institutional questions remain.

Much of the secretary of defense's authority for intelligence usually devolves to the USDI, who became, in effect, the chief operating officer for defense intelligence. DOD traditionally has tended to look at the intelligence community warily, worrying that the community managers might not be looking after DOD needs and that they might be assuming too much power over defense intelligence. The key to this relationship is the credibility of the DNI and his or her office with the Office of the Secretary of Defense (OSD); that is, the ODNI should have a working knowledge of defense intelligence programs and needs and of the defense budget process. The DNI and OSD have an unbalanced relationship, with OSD the stronger partner. If officials in OSD have the sense that the DNI is not paying adequate attention to DOD needs and privileges, they can stymie much that the DNI wants to do.

The relationship between DHS and the intelligence community continues to evolve. Critics of the imbalance between defense and intelligence sometimes refer to DOD as the 800-pound gorilla. Some observers initially thought that DHS might become the other 800-pound gorilla, but this has not happened to date, mainly because of DHS's large and unwieldy structure. The relationship of the DNI and the director of the NCTC with the secretary of DHS is important. However, DHS has found itself to be an awkward department to manage because of its size, complexity, and diversity. At least twenty-two separate agencies or major components were brought together into DHS in 2002. The structure of the DHS intelligence budget is illustrative. As noted, two DHS components, the Coast Guard and Intelligence and Analysis (I&A), are part of the intelligence community and funded by the NIP, coming under the DNI. However, many other DHS components have what might be termed an intelligence function or responsibility but are not considered part of the intelligence community and are not in the NIP. These include the Secret Service, Customs and Border Protection, Immigration and Customs Enforcement, and the Transportation Security Administration.

In addition, DHS is responsible for the sharing and coordination of terrorist-related information across all levels of government in the United States. Because the United States is a federal republic, there is a large state-by-state counterterrorist substructure in which DHS either has to coordinate or take part. This includes joint terrorism task forces (JTTFs), which are federal and operate in more than 100 cities, and fusion centers, of which there are seventy-two state and local intelligence-sharing bodies. DHS has been criticized for how it manages intelligence sharing in this difficult structure. This large JTTF and fusion center structure has come under criticism as being too large, duplicative, and perhaps more than is needed. (See chap. 12.) Francis X. Taylor, who became the DHS under secretary for intelligence and analysis in 2014, acknowledged problems in his office's information sharing with both the intelligence community and state and local law enforcement.

The relationship between the DNI and Congress has three key components. The first is the power of the purse. Congress not only funds the intelligence community (and the rest of the government) but also can, through its funding decisions, affect intelligence programs. Although it is generally believed that Congress reduces presidential budget requests, it has in many instances championed programs and funded them despite opposition from the executive branch.

The second is personal. Past DCIs have occasionally not gotten along with their overseers, to the ultimate detriment of the DCIs and the intelligence community. William J. Casey (1981–1987) was fairly contemptuous of the oversight process, which cost him support, even among his political allies. James Woolsey (1993–1995) ended up in a constant public squabble with the chairman of the Senate Intelligence Committee, Dennis DeConcini, D-AZ. John M. Deutch (1995–1997) had a difficult relationship with the House Intelligence Committee. The question of the rights and wrongs in each of these cases is irrelevant. Simply put, the DCI or DNI can only lose in the end. Also, having created the DNI to solve a set of perceived problems, Congress watches closely to see if the DNI meets expectations.

The third is the public perception of intelligence and support for it. Because of the secrecy surrounding intelligence, citizens get a glimpse of it mainly through congressional activities. Even without knowing the details of hearings, the fact that a congressional committee is investigating an intelligence issue affects media and public perceptions. After all, if the intelligence community is doing its job, why have a hearing or an investigation? And, as is usually the case, bad news tends to get reported more often than good news. In a representative democracy, legislators are seen as surrogates for the people at large. This includes the area of intelligence oversight. However, there have been issues, such as the NSA metadata mining program revealed in 2013, about which critics believed that the degree to which Congress was informed was insufficient.

At various junctures in the development of the investigation into Russia's meddling in the 2016 presidential election, members of Congress, predominantly Republicans, have demanded access to intelligence and Justice Department materials in details not previously seen, largely as a means of questioning the need for an inquiry. This has strained the relationship between the branches, even though the Republican Party controlled both branches in the 115th Congress.

USDI and the Defense Intelligence Agencies. USDI was created by Congress in 2002 at the behest of Secretary of Defense Rumsfeld (2001–2006), who felt that he had too many people reporting to him on various aspects of defense intelligence and wanted the information funneled to one office. (This was similar to President Truman's desire for one official—the DCI—to be responsible to him for all national intelligence issues.) The USDI is limited by law to a small staff. It is entirely a management oversight function as it has no direct control over any line intelligence assets—collectors, operators, or analysts. Still, it is an extremely influential position in terms of defense intelligence policies, requirements, and budgets.

Tension had arisen between USDI and the heads of NSA and NGA, both of whom also had a responsibility to the DCI and now have one to the DNI. Although they head combat support agencies and although their budgets still come through DOD channels, the directors of these agencies struggle with their two masters within the executive branch—DOD and the DNI. During the congressional hearings about the 2004 intelligence legislation, the directors of NSA and NGA (Hayden and Clapper, respectively) testified that they could come under the new DNI, a view that was not pleasing to DOD officials. However, neither the DNI nor USDI can issue orders or directives to NSA or NGA without taking into account the sensibilities of the other office.

The EXCOM established by DNI McConnell again raised the issue of the relationship between USDI and the defense intelligence agencies, all of whom are members of the EXCOM. To clarify the hierarchy, the USDI has been designated as the director of defense intelligence to make it clear that the USDI continues to have a position superior to the defense intelligence agencies even though they all sit on the same committee. The USDI carries out his or her director of defense intelligence function under the DNI, signaling a closer working relationship than had previously existed. However, this DNI defense function for the USDI has no legal status and could be suspended or eliminated should any DNI or secretary of defense wish to do so.

In October 2014, the Defense Department issued a new directive broadening the scope of USDI's portfolio. In addition to the expected areas of concern, such as WMD, terrorism, and so on, new issues were added: cybersecurity, insider threats, unauthorized disclosures of classified information, and biometrics, each reflecting more recent security issues.

Another internal Defense set of relationships that matter are those between the Combatant Commands (formerly called COCOMs but redesignated CCMDs) and the national intelligence agencies. Rivalry most often arises concerning control over collection assets between the regional CCMDs (there are also functional CCMDs) and national agencies. CCMDs, of necessity, are more responsive to crises in their geographic areas of responsibility (AORs), although these may not loom as large when seen from Washington. Thus, CCMDs are likely to demand intelligence collection that may not be supported by the national collection agencies or policy makers in Washington.

There has been a change in how intelligence functions at the CCMDs. Each CCMD now has a Joint Intelligence Operations Center (JIOC—pronounced jye-ock). The JIOC concept derives from the recognition that operations and intelligence work much more closely now than they have in the past and that part of U.S. military superiority in combat stems directly from superior intelligence support (or battlefield awareness). The so-called thunder run of U.S. forces into Baghdad in 2003 typifies this type of operation. The closer integration of planning, intelligence, and operations is undoubtedly a good idea; whether it will foster improved relations with the CCMDs is less certain.

USDI and Its Relationship With Congress. The USDI is one of two main conduits through which defense intelligence issues reach Congress, the other being DIA itself. But given the principle of civilian control of the military, USDI is more powerful and more important than DIA. The USDI has jurisdiction over defense intelligence requirements, the various defense intelligence agencies (among them NSA, DIA, and NGA), and some defense collection programs—called the air breathers. The USDI deals with the House and Senate Armed Services Committees. Furthermore, the USDI staff functions as a guardian of the authority of the secretary of defense over defense intelligence, watching warily for any possible encroachments, such as from the DNI.

INR and the Secretary of State. The Department of State's INR is the smallest of the three all-source analytical components (compared with the CIA and DIA) and is often thought of as the weakest. A great deal of INR's ability to get things done, both in its own department and as a player in the intelligence community, depends on the relationship between the INR assistant secretary and the secretary of state and one or two other senior State officials, who often are referred to collectively as the seventh floor, where they are situated at the Department of State. In some respects, the relationship among these State officials parallels that between the DNI and the president. If INR has access to the seventh floor, then it plays a greater role and has greater bureaucratic support when needed. But it is a highly variable relationship, depending on the preferences of the secretary and key subordinates. For example, Secretary of State George P. Shultz (1982–1989) met with all of his assistant secretaries regularly; James A. Baker III (1989–1992) did not, preferring to meet with a few senior subordinates, who then dealt with the rest of the department. Thus, under Shultz, INR had more opportunities to gain access; under Baker, most of INR's clients were other bureaus, but less so the vaunted seventh floor.

INR has taken a number of steps to increase its visibility in the State Department and to involve other bureaus more actively in setting intelligence requirements.

The goal has been to increase the bureaus' appreciation of the role of intelligence and of INR, thus making them potential sources of support.

New Areas of Rivalry. Increased rivalry has been evident among agencies both before and after the passage of the 2004 intelligence legislation. The war on terrorists has been a major impetus for this rivalry for at least two reasons. First, the war on terrorists has blurred distinctions between different types or fields of activity that were kept distinct, at least in U.S. practice. Most prominent are those between foreign and domestic intelligence issues and between intelligence and military operations. As became evident in 2001, terrorists could place themselves in the United States legally to plan and conduct attacks, creating what is both a foreign and domestic intelligence issue. The war against terrorists, particularly in places such as Afghanistan, called for greater intelligence-military cooperation but also blurred some of the distinctions between the areas in which both operated. For example, the initial liaison with and support of the Northern Alliance, which was fighting the Taliban, came via the CIA. The campaign against the Taliban had conventional and nonconventional (that is, special operations forces) aspects, as well as a large intelligence component—both of which were in evidence in the May 2011 operation that killed Osama bin Laden. The second reason for increased rivalry has been the natural tendency of most organizations to increase activities, particularly during periods of crisis or war.

Rivalry has been an issue between the FBI and the CIA. The FBI, beginning well before 2001, sought to increase its role both within the United States and overseas. In the mid-1990s, the FBI was aggressive about expanding the role of its legal attachés, who work out of U.S. embassies to foster greater cooperation with foreign law enforcement agencies. Press stories alleged that the FBI had, on occasion, conducted overseas activities without informing the CIA. Within the United States, increased rivalry emerged over the recruitment of foreigners who are in the United States and are then sent overseas to collect intelligence. Although the CIA cannot conduct intelligence within the United States or on U.S. citizens, this type of activity has been allowed as the recruited individuals are foreigners and their collection takes place outside of the country. The FBI reportedly sought to take over this activity, arguing that it is domestic intelligence (as recruitment takes place in the United States), and sought to be responsible for disseminating intelligence produced by foreigners in the United States. The CIA resisted the FBI efforts. Some observers noted that the FBI had little experience in this type of intelligence recruitment and that its own intelligence analytic effort just began in 2003 and thus it was not ready to take over reporting of this type. Concern also arose that both agencies could end up controlling some portion of overseas collection, resulting either in duplication or in the two working at cross-purposes if they are not aware of the other's activities. In 2012, DNI Clapper expanded the FBI's role as the coordinator for domestic intelligence, meaning federal, state, local, and tribal, when he designated FBI special agents in charge (SACs) in certain cities as DNI representatives, in effect making them the domestic equivalent of the chiefs of station overseas. Rivalry also exists between DOD and the CIA. This relationship had always been difficult because of the imbalance between the DCI's intelligence community responsibilities and the day-to-day control that the secretary of defense exercised over some 75 to 80 percent of the intelligence community. Even though the DCIA is responsible for only one agency, areas of rivalry remain. The blurring of intelligence and military roles in the war on terrorists has been one source. There are both overt and covert military aspects to this war. The CIA can claim to have a stake only in the covert aspect, as in its work with the Northern Alliance against the Taliban in Afghanistan in 2001. But the military can claim to have responsibilities in both spheres and appears to want to expand its activities in the covert sphere. (See the discussion of paramilitary operations in chap. 8.)

A second source of CIA-DOD competition was the apparent desire of DOD to gain greater control over any and all intelligence related to its missions. Several observers have noted that, once President George W. Bush decided to attack al Qaeda in its Afghan sanctuary, Secretary of Defense Rumsfeld was frustrated by the relative speed with which DCI Tenet was able to respond and begin inserting officers to link up with the Northern Alliance. DOD needed a much longer time span to plan and to deliver military combat units to Afghanistan. Rumsfeld was also reportedly displeased that the military had to depend largely on the CIA for human intelligence support.

In late 2004 and early 2005, a series of press reports indicated a unilateral expansion of DOD activities in intelligence. The fiscal year (FY) 2005 defense authorization bill included a provision allotting $25 million to the Special Operations Command (SOCOM) to support foreign forces, irregular forces, groups, or individuals. Some believed this sounded like what the CIA has done and certainly did in Afghanistan. Some questioned whether this would put DOD into the business of covert actions without the attendant legal apparatus of presidential findings and reports to Congress. (For additional discussion, see chap. 8.) The consensus is that the situation also raised the possibility that some of these foreigners might double dip, that is, solicit payments from both DOD and the CIA. The WMD Commission had recommended that DOD be given greater authority for conducting covert action. However, according to press reports in June 2005, the Bush administration decided against the proposal. Within the DO, there is now an assistant director who coordinates all clandestine overseas HUMINT collection.

This issue resurfaced in 2012, when SOCOM sought new authority to train and equip internal security forces in places like Yemen and Kenya, where many counterterrorism activities took place. The State Department, which controls security assistance, objected as did congressional committees, resulting in the concept's being rejected. In 2014, Congress rejected Obama administration efforts to shift more responsibility for the UAV programs from CIA to Defense. Press reports stated that congressional concern that SOCOM would handle these missions was one of reasons for the rejection.

More controversial were reports that DIA had created a Strategic Support Branch to augment its HUMINT capabilities. Again, this was seen as a way of minimizing DOD's need to rely on the CIA for HUMINT. Some observers agreed that there could be unique defense HUMINT requirements related to planned or ongoing operations that the CIA might not be able or willing to fulfill if they competed with other priorities. But this activity raised questions about congressional oversight (including whether Congress had been informed about the creation of this new capability), the degree to which it overlapped with or encroached upon the CIA's role, and whether sufficient coordination mechanisms were in place.

These questions became moot as Secretary Gates began to scale back some of these initiatives, such as in the area of HUMINT. In 2012, DNI Clapper and Secretary of Defense Panetta announced the creation of the Defense Clandestine Service (DCS), to expand Defense human intelligence. Some saw this as another effort to create a rival capacity to the CIA's, although press reports indicated that CIA favored the idea as a means of expanding HUMINT collection beyond areas where the CIA had to concentrate, especially those focused on military capabilities. The DCS would also train with the DO at its facility. However, the DCS ran into trouble in Congress. In December 2012, the Senate Armed Services Committee barred DCS from the personnel expansion it envisaged. In May 2013, the House Armed Services Committee withheld half of DCS's funding until DOD could show that this was a unique capability and not a duplicative one.

Congressional Relationships. Also of great importance are the relationships of the two intelligence committees with each other and with the other House and Senate committees with which they must work. The oversight responsibilities of the House and Senate Intelligence Committees are not identical, which accounts for their differing sets of relationships. (See chapter 10 for more details.) The Senate Intelligence Committee has sole jurisdiction over only the DNI, the CIA, and the NIC. The Senate Armed Services Committee has always jealously guarded its oversight of all aspects of defense intelligence. The relationship between Senate Intelligence and Senate Armed Services has been standoffish at best and hostile at worst. Antagonism has usually stemmed from the Senate Armed Services Committee's reactions to real or imagined efforts by Senate Intelligence to step beyond its carefully circumscribed turf. Senate Armed Services has usually responded with punitive actions of varying degrees (such as delaying action on the annual intelligence authorization bill).

Both intelligence committees also jealously and successfully guarded their oversight role against possible intrusions by the then Senate Governmental Affairs Committee (SGAC). However, legislation dealing with the reorganization of the intelligence community was referred to SGAC because of its role in government organization. This move was seen by some observers as a slap at the Senate Intelligence Committee, whose chairman, Pat Roberts, R-KS, had offered a much more radical proposal for intelligence organization earlier in 2004.

The House Intelligence Committee has exclusive jurisdiction over the entire NIP—all programs that transcend the bounds of any one agency or are nondefense—as well as shared jurisdiction with the House Armed Services Committee over the military intelligence programs. This arrangement has fostered a better working relationship between the two House committees than exists between their Senate counterparts. This is not to suggest that moments of friction do not arise, but the overall relationship between the House committees has not approached the hostility exhibited in the Senate. However, the House Armed Services Committee was the strongest advocate for DOD interests in the debate over the 2004 legislation and in the 2005 intelligence authorization legislation.

Good relationships between the two intelligence committees and the House and Senate Defense Appropriations subcommittees are important for avoiding disjunctions between authorized programs and appropriated funds. Generally speaking, all appropriators tend to resent (and would sometimes like to ignore) all authorizers. Once again, the relationship between intelligence authorizers and appropriators has tended to be smoother in the House than in the Senate. From 2005 to 2010, the intelligence committees failed to pass an authorization bill that became law, weakening their overall role in the process.

The House Foreign Affairs and Senate Foreign Relations Committees oversee State Department activities, but the relationship with their respective intelligence committee tends to be less fractious than the relationship between the intelligence and appropriations committees. Finally, the two judiciary committees oversee the FBI.

The two intelligence committees themselves have an important relationship. The House committee's jurisdiction is broader than the Senate's. However, the Senate Intelligence Committee has the exclusive and important authority to confirm the nominations of the DNI, the DNI's principal deputy, a few other subordinates, and the DCIA. The two committees often choose to work on different issues during the course of a session of Congress, apart from their work on the intelligence authorization bills. Despite differences of style and emphasis, hostility or rancor intruded only occasionally, even in the face of divergent viewpoints. Beginning in roughly 2005, the relationship between the two intelligence committees became more fractious, resulting in the inability to pass an intelligence authorization bill, as noted earlier. The FY2010 authorization bill was passed and signed by President Obama, although not until FY2011 had actually begun. (See chap. 10 for more details.) The two committees took very different approaches to the investigation of Russian interference in the 2016 election. In the Senate, Chairman Richard Burr, R-NC, and Vice Chairman Mark Warner, D-VA, have maintained a collegial relationship and overseen a less fractious investigation, and they have supported the intelligence community assessment that Russia did interfere. The House committee essentially ceased to function as a coherent committee because of the extreme partisanship stemming from the issue. Republican members largely supported Trump in opposing the investigation and trying to stymie it in various ways, while Democratic members supported the investigation. With the change in political control of the House in 2019 going over to the Democrats, the House committee will put more emphasis on the issue but will still face divisive partisan rancor.

THE INTELLIGENCE BUDGET PROCESS

The love of money is not only the root of all evil; money is also the root of all government. How much gets spent and who decides are fundamental powers. The intelligence budget is somewhat complex, although it has been simplified. The budget now has two components: the NIP and the MIP, which combines the Joint Military Intelligence Program and Tactical Intelligence and Related Activities.

The NIP comprises programs that either transcend the bounds of an agency or are nondefense in nature. The DNI is responsible for the NIP. The MIP consists of defense and service intelligence programs. The secretary of defense is responsible for the MIP. For many years, the rough rule of thumb was that the NIP was twice as large as the MIP. Recently, this ratio has shifted further in the NIP's favor, as the MIP has been reduced at a much greater rate than the NIP. The intelligence budget initially peaked at $80.1 billion ($53.1 billion NIP; $27 billion MIP) in FY2010, declining slowly to $66.8 billion in FY2015. However, since then it has begun to increase, with the FY2020 request totaling $85.75 billion ($62.8 billion NIP; $22.95 billion MIP). (Details of NIP and MIP spending, 2007–2020, are in chap. 10.) This would seem to suggest that the DNI has power with respect to NIP responsibility. However, given that the DNI does not have budget execution authority over NIP agencies, DNI power is again limited.

The following programs make up the NIP:

Civilian Programs	Defense Programs	Community-wide Program
CIA (CIAP)	Consolidated Cryptologic Program (CCP)	ODNI Community Management Account (CMA)
CIA Retirement and Disability System (CIARDS)		
Counterintelligence (FBI)	General Defense Intelligence Program (GDIP)	
Department of Homeland Security Program	National Geospatial-Intelligence Program	
INR (State Department)	National Reconnaissance Program (NRP)	
National Counterterrorism Program		
Office of Intelligence Support (Treasury Department)		

MIP is composed of intelligence programs that support DOD or its components that are not confined to any one military service. As the titles of some MIP programs indicate, many parallel NIP categories:

Air Force intelligence

Army intelligence

Defense Airborne Reconnaissance Program (DARP)

Defense Cryptologic Program (DCP)

Defense General Intelligence Applications Program (DGIAP)

Defense Geospatial-Intelligence Program

Defense Intelligence Counterdrug Program (DICP)

Defense Intelligence Special Technologies Program (DISTP)

Defense Intelligence Tactical Program (DITP)

Defense Space Reconnaissance Program (DSRP)

Marine intelligence

Navy intelligence

Special Operations Command (SOCOM)

Figure 3.4 arranges the components of the intelligence community by budget sectors. Not all of the agencies within a budget sector are controlled by the same authority. The solid lines denote direct control. The two double vertical lines show which part of the budget and agencies are national and which are DOD. There is an overlap, as some agencies are both national and defense, even if they fall into NIP or MIP. DIA straddles the line, containing both NIP and several of the MIP programs. Even within NGA, NRO, and NSA, there are programs and personnel paid out of the MIP. Figure 3.4 also indicates the secretary of defense's preponderant control over intelligence community resources.

There are significant differences in how the NIP and MIP are managed both internally and in terms of their relationship to other budget areas. NIP funds are all fenced from other funds—that is, they cannot be traded to support non-intelligence activities within an NIP agency, although trades can be made within the NIP. MIP funds are not fenced within their respective agencies or, more important, in the military services. Thus, MIP funds can be used for non-intelligence needs if so desired. The majority of NIP funds are within intelligence agencies; the majority of MIP funds are in non-MIP and non-intelligence Defense entities, the four military services and SOCOM being of note. Finally, trade-off discussions within the NIP are all about intelligence versus intelligence trades; in the MIP, intelligence programs must defend themselves against non-intelligence programs (weapons, personnel, etc.), which may be seen as having higher value.

The intelligence budget is shaped by a process that is lengthy and complex. (See Figure 3.5.) The budget-building process within the executive branch takes more than a year, beginning around November when the DNI provides guidance to the intelligence program managers. The **crosswalks** between the DNI and DOD— efforts to coordinate programs and to make difficult choices between programs—are major facets of the budget process. Crosswalks can take place at the program level or below and can go as high as the DNI and the secretary of defense. The budget process in the executive branch ends the following December, thirteen months after it began, with the DNI sending a completed intelligence budget to the president for final approval.

Figure 3.4 Alternative Ways of Looking at the Intelligence Community: A Budgetary View

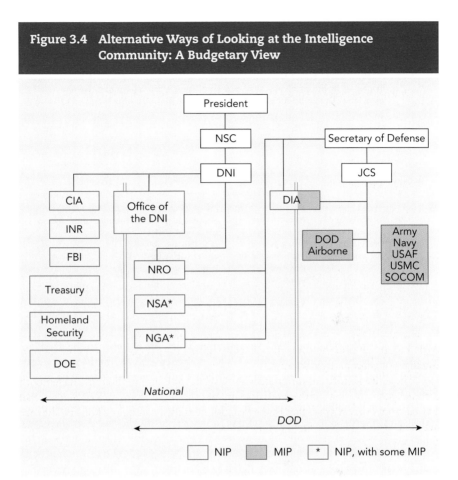

Note: The secretary of defense controls much more of the intelligence community on a daily basis than does the DNI. CIA = Central Intelligence Agency; DIA = Defense Intelligence Agency; DNI = director of national intelligence; DOD = Department of Defense; DOE = Department of Energy; FBI = Federal Bureau of Investigation; INR = Bureau of Intelligence and Research; JCS = Joint Chiefs of Staff; MIP = Military Intelligence Program; NGA = National Geospatial-Intelligence Agency; NIP = National Intelligence Program; NRO = National Reconnaissance Office; NSA = National Security Agency; NSC = National Security Council; SOCOM = Special Operations Command; USAF = U.S. Air Force; USMC = U.S. Marine Corps.

It takes about three years to develop a budget and then spend the money, beginning in March of any year and continuing until September two-and-a-half years later. The figure shows the activity for each phase and the time during which it happens.

The following February, the president's budget goes to Congress, where a new, eight-month process begins. It consists of hearings in the authorization and appropriations committees, committee markups of the bills, floor action, conference committee action between the House and Senate to work out differences (both houses

Figure 3.5 The Intelligence Budget: Four Phases Over Three Years

It takes about three years to develop a budget and then spend the money, beginning in March of any year and continuing until September two-and-a-half years later. The figure shows the activity for each phase and the time during which it happens.

Year 1	March–September	October ↓		
Year 2		August	August ↓	
Year 3			September	October ↓
Year 4				September
Activity	Planning	Programming	Budgeting	Execution
	Guidance	*Request and review*	*Build and submit*	*Obligate and spend*
	Broad guidelines of planning, programming, and budgeting are established.	Program resources are projected for future year requirements for dollar and manpower resources—a multiyear request.	Money or authority available to purchase goods and services or to hire people—for one or two years— is set.	Money on authorized programs is committed and spent.

must pass identical bills), and final passage, after which the bill goes to the president to be signed. By this time, the executive branch is already working on the next budget. A major difference between the president's budget and Congress's should be kept in mind. The president's budget is serious and detailed, but it is only a recommendation. Congress's budget allocates money. Or, as the old saying goes, "The president proposes and Congress disposes." Beyond this formal process is the use of supplemental budget bills, which are appropriations above the amount approved by Congress in the regular budget process. Supplementals tend not to be favored by executive agencies as they may provide one-year money that is not sustained in the following years. (See chap. 10 for more detail.) For Congress, however, **supplementals** are a way to take care of agreed-on needs without making long-term budget commitments. Supplementals, like all other appropriations bills, must be approved by Congress. For many years, a great deal of the military activity in Iraq and then Afghanistan was funded by OCO, overseas contingency operations, which can be thought of as a wartime supplemental. As the active combat declines, OCO funding will disappear rather than be returned to the budget "base." Intelligence activities at the CCMDs are especially hard hit by the loss of OCO funding.

This seemingly endless process points up another important aspect of the intelligence budget. At any time during the year, as many as eight different fiscal year (October 1–September 30) budgets are in some form of use or development. (*See box,* "*Eight Simultaneous Budgets.*") Two past fiscal-year budgets are still in use, in the form of funds that had been appropriated previously but have not been completely spent. Although funds for salaries and similar expenses are spent in a single fiscal year, other funds—such as those to build highly complex technical collection systems—are spent over the course of several years. Funds also are being spent for the current fiscal year.

EIGHT SIMULTANEOUS BUDGETS

Over the course of a fiscal year (October 1 to September 30), eight concurrent budgets are in some state of being. This shows the situation during FY2018 to FY2025.

FY2018 and FY2019: Past fiscal years; some funds still being spent

FY2020: Current fiscal year (Oct. 1, 2019–Sept. 30, 2020); funds being spent

FY2021: Budget for the next fiscal year being developed by executive branch and Congress

FY2022: Intelligence program nearing completion

FY2023: Budget in early development in executive branch

FY2024 and 2025: Budgets in long-range planning in executive branch

The budget for the following fiscal year is going through the political processes. The budget for the year after that is being formulated by the executive branch and Congress. Finally, two future-year budgets are in various states of planning. A great deal of influence accrues to those individuals in both branches of government who can master the process and the details of the budget.

KEY TERMS

budget execution authority 41
crosswalks 62
Deputies Committee 51

National Intelligence Priorities
     Framework 42
Principals Committee 51
supplementals 64

FURTHER READINGS

The following readings provide background on the current organization and structure of the U.S. intelligence community. The list includes some studies of proposed changes that would enable the intelligence community to deal more effectively with the challenges it will face in the future.

Commission on the Intelligence Capabilities of the United States Regarding Weapons of Mass Destruction. Report to the president, March 31, 2005. (Available at http://www.gpo.gov/fdsys/search/pagedetails.action?granuleId=&packageId=GPO-WMD&fromBrowse=true.)

Elkins, Dan. *Managing Intelligence Resources.* 4th ed. Dewey, AZ: DWE Press, June 2014.

George, Roger Z., and Harvey Rishikof, eds. *The National Security Enterprise: Negotiating the Labyrinth.* Washington, D.C.: Georgetown University Press, 2011.

Johnson, Loch K. *Secret Agencies: U.S. Intelligence in a Hostile World.* New Haven, Conn.: Yale University Press, 1996.

Lowenthal, Mark M. *U.S. Intelligence: Evolution and Anatomy.* 2d ed. Westport, Conn.: Praeger, 1992.

McConnell, Mike. "Overhauling Intelligence." *Foreign Affairs* (July/August 2007). (Available at www.foreignaffairs.org/20070701faessay86404/mike-mcconnell/overhauling-intelligence.html.)

National Commission on Terrorist Attacks Upon the United States [9/11 Commission]. *Final Report.* New York: W. W. Norton, 2004.

Office of the Director of National Intelligence. *National Intelligence: A Consumer's Guide.* Washington, D.C.: Office of the Director of National Intelligence, 2009. (Available at www.odni.gov.)

———. *The National Intelligence Strategy of the United States of America 2019.* Washington D.C.: Office of the Director of National Intelligence, 2019. (Available at www.odni.gov.)

———. United States Intelligence Community (IC) 100 Day Plan for INTEGRATION and COLLABORATION. Washington, D.C., April 11, 2007. (Available at www.odni.gov.)

———. U.S. National Intelligence: An Overview, 2013. 2013. (Available at www.odni.gov.)

Office of the Inspector General. *Critical Intelligence Community Management Challenges.* Washington, D.C., November 12, 2008. (Available at www.fas.org.)

Posner, Richard. "The 9/11 Report: A Dissent." *New York Times Book Review,* August 29, 2004, 1.

Richelson, Jeffrey T. *The U.S. Intelligence Community.* 4th ed. Boulder, Colo.: Westview Press, 1999.

Treverton, Gregory F. *Reorganizing U.S. Domestic Intelligence: Assessing the Options.* Santa Monica, Calif.: RAND Corporation, 2008.

U.S. Commission on the Roles and Responsibilities of the United States Intelligence Community. *Preparing for the 21st Century: An Appraisal of U.S. Intelligence.* Washington, D.C.: U.S. Government Printing Office, 1996.

U.S. House Permanent Select Committee on Intelligence. *IC21: The Intelligence Community in the 21st Century.* Staff study, 104th Cong., 2d sess., 1996.

CHAPTER FOUR

THE INTELLIGENCE PROCESS—
A MACRO LOOK
Who Does What for Whom?

The term "intelligence process" refers to the steps or stages in intelligence, from policy makers perceiving a need for information to the community's delivery of an analytical intelligence product to them. This chapter offers an overview of the entire intelligence process and introduces some of the key issues in each phase. Succeeding chapters deal in greater detail with the major phases. Intelligence, as practiced in the United States, is commonly thought of as having five steps, to which this book adds two. The seven phases of the intelligence process are (1) identifying requirements, (2) collection, (3) processing and exploitation, (4) analysis and production, (5) dissemination, (6) consumption, and (7) feedback.

Identifying **requirements** means defining those policy issues or areas to which intelligence is expected to make a contribution, as well as decisions about which of these issues has priority over the others. It may also mean specifying the collection of certain types of intelligence. The impulse is to say that all policy areas have intelligence requirements, which they do. However, intelligence collection and analytical capabilities are always limited, so priorities must be set, with some requirements getting more attention, some getting less, and some perhaps getting little or none at all. The key questions that determine these priorities include the following: Who sets these requirements and priorities and then conveys them to the intelligence community? What happens, or should happen, if policy makers fail to set these requirements on their own?

Once requirements and priorities have been established, the necessary intelligence must be collected. Some requirements will be better met by specific types of collection; some may require the use of several types of collection. Making these decisions among always-constrained collection capabilities is key, as is the question of how much can or should be collected to meet each requirement.

Collection produces intelligence, just not finished intelligence. That collected intelligence must undergo **processing and exploitation** (usually referred to as P&E) before it can be given to analysts. In the United States, constant tension exists over the allocation of resources to collection versus processing and exploitation, with collection inevitably coming out the winner; the result is that much more intelligence is collected than can be processed and exploited.

Identifying requirements, conducting collection, and processing and exploitation are meaningless unless the intelligence is given to analysts who are experts in their respective fields and can turn the intelligence into reports that respond to the needs of the policy makers. The types of products chosen, the quality of the **analysis and production**, and the continuous tension between current intelligence products and longer range products are major issues.

The issue of moving the analysis to the policy makers stems directly from the multitude of analytical vehicles available for disseminating intelligence. **Dissemination** decisions must be made about how widely intelligence should be distributed and how urgently it should be passed or flagged for the policy maker's attention.

Most discussions of the intelligence process end here, with the intelligence having reached the policy makers whose requirements first set everything in motion. However, two important phases remain: **consumption** and **feedback**.

Policy makers are not blank slates or automatons who are impelled to action by intelligence. How they consume intelligence—whether in the form of written reports or oral briefings—and the degree to which the intelligence is used are important.

Although feedback does not occur nearly as often as the intelligence community might desire, a dialogue between intelligence consumers and producers should take place after the intelligence has been received. Policy makers should give the intelligence community some sense of how well their intelligence requirements are being met and discuss any adjustments that need to be made to any parts of the process. Ideally, this should happen while the issue or topic is still relevant so that improvements and adjustments can be made. Failing that, even an ex post facto review can be tremendously helpful.

REQUIREMENTS

Each nation has a wide variety of national security and foreign policy interests. Some nations have more than others. Of these interests, the primacy of some is self-evident—those that deal with large and known threats; those that deal with neighboring or proximate states, especially potentially hostile ones; and those issues or conditions that are more severe. But the international arena is dynamic and fluid, so periodic readjustments of priorities are likely even among the agreed key interests. For example, the Soviet Union was the overwhelming top priority of U.S. intelligence from 1946 to 1991, after which that country as we knew it ceased to exist. The problems associated with its fifteen successor states were very different and required different intelligence strategies. In the early years of the twenty-first century, there has been a resurgence of Russian power, based initially on its oil and natural gas assets and then on a much more aggressive foreign policy with neighboring states and in the Middle East. Also, terrorism has been a concern of U.S. national security policy since the 1970s, but the nature of the terrorism issue changed dramatically in 2001. So even for issues that have long been on the national security agenda, there are shifts in priorities, in the intrinsic importance of the issues, and in the internal dynamics of issues.

Given that intelligence should be an adjunct to policy and not a policy maker in its own right, intelligence priorities should reflect policy priorities. Policy makers should have well-considered and well-established views of their own priorities and convey these clearly to their intelligence apparatus. Some of the requirements may be obvious or so long-standing that no discussion is needed. The cold war concentration on the Soviet Union was one such priority.

But what happens if the policy makers do not decide, find that they cannot decide, or fail to convey their priorities to the intelligence community? Who sets intelligence priorities then? These questions are neither frivolous nor hypothetical. Senior policy makers often assume that their needs are known by their intelligence providers. After all, the key issues are apparent. A former secretary of defense, when asked if he ever considered giving his intelligence officers a more precise definition of his needs, said, "No. I assumed they knew what I was working on." There is strong reason to believe that his view was not unique.

An obvious way to fill the requirements gap left by policy makers would be for the intelligence community to assume this task on its own. However, in a system such as that of the United States, where a strict line divides policy and intelligence, this solution may not be possible. Intelligence officials may feel that the limits on their role preclude making the decision; policy makers may view intelligence officials who seek to fill the requirements void as a threat to their function and may even react with hostility, especially if their issues are not high on the list.

The intelligence community thus faces two unpalatable choices. The first is to fill the requirements vacuum, running the risk of being wrong or accused of having overstepped into the realm of policy. The second is to overlook the absence of defined requirements and to continue collection and the phases that follow, based on the last-known priorities and the intelligence community's own sense of priorities, fully realizing that they may be accused of making the wrong choices or of working on outdated issues.

Some intelligence managers might take issue with this interpretation of their choices. They would note, correctly, that one function of intelligence is to look ahead, to identify issues that are not high priority at present but may be so in the future. But, as important as this function is, it is difficult to get policy makers to focus on issues that are far off or only possibly significant. They are hard-pressed to work on the issues demanding immediate attention. Intelligence officers may be tempted to shop an issue, that is, to look for some policy maker who will take interest in it and thus enhance its priority, but this comes very close to breaching the intelligence-policy barrier once again. Thus, the requirements conundrum remains.

Conflicting or competing priorities are also an issue. Although some sense of order may be easily imposed on certain issues, others may end up claiming equal primacy. Again, policy makers should make the difficult choices. In reality, most governments are large enough to have various competing sectors of interest either between or within departments or ministries. The result is that, once again, the intelligence community may be left to its own devices. In an intelligence community such as that of the United States, parts of the community may reflect the preferences of the policy makers to whom they are most closely tied. In some cases, there may be no final adjudicating authority, leaving the intelligence community to do the best that it can. In the U.S. system, the National Security Council (NSC) sets the policy and intelligence priorities. The director of national intelligence (DNI) should be the final adjudicator within the intelligence community, but the director's ability to impose priorities on a day-to-day basis across the entire intelligence community remains questionable, especially for Defense. All issues tend to get shorter shrift when too many are competing for attention.

One intellectual means of assessing requirements is to look at the likelihood of an event and its relative importance to national security concerns. Of great concern will be high-likelihood and high-importance events. It should be easier to assess importance (which should be based on known or stated national interests) than it is to assess likelihood (which is itself an intelligence judgment or estimate). Likelihood, however, is not a prediction; it is an estimate. (See the discussion in chap. 6.) For example, during the cold war a Soviet nuclear attack would have been judged a high-importance but low-likelihood event. Italian government instability would be judged a high-likelihood but low-importance event. Of the two, the Soviet issue would rank higher as a priority or intelligence concern because of its potential effect, even though an attack seemed even remotely possible in only a few instances and an Italian government fell several dozen times.

In both Panel A and Panel B of Figure 4.1, the issues that fall closer to the upper right reflect more important intelligence requirements. However, there may not be startling clarity as to likelihood or there may be a debate as to issues' relative importance.

The hidden factor that drives priorities is resources. It is impossible to cover everything. The United States, for example, has long had interests in every part of the globe, although some are more significant and more central than others. For decades, the U.S. intelligence community has used a variety of processes to set priorities. The current priority system is based on the National Intelligence Priorities Framework (NIPF), which came into effect under President George W. Bush in February 2003.

Figure 4.1 Intelligence Requirements: Importance Versus Likelihood

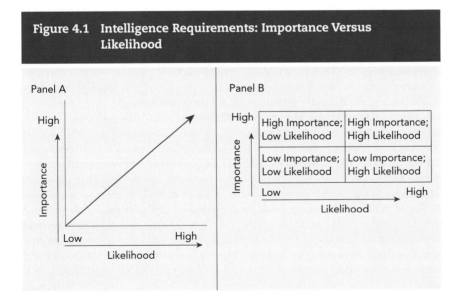

The NIPF seeks to obtain priorities from the highest level of government, the NSC. These senior policy makers review NIPF priorities annually; the DNI and the intelligence community review the NIPF each quarter and also can make changes based on ongoing events or new requirements. Director of Central Intelligence (DCI) George J. Tenet (1997–2004) described the NIPF, which was developed during his tenure, as being more flexible and more precise than any previous intelligence priority system. The NIPF is connected directly to analytic and collection resources to ensure that the most urgent needs are being covered and that gaps can be identified quickly. The system is also used for planning in the five-year budget cycle. Other congressional testimony revealed that each topic in the NIPF has an intelligence topic manager, now often the national intelligence managers created under DNI James Clapper (2010–2017), who helps determine collection requirements. The NIPF appears to be a more pervasive system in terms of overall intelligence community functions and a more flexible system than has been used in the past. The NIPF has survived into the Obama and Trump administrations. Longtime observers of the national security policy process found this carryover interesting, as each new administration, when it takes over the NSC system, typically renames various committees and memos, largely as a rebranding operation, to show that there are new people in charge. One of the other problems that the NIPF addressed was the division of intelligence issues into either geographic-based issues or functionally based issues. Neither means works very well, but this is how virtually all intelligence services array their priorities and analysis. The NIPF seeks to overcome this problem by relating each issue to each of the countries or non-state actors where it is important or, conversely, by showing which issues are relevant for a given country or non-state actor, because not every issue will matter for each country or non-state actor. The country/actor-issue nexus thus becomes a crucial focusing tool, allowing one to span the geography-functionality divide. In other words, one must be able to identify both an issue and the state or non-state actors who are taking part. As DNI Clapper once observed, "Intelligence is not just things and it is not just places. It is things in places."

One concern that has been expressed, especially in Defense service intelligence components, is that the NIPF may not reflect their needs when responding to military commanders. No priority system can adequately reflect all policy makers, especially in a government as large and as diverse as the United States. The NIPF has been a success in getting overall priority guidance from the most senior policy makers on a consistent basis, which was its intended goal.

All priority systems must address the issue of **priority creep**. Issues can and do move up and down in a priority system. This is actually a positive occurrence as it shows that the priority system is dynamic and responsive to changes in the international situation. The problem is that issues customarily do not receive significant attention until after they have begun moving up to the higher priority levels, at which point they must compete with the issues already in that bracket. Priority creep can become a problem as analysts or policy makers seek higher priority for certain issues. Priority creep is further exacerbated by the difficulty encountered in returning issues to lower priority status once they have become less urgent. Neither the intelligence analysts working on that issue nor the policy makers whom they support are eager to admit that the issue is no longer as important. After all, it is their issue.

This underscores the problem with any intelligence requirements system. Such a system is, of necessity, static between reviews or updates. Even if the requirements are reviewed and re-ranked periodically, such as the quarterly review in the NIPF, they remain snapshots in time of policy maker interests. Policy makers or intelligence officials must decide on the requirements and resources to be applied to them. However, the nature of international relations is such that unexpected issues inevitably crop up with little or no warning. These are sometimes referred to as **ad hocs**. When an issue like this arises, some policy makers and intelligence officers exert pressure to give the new issue a priority high enough to compete with other high-priority issues. Some resistance is felt, usually from those whose access to intelligence resources is threatened. Not every ad hoc merits higher priorities. (Some intelligence analysts speak of the **tyranny of the ad hocs**.) Moreover, a system that constantly responds to each ad hoc soon has little control over priorities and quickly breaks down. Thus, the system that preserves a modicum of flexibility or a modest reserve capability is more responsive to the realities of intelligence requirements. Policy makers often have little time or inclination to conduct periodic reviews of intelligence priorities, even as infrequently as annually. As a result, static, potentially outdated requirements and the necessity to make requirements decisions can be problems for the intelligence community. This was apparently the problem with the priority tier system used under President Bill Clinton. Once the system was introduced near the middle of his presidency, Clinton was not interested in visiting the relative rankings again. Without his input, the priorities could not be changed, resulting in a set of priorities that were increasingly divorced from international realities and that came to be dominated by issues pushed to higher priorities by their intelligence managers or policy clients.

Moreover, if a requirement cannot be met with current collection systems, developing the technical systems or the human sources will take time. Thus, uncertainty about requirements or lower priorities for some of them will affect the development of collection capabilities.

It is important to understand that a properly managed priority system is not attempting to forecast which issues will be the major ones over the next period of time. The system is trying to reflect those issues that policy makers said were most important to them so that intelligence can pay greater attention to those with the higher priorities. Policy makers may still feel ill-served when an unexpected issue crops up that was not part of the previous priority discussion.

One can think of the National Intelligence Strategy as an adjunct to the priority process, setting forth the major guiding principles for U.S. intelligence. In the FY2015 intelligence authorization, Congress mandated that, beginning in 2017, the DNI will "develop a comprehensive national intelligence strategy" every four years. This will be a more macro-level document, with priorities still reflecting more current concerns.

COLLECTION

Collection derives directly from requirements. Not every issue requires the same types of collection support. The requirements depend on the nature of the issue and on the types of collection that are available. For example, concerns over possible threats from cyberattacks likely derive little useful intelligence from imagery as the locus of the threat cannot initially be captured in a photo. Much better intelligence might be derived from signals intelligence, which can reveal capabilities or intentions. Collection is also the first—and perhaps the most important—facet of intelligence where budgets and resources come into play in precise terms (as opposed to broader discussions when priorities are at issue). Technical collection is extremely expensive and, because different types of systems offer different benefits and capabilities, the administration and Congress must make difficult budget choices. Also, the needs of agencies vary, further complicating the choices.

How much information should be collected? Or, put another way, does more collection mean better intelligence? The answer to these questions is ambiguous. On the one hand, the more information that is collected, the more likely it will include the required intelligence. On the other hand, not everything that is collected is of equal value. Collection analysts (sometimes referred to as **single-source analysts** as opposed to **all-source analysts**) must wade through the material—to process and exploit it—to find the intelligence that is really needed. This is often referred to as the wheat versus chaff problem. In other words, increased collection also increases the task of finding the truly important intelligence. If you have more haystacks, you do not necessarily get more needles.

An interesting phenomenon, found at least in the U.S. intelligence community, is that different analytical groups may prefer different types of intelligence. For example, the Central Intelligence Agency (CIA) may put greater store in clandestine human intelligence (espionage), in part because it is a product of CIA activities. Meanwhile, other all-source analysts may place greater emphasis on signals intelligence.

PROCESSING AND EXPLOITATION

Intelligence collected by technical means (imagery, signals, test data, and so on) does not arrive in ready-to-use form. It must be processed from complex digital signals into images or intercepts, and these must then be exploited—analyzed if they are images; perhaps decoded, and probably translated, if they are signals. Processing and exploitation are key steps in converting technically collected information into intelligence.

In the United States, collection far outruns processing and exploitation. Much more intelligence is collected than can ever be processed and exploited. Furthermore, technical collection systems have found greater favor in the executive branch and Congress than the systems and personnel requirements for processing and exploitation. One reason for this appeal is emotional. A similar circumstance, for example, exists in formation of the defense budget. Les Aspin, chairman of the House Armed Services Committee (1985–1993) and later the secretary of defense (1993–1994), once observed that both Congress and the executive branch were more interested in procurement (buying new weapons) than operations and maintenance (keeping already purchased systems functioning). Buying new systems was more attractive to decision makers in both branches and, more important, to defense contractors. Operations and maintenance, although important, are less exciting and less glamorous. Collection is akin to procurement and is much more appealing than processing and exploitation.

Collection advocates argue, usually successfully, that collection is the bedrock of intelligence, that without it the entire enterprise has little meaning. Collection also has support from the companies (prime contractors and their numerous subcontractors) who build the technical collection systems and who lobby for follow-on systems. Processing and exploitation are in-house intelligence community activities. Although these **downstream activities** (the steps that follow collection) are also dependent on technology, the technology is not in the same league, in terms of contractor profit, as collection systems.

The large and still growing disparity between collection versus processing and exploitation results in a great amount of collected material never being used. It simply dies on the cutting-room floor, to speak metaphorically. Advocates of processing and exploitation therefore argue that the image or signal that is not processed and not exploited is identical to the one that is not collected—it has no effect at all.

No proper ratio exists between collection versus processing and exploitation. In part, the ratio depends on the issue, available resources, and policy makers' demands. But many who are familiar with the U.S. intelligence community believe that the relationship between these two phases has been, and remains, badly out of balance. The congressional committees that oversee intelligence have increasingly expressed concern about this imbalance, urging the intelligence community to put more money into processing and exploitation. This is often referred to as the TPEDs (pronounced "tee-peds") problem. TPEDs refers to tasking, processing, exploitation, and dissemination. Tasking is the assigning of collectors to specific tasks. Of the four parts of TPEDs, tasking and dissemination are the least problematic for the intelligence community or for Congress. The processing and exploitation (P&E) gap is of highest concern to Congress.

Actual choices about P&E will depend on the relative priority of the issues themselves, available resources to conduct P&E, and, sometimes, the ability to process and exploit some collected intelligence—particularly signals—more quickly than others, depending on levels of encryption, the language being spoken, and so forth.

ANALYSIS AND PRODUCTION

Major, often daily, tension is evident between current intelligence and long-term intelligence. Current intelligence focuses on issues that are at the forefront of the policy makers' agenda and are receiving their immediate attention. Long-term intelligence deals with trends and issues that may not be an immediate concern but are important and may come to the forefront, especially if they do not receive some current attention. The skills for preparing the two types of intelligence are not identical, and neither are the intelligence products that can or should be used to disseminate them to policy makers. But a subtle relationship exists between current and long-term intelligence. Like collection versus processing and exploitation, a proper balance—not necessarily 50–50—should be the goal.

The U.S. system of competitive analysis—that is, having the same issue addressed by several different analytical groups—entails some analytical costs. Although the goal is to bring disparate points of view to bear on an issue, intelligence community products written within this system run the risk of succumbing to groupthink, with lowest common denominator language resulting from intellectual compromises. Alternatively, agencies can indulge in endless and—at least to the policy consumers—meaningless **footnote wars**, the only goal of which is to maintain a separate point of view regardless of the salience of the issue at stake. In the aftermath of critiques about intelligence performance on 9/11 and Iraqi weapons of mass destruction (WMD), the intelligence community put greater emphasis on collaboration, which usually means greater sharing among analysts both of their sources and their analyses. This new emphasis raises additional concerns as well, the most obvious of which is the potential for greater groupthink. (See chap. 6 for a fuller discussion.)

Analysts should have a key role in helping determine collection priorities. Although the United States has instituted a series of offices and programs to improve the relationship between analysts and the collection systems on which they are dependent, the connection between the two has never been particularly strong or responsive. Improving this relationship has been one of the goals of the NIPF. It was also one of the stated goals of DNI Clapper. The ideal state is one in which there is **analytically driven collection**—that is, collectors act in response to analytic needs and not more independently or opportunistically. This is the core of "intelligence integration," bringing collection and analysis (and counterintelligence) together at a strategic level, which will then permeate the intelligence community. It was also one of the motives for DCIA John Brennan's creation of CIA mission centers staffed by both analysts and operators. Similarly, in February 2016, National Security Agency (NSA) director Adm. Mike Rogers announced a reorganization, NSA21, to combine its major offensive and defensive arms—the Signals and Information Assurance Directorates—into a Directorate of Operations.

The training and the mind-sets of analysts are important. Analysts must often deal with intelligence that is contradictory, both internally and when viewed in light of their strongly held professional beliefs and perhaps their own past work. The way in which analysts deal with these contradictions depends on their training and the nature of the broader analytical system, including the review process.

Finally, analysts are not intellectual ciphers. They are likely to have ambitions and want their issues to receive a certain degree of high-level attention. This is not meant to suggest that they will resort to intellectually dishonest means to gain attention, but that possibility must be kept in mind by their superiors within the intelligence community and by policy makers.

DISSEMINATION AND CONSUMPTION

The process of dissemination, or moving the intelligence from the producers to the consumers, is largely standardized. The intelligence community has a set product line to cover the types of reports and customers with which it must deal. The product line ranges from bulletins on fast-breaking and important events to studies that may take a year or more to complete.

President's Daily Brief. The President's Daily Brief (PDB) is theoretically delivered every morning to the president and some of the president's most senior advisers by the PDB staff, but this depends on the availability of the president, not all of whom have made time for daily sessions. Formerly this was a CIA function but now comes under the DNI. The PDB is formatted to suit the preferences of each president in terms of length, display, detail, use of graphics, and so on. CIA, the Defense Intelligence Agency (DIA), State/INR, NSA, NGA, and the NIC all review articles that will go into the PDB, emphasizing its community nature.

Worldwide Intelligence Review. The Worldwide Intelligence Review (WIRe) is an electronically disseminated analytical product, the successor to the CIA's Senior Executive Intelligence Brief and the National Intelligence Daily, both of which were viewed as early morning intelligence "newspapers." WIRe articles vary in length and detail and include links and graphics that allow readers to drill down for more information.

DIA/J2 Executive Highlights. Executive Highlights are prepared by DIA. Although it is produced primarily for Department of Defense (DOD) policy makers, this product is also circulated elsewhere in the executive branch. Thus, in the sense of offering a different array of issues and perhaps different analyses, the Executive Highlights is a counterpart to the WIRe. On any given day, the WIRe and Executive Highlights cover some of the same issues, as well as issues that are of particular interest to their primary readers. Senior policy makers across the government will have access to both publications. The State Department Bureau of Intelligence and Research (INR) had long produced a similar morning report of its own, the Secretary's Morning Summary (SMS). In 2001, INR abandoned the SMS, relying on other vehicles to communicate with its major policy customers.

National Intelligence Estimates. National intelligence estimates (NIEs) are the responsibility of national intelligence officers (NIOs), who are members of the National Intelligence Council (NIC), which now comes under the DNI. (The NIC had come directly under the DCI but was considered separate from the CIA.) NIEs represent the considered opinion of the entire intelligence community and, once completed and agreed to, are signed by the DNI for presentation to the president and other senior officials and to Congress. The drafting of NIEs can take anywhere from a few months to a year or more. Special NIEs, or SNIEs (pronounced "sneeze"), are written on more urgent issues and on a fast-track basis.

The PDB, WIRe, and Executive Highlights are all current intelligence products, focusing on events of the past day or two at most and on issues that are being dealt with at present or will be dealt with over the next few days. NIEs are long-term intelligence products that attempt to estimate (not predict) the likely direction an issue will take in the future. Ideally, NIEs should be anticipatory, focusing on issues that are likely to be important in the near future and for which sufficient time exists to arrive at a communitywide judgment—as the Alan Breakspear definition of intelligence cited in chapter 1 suggests. This ideal cannot always be met, and some NIEs are drafted on issues that are already on policy makers' agendas. If these same issues demand current analysis, this analysis is distributed through other analytical vehicles or via a SNIE.

Beyond these types of intelligence analysis are various memos, reports, and briefs that are produced across the intelligence community on a daily basis, often with fairly wide distribution.

The following are questions the intelligence community must consider in the dissemination of information:

- Among the large mass of material being collected and analyzed each day, what is important enough to report?

- To which policy makers should it be reported—the most senior or lower ranking ones? To many or just a few?

- How quickly should it be reported? Is it urgent enough to require immediate delivery, or can it wait for one of the reports that senior policy makers receive the next morning?

- How much detail should be reported to the various intelligence consumers? How long should the report be?

- What is the best vehicle for reporting it—one of the items in the product line, a memo, a briefing? Are different vehicles needed for different policy makers, based on their preferences for consuming intelligence, their own depth of expertise on the issue, and so on?

The intelligence community customarily makes these decisions taking into account a number of factors and making the occasional trade-offs between conflicting goals. Ideally, the community employs a layered approach, using a variety of intelligence products to convey the same intelligence (in different formats and degrees of detail) to a broad array of policy makers. These decisions should also reflect an understanding of the needs and preferences of the policy makers and should be adjusted as administrations change.

Most discussions of the intelligence process do not include the consumption phase, given that the intelligence is complete and has been delivered. However, this approach ignores the key role played by the policy community throughout the entire intelligence process.

FEEDBACK

Communications between the policy community and the intelligence community are at best imperfect throughout the intelligence process. This is most noticeable after intelligence has been transmitted. Ideally, the policy makers should give continual feedback to their intelligence producers—detailing what has been useful, what has not, which areas need continuing or increased emphasis, which can be reduced, and so on. This is one of the advantages of the PDB and the early morning interchange with the president and other senior officials, seeing how they react to intelligence and getting firsthand knowledge of their concerns. However, given the extreme near-term focus of the PDB, this remains a fairly narrow field for feedback and may not be of great use to the larger intelligence community. It is also less than a systematic feedback mechanism.

In reality, however, the community receives feedback less often than it desires, and it certainly does not receive feedback in any systematic manner, for several reasons. First, few people in the policy community have the time to think about or to convey their reactions. They work from issue to issue, with little time to reflect on what went right or wrong before pushing on to the next issue. Also, few policy makers think feedback is necessary. Even when the intelligence they are receiving is not exactly what they need, they usually do not bother to inform their intelligence producers. The failure to provide feedback is analogous to the policy makers' inability or refusal to help define requirements.

THINKING ABOUT THE INTELLIGENCE PROCESS

Given the importance of the intelligence process as both a concept and an organizing principle, it is worth thinking about how the process works and how best to conceptualize it.

Figure 4.2, published by the CIA in *A Consumer's Handbook to Intelligence*, presents the intelligence cycle (as the guide calls it) as a perfect circle. Beginning at the top, policy makers provide planning and direction, and the intelligence community collects intelligence, which is then processed and exploited, analyzed and produced, and disseminated to the policy makers.

Although meant to be little more than a quick schematic presentation, this circular representation of the process is rather pervasive: The Federal Bureau of Investigation (FBI), DIA, and many foreign intelligence services all use the same schematic model. The CIA diagram misrepresents some aspects and misses many others. First, it is overly simple. Its end-to-end completeness misses many of the vagaries in the process. It is also oddly unidimensional. A policy maker asks questions and, after a few steps, gets an answer. There is no feedback, and the diagram does not convey the possibility that the process might not be completed in one cycle.

A more realistic diagram would show that at any stage in the process it is possible—and sometimes necessary—to go back to an earlier step. Initial collection may prove unsatisfactory and may lead policy makers to change the requirements; processing and exploitation or analysis may reveal gaps, resulting in new collection requirements; policy makers may change their needs or ask for more intelligence; and, on occasion, intelligence officers may receive feedback.

This admittedly imperfect process can be portrayed as in Figure 4.3. This diagram, although better than the CIA's, remains somewhat unidimensional. A still better portrayal would capture the more than occasional need to go back to an earlier part of the process to meet unfulfilled or changing requirements, collection needs, and so on.

Figure 4.4 shows how in any one intelligence process issues likely arise (the need for more collection, uncertainties in processing, results of analysis, changing requirements) that cause a second or even third intelligence process to take place. Ultimately, one could repeat the process lines over and over to portray continuing changes in any of the various parts of the process and the fact that policy issues are rarely resolved

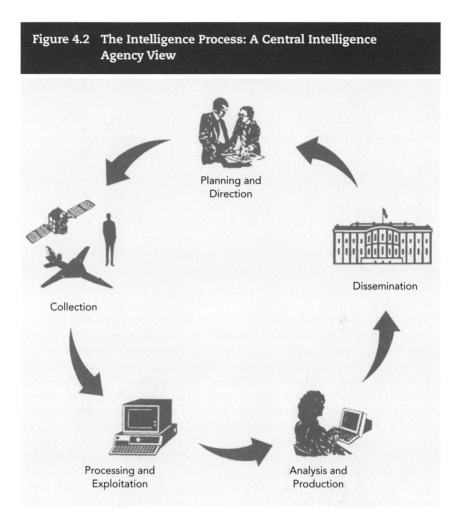

Figure 4.2 The Intelligence Process: A Central Intelligence Agency View

Planning and Direction

Dissemination

Collection

Processing and Exploitation

Analysis and Production

Source: Central Intelligence Agency, *A Consumer's Handbook to Intelligence* (Langley, Va.: Central Intelligence Agency, 1993).

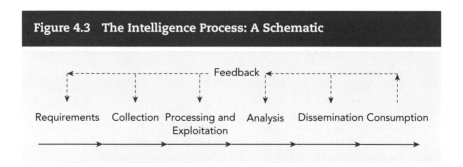

Figure 4.3 The Intelligence Process: A Schematic

Feedback

Requirements   Collection   Processing and Exploitation   Analysis   Dissemination   Consumption

Figure 4.4　The Intelligence Process: Multilayered

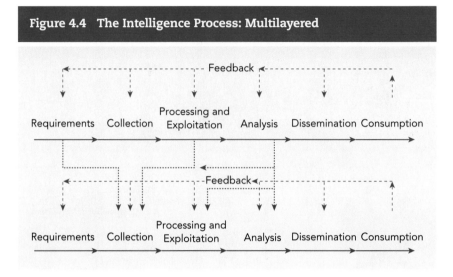

in a single neat cycle. This diagram is a bit more complex, and it gives a much better sense of how the intelligence process operates in reality, being linear, circular, and open-ended all at the same time.

Some observers have suggested that it is time to abandon or rethink the intelligence process as we have known it for the past seventy-plus years. They argue that it is outdated, almost an "Industrial Age" model in the age of computers. The answer depends to a large degree on how one views the process. If one sees this as a hard-and-fast set of steps that must be done fully and in order, then there is much to be said for rethinking the process. But if one sees it as a general guideline as to how to proceed, with enough inherent flexibility to account for shortcomings and vagaries, then the process as we know it probably remains a good guide. This latter view is how it has been presented here. Moreover, it is very difficult to suggest which steps in the process can be omitted and still result in a coherent process. Parts of some steps have become more automated—especially in collection and processing and exploitation. There are also ongoing efforts to apply information technology more to analysis (see chap. 6). But the intelligence process as long conceived remains an orderly way to go from policy makers' requirements to finished intelligence and, one hopes, feedback.

KEY TERMS

ad hocs 72
all-source analyst 73
analysis and production 68
analytically driven collection 75

collection 67
consumption 68
dissemination 68
downstream activities 74

FURTHER READINGS

The intelligence process in the United States has become so routinized in its basic steps and forms that it is not often written about analytically as an organic whole. These readings are among the few that attempt to examine the process on some broader basis.

Central Intelligence Agency. *A Consumer's Handbook to Intelligence.* Langley, Va.: CIA, 1993.

Davies, Philip H. J., Kristian C. Gustafson, and Ian Rigden. "The Intelligence Cycle Is Dead, Long Live the Intelligence Cycle: Rethinking Intelligence Fundamentals for a New Intelligence Doctrine." In *Understanding the Intelligence Cycle.* Ed. Mark Phythian. London: Routledge, 2013.

Hulnick, Arthur S. "The Intelligence Cycle." In *Intelligence: The Secret World of Spies.* Ed. Loch K. Johnson and James J. Wirtz. New York: Oxford University Press, 2015.

Johnson, Loch. "Decision Costs in the Intelligence Cycle." In *Intelligence: Policy and Process.* Ed. Alfred C. Maurer and others. Boulder, Colo.: Westview Press, 1985.

———. "Making the Intelligence 'Cycle' Work." *International Journal of Intelligence and Counterintelligence* 1 (winter 1986–1987): 1–23.

Kringen, John A. "Rethinking the Concept of Global Coverage in the U.S. Intelligence Community." *Studies in Intelligence* 59 (September 2015): 3–32.

Krizan, Lisa. *Intelligence Essentials for Everyone.* Joint Military Intelligence College, Occasional Paper No. 6. Washington, D.C.: Government Printing Office, 1999.

Omand, David. "The Intelligence Cycle." In *Routledge Companion to Intelligence Studies.* Ed. Robert Dover et al. New York: Routledge, 2014.

Phythian, Mark, ed. *Understanding the Intelligence Cycle.* New York: Routledge, 2013.

CHAPTER FIVE

COLLECTION AND THE COLLECTION DISCIPLINES

ollection is the bedrock of intelligence. Intelligence collection has been written about since the biblical references to spies in Numbers, chapters 13 and 14, and the Book of Joshua. Without collection, intelligence is little more than guesswork— perhaps educated guesswork, but guesswork nonetheless. The United States and several other nations use multiple means of collecting the intelligence they require. The means are driven by two factors: the nature of the intelligence being sought and the ability to acquire it in various ways. In the United States, the means of collecting intelligence are sometimes referred to as **collection disciplines** or INTs. This chapter discusses the overarching themes that affect all means of collection; it then addresses what the various INTs provide as well as their strengths and weaknesses.

Primarily in the military, collection is sometimes spoken of as ISR: intelligence, surveillance, and reconnaissance. The term covers three different types of activities.

1. Intelligence: a general term for collection

2. Surveillance: the systematic observation of a targeted area or group, usually for an extended period of time

3. Reconnaissance: a mission to acquire information about a target, sometimes meaning a one-time endeavor

OVERARCHING THEMES

Several themes or issues cut across the collection disciplines and tend to drive many of the debates and decisions on intelligence collection. These themes point out that collection involves more than questions such as, "What can be collected?" or "Should that be collected?" Collection is a highly complex government activity that requires numerous decisions and has many stress points.

Budget. Technical collection systems, many of which are based on satellites, are very expensive. The systems and programs are a major expenditure within the U.S. intelligence budget. Thus, costs always constrain the ability to operate a large number of collection systems at the same time. Moreover, because different types of satellites are employed for different types of collection (imagery versus signals, for example) or may be equipped to carry multiple sensors, policy makers and collection managers have to make difficult trade-offs. Significant costs are also associated with launching satellites. The larger the satellite, which is driven in large part by the nature of its sensor package, the equipment needed to power the satellite and to transmit the data, and the planned life span of the system, the larger the rocket required to put it into orbit. Finally, the costs of **processing and exploitation (P&E)**, without which collection is meaningless, should be factored into the total expense. Builders of collection systems often ignore P&E and launch costs as part of their estimates for collection. It is somewhat akin to calculating the price of a new automobile without thinking about fuel, maintenance, and insurance.

During the cold war, cost issues for technical collection rarely surfaced. The sense of threat, coupled with the fact that no better way existed to collect intelligence on the Soviet Union, tended to support the high costs of the systems. Also, decision makers placed greater emphasis on collection systems than on the processing and exploitation needed to deal with the intelligence collected. In the immediate post–cold war period, given the absence of any large and potentially overwhelming threat, collection costs became more vulnerable politically. The terrorist attacks in 2001 raised additional questions about the utility of these large overhead systems, as terrorist targets are less susceptible to collection via large-scale technical means (as opposed to unmanned aerial vehicles, that is, UAVs or drones) and may require greater use of human intelligence. More recently, renewed concerns about nation-state targets, such as China, Russia, Iran, and North Korea have likely reversed this trend to some degree.

A series of decisions since 2005 underscore the increased difficulty in sustaining the costs of technical collection. In June 2005, Rep. Peter Hoekstra, R-MI, chairman of the House Intelligence Committee, argued that too much money was being spent on satellites and not enough on human collectors and on analysts with language skills. Advocates for both views exist, but this is the sort of argument that rarely would have been made during the cold war. One of Director of National Intelligence (DNI) John Negroponte's major collection decisions came in September 2005, when he ordered the Boeing Company to stop work on a system known as the Future Imagery Architecture (FIA), widely thought to be the next generation of imagery satellites. FIA had fallen way behind schedule and had also incurred severe cost overruns. (According to detailed press accounts, FIA had gone from a program bid at $5 billion to more than $18 billion and was still $2 billion to $3 billion short.) This move was also seen as an attempt by the DNI to have a greater say in satellite decisions, which have customarily been dominated by the Department of Defense (DOD). Two years later, in August 2007, National Reconnaissance Office (NRO) director Donald Kerr testified publicly (during his nomination hearings to be the new principal deputy DNI) that he had recommended terminating two other satellite collection programs because he believed they could not be successfully completed. A decision on a new imagery constellation was not reached until April 2009, by which time press reports suggested the possibility of an imagery gap. The agreement reached between DNI Dennis Blair (2009–2010) and Secretary of Defense Robert M. Gates (2006–2011) was called "2+2," as it planned for two satellites built under the direction of the NRO and two provided by commercial satellite firms. Even then, the leaders of the Senate Intelligence Committee continued to resist building another large imagery satellite, championing smaller satellites instead.

The cost of launching satellites, which can range anywhere from $300 million to $500 million per launch, became an issue in 2014 as the Air Force looked for alternatives to its two dominant providers, Boeing and Lockheed. The issue was made more complex by the use of Russian-built engines for some launches, which was being curtailed after the Russian seizure of the Crimea in March 2014. However, Russian-based rockets have continued to be used for U.S. commercial satellite launches. Private firms, such as Space X, have also been used to launch classified payloads.

An added complication in building future technical collection systems is the shrinking industrial base that occurred in the 1990s. Secretary of Defense William Perry (1994–1997) had urged defense contractors to consolidate, arguing that there were too many firms competing for declining defense dollars. A period of consolidation followed, with firms either merging or acquiring one another. In the late 1990s, it became apparent that there were now actually very few firms left, especially in such high-specialty areas as technical collection systems. Thus, in the case of FIA there were only two industrial teams bidding on the contract. In 2012, U.S. Africa Command leased a Chinese commercial satellite to provide communications support.

The intelligence budget is also important because it is a major means by which Congress influences and even controls intelligence activities. Congress tended to be supportive of collection requirements throughout the cold war, but it was also inclined to support the disparity between collection and the less-favored processing and exploitation. Some changes in emphasis began to appear in the mid-1990s, after the end of the cold war. The House Intelligence Committee, for example, advocated the use of some smaller imagery satellites, both to have greater flexibility and to save on building and launching costs. This committee also tried to redress the collection and P&E balance, emphasizing the importance of TPEDs (tasking, processing, exploitation, and dissemination). However, the TPEDs problem remains and grew worse as new collection systems—especially UAVs—were launched, as these have increased collection capabilities. It has become increasingly difficult to get congressional backing for new collection systems without promising to improve the amount of intelligence that is processed and exploited.

Long Lead Times. All technical collection systems are extremely complex. They have to be able to collect the desired data, perhaps store it, and then send it to a remote location where it can be processed. All systems have to be rugged enough to endure difficult conditions, whether Earth-bound or space-based, although those in space face more austere challenges. No matter how satisfactory current collection capabilities are, there are several impetuses to build new systems: to improve collection capabilities, to take advantage of new technologies, and to respond to changing intelligence priorities.

The technological challenges alone are daunting and are a significant factor in the time required to build and launch a new system. The time period from the point that a decision is made to acquire such new technology to the actual launch of a large overhead collection system can be as long as ten to fifteen years. Reaching the decision to build a new system involves additional time (sometimes several years) as intelligence agencies and their policy customers debate which intelligence needs should take priority, which technologies should be pursued, and what trade-offs should be made among competing systems in an always constrained budget. Getting congressional approval can also take several years, especially if there is disagreement on which systems should have funding priority. DNI Mike McConnell (2007–2009) expressed his frustration with the satellite acquisition system, comparing the U.S. system with that of Europe, where a satellite can be developed in five years and cost less than $1 billion. But McConnell also admitted that U.S. satellites are built to collect against a more diverse set of targets and have longer orbital lives, and that there is now a higher degree of risk aversion prevalent in the U.S. system. This last point is important. Collection satellites are extremely complex to build, orbit, and manage, and launching them into a proper orbit really is rocket science. It is interesting to contrast the risk-averse atmosphere that DNI McConnell noted with the early history of U.S. intelligence satellites. According to the NRO, there were twelve CORONA satellite launches in 1959–1960 before the first successful recovery and thirteen before the first image was taken in space. Neither the budget nor the political system has such tolerance at present.

The net result of the lead times involved (not even taking into account the decision time) is that, by the time a system is launched, its technology may be dated and a whole new set of intelligence priorities may have emerged that the system was not designed to address. For example, if you were designing a U.S. intelligence satellite in 1984, the main target would likely have been the Soviet Union. Assuming the satellite was built very quickly, it would have been ready to orbit in 1995 or 1996, by which time the Soviet Union had ceased to exist. But at that point it would have been very costly to redesign the satellite, not to mention the time delays that would have been incurred. There are no shortcuts in system development if a commitment has been made to improving capabilities on a regular basis, which remains the best choice. Advances have been made in building smaller satellites more quickly, in part by relying on 3-D printing and automated testing of components. Boeing, a major satellite manufacturer, plans to apply these techniques to high-end commercial and military satellites. An array of many small satellites, perhaps as many as thirty-six, is seen as one way to deal with issues like mobile missiles, where more continuous coverage is required than can be had with one or a few large satellites.

Collection Synergy. One of the major advantages of having multiple means of collection is that one system or discipline can provide tips or cues that can be used to guide collection by other systems. For major requirements, more than one type of collection is used; the collectors are designed to be cooperative when the system is working correctly. The ultimate goal of the U.S. intelligence community is to produce **all-source intelligence**, or fusion intelligence—in other words, intelligence based on as many collection sources as possible to compensate for the shortcomings of each and to profit from their combined strength. Under the 2004 IRTPA (Intelligence Reform and Terrorism Prevention Act), the DNI is responsible for ensuring that "finished intelligence [is] based upon all sources of available intelligence." This is a somewhat odd provision, akin to a DNI collection seal of approval. It is also ambiguous, as it can be interpreted to mean all sources that should be brought to bear on an issue or all sources that are available, taking into account other priorities as well. All-source intelligence reflects collection in depth. At the same time, the diverse array allows collection managers to increase collection in breadth, that is, to increase the number of issues being covered, albeit with less depth for a particular issue.

An excellent example of collection synergy is the Cuban Missile Crisis of 1962. Although analysts were slow to understand Soviet premier Nikita Khrushchev's willingness to make such a risky move as deploying medium- and intermediate-range missiles in Cuba, the intelligence community brought a variety of collection means to bear. Anti–Fidel Castro Cubans still on the island provided some of the first reliable evidence that missiles were being deployed. A human source provided the data that targeted the U-2 flights over a trapezoid-shaped area bounded by four towns in western Cuba. Imagery then provided crucial intelligence about the status of the missile sites and the approximate time before completion, as did Soviet technical manuals turned over to the United States by Soviet colonel Oleg Penkovsky, a spy in the employ of the United States and Britain. Imagery and naval units gave the locations of Soviet ships bringing the missiles to the almost-completed sites. Finally, Penkovsky provided the United States with excellent authoritative information on the state of Soviet strategic forces, which indicated overwhelming U.S. superiority. That said, U.S. intelligence missed the fact that the Soviets had already deployed tactical (as opposed to intermediate-range) nuclear weapons to Cuba and had given local Soviet commanders authority to use these weapons as they saw fit if the United States attacked. This only became known in 1992.

A more recent example of collection synergy was the May 2011 operation that led to the death of Osama bin Laden. There was a human intelligence component—the interrogation of captured terrorists, which helped identify the courier who then unwittingly led them to bin Laden's house. There were also, according to DNI James Clapper (2010–2017), strong signals and geospatial intelligence components, presumably to keep the house under surveillance as well as to help rehearse the operation, in addition to human surveillance of the house until the operation was launched. It is also important to remember that any intelligence supporting a policy decision or an operation, whether single source or multisource, must also be processed, exploited, and analyzed before it can be of use.

In the last several years increased attention has been paid to **multi-int** or multi-int fusion. Multi-int refers to bringing together different types of technical collection, most often imagery and signals. These can be very powerful when fused. Problems can arise when multi-int is passed along to the policy maker, who may not recognize that it is not finished all-source intelligence. In other words, multi-int is more than a single INT but less than all-source. There are also analytical issues with multi-int. (See chap. 6.)

The Vacuum Cleaner Problem. Those familiar with U.S. technical collection systems often note that they have more in common with vacuum cleaners than they do with microscopes. In other words, collectors sweep up a great deal of information, within which may be the intelligence being sought. This problem is sometimes also referred to as **wheat versus chaff**. Roberta Wohlstetter, in her classic study *Pearl Harbor: Warning and Decision*, refers to the problem as **noise versus signals**, noting that the signals one wishes to receive and to know are often embedded in a great deal of surrounding noise.

No matter which metaphor one uses, the issue is the same: Technical collection is less than precise. The problem underscores the importance of processing and exploitation.

The issue then becomes how to extract the desired intelligence from the mountain of information. One answer would be to increase the number of analysts who deal with the incoming intelligence, but that raises additional demands on the budget. Another possible response, even less palatable, would be to collect less. But, even then, there would be no assurance that the "wheat" could be found within the smaller volume being collected. As Robert Litt, the Office of the Director of National Intelligence (ODNI) general counsel, noted with regard to the NSA metadata collection program that was revealed in 2013, "If you want to look for needles in a haystack, you first have to have a haystack."

The Processing and Exploitation Imbalance. As noted, a large imbalance exists between the amount of images or signals that are collected and the amount that are processed and exploited. This reflects, in part, the sheer amount of intelligence that is collected. It also reflects years of budget choices by the intelligence community and Congress that have favored new collection systems over improving P&E capabilities. According to DOD, for example, the National Security Agency (NSA) records 650 million events daily (apart from the metadata program), which eventually culminates in 10,000 reports. Although methodologies are in place to ensure that the most important intelligence is processed and exploited, an important image or message could be overlooked. DOD considered posting all collected intelligence in a single repository and then processing those items selected by analysts. This would, in theory, ensure that only the intelligence that was needed would be processed and analyzed, but it would also increase the burden on analysts to find the intelligence they needed instead of having it sent to them. The Central Intelligence Agency (CIA) is evaluating technology that would automatically examine digital images or video clips to look for details (such as a car) that are the same as those stored in an imagery library. Neither of these suggestions gets at the central issue—that P&E requires more manpower and more funding for technology if it is to have a better chance of getting the necessary intelligence out of the vast amount of information that is collected. Again, the increased reliance on UAVs with longer flight endurance and multiple sensors (see the discussion that follows) exacerbated this problem.

The P&E imbalance has been a political issue when Congress makes budget decisions. As noted, the intelligence committees find it difficult to put money into new collection systems when they are told that only as many images or signals will be processed and exploited as was the case for the previous generations of collectors. Although there may be valid explanations for this outcome, Congress—as might be imagined—would rather see increasingly expensive systems result in more collected intelligence that can be used by analysts.

Intelligence managers have been looking at **artificial intelligence (AI)** as a means of improving processing and exploitation. In simplest terms, AI is a computing technique, most useful when dealing with large sets of data. (See below regarding big data.) The literature speaks about "narrow AI," meaning algorithms that address specific problem sets, and "general AI," meaning systems capable of human-level intelligence across a broad range of tasks. The current focus is on narrow AI. Writers on the AI topic also describe an ongoing "AI arms race" among the United States, China, and Russia, although there is little barrier to entry for other states beyond adept personnel and capable computers.

Current examples of the application of AI to collection processing include the xView Detection Challenge, a $100,000 prize for the best algorithm that identifies in imagery objects of interest for disaster relief and humanitarian missions. The goal is for the algorithm to tag and annotate high-resolution imagery accurately (see p. 104). Similarly, the Defense Department's Project Maven seeks to identify objects from photos and from video, a key attribute when dealing with UAVs. However, this project has become controversial. In 2018, Google announced it would not renew its work on Maven, as many Google employees did not want to work in support of drone strikes.

AI still requires human intervention. First, someone has to write the algorithm. Then, the result of the AI has to be checked for accuracy and any errors must be corrected and "taught" to the program. However, the programs cannot self-correct, as humans do. Still, success in AI would both improve the amount of intelligence that can be processed and exploited, and free analysts for other tasks.

Competing Collection Priorities. Given that the number of collection platforms, or **spies**, is limited, policy makers must choose among competing collection requirements. They use various systems to set priorities, but some issues inevitably get shorter shrift, or may be ignored altogether, in favor of those that are seen as more pressing.

Both policy makers and the intelligence officers acting on their behalf request increased collection on certain issues. However, their requests are made within a system that is inelastic in terms of both technical and human collectors. Every collection request fulfilled means another collection issue or request goes wanting; it is a zero-sum game. That is why a priority system is necessary in the first place. Moreover, the system has little or no surge capacity; few collection systems (airplanes, drones, and ship-based systems) or spies are waiting in reserve for an emergency. Even if additional satellites have already been built, launching them requires a ready rocket of the appropriate size, an available launch pad, and other resources. (The Soviet Union used a different collection model. Soviet satellites lacked the life spans of their U.S. counterparts. During crises, the Soviets supplemented current collection assets with additional, usually short-lived, satellites, which were kept on hand with launch vehicles ready.) Similarly, one does not simply tap a clandestine services officer and send him or her off to a new assignment. Cover stories need to be created, along with the inevitable paraphernalia; training may be necessary; and a host of other preparations must be made. Inelasticity of collection resources makes the priorities system difficult at best. Finally, even though drones and aircraft can be redirected, the target area has to be one in which these collectors can fly without being shot down, what is sometimes called "permissive airspace." The shifting or nonshifting of collection resources in the face of novel situations or emergencies is always subject to 20/20 hindsight. For example, in May 1998 the newly elected government of India resumed testing nuclear weapons, as it had promised in its election campaign. The U.S. intelligence community had not detected the test preparations. As a result, Director of Central Intelligence (DCI) George J. Tenet (1997–2004) asked retired admiral David Jeremiah to review the intelligence community's performance on this hard-target issue— preventing the proliferation of nuclear weapons.

Jeremiah reported several findings, including the fact that—given the Indian government's publicly avowed intention to test, which required no clandestine collection to learn—intelligence performance could have been better. But he noted that collection assets that might have picked up indications of the impending test were focused on the Korean demilitarized zone (DMZ), at the request of the commander of U.S. forces in Korea. As an NSA director put it, the Korean DMZ was the only place in the world in the late 1990s where someone else could decide if the United States would go to war. Although the Korean DMZ remains a constant concern, for a brief period in 1998, Indian test activities perhaps should have been accorded a higher priority.

Collection Swarm Ball. A major problem that occurs in managing collection is the phenomenon known as collection **swarm ball**. This refers to the tendency of all collectors or collection agencies to collect on an issue that is deemed to be important, whether or not they bring anything useful to the table or can offer an appropriate type of collection. It is called "swarm ball" because it resembles the tactics of small children playing soccer, in which both teams converge on the ball en masse regardless of their assigned positions. Swarm ball has usually involved high-priority issues. For example, if a high-priority issue was the cyberspace attack capabilities of a hostile state, little value would be gained by imagery, although imagery collection managers might be tempted to contribute to the issue based solely on its priority. The impetus for swarm ball is clear: It allows collectors to show that they are working on high-value issues, regardless of their contribution, which will be important for their continued success in the next round of budget allocations.

The solution to swarm ball is twofold. First, agreement must be reached on which INTs are responsible for collecting on specific issues or priorities and which may not be. This is not a difficult agreement to reach, although it is time consuming, as the attributes of most issues can be delineated (locations, facilities, people involved, likelihood of communications, types of intelligence needed, and so on) and then matched against current or impending collection capabilities. Second, the agreement must be rigorously enforced, and agencies must not be penalized for not collecting against issues not suited to them, regardless of the issues' importance, and must be recognized for concentrating on the issues about which they can collect needed intelligence. The National Intelligence Priorities Framework (NIPF) has been seen as a significant advance in fending off the swarm ball issue by making clear which INTs are and are not expected to contribute to each issue. The unifying intelligence strategies begun under DNI Clapper also support this effort.

Protecting Sources and Methods. The details of collection capabilities—and even the existence of some capabilities—are among the most highly classified secrets of any state. In U.S. parlance, classification is referred to as the protection of intelligence **sources and methods**. It is one of the primary concerns of the entire intelligence community and a task specifically assigned by law to the director of national intelligence.

Several levels of classification are in use, reflecting the sensitivity of the intelligence or intelligence means. (*See box, "Why Classify?"*) The security classifications are driven by concerns that the disclosure of capabilities will allow those nations that are collection targets to take steps to prevent collection, thus effectively negating the collection systems. However, the levels of classification also impose costs, some of which are financial. The physical costs of security—guards, safes, and special means of transmitting intelligence—are high. Added to these is the expense of security checks for individuals who are to be entrusted with classified information. (See chap. 7 for details.)

WHY CLASSIFY?

Numerous critics of the U.S. classification system have argued—not incorrectly—that classification is used too freely and sometimes for the sake of denying information to others who have a legitimate need for it.

However, a rationale and some sense are behind the way in which classification is intended to be used. Classification derives from the damage that would be done if the information were revealed. Thus, classification related to intelligence collection underscores both the importance of the information and the fragility of its source—something that would be difficult to replace if disclosed.

The most common classification is SECRET (CONFIDENTIAL is rarely used any longer), followed by TOP SECRET. Within TOP SECRET are numerous TOP SECRET/CODEWORD compartments—meaning specific bodies of intelligence based on their sources. Admission to any level of classification or compartment is driven by an individual's certified need to know that specific type of information.

Each classification level is defined; current definitions are found in Executive Order 13526 of December 29, 2009:

- CONFIDENTIAL: information whose unauthorized disclosure "could be expected to cause damage to the national security."

- SECRET: information whose unauthorized disclosure "could be expected to cause serious damage to the national security."

- TOP SECRET: information whose unauthorized disclosure "could be expected to cause exceptionally grave damage to the national security."

Executive Order 13526 also created a National Declassification Center within the National Archives to streamline and standardize declassification processes.

Higher levels of access are useful bureaucratic levers for those who have them in contrast to those who do not.

The Obama administration created a category called Controlled Unclassified Information (CUI) to handle information that is sensitive but not classified and to create uniform standards for handling unclassified information (Executive Order 13556, November 4, 2010).

Critics maintain that the classification system is sometimes used inappropriately and even promiscuously, classifying material too highly or, in some cases, classifying material that does not deserve to be classified. Critics are also concerned that the system can be abused to allow the intelligence community to hide mistakes, failures, or even crimes.

Beyond the costs of the classification system and its potential abuse, the need to conceal sources and methods can limit the use of intelligence as a policy tool. For example, in the late 1950s Khrushchev broke a nuclear test moratorium and blustered about the Soviet Union's growing strategic nuclear forces. President Eisenhower, bolstered by the first images of the Soviet strategic forces taken by U-2 overflights, knew that the United States enjoyed a strong strategic superiority. But, to protect sources and methods, Eisenhower did not reply to Khrushchev's empty boasts. What might have been the results if the United States had released imagery to counter the Soviet claims? Would the release have spurred the Soviets to greater weapons-building efforts? Would it have severely undercut Soviet foreign policy? Would it have affected U.S. intelligence capabilities, even though the Soviets already knew their country was being overflown by U-2s and later by satellites? These questions are not answerable, but they provide a good insight into the problem.

In the post–cold war period, the U.S. intelligence community grew concerned about protecting intelligence sources and methods during military operations that involve cooperation with nations that are not U.S. allies. Even among allies the United States employs gradations of intelligence sharing, having the deepest such relationship with Britain, followed closely by Australia, Canada, and New Zealand, the intelligence sharing group collectively known as the **Five Eyes**. Intelligence relations with other North Atlantic Treaty Organization (NATO) allies are close, albeit less so than with the "Commonwealth cousins." But some operations, such as in Bosnia in the 1990s, involved military operations with nations that are viewed with lingering suspicion, such as Russia and Ukraine. In these cases, the need to protect intelligence sources and methods must be balanced against the need to share intelligence—not only for the sake of the operation but also to ensure that military partners in the operation are not put in a position in which their actions or inactions prove to be dangerous to U.S. troops. The multinational air campaign against the Islamic State in Syria can raise the same issues.

Another intelligence-sharing issue arose in 2002–2003, in the months before Operation Iraqi Freedom. The United States and Britain said they would provide intelligence on Iraq weapons of mass destruction (WMD) to United Nations (UN) inspectors but not necessarily all available intelligence. Some controversy arose after DCI Tenet said the United States was cooperating fully, but the CIA later revealed that it had shared intelligence on 84 of 105 suspected priority weapons sites, which some members of Congress felt was not what they had understood to be the agreed level of intelligence sharing.

The proliferation of and increased dependence on information technology systems to store and to share intelligence have now raised new sources and methods concerns. Information sharing often means putting the intelligence in locations where many intelligence officers can have access to it. Intelligence tends to be aggregated in very large soft-copy repositories under this scheme. However, as the confessed

WikiLeaks activity of Pvt. Bradley Manning and the leak of the NSA metadata program by Edward Snowden have shown, these same practices also increase the possibility of massive leaks and their attendant effect on sources and methods. In both of the cases cited above, questions were raised about why so much information was so easily accessible, how Manning and Snowden were able to remove the intelligence from classified systems and from classified office spaces, and why these individuals were hired and given clearances.

Limitations of Satellites. All satellites are limited by the laws of physics. Most orbiting systems can spend only a limited time over any target. On each successive orbit, the satellites shift to a slightly different coverage pattern. (Satellites correspond to the motion of the Earth, as they operate within Earth's gravitational pull. Thus, satellites' orbits move from west to east with each pass.) Moreover, satellites travel in predictable orbits. Potential targets of a satellite can derive the orbit from basic knowledge about its launch and initial orbit. For a variety of reasons, some individuals and organizations attempt to publicize this information. This enables nations to take steps to avoid collection—in part by engaging in activities they wish to keep secret only when satellites are not overhead.

There are several different types of orbits, depending on the mission of the satellite. **Low earth orbit (LEO)** ranges from roughly 200 miles to nearly 1,000 miles (320–1,600 kilometers [km]). (These ranges are all approximate and not strict dividing lines, except for GEO; see below.) LEO is used by imagery satellites as this allows a more detailed view of the Earth. **Medium earth orbit (MEO)** is the range between LEO and **geosynchronous orbits (GEO)**, or 22,000 miles (35,400 km). Satellites that are in geosynchronous orbit stay over the same spot on Earth at all times. For example, the United States uses GEO for early-warning satellites over both oceans. The great distance between the collectors and their targets raises the problem of transmitting collected information back to Earth. Collection can be precise only up to a point, thus explaining the vacuum cleaner problem. Satellites can also be flown in sun-synchronous orbits, that is, moving in harmony with the Earth's rotation so as to always remain where there is daylight, but this produces an easily tracked orbit. **Sun-synchronous orbit** is better for commercial satellites than for national imagery satellites.

Another interesting orbit is the "Molniya" orbit, named after the Soviet communications satellites that first used it. The Molniya orbit is highly elliptical (sometimes referred to as a **HEO, highly elliptical orbit**), coming close to the Earth over the southern hemisphere (perhaps 300 miles; 480 km) and then much farther away from the Earth over the northern hemisphere (perhaps 25,000 miles; 40,200 km). In this pattern, a satellite revolves around the Earth twice in a day. It is important to remember that the Earth's land mass is not evenly distributed; much more of it lies north of the equator than south of it. The advantage of the Molniya orbit is that it moves very quickly across the southern hemisphere, where there are likely to be fewer targets, because it is close to the Earth's gravitational pull, but then "lingers" as it moves across the northern hemisphere when it is farther away. Approximately eight of the twelve hours of one revolution will be spent over the northern hemisphere. This allows increased collection over the larger area of land. But the satellite's greater distance over the northern hemisphere also dictates that it does broad area collection as opposed to close-in or "spot" collection.

The Stovepipes Problem. Intelligence practitioners often talk about collection "stovepipes." This term is applied to two characteristics of intelligence collection. First, all of the technical collection disciplines—geospatial intelligence (GEOINT, formerly imagery or IMINT), signals intelligence (SIGINT), and measurement and signatures intelligence (MASINT)—and the nontechnical human intelligence (HUMINT), or **espionage**, have end-to-end processes, from collection through dissemination. (Some open-source intelligence—OSINT—has end-to-end processes, but some does not.) Thus, a pipeline forms from beginning to end. Second, the collection disciplines are separate from one another and are often competitors. The INTs sometimes vie with one another to respond to requests for intelligence—largely as a means of ensuring continuing funding levels—regardless of which INT is best suited to provide the required intelligence—the "swarm ball" problem. Often, several INTs respond, regardless of their applicability to the problem, thus creating the swarm ball. Within the U.S. intelligence system, a variety of positions and fora have been designed to coordinate the INTs, but no single individual exercises ultimate control over all of them. During testimony about the 2004 intelligence legislation, some of the tension between the DCI and Defense over control of the National Geospatial-Intelligence Agency (NGA) and NSA was evident. These agencies are, as the names indicate, national intelligence agencies and come under the DNI (or the DCI at the time of the hearings). But NGA and NSA are also DOD agencies and are designated as combat support agencies, thus indicating a degree of control by the secretary of defense as well. The legislation creating the DNI does not clarify this situation. The stovepipes are therefore complete but individual and separate processes.

Intelligence officers also sometimes talk about the "stovepipes within the stovepipes." Within specific collection disciplines, separate programs and processes likely work somewhat independently of one another and do not have insights into one another's operations, but they have an aggregate competitive effect that influences a particular INT. This is, in part, the natural result of the compartmentalization of various programs for the sake of security, but it further exacerbates the stovepipes issue and makes cross-INT strategies more difficult. As we will discuss, the technical INTs each involve many different types of collection, thus creating the stovepipes within the stovepipes.

The Opacity of Intelligence. The U.S. intelligence process seeks to have analysis-driven collection. This is a shorthand way of recognizing that collection priorities should reflect the intelligence needs of those crafting the analysis, who depend upon the collected intelligence. It further reflects the expectation, occasionally misplaced, that analysts have received a sense of the priorities from policy makers. In reality, the collection and analytical communities do not operate as closely as some expect, although there have been major improvements over the past 15 years. One of the most striking aspects of this is the view held by many analysts, including veteran ones, that the collection system is a black box into which analysts have little insight. Analysts say that they have no real sense of how collection-tasking decisions are made, what gets collected for which reasons, or how they receive their intelligence. To many analysts, the collection process is something of a mystery. This could simply be dismissed as the failure of one professional group to understand the methods of another group. But the divide goes to the heart of collection, often leaving analysts believing that they have no influence on collection and that whatever sources they do get are somewhat random and fortuitous. This view is significant because the intelligence community does spend some time educating analysts about collection, but often with little apparent return on the investment. This perceived opacity of collection also undercuts the goal of having analysis drive collection. It is difficult to know how to task a system that one does not fully understand.

DNI Clapper made the better integration of collection and analysis one of his major goals, and his restructuring of the office of the DNI was based on this, relying on national intelligence managers (NIMs), who are responsible for specific geographic or functional issues and for coordinating collection and analytic efforts for these issues. This is also the rationale for the unifying intelligence strategies that each NIM must write. Director of the CIA (DCIA) John Brennan's reorganization of the CIA likely addresses this issue as well, although on a more limited basis—that is, primarily between analysts and HUMINT collectors—although this proved to be a factor during the 2002 analysis of Iraqi WMD.

Denial and Deception. A targeted nation can use knowledge about the collection capabilities of an opponent to avoid collection (known as **denial**); the target can use the same knowledge to transmit information to a collector. This information can be true or false; if the latter, it is called **deception**. For example, a nation can display an array of weapons as a means of deterring attack. Such a display may reveal actual capabilities or may be staged to present a false image of strength. A classic example was when the Soviet Union sent its limited number of strategic bombers in large loops around Moscow during military parades so that they could be repeatedly counted by U.S. personnel in attendance, thus inflating Soviet air strength. The use of decoys or dummies to fool imagery, or false communications to fool SIGINT, also falls into this category. In World War II, the Allies exploited these techniques prior to D-Day in Operation Fortitude to raise German concerns about an invasion in the Pas de Calais instead of Normandy. The Allies created a nonexistent invasion force, replete with inflatable dummy tanks and streams of false radio traffic, all under the supposed command of Gen. George S. Patton. In August 2006, the British Ordnance Survey, which is responsible for all official British maps (and traces its heritage back to 1791), announced that it would end an eighty-year program of falsifying maps. During World War II, sensitive sites had been deleted from official British maps to thwart German bombing targets. The British government noted that this deception policy had been made obsolete by commercially available high-resolution satellite imagery and sources available on the World Wide Web.

The intelligence community has devoted ever-increasing resources to the issue of denial and deception, also known as D&D. Intelligence officials seek to know which nations are practicing D&D, determine how they may have obtained the intelligence that made D&D possible, and then seek to design countermeasures to circumvent D&D. As more information about U.S. intelligence sources and methods becomes publicly available, D&D is an increasing constraint on U.S. collection.

However, D&D is also a complex analytical issue and must be approached carefully. Assume, for example, that a potentially hostile state, which has practiced D&D, is believed to be fielding a new weapons system. Collectors are tasked to find it, if possible, but they cannot. Why? Is it a case of D&D, or is there no system to find? One cannot simply assume that failed collection is a result of D&D. The completely innocent state and the state with very good D&D both look identical to the observer. Thus, within D&D analysis lies the potential pitfall of self-deception. (One intelligence community wag put it this way: "We have never discovered a successful deception activity.")

A current concern has been the reported North Korean efforts to hide ongoing nuclear activities despite—or perhaps because of—the several meetings between Kim Jong Un and Donald Trump, which focused on the status and future of North Korea's nuclear weapons program. (See chaps. 11 and 12.)

Reconnaissance in the Post–Cold War World. The U.S. intelligence collection array was largely built to respond to the difficulties of penetrating the Soviet target, a closed nation-state with a vast land mass, frequent bad weather, and a long-standing tradition of secrecy and deception. At the same time, the primary targets of interest—military capabilities—existed in extensive and well-defined bases with a large supporting infrastructure and exercised with great regularity, thus alleviating the problem to some extent.

The end of the cold war called into question the utility of this collection array. On the one hand, the strategic threat to the United States had lessened. On the other hand, intelligence targets were more diffuse and more geographically disparate than before. Also, some of the leading intelligence issues—the so-called transnational issues such as narcotics, terrorism, and crime—are often less susceptible to the technical collection capabilities built to deal with the Soviet Union or other classic political-military intelligence problems. Many of the current collection targets are non-state actors with no fixed geographic location and no vast infrastructure that offers collection opportunities. These transnational issues may require greater human intelligence, albeit in geographic regions where the United States has fewer capabilities. At the same time, nation-state problems remain and may be growing in North Korea, Iran, Russia, and China. Thus, it does not make sense to abandon entirely the old method of collection, and doing so would be fiscally impractical as well. But it does seem to argue for a more hybrid approach, which again raises issues of cost.

Commercial overhead imagery capabilities can be used to augment national systems, as is evident in the "2+2" imagery plan mentioned earlier. Systems such as IKONOS, LANDSAT, and SPOT have ended the U.S. and Russian monopoly on overhead imagery. Any nation—or transnational group—can order imagery from commercial vendors. They may even do so through false fronts to mask their identity. Commercial imagery offers opportunities, freeing classified collection systems for the truly hard targets. In 2010, NGA awarded contracts to commercial firms for radar imagery to supplement government-owned systems, somewhat like the decision on electro-optical (EO) imagery in "2+2." The winning firms can sell foreign commercial radar data to NGA, as there are no U.S. firms in this area, in part because the government had placed restrictions on such work. In 2018, NGA released its new Commercial GEOINT Strategy, to allow it to make better use of commercial technology as part of its overall mission.

In 2007, Lt. Gen. David Deptula, the senior intelligence officer in the U.S. Air Force, noted that commercial imagery and online mapping software could give anyone detailed knowledge of potential targets. Deptula also acknowledged that this capability could not be controlled or reversed. A sense of the power of these commercially available capabilities can be had from the WorldView-1 satellite, launched by DigitalGlobe, a U.S. commercial system, in September 2007. This satellite can revisit a site every 1.7 days and can take images of up to 290,000 square miles (750,000 square km) a day, with a resolution (see p. 104) of 0.5 meters (roughly 20 inches). Interestingly, WorldView was developed in cooperation with NGA to ensure continued access to high-quality commercial imagery. Shutter control (that is, who controls what the satellites will photograph) is already an issue, for example, between those in the U.S. government who seek to limit photography of Israel and those who own the satellites. Dramatic changes occurred in the U.S. use of commercial imagery during the Afghanistan campaign (2001–), affecting each of these issues and perhaps suggesting a new relationship between the intelligence community and these commercial providers.

However, the commercial imagery market has proved to be less robust than advocates had hoped. In 2012, the two leading U.S. firms, GeoEye and DigitalGlobe, announced a merger after federal contracts were reduced. The following year, the U.S. relaxed satellite export controls, with the exceptions of China, North Korea, Iran, Cuba, Syria, and Sudan. (In 2017, DigitalGlobe was acquired by a Canadian firm now known as Maxar Technologies.)

Finally, open-source information is growing rapidly. The collapse of a number of closed, Soviet-dominated societies drastically reduced the **denied targets** area, that is, target areas to which one does not have ready access. As noted, the cold war paradigm that 80 percent of the information that the U.S. required was secret and 20 percent was open had reversed in the post–cold war world. Theoretically, the greater availability of open-source intelligence should make the intelligence community's job easier. However, this community was created to collect secrets; collecting open-source information is not a wholly analogous activity. The intelligence community has had difficulties assimilating open-source information into its collection stream. Moreover, the intelligence community harbors some institutional prejudice against open-source intelligence, as it seems to run counter to the purposes for which the intelligence community was created.

Satellite Vulnerability. Given that technical collection satellites are national security assets, they also represent points of vulnerability. During the cold war, the

United States and the Soviet Union both considered deploying **anti-satellite weapons (ASATs)**, and both nations tested ASATs. Efforts to negotiate a specific ASAT arms control treaty did not prove productive. However, in a series of treaties limiting or reducing strategic nuclear weapons (the strategic arms limitation talks [SALT] agreement, Antiballistic Missile [ABM] Treaty, SALT I and II Treaties, and the Strategic Arms Reduction Treaty [START]), both nations agreed not to interfere with one another's "national technical means" of collection (NTMs), a euphemism for the satellites. Both nations appeared to agree that strategic stability depended on knowing what the other state was doing rather than operating blindly in a crisis.

In the period after the collapse of the Soviet Union there were frequent press reports that an apparently impoverished Russia had, at best, only a few operational imagery satellites. Some reports suggested that, for periods of time, the Russians were "blind." This could be seen as dangerous not only by Russia but by other states as well, again fearing miscalculations during a crisis.

The United States is extremely dependent on satellites for intelligence collection, for communications, and for a host of commercial applications. Much of the U.S. military advantage depends on accurate, timely intelligence being fed to U.S. forces on a continuous basis. According to the National Air and Space Intelligence Center (NASIC), the United States has 353 intelligence, surveillance, reconnaissance, and remote sensing satellites in orbit. (China has 122; Russia has 23.) The United States also has 31 navigation satellites and 94 scientific satellites in orbit. Although no state is likely to be able to compete with the United States militarily for some time to come, U.S. forces could be hobbled by attacks on satellite systems. That is why the Chinese ASAT tests beginning in 2007 have raised concerns in the United States and among U.S. allies. There are also concerns about ongoing Chinese missile defense tests, which some believe could also be used to attack satellites. According to press accounts, U.S. intelligence had discovered indications of the 2007 Chinese ASAT preparations, but the Bush administration chose not to say anything until after the test, although it is not clear that a U.S. intervention would have led to the test's cancellation. There have also been press reports alleging that China has fired lasers in an effort to disable U.S. satellites when they pass over China. DIA has said that China will deploy a laser ASAT capable of attacking satellites in low earth orbit in 2020. The State Department raised concerns about a satellite that Russia said was a "space apparatus inspector." The U.S. said the satellite's behavior was not consistent with that mission. Russia has also been working on ASATs and claimed to have developed an aircraft-mounted laser that could disable satellites. Russia has also test ASAT missiles. According to press reports, the Russian MiG-31 jet fighter can carry a small missile that can be used either as an ASAT or to place a small satellite into orbit, which could be useful during hostilities as satellites become targets. Russia reportedly carried out a successful ASAT test in January 2019. India conducted a successful ASAT test in March 2019, raising concerns about an ASAT arms race, as well as the debris field created by India's test.

The United States is also concerned about sub-standard or defective parts getting into satellites because of intrusions into the supply chain, an issue closely related to cyber. (See chap. 12.)

In his 2019 Worldwide Threat Assessment, DNI Coats noted the continued Russian and Chinese development of ASATs, specifically to reduce U.S. and allied military effectiveness. Coats said that both countries would likely have initially operational ASAT systems in the next few years. He also noted the development of advanced directed energy weapons that could blind or disable sensors. A 2019 report by DIA echoed these concerns and also noted ASAT threats posed by Iran and North Korea, such as satellite jamming. Some analysts have raised concerns about "proximity operations," in which stalking satellites could be placed in orbit in peacetime near potential target satellites and then activated as weapons during a crisis or as a pre-emptive action.

There have also been concerns about who is responsible for satellite operations in the United States, especially if there are growing ASAT threats or attacks. Many of the most important assets are intelligence satellites, but they are operated on behalf of agencies that are also Defense components, such as NGA and NSA. In June 2015, the Defense Department announced the creation of a joint Defense-intelligence satellite and space operations center, now called the National Space Defense Center, to track intelligence and Defense satellites from one location and to serve as a backup for the Joint Space Operations Center at Vandenberg Air Force Base. The new center creates some redundancy in operations but does not resolve the issue of Defense versus intelligence control under ASAT attack.

There are few available remedies to a hostile ASAT capability. There are no alternatives to the roles played by satellites. Hardening satellites to enable them to withstand attack is difficult and makes them that much heavier, requiring a trade-off against collection or fuel payloads. It would be possible to build additional reserve satellites that could be launched if existing ones were disabled, but this requires an additional large investment that might never be used. Even with additional satellites, there would be periods in which the lost capability could not be replaced immediately if weather or technical issues delayed a launch—again assuming that the reserve satellites were loaded on a rocket and placed on a launch pad, ready to go (an eventuality that raises maintenance and reliability questions). The U.S. Air Force is looking at the possible creation of minisatellites that could navigate autonomously and be used to inspect satellites or spacecraft for damage. This program could be useful in the event of an ASAT attack or presumed ASAT attack. Critics of the program have argued that these satellites could also be used to disable hostile satellites. In May 2013, the Defense Department announced an initiative both to understand better the ASAT threat and to look at how the United States might operate without satellites if need be. In 2014, a Defense space policy official said the United States was looking at using smaller but more survivable satellites, in a policy called "disaggregation." The year 2025 was stated as the first launch of these "disaggregated" satellites. The budget to defend space systems has also increased. The U.S. Air Force is also looking at a concept called "hosted payload," meaning putting U.S. sensors on allied spacecraft as a way of spreading out sensors to deter the likelihood of attack as enough sensors would survive, and to ensure survivability if an ASAT attack occurred.

Some might argue that an ASAT attack would be an act of war. However, even if one were able to determine who had conducted the ASAT attack, the attack itself would limit the ability to command, control, and target a military retaliation.

The Chinese 2007 ASAT test also highlighted—and added to—another problem for all satellites. The destroyed weather satellite resulted in a **debris field** of some 3,400 pieces, ranging in size from less than an inch to several inches across. This debris orbits at the same speed as all other objects in space (roughly 4–5 miles/second—or 14,400–18,000 miles/hour—in low earth orbit) and thus becomes a hazard for all other satellites. In February 2009, a defunct Russian intelligence satellite collided with a U.S. commercial communications satellite, resulting in a debris field that some have estimated to be three times larger than the Chinese ASAT test, or 10,000 pieces of debris in low earth orbit. There are also some 1,000 active satellites in orbit, as well as inactive ones that have not been de-orbited. Given its dependence on space-based systems, the United States has begun to deploy a Space Surveillance System, relying, in part, on a space-based surveillance satellite (SBSS). Underscoring the risk, in January 2013 a Russian experimental satellite was rendered useless after colliding with debris from the 2007 Chinese ASAT test. The U.S. Air Force reportedly tracks over 22,000 pieces of space debris. In 2014, the United States announced plans to launch two satellites in the Geosynchronous Space Situational Awareness Program to keep track of satellites in geosynchronous orbit (approximately 23,000 miles) and to supplement Earth-based sensors that track space debris. NASA noted that as nations and firms look at launching constellations of smaller satellites, some thought has to be given to the crowding in orbital space that will take place and also to plans to de-orbit satellites once their mission is completed. Several national and international efforts are underway to create means to capture or reduce space debris but none has become operational. At the same time, several firms have plans to deploy thousands of satellites as part of the 5G (fifth-generation) network, which will make orbits even more crowded.

There is also a nexus between ASAT concerns and cyber. Instead of physically attacking a satellite, one can choose to attack the computer infrastructure on which the satellite is dependent for its operation, for transmitting data, and so on. As will be discussed in more detail (see chap. 12), this would raise even more complex issues to determine what had caused the problem and, if it was determined to be a cyberattack, attribution and an appropriate response. Alternatively, some have suggested that older satellites that have been junked but remain in orbit and have some fuel remaining could be hacked and then used to collide with intelligence-gathering satellites. Such an attack might look accidental, and it would be difficult to determine attribution for the attack.

Domestic Intelligence Collection. Although the DNI was created, in part, to bridge the gap between foreign and domestic intelligence, issues remain about how domestic collection is conducted. The central issue is still the balance between civil liberties and security.

Primary responsibility for domestic intelligence collection falls to the Federal Bureau of Investigation (FBI). The FBI is unique, as it is both a law enforcement agency and an intelligence agency, which gives it two very different sets of authorities. One issue has been FBI monitoring of Muslim Americans to prevent terrorist attacks. Although Justice Department rules prohibit racial profiling, the FBI is allowed to use nationality to identify neighborhoods to recruit informers or to look for foreign agents, which civil rights advocates still find objectionable.

The FBI has also used video and surveillance equipment on small aircraft that it flies, again some for criminal cases and some for national security. According to press reports, court orders are required for surveillance but not video.

Concerns about terrorists using various computer messaging applications and other computer-based means have led the FBI to seek broader authority to conduct surveillance. According to a 2012 report by the inspector general of the Justice Department, the FBI has been receiving copies of "unprotected" communications gathered by NSA (meaning those that did not require a court order) since 2009 and in 2012 began nominating e-mails and telephone numbers for NSA to target. In 2015, the Justice Department obtained a change in criminal procedure rules, allowing federal judges to grant warrants for remote searches of computers beyond the geographic bounds of a judge's jurisdiction. Again, civil liberties groups raised objections.

The Department of Homeland Security (DHS) stated in April 2015 that it planned to increase its HUMINT capabilities by 50 percent. DHS collects overt HUMINT. A DHS program, Enhanced Cybersecurity Services, designed to alert Internet service providers (ISPs) to identify and analyze malicious activity on their networks, has raised concerns among civil liberties groups. DHS says that it provides anonymized data, including metadata, to the ISPs, which can cross-reference it against customer records. In 2014, the U.S. Postal Service said that it approved requests from law enforcement agencies to monitor the mail of 50,000 U.S. persons for use in criminal or national security investigations.

Finally, a 2016 report by the Defense Department inspector general cited instances where Defense drones have been used domestically, to assist in search and rescue, natural disasters, or National Guard exercises. This use has always been approved by the secretary of defense.

STRENGTHS AND WEAKNESSES

Each of the collection disciplines has strengths and weaknesses. But when evaluating them—especially the weaknesses—it is important to remember that the goal of intelligence is to focus as many collection disciplines as possible on the major issues. This should allow the collectors to gain advantages from mutual reinforcement and from individual capabilities that can compensate for shortcomings in the others.

Geospatial Intelligence. GEOINT is a collection discipline that used to be called imagery or IMINT, also referred to as PHOTINT (photo intelligence). It is a direct descendant of the brief practice of sending soldiers up in balloons, first used by the French army at Fleurus in 1794. In World War I (1914–1918) and World War II (1939–1945), both sides used airplanes to obtain photos. Airplanes are still employed, but several nations now use imagery satellites. NGA (which until 2003 was the National Imagery and Mapping Agency, NIMA) has overall responsibility for GEOINT, including processing and exploitation. Some imagery also comes via DOD's airborne systems, such as unmanned aerial vehicles (UAVs), or drones. Handheld cameras also are considered part of imagery collection.

▶ These satellite photos of San Diego, California, illustrate differences in resolution. (Resolution numbers indicate the size of the smallest identifiable object.) They also show recent advances in commercial satellite imagery. The top photo has 25-meter (75-foot) resolution; major landforms—the hills and Mission Bay—are identifiable at lower center. Larger man-made objects—piers, highways, runways at North Island U.S. Naval Air Station—can be seen on the peninsula to the right.

▶ At 5-meter (15-foot) resolution, clarity improves dramatically. North Island and San Diego International Airport are visible, as are rows of boats in the marinas and wakes of boats in the bay. Taller buildings in downtown San Diego can be seen at upper center. Shadows indicate this image was taken in mid- to late morning.

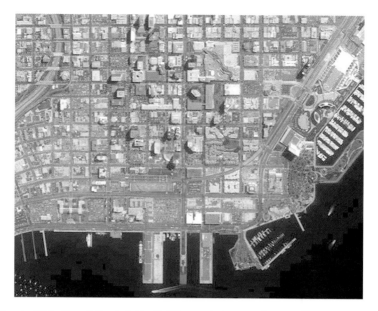

▶ At 4-meter (12-foot) resolution, individual buildings and streets can be seen, along with each boat in the marinas. At the bottom, a cruise ship is docked at the terminal. Individual cars can be seen in the parking lot above the piers.

▶ At 1-meter (39-inch) resolution, each building stands out. Individual cars are seen in parking lots and streets. Railroad tracks are visible on a diagonal at the top right, as are paths and small groups of trees in the Embarcadero Marina Park, just below the marina at the upper right. Photos courtesy of Space Imaging, Inc.

NGA defines GEOINT as "information about any object—natural or man-made—that can be observed or referenced to the Earth, and has national security implications." For example, an image of a city includes natural objects (rivers, lakes, and so on) and man-made objects (buildings, roads, bridges, and so on) and can have overlaid on it utility lines, transport lines, and so on. It may also include terrain or geodetic data. Thus, a more complete picture is drawn that may be of greater intelligence value.

The term "imagery" is somewhat misleading in that it is generally considered to be a picture produced by an optical system akin to a camera. Some imagery is produced by optical systems, usually referred to as electro-optical (EO) systems. Early satellites contained film that was jettisoned in capsules and subsequently recovered and developed. Modern satellites transmit their images as signals, or digital data streams, which are received and reconstructed as images. Radar imagery sends out pulses of radio waves that reflect back to the sensor in varying degrees of brightness, depending on the amount of reflected energy. Radar is thus not dependent on light and therefore can be used in bad weather or at night.

Infrared imagery (IR) produces an image based on the heat reflected by the surfaces being recorded. IR provides the ability to detect warm objects (for example, engines on tanks or planes inside hangars). Some systems, referred to as multispectral or hyperspectral imagery (MSI and HSI, respectively), derive images from spectral analysis. These images are not photographic per se but are built by reflections from several bands across the spectrum of light, some visible, some invisible. They are usually referred to as MASINT and have been called advanced geospatial intelligence (AGI).

Massachusetts Institute of Technology (MIT) scientists have reported the development of a camera that can reconstruct three-dimensional images from reflected photons, meaning that images could be captured in almost complete darkness.

The level of detail provided by imagery is called **resolution**. Resolution refers to the smallest object that can be distinguished in an image, expressed in size. Designers of imagery systems must make a trade-off between the resolution and the size of the scene being imaged. The better the resolution, the smaller the scene. The degree of resolution that analysts desire depends on the nature of the target and the type of intelligence sought. For example, a resolution of 1 meter allows fairly detailed analysis of man-made objects or subtle changes to terrain. A 10-meter resolution loses some detail but allows the identification of buildings by type or the surveillance of large installations and associated activity. Similarly, 20- to 30-meter resolution covers a much larger area but allows the identification of large complexes such as airports, factories, and bases. Thus, the degree of resolution has to be appropriate to the analyst's needs. Sometimes high resolution is the correct choice; sometimes it is not.

During the cold war, it was often popular to refer to the ability to "read the license plates in the Kremlin parking lot"—a wholly irrelevant parameter. Different collection needs have different resolution requirements. For example, keeping track of large-scale troop deployments requires much less detail than tracking the shipment of military weapons. The U.S. intelligence community developed the science of crateology, by which analysts were able to track Soviet arms shipments based on the size and shape of crates being loaded or unloaded from Soviet-bloc cargo vessels. (This analytical practice was subject to deception simply by purposely using misleadingly sized crates to mask the nature of the shipments.)

Several press accounts say that U.S. satellites now have resolutions of 10 inches. Commercial imagery is available at a resolution of 25 to 31 centimeters (cm) (or 10–12 inches), meaning that an object 10 to 12 inches in size can be distinguished in an image. By previous agreement with the U.S. government, U.S. commercial vendors were subject to a twenty-four-hour delay from the time of collection before they could release any imagery with a resolution better than 0.82 meters, or just over 32 inches. In 2014, DNI Clapper announced that the intelligence community had approved the sale of 25- to 31-cm-resolution imagery by commercial providers and was waiting for concurrence from other agencies.

GEOINT offers a number of advantages over other collection means. First, it is sometimes graphic and compelling. When shown to policy makers, an easily interpreted image can be worth the proverbial thousand words. Second, imagery is easily understood much of the time by policy makers. Even though few of them, if any, are trained imagery analysts, all are accustomed to seeing and interpreting images. From family photos to newspapers, magazines, and news broadcasts, policy makers, like many people, spend a considerable part of their day not only looking at images but also interpreting them. Imagery is also easy to use with policy makers in that little or no interpretation is necessary to determine how it was acquired. Although the method by which images are taken from space, transmitted to Earth, and processed is more complex than using a digital camera, policy clients are sufficiently informed to trust the technology and take it for granted.

Another advantage of imagery is that many of the targets "**self-reveal**" or make themselves available. Military exercises in most nations are conducted on regular cycles and at predictable bases and exercise areas, making them highly susceptible to GEOINT. Finally, an image of a certain site often provides information not just about one activity but about some ancillary ones as well. A distinction must be made, though, between these military targets, which are familiar to the intelligence community, and the challenges posed by terrorism. In brief, terrorism presents a smaller imagery target. Although training camps may have been set up, as was the case of al Qaeda in Afghanistan, terrorist cells or networks are far smaller, are less elaborate, and have much less visible infrastructure, if any, than do the traditional political-military targets.

Imagery also suffers from a number of problems. The graphic quality that is an advantage can also be a disadvantage. An image can be too compelling, leading to hasty or ill-formed decisions or to the exclusion of other, more subtle intelligence that is contradictory. Also, the intelligence on an image may not be self-evident; it may require interpretation by trained photo interpreters who can discern things that the untrained person cannot. At times, the policy makers must take it on faith that the skilled analysts are correct. (*See box, "The Need for Photo Interpreters."*)

Another disadvantage of satellite and some airborne imagery is that it is only a snapshot, a picture of a particular place at a particular time. This is sometimes referred to as the "where and when" phenomenon. This imagery is a static piece of intelligence, revealing something about where and when it was taken but nothing about what happened before or after or why it happened. Analysts perform a **negation search**,

THE NEED FOR PHOTO INTERPRETERS

Two incidents underscore the difficulty of interpreting even not-so-subtle images. A convincing sign of planned Soviet missile deployments in Cuba in 1962 was an image of a peculiar road pattern called "the Star of David" because of its resemblance to that religious symbol. To the untrained eye it looked like an odd road interchange, but trained U.S. photo interpreters recognized it as a pattern they had seen before—in Soviet missile fields. Without explaining the image, and perhaps without showing photos of Soviet missile fields, interpreters could have faced ridicule from policy makers.

In the late 1970s and early 1980s, when Cuba was sending expeditionary forces to various countries in Africa, newly constructed baseball fields indicated their arrival. To understand the significance of these fields, policy makers needed to know that Cuban troops play baseball for recreation. Interpreters would have to supply supporting analysis, perhaps a note explaining how seriously Cubans take baseball, to avoid being dismissed out of hand. New fields, in this case, could have meant large troop concentrations.

looking at past imagery to determine when an activity commenced. This can be done by computers comparing images in a process called **automatic change extraction**. The site can be revisited to watch for further activity. But a single image does not reveal everything. As will be discussed later, UAVs can collect video, which solves some of the "where and when" problem but raises other issues of its own.

Because details about U.S. imagery capabilities have become better known, states can take steps to deceive collection—through the use of camouflage or dummies—or to preclude collection by conducting certain activities at times when they are unlikely or less likely to be observed or by using underground facilities, which seems to be common in the case of WMD proliferation.

The war against terrorists led to four major developments in the use of imagery. First, the government greatly expanded its use of commercial imagery. In October 2001, NGA (then known as NIMA) bought exclusive and perpetual rights to all imagery of Afghanistan taken by the IKONOS satellite, operated by the Space Imaging Company. This satellite has a resolution of 0.8 meter (approximately 31.5 inches). The agency's actions expanded the overall collection capability of the United States and allowed it to reserve more sophisticated imagery capabilities for those areas where they were most needed, while IKONOS took up other collection tasks. As noted earlier, use of this commercial imagery makes it easier for the United States to share imagery with other nations or the public without revealing classified capabilities. At the same time, foreign governments that may be hostile to the United States or may see the Afghanistan campaign as a means of gauging U.S. military capabilities were denied access to imagery. The purchase also denied the use of this commercial imagery to news media, which might be eager to use it as a means of reporting on and assessing the conduct and success of the war.

DOES GEOINT HAVE TO BE AN IMAGE?

When we think of GEOINT, we typically think of an image, a photo. But there are other ways to use GEOINT. If we think of GEOINT as intelligence related to location, then there are other ways to display GEOINT. For example, if we were to plot patterns of Twitter postings, we could determine where there were major aggregations of active Twitter users. We might then be able to draw conclusions about the economics or demographics of those most concerned about this issue or most active in a debate or protest. This would be GEOINT, but it would not be an image. It would be a representation of where an activity was most or least prominent. For example, NGA has used social media to map refugees fleeing Syria.

An ancillary effect of the purchase of commercial imagery was to circumvent the **shutter control** issue. The United States can impose shutter control over commercial satellites operated by U.S. companies for reasons of national security. Concerns arose that civil liberties groups or the news media would mount a legal challenge to an assertion of shutter control, the outcome of which was uncertain. By simply purchasing the imagery, NIMA avoided the entire issue. (The French Ministry of Defense banned the sale of SPOT images of the Afghan war zone. The French commercial satellite SPOT has a 10-meter resolution.) Increased use of commercial imagery to support intelligence has become official U.S. intelligence policy. In June 2002, DCI Tenet ordered that commercial imagery would be "the primary source of data for government mapping," with government satellites to be used for this purpose only in "exceptional circumstances." Tenet had two goals: to reserve higher resolution satellites for collection tasks more demanding than map making and to provide a base for a continuing U.S. commercial satellite capability. This policy was expanded in April 2003, when President Bush signed a directive stating that the United States would rely on commercial imagery "to the maximum practical extent" for a wider range of requirements: "military, intelligence, foreign policy, homeland security and civil uses." Again, U.S. government systems are to be reserved for the more demanding collection tasks. However, as noted above, federal spending on commercial imagery has decreased in the past few years. A further development in this direction has been the increased emphasis by NGA, starting in 2015, on imagery and imagery analysis that can be released publicly. Relying on commercially provided imagery, NGA made available intelligence related to the Ebola outbreak in West Africa. Human rights organizations also used commercial imagery to get more accurate information about Boko Haram's depredations in Nigeria, which ran counter to official Nigerian government reports.

NGA created a project called GEOINT Pathfinder, which sought to answer key intelligence questions from unclassified sources only. One result has been NGA Tearline, which involves NGA partnering "with expert private groups to create public-facing and authoritative open source intelligence on various strategic, economic, and humanitarian intelligence topics that tend to be under-reported within in-depth or long-form formats."

As noted, in April 2018, NGA released its latest Commercial GEOINT Strategy, which essentially seeks to enhance NGA capabilities by deepening NGA's relationship with and use of various commercial imagery vendors of all sorts, including imagery, processing and evaluation, and analysis. A key aspect is utilizing a diverse range of these partners for the sake of "GEOINT assurance." As with the previous strategy, a key driver is growing demands by policy makers for "persistent" imagery capabilities and for greater speed in having their imagery needs met, and the growing ubiquity of geospatial data from an ever-wider number of suppliers. In 2018, NGA and the NRO created the Commercial GEOINT Activity to improve discussions with commercial imagery firms about future needs.

Some commercial providers have begun looking at the eventual (around 2021) ability to provide near-real-time imagery from commercial satellites, moving imagery from ground stations to the cloud much more quickly than is now the case. This would make it possible to provide the imagery to those who need it more quickly, such as firefighters or first responders. There may be advantages in this for these types of immediate needs, but it also sidesteps or ignores other situations where an imagery analyst first has to make sense of what is seen before passing along the imagery to a potential user.

In addition to shutter control, the U.S. government reserves the right to limit collection and dissemination of commercial imagery. (The secretary of commerce regulates and licenses the U.S. commercial imagery industry. The secretaries of state and defense determine policy with regard to protecting national security and foreign policy concerns.) U.S. policy also allows the use of foreign commercial imagery. NGA's contracts with commercial imagery firms called for 0.5-meter (19.7-inches) resolution by 2006. One U.S. company applied to the Department of Commerce for permission to deploy a satellite with a 0.25-meter (less than 10-inch) resolution. Several non-U.S. firms now offer imagery in the 1- to 1.5-meter (40- to 60-inch) resolution range.

A second major imagery development has centered on UAVs. The use of pilotless drones for imagery is not new, but their role and capability have expanded greatly. UAVs offer two clear advantages over satellites and manned aircraft. First, like airplanes but unlike satellites, they can fly closer to areas of interest and loiter over them instead of making a high-altitude orbital pass. Second, unlike manned aircraft, UAVs do not put pilot lives at risk, particularly from surface-to-air missiles (SAMs). Not only are UAVs unmanned, but operators also can be safely located great distances (even thousands of miles) from the area of operation, linked to the UAV by satellite. A third advantage is that the UAVs produce real-time images—they carry high-definition television and infrared cameras—that is, video images are immediately available for use instead of having to be processed and exploited first. This capability helps obviate the "snapshot" problem. In 2006, the Senate Intelligence Committee stated that it wanted NGA to be able to provide video and images to troops via laptop computers, thus increasing tactical imagery support.

Drones also have vulnerabilities. Like all fixed-wing aircraft, drone operations can be affected by weather. Lower flying drones are susceptible to SAMs. UAVs are also susceptible to being hacked, either having their video feeds intercepted or having hackers tamper with their overall operations. The terrorist group Islamic Jihad reportedly hacked an Israeli drone; insurgents in Iraq intercepted the feed from a U.S. drone. Narco-traffickers have also hacked into Customs and Border Protection drones over the Mexican border, jamming them or spoofing their locations. Efforts are underway to rewrite and safeguard U.S. UAV software with the goal of having "hacker-proof" UAVs.

It is possible to create a "**geofence**," a virtual barrier to prevent drone flights within a certain area via GPS, radio frequencies, or other technologies. According to press reports, the Chinese firm DJI (Dà-Jiāng Innovations) created a geofence over parts of Syria and Iraq to prevent Islamic extremists from using DJI drones in these contested areas.

The United States relies on several UAVs: the Global Hawk and the Reaper. (DOD retired the Predator drone in March 2018, but they continue to be used by the Border Patrol.) UAVs can conduct long-term surveillance over a target area and can armed be with Hellfire missiles, which are guided to the target by a laser. Thus, once a target has been located and identified, no time is lost in calling in an air strike. The U.S. government had a policy of neither commenting on nor confirming UAV-based attacks, but President Obama confirmed the death of Anwar al-Awlaki in Yemen and the use of drone strikes in Pakistan. However, in July 2016, the ODNI released a report on the results of drone strikes outside of areas of active hostilities, which are Iraq, Afghanistan, and Syria. The report stated that from January 20, 2009, to December 31, 2015, there had been 473 drone strikes, killing 2,372–2,581 enemy combatants and also resulting in 64 to 116 noncombatant deaths. The Obama administration also publicly committed the United States to using drones along the U.S.-Mexican border in February 2011 to support counternarcotics efforts and, in April 2011, two UAVs to support NATO operations against Libya. Global Hawk operates at up to 65,000 feet (19.8 km) at a speed of up to 400 miles per hour (644 km/h). It can be based 3,000 miles (4,800 km) from the target and can operate over the target for twenty-four hours. Global Hawk is designed to conduct both broad area and continuous spot coverage. Reaper operates at 25,000 feet but can fly as high as 50,000 feet (15.2 km), with a flight time of up to forty hours, depending on the loading. Reaper can carry fourteen Hellfire missiles or four Hellfire missiles and two 500-pound laser-guided bombs. Reaper can collect and send multiple video streams. One aerospace firm has created the design for a UAV that could fly at 65,000 feet and stay aloft for up to five years using solar power to recharge its battery.

The number of UAVs being deployed and flown has become an important issue, reflecting the utility of the systems and the operational tempo (OPTEMPO) at which they are used. There has been widespread reporting about increased strain and fatigue among Air Force drone pilots, to the point where operations were cut back to allow time to refresh the pilot force. There are also reports about the greater number of UAV pilots leaving the service, as opposed to those entering. One solution is retention bonuses, which are being offered. The Defense Department plans on flying sixty UAV missions daily by 2019, but this will require other services to contribute to the overall effort.

The use of UAVs and their extended collection capabilities have given rise to several new concepts. **Full motion video (FMV)** refers both to the long-duration, close-in video that can be collected by UAVs and to capabilities designed to derive as much intelligence as possible from this video. **Activity-based intelligence (ABI)** (sometimes also called **pattern of life**) means intelligence collection based on observed behaviors that are more likely to indicate that an activity of interest is taking place in that location. ABI can look either for activities that seem to differ from the norm in a given location or for patterns that indicate an activity—such as teams planting IEDs (improvised explosive devices). Therefore, ABI must depend on a large amount of collected data to establish either the norms or the patterns deemed hostile. There is an obvious connection between ABI and FMV. DARPA (the Defense Advanced Projects Research Agency) is looking at the possibility of creating an artificial intelligence system to predict a person's likely future actions based on various real-time video surveillance feeds. The use of FMV and ABI in counterterrorism is evident. It is less clear how useful they can be against traditional nation-state issues where UAVs may not be in use.

Extended range and duration is one direction for drone development. Another is drones that are smaller, lighter, and faster. DARPA announced the successful test flight of a drone (FLA—fast lightweight autonomy) that can fly 45 mph while carrying a suite of sensors. The goal is to have the drone fly autonomously, without using GPS. Several countries and firms are developing very small drones several inches (2.5–10 cm) in size, which could also be operated in swarms. The U.S. Army is also looking at minidrones that could be 3-D printed where and when needed. Again, these technologies are unlikely to remain limited to nation-states and will be available through various means to terrorists, narco-traffickers, and the like.

These UAV operations have raised many issues:

- *Processing and exploitation.* A UAV operating for up to a day at a time and shooting video produces a great deal of imagery. Again, this video has to undergo P&E if it is to be useful. But this volume of video (known to some as "Preda-porn") is a much more daunting task than even hundreds of single images. In 2009, UAVs collected 200,000 hours of video, a number that will continue to rise. All of this collection is of little use if it is not processed and exploited. An interesting analogous capability being examined is how professional baseball and football retain and tag the video from every game played. The volume in these sports is much less than in intelligence, but the techniques would be similar. UAV operators have complained about data overload and data fatigue.

- *UAVs as weapons platforms.* UAVs are not only collection platforms; they are also weapons platforms. The tempo of drone strikes increased dramatically in the Obama administration, increasing four times over that in the Bush administration. Questions have been raised about the propriety of having intelligence officers conduct these strikes, as opposed to military personnel. A 2010 UN investigation raised this issue, as have U.S. government officials. Closely related to this is the use of drones to kill U.S. citizens. (See chap. 8 for both issues.)

- *UAV vulnerabilities.* Because they are piloted remotely, UAVs depend on a computer infrastructure, which raises concerns about cyberattacks and hacking. In 2009, for example, there were press reports that Iraqi insurgents backed by Iran had been able to hack into UAVs and capture the video feeds.

- *Unilateral advantage and permissive environments.* The United States has operated UAVs as a unilateral advantage in "permissive" environments—that is, airspace where the UAVs cannot be challenged. Many of the nation-state issues that are of increasing importance to the United States—Russia, China, Iran, and North Korea—involve areas that are not permissive and therefore not suitable for UAV missions. Therefore, for these targets, the United States will have to put greater emphasis on satellite collection. This was the case during the Russian incursion into Ukraine, for example. The United States released DigitalGlobe photos showing Russian troop activities. The U.S. unilateral advantage will inevitably disappear as other nations produce UAVs of their own. Many other states—such as China, Iran, Israel, and Pakistan—already have drones, as do some non-state actors, such as Hezbollah and other terrorist and criminal groups. According to captured documents, the terrorist group ISIS or ISIL had a rather robust UAV program before losing much of the territory it controlled. Several nations, including the United States and Israel, are exploring various technologies, including lasers and radars, to defeat drones.

- *UAV operations in the United States.* In June 2013, the FBI said that it had operated drones within the United States on several occasions but provided no more details. The Border Patrol owns ten Predators and has made them available for use by other domestic law enforcement agencies. According to press reports, the Border Patrol has also considered asking for authorization to put "nonlethal weapons" on its drones intended to immobilize people. Other state and local law enforcement agencies have also used drones in the United States, as have private institutions and a growing number of individuals, raising issues concerning privacy and air safety as these systems proliferate. More recently, the Border Patrol has been examining the use of smaller, hand-launched drones. The Federal Aviation Administration (FAA) Modernization and Reform Act of 2012, which became law in 2013, requires the FAA to begin integrating drones and UAVs into the national airspace. In July 2013, the FAA certified two drones for commercial use. Initial users of these drones appear to include energy exploration firms and environmental emergency response teams.

The United States has been expanding its use of UAVs overseas. Drones were used in support of French forces against radical Muslim rebels in Mali in 2013 and are reported to have been used to keep track of other potential hotspots, such as the Kurdish regions of Turkey, Iraq, Syria, and sub-Saharan Africa. After an initial false start, the State Department accepted the use of UAVs for embassy security and diplomatic travel routes in potentially dangerous areas, reflecting the Benghazi U.S. mission attack in 2012.

U.S. UAV operations have been supported by an extensive overseas basing structure. Press reports have stated that there is a virtual belt of UAV bases in the Middle East, East Africa, and the Sahel region of Africa. Such bases always depend on the support of the local government. In May 2013, the U.S. Navy launched and landed an experimental drone, the XB-47 UCAS (unmanned combat air system) from an aircraft carrier. In April 2015, an XB-47 underwent successful aerial refueling. The full development of such a capability would give increased flexibility and reach to U.S. UAVs. In May 2017, the Air Force recovered its robotic space plane, X-37B (also known as Orbital Test Vehicle-2), which had been in orbit for almost two years, its fourth mission. DARPA is examining "sleeper" drones (UFPs, or upward falling payloads) that could be deployed on the ocean floor and then activated as needed.

A growing number of much smaller UAVs (some weighing as little as 2 kilograms [kg] or 4.5 pounds) can be carried and launched by individuals. These UAVs (sometimes called TUAVs—tactical UAVs) have smaller operating ranges and shorter flight times but are useful for tactical intelligence collection. Some UAV advocates have shown interest in stealth UAVs that could begin collection close to a presumed enemy without detection prior to hostilities. Critics argue that overflights of territory by UAVs would be precluded prior to hostilities (an incursion being a violation of international law) and that therefore stealth is unnecessary. The U.S. military has examined using blimps, but the future of these programs is uncertain. Some have been curtailed; others continue in experimental modes.

The United States is not the only nation manufacturing drones. According to press reports, China has been especially active in developing its drone capabilities, some of which closely resemble the U.S. Reaper, and there are concerns that the design may have been copied, perhaps through cyber espionage. Among the areas China is exploring is the use of swarms of smaller drones, as well as drones that can operate in the lower boundaries of "near space," meaning roughly at 18 to 25 km (60,000–82,000 feet), similar to Global Hawk and Reaper. China has also taken advantage of U.S. policy that had restricted the sale of its UAVs as part of the Missile Technology Control Regime (MTCR), the 1987 multilateral export control regime to prevent missile proliferation. China is not an MTCR signatory and has sold drones to several Middle East nations. In 2018, the Trump administration announced a change in policy, allowing U.S. manufacturers to make direct commercial sales of drones, reversing a 2016 Obama administration policy.

In a related UAV development, IARPA (the Intelligence Advanced Research Projects Agency), the DNI's technical research and development agency, announced that it was interested in developing improved means for watching maritime traffic and international sea chokepoints. One possible response could be networks of UUVs (unmanned underwater vehicles), in effect squadrons of unmanned submarines that would operate much as UAVs do.

A third major imagery development is the utility of very small satellites, sometimes referred to as microsatellites (approximately 20 inches high and 41 inches in diameter) or nanosatellites, such as CubeSat, which is a 10-cm (4-inch) cube weighing 1.3 kg (2.9 pounds), and pico satellites that are even smaller. These smaller satellites can be launched as demands for collection increase. They do not have the multiyear orbital lives of the more traditional large satellites and do not carry as large a payload of sensors, but they provide a more flexible collection array and might be useful if satellites were lost to ASATs. Because of their small size, nanosatellites can be launched in swarms of a dozen or more at a time, which compensates for their more limited capabilities. Google purchased the small satellite firm Skybox and planned to be able to revisit any place on Earth twice daily by 2016 and three times daily by 2018, when all twenty-four of its satellites were in orbit. However, in 2017, Google sold this capability to Planet but also agreed to buy data from the new owners—thus giving Google the data it wanted without having to operate a satellite fleet. Planet has launched several "flocks" of satellites, meaning multi-satellite constellations, including an eighty-eight-satellite flock launched on an Indian rocket in 2017. Planet has provided NGA with imagery of most of the Earth's landmass that is refreshed every fifteen days. DARPA has a program called Phoenix, which would mine old orbiting satellites for parts and construct a new satellite around them. DARPA is also examining a lightweight optics array made of a flexible membrane that would function as a large telescope in space.

There have also been several press articles about the possibility of creating microdrones. These are typically compared to dragonflies and can be as small as 15 cm (6 inches) in wingspan. Microdrones are powered so that their flight can be controlled and they can be equipped with tiny cameras. Microdrones are still experimental, and no U.S. agency will acknowledge such a program. These platforms would have the advantage of being relatively inexpensive and could access locations that even UAVs could not target.

All of these various new or experimental systems have two goals. The first is to enhance the overall flexibility of the GEOINT collection system, especially in the ability to respond to sudden needs for geospatial intelligence in areas where assets had not been operating before but on a much more localized basis than by launching another satellite. The second is the drive to achieve what some call "persistent surveillance," in other words, as close to around-the-clock collection as is possible. This obviously represents a large investment in collectors and would also create further P&E burdens and strains.

As noted, the war on terrorists has led to the use of NGA imagery platforms on potential terrorist targets within the United States as a security measure. These have included the 2002 Olympics in Utah, the quadrennial political conventions, and other public events that would attract large crowds or locations (such as nuclear power plants) that might be targets. Unlike the CIA and NSA, NGA can operate within the United States, although as a defense component, NGA cannot be used to support law enforcement. In August 2007, however, the Bush administration announced that it would allow greater access to imagery by state and local officials. Officials argue that this is necessary both to improve homeland security (in such areas as seaport and border security) and to help with disaster planning or relief. They also argue that these uses do not violate the law enforcement restrictions. Still, various groups that are concerned about intrusive government activities have raised questions about this domestic imagery collection, as have some members of Congress. A plan by DHS to transfer the Commerce Department's Civil Applications Office, which oversees domestic satellite imagery, to DHS's National Applications Office, was abandoned by the Obama administration in the face of congressional opposition. In March 2011, press reports stated that the United States was flying UAVs "deep" into Mexico to gather narcotics-related intelligence. DHS's Customs and Border Protection has also used drones to monitor illegal entry into the United States along the southern border. The effectiveness of this effort is uncertain.

Finally, space-based imagery capabilities have proliferated. Once the exclusive preserve of the United States and the Soviet Union, this field has expanded rapidly. France, Japan, and Israel have independent imagery satellites. India relies on Israeli-made radar-imaging satellites, which show a concern over indications and warning. As of 2018, China had four high-resolution imagery satellites and announced that it is building a national engineering and research center to design small satellites, hoping to produce six to eight annually. China plans on launching more than 100 satellites by 2020 for a variety of monitoring tasks within China itself—economic, ecological, and others. Germany has decided to create its own satellite capability. Furthermore, cooperation among current and would-be imagery satellite powers has increased. Israel is reported to have cooperative imagery relationships with India, Taiwan, and Turkey. Brazil and China are cooperating on satellites; South Korea and Germany are considering a cooperative venture. Russia, eager for cash, has helped several nations launch satellites, including Israel, Japan, and Iran. Some experts believe that the Iranians seek an independent launch capability, which could be part of their overall missile development program. Perhaps more significant, France is working with several European partners—Belgium, Italy, and Spain—on its next generation of imagery satellites. This independent capability within NATO could prove troublesome, as the United States may have to deal with allies having their own imagery and different interpretations of events. This apparently happened in 1996, when France refused to support a U.S. cruise missile attack on Iraq because the French maintained that their imagery did not show significant Iraqi troop movements into Kurdish areas. France, Germany, and Israel also have indigenous UAV programs. In 2004, Iran admitted supplying eight UAVs to the Hezbollah terrorist group, one of which penetrated Israeli airspace. In 2017, German intelligence received funding for its own high-resolution satellite. This would be the first satellite controlled by a German intelligence agency.

Imagery proliferation also has a commercial aspect. A British firm, Surrey Satellite Technology (now owned by Airbus, with a U.S. subsidiary), has pioneered a range of imagery satellites, including nanosatellites and microsatellites weighing as little as 6.5 kg, or just over 14 pounds. These satellites do not approach resolutions of the best national systems, but they are sufficient for many nations' needs. Among the firm's clients are Algeria, Britain, China, Nigeria, and Thailand. These satellites also have the ability to get close to other satellites and image them, which is of concern to the United States because of their potential to be used as ASATs. Several nations, including Australia, Malaysia, and South Korea, as well as some current Surrey customers, are looking at small satellite demonstration projects. More recently, two U.S. firms have begun developing microsatellites, weighing between 10 and 100 kg (22–220 pounds). Microsatellites are launched more easily and, given their small size, can "piggyback" on other launch vehicles. Their small size obviously limits the size and number of sensors they can carry, which is why they are launched in flocks or **constellations**.

The proliferation of imagery capabilities could be a problem for the United States should it become engaged in hostilities with a state that has access to space-borne imagery satellites. Therefore, DOD has considered countermeasures. One such system, Counter Surveillance Reconnaissance System (CSRS, pronounced "scissors"), would have blinded or dazzled imagery satellites with directed energy. However, Congress refused to fund the program.

Signals Intelligence. SIGINT is essentially a twentieth-century phenomenon. (There was some tapping of telegraph lines by both sides during the U.S. Civil War, but this appears to have been fairly minor.) British intelligence pioneered the field during World War I, successfully intercepting German communications by tapping underwater cables. The most famous product of this work was the Zimmermann Telegram, a 1917 German offer to Mexico of an anti-U.S. alliance, which Britain made available to the United States without revealing how it was obtained. With the advent of radio communications, cable taps were augmented by the ability to pluck signals from the air. The United States also developed a successful signals intercept capability that survived World War I. Prior to World War II, the United States broke Japan's Purple Code; Britain, via its ULTRA decrypting efforts, read German codes.

Today, signals intelligence can be gathered by Earth-based collectors—ships, planes, ground sites—or satellites. NSA is responsible for both carrying out U.S. signals intelligence activities and protecting the United States against hostile SIGINT. UAVs, which had initially been GEOINT platforms, are being used for SIGINT as well. Global Hawk can be configured to carry electronic intelligence (ELINT) and communications intelligence (COMINT) payloads. This enhances the utility of the UAV, as it allows collection synergy between GEOINT and SIGINT on a single platform that can be targeted or retargeted during flight. To enhance cooperation, NSA and NGA created a Geocell, a jointly manned unit that allows quick handoffs between the two INTs, which can be especially important when tracking fast-moving targets, such as suspected terrorist activities.

As with GEOINT, the United States seeks ways to deny enemies their own SIGINT capabilities. Although the CSRS against imagery was not funded, DOD has declared the Counter Communications System operational. The system temporarily jams communications satellites with radio frequencies.

SIGINT consists of several different types of intercepts. The term is often used to refer to the interception of communications between two parties, or COMINT. SIGINT can also refer to the pickup of data relayed by weapons during tests, which is sometimes called telemetry intelligence (TELINT). Finally, SIGINT can refer to the pickup of electronic emissions from modern weapons and tracking systems (military and civil), which are useful means of gauging their capabilities, such as range and frequencies on which systems operate. This is sometimes referred to as ELINT (electronic intelligence) but is more customarily referred to as FISINT (foreign instrumentation signals intelligence).

The ability to intercept communications is highly important because it gives insight into what is being said, planned, and considered. It comes as close as one can, from a distance, to reading the other side's mind, a goal that cannot be achieved by imagery. Reading the messages and analyzing what they mean is called **content analysis**. Tracking communications also gives a good **indication and warning**. As with imagery, COMINT relies to some degree on the regular behavior of those being collected against, especially among military units. Messages may be sent at regular hours or regular intervals, using known frequencies. Changes in those patterns—either increases or decreases or switching frequencies—may be indicative of a larger change in activity. Monitoring changes in communications is known as **traffic analysis**, which has more to do with the volume and pattern of communications than it does with the content. (*See box, "SIGINT Versus IMINT."*) Traffic analysis is now called geospatial metadata analysis, emphasizing the importance of pinpointing the location of the signal as a means of attacking the sender or recipient, if necessary. One other important aspect of COMINT is that it provides both content (what is being said) and what might be called texture, meaning the tone, the choice of words, or the accent (such as when distinguishing one type of French or Spanish or Arabic speaker). Texture is like listening to the tone or watching the facial expression of a speaker. This can tell you as much as—or sometimes more than—the words.

SIGINT VERSUS IMINT

An NSA director once made a distinction between IMINT—now called GEOINT—and SIGINT: "IMINT tells you what has happened; SIGINT tells you what will happen."

While an exaggeration—and said tongue in cheek—the statement captures an important difference between the two collection disciplines.

COMINT has some weaknesses. First and foremost, it depends on the presence of communications that can be intercepted. If the target goes silent or opts to communicate via secure landlines instead of through the air or lines that can be intercepted, then the ability to undertake COMINT ceases to exist. Perhaps the landlines can be tapped, but doing so is a more difficult task than remote interception from a ground site or satellite. The target also can begin to **encrypt**—or code—its communications. Within the offensive-defensive struggle over SIGINT is a second struggle, that between encoders and codebreakers, or **cryptographers**. Crypies, as they are known, like to boast that any code that can be constructed can also be solved. But the present day is far removed from the Elizabethan age of relatively simple ciphers. Computers greatly increase the ability to construct complex, onetime-use codes. Meanwhile, computers also make it more possible to attack these codes. Finally, the target can use false transmissions as a means of creating less compromising patterns or of subsuming important communications amid a flood of meaningless ones—in effect, increasing the ratio of noise to signals.

The use of computers has also enhanced the uses of **steganography**, which means concealed writing, a technique that is centuries old. A major difference between cryptography and steganography is that in cryptography, the existence of the message is known but it may not be in a format that can be read. In steganography, the message itself is hidden, so its existence is uncertain at best. Information technology allows messages to be hidden on web pages or within other packets of data.

Another issue is the vast quantity of communications now available: telephones of all sorts, faxes, e-mails, and so on. As of 2013, there were some 7 billion telephones worldwide (mobile and fixed) or more than the total world population, generating some 12.4 billion calls every day. Newer communications channels add to the total. In 2017, on a daily global basis, there were 23 billion text messages, 60 billion WhatsApp messages, and 500 million tweets. As communications switch to fiber-optic cable, the available volume will increase. Also, more phone calls are going over the Internet using the Voice-over-Internet Protocol (VoIP) technology.

Even a focused collection plan collects more COMINT than can be processed and exploited. One means of coping with this is the **key-word search**, in which the collected data are fed into computers that look out for specific words or phrases. The words are used as indicators of the likely value of an intercept. The system is not perfect, but it provides a necessary filter to deal with the flood of collected intelligence. TELINT and ELINT offer valuable information on weapons capabilities that would otherwise be unknown or would require far more risky human intelligence operations to obtain. However, as the United States learned from its efforts to monitor Soviet arms, the weapons tester can employ many techniques to maintain secrecy. Like communications, test data can be encrypted. It can also be encapsulated—that is, recorded within the weapon being tested and released in a self-contained capsule that will be recovered—so that the data are never transmitted as a signal that would be susceptible to interception. If the data are transmitted, they can be sent in a single burst instead of throughout the test, greatly increasing the difficulty of intercepting and reading the data. Or the data can be transmitted via a spread spectrum, that is, using a series of frequencies through which the data move at irregular intervals. The testing nation's receivers can be programmed to match the frequency changes, but such action greatly increases the difficulty of intercepting the full data stream.

One issue that arises in SIGINT, especially in COMINT, is **risk versus take**. This refers to the need to consider the value of the intelligence that is going to be collected (the take) against the risk of discovery—either in political terms or in the collection technology that may then be revealed to another nation.

The war against terrorists has underscored a growing concern for SIGINT. As with the other collection disciplines, SIGINT was developed to collect intelligence on the Soviet Union and other nations. Terrorist cells offer much smaller signatures, which may not be susceptible to interception by remote SIGINT sensors. Therefore, a growing view is that future SIGINT will have to rely on sensors that have been physically placed close to the target by humans. In effect, HUMINT will become the enabler for SIGINT. Signs also are evident that terrorist groups have increasing knowledge about U.S. SIGINT capabilities and therefore take steps to evade SIGINT detection by such means as using cell phones only once or avoiding cell phones and other telecommunications altogether.

Another SIGINT weakness is found within COMINT—foreign language capabilities. During the cold war, the United States emphasized the need for Russian speakers through a series of government-sponsored educational programs. Today, different languages are at issue: Arabic (which has many spoken varieties), Farsi, Pushto, Dari, Hindi, Urdu, and other languages common to the Middle East and South Asia, to which we can add various African languages or dialects. None of these languages has much academic support in the United States, and many have the added difficulty of not being written in the Roman alphabet (which is also true of Russian, Chinese, and some 6,000 other languages). It takes about three years (full time) to train someone to the desired capability in a non–Roman alphabet language. The United States suffers in its language capabilities because of the decline in language requirements in colleges and universities. According to the Modern Language Association, only 8 percent of schools have language requirements, down from 87 percent in the 1950s through the early 1970s. The United States, being an immigrant nation, has among its citizens speakers of most languages. But they need to be recruited, cleared, and trained. Clearing such candidates was a major motivation in DNI McConnell's efforts to improve the security clearance process. In some cases, the native language skills of these people are very good, but their ability to translate into English, which is the required outcome, is poor. For the foreseeable future, language skills will be a major problem for COMINT and for all intelligence activities.

A more fundamental issue for SIGINT collection in U.S. intelligence has been the capability of NSA and the FBI to keep pace with the technological changes. It is important to understand that NSA has two roles: offense and defense. NSA intercepts foreign communications but also acts to prevent the interception of U.S. communications. These two roles are very closely allied—in effect, they are opposite sides of the same coin. This explains Adm. Mike Rogers's decision in his NSA21 plan to merge his offensive and defensive capabilities (Signals and Information Assurance) into a single Operations Directorate. One major change came in 2017, when China tested the Micius communications satellite, which sends messages by light—photons—rather than radio waves. This **quantum cryptography** is much more difficult to intercept. In effect, the sender will know if a message has been intercepted and it cannot be hacked as the message self-destructs upon identifying an interception attempt.

The offense role is made more difficult by the ongoing explosion in the amount of communications worldwide. Again, NSA does not have to track all of these communications, but it does have to find the intercepts it needs inside this vast communications haystack. The FBI, which conducts electronic surveillance within the United States, faces a similar problem. In 2009, the FBI, responding to a report by its inspector general, said that it had an audio backlog of more than 200 days (the inspector general report said the backlog was ten times larger) and that it reviewed about 25 percent of recordings made related to counterintelligence. As with other P&E issues, not every recording needs to be listened to, but even processing a significant fraction remains daunting.

Encryption, which used to be the prerogative of states, is now an integral part of information technology. Intelligence and law enforcement officials have expressed concern about communications "going dark." The privacy of communications and the security of commercial and financial transactions is a positive aspect, but there is also the problem of terrorists or criminals using these same encrypted devices to communicate. This came to a head when the FBI sought Apple's assistance in unlocking the phone used by the couple who carried out the 2015 San Bernardino shooting to determine if anyone else was involved and if there were links to terrorist groups. Although Apple had helped the government in previous cases, it balked now. Apple expressed concern about the effect on its brand and on other American technology, especially overseas. Among Apple's more curious arguments was that to comply would send a signal to foreign nations that it was acceptable to break into Apple phones, as if foreign services were waiting for U.S. legal permission. The FBI sued Apple for access but, before a final judicial decision, found a way into the phone. Somewhat ironically, Apple then asked the FBI to explain how the entry was made so that Apple could secure its devices. The positions of technology firms and civil liberties advocates versus law enforcement and intelligence officials on the encryption issue remain unchanged.

Likewise, the defensive role is made more difficult by the increasing number of hacking attempts against government computers. Several new procurement programs designed to upgrade NSA infrastructure ran into cost overruns and failed to produce the needed improvements. In 2017, there were many press reports that a group called Shadow Brokers had hacked into NSA computers and stolen an NSA hacking tool, which they then used for criminal purposes. Several nations have claimed to have alerted the United States to this activity, which originated in Russia. This raised obvious questions about NSA security, especially in the aftermath of the Snowden leaks. In July 2018, the NSA inspector general flagged "significant" issues related to employees obeying rules and relations intended to safeguard "computer networks, systems and other data." (See chap. 7.) There have even been concerns that NSA's obviously high demands for electrical power will soon outstrip available supplies in its home state of Maryland.

The defense role has received increased attention as the number of attacks on U.S. government computers has increased sharply. Defense not only seeks to protect U.S. codes and communications but also the vast array of computers on which the nation relies. In January 2008, President Bush signed a directive authorizing the intelligence community—especially NSA—to monitor the networks of all federal computers as a means of detecting and defending against external attacks.

An important aspect of SIGINT operations for the United States in combating terrorists is the legal issues involved. Under pre-2001 rules, if the SIGINT target was within the United States, the operation became the responsibility of the FBI, not NSA. To undertake wiretaps in the United States, the FBI must get a court order. Foreign intelligence wiretaps (as opposed to criminal case wiretaps) come under the jurisdiction of the Foreign Intelligence Surveillance Court or FISC, created in 1978 by the Foreign Intelligence Surveillance Act (FISA, pronounced "fy-za"). This was not seen as a major legal barrier, as the FISC has reportedly approved almost 34,000 requests and denied only 12 since its inception. Several hundred were also modified. (See chap. 10 for more details on the court.)

The changing nature of communications and the campaign against terrorists also led to requests by U.S. intelligence to change the rules under which they collect SIGINT within the United States. Since 1978, these activities had been conducted under FISA. Although FISA allowed for warrantless wiretaps under certain conditions (a one-year limit, conducted on foreign powers only, authorized by the president via the attorney general), press stories in December 2005 revealed a more extensive use of warrantless wiretaps since 2002. The new warrantless taps President Bush allowed after the September 11, 2001, attacks were placed on calls between people in the United States and terrorist suspects abroad. The Bush administration argued that the new program was necessary as the taps had to be placed quickly and this did not allow time to go to the FISA court. Judge Royce C. Lamberth, who headed the court from 1995 to 2002, refuted this argument, saying that court procedures had been streamlined in 2001 to make the court more responsive. In August 2007, DNI McConnell revealed that legal changes were necessary because a judge on the FISA court had ruled that court-sanctioned warrants were required on any communications traveling through the United States, even if the two parties involved in the exchange were both overseas. This was seen as a major setback for surveillance, as many Internet communications will pass through the United States, even if they are between foreign locations, simply because there is more bandwidth in the United States. According to press reports, intelligence officials said this ruling had resulted in a 25 percent drop in intercepts. McConnell also revealed that 100 or fewer individuals in the United States were under surveillance. He also acknowledged that some telecommunications companies had assisted the warrantless surveillance program.

After an intense and partisan debate that lasted almost a year, Congress passed a new law in July 2008 that was largely seen as a victory for the Bush administration, allowing emergency wiretaps on American targets for one week without a warrant to preclude losing important intelligence and if there is strong reason to believe that the target is linked to terrorism. There was a similar one-week provision for foreign targets. Broad warrants, versus specific ones, are allowed against foreign communications. The law also grants legal immunity to telecommunications firms that cooperated with the earlier warrantless program, which had been a major issue. The new law also makes clear that changes can only be made in the wiretap program within the law and not solely on order of the president. Various oversight provisions by the FISA court and by inspectors general were laid out as well.

The surveillance controversy flared anew in June 2013, when Edward Snowden, an NSA contract employee, leaked documents revealing the details of two programs that had been created in legislation. One program monitored the metadata of telephone calls, collected under the provisions of Section 215 of the USA PATRIOT Act (Uniting and Strengthening America by Providing Appropriate Tools Required to Intercept and Obstruct Terrorism Act). This program collected the numbers of the telephones involved in the call and the date, time, and length of the call. The program was covered by FISA court orders, which compelled telephone companies to provide the requested metadata. NSA and ODNI personnel stated that no telephone conversations were intercepted as part of this program. An internal NSA audit that was released showed just under 2,800 violations, of which 1,900 did not involve U.S. citizens. Defenders of the program argued that the majority of violations were inadvertent, that NSA was overseeing the program for violations, and that the actual number was minuscule given the large number of records being search. Critics of the program argued that the number of reported violations was still large and that the violations underscored the potential for abuse.

The scale of surveillance versus the number of errors remains controversial. For example, according to the DNI's Statistical Transparency Report, in 2017 NSA collected 534 million telephone calls and text message records. This was more than three times the 2016 total but less than under the previous bulk collection program. But in June 2018, NSA announced that it had deleted 685 million call records obtained from telecommunications companies going back to 2015, after determining that "technical irregularities" had resulted in NSA obtaining some data that had not been authorized. All of these data indicate both the scope of the collection problem that NSA faces and the difficulty of adhering to legal requirements at the same time. In July 2018, the NSA inspector general cited "many issues of non-compliance" in protecting data gathered from U.S. citizens but said these were not flagrant or willful violations.

There is a second court order establishing limits on what can be done with the collected data. According to Robert Litt, then the ODNI general counsel, the data can "be queried" only if there is "reasonable suspicion" that a telephone number is associated with "specified foreign terrorist organizations." Litt also said that only 300 of the vast number searched were approved for further search.

The second program, sometimes called PRISM—although this is the name of the database and not the program—targets various Internet communications of foreigners outside the United States, under the provisions of Section 702 of the FISA. Again, this requires an order from the FISC.

The Section 215 program is sometimes referred to as "bulk collection," but this can somewhat be misleading. Although telephone records were collected in bulk, in 2013, these resulted in specific queries about 248 "known or presumed U.S. persons." In other words, a very large initial collection was then significantly narrowed to specific targets. (In 2018, the Supreme Court ruled that the government generally needs a warrant to collect cell phone location data from telecommunications firms.)

The revelation of these two programs raised multiple issues. An obvious one was how Snowden was able to access this material and then release it, as well as the related issue of the role of contractors in the intelligence community and how they are granted clearances. (See chap. 7 for a fuller discussion.) Another issue was judicial and congressional oversight, although here many members of Congress, particularly those on the two intelligence committees, rallied around the programs and the extent to which they had been informed. (See chap. 10.) However, other members, mostly not on these committees, found the oversight of these programs wanting and forced a vote on ending this collection that failed by a very narrow margin. Finally, there is the larger question of the tension between civil liberties and national security. (See chap. 13.) Some observers questioned the legality of the programs despite the claims of legal and judicial authorization. Various federal judges made contradictory rulings about the legality of the NSA program.

In August 2013, President Obama created the President's Review Group on Intelligence and Communications Technologies, tasked with reviewing how the United States could employ technical collection capabilities to safeguard both national security and civil liberties. The review group reported in December 2013, making forty-six recommendations to the president. In January 2014, Obama defended the legality of the NSA programs and the manner in which they were conducted. Among the changes Obama announced were the following:

- Requiring a court order for each search of the collected telephone metadata
- Reducing the secrecy of national security letters (NSLs; see below)
- No monitoring of friendly and allied foreign leaders unless there is a compelling national security purpose
- Develop safeguards for collection against foreigners similar to those accorded to U.S. persons
- Asking Congress to create a panel of privacy advocates for FISC cases but apparently only in limited circumstances

Many of the other issues raised by these leaks—such as who should hold the repositories of collected metadata, the government or the private sector—either were not addressed or were remanded for further study.

In the aftermath of the Snowden leaks in 2013, Congress considered several bills related to the NSA programs. The USA FREEDOM Act (Uniting and Strengthening America by Fulfilling Rights and Ensuring Effective Discipline Over Monitoring Act), passed in 2015, made minimal changes to the NSA programs. The law generally prohibits the Section 215 bulk-collection program for collection not limited as much as possible by "specific selection terms," meaning a person, account, address, specific device, or other identifier. There are provisions for emergency coverage in advance of a court order. Private firms have greater latitude to report publicly on FISA orders, which had become an issue for major information technology and communications firms, some of which took steps to put "unbreakable encryption" in place to thwart NSA collection. The DNI and attorney general will review FISA court opinions that contain significant legal interpretations for possible redacted declassification. Finally, the act requires the FISA court to designate "friends of the court" panels to represent the public interest in cases involving new or significant legal issues (see chap. 10). Interestingly, the new law does not speak of SIGINT collection per se but uses the euphemism "tangible things." In July 2015, DNI Clapper's office said that NSA analysts would no longer be able to search a database holding five years of U.S. domestic calling records.

In 2017, Congress began reconsideration of Section 702, whose legislative authorization would expire at the end the year. Debate over this legislation was made more complex by the Snowden leaks and by Donald Trump's erroneous claims that the act had been used to spy on his presidential campaign. As Congress neared final passage in January 2018, Trump sent mixed signals regarding his support or opposition. The final act, which Trump did sign, reauthorized the program for six years. Among the key provisions are the following:

- The attorney general and DNI must adopt procedures "consistent with . . . the 4th amendment" for querying information collected under Section 702 in order to retrieve U.S. persons communications. The FISC must review these procedures.

- There are restrictions placed on U.S. person information obtained under Section 702 for use in criminal cases.

- Section 103 concerns **"about"** collection—meaning messages taken from the Internet that may not be going to or from a specific target but contain key selectors (search terms) in the body. This is also known as "upstream collection." NSA had ceased "about" collection in 2017. The attorney general and DNI can resume this collection, but they must give Congress thirty days to review the program and must also include a FISC decision approving it.

- NSA and FBI must appoint privacy and civil liberties officers.

- The attorney general and DNI must report to Congress "on current and future challenges to the effectiveness of the foreign intelligence surveillance activities of the United States authorized under [FISA]" and recommended changes, particularly in light of technological developments.

- Whistle-blower protection is extended to intelligence community and FBI contract employees.

U.S. intelligence officials have stated that these programs stopped more than fifty terrorist plots worldwide, which some senators have disputed. Subsequent revelations disclosed that some of the NSA collection was against communications in many other nations, some of them—France, Germany, Japan, and Turkey—U.S. allies. Most of the nations that discovered they were targets protested, as did the European Union (EU). There were also reports alleging that some of this collection had taken place against the UN. By treaty, the UN is supposed to be sacrosanct from intelligence collection even though many countries disregard this and, indeed, see the UN as a major field for collection given the multiplicity of targets available.

In September 2013, Judge Claire Eagan, a member of the FISC, released an opinion that offered insights into how these two programs are managed. Although the programs are based on provisions of law, the government must apply to the FISC for permission to conduct surveillance. The programs have to be reauthorized by the court every ninety days. Judge Eagan also noted that no telecommunications company had ever invoked its legal right to challenge a court order to turn over bulk records of metadata.

One other result of the Snowden leaks has been the decision by several information technology and telecommunications firms—such as Apple and Google—to put encryption on their devices that has no key or backdoor and therefore cannot be accessed or broken into on a timely basis. FBI Director James Comey was especially vocal about the risks entailed in these corporate decisions and the advantage that this gives to terrorists, criminals, and so on. In the aftermath of the November 2015 terrorist attacks in Paris, Comey, joined by DCIA Brennan, again made the case for some sort of controlled access, but the firms did not agree. In December 2015, EU officials took a similar stance, which was striking, as it represented a change after European reactions to the Snowden revelations.

Interestingly, the United States entered into negotiations with Britain to allow that country to serve orders on U.S. companies for live intercepts and stored data in criminal and terror investigations. Investigated accounts would not include U.S. citizens or people in the United States. The two nations have a mutual legal assistance treaty. Congressional approval for a pact would also be needed.

Finally, in 2017 the concept and process of "**unmasking**" U.S. individuals named in surveillance reports became controversial. Typically, U.S. persons are not specifically identified in surveillance reporting but are identified as "U.S. person" or "U.S. person 1" if there are several. In other words, their identity is masked. There are procedures by which certain officials can request, in writing, that the person be "unmasked" for specific intelligence purposes, such as to understand better the reporting. The controversy centered, initially, on reporting concerning Michael Flynn's contacts with Russian ambassador Sergei Kislyak during the presidential transition period in 2016–2017. Flynn, who had been named Trump's national security adviser, resigned after reports containing his name leaked and it was evident that he had misrepresented to Vice President Mike Pence the nature of his contacts with Kislyak. Susan Rice, Flynn's predecessor in the NSC job, had requested the unmasking. The names of other Trump campaign personnel who might have had contacts with Russians were also requested, leading some Republicans to claim that the Obama administration had been spying on the Trump campaign for political purposes. In January 2018, DNI Dan Coats issued a policy guidance detailing procedures for requesting and safeguarding "unmasking" information, including specific rules for periods between elections and presidential inaugurations that may include transition team personnel.

Measurement and Signatures Intelligence. FISINT and ELINT are both major contributors to a little-understood branch of collection known as MASINT. MASINT focuses primarily but not exclusively on weapons capabilities and industrial activities. Multispectral and hyperspectral imagery (MSI and HSI) also contribute to MASINT.

An arcane debate rages between those who see MASINT as a separate collection discipline and those who see it as simply a product, or even a by-product, of SIGINT and other collection capabilities. For our purposes, it is sufficient to understand that MASINT exists and that, in a world increasingly concerned about such issues as proliferation of weapons of mass destruction and pollution, it is of growing importance. For example, MASINT can help identify the types of gases or waste leaving a factory, which can be important in chemical weapons identification. It can also help identify other specific characteristics (composition, material content) of weapons systems.

MASINT practitioners think of their INT as having six disciplines:

1. Electro-optical (EO): the properties of emitted or reflected energy in the infrared to ultraviolet part of the spectrum, including lasers and various types of light—infrared, polarized, spectral, ultraviolet, and visible

2. Geophysical: the disturbance and anomalies of various physical fields at, or near, the surface of Earth, such as acoustic, gravity, magnetic, and seismic

3. Materials: the composition and identification of gases, liquids, or solids, including chemical-, biological-, and nuclear-related material samples

4. Nuclear radiation: the qualities of gamma rays, neutrons, and x-rays

5. Radar: the properties of radio waves reflected from a target or objects, including various types of radars such as line-of-sight and over-the-horizon and synthetic apertures

6. Radio frequency: the electromagnetic signals generated by an object, either narrow- or wide-band

MASINT can be used against a wide array of intelligence issues, including WMD development and proliferation, arms control, environmental issues, narcotics, weapons developments, space activities, and denial and deception practices. At its core, MASINT consists of collecting and identifying certain physical "signatures"—that is, indicators of an activity or process—so that when these signatures are seen again, it is quickly understood what has happened. For example, the seismic waves set off by an earthquake and those by an underground nuclear test are different and will appear different on a seismograph, allowing scientists to determine which event has occurred. In 2013, the Air Force Technical Applications Center (AFTAC) proposed upgrading the system that detects and characterizes nuclear tests, likely a response to the growing concern about WMD proliferation. MASINT sensors can be used to distinguish between real armored vehicles and rubber ones that are used for deception. MASINT can also be used to defeat camouflage.

In Afghanistan, the U.S. military has used very small (palm-sized) acoustic and seismic sensors to detect motion. These **unattended grounds sensors (UGSs)** can be disguised to blend with their surroundings and can be linked into a network. According to press accounts, many UGSs will be left behind after U.S. troops leave Afghanistan. DARPA is investigating UGSs and underwater sensors that would draw very little power and thus might be effective for long periods of time.

MASINT has suffered as a collection discipline because of its relative novelty and its dependence on the other technical INTs for its products. Often, analysts or policy makers look at a MASINT product without knowing it. MASINT is a potentially important INT still struggling for recognition. It is also more arcane and requires analysts with more technical training to be able to use it fully. At present, policy makers are less familiar—and probably less comfortable—with it than they are with GEOINT or SIGINT. Responsibility for MASINT is shared by DIA and NGA; it is not a separate agency. Some of its advocates believe that MASINT will never make a full contribution until it has more bureaucratic clout. Others, even some sympathetic to MASINT, do not believe this INT needs the panoply of a full agency.

Human Intelligence. HUMINT is espionage—spying—and is sometimes referred to as the world's second-oldest profession. Indeed, it is as old as the Bible. First Moses and then Joshua sent spies into Canaan before leading the Jewish people across the Jordan River. Spying is what most people think about when they hear the word "intelligence," whether they conjure up famous spies from history such as

Nathan Hale or Mata Hari (both failures) or fictional agents such as James Bond. In the United States, HUMINT is largely the responsibility of the CIA, through the Directorate of Operations (DO). DIA also has a HUMINT capability with the renamed Defense Clandestine Service (DCS). The FBI and the Drug Enforcement Administration (DEA) also have officers who operate overseas. (Foreign Service officers and commercial attachés are also HUMINT collectors, but their collection is overt. Defense attachés are overt, but some of their collection may be clandestine.) The DO has three branches: CIA HUMINT, Community HUMINT, and Technology. The Community HUMINT office serves to coordinate among the various agencies conducting HUMINT, a necessary task to avoid duplication of effort or operations that run at cross-purposes. The director of the CIA (DCIA) is the HUMINT program manager.

As noted earlier (see chap. 3), the shift from the Defense HUMINT Service to the DCS also envisaged an expansion in the number of DCS officers deployed, as well as closer training and coordination with the CIA's DO. DO officers apparently supported this, as the DCS could cover military HUMINT requirements for which they were better suited, which would also free DO officers for other targets. DCS officers were not to be engaged in covert action. However, some members of Congress saw this as being largely duplicative and scaled back the DCS plans from 1,000 to 500 undercover case officers overseas.

HUMINT largely involves sending clandestine service officers to foreign countries, where they attempt to recruit foreign nationals to spy. The process of recruiting spies has several steps and a unique vocabulary. The process of managing spies is sometimes referred to as the **agent acquisition cycle**. The cycle has five steps:

1. Targeting or spotting: identifying individuals who have access to the information that the United States may desire.

2. Assessing: gaining their confidence and assessing their weaknesses and susceptibility to be recruited; done via the **asset validation system**.

3. Recruiting: making a **pitch** to them, suggesting a relationship; a **source** may accept a pitch for a variety of reasons: money, disaffection with their own government, or thrills. U.S. clandestine service officers state very firmly that blackmail is not used, at least by them, to recruit spies.

4. Handling: managing of the asset.

5. Termination: ending the relationship for any of several reasons—unreliability, a loss of access to needed intelligence, a change in intelligence requirements, and so on.

Another HUMINT term of art is the **developmental**, a potential source who is being brought along—largely through repeated contacts and conversations to assess his or her value (validation) and susceptibilities—to the point where the developmental can be pitched. If and when the pitch has been accepted, the officer must meet with this new source regularly to receive information, holding meetings in a manner and in places that reduce the risk of being caught and then transmitting the information back home. The source may rely on sources of his or her own, known as **sub-sources**, to provide intelligence that the original source then conveys to the agent.

Some intelligence veterans expressed the view that President Trump's ban on immigrants from certain Muslim nations would hurt HUMINT efforts. First-generation recruits can be extremely useful in creating relationships with potential human sources, having an affinity and a rapport that will elude nonnative officers. Also, some human sources are recruited by the promise of eventual resettlement in the United States, which could be problematic under the ban.

Diplomatic reporting is a type of HUMINT, although it tends to receive less credibility in some circles because of its overt nature. After all, the foreign government official knows, when speaking to a diplomat, that his or her remarks are going to be cabled to that diplomat's capital. An espionage source is likely to be thinking the same thing. Nonetheless, some people prefer more traditional HUMINT, even if the source's reliability remains uncertain, rather than diplomatic reporting. One of the revelations in WikiLeaks was apparent orders to U.S. diplomats to collect various types of information on their foreign counterparts. Although some of the requested material, such as biometric data, may be beyond the norm, much of the other tasking for biographic data would not be unusual for diplomats to gather as they are most likely to have contact with other diplomats. Policy makers are usually keen to know their opposite numbers in foreign countries at a human level as an aid to dealing with them.

HUMINT requires time to be developed. Clandestine service officers need to learn a variety of skills (foreign languages; conducting, detecting, or evading surveillance; recruiting skills and other aspects of HUMINT tradecraft; the ability to handle various types of communications equipment; weapons training; and so on). Like all other professions, it takes time to become adept. In the case of HUMINT officers, it takes up to seven years, according to some accounts. This factor causes some intelligence officers to question the wisdom of tit-for-tat intelligence officer expulsions, such as those between the United States, Britain, and several other nations together versus Russia after the Novichok nerve gas incident in Britain in 2018. (See chap. 15.) The concern is that agents cannot simply and immediately replace expelled agents, especially in a hostile target like Moscow. The issues of suitability, training, expertise, and so on may limit the ability to replace the expelled agents, resulting in at least a temporary loss of HUMINT capability.

In addition to gaining the skills required for this activity, officers have to maintain their cover stories—the overt lives that give them a plausible reason for being in that foreign nation. There are two types of cover: official and nonofficial. Officers with **official cover** hold another government job, usually posted at the embassy. Official cover makes it easier for the agent to maintain contact with his or her superiors but raises the risk of being suspected as an agent. Also, if a clandestine officer under official cover is compromised, he or she has diplomatic status and is immune from prosecution. More likely the officer will be declared *persona non grata* (or "PNG-ed") and expelled from the country. A recent example was Ryan Fogle, a U.S. embassy officer who was arrested in Moscow in May 2013 when he was allegedly meeting with a prospective source. Fogle was ordered to leave Russia. According to Russian authorities, Fogle was attempting to recruit a source in Russian intelligence. In retaliation, Russia revealed the name of the CIA chief of station in Moscow.

Nonofficial cover (NOC, pronounced "knock") avoids any overt connection between the officer and his or her government but can make it more difficult to keep in contact. NOCs need a full-time job that explains their presence; they cannot make contact with superiors or colleagues overtly. (This led to a bureaucratic problem for the CIA in that NOCs had to at least appear to be paid at a level commensurate with their cover job, which was sometimes higher than their government salary. This then raised the issue of being liable for taxes higher than their actual salary. Congress authorized the CIA to pay NOCs "in a manner consistent with their cover.") The U.S. government does not discuss cover arrangements, but it is widely believed that NOCs do not have diplomatic status and therefore are in greater danger if they are compromised. They can be arrested and jailed, although, typically, they will be traded for someone being held by the other country. (This courtesy does not extend to one's own citizens who are caught spying.) Thus, within HUMINT there are trade-offs between ease of command and control, access, degree of cover, and relative exposure.

For the CIA, at least, some limits exist on the jobs that NOCs can hold. Clergy and Peace Corps volunteers are off limits. Journalism is an ideal cover for a NOC, as journalists have a plausible reason for being in a foreign country, for seeking out officials, and for asking questions. However, professional journalists have long protested any such use of cover, arguing that if one agent posing as a journalist were to be unmasked, then all journalists would be suspect and perhaps in danger. Proponents counter that journalism is a profession like any other and should be available for use. All told, the use of NOCs is more complex than is official cover for agents. However, NOCs should be able to get out beyond the "diplomatic cocktail circuit" and thus have a wider base from which to recruit. According to press accounts, efforts to expand the number of NOCs has run into some difficulties and did not produce as much additional high-value HUMINT as had been hoped.

Using NOCs, if they are exposed, can also have unintended consequences. The CIA had created a hepatitis vaccination program in Pakistan as a means of attempting to obtain DNA from the residents of the compound in Abbottabad where bin Laden was thought to be living. The effort was not successful, but as a result of its becoming known, Pakistani Islamic militants killed dozens of public health workers, none of whom was involved in the DNA effort. As a result, President Obama's senior counterterrorism advisor sent a letter to U.S. public health schools assuring them that the CIA would no longer make "operational use" of vaccination programs and would also not try to access or use any DNA obtained through such programs.

The entire issue of cover is likely becoming more difficult. Many officers being recruited into the clandestine service will likely already have extensive "public" profiles because of their participation in social networks from a relatively young age. For the sake of their cover, they will likely have to continue this activity, albeit in a reduced and more circumspect manner. But they may have to create an entire second social networking profile to accommodate their cover story. It is possible to have more than one Facebook page, for example, but facial recognition software could be a problem. Also, new technologies such as biometric passports will also make cover more difficult. As closed-circuit televisions proliferate in many cities, combined with facial recognition software, operations will become more difficult, as it becomes easier to track and identify people on the street. This was how the two Russians who attempted to poison

Sergei Skripal in Britain in 2018 were identified. (See chap. 15.) At the same time, not having social media accounts of any sort would seem so anomalous that it might raise suspicions that an individual is an intelligence agent. One of the keys to being a successful agent is the ability to blend in, not to stand out. Thus, the key would be to use social media in a way that enhances and is consistent with cover, rather than avoid it entirely.

HUMINT officers may be active as soon as they arrive at their duty station or they may be **sleepers**. Sleepers are inserted into the target country but spend time—sometimes years—integrating themselves and do not become active immediately. They maintain regular lives. This allows them to become much more comfortable in and familiar with the target country and also keeps them away from the target's counterintelligence activities. In 2010, the United States arrested ten Russian sleepers who lived and worked in various locations in the eastern United States. Although none of these sleepers had diplomatic status, they were exchanged for four Russians who had been convicted of espionage.

Some HUMINT sources volunteer. They are called **walk-ins**. Spies Oleg Penkovsky of the Soviet Union, Aldrich Ames of the CIA, and Robert Hanssen of the FBI were all walk-ins. Walk-ins raise a host of other issues: Why have they volunteered? Do they really have access to valuable intelligence? Are they real volunteers or a means of entrapment—called **dangles**? Dangles can be used for a number of purposes, including identifying hostile intelligence personnel or gaining insights into the intelligence requirements or methods of a hostile service. According to press accounts reporting on the investigation led by former FBI director (1978–1987) and DCI (1987–1991) William Webster, the Soviet Union suspected that Hanssen was a dangle and protested to the United States. The United States denied the charge but did not follow up as to why the Soviets thought they had been sent a dangle.

In addition to recruiting foreign nationals, HUMINT officers may undertake more direct spying, such as stealing documents or planting sensors. Some of their information may come through direct observation of activity. Thus, HUMINT can involve more INTs than just espionage.

Important adjuncts to one's own HUMINT capabilities are those of allied or friendly services—or even services that are simply useful because of their location. Known as **foreign liaison** relationships, these offer several important advantages. First, the foreign intelligence service has greater familiarity with its own region. Second, its government may maintain a different pattern of relations with other states, friendlier in some cases or even having diplomatic relations where one's own government does not. These HUMINT-to-HUMINT relationships are somewhat formal in nature and are often symbiotic. They also entail risks, as one can never be entirely sure of the liaison partner's security procedures. For example, in 2015, Iraq entered into an intelligence-sharing agreement with Russia as Russia intervened in the Syrian civil war. U.S. officials were concerned that Iraq might share intelligence that the United States had provided earlier. Thus, there are different degrees of liaison, depending on past experience, shared needs, the sense of security engendered, the depth and value of the intelligence being shared, and so forth. Furthermore, some liaison relationships may be with intelligence services that do not have the same standards in terms of operational limits, acceptable activities, and other criteria. There have been press reports, for example, that U.S. and U.K. intelligence agencies shared intelligence with Libya's Muammar Qaddafi after he gave up his WMD in 2003; there are also reports about U.S. and U.K. intelligence cooperation with Syrian rebels. According to press reports, the United States was reluctant to share intelligence with the Nigerian military regarding the radical Boko Haram insurgents because of the Nigerian military's apparent reluctance to engage in serious operations. These concerns were apparently overcome, but this again is illustrative of some of the issues involved in foreign liaison. A choice therefore has to be made between the value of the information being sought or exchanged and the larger question of the propriety of a relationship with this service. Nevertheless, liaison is an important means of increasing the breadth and depth of available HUMINT.

The United States and its liaison partners practice the **"third party rule,"** meaning that a nation receiving foreign liaison intelligence will not share it with a third party without permission. U.S. intelligence veterans expressed concern in May 2017, when President Trump shared sensitive intelligence, apparently originating from Israel, with Russian foreign minister Sergei Lavrov and in violation of the third party rule. Officially, Israel expressed its continued confidence in its intelligence relationship with the United States, but there were also press reports about concerns being raised privately by several intelligence partners about the security of intelligence that they shared with the United States.

Liaison is also not the exclusive preserve of HUMINT. There are also GEOINT and SIGINT liaison relationships that will be conducted by their respective agencies. Foreign intelligence liaison is carried out on an agency-by-agency basis instead of by the intelligence community as a whole. The CIA, DIA, NGA, and NSA create and conduct their own liaison relationships, which does raise questions about the possible need for better coordination to avoid duplication. In October 2015, DIA announced the creation of a deputy director for commonwealth integration (DDCI), to serve as the DIA director's senior adviser on Five Eyes (U.S., Britain, Australia, Canada, and New Zealand) defense and intelligence issues. The DDCI will be a rotational flag officer position among the five allies. The first DDCI was a British air vice marshal; the second is a New Zealand major general.

Thus, the stovepipes problem carries over into foreign liaison. This has proved to be a problem for the DNI, who is charged with overseeing the coordination of these relationships and who conducts some foreign liaison of his or her own but does not control other agencies' foreign liaison relationships. Press reports stated that DNI Blair's unilateral effort to improve relations with French intelligence also helped undercut his position with the Obama administration.

In the war against terrorists, several nations have apparently offered intelligence support to the United States, including some whose services may be considered occasionally hostile. These types of liaison relationships call for extra caution regarding intelligence sharing, and questions may arise about the depth and detail of the intelligence received. However, exchanging useful intelligence is a good way for nations to build confidence in one another. For example, according to press accounts, Russian officers placed nuclear detection equipment in North Korea at the request of the United States to help track possible nuclear developments. By contrast, U.S. intelligence relations with Pakistan have been difficult at best. According to press accounts,

U.S. officials have been displeased with Pakistani efforts to combat extremists in their own country, as well as Pakistan's ongoing relations with Taliban elements in Afghanistan. Pakistan, at the same time, has objected to the use of UAVs against suspected terrorist targets in Pakistan and has asked for greater transparency on the part of the United States. The May 2011 operation to kill bin Laden, conducted on Pakistani soil without notifying Pakistan, exacerbated tensions on both sides. Pakistan objected to the breach of its sovereignty; U.S. officials stated that bin Laden could not have lived where he did, away from the tribal areas in western Pakistan for so many years, without someone in the government at some level being aware of his presence. Pakistan was embarrassed by the fact that they had not been informed of the operation, they were unable to detect the operation, and bin Laden had been living for years in a relatively open place near a major military installation. Finally, according to press reports, the two successive U.S. chiefs of station in Pakistan have been identified by Pakistani officials, forcing them to return to the United States. This sort of action also greatly undermines trust, although later press reports suggested that the intelligence relationship had improved.

Espionage provides a small part of the intelligence that is collected. GEOINT and SIGINT produce a greater volume of intelligence. But HUMINT, like SIGINT, has the major advantage of affording access to what is being said, planned, and thought. Moreover, clandestine human access to another government may offer opportunities to influence that government by feeding it false or deceptive information. For intelligence targets in which the technical infrastructure may be irrelevant as a fruitful target—such as terrorism, narcotics, or international crime, where the signature of activities is small—HUMINT may be the only available source.

HUMINT also has disadvantages. First, it cannot be done remotely, as is the case with various types of technical collection. It requires proximity and access and therefore must contend with the counterintelligence capabilities of the other side. It is also far riskier, as it jeopardizes individuals—both the agents and the spies—and, if they are caught, can have political ramifications that are less likely to occur with technical collectors. For example, press reports asserted that U.S. espionage efforts in China had been severely damaged when a dozen sources were jailed or killed, beginning in 2010, apparently because of a compromised CIA communications program.

HUMINT is far less expensive than the various technical collectors, although it still involves costs for training, special equipment, and the accoutrements clandestine officers need to build successful cover stories.

Like all the other collection INTs, HUMINT is susceptible to deception. Some critics argue that it is the most susceptible to deception. The bona fides of human sources are always subject to question initially and, in some cases, may never be wholly resolved. Many questions arise and linger. Why is this person offering to pass information—ideology, money, vengeance? The person will claim to have good access to valuable information, but how good is it? Is it consistent, or is this a single event? How good is the information? Is this person a dangle, offered as a means of passing information that the other side wants to have passed—either because it is false or because it will have a specific effect? Is this person a double agent who is collecting information on your intelligence agency's HUMINT techniques and capabilities even as he or she passes information to you?

HUMINT is also an extremely fragile INT, in large part because it is based on human relationships. The dynamics of interpersonal relationships do not affect the technical collections INTs (GEOINT, SIGINT, and MASINT). The personal aspect of HUMINT also increases sensitivities about its use. According to press reports, in the aftermath of leaks by Edward Snowden about collection in allied countries, the CIA curtailed "unilateral operations" in Western Europe, meaning recruitments of or meetings with sources in allied countries—as opposed to operations to which host nations are privy. DNI Clapper said that the United States had stopped spying on "specific targets."

HUMINT officers must walk a fine line between prudent caution and the possibility that too much caution will lead them to deter or reject a promising source. For example, the United States initially rejected the services of Penkovsky, who then turned to the British, who accepted him. Only later did the United States take on this valuable spy. Deception is particularly difficult to deal with, because people naturally are reluctant to accept that they are being deceived. However, people might slip into a position where they trust no one, which can result in turning away sources who might have been valuable. The inherent danger in dealing with human sources was underscored by the death of seven CIA officers in Khost, Afghanistan, in December 2009, when a Jordanian who had been an intelligence source staged a suicide attack. (See chap. 7 for more details.)

HUMINT's unique sources and methods raise another issue. These sources are considered to be extremely fragile, given that good human penetrations take so long to develop and risk the lives of the case officers, their sources, and perhaps even the sources' families. Therefore, the intelligence analysts who receive HUMINT reports may not be told the details of the source or sources. Analysts are not informed, for example, that "this report comes from a first secretary in the Fredonian Foreign Ministry." Instead, the report includes information on the access of the source to the intelligence, the past reliability of the source, or variations on this concept. Sometimes several sources may be blended together in a single report. Although the masking of HUMINT sources promotes their preservation, it may have the unintended effect of devaluing the reports for analysts, who may not fully appreciate the value of the source and the information. This became an issue in the aftermath of the Iraq WMD experience, when it was recognized that some sources had been of questionable reliability and that analysts were not always given as much information as would have been desirable about the nature of some of the HUMINT reporting. It also denies all-source analysts the ability to make an independent judgment of the HUMINT source when compared with the other sources to which they have access. (HUMINT reports come with captions provided by reports officers as to the nature of the source: a reliable source, an untested source, a source with proven access, a source with unknown access, and so on.) DCIA Brennan's creation of CIA mission centers, in which analysts and DO officers are working together, may help overcome this problem.

Also, as DCI Richard Helms (1966–1973) observed, most HUMINT sources are recruited for a specific assignment or requirement, based on their access to the desired intelligence. They cannot be assigned from issue to issue as they are extremely unlikely to have access to other intelligence. Helms also believed that spies who no longer had the desired access should not be held in reserve but should be dropped. He said that a well-run station (the base from which officers operate overseas) "does not cling to spent spies." Thus, even successful HUMINT, although extremely valuable, is narrow in focus.

HUMINT also puts one in contact—and perhaps into relationships—with unsavory individuals such as terrorists and narco-traffickers. If one is going to penetrate such groups or develop other types of relationships with them, some may become recipients of money or other forms of support. These types of relationships raise moral and ethical issues for some people. (See chap. 13.) In the aftermath of the September 2001 attacks, special attention was given to the so-called Deutch rules about HUMINT recruitment. In 1995, DCI John Deutch (1995–1997) ordered a scrub of all HUMINT assets, with a particular focus on persons who in the past had been involved in serious criminal activity or human rights violations. The scrub was the result of revelations that some past CIA assets in Guatemala had violated human rights, including those of some Americans resident in that country. New rules were promulgated requiring headquarters' approval of any such recruitments in the future. After the terrorist attacks, the rules were widely criticized, with many people asserting that they had limited the CIA's ability to penetrate terrorist groups. CIA officials maintained that no valuable relationship was ever turned down because of the Deutch rules. Critics countered, however, that the very existence of the rules bred timidity in the DO, as officers would be more cautious about whom they recruited, running the risk of losing useful sources, rather than have these recruitments be scrutinized on the basis of changing standards. By the end of 2001, the Deutch rules were no longer considered an operational factor as field stations were told they could be ignored. In July 2002, they were formally rescinded. Writing in the aftermath of the September 2001 attacks, Deutch defended his rules, arguing that they allowed DO officers to recruit with clear guidelines and focused on acquiring high-quality agents.

In the United States, constant tension exists between HUMINT and the other collection disciplines. The dominance of technical collection periodically gives rise to calls for a greater emphasis on HUMINT. So-called intelligence failures, such as the fall of the shah of Iran in 1979, the unexpected Indian nuclear tests in 1998, and the 2001 terrorist attacks have led to demands for more HUMINT. There is something odd about this recurring call for more HUMINT in that successful HUMINT is not a question of the mass of agents being assigned to a target. Some targets, such as terrorist cells or the inner sanctum of totalitarian regimes, will always be difficult to penetrate. There is no reason to believe that the twentieth agent who is sent will succeed when the first nineteen have not. It is not possible to swarm agents against a difficult HUMINT target in terms of the agents' availability and, more important, the risk. Such an effort would be more likely to alert the target to possible penetration attempts, further hampering HUMINT.

Again, no right balance can be struck between HUMINT and the other collection disciplines. Such an idea runs counter to the concept of an all-source intelligence process that seeks to apply as many collection disciplines as possible to a given intelligence need. But not every collection INT makes an equal or even similar contribution to every issue. Clearly, having a collection system that is strong and flexible and can be modulated to the intelligence requirement at hand is better than one that swings between apparently opposed fashions of technical and human collection.

As with all other INTs, it is difficult, if not impossible, to put an ultimate value on HUMINT. It is one of the two most democratic INTs (along with OSINT), because any nation or group can conduct HUMINT. Clearly, it would be preferable to have good HUMINT access for key issues. But cases such as those involving Ames and Hanssen also raise questions about HUMINT's value. These two spies provided the Soviet Union and post-Soviet Russia with invaluable information, largely about U.S. spy penetrations in that country but also, in the case of Hanssen, about technical collection operations and capabilities. When their activities are added to past espionage revelations—such as William Kampiles, a CIA officer who gave the Soviets satellite details; John Walker and his confederates, all of whom had served in the U.S. Navy, who gave the Soviets cryptographic data; and Ronald Pelton, an NSA employee who gave the Soviets details on signals collection—the Soviet Union and post-Soviet Russia gained substantial knowledge about U.S. collection capabilities. Yet the Soviet Union lost the cold war and ceased to exist as a state. One could argue, on the one hand, that all of this HUMINT ultimately proved to be of no value, thus raising questions about HUMINT's utility. On the other hand, one could argue that no amount of HUMINT—or any other INT—can save a state that has profound internal problems.

Critics of HUMINT argue that the most important spies (Penkovsky, Ames, Hanssen, and many others) have tended to be walk-ins rather than recruited spies, which raises a serious question about HUMINT capabilities. If one accepts the idea that collection is a synergistic activity, then even the recruitment of lower level spies adds to one's overall knowledge. Also, even if the most productive spies are walk-ins, some sort of apparatus is needed to handle them, to get out the intelligence they provide, and so on.

One of the major concerns in HUMINT is the possibility that a clandestine officer will be caught and unmasked, with attendant personal risk for the officer and political embarrassment for the state that sent the officer. Even a successful long-term espionage penetration can prove costly. The case of Gunter Guillaume is illustrative. Guillaume was an East German spy who was able to penetrate the West German government, rising to a senior position in the office of Chancellor Willy Brandt. When Guillaume's espionage was uncovered in 1974, Brandt was forced to resign. Many people believed that the political cost of the operation exceeded any gains in intelligence. Brandt's Ostpolitik—or favorable policy toward East Germany—was never resumed by his successors, at great cost to East Germany, perhaps even greater than any intelligence that Guillaume produced over the years. Similarly, the fate of Jonathan Pollard (see chap. 15 for more details), who passed classified intelligence to Israel, became a constant irritant in U.S.-Israeli relations, again outweighing the value of the intelligence that Pollard provided.

The state of HUMINT remains a concern in the U.S. intelligence community. HUMINT suffered from budget cuts through the 1990s, as did all aspects of intelligence. Several officials have noted that the FBI had more agents assigned to New York City than did the DO worldwide prior to the 2001 attacks. President Bush ordered a 50 percent increase in the number of DO officers. As noted, it would take seven years from their entry on duty (EOD) before these officers were considered fully operational. Goss's tenure as DCI and then DCIA (2004–2006) saw the departure of many DO veterans, owing to friction with Goss's staff. This eased under DCIA Michael Hayden (2006–2009), but press reports indicated that attrition rates in the DO remained high, especially in the five- to ten-year cadre.

For the United States, at least, it remains important to view HUMINT as part of a larger collection strategy instead of as the single INT that meets the country's most important intelligence needs. To place that sort of expectation on any one INT is bound to set it up for disappointment at best and perhaps even failure.

Just as the boundary between foreign and domestic intelligence has created issues in SIGINT, the same has happened, on a smaller scale, in HUMINT. The CIA sent several officers to work with the Intelligence Division of the New York Police Department (NYPD). NYPD had been accused of ethnic and racial profiling in Muslim neighborhoods. The Intelligence Division was run for several years by two retired CIA officers. The National Security Act states that the CIA "shall have no police, subpoena, or law enforcement powers or internal security functions." Some observers felt this made the CIA-NYPD liaison highly questionable. The CIA's inspector general reviewed the partnership in 2011 and found no violation of law or executive order but also found management issues in the program and risks to the CIA arising from public misperceptions.

HUMINT is a very specialized skill that takes years to develop to a suitable degree of proficiency. It is also, as DCI Helms pointed out, one of the two most dangerous actions undertaken by intelligence. (The other is covert action. See chap. 7.) One of the concerns raised about DCIA Brennan's mission centers is the possibility that the DO—and the DA—will lose some of their unique aspects as they operate together and perhaps become somewhat homogenized culturally. There is also the question of who will manage CIA's HUMINT. The DCIA is the national HUMINT manager, and the DCIA has, in the past, exercised most of this function via the DO. With the DO no longer a "line" (that is, operational) entity, does this mean that HUMINT will be directed by each of the assistant directors in charge of the mission centers? Moreover, as some of these assistant directors will be DA officers, will they then be responsible for HUMINT (and covert action) by their DO subordinates?

Finally, it is possible to think of cyber as a means of conducting HUMINT. Using false identities, one can contact individuals in a foreign intelligence service and then go through the same recruitment process as with traditional HUMINT. This may have been part of the process by which Bradley Manning provided thousands of cables to WikiLeaks. In some ways, cyber offers additional benefits for HUMINT, as one can stay in fairly constant contact with the source or potential source and yet run lower risk of exposure. Even if "caught" online, the source can still be masked in terms of true identity and location and also be remote from the source, running less risk of capture. This type of online recruitment apparently was used by Iranian intelligence with former Air Force counterintelligence officer Monica Witt, who defected to Iran in 2013 and provided Iran with intelligence on U.S. capabilities.

Open-Source Intelligence. To some observers, OSINT may seem like a contradiction in terms. How can information that is openly available be considered intelligence? This question reflects the misconception that intelligence must inevitably be about secrets. Much of it is, but not to the exclusion of openly available information.

Even during the height of the cold war, according to one senior intelligence official, at least 20 percent of the intelligence about the Soviet Union came from open sources.

OSINT includes a wide variety of information and sources:

- Media: newspapers, magazines, radio, television, and computer-based information, including social media (see below).

- Public data: government reports, official data such as budgets and demographics, hearings, legislative debates, press conferences, and speeches.

- Professional and academic: conferences, symposia, professional associations, academic papers, and experts.

- In addition to these open sources, each of the classified INTs has an OSINT component. The most obvious is commercial imagery. One can also conduct a variety of SIGINT-type activities on the World Wide Web, such as traffic analysis (the number of people who visit a website) or changes in websites. Given that some aspects of MASINT are related to geophysical phenomena, there are open aspects of MASINT. Finally, there is open HUMINT—the use of overt experts for their own knowledge or as sources of elicitation. This list is by no means exhaustive, but it does give a feel for the range of OSINT within the other INTs. (*See box, "Some Intelligence Humor."*)

One of the hallmarks of the post–cold war world is the increased availability of OSINT. The number of closed societies and **denied areas** has decreased dramatically. With the exception of Russia and the other former Soviet states, all of the former Warsaw Pact states are now NATO allies. This does not mean that classified collection disciplines are no longer needed; instead, the areas in which OSINT is available have expanded.

The major advantage of OSINT is its accessibility, although it still requires collection. OSINT needs less processing and exploitation than the technical INTs or HUMINT, but it still requires some P&E. For example, most newspapers and news outlets have a distinct point of view (think of Fox News and MSNBC) and some are more reliable than others. A good OSINT officer or analyst would want to know this and to convey it to others using this newspaper as a source. Given the diversity of OSINT, it may be more difficult to manipulate for the purpose of deception than are other INTs, at least on a broad basis as opposed to a few outlets. Beyond the issue of understanding the viewpoint of various OSINT sources, an analyst now must also be more alert to the problem of "fake news," meaning reporting that is being deliberately manipulated. No news source is completely free from bias. (There is a CIA saying: "In newspapers, only the weather and the sports results are printed for information. Everything else is printed for effect.") But the ability to manipulate or alter stories, or to broadcast false stories, has complicated the problem.

OSINT is also useful for helping put the secret information into a wider context, which can be extremely valuable. Harvard professor Joseph Nye, who served as chairman of the National Intelligence Council and as an assistant secretary of defense, compared OSINT to the outer edges of a jigsaw puzzle, which give a sense of boundary and some of the pattern while the other INTs are used to fill in the center of the puzzle. DNI McConnell referred to OSINT as the starting point for collection, as have others before him—in other words, looking for the needed intelligence in open sources first before tasking classified collection sources, either technical or human. Putting this seemingly obvious plan into practice has proved difficult over the years for a number of reasons, including preferences within the intelligence community and among policy makers for classified sources and the difficulty that the intelligence community's open-source activity has had in keeping pace with the explosion of open sources.

SOME INTELLIGENCE HUMOR

In addition to GEOINT, SIGINT, HUMINT, OSINT, and MASINT, intelligence officers, in their lighter moments, speak of other INTs (collection disciplines). One of the most famous is PIZZINT—pizza intelligence. This refers to the belief that Soviet and now Russian officials based in Washington, D.C., keep watch for large numbers of pizza delivery trucks going late in the evening to the CIA, DOD, the State Department, and the White House as an indication that a crisis is brewing somewhere. The notion is that, after seeing many trucks making deliveries, the officials would hurry back to the Soviet/Russian embassy to alert Moscow that something must be going on somewhere in the world.

Some other INTs that intelligence officers talk about are

- LAVINT: lavatory intelligence, such as is heard in restrooms

- RUMINT: rumor intelligence

- REVINT: revelation intelligence

- DIVINT: divine intelligence

The main disadvantage of OSINT is its volume. In many ways, it represents the worst wheat-and-chaff problem. Some observers argue that the so-called information revolution has made OSINT more difficult without a corresponding increase in usable intelligence. Computers have increased the ability to manipulate information; however, the amount of derived intelligence has not increased apace.

The OSINT phenomenon called **echo** or **circular reporting** is the effect of a single media story being picked up and repeated by other media sources until the story takes on a much larger life of its own, appearing more important than it actually is. In other words, there is repeated reporting on the reporting. Echo is difficult to deal with unless one is aware of the original story and can therefore knowingly discount its effect. Echo or circular reporting can happen under the other INTs as well.

Popular misconceptions about OSINT persist, even within the intelligence community. OSINT is not free. Buying print media costs the intelligence community money, as do various other services that are useful—if not essential—in helping analysts manage, sort, and sift large amounts of data more efficiently. Another misconception is that the Internet or, more properly, the World Wide Web, is the main fount of OSINT. Experienced intelligence practitioners have discovered that the Internet—meaning searches among various sites—yields no more than 3 to 5 percent of the total OSINT take. That is why practitioners spend much time on what is called the "Deep Web," meaning that much larger portion of the Web that has not been indexed by search engines. Some experts estimate that the Deep Web is roughly 500 times bigger than the easily accessible Web.

The availability of open source via computer technology has raised new issues: copyrighted material and privacy of information that may be posted but is still considered personal. The DNI's open-source office is creating guidelines to deal with these issues as part of its larger program to certify individuals as open-source intelligence professionals. There is also the problem of an intelligence analyst tipping off potential adversaries by conducting deep open-source searches from a government account. Thus, even open source may require occasional cover for its collectors.

Even though OSINT has always been used, it remains undervalued by significant segments of the intelligence community. This attitude derives from the fact that the intelligence community was created to discover secrets. If OSINT could largely meet U.S. national security needs, the intelligence community would look very different. Some intelligence professionals have mistakenly equated the degree of difficulty involved in obtaining information with its ultimate value to analysts and policy makers. Contributing to this pervasive bias is the fact that OSINT has always been handled differently by the intelligence community. All of the other INTs have dedicated collectors, processors, and exploiters. With the exception of the Open Source Center (formerly the DNI's Open Source Center and before that the Foreign Broadcast Information Service, FBIS), which is housed in the CIA and monitors foreign media broadcasts, OSINT does not have dedicated collectors, processors, and exploiters. Instead, analysts are largely expected to act as their own OSINT collectors, a concept that other INTs would consider ludicrous. This is unfortunate, because OSINT is, as DNI McConnell noted, the perfect place to start any intelligence collection. By first determining what material is available from open sources, intelligence managers could focus their clandestine collectors on those issues for which such means were needed. Properly used, OSINT could be a good intelligence collection resource manager.

The 2015 shift of the DNI Open Source Center to the CIA and its later incorporation into the new Digital Innovation Directorate would appear to end its quasi-independent existence under the DNI and return open source to an activity within CIA. The past issue with this arrangement has been that the CIA focuses most heavily on its clandestine and covert activities (espionage, covert action), along with all-source analysis derived from many INTs—most of them classified. OSINT tended to be treated as a less central and less important activity, struggling for recognition. Whether this is again an issue will depend to a great extent on the overall mission and outlook of the Digital Innovation Directorate and the degree to which it carves out significant space and support for OSINT alongside its broader cyber mission.

Cyber Espionage: SIGINT, HUMINT, or Something Else? The use of cyberspace to conduct espionage is problematic in terms of trying to categorize it within the five collection disciplines. It can be thought of as SIGINT, as one is using similar technology to access and to exfiltrate intelligence.

In some respects, cyber espionage also resembles HUMINT. Maloy Krishna Dhar, an Indian intelligence officer, compared the steps in the HUMINT process to analogous cyber activities:

- Spotting and assessing is similar to looking for computers with the information or access that is desired.

- Asset validation in cyber includes detecting "honeypots"—a computer set up to detect and track unauthorized access attempts.

- Recruitment can include the use of false-front e-mails, such as spearphishing.

- Cover can include the use of botnets to hide the origin of the infiltrator.

In other aspects, cyber espionage differs from HUMINT. The risk in cyber espionage is obviously much lower. Also, in cyber espionage, it is possible, if one desires, to stay in constant contact with the source computer, as opposed to the greater distance and less frequent contact kept between an agent and his or her assets. Finally, if discovered, it is easier to deny culpability in cyber espionage, as opposed to an agent or asset who is caught in the act.

As will be discussed in more detail later (see chap. 12), some computer intrusions can be viewed as espionage through other means, rather than attempts to control, alter, or create effects via unauthorized computer access. For example, DNI Clapper said the entry into the Office of Personnel Management (OPM) records—which China admitted was conducted by its nationals, albeit claiming it was criminals and not government employees—was a classic espionage effort, in this case through other means. This does not ameliorate concerns about the lost data, but it should put some perspective on certain cyber activities.

The view here is that cyber in and of itself is not an INT. It is a technology that makes various types of intelligence available, just as satellites do, for example. The types of intelligence provided by cyber may fall into several different categories, but cyber itself does not define an INT.

SOCMINT and Data-Int? There is nothing sacred about the five current INTs and it may be necessary to consider adding to them as intelligence sources evolve. Decisions of this sort should be based on the relative value of the proposed INT and the degree to which it differs from other INTs.

Two possible candidates are **social media** intelligence (SOCMINT) and data intelligence (data-int). Social media are currently treated as part of OSINT as they are neither classified nor proprietary, although in some cases (Facebook and Twitter, for example) one has to enroll in the network. "Social media" refers to the sharing of information, views, and ideas via virtual communities and networks. Sir David Omand, former director of Britain's Government Communications Headquarters (GCHQ, NSA's sister organization), has argued that social media should be a separate INT and coined the term "SOCMINT."

The 1999 Kosovo air war produced what may be considered an early social media stream. Individuals in Serbia who said they were opposed to the Slobodan Milosevic government sent e-mails to private-sector intelligence firms in the United States, giving reports on the relative success of NATO air strikes, the mood in Belgrade, and related matters. Dealing with such reports is problematic as no assured means exists of authenticating them. The most reliable reports would come from known and trusted sources, probably based on past reporting. Establishing an independent capability to accomplish this may not be possible during hostilities. Some sources may prove to be reliable over time. But one has to be on guard for the possibility, if not the likelihood, of at least some level of disinformation from the targeted regime. In the case of Kosovo, at least some of the sources proved to be reliable, thus establishing a new OSINT stream.

Although these social networks have been in use for some time, they first achieved significant notice as an intelligence source during the Arab Spring revolt against President Hosni Mubarak of Egypt in February 2011. Antigovernment demonstrators in Tahrir Square in Cairo used text messaging and Twitter as a means of communicating. Apparent leaders of the demonstrators were identified by the number of Twitter followers. From this high point of social media as an intelligence tool, we come to a low point in April 2013. In the immediate aftermath of the Boston Marathon bombing, some social media initially misidentified a Pakistani American as a possible suspect. Also, CNN, in an attempt to stay abreast of Twitter feeds, aired several reports that turned out to be erroneous, hurting the network's credibility.

Mining social media for intelligence has obvious attractions, although it raises issues of privacy. Given the extensive use of social media (2.19 billion Facebook users and 336 million active Twitter users per month, for example), using some sort of high-level bulk-scanning approach may seem useful. But this then runs into privacy concerns, although it can also be argued that anyone posting something online can have no real expectation of privacy. Sen. Dianne Feinstein, D-CA, in the aftermath of the December 2015 San Bernardino shooting, introduced legislation requiring social media firms to report "knowledge of any terrorist activity."

The European Union (EU) enacted General Data Protection Regulations (GDPR) in May 2018, which essentially states that individuals continue to have the right to control their personal information, including items they may post on the World Wide Web or social media.

Another issue with social media is the relative ease with which they can be manipulated in terms of content, offering major opportunities for **disinformation** campaigns. Collectors and analysts have to be able to distinguish between genuine and witting false posts on social media, which is somewhat akin to determining the veracity of a human source. (See chap. 8 for a fuller discussion.)

Exploiting social media as a collection tool begins to branch off into other collection disciplines. For example, the prevalence of photos, including selfies, is a type of GEOINT. In this case, facial recognition software may also become important. Social media also provide the potential to create or sway opinion, moving into aspects of both public diplomacy and covert action (see chap. 7). According to press accounts, DARPA has conducted studies about social media, not only tracking how it is used but also taking part in social media exchanges to record and track responses. This could raise civil liberties concerns.

There are also severe authentication issues, as was seen during the 2016 U.S. election. It is important to remember that social media users willingly post their views, photos, and so on to the World Wide Web. Therefore, are manipulative social media efforts merely surreptitious but not intrusive in the intelligence sense? These doctrinal and legal questions may not be resolved for some time.

There may be several lessons regarding the use of social media as an intelligence collection source:

- First, the fact of the social media itself is not important. In a case like Tahrir Square, key questions would be these: Who are the most influential people on social media, and why are they so influential? The answers can be determined at a gross level by numbers of followers, after which one must begin to look at the content of their messages.

- But this leads to the second lesson: Social media, like all other collection sources, are subject to deception. A person need not have social media accounts in one's true name. Individuals can have multiple Twitter accounts. Moreover, in the case of Twitter, it is possible to buy fake followers (such as 100,000 followers for $399). Twitter says that it tries to police such efforts, but this seems rather difficult. Also, it is a very raw source. Twitter feeds cannot be geolocated as sent, although these data can be derived through certain technologies. Therefore, analysts have to rely largely on the language of origin. That may be useful for those languages spoken in relatively few places, such as Farsi or Korean, or those located predominantly in one place (Chinese), but in the case of a language like Arabic, which is an officially recognized language in twenty-four countries, more analysis must be brought to bear, looking for names, context, and so on.

- Third, social media represent an evolving intelligence source. For example, the U.S. Special Operations Command (SOCOM) has run successful experiments with Twitter and other social media that could be used to disrupt terrorist financial networks.

- Finally, as the initial reports about the possible perpetrators of the Boston Marathon bombing showed, most social media are very raw intelligence and must be assessed—just like any other intelligence—before becoming the basis for substantial reporting.

Turning to data-int, it is fashionable, when discussing any endeavor that deals with information, to mention big data, which typically refers to voluminous sets of data generated by communications, social media, business, and so on. Big data evangelists argue that there is potentially useful intelligence in these data sets, perhaps revealing relationships or details that are otherwise not easily known.

The intelligence community has always relied on various types of data. Each of the technical INTs provides data, as can HUMINT and OSINT. Data, like all other intelligence, must deal with the possibility of false data, either accidental or purposeful. Data have to be validated. One of the goals of the CIA's Directorate of Digital Innovation (DDI) is to understand better how to use digital information, including the data that people accumulate or leave behind and the relationship of these data to HUMINT.

But there are also distinct differences between the use of data as envisaged by big data evangelists and how intelligence agencies operate:

- Big data advocates talk about "all the data," meaning any and all data that can be examined. But intelligence uses the data that will answer its requirements, clearly a smaller set. Therefore, there has to be a means of examining and then winnowing the data to what is actually relevant.

- Also, much of the data that are discussed are either proprietary or U.S. citizen data. This runs into issues of how such data can be collected legally, and how data that should not be examined can be minimized or eliminated from the collection set.

- Big data advocates also say "collect now, analyze later." The idea is that the more data that is accumulated, the better the possible outcome. However, intelligence officers do not have this luxury. They need to collect now, analyze now.

Data are inert, sitting in repositories. They have to be acted upon in order to be of use. Algorithms matter. The choice of algorithms can affect the outcome of a data search. Also, different types of data—pandemic data, financial data, social media data, and so on—require different algorithms and possibly different types of expertise to interpret and understand them.

It may be more useful to think of data as an INT, akin to a foreign language, or multiple languages. Just as the other INTs produce intelligence that has to be processed and exploited before being passed on to analysts, we can think of data in the same manner, with a major goal of "translating" the data into a form or content that will have meaning for analysts who do not "speak" or read data. Different types of data also may not be compatible with one another when trying to fuse them. These are called heterogeneous data. For example, researchers are experimenting with geospatial data and social media data as a means of tipping, cuing, and verifying the two disparate data streams. The concept shows promise in terms of improved intelligence, but the issue of fusing the two types of data remains to be solved.

CONCLUSION

Each collection discipline is made up of several distinct types of sources (see Figure 5.1), and each offers unique advantages that are well suited to some types of intelligence requirements but brings with it certain disadvantages as well (see Table 5.1). By deploying a broad and varied array of collection techniques, the United States derives two advantages. First, it is able to exploit the advantages of each type

Figure 5.1 Intelligence Collection: The Composition of the INTs

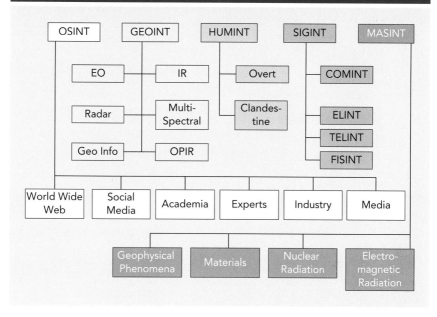

Note: This schematic provides a guide to the types of intelligence within each of the five major INTs. COMINT = communications intelligence; ELINT = electronic intelligence; EO = electro-optical; FISINT = foreign instrumentation signals intelligence; HUMINT = human intelligence; Geo Info = geospatial information; GEOINT = geospatial intelligence; IR = infrared imagery; MASINT = measurement and signatures intelligence; OPIR = overhead persistent infrared; OSINT = open-source intelligence; SIGINT = signals intelligence; TELINT = telemetry intelligence.

Table 5.1 A Comparison of the Collection Disciplines

INT	Advantages	Disadvantages
GEOINT	Graphic and compelling	Perhaps overly graphic and compelling
	Use seems familiar to policy makers	Still requires interpretation
	Ready availability of some targets—particularly military exercises	Images are literally a snapshot of a moment; very static; UAV video can overwhelm P&E
	Can be done remotely	Subject to problems of weather, spoofing
		Expensive

(Continued)

Table 5.1 (Continued)

INT	Advantages	Disadvantages
SIGINT	Offers insights into plans, intentions	Signals may be encrypted or encoded—requiring them to be broken
	Voluminous material	Voluminous material
	Military targets tend to communicate in regular patterns	May encounter communications silence, use of secure lines, spoofing via phony traffic
	Can be done remotely	Expensive
MASINT	Extremely useful for issues such as proliferation	Expensive
	Can be done remotely	Little understood by most users
		Requires a great deal of processing and exploitation
HUMINT	Offers insights into plans, intentions	Riskier in terms of lives, political fallout
	Relatively inexpensive	Requires more time to acquire and validate sources
		Problems of dangles, false feeds, double agents
OSINT	More readily available	Voluminous
	Extremely useful as a place to start all collection	Less likely to offer insights available from clandestine INTs

Note: INT = collection discipline; GEOINT = geospatial (formerly imagery) intelligence; SIGINT = signals intelligence; MASINT = measurement and signatures intelligence; HUMINT = human intelligence; and OSINT = open-source intelligence.

of INT, which, ideally, will compensate for the shortcomings of the others. Second, it is able to apply more than one collection INT to an issue, which enhances the likelihood of meeting the collection requirements for that issue. However, the intelligence community cannot provide answers to every question that is asked, nor does it have the capability to meet all possible requirements at any given time. The collection system is simultaneously powerful and limited.

The cost of collection was rarely an issue during the cold war because of the broad political agreement on the need to stay informed about the Soviet threat. In the post–cold war world, prior to the September 2001 attacks, the absence of any overwhelming strategic threat made the cost of collection systems more difficult to justify. As a result, some people questioned whether a need existed for the level of collection capability that the United States maintained during the cold war. Prior to the terrorist attacks, the United States experienced greatly diminished threats to its national security but faced ongoing concerns that are more diverse and diffuse than was the largely unitary Soviet problem, raising new collection challenges. As horrific as the September 2001 attacks were, terrorism still does not pose the same potentially overwhelming threat to the existence of the United States as did a hostile nuclear-armed Soviet missile force. Ultimately, no yardstick can measure national security problems against a collection array to determine how much collection is enough. For the near future, collection requirements likely will continue to outrun collection capabilities.

KEY TERMS

"about" collection 123
activity-based intelligence (ABI) 110
agent acquisition cycle 126
all-source intelligence 86
anti-satellite weapons (ASATs) 98
artificial intelligence (AI) 88
asset validation system 126
automatic change extraction 106
circular reporting 137
collection disciplines 83
constellation 115
content analysis 116
cryptographers 116
dangles 129
debris field 100
deception 95
denial 95
denied areas 136
denied targets 97
developmental 126
disinformation 140
echo 137
encrypt 116
espionage 94
Five Eyes 92
flock 113
foreign liaison 129
full motion video (FMV) 110

geofence 109
geosynchronous orbit (GEO) 93
highly elliptical orbit (HEO) 93
indication and warning 116
key-word search 117
low earth orbit (LEO) 93
medium earth orbit (MEO) 93
multi-int 87
negation search 105
noise versus signals 87
nonofficial cover 128
official cover 127
pattern of life 110
pitch 126
processing and exploitation (P&E) 84
quantum cryptography 118
resolution 104
risk versus take 117
self-reveal 105
shutter control 107
sleepers 129
social media 139
source 126
sources and methods 90
spies 89
steganography 117
sub-sources 127
sun-synchronous orbit 93

FURTHER READINGS

For ease of use, these readings are grouped by activity. Although there are numerous books by spies and about spying, few of them have good discussions of the craft of espionage and the role it plays, as opposed to its supposed derring-do aspects.

General Sources on Collection

Best, Richard A., Jr. *Intelligence, Surveillance, and Reconnaissance (ISR) Programs: Issues for Congress.* Washington, D.C.: Congressional Research Service, updated August 24, 2004.

Burrows, William. *Deep Black: Space Espionage and National Security.* New York: Random House, 1986.

Clark, Robert M. *The Technical Collection of Intelligence.* Washington, D.C.: CQ Press, 2011.

Lowenthal, Mark M., and Robert M. Clark, eds. *The Five Disciplines of Intelligence Collection.* Washington, D.C.: CQ Press, 2016.

Wohlstetter, Roberta. *Pearl Harbor: Warning and Decision.* Stanford, Calif.: Stanford University Press, 1962.

Artificial Intelligence

Allen, Greg, and Taniel Chan. *Artificial Intelligence and National Security.* Cambridge, Mass.: Belfer Center for Science and International Affairs, Harvard Kennedy School, July 2017. (Available at https://www.belfercenter.org/sites/default/files/files/publication/AI%20NatSec%20-%20final .pdf.)

Hoadley, Daniel S., and Nathan J. Lucas. *Artificial Intelligence and National Security.* CRS Report R45178. Washington, D.C.: U.S. Congressional Research Service, April 26, 2018.

Cyber Espionage

Dhar, Maloy Krishna. *Intelligence Tradecraft: Secrets of Spy Warfare.* New Delhi, India: Manas Publications, 2011.

Price, Douglas R. "A Guide to Cyber Intelligence." *The Intelligencer* 21 (winter 2014–2015): 55–60. (Available at http://www.afio.com/publications/PRICE_A_Guide_to_Cyber_Intelligence_%20 from_AFIO_INTEL_WINTER2014-15_Vol21_No1.pdf.)

Denial and Deception

Bennett, Michael, and Edward Waltz. *Counterdeception Principles and Applications for National Security.* Norwood, Mass.: Artech House, 2007.

Godson, Roy, and James Wirtz, eds. *Strategic Denial and Deception.* New Brunswick, N.J.: Transaction Books, 2002.

Espionage

Crumpton, Henry A. *The Art of Intelligence: Lessons From a Life in CIA's Clandestine Service.* New York: Penguin Books, 2012.

Hitz, Frederick P. "The Future of American Espionage." *International Journal of Intelligence and Counterintelligence* 13 (spring 2000): 1–20.

———. *The Great Game: The Myth and Reality of Espionage.* New York: Alfred Knopf, 2004.

———. *Why Spy? Espionage in an Age of Uncertainty.* New York: Dunne Books, 2008.

Hulnick, Arthur S. "Intelligence Cooperation in the Post–Cold War Era: A New Game Plan?" *International Journal of Intelligence and Counterintelligence* 5 (winter 1991–1992): 455–465.

Lord, Jonathan. "Undercover Under Threat: Cover Identity, Clandestine Activity, and Covert Action in the Digital Age." *International Journal of Intelligence and Counterintelligence* 28 (winter 2015–2016): 666–691.

Phillips, David Atlee. *Careers in Secret Operations: How to Be a Federal Intelligence Officer.* Frederick, Md.: Stone Trail Press, 1984.

Wallace, Robert, and H. Keith Melton, with Henry Robert Schlesinger. *Spycraft: The Secret History of the CIA's Spycraft From Communism to Al-Qaeda.* New York: Dutton, 2008.

Walsh, James Igoe. *The International Politics of Intelligence Sharing.* New York: Columbia University Press, 2009.

Weiser, Benjamin. *A Secret Life: The Polish Colonel, His Secret Mission, and the Price He Paid to Save His Country.* New York: PublicAffairs, 2004.

Wippl, Joseph W., with Donna D'Andrea. "The CMO [Collection Management Officer] in the CIAs National Clandestine Service." *International Journal of Intelligence and Counterintelligence* 23 (fall 2010): 521–533.

Wirtz, James J. "Constraints on Intelligence Collaboration: The Domestic Dimension." *International Journal of Intelligence and Counterintelligence* 6 (spring 1993): 85–89.

Imagery/GEOINT

Baker, John C., Kevin O'Connell, and Ray A. Williamson, eds. *Commercial Observation Satellites: At the Leading Edge of Transparency.* Washington, D.C.: RAND Corporation, 2001.

Best, Richard A., Jr. *Airborne Intelligence, Surveillance, and Reconnaissance (ISR): The U-2 Aircraft and Global Hawk UAV Programs.* Washington, D.C.: Library of Congress, Congressional Research Service, 2000.

Bowden, Mark. "The Killing Machines: How to Think About Drones." *The Atlantic,* August 14, 2013. (Available at http://www.theatlantic.com/magazine/archive/2013/09/the-killing-machines-how-to-think-about-drones/309434/.)

Brugioni, Dino A. "The Art and Science of Photo Reconnaissance." *Scientific American* (March 1996): 78–85.

———. *Eyeball to Eyeball: The Inside Story of the Cuban Missile Crisis.* Ed. Robert F. McCort. New York: Random House, 1990.

———. *Eyes in the Sky: Eisenhower, the CIA and Cold War Aerial Espionage.* Annapolis, Md.: U.S. Naval Institute Press, 2010.

———. *From Balloons to Blackbirds: Reconnaissance, Surveillance, and Imagery Intelligence—How It Evolved*. McLean, Va.: Association of Former Intelligence Officers, 1993.

Day, Dwayne A., and others, eds. *Eye in the Sky: The Story of the CORONA Spy Satellites*. Washington, D.C.: Smithsonian Institution Press, 1998.

Dolan, Alissa M., and Richard M. Thompson II. *Integration of Drones Into Domestic Airspace: Selected Legal Issues*. Washington, D.C.: Library of Congress, Congressional Research Service, 2013.

Lindgren, David T. *Imagery Analysis in the Cold War*. Annapolis, Md.: U.S. Naval Institute Press, 2000.

Long, Letitia. "ABI: Activity Based Intelligence, Understanding the Unknown." *The Intelligencer* 20, no. 2 (fall/winter 2013): 7–15.

Peebles, Christopher. *The CORONA Project: America's First Spy Satellite*. Annapolis, Md.: U.S. Naval Institute Press, 1997.

Richelson, Jeffrey T. *America's Secret Eyes in Space: The U.S. Keyhole Spy Satellite Program*. New York: Harper and Row, 1990.

———. "'High Flyin' Spies." *Bulletin of the Atomic Scientists* 52 (September–October 1996): 48–54.

Shulman, Seth. "Code Name CORONA." *Technology Review* 99 (October 1996): 23–25, 28–32.

SPOT Image Corporation. *Satellite Imagery: An Objective Guide*. Reston, Va.: SPOT Image Corporation, 1998.

Taubman, Philip. *Secret Empire: Eisenhower, the CIA, and the Hidden Story of America's Space Espionage*. New York: Simon and Schuster, 2003.

U. S. Central Intelligence Agency. *CORONA: America's First Satellite Program*. Ed. Kevin C. Ruffner. Washington, D.C.: CIA, 1995.

U.S. Government Accountability Office. *Unmanned Aircraft Systems: Use in the National Airspace System and the Role of the Department of Homeland Security*. Washington, D.C.: Government Accountability Office, 2012.

U.S. National Geospatial-Intelligence Agency. *Commercial GEOINT Strategy*. Washington, D.C.: NGA, 2018. (Available at https://www.nga.mil/Partners/Pages/Commercial-GEOINT-Strategy.aspx.)

Open-Source Intelligence

Bazzell, Michael. *Open Source Intelligence Techniques*. 6th ed. CreateSpace (Amazon), 2018.

Best, Richard A., Jr., and Alfred Cumming. *Open Source Intelligence (OSINT): Issues for Congress*. Report RL34270. Washington, D.C.: Library of Congress, Congressional Research Service, December 5, 2007.

Eldridge, Christopher, Christopher Hobbs, and Matthew Moran. "Fusing Algorithms and Analysts: Open-Source Intelligence in the Age of Big Data." *Intelligence and National Security* 33 (April 2018): 391–406.

Hobbs, Christopher, Matthew Moran, and Daniel Salisbury, eds. *Open Source Intelligence in the Twenty-First Century: New Approaches and Opportunities*. London: Palgrave Macmillan, 2014.

Leetaru, Kalev. "The Scope of FBIS and BBC Open-Source Media Coverage, 1979–2008." *Studies in Intelligence* 54 (March 2010): 17–37.

Lowenthal, Mark M. "Open Source Intelligence: New Myths, New Realities." *Defense Daily News*, November 1998. (Available at http://www.oss.net/dynamaster/file_archive/040319/ca06aacb07e5 cb9f25f21babf7ef2bf0/OSS1999-P1-08.pdf.)

———. "OSINT: The State of the Art, the Artless State." *Studies in Intelligence* (fall 2001): 61–66.

Mercado, Stephen C. "Sailing the Sea of OSINT in the Information Age." *Studies in Intelligence* 48 (2004). (Available at www.cia.gov.csi/studies.)

Olcott, Anthony. *Open Source Intelligence in a Networked World*. New York: Continuum, 2012.

Omand, David, Jamie Bartlett, and Carl Miller. "Introducing Social Media Intelligence (SOCMINT)." *Intelligence and National Security* 27 (December 2012): 801–823.

Thompson, Clive. "Open-Source Spying." *New York Times Magazine*, December 6, 2006, 54.

Satellites

Berkowitz, Bruce. *The National Reconnaissance Office at 50 Years: A Brief History*. Chantilly, Va.: U.S. National Reconnaissance Office, Center for the Study of National Reconnaissance, 2011.

Klass, Philip. *Secret Sentries in Space*. New York: Random House, 1971.

National Academies of Science. *National Security and Space Defense Protection*. Washington, D.C.: The National Academies Press, 2016.

Taubman, Philip. "Death of a Spy Satellite." *New York Times*, November 11, 2007, 1.

U.S. Defense Intelligence Agency. *Challenges to Security in Space*. Washington, D.C.: DIA, January 2019. (Available at http://www.dia.mil/Portals/27/Documents/News/Military%20Power%20 Publications/Space_Threat_V14_020119_sm.pdf.)

U.S. Department of Defense. Defense Science Board. *Task Force on Military Satellite Communication and Networking*. Washington, D.C.: DOD, March 2017. (Available at https://www.acq.osd.mil/dsb/ reports/2010s/DSB-MilSatCom-FINALExecutiveSummary_UNCLASSIFIED.pdf.)

U.S. Department of Defense and Office of the Director of National Intelligence. *National Security Space Strategy: Unclassified Summary*. Washington, D.C.: DOD and ODNI, 2011.

U.S. National Air and Space Intelligence Center. *Competing in Space*. Wright-Patterson AFB, Ohio: U.S. National Air and Space Intelligence Center, December 2018. (Available at https://media .defense.gov/2019/Jan/16/2002080386/-1/-1/1/190115-F-NV711-0002.PDF.)

U.S. National Commission for the Review of the National Reconnaissance Office. *Report: The National Commission for the Review of the National Reconnaissance Office*. Washington, D.C.: U.S. Government Printing Office, November 14, 2000. (Available at https://www.fas.org/irp/nro/ commission/nro.pdf.)

Zenko, Micah. *Dangerous Space Incidents*. New York: Council on Foreign Relations, 2014.

Secrecy

Moynihan, Daniel Patrick. *Secrecy: The American Experience*. New Haven, Conn.: Yale University Press, 1998.

Secrecy. Report of the Commission on Protecting and Reducing Government Secrecy, Senate Document 105–2. Washington, D.C.: U.S. Government Printing Office, 1997.

Signals Intelligence

Aid, Matthew M. *The Secret Sentry: The Untold History of the National Security Agency*. New York: Bloomsbury Press, 2009.

Aid, Matthew M., and Cees Wiebes. *Secrets of Signals Intelligence During the Cold War and Beyond*. Portland, Ore.: Frank Cass, 2001.

Bamford, James. *Body of Secret: Anatomy of the Ultra-Secret National Security Agency—From the Cold War Through the Dawn of a New Century*. New York: Doubleday, 2001.

———. *The Puzzle Palace: A Report on America's Most Secret Agency*. Boston: Viking, 1982.

Brownell, George A. *The Origin and Development of the National Security Agency*. Laguna Hills, Calif.: Aegean Park Press, 1981.

Harris, Shane. *The Watchers: The Rise of America's Surveillance State*. New York: Penguin Press, 2010.

Kahn, David. *The Codebreakers*. Rev. ed. New York: Scribner, 1996.

National Security Agency and Central Intelligence Agency. *VENONA: Soviet Espionage and the American Response, 1939–1957*. Ed. Robert Louis Benson and Michael Warner. Washington, D.C.: NSA and CIA, 1996.

Presidential Policy Directive 28 (PPD-28), Signals Intelligence Activities, January 17, 2014. (Available at http://www.whitehouse.gov/sites/default/files/docs/2014sigint_mem_ppd_rel.pdf.)

Warner, Michael, and Robert Louis Benson. "VENONA and Beyond: Thoughts on Work Undone." *Intelligence and National Security* 12 (July 1996): 1–13.

CHAPTER SIX

ANALYSIS

D irector of Central Intelligence (DCI) Richard Helms (1966–1973) spent most of his career in operations, but in his memoirs he noted that "the absolute essence of the intelligence profession" rests in the production of various analytic products "on which sound policy decisions can be made." Intelligence analysis provides civil and military policy makers with information directly related to the issues they face and the decisions they have to make. Intelligence products do not arrive on policy makers' desks once or twice a day, but in a steady stream throughout the day. Certain products, particularly the daily intelligence reports and briefings, are often received first thing in the morning, but other intelligence reports can be delivered when they are ready or may be held for delivery at a specific time. As Helms observed, despite all the attention lavished on the operational side of intelligence (collection and covert action), analysis is the mainstay of the process. Intelligence analysis provides civil and military policy makers with information directly related to the issues they face and the decisions they have to make.

Although not all intelligence practitioners agree, the ongoing production and delivery of intelligence can have a numbing effect on policy makers. Intelligence analysis can become part of the daily flood of information—intelligence products; commercially provided news; reports from policy offices, embassies, and military commands; e-mails; and so on. One of the challenges for intelligence is to make itself stand out from this steady stream of information.

Intelligence can be made to stand out in two ways. One is to emphasize the unique nature of the intelligence sources. But this option is not the preferred choice of intelligence officials, who believe that they are much more than just conduits for their sources. The other way for intelligence to achieve prominence is to produce analysis that stands out on its own merits by adding value. The value added includes the timeliness of intelligence products, the ability of the community to tailor products to specific policy makers' needs, and the objectivity of the analysis. One analyst who had been a presidential briefer put it this way: "My value was telling the president something he didn't already know about something he needed to know." But the fact that value-added intelligence is discussed as often as it is within the intelligence community suggests that it is not achieved as often as desired.

MAJOR THEMES

Prescribing how to produce value-added intelligence—or how to measure the frequency with which it is produced—is difficult because intelligence officers and their policy clients do not agree on what adds value. For policy clients, value added is an idiosyncratic and personal attribute.

Analysis is much more than sitting down with the collected material, sifting and sorting it, and coming up with a brilliant piece of prose that makes sense of it all. Major decisions have to be made in the analytical process, and several areas of controversy have proved to be resilient or recurrent.

Formal Requirements. In the ideal intelligence-process model, policy makers give some thought to their main requirements for intelligence and then communicate them to the intelligence managers. Such a formal process has not appeared often in the history of the intelligence community, leaving managers to make educated guesses about what intelligence is required.

Some people argue that a less formal process is, in reality, much better than the presumed ideal one, because most of the requirements of intelligence are fairly well known and do not need to be defined. For example, most people, if asked to name the main U.S. intelligence priorities during the cold war, would mention a number of Soviet-related issues. Even in the less clear post–cold war period before the September 2001 terrorist attacks, a similar exercise would have yielded such answers as narcotics, terrorism, proliferation, Russia's reform and stability, and the regional trouble spots of the moment, such as Iran, the Middle East, and North Korea. The list parallels the U.S. intelligence priorities as stated in the Bill Clinton administration's Presidential Decision Directive 35. After September 2001, terrorism became the primary, but not the sole, focus of intelligence.

The real importance of the requirements process may lie in giving the intelligence community some sense of priority among the requirements, many of which are known. Formal discussions about priorities between senior policy makers and intelligence officers tend to revolve around relative degrees of importance instead of issues that have been added to the priorities list or overlooked. Assigning priorities is especially important and difficult in the absence of a single overwhelming issue, as was the case from roughly 1991 (the end of the Soviet Union) until 2001 and even after, albeit it to a lesser degree. When several issues are considered to be of roughly equal importance, no single one of them has complete priority. However, this seeming lack of focus may reflect the reality of national security interests. In such a circumstance the intelligence managers must then make critical decisions about the allocation of collection and analytical resources among several equally important and competing issues.

Some people also misunderstand the goal of the priority process and view it as a forecast of the issues that will be important in the near future. A priorities process is an expression of areas of policy maker interest and their relative importance to one another, not a forecast of which of these issues will be most prominent. Indeed, most people who manage priorities systems recognize that unforeseen issues will inevitably arise. A good priority system should be able to adjust for these new issues and have some sense of which other issues can be given less attention instead, even if only for a short period. The Arab Spring unrest in the Middle East is an excellent example of the problem. The United States clearly had a stake in the stability of friendly Arab states, such as Tunisia and Egypt. This does not mean that analysts were blind to the negative aspects of the Zine El Abidine Ben Ali and Hosni Mubarak governments or the inevitability of regime change given the age of the leaders. But there would be little reason, in late 2010, to give Tunisia the priority it likely assumed in early 2011 after the Arab Spring revolts began. Egypt was already a nation of greater importance to U.S. national security. There was nothing in the decades that had passed in either country to suggest a sudden turn into instability, as opposed to the inevitability of a transfer of power at some unknown point as the autocrats aged.

Another issue in setting priorities is the fact that very few, if any, national security issues or threats are completely independent issues. Instead, there are interconnections among many issues. For example, the nexus between terrorism and weapons of mass destruction (WMD) is a constant concern. Terrorism is also connected to narcotics, as narcotics trafficking is a primary means of funding terrorism. In addition, terrorism and other transnational issues (crime, narcotics, human trafficking, etc.) thrive in failed states, which have little law and order or control over their borders. The issues in such failed states are not equally important, or threatening, but it is necessary to take into account the interconnections when determining priorities. Thus, a lesser issue may get more attention because of its relationship to a more pressing issue. However, one cannot state that any issue that is related to a high-priority issue therefore also requires a high priority. If we did that, then almost every issue would end up with a relatively high priority, effectively undoing the entire priority system. One must recall the warning: "When everything is important, nothing is important."

It is also important to understand that issues do not exist in an abstract realm: All issues have a geographic aspect. This may be broad or narrow, but every issue can be tied to specific locations. In determining priorities, it may be useful to differentiate based on the importance of the geographic aspect of the issue. For example, drugs being produced in Afghanistan may be seen as more problematic than those produced in Southeast Asia because of the Afghan–Taliban–al Qaeda connection. This geographic differentiation may also be useful in determining which supporting issues are more or less important.

Finally, issues are not monolithic. Every nation in which the United States has intelligence interests comprises several issues (e.g., political, military, social, economic) that will be of varying importance depending on the nation and its relationship to the United States. For example, U.S. interest in the state of the British military is that of assessing the capabilities of a close ally, while in North Korea we focus on the capabilities of a potential enemy. Although both are capabilities issues, the basis of our intelligence interest in each is quite different. Similarly, when dealing with a transnational issue, such as terrorists, it is important to differentiate among the various groups, their capabilities, their locations, and their interrelationships. Not every group will pose the same level of threat or of interest. It is important for intelligence managers to be able to make these distinctions to achieve the optimal allocation of both collection and analytical resources, even when examining the same issues.

Current Versus Long-Term Intelligence. The competition between current and **long-term intelligence** is a perennial analytical issue. Current intelligence—reports and analysis on issues that may not extend more than a week or two into the future—is the mainstay of the intelligence community, the product most often requested and seen by policy makers. In many respects, **current intelligence** pays the rent for the intelligence community. Current intelligence always predominates over other types, but the degree of this predominance varies over time. During a crisis or war, current intelligence increases, as many of the decisions made during these periods are tactical in nature—even among senior policy makers—thus demanding current intelligence.

But some intelligence analysts are frustrated by the emphasis on current intelligence. Having developed expertise in an area and analytical skills, they wish to write longer range analyses that look beyond current demands. However, few policy makers are likely to read papers with very long time horizons—owing not to lack of interest but to lack of time and the inability to pull away, even briefly, from pressing matters. Thus, a conflict arises between what the policy makers need to read and what many analysts wish to produce. Current intelligence products also tend to be shorter by their nature and goals, further limiting the ability of analysts to add the depth or context that they deem valuable. An additional concern is that if current intelligence represents the majority of what analysts produce, then a risk arises that they will largely become reporters of that day's collection instead of true analysts. Building true depth of expertise is difficult on a steady diet of current intelligence analysis.

Some middle ground exists simply because the intelligence community does not make a stark choice between one type of analysis and another on any given day. A range of analysis is produced. But because of the limited number of analysts, managers have to decide where to put their resources, and the fact remains that the current intelligence products predominate in terms of resources and the way policy makers perceive the intelligence community.

The current versus mid-term or long-term intelligence conundrum is not the only way to think about allocation issues, although it is the most common. Instead of thinking about intelligence as a matter of time, think about it as a depth versus breadth issue, or a tactical versus strategic issue. By its nature, most current intelligence tends to emphasize breadth over depth. However, one's analytical sights can be raised to create intelligence that is current as well as strategic. Intelligence may be current in that it is focused on issues on the agenda right now or in the near future, but it also may attempt to give the policy maker a deeper look at the issues involved—for example, by providing more context, more interconnection with other issues or possible solutions, and so on. A more strategic current intelligence is not produced often, but it can be done without pushing the analysis into areas that policy makers are less likely to find useful. But a relationship exists between the two types of intelligence that is important both to analysts and to policy makers. One can think of current intelligence on issues as providing the building blocks for the more strategic intelligence, knowing the details as issues develop over time. This is especially important during a crisis, when it is much more difficult to come up to speed on issues that are moving quickly. This explains why some intelligence professionals were taken aback when President-elect Trump said he did not need daily briefings that said "the same thing in the same words every single day." This showed a misunderstanding of how intelligence develops. Trump later changed his mind and does get regular, if not daily, briefings.

The problem of current versus long-term intelligence also reflects yet another difference in outlook between policy makers and intelligence officers. Policy makers in the United States think in four-year blocks of time, the length of any presidential administration—which at best can be extended to eight years with reelection. Therefore, policy makers have difficulty thinking in larger blocks of time because of their more limited ability to influence events beyond their tenure. Another problem for long-term analytical products is the inherent "softness" of their judgments as their time frame increases. Trying to gauge likely conditions or outcomes is always difficult, but as the period being examined gets longer, the judgments become much less reliable. There is no absolute gauge about how far out analysis can be done and still be seen as reliable, but once the analysis ranges beyond a few years, the fidelity is likely to drop off markedly. Long-range analysis may be interesting intellectually, but it is unlikely to be seen as useful by policy makers. Indeed, it could even have a negative effect on the intelligence community at large if some policy makers question why resources are being devoted to this type of work rather than to more pressing and clearly identified issues that are on the current agenda.

Briefings. Briefings for policy makers are a form of current intelligence. Many are routine and take place first thing in the morning. Briefings are one of the main ways in which current intelligence is conveyed. One of the main advantages of briefings is the intelligence officer's ability to interact directly with the policy maker, to get a better idea of the policy maker's preferences and reactions to the intelligence, thus overcoming the absence of a formal feedback mechanism. Risks also are involved, though. Briefings, as their name indicates, tend to be brief. Given policy makers' schedules, most briefings are limited by the time allotted for them. Moreover, the morning briefings usually must cover several topics—although both President George W. Bush and President Barack Obama had regular in-depth briefings on a single issue, known as "deep dives." Providing the necessary context and depth in a briefing can be difficult in a time-constrained environment. Briefings are not necessarily restricted to oral presentations. Items that back up or underscore a briefing point—such as a signals intelligence (SIGINT) or human intelligence (HUMINT) report—may also be used. Part of this depends on the preference of the policy maker. For example, President Trump's briefs reportedly are mostly oral, with little use of supporting material, which can increase the difficulty in conveying detail and nuance.

At their best, briefings can be a give-and-take between the policy maker and the intelligence officer. This sort of exchange can be stimulating, but it runs risks. The briefer must be sure of his or her information, some of which may not be in the material that was prepared for the briefing. Briefers have to be taught to say, "I don't know," and offer to get the desired information later, not hazard guesses. Furthermore, the briefing has an ephemeral quality. The briefer may not be able to recapture all that was said after the fact.

Briefings raise issues associated with analysts' more proximate relationship with policy makers, particularly the ability to and necessity of keeping some distance from policy to maintain analytic objectivity. The regularly assigned briefers have a two-way role, conveying intelligence to the policy makers and conveying the policy makers' needs or reactions back to the intelligence community. The briefers must avoid slipping into a role of advocacy or support for the policy makers' policies, either writ large or in bureaucratic debates.

An area of controversy that arose in the aftermath of the terrorist attacks in 2001 was the nature of the Central Intelligence Agency (CIA) briefing for the president and senior officials. The briefing, which centers on the President's Daily Brief (PDB), was a CIA publication, conducted exclusively by the CIA. Although senior officials in the executive departments and in the intelligence community are privy to the PDB, this group is very small. Thus, other intelligence agencies did not necessarily know what the president or their own departmental senior policy makers were being told. This engenders a certain amount of jealousy and can lead to a situation in which analytic components of the intelligence community are working at cross-purposes.

After the passage of the 2004 Intelligence Reform and Terrorism Prevention Act (IRTPA), control of the PDB shifted. The PDB staff became part of the Office of the Director of National Intelligence (ODNI). For the CIA, control over the PDB was one of its crown jewels, giving it an assured level of access. However, responsibility for conducting the morning briefing has passed to the director of national intelligence (DNI). Under the DNI, the PDB is open to contributions from many analytic components. This makes it more of a community product and may also add greater breadth, but it highlights a problem in the DNI structure. PDB articles are all cleared—that is, reviewed for publication—by CIA, DIA, INR, the NIC, NSA, and NGA. When the DCI controlled the CIA and the PDB, the DCI had a greater sense of who was behind the PDB articles and, perhaps, a greater sense of ownership than the DNI. The DNI controls no analysts beyond the National Intelligence Council (NIC), so the DNI is, in effect, presenting the work of other agencies. In theory, and in law, the DNI has responsibility for all intelligence components but has authority over very few of them. Also, in terms of content, the CIA continues to be the main contributor to the PDB (some estimate on the order of 75 percent) as it has the largest number of all-source analysts and thus the greatest depth and breadth of analytic capability, writ large.

Some observers believe that too much emphasis has been placed on the PDB, which has had a negative effect on overall analytic efforts. Spending time with the chief executive on a regular basis and being able to put an intelligence product before the president routinely are valuable assets. No intelligence manager would decline these opportunities. But decisions still have to be made about how much effort to put into preparing one discreet entity (the PDB) and how much goes into broader and perhaps deeper products. Analyses that go into the PDB or any other morning intelligence publication are nonurgent enough to wait until the next day. If the items reported on were crucial, they would be briefed to the president and other senior officials at once. This ongoing emphasis on the PDB also skews the work of analysts, many of whom seek to write something that goes into the PDB or a deep dive, when this is hardly a significant indicator of analytic capability. An example of this overemphasis on the PDB is a result of the fact that other agencies may now contribute to it. In some intelligence agencies, managers set targets of how many PDB articles they should have in a given week or keep tallies of how many PDB articles their offices produced. Having an article in the PDB, while rewarding, is hardly a metric of analytic success.

Crises Versus the Norm. One way in which requirements are set is in response to crises. Crisis-driven requirements represent the ultimate victory of current over long-range intelligence needs.

Given the limited nature of collection and analytical resources, certain issues inevitably receive short shrift or even no attention at all. And, just as inevitably, annual or semiannual requirements planning regularly fails to predict which of the seemingly less important issues may erupt into a crisis. Indeed, as noted, this is not the purpose of the requirements process. Thus, the planning exercises are to some degree self-fulfilling—or self-defeating—prophecies.

Analytical managers must find a way to create or preserve some minimal amount of expertise against the moment when a seemingly less important issue erupts and suddenly moves to the top of policy makers' concerns. The intelligence community has only a small collection reserve, no analytical reserve, and a limited capacity to move assets to previously uncovered but now important topics. Assets therefore move from hot topic to hot topic, with other matters receiving little or no coverage.

Despite the problem of defining requirements and the vagaries of international relations, the intelligence community is put on the spot when it misses an issue—that is, fails to be alert to its eventuality or is unprepared to deal with it when it occurs. In part, the high expectations are deserved, given that one function of intelligence is strategic warning. But strategic warning is usually taken to mean advance notice on issues that would pose a threat to national security, not regional crises that might require some level of involvement. Such crises strain the image of the intelligence community as well as its resources, because policy makers in both branches and the media tend to be harsh—sometimes fairly, sometimes not—in their view of misses. For example, in the autumn of 2015, press reports stated that members of Congress wanted to investigate why the intelligence community had failed to warn policy makers that Russia might intervene in Syria. First, it would have to be established that the intelligence community did, indeed, fail to warn. But assuming that there was a failure to warn, there is a second question: Did this make any difference in terms of U.S. policy? President Obama had been very clear that he did not want to get more deeply involved in the Syrian civil war. Would a warning about possible Russian intervention have changed the president's calculus? Indeed, repeated intelligence warnings could be interpreted as an effort by the analyst or managers to get the president to change his policy. Why else keep sending in analysis that runs counter to his stated preferences? There is an unstated assumption that intelligence somehow forces policy makers to act regardless of the policy maker's preferences. As noted earlier, policy makers are free to ignore or reject intelligence and will do so, especially if it runs contrary to their policy preferences.

One difficult aspect of dealing with crises that has arisen has been the demands of the combatant commanders (now called CCMDs, formerly called COCOMs—the four-star officers who command U.S. forces in Europe, the Pacific, and so on) for intelligence support from national intelligence collection assets. The issue is one of conflicting priorities. The CCMDs are responsible for huge swaths of the globe and react to unrest in any of the countries in their area of responsibility (AOR). However, policy makers and intelligence officers in Washington, D.C., may not have the same sense of urgency about events in some of the smaller states and those that have less affiliation to the United States. Thus, there is a difference of perspective and perception. Efforts have been made to wean the CCMDs off their desire to call upon national assets for any and all emergencies in their AOR and to rely more on their own, admittedly less capable, theater intelligence assets.

The fact that the United States has been engaged in three hostile situations—terrorists, Iraq, and Afghanistan—tends to exacerbate the crises versus the norm issue. Active combat or active intelligence operations tend to overwhelm other issues and activities. No one questions the importance of supporting either the military or intelligence operators, but these demands can become overwhelming, crowding out other issues. Also, for the intelligence community, a lot of these demands are tactical in nature, calling for support for an ongoing operation. This makes it more difficult for the intelligence analysts to "pull up to a higher altitude" and try to take a strategic view of the overall campaign.

The Wheat Versus Chaff Problem. The wheat versus chaff problem, although part of collection, ultimately becomes an analytical issue. Although much that is collected does not get processed and exploited, the amount that does is still formidable. Even in the age of computers, few technical shortcuts have been found to help analysts deal with the problem to any significant degree. The intelligence community has adopted some software programs to assist in parts of information management, such as text mining and data mining, and has examined many others, but no major breakthroughs have been made. The DNI's office has sponsored several of these, such as the "Xpress" Automated Analysis Challenge, a $500,000 competition to find artificial intelligence approaches to improve intelligence research and report generation. However, to a large degree, the analysts' daily task of sifting through the incoming intelligence germane to their portfolios remains a grind, whether done electronically or on paper. Sifting is not just a matter of getting through the accumulated imagery, signals, open-source reporting, and other data. It is also the much more important matter of seeing this mass of material in its entirety, of being able to perceive patterns from day to day and reports that are anomalous. There are no shortcuts. Sifting requires training and experience. Although some intelligence practitioners think of analysts as the human in the loop, the analysts' expertise should be an integral part of collection sorting as well.

Data Versus Knowledge. Closely related to the wheat versus chaff issue are the issues of data and of data versus knowledge. The ability to amass and manipulate large amounts of data on computers offers, to some, tantalizing possibilities for analysis and forecasting that did not exist before. There has been a great deal of discussion about big data, which in essence means the possibility of gaining new insights and connections from the reams of new data created every day (see chap. 5). Part of the problem is in the counting rules. Most big data enthusiasts count all of the telephone calls, e-mails, tweets, blog posts, and so on created every day to prove how rich the field is. These data certainly exist, but how many of them are of interest or utility to intelligence analysts? For example, of the millions of telephone metadata records searched by the National Security Agency (NSA), 300 led to further inquiries. The argument can be made that without the NSA metadata program these leads might not have existed at all, but a means-and-ends argument remains over the larger big data claims. Moreover, many of these data troves are proprietary—belonging to Google, Facebook, Amazon, and so on, whose goal is to monetize these data. They are not going to share much of them. Also, much of these data contain U.S. persons information, which immediately creates legal limits and requirements related to how they can be used.

There are clearly intelligence issues that rely on large data inputs: the terrorism connections noted earlier, the details of weapons systems, or economic data. However, no amount of data will get at some of the key questions uppermost on the minds of policy makers: intentions. What North Korea or Iran or any other nation or leader will do next is not very susceptible to data. Moreover, as one senior policy official remarked, "I do not want data. I want knowledge and insight."

There has also been some pushback on the utility of big data. As several analysts have noted, correlation, which is relatively easy with data, does not equal causation. (The Iraq WMD experience is a good illustration of this pitfall.) It is easy to confuse large amounts of data with in-depth knowledge and expertise. To a certain degree, data are much easier to deal with as they are almost mechanical and can give the illusion of useful insights when they may instead be somewhat ephemeral. As Kenneth Cukier and Viktor Mayer-Schoenberger noted in a 2013 article in *Foreign Affairs:* "Big data is a resource and a tool. It is meant to inform, rather than explain."

Analytical managers will therefore have to be on guard to assure themselves that their analysts also continue to be "knowledge workers," a term coined by Peter Drucker around 1959 to connote someone who works primarily with information or who develops and uses knowledge in the workplace. Indeed, one of the main functions of the intelligence community in the past had been the creation, preservation, and transmission of knowledge. Some people argue that this function has atrophied as analysts and managers focus more on data and as the overall experience level within the intelligence community has declined in the years since 2001 as senior analysts retired and there was also a huge influx of new analysts.

The CIA's Directorate of Digital Innovation (DDI) seeks to find ways to use data with analytical models as a means of identifying emerging trends and reportedly has had some success forecasting initial unrest or societal instability several days before they actually occurred. In a related development, IARPA (the DNI's Intelligence Advanced Research Projects Agency) has begun a Geopolitical Forecasting Challenge to develop methodologies to attempt to anticipate events in real time.

Analyst Fungibility. When requirements change or when crises break out, analysts must be shifted to areas of greater need. As with collection, they are participating in a zero-sum game. The analysts have to come from some other assignment, and not every analyst can work on every issue. Each analyst has strengths, weaknesses, and areas that he or she simply does not know. Even though analysts far outnumber collection systems, analysts are less fungible—that is, easily interchanged or replaced—than the technical collection systems. A SIGINT satellite that has been collecting against a French-speaking target will not plead ignorance or inability if redirected against an Arabic-speaking target. Significant issues of targeting, access, frequencies, and so on come up, but no language barrier exists per se. Streams of digital communications data do not have indecipherable accents or abstruse grammar. However, not every analyst has the requisite language, regional, or topical skills to move to an area of greater need. Very real limits exist on **analyst fungibility**, which is a major management concern. This is also sometimes referred to as **analyst agility**, again meaning the need for analysts who have more than one (or two) areas of expertise and therefore can be shifted to higher priority accounts during times of need. Fungibility or agility relies on three factors: the talents and background of the analysts when they are recruited; their training and education within the intelligence community; and the management of their careers, which should give them sufficient opportunities to develop this expertise in a few areas.

U.S. intelligence managers often speak about **global coverage**, which can be a dangerous and misleading term. By global coverage, intelligence officers mean their acknowledged requirement to cover any and all issues. Members of the intelligence community cannot say to a policy maker, for example, that they do not have much capability to analyze the current crisis in Mali but they are very good on Mexico. No bait and switch is allowed. If the situation in a country or region becomes a matter of concern, the intelligence community is expected to cover it. The pitfall in the term "global coverage" is the real possibility that it leaves the impression among policy makers of more depth and breadth than is available in the intelligence community. Intelligence managers understand the resource limitations within which they are working, but by using the term "global coverage" they may be misinterpreted as promising more than they can deliver.

Part of the problem stems from the limitations of the analyst hiring process. In the United States, recruiters go to colleges and universities looking for potential analysts. Other candidates simply apply on their own. But this is a seller's market. The intelligence agencies can hire only those people who evince an interest. Certain schools may have programs that tend to produce more analysts with a certain interest or skill, but this does not appreciably solve the problem. Congress has given the intelligence community a limited ability to offer scholarships for analysts with particular skills, in return for which the analysts must work for the intelligence community for a set number of years. Although a valuable change, such ability does not solve the recruitment problem. It is also very difficult to forecast analytical needs several years out. Analysts tend to be hired against current needs in terms of skill sets, areas of expertise, and languages. This can create imbalances when issues shift dramatically. For example, the Soviet Union remained a priority until its collapse, but once it was gone there was a surplus of Russian language speakers, not all of whom could easily be shifted to other issues. However, interest in Russia increased again after Vladimir Putin resumed the presidency in 2012 and began to pursue a more aggressive foreign policy. The old "Soviet hands" were long gone, along with their accumulated expertise. Similarly, in the aftermath of the terrorist attacks in 2001, there was an urgent and very difficult-to-fill need for speakers and readers of Arabic and then for the many non-Roman alphabet languages spoken in southwestern Asia.

Thus, the intelligence community has greater analytic capabilities in some areas than in others. The situation can be ameliorated to some extent by moving analysts around from issue to issue, but sacrificing depth for breadth can result. Moreover, during a crisis, what is wanted most from analysts is depth. The point remains that all analysts have limitations that can curtail the ability of the intelligence community to respond as expected and as the community would prefer.

Analyst Training. The intelligence community's approach to training has been somewhat idiosyncratic, with each major component creating unique training programs. Training is most useful in giving incoming analysts a sense of what is expected of them, how the larger community works, and its ethos and rules. No amount of training, however, can obviate the fact that much of what an analyst needs to know is learned on the job. Analysts arrive with certain skills garnered from their college or graduate school studies or their work experience (a significant number of analysts now come to the intelligence community after having begun careers in other areas) and then are assimilated into their specific intelligence agency or unit. They learn basic processes and requirements, the daily work schedule, and preferred means of expression, which vary from agency to agency. They become familiar with the types of intelligence with which they will be working.

The minimum skills for all analysts are knowledge of one or more specific fields, appropriate language skills, and a basic ability to express themselves in writing. A senior official used to ask his subordinates two questions about new analysts they wished to hire: Do they think interesting thoughts? Do they write well? This official believed that, with these two talents in hand, all else would follow with training and experience.

The basic skills are a foundation on which better skills must be built. Some of the new skills to be mastered are parochial. Each intelligence agency has its own corporate style that must be learned. More important, analysts must learn to cope with the wheat versus chaff problem and to write as succinctly as possible. These two skills reflect the demands of current intelligence and the fact that policy makers are busy and prefer economies of style. The bureaucratic truism remains that shorter papers will usually best longer papers in the competition for policy makers' attention. They must also learn how to manage their time so that their analysis is ready when needed or expected.

Training analysts about collection systems appears to fall short of desired goals, given the ignorance expressed by even some senior analysts about this important topic. This means that some analysts are hard put to understand the true nature and relative reliability of intelligence sources because they do not have a very deep appreciation of how they are collected. This does not mean that every analyst has to be deeply versed in each of the collection disciplines, but something more than a superficial knowledge is an analytical advantage. Another important skill that analysts must learn is objectivity, or overcoming **analyst bias**. Although intelligence analysts can and often do have strong personal views about the issues they are covering, their opinions have no place in intelligence products. Analysts are listened to because of their accumulated expertise, not the forcefulness of their views. Presenting personal conclusions would cross the line between intelligence and policy. Still, analysts need training to learn how to recognize when they have strong biases on issues they are writing about and to filter out their views, especially when they run counter to the intelligence at hand or the policies being considered.

A more subtle and difficult skill to master is cultivating the intelligence consumer without politicizing the intelligence as a means of currying favor.

Finally, there is the question of how far training (or experience) can take a given analyst. Any reasonably intelligent individual with the right skills and education can be taught to be an effective analyst. But the truly gifted analyst—like the truly gifted athlete, musician, or scientist—is inherently better at his or her job by virtue of inborn talents. Being able to analyze and synthesize intuitively and quickly and having a good nose for the subtext of a situation are innate skills that are difficult to acquire. In all fields, such individuals are rare. They must be nurtured. But the benefits they derive from training are different from those that accrue to less gifted analysts.

Part of the underlying problem in analyst education and training has been the rather vague sense across the intelligence community of what an analyst's career progression of skills should look like. There has been some general agreement, but it has not been specific enough or accepted across all agencies. It is extremely difficult to create an education program if the levels of achievement are not described with some precision. A recent, more detailed effort by the CIA's Sherman Kent School has been the intelligence analyst training program, which describes the skills required at progressive levels—first year: career analyst program; one-plus years: essential skills; four-plus years: advanced analyst; ten-plus years: expert.

Managing Analysts. Managing intelligence analysts presents a number of unique problems. A major concern is developing career tracks. Analysts need time to develop true expertise in their fields, but intellectual stagnation can set in if an analyst is left to cover the same issue for too long. Rotating analysts among assignments quickly helps them avoid becoming stale and allows them to learn more than one area. But this career pattern raises the possibility that analysts will never gain expertise in any one area, instead becoming generalists. Ideally, managers seek to create some middle ground—providing analysts with assignments that are long enough for them to gain expertise and substantive knowledge while also providing sufficient opportunities to shift assignments and maintain intellectual freshness. Nor is there any specific time frame for assignments; the length depends on the individual analyst, the relative intensity of the current assignment, and the demands generated by intelligence requirements at the time. More intense jobs tend to argue for somewhat shorter tours to avoid burnout. But more urgent issues also tend to have higher priority, demanding greater expertise and consistency of staffing. Thus, there are again competing needs.

The criteria for promotion are another management issue. As government employees, intelligence analysts are generally assured of promotions up to a level that can be described as high-middle. The criteria for promotion through the grades are not overly rigorous. Promotions should come as a result of merit, not time served. But what criteria should a manager consider in evaluating an intelligence analyst for merit promotion: accuracy of analysis over the past year, writing skills, increased competence in foreign languages and foreign area knowledge, participation in a specific number of major studies, intellectual growth in mastering new areas? And how should a manager weigh the various criteria?

The competition is stronger for more senior assignments than for those at the lower level, and the criteria for selection are different. The qualities that first merit promotion—keen analytical abilities—are the ticket to management positions, where responsibilities and pay are greater. Ironically, or perhaps sadly, analytical skills have little to do with, and are little indication of, the ability to carry out managerial duties. But, with few exceptions, management positions have been the only route to senior promotion. The CIA has created a Senior Analytical Service, which allows analysts to reach the first rungs of senior ranks solely on the basis of their analytic capabilities.

Analysts' Mind-Set. Analysts, as a group, exhibit a set of behaviors that can affect their work. Not all analysts exhibit each of these characteristics all of the time, and some analysts may never display any of them. Still, many of these traits are common among large segments of this population.

One of the most frequent flaws of analysts is **mirror imaging**, which, as described earlier, assumes that other leaders, states, and groups share motivations or goals similar to those most familiar to the analyst. "They're just like us" is the quintessential expression of this view. The prevalence of mirror imaging is not difficult to understand. People learn, from an early age, to expect certain behavior of others. The golden rule is based on the concept of reciprocal motives and behavior. Unfortunately, as an analytical tool, mirror imaging fails to take into account such matters as differences of motivation, perception, or action based on national differences, subtle differences of circumstance, different rationales, and the absence of any rationale.

Simon Montefiore (*Stalin: The Court of the Red Tsar*) quotes Josef Stalin as saying, "When you're trying to make a decision, NEVER put yourself in the mind of the other person because if you do, you can make a terrible mistake." For example, during the cold war, some Kremlinologists and Sovietologists talked about Soviet hawks and doves and tried to assess which Soviet leaders belonged to which group. No empirical evidence existed to suggest that there were Soviet hawks and doves. Instead, the fact that the U.S. political spectrum included hawks and doves led to the facile assumption that the Soviet system must have them as well. More recently, some commentators and analysts working on Iran speak of Iranian extremists and moderates. When pressed by skeptical peers as to their evidence for the existence of moderates, the response is often this: If there are extremists, there must be moderates. Again, they reflect other political systems they know, as well as making a faulty assumption. It could be argued that in Iranian politics there are ultra-extremists and extremists but that someone who is considered moderate within the context of Tehran might not fit that definition in the wider world.

To avoid mirror imaging, managers must train analysts to recognize it when it intrudes in their work and must establish a higher level review process that is alert to this tendency.

Clientism is a flaw that occurs when analysts become so immersed in their subjects—usually after working on an issue for too long—that they lose their ability to view issues with the necessary criticality. (In the State Department this phenomenon is called "clientitis," which should be defined as "an inflammation of the client," although the term is used when referring to someone who has "gone native" in his or her thinking.) Analysts can spend time apologizing for the actions of the nations they cover instead of analyzing them. The same safeguards that analysts and their managers put in place to avoid mirror imaging are required to avoid **clientism**.

The issue of "**layering**" arose largely as a result of the Iraq WMD experience. Layering refers to the use of judgments or assumptions made in one analysis as the factual basis for judgments in another analysis without also carrying over the uncertainties that may be involved. This can be especially dangerous if the earlier judgments were based on meager collection sources. Analysts are allowed—and are expected—to make assumptions; they are not allowed to use these assumptions as the factual basis for additional assumptions. Layering tends to give these earlier judgments greater certainty and can mislead analysts and, more important, policy makers. Both the Senate Intelligence Committee and the WMD Commission (Commission on the Intelligence Capabilities of the United States Regarding Weapons of Mass Destruction) accused intelligence analysts of layering when they analyzed Iraq's alleged possession of WMD.

Finally, there is the issue of linear thinking. Most people think linearly since most days pretty much resemble those days before and after, with some minor variations. Thus, it is easy for linearity to creep into analysis. The problem is that analysts need to be constantly on the watch for discontinuities, for nonlinear events. This is a fairly constant requirement, albeit a difficult one. An analyst has to walk a fine line between being blasé and being a doomsayer. However, it is the discontinuities that prove to be most problematic for policy makers. The collapse of the Soviet Union, the crisis of the euro in 2010–2011, and the so-called Arab Spring are all good examples of nonlinear events. Baseball icon Yogi Berra was correct when he said, "The future will be just like the past, only different." A good analyst should look at the issues in his or her brief and constantly ask, "What might arise to put this on a different path?" The chances of coming up with the precisely right answer may be small, but the questions help counter linearity and complacency.

On-the-Ground Knowledge. Analysts have varying degrees of direct knowledge about the nations on which they write. During the cold war, U.S. analysts had difficulty spending significant amounts of time in the Soviet Union or its satellites, and they were unable to travel widely in those nations. Similarly, intelligence analysts may have less contact with the senior foreign officials about whom they write than do the U.S. policy makers who must deal with these foreigners. Analysts' distance from the subjects being analyzed can occasionally be costly in terms of how their policy consumers view the intelligence they receive. Some policy clients also may have more in-country experience than do the intelligence analysts.

This problem can be compounded when dealing with terrorists, with whom few opportunities arise for direct or prolonged contact and perhaps little shared basis of rationality by which to gauge their motives or likely next actions. Recent studies of intelligence analysis by then-Maj. Gen. Michael Flynn in Afghanistan and by former National Security Council (NSC) Asia director Kenneth Lieberthal offer the same critique about the paucity of on-the-ground knowledge and the effects this has on policy and how policy makers view intelligence.

Analysts, like everyone else, are proud of their accomplishments. Once they have mastered a body of knowledge, they may look for opportunities—no matter how inappropriate—to display that knowledge in detail. Analysts can have difficulty limiting their writing to those facts and analyses that may be necessary for a specific consumer need. Analysts may want the consumer to have a greater appreciation for where the issues being discussed fit in some wider pattern. Unfortunately—and perhaps too frequently—the policy client wants to know "only about the miracles, and not the lives of all the saints who made them happen." Analysts require training, maturity, and supervision to cure this behavior. Some analysts get the message sooner than others; some never get it and produce analysis that requires greater editing to get to the essential message, which can cause resentment on the part of either analysts or their editors. Furthermore, the intelligence provider may lose the attention of the policy client if he or she gives too much material, large portions of which do not seem relevant to the policy maker's immediate needs.

Just as analysts want to show the depth of their knowledge, so, too, they want to be perceived as experienced—perhaps far beyond what is true. Again, this is a common human failing. Professionals in almost any field, when surrounded by peers and facing a situation that is new to them but not to others, are tempted to assert their familiarity, whether genuine or not. Given the choice between appearing jaded ("been there, done that") and naïve ("Wow! I've never seen that before!"), analysts usually choose jaded. The risk of being caught seems small enough, and it is preferable to being put down by someone else who displays greater experience.

Sometimes, however, much is at stake. For example, in April 1986 the operators of the Chernobyl nuclear reactor in the Soviet Union, while running an unauthorized experiment, caused a catastrophic explosion. The next afternoon, Sweden reported higher than normal radioactive traces in its air monitors, which had been placed in many cities. In the United States, an intelligence manager asked a senior analyst what he made of the Swedish complaints. The analyst played them down, saying the Swedes were always concerned about their air and often made such complaints for the smallest amounts of radiation. On discovering what was actually going on, analysts spent the following day frantically trying to catch up with the facts about Chernobyl. The jaded approach precluded the analysts from making the simplest inquiries, such as what types of radiation Sweden detected. The answer would have identified the source as a reactor and not a weapon. And the prevailing winds over Sweden could have been surveyed to identify the source. (Some years later the intelligence manager met with some of his Swedish counterparts. They had initially concluded, based on analysis of the radiation and wind conditions, that a reactor at nearby Ignalina, across the Baltic Sea in Soviet territory, was leaking. Although they misidentified the source, which was a reactor much farther away, they were much closer to the truth than were U.S. intelligence analysts.)

The costs of the jaded approach are threefold. First, this approach represents intellectual dishonesty, something all analysts should avoid. Second, it proceeds from the false assumption that each incident is much like others, which may be true at some superficial level but may be false at fundamental levels. Third, it closes the analyst's thinking, regardless of his or her level of experience, to the possibility that an incident or issue is entirely new, requiring wholly new types of analysis.

Credibility is one of the most highly prized possessions of analysts. Although they recognize that no one can be correct all of the time, they are concerned that policy makers are holding them accountable to an impossible standard. Their concern about credibility—which is largely faith and trust in the integrity of the intelligence process and in the ability of the analysts whose product is at hand—can lead them to play down or perhaps mask sudden shifts in analyses or conclusions. For example, suppose intelligence analysis has long estimated a production rate of fifteen missiles a year in a hostile state. One year, because of improved collection and new methodologies, the estimated production rate (which is still just an estimate) goes to forty-five missiles per year. Policy makers may view this increase—on the order of 300 percent—with alarm. Instead of presenting the new number with an explanation as to how it was derived, an analyst might be tempted to soften the blow. Perhaps a brief memo is issued, suggesting changes in production. Then a second memo, saying that the rate is more likely twenty to twenty-five missiles per year, and so on, until the policy maker sees a more acceptable analytical progression to the new number and not a sudden spike upward. Playing out such a scenario takes time, and it is intellectually dishonest. Intelligence products that are written on a recurring basis—such as certain types of national intelligence **estimates**—may be more susceptible than other products to this type of behavior. They establish benchmarks that can be reviewed more easily than, say, a memo that is not likely to be remembered unless the issue is extremely important and the shift is dramatic.

At the same time, there are risks inherent in sudden and dramatic shifts in analysis. In November 2007, DNI Mike McConnell (2007–2009) released unclassified key judgments of a new national intelligence estimate (NIE) on Iran's nuclear intentions and capabilities. The NIE estimated that Iran had ceased its weaponization program in 2003, reversing views held in a 2005 estimate. Officials explained that recently collected intelligence had led to the new position. But observers and commentators questioned why this had not been known earlier, failing to understand the nature of intelligence collection. Some wondered if the new conclusions were "compensation" (or penance) for the mistaken conclusions in the 2002 Iraq WMD estimate. And some wondered if the intelligence community was trying to prevent the Bush administration from using force against a recalcitrant Iran. Interestingly, few commentators took the NIE at face value, accepting the possibility that analytic views had changed. A 2015 analysis by the IAEA (International Atomic Energy Agency), based on partial Iranian responses to questions about its past activities, said Iran was actively designing a nuclear weapon until 2009 but that coordinated efforts to create a weapon stopped after 2003, largely agreeing with the NIE.

Although policy makers have taken retribution on analysts for sudden changes in estimates, more often than not the fear in the minds of analysts is greater than the likelihood of a loss of credibility. Much depends on the prior nature of the relationship between the analyst and the policy maker, the latter's appreciation for the nature of the intelligence problem, and the intelligence community's past record. If several revisions have been made in the recent past, there is reason to suspect a problem. If revision is an isolated phenomenon, it is less problematic. The nature of the issue, and its importance to the policy maker and the nation, also matters.

For example, the level of Soviet defense spending—then usually expressed as a percentage of gross national product (GNP)—was a key intelligence issue during the cold war. At the end of the Gerald Ford administration (1974–1977), intelligence estimates of Soviet GNP going to defense rose from a range of 6 to 7 percent to 13 to 14 percent, largely because of new data, new modeling techniques, and other factors unrelated to Soviet output. The revision was discomforting to the incoming Jimmy Carter administration. In his inaugural address, Carter signaled that he did not want to be constantly concerned with the Soviet issue, that he had other foreign policy issues to pursue. A more heavily armed Soviet Union was not good news. Carter prided himself on his analytic capabilities. When faced with the revised estimates, he reportedly chided the intelligence community, noting that they had just admitted to a 100 percent error in past estimates. That being the case, why should he believe the latest analyses?

Few intelligence products are written by just one analyst and then sent along to the policy client. Most have peer reviews and managerial reviews and probably the input of analysts from other offices or agencies. This is especially true for the intelligence products (analytical reports) that agencies call estimates in the United States or **assessments** in Australia and Britain. Participation of other analysts and agencies adds another dimension to the analytical process—bureaucratics—which brings various types of behaviors and strategies.

More likely than not, several agencies have strongly held and diametrically opposed views on key issues within an estimate. How should these be dealt with? The U.S. system in both intelligence and policy making is consensual. No votes are taken; no lone wolves are cast out or beaten to the ground. Everyone must find some way to agree. But if intellectual arguments fail, consensus can be reached in many other ways, few of which have anything to do with analysis:

- Back scratching and logrolling. Although usually thought of in legislative terms, these two behaviors can come into play in intelligence analysis. Basically, they involve a trade-off: "You accept my view on p. 15 and I'll accept yours on p. 38." Substance is not a major concern.

- False hostages. Agency A is opposed to a position being taken by Agency B but is afraid its own views will not prevail. Agency A can stake out a false position on another issue that it defends strongly, not for the sake of the issue itself, but so that it has something to trade in the back scratching and logrolling.

- Lowest common denominator language. One agency believes that the chance of something happening is high; another thinks it is low. Unless these views are strongly held, the agencies may compromise—a moderate chance—as a means of resolving the issue. This example is a bit extreme, but it captures the essence of the behavior—an attempt to paper over differences with words that everyone can accept.

- Footnote wars. Sometimes none of the other techniques works. In the U.S. estimative process, an agency can always add a "footnote" in which it expresses alternative views. (In estimates, these are not actually footnotes, that is, text at the very bottom of the page. They are successive paragraphs in the main text that express alternative views but are flagged as not being the majority or consensus opinion.) Or more than one agency might add a footnote, or agencies may take sides on an issue. This can lead to vigorous debates as to whose view appears in the main text and whose in the footnote.

In U.S. practice, an estimate may refer to "a majority of agencies" or a "minority." This is an odd formulation. First, it is vague. How many agencies hold one view or the other? Is it a substantial majority (say, eleven of the sixteen agencies) or a bare one? Second, the formulation strongly implies that the view held by the majority of agencies is more likely the correct one, although no formal or informal votes are taken in the NIE process. The British practice is different. In Britain, if all agencies participating in an assessment cannot agree, then the views of each are simply laid out. This may be more frustrating for the policy maker reading the assessment, but it avoids false impressions about consensus or correct views based on the vague intellectual notion of a majority.

One critique of the intelligence community's analysis of Iraq WMD was the absence of different views on most issues and the problem of **groupthink**. The Senate Intelligence Committee held that the analysts did not examine their assumptions rigorously enough and thus lapsed too easily into agreement. The case highlights a conundrum for managers and analysts, particularly those involved in estimates. As a rule, policy makers prefer consensus views, which save them from having to go through numerous shades of opinion on their own. After all, isn't that what the intelligence community is supposed to be doing? Thus, there has always been some impetus to arrive at a consensus, if possible. In the aftermath of Iraq, however, most consensus views—even if arrived at out of genuine agreement—could be viewed with suspicion. How does one determine, when reading intelligence analysis, the basis on which a consensus has been achieved? How does one determine if it is a true meeting of minds or some bureaucratic lowest common denominator?

Analytical Stovepipes. Collection stovepipes emerge because the separate collection disciplines are often based on different technologies, are managed independently, and often are rivals to one another. Analytical stovepipes also appear in the U.S. all-source community. The three all-source analytical groups—the CIA's Directorate of Analysis, Defense Intelligence Agency's Directorate of Intelligence, and the State Department's Bureau of Intelligence and Research (INR)—exist to serve specific policy makers. They also come together on a variety of community analyses, most often the NIEs. Efforts to manage or, even more minimally, to oversee and coordinate their activities reveal a stovepipe mentality not unlike that exhibited by the collection agencies. The three all-source agencies tend to have a wary view of efforts by officials with community-wide responsibilities to deal with them as linked parts of a greater analytical whole. The analytical agencies manifest this behavior less overtly than do the collectors, so it is more difficult to recognize. It thus may be surprising to some people, perhaps more so than when collectors exhibit this behavior. After all, each of the collectors operates in a unique field, with a series of methodologies that are also unique. The analytical agencies, however, are all in the same line of work, often concerned with the same issues. But bureaucratic imperatives and a clear preference for their responsibilities in direct support of their particular policy clients, as opposed to interagency projects, contribute to **analytical stovepipes**.

All of these behaviors can leave the impression that the estimative process—or any large-group analytical effort—is false intellectually. That is not so. However, it is important to note that intelligence analysis is not a purely academic exercise. Other behaviors intrude, and more than just analytical truths are at stake. The estimative process yields winners and losers, analysts whose papers go forward and those whose do not, and careers may rise and fall as a result.

ANALYTICAL ISSUES

In addition to the mind-set and behavioral characteristics of analysts, several issues within analysis need to be addressed.

Competitive Versus Collaborative Analysis. As important as the concept of **competitive analysis** is to U.S. intelligence, a need has been seen to bring together analysts of agencies or disciplines to work on major ongoing issues, in addition to the collaborative process of NIEs. DCI Robert M. Gates (1991–1993) created centers, most of which focused on transnational issues—terrorism, nonproliferation, narcotics, and so on. DCIA John Brennan (2013–2017) reorganized CIA based on the same mission centers concept.

The intelligence community also forms task forces to deal with certain issues. Among these was the Balkans task force, which during the 1990s monitored the range of issues related to the breakup of Yugoslavia.

The 9/11 Commission (National Commission on Terrorist Attacks upon the United States) recommended organizing all analysis around either regional or functional centers. The 2004 intelligence law mandated the establishment of the National Counterterrorism Center (NCTC), which was basically an expansion of the Terrorism Threat Integration Center that DCI George J. Tenet (1997–2004) had created. The law also required that the DNI examine the utility of creating a National Counterproliferation (NCPC), which was done and gives the DNI the authority to create other centers as necessary. The problem with the center approach for all analysis is that it becomes somewhat inflexible. Inevitably, some issues or some nations do not fit easily into the center construct. What happens to them? Also, although creating a center is easy, centers—like all other offices—do not like to share or lose resources. Centers therefore run counter to the desire for analytic workforce agility. To date, centers have been organized along functional lines and are staffed by analysts who tend to be more expert in the issue than in the national or regional context within which that issue has been raised. (The new CIA structure has both functional and regional centers.) A functional center therefore runs the risk of providing technical analysis that is divorced from its political or cultural context. For example, analyzing the state of WMD development in a nation is not enough. One should also analyze the internal or regional political factors driving the program, as these will give important indicators as to its purpose and scope. This gap was one of the flaws in the 2002 Iraq WMD estimate. Being housed in a center does not preclude a functional analyst from seeking out his or her regional counterparts. Analysts do this on a regular basis. But it requires some effort and can be dropped during the press of the day's work. The center concept can make collaboration beyond the bounds of the center itself more difficult, in effect creating analytical stovepipes.

Centers can become competitors for resources with offices in agencies. This appears to have been the case with the NCTC and CIA's Counterterrorism Center, according to the WMD Commission. As has been seen from the time that DCI Gates began creating centers in the early 1990s, the heads of agencies are not willing to siphon away scarce resources to an activity over which they will have no control (centers fell under the jurisdiction of the DCI and now are under the DNI) and from which they will receive no direct results. The creation of centers does not relieve the analytical agencies of responsibility for those same issues. The WMD Commission recommended the creation of an additional center, the National Counterproliferation Center, which has a managerial role in line with the commission's concept of mission managers to coordinate collection and analysis on specific issues or topics but not to produce its own analysis.

A bureaucratic debate ensued on the nature of the centers. Although their goal is to bring the intelligence components into a single place, most centers had been located in and dominated by the CIA. A 1996 review by the House Intelligence Committee staff validated the concept of the centers but urged that they be less CIA-centric. Several of the centers (Terrorism, Counterproliferation, Counterintelligence and Security, Cyber) are now DNI centers. Given the location of the centers, however, other agencies are sometimes loath to assign analysts to them, fearing that they will be essentially lost resources during their center service. (A similar problem used to occur on the Joint Staff, which supports the Joint Chiefs of Staff. The military services—Army, Navy, Air Force, Marines—naturally preferred to keep their best officers in duties directly related to their service. This ended when Congress passed the Goldwater-Nichols Act in 1986, which mandated a joint service tour as a prerequisite for promotion to general or admiral.) However, the DNI centers face the issue about how they will be staffed when the DNI has no direct control over any analytic components comparable to the control that the DCI had over the CIA. DNI McConnell created the requirement that intelligence officers have "joint duty" assignments before being promoted to senior ranks (similar to the requirement for the military) to make assignments to centers more attractive, especially for one's most talented officers, as a means of ensuring their continued promotion. Another issue for the centers is their longevity. In government—in all sectors—ostensibly temporary bodies have a way of becoming permanent, even when the reasons for their creation have long since ended. A certain bureaucratic inertia sets in. Some people wish to see the body continue, as it is a source of power; others fear that by being the first to suggest terminating it they will look like shirkers. The situation has a comic aspect to it, but also a serious one, as these temporary groups absorb substantial amounts of resources and energy.

Thus, the question for the centers—or any other groups—is this: When are they no longer needed? Clearly, the transnational issues are ongoing, but even they may change or diminish over time. One former deputy DCI suggested a five-year sunset provision for all centers, meaning that every five years each center would be subject to a hard-nosed review of its functions and the requirement for its continuation. Regional centers are less problematic in this regard, but their relative staffing levels should be revisited periodically.

Finally, some critics question the focus of the centers, arguing that they are concentrating tactically on operational aspects of specific issues instead of on the longer term trends. Center proponents note the presence of analysts and the working relationship between the centers and the national intelligence officers (NIOs), who can keep apprised of the centers' work and offer advice, and are responsible for the production of NIEs.

The WMD Commission, reporting in March 2005, recommended the creation of mission managers to "ensure a strategic, Community-level focus on priority intelligence missions." The commission envisioned these managers overseeing both collection and analysis on a given issue, as well as fostering alternative analyses on their issues. However, the mission managers would not conduct actual analysis; rather, they would facilitate analysis. The commission also posited that the mission managers offered a more flexible approach than the centers. The commission recommended that mission managers oversee target development and research and development for their issues.

The portfolios of the **national intelligence managers (NIMs)** have been somewhat fluid. As of 2019, there were seventeen NIMs: six regional (Africa; East Asia; Russia, Europe and Eurasia; Near East; South Asia; Western Hemisphere) and ten transnational (Counterterrorism, Counterproliferation, Counterintelligence, Cyber, Economic Security and Threat Finance, Space and Technical Intelligence, Aviation, Maritime, Transnational Crime, and Homeland). Transnational Crime and Homeland come under the Western Hemisphere NIM. The NIM concept raises several issues, as did the mission managers. First, and most obvious, is their authority to target collection or facilitate analysis. These activities occur in the various intelligence agencies, where the DNI faces very real limits on his or her authority, as did the DCI. Second, it is exceedingly difficult for managers to maintain awareness of all of the analysis being produced on certain issues. The NIMs must also have knowledge of the analysts working on an issue across the community. Each NIM is responsible for creating a **unifying intelligence strategy (UIS)** for his or her portfolio to integrate relevant collection and analysis. Annually, each NIM is expected to write a "State of the Mission" letter to the DNI, discussing how integration and other issues are progressing in his or her mission. Finally, creation of the NIMs led to questions about their roles versus that of the NIOs, which appear to be similar in some respects. The NIOs had been seen as the intellectual leaders for their issues in the intelligence community, and they had some sense of lost status vis-à-vis the NIMs, especially as each NIO is part of the NIM team as the analytical expert. (There is also a national intelligence collection officer—NICO—and a national counterintelligence officer—NCIO—on each NIM team.)

The impetus to create a center can also come from policy makers. In February 2015, President Obama ordered the DNI to create a Cyber Threat Intelligence Integration Center (CTIIC) despite the fact that senior intelligence officers with cyber responsibilities held that this was not necessary. The impetus to create CTIIC came from the NSC staff, reflecting either dissatisfaction with intelligence support on cyber or the political need to be seen as "doing something" about cyber, or both. CTIIC is charged with all-source analytic support to U.S. cyber efforts, although details of what it would do and how it would do it remained vague, which became an issue between the administration and the House Intelligence Committee during 2015 budget deliberations.

In its report on the FY2016 intelligence authorization bill, the Senate Intelligence Committee expressed concerns that there were too many finished analytic products, which fostered confusion on the part of policy makers, including Congress. Although recognizing the value of competitive analysis, the committee was concerned about this analytic "redundancy" and directed the ODNI to pilot a "repeatable methodology" to reduce it. The boundary between fewer reports on the same issue and a more homogenized analysis overall may prove to be difficult to define and may not work to the advantage of policy makers.

Ultimately, there is no best way to organize analysts. Each scheme has distinct advantages and disadvantages. Each scheme still revolves around either functional or regional analysts. The goal should be to ensure that the right analysts of both types are brought to bear on topics as needed—on either a permanent or a temporary basis, depending on the issue and its importance. Flexibility and agility remain crucial. (*See box, "Metaphors for Thinking About Analysis."*)

METAPHORS FOR THINKING ABOUT ANALYSIS

Metaphors are often used to describe the intelligence analysis process. Thomas Hughes, a former director of the Department of State Bureau of Intelligence and Research, wrote that intelligence analysts were either butchers or bakers. Butchers tend to cut up and dissect intelligence to determine what is happening. Bakers tend to blend analysis together to get the bigger picture. Analysts assume both roles at different times. In the aftermath of the September 11 terrorist attacks, the phrase "connect the dots" became prevalent as a means of describing an analytic intelligence failure. It is an inapt metaphor. Connecting the dots depends on all of the dots being present to draw the right picture. (The dots also come numbered sequentially, which helps considerably.) As a senior intelligence analyst pointed out, the intelligence community was accused of not connecting the dots in the run-up to September 11 but was accused of connecting too many dots regarding the alleged Iraqi weapons of mass destruction. Two more useful descriptions are mosaics or pearls. Intelligence analysis is similar to assembling a mosaic, but one in which the desired final picture may not be clear. Not all of the mosaic pieces may be available. Further complicating matters, in the course of assembling the mosaic, new pieces appear and some old ones change size, shape, and color. The pearl metaphor refers to how intelligence is collected and then analyzed. Most intelligence issues are concerns for years or even decades. Like the slow growth of a pearl within an oyster, there is a steady aggregation of collected intelligence over time, allowing analysts to gain greater insight into the nature of the problem. Why do these metaphors matter? They matter because they will affect how one views the analytical process and the expectations one has for the outcomes of that process.

Dealing With Limited Information. Analysts rarely have the luxury of knowing everything they wish to know about a topic. In some cases, little may be known. How does an analyst deal with this problem?

One option is to flag the problem so that the policy client is aware of it. Often, informing policy consumers of what intelligence officials do not know is as important as communicating what they do know. Secretary of State Colin Powell (2001–2005) used the formulation: "Tell me what you know. Tell me what you don't know. Tell me what you think." Powell went on to say that he held intelligence officers responsible for what they knew or did not know but that he was responsible if he took action based on what they think. But admitting ignorance may be unattractive, out of concern that it will be interpreted as a failing on the part of the intelligence apparatus. Alternatively, analysts can try to work around the problem, utilizing their own experience and skill to fill in the blanks as best they can. This may be more satisfying intellectually and professionally, but it runs the risk of giving the client a false sense of the basis of the analysis or of the analysis being wrong.

Another option is to arrange for more collection, time permitting. Yet another is to widen the circle of analysts working on the problem to get the benefit of their views and experience.

A reverse formulation of this same problem has arisen in recent years. To what degree should analysis be tied to available intelligence? Should intelligence analyze only what is known, or should analysts delve into issues or areas that may be currently active but for which no intelligence is available? Proponents argue that the absence of intelligence does not mean that an activity is not happening, only that the intelligence about it is not available. Opponents argue that this sort of analysis puts intelligence out on a limb, where there is no support and the likely outcome is highly speculative worst-case analysis. On the one hand, intelligence analysis is not a legal process in which findings must be based on evidence. On the other hand, analysis written largely on supposition is not likely to be convincing to many and may be more susceptible to politicization. For many years, the intelligence community has stressed the importance of **analytic penetration**, as an intellectual means of trying to overcome a dearth of intelligence sources. Analytic penetration means thinking longer and harder about the issue, perhaps making suppositions of what is most likely, and perhaps laying out a range of outcomes based on a set of reasonable assumptions. The underlying premise in analytic penetration is that the analytic community does not have the luxury of simply throwing up its hands and saying, "Sorry, no incoming intelligence; no analysis." But if analysis is required and the sources are insufficient, there has to be rigor applied to the analysis that attempts to make up for these missing sources. This is an area where greater collaboration across offices and agencies would be most useful.

The concerns about dealing with limited intelligence arose in the reviews of intelligence performance before the 2001 terrorist attacks and of intelligence before the Iraq war (2003–2011). The problems in each case were different. In the case of the September 11 attacks, some people criticized analysts for not putting together the intelligence they did have to get a better sense of the al Qaeda threat and plans. Intelligence officials were also criticized for not being more strident in their warnings—a charge that intelligence officials rebutted—and policy makers were criticized for not being more attuned to the intelligence they were receiving. However, no one has been able to make the case that sufficient intelligence existed to forecast the time and place of the attacks. The admonition about strategic versus tactical surprise is apropos. (See chap. 1.) Stopping a terrorist attack requires tactical insights into the terrorists' plans.

In the case of Iraq, the critique is just the opposite, that is, that intelligence analysts made too many unsubstantiated connections among various pieces of collected intelligence and created a false picture of the state of Iraq WMD programs. Implicit in this critique is the view, held by some, that analysts should not analyze beyond the collected intelligence lest they draw the wrong conclusions. This would be a deviating and alarming practice from the norm, given the likelihood at all times of less than perfect collection. Analysts are trained to use their experience and their instinct to fill in the collection gaps as best they can. That is one of the value-added aspects of analysts.

If a lesson is to be drawn from these two analytical experiences, it may be no more than that the analytical process is imperfect under any and all conditions. No Goldilocks formula has been devised as to the right amount of intelligence on which analysis should be based. The quality of that intelligence matters a great deal, as does the nature of the issue being analyzed.

The ODNI addressed the sourcing issue in an intelligence community directive (ICD) in 2007. ICD 206 establishes sourcing and reference citation requirements for analytic products. This ICD was a response to some of the problems encountered in the Iraq WMD estimate, where judgments were not always clearly associated with the underlying intelligence, making it difficult for readers to determine the substantive basis for these judgments. Although intended as a guideline, ICD 206 is written in fairly adamant terms, establishing a "requirement that disseminated analytic products must contain consistent and structured sourcing for all significant and substantive reporting." It allows for few exceptions. Many analytic managers took this to mean that if the analysis could not be sourced, then it could not go forward. Others argued that this was not the intent of the ICD, as that approach left no room for analysts to make judgments based on their expertise and experience, especially in cases where sufficient sources might not be available. This takes us back to the role of analysis: Is it simply to pass on collected intelligence or to try to add value based on the analyst's knowledge? Whatever the original intent, as of 2018, ICD 206 was still seen as a significant straitjacket by many analytic managers. One of the distinctions that analysts like to make—and that also helps underscore the issue of dealing with limited information—is the difference between secrets and mysteries, noted earlier. Secrets are items of knowledge that are known to someone, just not to us. For example, there are Iranians who know the details and intent of their nuclear program. Mysteries are things that are not known and probably not knowable. For example, how were the pyramids built? Intelligence agencies exist to resolve secrets—either by penetrating them outright or by collecting against them and providing analysis. Mysteries fall into a different category. But there are times when the question being asked by the policy maker is more of a mystery than a secret. The analyst would like to beg off but often cannot.

Finally, there has been an increased emphasis, among policy makers and observers of the intelligence community, on ensuring that analysts have access to and check all available data. This preference is an outgrowth of the failure among some agencies to share information prior to 9/11 and the "connect the dots" metaphor. After all, if one just connects all of the dots, then the answer should be there. (This is similar to the belief of big data advocates that the answer must lie somewhere in the data, if we just analyze enough of it.) As an example, in the aftermath of the failed Christmas 2009 airline bombing attempt in Detroit, President Obama excoriated the intelligence community for not sharing all of the available intelligence. In reality, few analysts will ever be sure that they have seen all of the available intelligence on a given issue unless it is relatively unimportant and therefore has little intelligence associated with it. But the emphasis on analysts seeing "everything" and checking all databases can lead to timidity on the part of analysts, who will become leery of publishing anything lest they are found to have missed some piece of intelligence. So, instead of learning to deal with limited information, one could end up with analysts who will not be willing to publish unless they are fairly certain that they have all of the information, largely to avoid being criticized should they miss something that leads to an unfortunate result.

Conveying Uncertainty. The ability to convey uncertainty accurately and clearly is important and not as oxymoronic as it may sound. After all, one of the main goals of intelligence analysis is to help bound policy makers' uncertainty, to give them a sense of different likely outcomes and to help them focus on the most pressing or urgent issues. Just as everything may not be known, so, too, the likely outcome may not be clear. Conveying uncertainty can be difficult. Analysts shy away from the simple but stark "We don't know." After all, they are being paid, in part, to make some intellectual leaps beyond what they do know. Too often, analysts rely on weasel words to convey uncertainty: "on the one hand," "on the other hand," "maybe," "perhaps," and so on. (President Harry S. Truman was famous for saying he wanted to meet a one-armed economist so that he would not have to hear "on the one hand, on the other hand" economic forecasting.) These words may unwittingly convey analytical pusillanimity, not uncertainty. (Conveying uncertainty seems to be a particular problem in English, which is a Germanic language and makes less use of the subjunctive than do the Romance languages.)

Some years ago, a senior analytical manager crafted a system for suggesting potential outcomes by using both words and numbers—that is, a 1-in-10 chance, a 7-in-10 chance. Such numerical formulations may be more satisfying than words, but they run the risk of conveying to the policy client a degree of precision that does not exist. What is the difference between a 6-in-10 chance and a 7-in-10 chance, beyond greater conviction? It is also important to remember that an event that has a 6-in-10 chance of occurring also has a 4-in-10 (40 percent) chance of not occurring. When presented this way, the event now may seem uncomfortably close to 50/50, which a 6-in-10 chance does not convey by itself. There are very few "sure things." In reality, the analyst is back to relying on gut feeling. (One chairman of the NIC became incensed when he read an analysis that assessed "a small but significant chance" of something happening.)

One way to help convey uncertainty is to identify in the analysis the issues about which there is uncertainty or the intelligence that is essentially missing but that would, in the analyst's view, either resolve the unknowns or cause the analyst to reexamine currently held views. This raises another issue: known unknowns (that is, the things one knows that one does not know) versus the unknown unknowns (that is, the things one did not know that one did not know). By definition, the second group cannot be bounded or reduced as it is unknown. But one's analysis must be examined constantly to identify known unknowns and to give attention to resolving these issues, if possible.

The use of language is important in all analysis. Analysts tend to use a stock set of verbs to convey their views: "believe," "assess," "judge." For some analysts, the words have distinct and separate meanings that convey the amount of intelligence supporting a particular view and their certainty about this view. However, the intelligence community did not reach a consensus as to what each verb meant until 2005. The NIC now publishes an explanatory page with each NIE that explains the use of estimative language. The text box, "What We Mean When We Say: An Explanation of Estimative Language," in the July 2007 NIE, *The Terrorist Threat to the Homeland,* is a useful example. Terms like "we judge" or "we assess" are used interchangeably. (This seems close to the British experience on this issue, according to the 2004 British Butler report on intelligence about Iraq WMD. The Butler report states that British policy makers assumed the different words had different meanings, but British analysts said they just wrote naturally, using the terms interchangeably.) Analytical judgments can be based on collected intelligence or previous judgments that serve as "building blocks." The use of "precise numerical ratings" is rejected as these "would imply more rigor than we intend." Instead, there is a range of likelihood outcomes:

- Remote

- Unlikely

- Even chance

- Probably, likely

- Almost certainly

Note that there is no certainty at either end of this range. An event that is known to have no chance of occurring will not be analyzed. Nor will an event that is certain to occur be analyzed in terms of likelihood, although its ramifications can be discussed. Phrases like "we cannot rule out" or "we cannot discount" reflect an event that is seen as being unlikely or even remote but "whose consequences are such that it warrants mentioning." These phrases are classic estimative language and can be interpreted by some readers, again, as a pusillanimous call. Finally, the use of "maybe" and "suggest" are defined as events the likelihood of which cannot be assessed because of a paucity of information.

Beyond these uses of language, there is the issue of the confidence that the analyst has in his or her judgments, called **confidence levels**. In NIEs, the confidence levels are "based on the scope and quality of information supporting our judgments":

- High confidence: judgments based on high-quality information, or the nature of the issue makes a solid judgment possible

- Moderate confidence: available information is susceptible to multiple interpretations; or there may be alternative views; or the information is "credible and plausible" but not sufficiently corroborated

- Low confidence: information is scant, questionable, or fragmented, leading to difficulties in making "solid analytic inferences"; or is based on sources that may be problematic

Publishing a text box of this sort is a major step forward in trying to get policy readers to understand the basis by which judgments are made. The usefulness of the box also depends on policy makers reading it, and even this will not preclude future misunderstandings about the use of estimative language. Those who do read it will get a much better idea of the layers of meaning inherent in an estimative judgment. There are few, if any, straightforward calls. Much of the text of "What We Mean When We Say" was repeated in the January 2017 Intelligence Community Assessment of Russian activities during the 2016 election, in order to give readers a better framework for understanding the paper.

An example of this issue of confidence levels came in 2013 when a DIA assessment of North Korea's ability to reduce a nuclear weapon to a size that would fit on a missile was inadvertently disclosed during a congressional hearing. The DIA analysis had "moderate confidence" that North Korea had this capability. Some participants in the hearing dismissed the DIA analysis because it was "only" moderate confidence, apparently not understanding the full meaning of that phrase as defined above. These participants apparently believed that anything less than high confidence can be dismissed, which shows a misunderstanding of how intelligence analysis is written. DNI Clapper later testified that the DIA confidence was higher than the rest of the intelligence community but also noted that these types of disagreements are typical in a competitive analysis process.

Indications and Warnings. **Indications and warnings**, or **I&W**, as it is known among intelligence professionals, is one of the most important roles of intelligence—giving policy makers advance warning of significant, usually military, events. The emphasis placed on I&W in the United States reflects the cold war legacy of a long-term military rivalry and the older roots of the U.S. intelligence community in Pearl Harbor, the classic I&W failure.

I&W is primarily a military intelligence function, with an emphasis on surprise attack. It relies, to a large extent, on the fact that all militaries operate according to certain regular schedules, forms, and behaviors, which provide a baseline against which to measure activity that may raise I&W concerns. In other words, analysts are looking for anything that is out of the ordinary, any new or unexpected activity that may presage an attack: calling up reserves, putting forces on a higher level of alert, decreasing or increasing communications activity, imposing sudden communications silence, or sending more naval units to sea. But none of these can be viewed in isolation; they have to be seen within the wider context of overall behavior.

During the cold war, for example, U.S. and North Atlantic Treaty Organization (NATO) analysts worried about how much warning they would receive of a Warsaw Pact attack against Western Europe. Some analysts believed that they could provide policy makers, minimally, several days' warning, as stocks were positioned, additional units were brought forward, and so on. Others believed that the Warsaw Pact had sufficient forces and supplies in place to attack from a standing start. Fortunately, the issue was never put to the test.

For analysts, I&W can be a trap rather than an opportunity. Their main fear is failing to pick up on indicators and give adequate warning, which in part reflects the harsh view about intelligence when it misses an important event. In reaction, analysts may lower the threshold and issue warnings about everything, in effect crying wolf. Although this may reduce the analyst's exposure to criticism, it has a lulling effect on the policy maker and can cheapen the function of I&W. A classic case of an I&W failure was Israeli I&W prior to the 1973 Yom Kippur War. Israeli military intelligence knew that the Egyptians would have to cross the Suez Canal to initiate war and established an elaborate I&W list. However, when the observed Egyptian activities did not conform to the established list, abetted by an Egyptian deception campaign, alarms were not raised, resulting in a surprise attack. In other words, the analysts became prisoners of their own I&W list.

Terrorism presents an entirely new and more difficult I&W problem. Terrorists do not operate from elaborate infrastructures, and they do not need to mobilize large numbers of people for their operations. One attraction of terrorism as a political tool is the ability to have a large effect with minimal forces. Thus, an entirely new I&W concept is needed to fight terrorism, one more likely to catch the much smaller signs of impending activity. In some respects, the I&W function for terrorism becomes very close to police work and keeping watch over neighborhoods or precincts, looking for things that "just don't look right." Terrorism also raises the duty-to-warn issue. If credible evidence indicates a potential attack, does the government have a responsibility to warn its citizens? A warning may tip off the terrorists to the fact that their plot has been penetrated, thus putting sources and methods at risk. Also, citizens may become inured to—if not downright cynical about—recurring changes in the level of warning, especially if the attacks do not occur. Some may come to believe that the government, and especially the intelligence agencies, is trying to cover itself in case an attack does occur. This phenomenon has been seen in the United States since 2001 as alerts have been issued and then withdrawn after the threat subsided or failed to materialize.

Opportunity Analysis. I&W is not only one of the most important analytic functions, but it is also one that comes naturally to intelligence analysts. A primary reason to have intelligence agencies is to avoid strategic surprise. (See chap. 1.) I&W is a means to that end. But I&W can become something of a trap, a theme that is reverted to too often lest something be missed.

Policy makers understand that I&W leaves them in the position of reacting to intelligence. But policy makers also want to be actors, to achieve goals and not just prevent bad things from happening. As more than one senior policy maker has said, "I want intelligence that helps me advance my agenda, that makes me the actor, not the reactor." This is often referred to as **opportunity analysis**.

Opportunity analysis is a sophisticated but difficult type of analysis to produce. First, it requires that the intelligence managers or analysts have a good sense of the goals that the policy maker seeks to achieve. Successful opportunity analysis may require some degree of specific and detailed knowledge of these goals. For example, knowing that a goal is arms control may not suggest many useful avenues of opportunity analysis beyond broad generalities. Knowing that the goals include certain types of weapons or restrictions, or that the goals are responding to certain political pressures would be more helpful. Thus, again, emphasis is placed on the importance of the intelligence analysts knowing the intended directions of policy. Second, opportunity analysis often seems more difficult or riskier as it requires positing how foreign leaders or nations will react to policy initiatives. Positing a foreign action and then describing either the consequences or possible reactions often seems easier than the reverse process. After all, an analyst often feels more comfortable understanding how a nation or its policy makers are likely to react even if the analyst is an expert in the politics of another country. Finally, opportunity analysis brings the intelligence community close to the line separating intelligence from policy. Writing good opportunity analysis without appearing to be prescriptive can be difficult even if that is not the intended message or goal.

In general, opportunity analysis is not engaged in often and is easily misunderstood when it is produced. However, opportunity analysis remains an important contribution to policy.

An excellent example of opportunity analysis was the intelligence support that helped President George W. Bush decide to negotiate with Muammar Qaddafi about Libya's covert WMD programs in 2003. The end result was the transfer of a variety of WMD components to the United States, which not only was important in its own right but also seemed even more important in 2011 when NATO began an air campaign against Libyan forces trying to suppress a revolt, secure in the knowledge that Libya had, at best, little WMD at its disposal.

Alternative Analysis. One critique of the intelligence community's performance on Iraq WMD was the alleged failure to examine alternative analytical lines. Even if true, it remains difficult in the case of Iraq to come up with analytically and intellectually sensible arguments that, in 2003, Saddam Hussein had come clean and had no WMD and was telling the truth when he made this case. Still, looking beyond the Iraq WMD case, the issue of alternative analysis is an important one. The 2004 intelligence law requires that the DNI create a process to ensure the effective use of alternative analysis.

The main driver is the concern that analysts can fasten on to one line of analysis, especially for issues that are examined and reexamined over the years, and then will not be open to other possible hypotheses or alternatives. (This behavior is called **premature closure**.) Should this happen, the analyst will then not be alert for changes, discontinuities, or surprises, even if they are not threatening. One way to attempt to avoid this potential intellectual trap is to create teams to draft alternative analyses, which are sometimes called red cells or red teams.

For several reasons, the intelligence community has not always embraced the concept. First, concerns arise that the process can be political in nature or can lead to politicization. The Team A and Team B example from the cold war (see chap. 11) remains a warning in this regard. The alternative analysis group (Team B) was made up of individuals who were more hawkish about dealing with the Soviet Union. Thus, it was no surprise that they found the NIEs on Soviet strategic goals wanting. The existence of an alternative analysis, especially on controversial issues, can lead policy makers to shop for the intelligence they want or cherry-pick analysis, which also results in politicization. Second, only so many analysts are available to deal with any issue or have the requisite expertise on any issue. Therefore, a decision has to be made as to which analysts are assigned to the mainstream and which to the alternative group. Their levels of expertise should be roughly equal. For analysts who have been on the losing side of issues in the area in the past, the chance to participate in alternative analysis may be an irresistible opportunity to reopen old arguments or settle scores. Finally, one of the prerequisites for alternative analysis is that it provides a fresh look at an issue. Therefore, as soon as this type of capacity is institutionalized and made a regular part of the process, it loses the originality and vitality that were sought in the first place.

Alternative analysis consists of more than simply asking a contrafactual question. As in the case of Iraq WMD, the contrafactual question (make the case that Saddam is telling the truth and has no WMD) would likely not have yielded a better analytical result. The analyst or the analytical manager has to be alert to the nature of the issue under consideration and the type of contrafactual question that will actually probe the generally held premise. It may be necessary to try several such questions before coming up with one that truly challenges the prevailing wisdom. In the case of Iraq WMD, a better question to ask might have been, What would Iraq look like if it did not possess WMD? Some analysts might have recognized that the Iraq they were analyzing could easily be viewed either way. This might not have changed the outcome of the NIE, as it still seemed more likely that Iraq did possess WMD, but at least the analysts would have probed alternatives.

The 2004 intelligence law puts great emphasis on alternative analysis, competitive analysis, and red teaming, which are all variants on the same theme—an effort to avoid groupthink. The DNI is responsible for institutionalizing processes for these other types of analysis.

The intelligence community has long sought analytic tools, which means both programs and techniques that will foster better analysis. The computer industry has advanced the intelligence community's ability to collect, manipulate, and correlate data, all of which eases part of the analyst's burden. But there have also been problems integrating the tools into the analytic process, in large part because of the intellectual disconnect between those responsible for designing the tools and the analysts. Programmers and analysts do not think along similar lines, and too many programs have been developed without regard to how analysts think or work. Also, too few of the tools have been tested by working analysts. The net result has often been a new program that sits unused on an analyst's computer desk top because it is either overly complex or not complementary to the analyst's working methods.

There are also a variety of analytic techniques available to analysts. One of the more popular ones, in the aftermath of 9/11 and Iraq, is alternative competing hypotheses (ACH). ACH offers a simple way to ensure that multiple plausible explanations for the known intelligence are considered and also allows for assessment of which hypotheses are more likely by building a matrix to consider alternative scenarios. The Defense Intelligence Agency (DIA) has experimented with "object-based production" (OBP)—that is, organizing available data from all INTs on the "object" of concern, meaning an issue or actor. The belief is that by organizing the intelligence in this way, the "knowns" will be more readily identified, as will, presumably, the unknowns. DIA also believes that OBP can be enhanced by applying some of the techniques and lessons learned in activity-based intelligence (ABI) in collection (see chap. 5), which will help associate discovered activities with "objects."

Various techniques have strong advocates both inside and beyond the intelligence community. But it is best to think about these like tools, no different than a homeowner's toolbox. No tool is right for every job. They key is to be conversant with the tools and to know which one is right for which analytical job.

Estimates. The United States creates and uses analytical products called estimates (or assessments in Britain and Australia). These serve two major purposes: to see where a major issue or trend will go over the next several years and to present the considered view of the entire intelligence community, not just one agency. In the United States, the NIE's community-wide basis is signified by the fact that the DNI signs completed estimates, just as DCIs did before.

Estimates are not predictions of the future but rather considered judgments as to the likely course of events regarding an issue of importance to the nation. Often, more than one possible outcome may be included in a single estimate. The difference between estimate and prediction is crucial but often misunderstood, especially by policy makers. Prediction foretells the future—or attempts to. Estimates are vaguer, assessing the relative likelihood of one or more outcomes. If an event or outcome were predictable—that is, capable of being foretold—one would not need intelligence agencies to estimate its likelihood. It is the uncertainty or unknowability that is key. To quote Yogi Berra again, "It is very difficult to make predictions, especially about the future."

The bureaucratics of estimates are important to their outcome. In the United States, national intelligence officers are responsible for preparing estimates. They circulate the terms of reference (TOR) among colleagues and other agencies at the outset of an estimate. The TOR may be the subject of prolonged discussion and negotiation, as various agencies may believe that the basic questions or lines of analysis are not being framed properly. Shaping the TOR is crucial to the outcome of the estimate. Drafting is not done by the NIOs but by someone from the NIO's office, or the NIO may recruit a drafter from one of the intelligence agencies. Once drafted, the estimate is coordinated with other agencies, that is, the other agencies read it and give comments, not all of which are accepted, because they may be at variance with the drafter's views. Numerous "coordination" meetings are held to resolve disputes, but the meetings may end with two or more views on some aspects that cannot be reconciled. The DNI chairs a final meeting, a National Intelligence Board, which is attended by senior officials from a number of agencies. After the DNI signs the estimate, signifying he or she is satisfied with it, the DNI owns the estimate. DCIs were known to change the views expressed in estimates with which they disagreed. This usually displeased the drafter but was within the DCI's authority.

In addition to the bureaucratic game playing that may be involved in drafting estimates, issues of process influence outcomes. Not every issue is of interest to every intelligence agency. But each agency understands the necessity of taking part in the estimative process, not only for its intrinsic intelligence value but also as a means of keeping watch on the other agencies. Furthermore, not every intelligence agency brings the same level of expertise to an issue. For example, the State Department is much more concerned on a day-to-day basis about human rights violations than are other agencies, and INR reflects this in its work for its specific policy makers and in the expertise it chooses to develop on this issue. Or, the Department of Defense (DOD) is much more concerned about the infrastructure of a nation in which U.S. troops may be deployed. Rightly or wrongly, however, estimates are egalitarian experiences in that the views of all agencies are treated as having equal weight. This ignores the Orwellian view of intelligence that holds, on certain issues, that some agencies are "more equal" than others.

Some issues are the subjects of repeated estimates. For example, during the cold war, the intelligence community produced an annual estimate (in three volumes) on Soviet strategic forces, NIE 11–3–8. For issues of long-term importance, regular estimates are a useful way of keeping track of an issue, of watching it closely and looking for changes in perceived patterns. However, a regularly produced estimate can also be an intellectual trap, as it establishes several benchmarks that analysts do not want to tinker with in the event of possible changes. Having produced a long-standing record on certain key issues, the estimative community finds it difficult to admit that major changes are under way that, in effect, undercut its past analysis.

This issue may be less crass than preserving one's past record. Having come to a set of conclusions based on collection and analysis, what does it take for an analyst or a team of analysts working on an estimate to feel compelled to walk away from their past work and come to an opposite conclusion? One can create a scenario in which some new piece of intelligence completely reverses analysts' thinking. Such an occasion is extremely rare. Is it possible to start from scratch and ignore past work? If one tries to, what is the cutoff point for old collection that is no longer of use? Although the influence of past analysis can be a problem, it is less easily solved than is commonly thought. Intelligence analysis is an iterative process that lacks clear beginning and end points for either collection or analysis. The case of the 2007 Iran nuclear estimate is again instructive. According to intelligence officials, newly available intelligence came to light only very late in the estimative process. The implications of the new intelligence were clear and stark. The first issue to be dealt with was the veracity of the new intelligence: Was it being fed by Iran? Although this question cannot be answered definitively, analysts who subjected the new intelligence to rigorous examination came away convinced that it was real. This meant that the conclusions of the estimate had to be revised, with all of the attendant reaction discussed earlier. Although those responsible for the Iran nuclear NIE stood by their analysis, they also admitted that it was not a certainty and would remain subject to change.

Some people question the utility of estimates. Both producers and consumers have had concerns about the length of estimates and their sometimes plodding style. Critics also have voiced concerns about timeliness, in that some estimates take more than a year to complete. One of the worst examples of poor timing came in 1979. An estimate on the future political stability of Iran was being written—including the observation that Iran was "not in a prerevolutionary state"—even as the shah's regime was unraveling daily. This incongruity led the House Intelligence Committee to observe that estimates "are not worth fighting over." In 2010, the NIC made a series of changes to the structure of NIEs to respond to some of these criticisms. Among these are limiting the main body text to twenty pages (down from an average length of fifty-four to sixty-eight pages), limiting Key Judgments (KJs) to two to three pages, and tightening the linkages between the KJs and the supporting analysis.

After the start of the Iraq war (2003–2011), the estimate process came under intense scrutiny and criticism, prompted by the Iraq WMD NIE. Among the concerns were the influence of past estimates, the groupthink issue, the use of language that seemed to suggest more certainty than existed in the sources, inconsistencies between summary paragraphs (KJs) and actual text, and the speed with which the estimate was written. This last criticism was interesting in that the Iraq WMD estimate was written at the request of the Senate, to meet its three-week deadline before voting on the resolution granting the president authority to use force against Iraq. Frequent leaks of NIEs on a variety of Iraq-related topics led some observers to charge that the intelligence community was at war with the Bush administration.

After the Iraq WMD NIE, there was increased political pressure, coming largely from Congress, to have at least the KJs of the estimates made public. The KJs for *Prospects for Iraq's Stability: A Challenging Road Ahead* (January 2007) and *The Terrorist Threat to the Homeland* (July 2007) were published. As could be expected, members of Congress who took issue with the Bush administration's policies used these published documents as confirmation of their own political stances. Although this does not contravene any rules or procedures, it does have the effect of immediately injecting the NIEs into a partisan debate. On October 24, 2007, DNI McConnell announced his judgment that declassified KJs should not be published and that he did not accept the recent publication as a precedent. However, the Iran nuclear NIE's KJs were published just seven weeks later, undercutting McConnell's stance. This practice actually ended after the Iran NIE. There are many costs in publishing NIEs, in whole or in part. It can affect the willingness of analysts or NIE managers to make strong calls because of their reluctance to be drawn into partisan debates. It also tends to misuse NIEs as factual refutations of administration policies, thus changing the very basis by which an estimate is crafted. Also, given the instant political analysis to which released NIEs are subject, this process has the odd effect of taking a strategic document and turning it into current intelligence.

In addition to shortening NIEs (twenty pages maximum), the NIC has made other changes to improve the rigor of NIEs. Judgments are now accompanied by assessments of likelihood or probability and confidence statements. NIEs also include risks and opportunities analysis, and they identify collection gaps and alternative scenarios.

It is also possible that too much emphasis has been put on estimates. Although they represent the collective views of the intelligence agencies and are signed by the DNI and given to the president, estimates are not the only form of strategic intelligence produced within the analytic community. However, estimates—or the lack of them—have come to be seen, incorrectly, as the only indicator of whether the intelligence community is treating an issue strategically. This certainly was the critique of the 9/11 Commission, whose report castigated the community for not producing an NIE on terrorism for several years before 9/11. Strategic intelligence analysis can take many forms and can be written either by several agencies or by one. NIEs are not the only available format, and their existence or absence does not indicate the seriousness with which the intelligence community views an issue.

Competitive Analysis. The U.S. intelligence community believes in the concept of competitive analysis—having different agencies with different points of view work on the same issue. Because the United States has several intelligence agencies—including three major all-source analytical agencies (CIA, DIA, and INR)—every relevant actor understands that the agencies have different analytical strengths and, likely, different points of view on a given issue. By having each of them—and other agencies as well on some issues—analyze an issue, the belief is that the analysis will be stronger and more likely to give policy makers accurate intelligence.

Beyond the day-to-day competition that takes place among the intelligence publications of each agency, the intelligence community fosters competition in other ways. Intelligence agencies occasionally form red teams, which take on the role of the analysts of another nation or group as a means of gaining insights into their thinking. A now-famous competitive exercise was the already noted 1976 formation of Teams A and B to review intelligence on Soviet strategic forces and doctrine. Team A consisted of intelligence community analysts, and Team B consisted of outside experts, but with a decidedly hawkish viewpoint. The teams disagreed little on the strategic systems the Soviets had built; the key issue was Soviet nuclear doctrine and strategic intentions. Predictably, Team B believed that the intelligence supported a more threatening view of Soviet intentions. However, the lack of balance on Team B largely vitiated the exercise, which could have been useful not only for gaining insight into Soviet intentions but also for validating the utility of competitive intelligence exercises.

Dissent channels—bureaucratic mechanisms by which analysts can challenge the views of their superiors without risk to their careers—are helpful but not widely used. Such channels have long existed for Foreign Service officers in the State Department. Although less effective than competitive analysis for articulating alternative viewpoints, they offer a means by which alternative views can survive a bureaucratic process that tends to emphasize mutual consent.

A broader issue is the extent to which competitive intelligence can or should be institutionalized. To some degree, in the U.S. system it already is. But the competition among the three all-source agencies is not always pointed. They frequently work on the same issue, but with different perspectives that are well understood, thus muting some of the differences that may be seen.

Competitive analysis requires that enough analysts with similar areas of expertise are working in more than one agency. This was certainly true during the zenith of competitive analysis, in the 1980s. But the capability began to dwindle as the intelligence community faced severe budget cuts and personnel losses in the 1990s, after the end of the cold war. As analytic staffs got smaller, agencies began to concentrate more on those issues of greatest importance to their policy customers. Thus, the ability to conduct competitive analysis declined. To rebuild the capability requires two things: more analysts and the time for them to become expert in one or more areas.

For competitive analysis to work well, analysts have to be willing to share their analysis with other analysts. One of the impediments to this had been the security concept "need to know," which could be used as justification not to share. In the aftermath of the 2001 terrorist attacks, there was a shift in intelligence community thinking. The new guidelines went from "need to know," to "need to share," to "responsibility to provide," under DNI McConnell. This changed the emphasis heavily in favor of sharing, which would be one way in which intelligence managers and analysts would be assessed. However, information sharing remains problematic. In March 2017, the inspector general of Justice and the Department of Homeland Security (DHS) noted a lack of unity and strategy in homeland security intelligence sharing.

Another impediment has been technical, finding common secure networks to facilitate sharing. There was a long history of incompatible and outdated technical systems across the community. One response to this has been the DNI program called ICITE (Intelligence Community Information Technology Enterprise), an ongoing effort to create a common community-wide IT platform. Another has been to rely on cloud technology, specifically the Amazon Web Services Secret Region, which allows sharing at various levels of classification as well as a place to test new software and applications. In October 2017, the Trump administration ordered the DNI, the attorney general, and the secretary of DHS to set up an information-sharing network that would correspond to national security threats. It was not clear if this would be separate from or linked to ICITE and other intelligence community efforts.

Not all firms are eager to assist U.S. intelligence efforts. Google employees objected to their firm's work on Project Maven (see chap. 5), moving Google to drop out. Twitter ended U.S. intelligence access to Dataminr, which allows a user to sift through that social media's entire output.

Although the intelligence community believes in competitive analysis, not all policy makers are receptive to the idea. Some see no reason why agencies cannot agree on issues, perhaps assuming that each issue has a single answer that should be knowable. One main reason that President Truman created the Central Intelligence Group (CIG) and its successor, the CIA, was his annoyance over receiving intelligence reports that did not agree. He wanted an agency to coordinate the reports so that he could work his way through the contradictory views. Truman was smart enough to realize that agencies might not agree, but he was not comfortable receiving disparate reports without some coordination that attempted to make sense of the areas of agreement and disagreement. Other policy makers lack Truman's subtlety and cannot abide having agencies disagree, thus vitiating the concept of competitive analysis.

Finally, those who are not familiar with the idea of competitive analysis, and even some who are, may regard the planned redundancy as more wasteful than intellectually productive.

Multi-Int Versus All-Source Analysis. As noted in chapter 5, there has been growing tension and some confusion about the differences between and the relative
benefits of multi-source intelligence (usually called multi-int) and all-source intelligence. To repeat, multi-int is a combining of two or more technical intelligence
sources, most often geospatial intelligence (GEOINT) and signals intelligence
(SIGINT). Again, multi-int is more than a single INT but less than all-source. To
be clear, this is not an all-or-nothing issue. There are times when a multi-int analysis
may be the sufficient, if not proper, response and times when all-source is required.
However, some problems have arisen, at least in the view of those responsible for
all-source. One concern is that the policy maker, who is less facile with these intelligence nuances, may be reading a multi-int product and not realize that it is not all-
source. This may or may not affect the value of the analysis, but for a policy maker,
the ability to make that judgment is difficult as he or she will not readily understand
the difference and what may be missing in a multi-int analysis that might have been
available in all-source. Another concern is that the analysts who contribute to multi-
int analyses are, in essence, single INT analysts and do not have the same analytic
depth that an all-source analyst is expected to have. There have been instances in
which multi-int analysts have gotten beyond their depth, especially when they venture into political analyses. At the same time, the managers of the analysts writing
multi-int are pleased to be bridging the stovepipes and sometimes take umbrage
when it is suggested that their analysts have some limitations.

There is a need for both types of analysis, but some "rules of the road" about who
does what would probably improve the products, as would some labeling so that policy
makers know at the outset the basis of the analysis they are reading.

Politicized Intelligence. The issue of **politicized intelligence** arises from the line
separating policy and intelligence. This line is best thought of as a semipermeable
membrane; policy makers are free to offer assessments that run counter to intelligence analyses, but intelligence officers are not allowed to make policy recommendations based on their intelligence. For example, in the State Department in the
late 1980s, the assistant secretary responsible for the Western Hemisphere, Elliot
Abrams, often disagreed with pessimistic INR assessments as to the likelihood that
the contra rebels would be victorious in Nicaragua. Abrams would often write more
positive assessments on his own that he would forward to Secretary of State George
P. Shultz (1982–1989). As Abrams did not purport to be writing intelligence, this
disagreement was with bounds.

Policy makers and intelligence officers have different institutional and personal
investments in the issues on which they work. The policy makers are creating policy
and hope to accrue other benefits (career advancement, reelection) from a successful
policy. Intelligence officers are not responsible for creating policy or for its success,
yet they understand that the outcomes may affect their own status, both institutional
and personal.

We can think of two types of politicization: positive and negative. The issue
of positive politicization arises primarily from concerns that intelligence officers
may intentionally alter intelligence, which is supposed to be objective, to support
the options or outcomes preferred by policy makers. These actions may stem from

a number of motives: a loss of objectivity regarding the issue at hand, a preference for specific options or outcomes, an effort to be more supportive, career interests, or outright pandering. This is the more familiar case. But there can also be negative politicization where, as noted before, intelligence is provided to influence policy makers so that they change or reverse their policy. We can also think of downward- or upward-flowing politicization. In the case of downward flowing, the policy maker tells the analyst the analytical outcome that is strongly preferred or desired. In the case of upward flowing, the analyst tells the policy maker what he or she wants to hear. In each of these cases—positive or negative, downward or upward—the action is wrong and has a warping effect on the role of analysis.

Intentionally altering intelligence is a subtle issue because it does not involve crossing the line from analysis to policy. Instead, the analyst is tampering with his or her own product so that it is received more favorably. The issue is also made more complex by the fact that, at the most senior levels of the intelligence community, the line separating intelligence from policy begins to blur. Policy makers ask senior intelligence officials for their personal views on an issue or policy, which they may give. It is difficult to conceive of a DNI or a DCI always abstaining when the president or the secretary of state asks such a question. (It should be kept in mind that politicization is different from analyst bias, which is occurring within the analyst's own process and without reference to the policy makers. Both have to be guarded against, but they are different.)

The size or persistence of the politicization problem is difficult to determine. Some who raise accusations about politicized intelligence are losers in the bureaucratic battles—intelligence officers whose views have not prevailed or policy makers (in the executive branch or Congress, either loyal to the current administration or in opposition) who are dissatisfied with current policy directions. Thus, their accusations may be no more objective than the intelligence that concerns them. Those unfamiliar with the process are often surprised to hear intelligence practitioners talk about winners and losers. But these debates—within the policy or the intelligence community—are not abstract academic discussions. Their outcomes have real results that can be significant and even dangerous. Analysts' careers can rise and fall as well as a result of which side of a debate they are on. Just as intelligence officers serve policy makers, career officers—both intelligence and policy—serve political appointees, who are less interested in the objectivity of analysis.

For example, in the late 1940s and early 1950s, many State Department experts on China (the "China hands") had their careers sidetracked or were forced from office over allegations that they had "lost" China to the communists. Numerous scholars and officials interpreted their treatment as a gross injustice. But, as Harvard University professor Ernest R. May pointed out, the U.S. public in the elections of the early 1950s largely repudiated the anti–Chiang Kai-shek views of the China hands by returning the pro-Chiang Republicans to power. So the China hands not only had ideological foes within the government, but they also had no political basis on which to pursue their preferred policies. Similarly, the careers of many intelligence officers and Foreign Service officers involved in crafting and promoting the strategic arms limitation talks (SALT II) treaty during the Carter administration failed to prosper when Ronald Reagan, who opposed the treaty, took office. Again, their careers suffered only because of an electoral victory. One can argue that these punishments were not what the electorate had in mind, but they underscore the fact that the government and the underlying policy processes are essentially political in nature.

Politicization by intelligence officers may also be a question of perception. A consensus could probably be reached on what politicized intelligence looked like, but much less agreement would emerge on whether a specific analysis fit the definition.

Thus, politicized intelligence remains a concern, albeit a somewhat vague one, which may make it more difficult and important. Many issues surrounding politicized intelligence came up in the hearings on Robert Gates's second nomination as DCI, when several analysts charged that Gates had altered analyses on the Soviet Union to meet policy makers' preferences. (Gates asked President Reagan to withdraw his first nomination in 1986, during the Iran-contra affair. He was subsequently renominated by President George H. W. Bush and confirmed in 1991.)

Politicization was also a concern in the Iraq WMD issue. In 2003, the press reported that Vice President Richard Cheney had been out to the CIA several times to receive briefings on Iraq. Critics saw the visits as an attempt to influence the analysts, even though intelligence officials and analysts maintained that they were not asked to alter their analyses. Is there a proper number of times a senior official should be briefed on a highly sensitive topic, after which it appears to be politicization? The answer likely is no. What matters is the substance of the exchange. Also, such exchanges are a primary reason for intelligence agencies—to help officials make decisions. In Britain, charges of politicization on Iraq centered on accusations that Prime Minister Tony Blair or his office asked Defence Ministry officials to "sex up" their intelligence on Iraq WMD, which the government denied. Three external reviews of intelligence on Iraq, by the Senate Intelligence Committee and the WMD Commission in the United States and by Lord Butler in Britain, all concluded that the intelligence had not been politicized. A fourth report, done for the Australian government, came to the same conclusion.

In August 2015, press reports alleged that many intelligence analysts at Central Command (CENTCOM) believed their analyses had been changed by superiors in order to offer a more optimistic view of U.S. operations against the Islamic State. The Defense Department inspector general issued a report in January 2017, which found no basis for the allegations of intelligence being skewed or falsified but did make recommendations on improving the atmosphere and procedures at CENTCOM's J-2 (intelligence directorate). An earlier report by a joint task force formed by the House Armed Services and Intelligence Committees was more critical. But the entire incident underscored the increased political atmosphere in which intelligence analysis has had to function since 9/11 and the Iraq WMD estimate.

A second type of politicized intelligence is caused by policy makers who may react strongly to intelligence, depending on whether it confirms or refutes their preferences for policy outcomes. For example, according to press accounts in November 1998, Vice President Al Gore's staff rejected CIA reports about the personal corruption of Russian premier Viktor Chernomyrdin. Staff members argued that the administration had to deal with Chernomyrdin, corrupt or not, and that the intelligence was inconclusive. Analysts countered that the administration set the standard for proof so high that it was unlikely to be met by intelligence. The analysts found that they were censoring their reports to avoid further disputes with the White House. Both policy and intelligence officers denied the allegations.

Policy makers may also use intelligence issues for partisan purposes. Two examples in the United States were the missile gap (1959–1961) and the window of vulnerability (1979–1981). In both cases, the party that was out of power (the Democrats in the first case, the Republicans in the second) argued that the Soviet Union had gained a strategic nuclear advantage over the United States, which was being ignored or not reported. In both cases, the accusing party won the election (not because of its charges) and subsequently learned that the intelligence did not support the accusations—which it then simply claimed had been resolved.

Analytical Standards. As this chapter has argued, there is a set of standards in intelligence analysis. Most of them are fairly well-known and accepted, although, until recently, little effort was made to codify them. This changed in the aftermath of the 2001 terrorist attacks and the Iraq WMD issue. The Intelligence Reform and Terrorism Prevention Act (IRTPA, 2004) includes a number of standards for intelligence analysis. The DNI's office has also issued standards for evaluating intelligence.

It is important to understand analytic standards for their own sake, but they cannot be wholly separated from the circumstances in which they are written. The twin events of 9/11 and Iraq WMD left most observers with the overwhelming impression that the analytical capacity of the intelligence community was flawed and performed badly. However, as has been noted earlier, the perceived "lessons" of the two events tend to run in opposite directions:

- Warning: The "lesson" of 9/11 was that the intelligence community failed to be strident enough in its warnings, leaving policy makers with an imprecise sense of the impending nature of the threat. Intelligence officers serving at the time deny this and also note that the tactical intelligence that would have been useful did not exist. In the case of Iraq WMD, the intelligence community is said to have overblown the threat based on very little new intelligence.

- Analytical process: In 9/11, analysts failed to make the necessary linkages between disparate pieces of intelligence (hence, the "connect the dots" metaphor), but for Iraq WMD they made too many linkages, resulting in a false image of the WMD programs. The analysis before 9/11 has also been attacked as a "failure of imagination," but in the case of Iraq, the analysis was seen as being perhaps too imaginative.

- Information sharing: The failure to discover the 9/11 plot is ascribed, in part, to the failure of the CIA and the Federal Bureau of Investigation (FBI) to share information. But in the case of Iraq WMD, the intelligence community was taken to task for sharing information (from the unreliable human source called CURVEBALL) that was not true, although those sharing it did not know that.

Therefore, when crafting the legislation creating the DNI, Congress went into unusual detail about what it expected of future analysis. The DNI must appoint an individual or office responsible for ensuring that finished intelligence produced by any intelligence community element is "timely, objective, independent of political considerations, based upon all sources of available intelligence, and employ[s] the standards of proper analytic trade-craft" (Section 1019). This individual or office can have no direct responsibility for the specific production of any finished intelligence and must prepare regular detailed reviews of analytic products, lessons learned, and recommendations for improvement. The criteria for these evaluations and reviews are detailed. Finally, the act calls for the creation of what has become an analytic ombudsman. (*See box, "How Right How Often?"*)

The analytic overseers in the ODNI also created a set of evaluation tradecraft standards for analysis, few of which are controversial. They deal mostly with the underlying aspects of intelligence: sources, assumptions, judgments, alternative analyses, logical argumentation, and so on. The final standard, accuracy, may not be known for some time. However, Josh Kerbel, a veteran intelligence analyst, argues that the standards represent an "industrial age craft" approach to analysis that can limit the ability of analysts to apply creativity and imagination.

Most observers would likely agree that these are among the necessary standards for good analysis. The real concern is how these standards are put into practice. It is noteworthy that the standards reflect more of the perceived lessons of Iraq WMD than of September 11. The ODNI has stated that these standards serve as community-wide guidelines, making them part of the training for all new analysts and for analytical managers. Given the paucity of community-wide courses, this training can capture only a small number of the analysts across the community in any given year and far fewer than the large numbers that have been recruited. Therefore, overseeing standards implementation requires insights into the analytic training being conducted at each agency. But, as noted regarding ICD 206 on sourcing, these standards also run the risk of being misinterpreted or having unintended consequences.

The use of these standards as an evaluation tool is more problematic. The congressional mandate for a broad review of finished intelligence products is impractical given the volume of intelligence produced daily. The most that can then be done is to sample, either by topic or by office, or both, and hope that some larger lessons can be drawn. This may prove difficult given the problems inherent in any sampling methodology.

The underlying question is the expectations of either Congress or the ODNI about how these standards might affect future analysis. It is possible, for example, to perform highly in each of the standards and still find, after the fact, that the judgments and assessments proved to be inaccurate—in other words, a victory of form over substance. Value is given to consistency, which can run counter to the desire for analytic insight and the avoidance of groupthink. If the highest standard for analysis is accuracy, then we face the problem that neither these standards nor any others will guarantee that outcome. Clearly, these standards are more likely to result in analytic products that are sound in terms of methodology, but this is not the same as accuracy. Also, these standards run the risk of creating a very mechanistic approach to what is, at its core, an intellectual process. For example, the truly gifted and occasionally insightful analyst could get poor grades in most of these criteria and still produce an accurate and useful analysis.

HOW RIGHT HOW OFTEN?

The Nature of the Question: A Baseball Analogy

One of the most persistent and unanswerable questions in intelligence analysis is this: How right should the analysts be how often? The answer depends, in part, on the available intelligence and the skills of the analyst. But there are also significant differences depending on the nature of the question being asked.

To use baseball as an analogy, consider two key activities happening in a ball game: fielding and hitting. The standards for these two activities are very different. Professional baseball fielders are expected to perform in the range of .950, or better, out of a thousand. But across the major leagues, the batting average is around .260. So, clearly, batting is more difficult than fielding.

In terms of analysis, sometimes there are fielding questions. For example: Who is the commander of the North Korean air force, and what do we know about him? But sometimes there are batting questions: What is Kim Jong Un going to do next?

Therefore, analytic performance is also driven by the nature of the question being asked.

The Analytic Workforce. The demographics of the analysts in U.S. intelligence are driven first by the contraction that the intelligence community endured during the 1990s, suffering deep budget cuts after the cold war. The so-called cold war peace dividend fell more heavily in proportional terms on intelligence than it did on defense. As DCI Tenet expressed it, the net result was the loss of 23,000 employees and positions across U.S. intelligence, meaning both people who left and—more significantly—people who were never hired. The second factor came in the aftermath of the 2001 terrorist attacks when all agencies began major hiring efforts. The result of these efforts has been a workforce of decreasing experience over time as new hires outnumber veterans, who continue to retire. In 2018, perhaps half of the analysts across the intelligence community had six years or less experience in their subject areas, leading some to observe that this is the least experienced analytic cadre since the formation of the intelligence community in 1947.

These demographic trends have several important implications for analysis:

- Experience: The most obvious issue is the relative inexperience of the workforce as analysts and subject matter experts. As discussed earlier, human intelligence (HUMINT) collectors need five to seven years to be considered seasoned. There is no agreed benchmark for analysts, but the five-year mark is probably a reliable one, give or take a year. This is sometimes referred to as the "green/gray" problem—that is, the analytic workforce is getting younger, not older. This is both a problem in and of itself and also a problem in terms of management. The cadre that should be moving into senior analytic management ranks is too thin to fill all of the necessary positions. This necessitates promoting more junior analysts sooner. Again, their lack of experience might become problematic.

- Work methods: The new cadre of analysts are more comfortable working in networks and working more collaboratively, both of which are positive attributes. They also are much more comfortable with information technology and working in a "softcopy" world. It is too soon to know, however, if they will be comfortable asserting themselves and their views when necessary or if they will default to lowest common denominator analyses as part of their collaborative instinct.

    It is also not clear how the new cadre of analysts will assess incoming intelligence. One of the charms of the World Wide Web is that it is a democratic institution: Anyone is free to post any of their views on any subject. This is also, from an intelligence viewpoint, a problem, as intelligence must address the issue of validity of sources: Who are they? What is their basis for saying this? Are they knowledgeable and credible? Do they have motives for saying this? If one thinks of the Web as a giant bulletin board where anything can be posted and shared, the ability to rise above that in working on intelligence becomes more evident. The Web may be an interesting metaphor for collaboration, but it can be dangerous when assessing views and information. Moreover, for a generation that uses social media as a major form of communication, will they bring enough critical faculties to bear when assessing intelligence derived from social media?

- Retention: A key issue for intelligence agencies is retaining as many of these new analysts, or at least the good ones, as possible. Poor retention rates will only replicate the current demographic problems that led to this issue. Retention goes to the issues of career management, career progression, and education and training. These have not been areas to which managers have given much attention until recently, but they will underpin much of the other efforts at transformation. There is a budgetary aspect to this that will also affect the experience levels, noted above. As the Afghan war wound down, the Defense budget lost funding for the Iraq and Afghan wars. This funding helped support literally hundreds of contractors who served as analysts at the various commands. Their contracts will not be renewed, thus hurting the experience levels once again and creating a "brain drain" as many of these analysts have more experience than their intelligence community colleagues.

In some respects, the workforce issues at the DHS Office of Intelligence and Analysis (I&A) are most problematic. I&A is the newest analytic component in the intelligence community, created in 2005. A 2014 study by the Government Accountability Office (GAO) found that I&A's analyses were not seen as useful by several of its customer sets. Some of I&A's problems stem from similar but broader issues in DHS, including an absence of clear purpose and strategic goals. The GAO study also noted that I&A had problems in hiring, retention, and morale.

A final workforce issue results from the long war against terrorists, buttressed to some degree by the campaigns in Iraq and Afghanistan and now Syria: the issue of counterterrorism and counterinsurgency (CT and COIN). Although there has been strategy guiding these efforts, for the analysts these have been largely tactical engagements, looking for small groups if not individuals. Thus, many of the analysts who joined in the surge after 2001 have spent a good deal of their careers on these tactical types of issues. The effect has probably been most telling in CIA and DIA. Former DCIA Michael Hayden (2006–2009) remarked that he had "targeteers" rather than analysts. DCIA Brennan spoke of the need to "demilitarize" the CIA, in part for operational rather than analytical reasons.

At DIA, there has been some of the same effect, although it is less pronounced there as DIA more often works on tactical issues in support of fighting forces. However, in the workforce transition noted above there has been a loss of analysts who had the substantive knowledge to help plan conventional military campaigns, which has not been passed on to those who followed and who have focused mostly on terrorism. But DIA faces another conundrum, framed by this question: Are we doing defense intelligence or intelligence for defense? What DIA managers and analysts mean when they ask this question is that their preference is to do "defense intelligence"—that is, a focus on defense-related intelligence issues. However, they are often required to become the more general intelligence support, especially for the CCMDs, on a host of political and economic issues because there is no one else in the intelligence community who will respond to these requests. Some DIA analysts believe these types of questions should more properly be answered by CIA, but CIA does not automatically respond to answer CCMD requests the way that DIA does. Both workforces, CIA and especially DIA, have also been stretched by the need to deploy analysts forward for long periods of time.

The problem facing the intelligence community is how to transition some analysts away from CT and COIN and back to more traditional political-military issues that are strategic, rather than tactical, in nature. DCIA Gina Haspel (2018–) signaled the need for this change in public remarks in September 2018. Many veteran analysts agree that it is more difficult to go from tactical issues to strategic issues than the other way around—but that is the task that now must be addressed.

This transition may be made more difficult if retention rates continue to decline, as they have done in recent years. For several years, intelligence managers were fairly callous about the retention issue, arguing that the recession made leaving government service very unattractive. However, as the economy has improved, there are more noticeable losses of personnel to the private sector, which again affects experience levels but without necessary budget authority to fill vacated positions. The retention issue is also seen as a reflection of poor management practices in some of the agencies. It may also reflect the burnout caused by working on relentlessly intense issues such as terrorism or supporting forces in active combat.

INTELLIGENCE ANALYSIS: AN ASSESSMENT

Sherman Kent, an intellectual founder of the U.S. intelligence community, especially of its estimative process, once wrote that every intelligence analyst has three wishes: to know everything, to be believed, and to influence policy for the good (as the analyst understands it). Kent's three wishes offer a yardstick by which to measure analysis. Clearly, an analyst can never know everything in a given field. If everything were known, the need for intelligence would not exist—nothing would be left to discover. But what Kent is getting at is the desire of the analyst to know as much as possible about a given issue before being asked to write about it. The amount of intelligence available varies from issue to issue and from time to time. Analysts must therefore be trained to develop some inner, deeper knowledge that enables them to read between the lines, to make educated guesses or intuitive choices when the intelligence is insufficient.

Kent's second wish—to be believed—goes to the heart of the relationship between intelligence and policy. Policy makers pay no price for ignoring intelligence, barring highly infrequent strategic disasters such as Josef Stalin's refusal to accept the signs of an imminent German attack in 1941. Intelligence officers see themselves as honest and objective messengers who add value to the process, who provide not just sources but also analysis. Their reward, at the end of the process, is to be listened to, which varies greatly from one policy maker to another.

Finally, and derived from his second wish, Kent notes that intelligence officers want to have a positive effect on policy, to help avert disaster and to help produce positive outcomes in the nation's interests. But analysts want to be more than a Cassandra, constantly warning of doom and disaster. Their wish to have a positive influence also indicates the desire to be kept informed about what policy makers are doing to enable the intelligence officers to play a meaningful role.

What, then, constitutes good intelligence? This is no small question, and one is reminded of Justice Potter Stewart's opinion in a court case involving obscenity and pornography: "[I can't define it,] but I know it when I see it." Good intelligence has something of the same indistinct quality. At least four qualities come to mind. Good intelligence is

- Timely: Getting the intelligence to the policy maker on time is more important than waiting for every last shred of collection to come in or for the paper to be pristine, clean, and in the right format. The timeliness criterion runs counter to the first of Kent's three wishes: to know everything. Time can change the perspective on an occurrence. Napoleon died on St. Helena in May 1821; word of his death did not reach Paris until July. Charles Maurice de Talleyrand, once Napoleon's foreign minister and later one of his foes, was dining at a friend's house when they heard of Napoleon's passing. The hostess exclaimed, "What an event!" Talleyrand corrected her: "It is no longer an event, Madam, it is news."

- Tailored: Good intelligence focuses on the specific information needs of the policy maker, to whatever depth and breadth are required, but without extraneous material. This must be done in a way that does not result in losing objectivity or politicizing the intelligence. Tailored intelligence products (those responding to a specific need or request) are among the most highly prized by policy makers.

- Digestible: Good intelligence has to be in a form and of a length that allow policy makers to grasp what they need to know as easily as possible. The requirement tends to argue in favor of shorter intelligence products, but it is primarily meant to stress that the message be presented clearly so that it can be readily understood. This does not mean that the message cannot be complex or even incomplete. But whatever the main message is, the policy maker must be able to understand it with a minimum of effort. Being succinct and clear is an important skill for analysts to learn. Writing a good two-page memo is much more difficult than writing a five-page memo on the same subject. As Mark Twain observed in a letter to a friend, "I am writing you a long letter because I don't have time to write a short one."

- Clear regarding the known and the unknown: Good intelligence must convey to the reader what is known, what is unknown, and what has been filled in by analysis, as well as the degree of confidence, including lack of confidence where appropriate, in the material. The degree of confidence is important because the policy maker must have some sense of the relative firmness of the intelligence. All intelligence involves risk by the very nature of the information being dealt with. The risk should not be assumed by the analysts alone but should be shared with their clients.

Adm. Mike Mullen, a former chairman of the Joint Chiefs of Staff, expressed similar intelligence requirements when he told the J-2, his senior intelligence officer: "Too late; too bad. Too long; too bad. Too complicated; too bad." Mullen understood the intricacies of intelligence but he also required intelligence that was easily accessible within the constraints in which he operated.

Objectivity is not one of the major factors defining good intelligence. Its omission is not an oversight. The need for objectivity is so great and so pervasive that it should be taken as a given. If the intelligence is not objective, then none of the other attributes—timeliness, digestibility, clarity—matters.

Accuracy also is not a criterion. Accuracy is a more difficult standard for assessing intelligence than might be imagined. Clearly, no one wants to be wrong, but everyone recognizes the impossibility of infallibility. Given these limits, what accuracy standard should be used? One hundred percent is too high and 0 percent is too low. Splitting the difference at 50 percent accuracy is still unsatisfactory. Thus, what is left is a numbers game—something more than 50 percent and less than 100 percent. Accuracy can also be difficult to assess as many issues do not have definitive endings. Here we are back to the current versus long-term problem. Short-term issues are more likely to have specific endings (elections; specific decisions or actions); longer term issues will not. Therefore, it becomes more difficult to assess accuracy. For example, during the cold war, the United States maintained its policy of containment for more than forty years, despite the fact that there were not many signs of its being successful.

Then, quite suddenly, between roughly 1989 and 1991, it worked. So, how would one have phrased assessments of containment over that period?

The issue of accuracy became more demanding in the aftermath of September 11 and the onset of the Iraq war. The political system seemed to have decreasing tolerance for the imperfection that is inherent in intelligence analysis. Even though all observers understand that perfection is not possible, each and every mistake seemed to incur a large political cost for the intelligence agencies. This can have an additional cost in the analytic system if analysts become risk-averse because of the political costs of being wrong. Even though most observers would agree that 100 percent accuracy is unachievable, they would also argue that the "big things" are the issues where accuracy matters. Examples of such "big things" would be the existence of Iraq WMD or the impending fall of the Soviet Union. But these are the very issues where intelligence is more likely to be wrong because they run counter to years of collected intelligence and presumably accurate analyses. Recall the pearl metaphor discussed under collection: the slow, steady accumulation of intelligence over time, often decades. This accumulative process has an effect on the analysts. It leads them to create what they believe are accurate pictures of behavior and more or less likely outcomes. But the "big things" tend to be hardest to foresee for the very reason that they run counter to all of that accumulated intelligence. Even today, long after the facts, it is difficult to make an analytical, intelligence-based case (1) that when a crisis erupts in the Soviet Union, the Communist Party will peacefully give up power, or (2) that Saddam Hussein is telling the truth and has no WMD on hand.

As unsatisfactory as this standard is, other metrics are not much better. For example, a batting average could be constructed over time—for an issue, for an office, for an agency, for a product line. Or the quality of intelligence could be assessed on the basis of the number of products produced—estimates, analyses, images. But these measures are inadequate, too. Furthermore, they are not meant to be as frivolous as they seem. They are meant to give a feel for the difficulty of assessing what is good intelligence.

However, producing good intelligence is not some sort of Holy Grail that is rarely achieved. Good intelligence is often achieved. But one must distinguish between the steady stream of intelligence that is produced on a daily basis and the smaller amount within that daily production that stands out for some reason—its timeliness, the quality of its writing, its effect on policy. The view here—and it is one that has been debated with the highest intelligence officials—is that effort is required to produce acceptable, useful intelligence on a daily basis, but that producing exceptional intelligence is much more difficult and less frequently achieved. A conflict arises between the goal of consistency and the desire to be exceptional. An entire intelligence community cannot be exceptional all the time, but it does hope to be consistently helpful to policy. Consistent intelligence and exceptional intelligence are not one and the same. (As a cynic once said, "Only the mediocre are at their best all the time.") Consistency is not a bad goal, but it allows analysis to fall into a pattern that lulls both the producer and the consumer. Thus, for all that is known about the distinctive characteristics of good intelligence, it remains somewhat elusive in reality, at least as a widely seen daily phenomenon. But, for analysts, that is one of the positive challenges of their profession.

In the aftermath of 9/11 and Iraq WMD and after the promulgation of analytic standards, there still has not been closure on the key questions: How good is intelligence supposed to be, how often is it to be supplied, and on which issues? There are both professional and political answers to these questions, but the inherent differences between them have not been resolved.

KEY TERMS

analyst agility 160
analyst bias 161
analyst fungibility 160
analytic penetration 173
analytical stovepipes 169
assessments 167
clientism 164
competitive analysis 169
confidence levels 176
current intelligence 154
estimates 166
global coverage 160

groupthink 168
indications and warnings (I&W) 177
layering 164
long-term intelligence 154
mirror imaging 163
national intelligence managers
    (NIMs) 171
opportunity analysis 179
politicized intelligence 186
premature closure 179
unifying intelligence
    strategy (UIS) 171

FURTHER READINGS

The literature on analysis is rich. These readings discuss both broad, general issues and some specific areas of intelligence analysis that have been particularly important. The CIA has declassified many of its estimates on the Soviet Union and related issues. (See chap. 11.)

Adams, Sam. "Vietnam Cover-Up: Playing With Numbers: A CIA Conspiracy Against Its Own Numbers." *Harper's* (May 1975): 41–44ff.

Bar-Joseph, Uri. "The Politicization of Intelligence: A Comparative Study." *International Journal of Intelligence and Counterintelligence* 26 (summer 2013): 347–369.

———. "The Professional Ethics of Intelligence Analysis." *International Journal of Intelligence and Counterintelligence* 24 (spring 2011): 22–43.

Bell, J. Dwyer. "Toward a Theory of Deception." *International Journal of Intelligence and Counterintelligence* 16 (summer 2003): 244–279.

Berkowitz, Bruce. "The Big Difference Between Intelligence and Evidence." *Washington Post*, February 2, 2003, B1.

Caldwell, George. *Policy Analysis for Intelligence.* Report by the Central Intelligence Agency, Center for the Study of Intelligence. Washington, D.C.: CIA, 1992.

Clark, Robert M. *Intelligence Analysis: Estimation and Prediction.* Baltimore, Md.: American Literary Press, 1996.

Cooper, Jeffrey R. *Curing Analytic Pathologies: Pathways to Improved Intelligence Analysis*. Washington, D.C.: Center for the Study of Analysis, CIA, December 2005.

Cukier, Kenneth Neil, and Viktor Mayer-Schoenberger. "The Rise of Big Data." *Foreign Affairs* (May–June 2013). (Available at www.foreignaffairs.com/articles/139104/kenneth-neil-cukier-and-viktor-mayer-schoenberger/the-rise-of-big-data.)

Davis, Jack. *The Challenge of Opportunity Analysis*. Report by the Central Intelligence Agency, Center for the Study of Intelligence. Washington, D.C.: CIA, 1992.

Frederichs, Rebecca L., and Stephen R. Di Rienzo. "Establishing a Framework for Intelligence Education and Training." *Joint Forces Quarterly* 2 (3rd quarter, 2011): 68–73.

Friedman, Jeffrey A., and Richard Zeckhauser. "Assessing Uncertainty in Intelligence." Faculty Research Working Paper RWP 12-027, June 2012. (Available at https://research.hks.harvard.edu/publications/workingpapers/citation.aspx?PubId=8427&type=WPN.)

Flynn, Michael T., Matt Pottinger, and Paul D. Batchelor. *Fixing Intel: A Blueprint for Making Intelligence Relevant in Afghanistan*. Washington, D.C.: Center for a New American Security, 2010.

Ford, Harold P. *Estimative Intelligence*. McLean, Va.: Association of Former Intelligence Officers, 1993.

———. *Estimative Intelligence: The Purposes and Problems of National Intelligence Estimating*. Washington, D.C.: Defense Intelligence College, 1989.

Gates, Robert M. "The CIA and American Foreign Policy." *Foreign Affairs* 66 (winter 1987–1988): 215–230.

———. "Guarding Against Politicization." *Studies in Intelligence* 36, no. 5 (1992): 5–13.

Gazit, Shlomo. "Estimates and Fortune-Telling in Intelligence Work." *International Security* 4 (spring 1980): 36–56.

———. "Intelligence Estimates and the Decision-Maker." *International Security* 3 (July 1988): 261–287.

Gentry, John A. "Assessing Intelligence Performance." In *The Oxford Handbook of National Security Intelligence*. Ed. Loch Johnson. Oxford, U.K.: Oxford University Press, 2010.

———. "Has the ODNI Improved U.S. Intelligence Analysis?" *International Journal of Intelligence and Counterintelligence* 28 (winter 2015–2016): 637–661.

George, Roger Z. "Beyond Analytic Tradecraft." *International Journal of Intelligence and Counterintelligence* 23 (summer 2010): 296–308.

———. "Fixing the Problem of Analytical Mind-Sets: Alternative Analysis." *International Journal of Intelligence and Counterintelligence* 17 (fall 2004): 385–404.

George, Roger Z., and James B. Bruce, eds. *Analyzing Intelligence: Origins, Obstacles, and Innovations*. Washington, D.C.: Georgetown University Press, 2008.

Heuer, Richards J., Jr. *Psychology of Analysis*. Washington, D.C.: Central Intelligence Agency, History Staff, 1999. (Available at www.cia.gov/library/center-for-the-study-of-intelligence/csi-publications/books-and-monographs/psychology-of-intelligence-analysis.)

Jervis, Robert. *Why Intelligence Fails*. Ithaca, N.Y.: Cornell University Press, 2010.

Johnson, Loch K. "Analysis for a New Age." *Intelligence and National Security* 11 (October 1996): 657–671.

Kerbel, Josh. "Are the Analytic Tradecraft Standards Hurting as Much as Helping?" National Intelligence University Research Short, November 1, 2017.

Kerbel, Josh, and Anthony Olcott. "Synthesizing With Clients, Not Analyzing for Customers." *Studies in Intelligence* 54 (December 2010): 1–13.

Lieberthal, Kenneth. *The U.S. Intelligence Community and Foreign Policy.* Washington, D.C.: Brookings Institution, 2009.

Lockwood, Jonathan S. "Sources of Error in Indications and Warning." *Defense Intelligence Journal* 3 (spring 1994): 75–88.

Lowenthal, Mark M. "The Burdensome Concept of Failure." In *Intelligence: Policy and Process.* Ed. Alfred C. Maurer and others. Boulder, Colo.: Westview Press, 1985.

———. "The Intelligence Time Event Horizon." *International Journal of Intelligence and Counterintelligence* 22 (fall 2009): 369–381.

Lowenthal, Mark M., and Ronald A. Marks. "Intelligence Analysis: Is It as Good as It Gets?" *International Journal of Intelligence and Counterintelligence* 28 (fall 2015): 662–665.

MacEachin, Douglas J. *The Tradecraft of Analysis: Challenge and Change in the CIA.* Washington, D.C.: Consortium for the Study of Intelligence, 1994.

Marrin, Stephen. "Evaluating the Quality of Intelligence Analysis: By What (Mis) Measure?" *Intelligence and National Security* 27 (December 2012): 896–912.

———. "Training and Educating U.S. Intelligence Analysts." *International Journal of Intelligence and Counterintelligence* 22 (spring 2009): 131–146.

Nye, Joseph S. *Estimating the Future.* Washington, D.C.: Consortium for the Study of Intelligence, 1994.

Pease, Bruce E. *Leading Intelligence Analysis: Lessons from CIA's Analytic Front Lines.* Thousand Oaks, CA: CQ Press, 2019.

Petersen, Martin. "What I Learned in 40 Years of Doing Intelligence Analysis for US Foreign Policymakers." *Studies in Intelligence* 55 (March 2011): 13–20.

Pillar, Paul. "The Perils of Politicization." In *The Oxford Handbook of National Security Intelligence.* Ed. Loch Johnson. Oxford, U.K.: Oxford University Press, 2010.

Pipes, Richard. "Team B: The Reality Behind the Myth." *Commentary* 82 (October 1986).

Price, Victoria. *The DCI's Role in Producing Strategic Intelligence Estimates.* Newport, R.I.: U.S. Naval War College, 1980.

Reich, Robert C. "Reexamining the Team A–Team B Exercise." *International Journal of Intelligence and Counterintelligence* 3 (fall 1989): 387–403.

Rieber, Steven. "Intelligence Analysis and Judgmental Calibration." *International Journal of Intelligence and Counterintelligence* 17 (spring 2004): 97–112.

Stack, Kevin P. "A Negative View of Comparative Analysis." *International Journal of Intelligence and Counterintelligence* 10 (winter 1998): 456–464.

Steury, Donald P., ed. *Sherman Kent and the Board of National Estimates.* Washington, D.C.: Center for the Study of Intelligence, History Staff, CIA, 1994.

Turner, Michael A. "Setting Analytical Priorities in U.S. Intelligence." *International Journal of Intelligence and Counterintelligence* 9 (fall 1996): 313–336.

U.S. Central Intelligence Agency. *The Collection of Presidential Daily Briefing Products from 1961 to 1969*. (Available at http://www.foia.cia.gov/collection/PDBs.)

———. *The President's Daily Brief: Delivering Intelligence to Kennedy and Johnson*. (Available at https://www.cia.gov/library/publications/intelligence-history/presidents-daily-brief/PDB_Kennedy_and_Johnson_public16Sep2015.pdf.)

———. *A Tradecraft Primer: Structural Analytic Techniques for Improving Intelligence Analysis*. March 2009. (Available at www.cia.gov/library/center-for-the-study-of-intelligence/csi-publications/books-and-monographs/Tradecraft%20Primer-apr09.pdf.)

U.S. Department of Defense. Inspector General. *Unclassified Report of Investigation on Allegations Relating to USCENTCOM Intelligence Products*. January 31, 2017. (Available at https://media.defense.gov/2017/Feb/01/2001714315/-1/-1/1/DODIG-2017-049.pdf.)

U.S. House of Representatives. *Initial Findings of the U.S. House of Representatives Joint Task Force on U.S. Central Command Intelligence Analysis*. August 10, 2016. (Available at https://intelligence.house.gov/uploadedfiles/house_jtf_on_centcom_intelligence_initial_report.pdf.)

U.S. House Permanent Select Committee on Intelligence. *Intelligence Support to Arms Control*. 100th Cong., 1st sess., 1987.

———. Iran: Evaluation of U.S. Intelligence Performance Prior to November 1978. 96th Cong., 1st sess., 1979.

U.S. Office of the Director of National Intelligence. *Background to "Assessing Russian Activities and Intentions in Recent U.S. Elections": The Analytic Process and Cyber Incident Attribution* [and] *Assessing Russian Activities and Intentions in Recent U.S. Elections*. Intelligence Community Assessment. January 6, 2017. (Available at https://www.dni.gov/files/documents/ICA_2017_01.pdf.)

U.S. Senate Select Committee on Intelligence. The National Intelligence Estimates A–B Team Episode Concerning Soviet Strategic Capability and Objectives. 95th Cong., 2d sess., 1978.

———. *Nomination of Robert M. Gates*. 3 vols. 102d Cong., 1st sess., 1991.

———. Nomination of Robert M. Gates to Be Director of Central Intelligence. 102d Cong., 1st sess., 1991.

———. Report on the U.S. Intelligence Community's Prewar Intelligence Assessments on Iraq. 108th Cong., 2d sess., 2004.

Walton, Timothy. *Challenges in Intelligence Analysis: Lessons From 1300 bce to the Present*. New York: Cambridge University Press, 2010.

Weiss, Charles. "Communicating Uncertainty in Intelligence and Other Professions." *International Journal of Intelligence and Counterintelligence* 21 (spring 2008): 57–85.

Wirtz, James J. "Miscalculation, Surprise, and American Intelligence after the Cold War." *International Journal of Intelligence and Counterintelligence* 5 (spring 1991): 1–16.

———. *The Tet Offensive: Intelligence Failure in War*. Ithaca, N.Y.: Cornell University Press, 1991.

CHAPTER SEVEN

COUNTERINTELLIGENCE

Counterintelligence (CI) refers to efforts taken to protect one's own intelligence operations from penetration and disruption by hostile nations or their intelligence services. Executive Order 12333 (1981; revised 2008) defines **counterintelligence** as "information gathered and activities conducted to identify, deceive, exploit, disrupt or protect" against espionage and other activities carried out by foreign states or non-state actors. It is both analytical and operational. Counterintelligence is not a separate step in the intelligence process. It should pervade all aspects of intelligence, but it is often pigeon-holed as a security issue. Counterintelligence does not fit neatly with human intelligence, although it is, in part, a collection issue. Nor does it fit with covert action. It is also more than security—that is, defending against or identifying breaches—because successful CI can also lead to analytical and operational opportunities. It is also much more than a law enforcement issue. In sum, CI is one of the most difficult intelligence topics to discuss.

Most nations have intelligence enterprises of some sort. As a result, these agencies are valuable intelligence targets for other nations. Knowing what the other side knows, does not know, and how it goes about its work is always useful. Moreover, knowing if the other side is undertaking similar efforts is extremely helpful. The widespread existence of intelligence agencies in virtually all nations and their intelligence collection activities does not preclude states from striking disingenuous poses of dismay and shock when it is revealed that they have been targeted, as was the case with many nations after Edward Snowden's revelations about National Security Agency (NSA) collection activities aimed at them. (*See box, "Who Spies on Whom?"*)

However, counterintelligence is more than a defensive activity. There are at least three types of CI:

- Collection: gaining information about an opponent's intelligence collection capabilities that may be aimed at one's own country

- Defensive: thwarting efforts by hostile intelligence services to penetrate one's service

- Offensive: having identified an opponent's efforts against one's own system, trying to manipulate these attacks either by turning the opponent's agents into double agents or by feeding them false information that they report home

Paul Redmond, a Central Intelligence Agency (CIA) officer who spent a large part of his career on counterintelligence issues, defined CI as a broad array of activities, all designed to support one's own efforts and to thwart hostile ones. Redmond's list includes **counterespionage** (countering penetrations of one's service), asset validation (confirming the bona fides of human intelligence, or HUMINT, sources), disinformation (putting out false information to support penetrations), and operational tradecraft. John Ehrman, another CIA counterintelligence veteran, defined CI as "the study of the organization and behavior of the intelligence services of foreign states and entities and the application of the resulting knowledge."

The world of spy and counterspy is murky at best. Like espionage, counterintelligence is a staple of intelligence fiction. But, like all other aspects of intelligence, it has less glamour than it does grinding, painstaking work. There has been a marked increase in hostile foreign intelligence activity against the United States and its allies, particularly from Russia, and against the United States from China on a very large scale (see chap. 15). This involves both HUMINT and cyber. There has also been an increase in leaks by intelligence officers, all of which puts increased emphasis on counterintelligence.

WHO SPIES ON WHOM?

Some people assume that friendly spy agencies do not spy on one another. But what constitutes "friendly"? The United States and its Five Eyes partners, or "Commonwealth cousins"—Australia, Britain, Canada, and New Zealand—enjoy a close intelligence partnership and do not spy on one another. Beyond that, all bets are off.

In the 1990s, the United States allegedly spied on France for economic intelligence. In the 1980s, Israel willingly used Jonathan Pollard, a U.S. Navy intelligence employee who passed sensitive U.S. intelligence that he believed Israel needed to know. Some people were surprised—if not outraged—that post-Soviet Russia would continue using Aldrich Ames to spy against the United States. (Subsequent revelations about the espionage of Robert Hanssen stirred less surprise—perhaps a sign of increased maturity gained through painful experience.) In the late 1990s, a House committee found that China stole nuclear secrets from the United States at a time when the two nations were strategic partners against the Soviet Union. In 2013, information leaked by Edward Snowden revealed that the United States collected intelligence against various European allies, the European Union (EU), and several Latin American nations.

In the 1970s, a "senior U.S. government official" (probably Secretary of State Henry A. Kissinger) observed, "There is no such thing as 'friendly' intelligence agencies. There are only the intelligence agencies of friendly powers."

INTERNAL SAFEGUARDS

All intelligence agencies establish a series of internal processes and checks, the main purposes of which are to weed out applicants who may be unsuitable and to identify current employees whose loyalty or activities are questionable. The vetting process for applicants includes extensive background checks, interviews with the applicants and close associates, and, in the United States at least, the use of the **polygraph** at most but not all agencies. The ideal candidate is not necessarily someone whose past record is spotless. Most applicants likely have engaged in some level of experimentation—either sexual or drugs, or both. Some may have committed minor criminal offenses. It is crucial, however, that applicants be forthcoming about their past and be able to prove that they are no longer exhibiting behaviors that are criminal, dangerous, or susceptible to blackmail. In May 2016, Director of National Intelligence (DNI) James Clapper (2010–2017) authorized examining "publicly available" social media pages of applicants as part of their suitability check. (Many commercial firms now routinely look at the social media pages of job applicants.)

The polygraph, sometimes mistakenly referred to as a lie detector, is a machine that monitors physical responses (such as pulse and breathing rate) to a series of questions. Changes in physical responses may indicate falsehoods or deceptions. The use of the polygraph by U.S. intelligence remains controversial, as it is imperfect and can be deceived. A 2002 study by the National Research Council found that polygraphs are more useful in criminal investigations, where specific questions can be asked, than for counterintelligence, where the questions are more general and therefore are more likely to yield false-positive responses.

At least three spies, Larry Wu-tai Chin, Aldrich Ames, and Ana Belen Montes, passed polygraph tests while they were involved in espionage against the United States. According to press reports, the Obama administration launched criminal investigations of individuals who claimed they could teach people how to "beat" polygraphs.

Advocates of the polygraph argue that it does serve as a deterrent. They are also quick to assert that the machine is only a tool that can point to problem areas, some of which may be resolved without prejudice. However, an individual's inability or failure to resolve such issues can lead to termination. In addition to new employees, current employees are polygraphed at intervals of several years; contractors are also subject to polygraphs; and the machines are used with new human sources defectors. Polygraphs are not used consistently throughout the national security structure, however. CIA, Defense Intelligence Agency (DIA), National Reconnaissance Office (NRO), and National Security Agency (NSA) all use polygraphs; the State Department and Congress do not. The Federal Bureau of Investigation (FBI) began using polygraphs in the aftermath of the 2001 Robert Hanssen espionage case, which revealed that polygraphs had not been in use at the FBI. This is not to suggest that some agencies are more rigorous or more lax than others. But it does underscore a range of standards in terms of personnel security.

Despite the fact that so many agencies use polygraphs as part of their security practice, there is no standard procedure for these tests. Each agency administers polygraphs to its own standards, which, according to press accounts, can lead to different results for the same subject. Also, agencies do not accept one another's polygraph results, which can be interpreted as either rigor or the lack of an agreed baseline.

Categorizing the different types of polygraph exams depends on the questions being asked and the information being sought. Thus, intelligence agencies have what they call the **lifestyle poly** (personal behavior) and the **counterintelligence poly** (foreign contacts, handling of classified information). In some instances, such as vetting an intelligence source, only a few pertinent questions are asked.

In 2012, DNI Clapper announced some changes in polygraph policy, including requiring agencies to accept each other's polygraph results; requiring that "relevant" law enforcement or national security information discovered during a polygraph be reported, such as criminal behavior; and requiring a polygraph question about leaking classified information. In 2015, the Office of the DNI (ODNI) announced that a question about "unauthorized disclosures of classified information" would be added to polygraph examinations. However, critics held that these changes did not address some perceived abuses, such as personal questions that had little relevance to the granting of a clearance.

Beyond taking a polygraph (known as "being put on the box"), employees and prospective employees are evaluated for other possible indicators of disloyalty. Changes in personal behavior or lifestyle—marital problems, increased use of alcohol, suspected use of drugs, increased personal spending that seems to exceed known resources, running up large debts—may be signs that an individual is spying or susceptible to being recruited or volunteering to spy. Any of these personal difficulties may befall an individual who would never consider becoming a spy, but past espionage cases indicate some reason for concern. For many years, individuals with security clearances would be leery about seeking mental health assistance out of concern that this might jeopardize their clearances. This was eventually changed to allow for a range of counseling, including counseling for family issues, grief, marital issues, and sexual assault. (*See box, "Why Spy?"*) The response of counterintelligence agents to the discovery of such problems depends on the suspect's larger patterns of behavior, how long the problem persists, and evidence of potentially hostile activity. In the aftermath of the Ames case—in which marginal performance, alcohol abuse, and a sudden increase in fairly ostentatious personal spending should have been taken as indicators of a problem—U.S. intelligence increased the amount of personal financial information that intelligence personnel must report on a regular basis. These financial-reporting forms assume, however, that ill-gotten gains show up in some way that is detectable with or without the cooperation of the recipient—cash, stocks, or new homes, cars, and so forth bought with cash received. However, as was learned from both the Ames and the Hanssen cases, the country supporting the espionage may be putting some or all of the money in escrow accounts that will not be detected—or even accessed—until years after the espionage is completed. Again, the cases of Ames and Hanssen are instructive. Ames's lifestyle clearly changed—new house, new car, better clothes, cosmetic dental work—but all this occurred before the financial-reporting forms were required. Outwardly, Hanssen's life showed no signs of increased wealth.

WHY SPY?

U.S. counterintelligence emphasizes personal financial issues in assessing security risks. Many people involved in the worst espionage cases suffered by the United States—Aldrich Ames, Robert Hanssen, the Walker spy ring, Ronald Pelton, Harold Nicholson—were motivated largely by greed, not ideology. Some exceptions were Julius Rosenberg and Alger Hiss (both for the Soviet Union), Larry Wu-tai Chin (for China), and Ana Belen Montes and Kendall Myers (both for Cuba). By contrast, many involved in the worst espionage cases in Britain—Kim Philby and his associates or George Blake, for example—spied because of ideological devotion to the Soviet Union.

Although espionage cases of either type (greed or ideology) can arise in either country, some observers have been struck by the difference. It can be explained, in part, by the fact that Britain has had (and still has) a class system that makes ideology a more likely reason for betrayal, although the most serious British spies have come from the upper class. In the United States, the main competition has always been based on economic status, not social class.

Spies may also be motivated by vengeance toward superiors or agencies, by blackmail against themselves or family members, by thrills, or by involvement with a foreign national. Still, until recently, most of the spies suffered by the United States have been motivated primarily by money. However, a Defense Department study released in April 2008 found that "divided loyalty" between the United States and the nation enlisting the spy had greatly increased as a motive for espionage.

Counterintelligence officers summarize the possible motives for espionage as MICE:

Money

Ideology

Compromise (or coercion)

Ego

David L. Charney, a psychiatrist who has interviewed several confessed spies, describes "injuries to pride and ego" and an "intolerable sense of personal failure" as key motivators for those who decide to spy.

Another internal means of thwarting espionage attacks is the classification system. In U.S. intelligence parlance, the system is **compartmented**. In other words, an employee being accorded the privilege of a clearance does not automatically get access to all of the intelligence information available. Admission to various compartments had been based on a **need to know**. Thus, someone working on a new imagery system is likely to have different clearances than someone involved in running

HUMINT. There are also compartments within compartments. For example, a clearance involving HUMINT may include only specific cases or types of HUMINT—perhaps proliferation or narcotics.

Although "need to know" was the standard for decades, in the aftermath of the 2001 terrorist attacks, many observers believed that this standard also served to impede the necessary sharing of intelligence. In 2003, the intelligence community began to stress the "need to share," an important shift in emphasis. Many also believed it was necessary to get away from the notion of various agencies—especially those that collect intelligence—"owning" the intelligence they produced. The clearest sign of this "data ownership" concept was the classification marking ORCON, or "originator controlled." ORCON means that any further distribution of intelligence or its inclusion in another document must be approved by the originating agency. ORCON reflects the concern that the intelligence could reveal a sensitive source or method, a sensitivity that those wishing to use the intelligence more broadly might not appreciate. ORCON, even if necessary, was also a major impediment in intelligence sharing. The Information Security Oversight Office (ISOO), which is part of the National Archives, reports annually to the president on the security classification system. For FY2012, ISOO reported a decrease in ORCON classification decisions, with the State Department the most active, ordering over half of the more than 73,000 ORCON actions.

In 2007, DNI Mike McConnell (2007–2009) signaled a change in emphasis by promulgating a **"responsibility to provide"** standard. In other words, officers and agencies now would be evaluated by the degree to which they actively seek to share intelligence. This is far from the old "need to know" standard but, as with all other DNI initiatives, the question remains as to how this new standard will be enforced and what sanctions can be imposed against those who fail to measure up. In the aftermath of the leak to WikiLeaks of thousands of State Department cables, all of which were easily accessible on a secret-level Defense Department system, and Snowden's revelations about NSA, and subsequent multiple leaks, there is more pressure to restrict access than to improve intelligence sharing.

In response to the Snowden leaks, NSA announced new security measures for systems administrators, which was Snowden's function. Now two systems administrators will have to be present to access or to move certain information, and data storage rooms with sensitive servers will also require two persons to gain access. This is similar to the rules for two-person crews controlling nuclear-armed land-based missiles, designed to prevent accidental or unauthorized launches. The irony is that the very information technology that enables many of the intelligence community's capabilities and achievements has also become a major source of vulnerability in terms of safeguarding intelligence information. It is much easier to access and remove large amounts of data that are stored digitally than it is with hardcopy material. The case of Harold Martin is illustrative. Martin was a contractor employee at NSA, who removed 50 terabytes of data, in both hard and soft copy, from NSA and was arrested in 2016. It was unclear if Martin had removed the material to commit espionage, for his own personal use, or because he was simply a unique hoarder. In 2018, Martin pleaded guilty to a felony of "willful retention of national defense information." The Martin case highlighted other issues as Martin had exhibited behaviors—falling into debt, binge drinking, and computer harassment—that should have raised security concerns.

Different problems in security classification and sharing have been raised by homeland security issues, where such information may have to be shared with state, local, tribal, or private-sector individuals who do not have clearances. This issue first arose in 2002 when the Department of Homeland Security (DHS) was created. Sen. Richard Shelby, R-AL, then chairman of the Senate Intelligence Committee, insisted that Director of Central Intelligence (DCI) George J. Tenet (1997–2004) share raw intelligence with DHS Secretary Tom Ridge. Tenet refused and was supported by Ridge, who said DHS did not need to see the raw intelligence but would work on the understanding that if the DCI passed along intelligence, it should be deemed serious and actionable. Still, in a federal system like the United States, sharing classified information remains an issue. In 2010, President Barack Obama signed an executive order (EO 13549) creating a program to allow for both sharing and safeguarding information with these nonfederal entities. Typically, access is granted at the secret level, although higher access can be granted on a case-by-case basis.

The clearance and classification system that remains in place limits access and in theory reduces the damage that can be caused by any one source of leaks, although the breadth of the Snowden and other leaks calls into question these assumptions. The system is not without costs. It may become an obstacle to analysis, either wittingly or inadvertently, by excluding some analysts from a compartment crucial to their work. Despite the "responsibility to provide" standard, intelligence sharing still has difficulties, some of which stem from the necessary safeguards. Administering such a system has direct costs: devising a system, tracking documents, running security checks on employees, and so forth. Indirect costs include safes, couriers, security officers to check officers' clearances, and color-coded or numerically tagged papers, to name a few. This list gives some sense of what is involved in a thorough classification scheme. Indeed, if such a scheme is not thorough, it is nothing more than annoying and wasteful. ISOO reported that the total cost of protecting classified information (government and industry) for FY2017 was $18.39 billion, which was an increase of 9 percent, from FY2016.

Other safeguards include the certified destruction of discarded material; the use of secure phones, which cannot be easily tapped, for classified conversations; and restricted access to buildings or to parts of buildings where sensitive material is used. These are called sensitive compartmented information facilities (SCIFs). Finally, employees and former employees with current or past access to classified materials are required by agreements they have signed, in the United States, to have anything they write submitted for "prepublication review." In 1980, the Supreme Court upheld the legality of these agreements. This decision had been prompted by the publication of a memoir by a former CIA officer, Frank Snepp, who was then sued by the CIA, which won the case and had Snepp's royalties attached. This sometimes leads to controversy either when authors do not agree with requested changes or when individuals do not submit their works for review. In 2010, the Defense Department purchased and destroyed 9,500 copies of a book written by a Reserve Army officer who had had his manuscript reviewed by the Army but not the Defense Department. In 2012, press reports said that the CIA was reviewing its publication review process in response to concerns that the process favored more positive works and was used to censor critics. The CIA did not comment on these reports. (As noted in the preface, the book you are now reading was submitted for prepublication review.)

The process by which individuals are vetted for hiring by the intelligence community has also come under scrutiny and some pressure for change, especially in the aftermath of Snowden's leaks. Much has been made of the fact that Snowden was a contractor. Although there are certain "inherently governmental functions" that contractors may not perform—such as prosecutions, obligating funds or acquisition decisions, and so on—beyond that, contractors are used interchangeably and seamlessly with government employees in many offices. One of the ironies of the Snowden case is that background security checks had been conducted by contractors rather than government employees. Once a contractor is given a clearance and is put in position, the degree of access will depend not only on his or her job but also on the way in which classified information is being handled overall in terms of access. Both Bradley Manning and Snowden appear to have been able to access fairly broad amounts of information. A 2012 study by the U.S. Government Accountability Office (GAO) found that the policies and procedures used to determine if a position requires a security clearance were not clear or consistent and called upon the DNI to improve this.

Ironically, one of the reasons contractors were used to conduct security clearances was congressional pressure to speed up the process, especially as hiring increased after the 2001 attacks. For private-sector firms conducting background investigations, the number of investigations completed and completed quickly were major means of increasing revenue. In the aftermath of Snowden and a non-intelligence case (Aaron Alexis, who killed twelve people at the Washington Navy Yard in September 2013 and had been granted a clearance despite apparently evident mental health issues), Congress moved to limit the use of contractors for security vetting. The firm that vetted Snowden and Alexis, USIS LLC, was accused by the Office of Personnel Management (OPM) of falsifying many of its investigations. In 2014, USIS's records were hacked. OPM dropped USIS as a contractor. OPM also resumed quality-control review for personnel investigations. In February 2014, the SCORE Act (Security Clearance Oversight and Reform Enhancement) was passed, giving the inspector general of OPM access to funds to increase oversight of background investigations. Issues like these are often pendulums, set in motion by political concerns that may have little to do with the function at hand.

The security clearance process has also come under scrutiny as a result of a cyber intrusion into the personnel records held by OPM. In June 2015, OPM said that the personnel records of 21.5 million current and former federal employees had been compromised. Many of these employees hold or held security clearances. Although federal officials were cautious not to fix attribution for the OPM breach, it is widely assumed to have been done by China, which China admitted, blaming criminals as opposed to government employees. An added concern is that China—or anyone else with access to the OPM data—could use it to identify U.S. clandestine service officers posted overseas under official cover if their records as stated in their cover job do not show up in the OPM data, a major counterintelligence problem. There are also concerns that given access to the OPM system, the data could be manipulated, raising issues about its future reliability. There have also been press reports about similar intrusions, again attributed to China, at other U.S. government agencies.

In January 2016, the Obama administration announced a new structure for handling personnel clearance information. The data itself would be kept by the Defense

Department, with greater security safeguards than had been the case in the past, and responsibility for conducting clearance checks was given to a new entity, the National Background Investigations Bureau, which was still part of OPM. However, concerns were now raised about the backlog of security investigations and the length of time required to complete a security background check, both of which delayed hiring new personnel in both the government and in private-sector firms that do classified work. In late 2018, the number of cases in the backlog was estimated to be around 500,000, some 70 percent of which are in Defense. However, this is not a stagnant number, as some 200,000 cases move in and out each year. The time required to complete a security background check in 2018 averaged 18 months. In April 2019, President Trump signed an executive order moving all security investigations into the Defense Department. This will allow the Defense Department to work to reduce its portion of the backlog, but some observers wonder if Defense understands, or is willing to take on, the broader responsibilities for security clearance activities across the civilian part of the government.

Many security experts urge the adoption of a continuous monitoring and evaluation system for cleared personnel, citing personnel policies in the financial sector as an example. Currently, cleared personnel are supposed to be reviewed every five years, but often the interval is longer. The DNI, working through the National Counterintelligence and Security Center (NCSC) has begun implementing a continuous evaluation program, in which databases, such as financial records, will be used to supplement the more traditional interviews and investigations. The National Geospatial-Intelligence Agency (NGA) is experimenting with "sentiment analysis" software, called SCOUT, that analyzes the emotional content of emails, work chats, and social media on work-related systems. A key, of course, will be to weed out false positives.

Major leak cases also revive the discussion of the number of people holding clearances. For FY2016, 4,080,728 government employees and contractors were eligible to hold clearances, a decrease 168,325 or 4 percent from 2015, according to the ODNI. Of the overall eligible total, 1,240,675 did not currently have access to classified material. It is important to understand that contractors hold clearances because the government requires this if they are going to do classified work. Therefore, the numbers are driven by government needs and not contractor desires. Indeed, contractors incur large costs for the infrastructure required to maintain clearances and classified work areas.

Another security clearance issue has been **reciprocity**, meaning the willingness—or unwillingness—of agencies to accept the validity of clearances granted by other agencies, thus requiring new investigations and adjudications of people who have already been cleared by one agency. As clearances have been managed on an agency-by-agency basis, several agencies claimed that their system or approach was more rigorous. In November 2018, DNI Dan Coats (2017–2019) issued a directive essentially mandating reciprocity across all relevant agencies, including the military. The issue will be the willingness of agencies to comply and the ability of the DNI to oversee the process and to enforce compliance, which has sometimes been an issue in the intelligence community.

Managers and applicants have all decried the time it takes to hire new personnel. It is also an expense for the intelligence community, costing perhaps as much as

$10,000 per potential employee. From a security point of view, it is likely preferable to be overly rigorous during the hiring process rather than take a chance on letting a potential security risk get inside the system. This has been characterized by many observers as a "risk-avoidance" approach. This approach has many results, some intended, some not. It means that the vetting process is more thorough but also longer. The intelligence community is aware that this has, on occasion, cost them would-be employees who could not afford to wait out the nine or more months needed to check backgrounds. It also means, in a period of greatly increased hiring, like the one that began across the intelligence community in 2001, that hiring delays will likely increase.

The risk-avoidance approach also means that some candidates who may not actually pose a security risk will not be hired because of the guiding cautious approach. DNI McConnell noted the need to improve the hiring of first-generation Americans "whose native language skills and cultural experiences" are most needed. There is evidence to suggest that these candidates face particular burdens under the risk-avoidance approach, out of fear of divided loyalties, family left behind whose influence is unknown or who could become subject to external pressure, and so on. FBI employees who were born overseas or who have relatives or friends overseas face more intense security scrutiny in the Post-Adjudication Risk Management (PARM) plan, which the FBI sees as a risk-management plan. FBI supervisors say there are no adverse effects to being in PARM and that it is simply a way to assess vulnerabilities. Employees who have been in PARM disagree. There is an irony here in that most of the worst espionage breaches suffered by the United States came from individuals whose families had been here for generations. This is not to discount the problem of **sleeper agents**—that is, agents sent to another nation to assume normal lives who then become active agents at some time later. The 2010 expulsion of ten Russian sleeper agents underscores the continuing problem.

DNI McConnell sought to move from the risk-avoidance security approach to a "risk-management" approach. This implies a willingness to give the benefit of the doubt to some applicants or employees rather than to try to run a system that wards off any potential risks, which clearly is not possible. As sensible as this approach may be, it can run into opposition from those people who are supposed to administer it, the individuals responsible for personnel security. These individuals are unlikely to see any benefit to clearing more people if this means they have also cleared the individual who becomes a security threat. The personnel security staff may also recognize that they will be the ones who are asked to explain how breaches got through in the first place. This personnel policy shift is another interesting test of the DNI's authority over intelligence officers who work in agencies that the DNI does not control directly. Finally, it is important to remember that security rules do not exist in a vacuum. Rather, they coexist with several other policy goals, at least in democracies. These goals include the necessity and desire of governments to be transparent and to give their citizens access to certain types of information. This does not equate to access to any and all information, but it does occasionally raise issues about where to draw the line, one way or the other, or how long information should remain classified and the rules for declassification. All of these tensions exist in the United States.

The security clearance issue became highly politicized with the advent of the Trump administration in 2017. First, there was the issue of clearances for the new White House staff, some of whom spent prolonged periods with interim clearances while their cases were adjudicated, including Trump's son-in-law and senior adviser, Jared Kushner. In 2018, White House chief of staff John Kelly took steps to improve the White House process by improving liaison with the FBI and expediting the transmission of "significant derogatory information." Kelly also banned any further use of interim clearances for new hires.

Second, and more controversial, was Trump's decision in August 2018 to remove the security clearances held by former DCIA John Brennan (2013–2017). Former senior national security officials retain clearances largely as a courtesy, so that they can offer advice when asked by their successors. Brennan repeatedly expressed his extreme discontent with Trump's tenure in a series of Twitter postings. As a result, Trump lifted Brennan's clearance. Although most observers believed Trump had the authority to do so, the action was unprecedented in that it was the White House taking this action and not the agency holding Brennan's clearances, in this case the CIA. Most of the former DCIs, DNIs, and their deputies signed a letter protesting Trump's action, as did several hundred former intelligence and national security officials. Although not necessarily supporting what Brennan said, they defended his right to do so. There are thirteen administrative reasons for which a clearance can be revoked (substance abuse problems, criminal activity, security violations, and so on). Disagreeing with or speaking harshly about a president and his policies is not among them.

EXTERNAL INDICATORS AND COUNTERESPIONAGE

Besides internal measures taken to prevent or to identify problems, counterintelligence agents look for external indicators of problems. They may be more obvious, such as the sudden loss of a spy network overseas, a change in military exercise patterns that corresponds to satellite tracks, or a penetration of the other service's apparatus that reveals the possibility of one's own having been penetrated as well. This apparently is how Robert Hanssen was detected. According to Russian press sources, the ten Russian sleepers arrested in the United States in 2010 were also identified by a Russian intelligence officer who had defected. The indicators may be more subtle—the odd botched operation or failed espionage meeting or a negotiation in which the other side seems to be anticipating one's bottom line. These are all murkier indicators of a leak or penetration—what some have described as a "wilderness of mirrors."

In 1995, the CIA and NSA published signal intelligence (SIGINT) intercepts (code-named VENONA) that had been used to detect Soviet espionage in the United States. From 1943 to 1957, VENONA products helped identify Alger Hiss, Julius Rosenberg, Klaus Fuchs, and others working for Soviet intelligence. As VENONA showed, SIGINT can offer indications of ongoing espionage, although the references to spying may be oblique and are unlikely to identify the spy outright. The VENONA intercepts used code names for the spies but often provided enough information to help narrow the search.

The serious problems resulting from having been penetrated by a hostile service also highlight the gains to be made by carrying out one's own successful penetration of the hostile service. Among the intelligence that may be gathered are the following:

- An opponent's HUMINT capabilities and targets, strengths, weaknesses, and techniques

- The identity of clandestine service officers

- An opponent's main areas of intelligence interest and current shortfalls

- Possible penetrations of one's own service or other services

- Possible intelligence alliances (for example, the Soviet-era KGB used Polish émigrés in the United States for some defense industry espionage and Bulgarian operatives for "wet affairs"—assassinations)

- Sudden changes in an opponent's HUMINT operations—new needs, new taskings, changed focuses, a recall of agents from a specific region—each of which can have a host of meanings

Discovering the presence of foreign agents may not lead automatically to their arrest. The agents also present opportunities, as they are conduits back to their own intelligence services, which takes us into the realm of counterespionage. At a minimum, efforts can be made to curtail some of their access without their becoming aware of it and then false information can be fed to them to send home to confuse their analyses. Alternatively, counterintelligence officers may try a more aggressive approach, attempting to turn them into **double agents** who, although apparently continuing their activities, then provide information on their erstwhile employer and knowingly pass back erroneous information. (Britain's Double Cross system was very effective at turning German agents into double agents during World War II. Fidel Castro apparently was also successful with U.S. agents sent against his regime in Cuba.) But just as there are double agents, so there are triple agents—agents who have been turned once, discovered, and then turned again by their own side. The effect, again, is a wilderness of mirrors.

Counterespionage also underscores the use of "dangles," discussed earlier. (See chap. 5, HUMINT.) One way to probe or to identify hostile counterintelligence activities is to dangle a supposed spy in front of a foreign service and see how they react and how they handle the dangle. (When Hanssen first approached the Soviets, they apparently protested about what they believed to be a dangle, which the United States denied doing but did not follow up as to why the Soviets had raised this at the time.)

PROBLEMS IN COUNTERINTELLIGENCE

Several problems arise in assessing counterintelligence operations. First, by its very nature, any CI penetration is going to be clandestine. Counterintelligence officers are unlikely to come across initially compelling evidence about a successful hostile penetration.

Second, the basic tendency within any intelligence organization (or any organization, for that matter) is to trust its own people, who have been vetted and cleared. They work with one another every day. Familiarity can lead to lowering one's guard or being unwilling to believe that one's own people may be disloyal. This appears to have been a problem in uncovering the espionage of Ames; the CIA was slow to look inward for the cause of severe losses of assets in Moscow. It was originally thought that Hanssen escaped detection for more than twenty years because of his familiarity with U.S. counterintelligence policy and techniques. However, a 2003 report by the inspector general of the Justice Department (the FBI is part of that department) found that internal laxity and poor oversight allowed Hanssen, who was portrayed as erratic and bumbling, to avoid detection. Most telling, the FBI first concentrated on a CIA officer when hunting for the spy who turned out to be one of their own—Hanssen. It is easier to believe that the problem lies in another agency. Similarly, fellow employees apparently did not ask why Edward Snowden, a systems administrator, was asking for their computer passwords.

But the alternative behavior—unwarranted suspicion—can be just as debilitating as having a spy in one's midst. James Angleton, who was in charge of the CIA's counterintelligence from 1954 to 1974, became convinced that a Soviet **mole**—a deeply hidden spy—had penetrated the CIA. Some believed that Angleton was reacting to the fact that his close British associate, Kim Philby, had turned out to be a Soviet agent. Angleton was unable to find the mole, and some believe that he tied the CIA in knots by placing virtually anyone under suspicion. Some suggested that Angleton himself was the mole and that he created a furor to divert attention. Angleton remains a controversial figure, but his activities give some indication of the intellectual issues that can be involved in spying and counterintelligence.

For many years, counterintelligence was a major source of friction between the CIA and the FBI. Some of the friction was a legacy of longtime FBI director J. Edgar Hoover's resentment toward the CIA and that agency's reciprocation of Hoover's feelings. The friction also stemmed from differing views of the problem. A discovered spy is a problem as well as a counterespionage opportunity that the CIA may wish to exploit. Counterespionage can be thought of as a subset of the larger counterintelligence issue. CI seeks to thwart or exploit any and all attempts to undercut or penetrate intelligence activities. Counterespionage works against the HUMINT aspects (both offensive and defensive) of the CI problem. For the FBI, spying is a prelude to prosecution. As late as the Ames case of the early 1990s, the CIA and the FBI were not coordinating their counterintelligence efforts, which probably prolonged Ames's activities. As a result of his arrest and the subsequent investigation, the CIA and the FBI created a jointly staffed counterintelligence office to correct the mistakes of the past.

Like so much else in intelligence, suspicions of espionage may not always be proved. The case of Wen Ho Lee, a scientist at Los Alamos National Laboratory, is instructive but complex. In brief, Lee's case came up hard on the heels of a congressional report put out by the Cox Committee (U.S. House Select Committee on U.S. National Security and Military/Commercial Concerns with the People's Republic of

China, 1999), which was headed by Rep. Christopher Cox, R-CA, and investigated a series of allegations about Chinese spying that largely targeted high-end technology, including U.S. nuclear weapons designs. Given the issues involved, the Department of Energy (DOE) and the national laboratories were likely places to look. (A series of nasty arguments also played out in public between current and former DOE intelligence and counterintelligence officers, as well as between some of them and the FBI, over the issue of responsibility.) Lee, who was born in Taiwan, had been under investigation since 1994, but the investigation was fitful and inconclusive. He had downloaded some 400,000 pages of classified nuclear data unrelated to his work at Los Alamos. In 2000, Lee was arrested, charged with fifty-nine counts, and held in jail for more than nine months, mostly in solitary confinement. However, the government was unable to discover evidence of espionage, that is, passing the material to a foreign power. A Justice Department report castigated the FBI's handling of the investigation, concluding that if Lee was a spy, the FBI let him get away, and if he was not a spy, the bureau failed to consider other lines of investigation. Lee was eventually released and agreed to plead guilty to one felony count of illegally downloading sensitive nuclear data. The case remains, at best, inconclusive. This calls to mind Scottish law, which gives a jury the option to return a verdict of "not proven," instead of either guilty or not guilty.

In intermediate cases, officers come under suspicion for reasons other than espionage but still pose risks. A good example is Edward Howard, a CIA Directorate of Operations (DO) officer who was slated to be posted to Moscow in the 1980s. Howard was revealed to have ongoing drug and criminal problems that made the posting impossible. He was suspected of being a counterintelligence problem, but handling the situation was difficult. If sending him to Moscow was not an option, he would have to be reassigned or fired. If he were reassigned, he would still be in a position to see classified material even though he remained a security risk because of his personal behavior. Moreover, he would most likely feel aggrieved because of the cancellation of his overseas posting, making him an ever bigger risk. Alternatively, to fire him was risky, as he had thorough knowledge of DO tradecraft plus information about operations in Moscow. Once fired, it would be difficult, if not impossible, to keep watch on him. Ultimately, Howard was fired, but he was kept under FBI surveillance. He eluded surveillance (using techniques he learned as a DO officer) and fled to Moscow, claiming that he had not been a spy but had been driven away by the CIA. David Wise, a veteran intelligence author and sometimes critic of U.S. intelligence, interviewed Howard in Moscow and came away convinced that Howard's disloyalty predated his flight.

Some who deal with counterintelligence make a distinction between **big CI** and **little CI**. If a spy is revealed in one's organization, it is important to determine the reasons why he or she went after specific information. Was this tied to some specific need or tasking or was it simply opportunistic? If one is able to answer this question, it will reveal the nature of the penetration and the goals of the nation running the spy. All of this comes under "big CI." Beyond this, there are still the specific issues surrounding the penetration: how it happened, how long it has been going on, who on the other side has been responsible for tasking and for running the penetration, what information may have been compromised, issues of tradecraft. All of these are "little CI" issues. It is like the distinction made in military operations between strategy (big CI) and tactics (little CI).

Once a spy has been identified and arrested (or, in the case of some foreigners with diplomatic status, expelled), the intelligence community conducts a **damage assessment** to determine what intelligence has been compromised. Having the cooperation of the captured spy would be useful. In the United States, this cooperation often becomes a major negotiating point between government prosecutors and the spy's attorney: cooperation in exchange for a specific sentence or for consideration for the spy's family. (The wives of Ames and Pollard also received short prison terms for their complicity in their husband's espionage, serving five years and three years, respectively. Hanssen's wife knew at least about his first period of espionage. However, she was allowed to keep the survivor portion of Hanssen's federal pension.) As with everything else in counterintelligence, however, issues always linger. The most obvious is the degree to which the spy is being honest and forthcoming. Those conducting the damage assessment must avoid the temptation to use the fact of a discovered spy to explain intelligence losses that are unrelated to that person's espionage. The focus must stay firmly on the intelligence to which the spy had access. More than one spy may have been operating at the same time, with access to the same intelligence. This appears to have been the case with Ames and Hanssen, whose espionage was contemporaneous and who had access to some of the same intelligence. Thus, the Hanssen damage assessment likely required a reexamination of the Ames damage assessment, perhaps without any definitive conclusions. The Soviets or, later, the Russians could have used one set of information to confirm the other, thus having Ames and Hanssen ironically confirming each other's bona fides as useful spies.

Double agents raise a host of concerns about loyalty. Have they been turned, or are they playing a role while remaining loyal to their own service? Investigations of U.S. citizens suspected of spying bring up legal issues because of constitutional safeguards on civil liberties. Domestic telephones can be tapped, but only after intelligence agents have obtained a warrant from a special federal court (the Foreign Intelligence Surveillance Court), which was set up by the Foreign Intelligence Surveillance Act of 1978 (FISA, pronounced "fy-za"). (See chap. 10 for a discussion of this court.) Agents also use other intrusive techniques, such as listening devices in the suspect's home or office; searches of home or office when the suspect is absent, including making copies of computer files; and going through garbage.

Prosecuting intelligence officers for spying was a major concern for the intelligence agencies, which feared that accused spies would threaten to reveal classified information in open court as a means of avoiding prosecution. This is known as **"graymail"** (as opposed to blackmail). To preclude this possibility, Congress in 1980 passed the Classified Intelligence Procedures Act (also known as the Graymail Law), which allows judges to review classified material in secret, so that the prosecution can proceed without fear of publicly disclosing sensitive intelligence.

In 1999, as part of a government-wide response to revelations about Chinese espionage, the FBI proposed splitting its National Security division into two separate units, one to deal with counterespionage and the other with terrorism. In 2003, the FBI created an Intelligence Division, concentrating primarily on terrorism. The 2004 intelligence legislation formally recognized the new office as the Intelligence

Directorate. The FBI also proposed broadening the National Security Threat List, on which it assesses counterespionage threats, to include corporations and international criminal organizations as well as foreign governments.

In June 2005, President George W. Bush ordered a restructuring of both the Justice Department and the FBI. The position of assistant attorney general for national security was created, overseeing counterterrorism, counterespionage, and intelligence policy. The FBI now has a National Security Branch, which oversees the new Directorate of Intelligence and the Counterterrorism and Counterintelligence Divisions, and the Weapons of Mass Destruction Division. The National Security Branch is headed by an executive assistant director, who is the FBI's primary liaison to the DNI for coordination of activities and budget. Interestingly, the branch deputy has been a senior CIA officer.

In addition to the FBI, which has the primary counterintelligence responsibility in the United States, and the CIA, the Defense Investigative Service and the counterintelligence units of virtually all intelligence agencies or offices share some CI responsibility. The diffusion of the CI effort reflects the organization of the community and also highlights why coordination on CI cases has been problematic. To remedy this, Congress, in 2002, passed the Counterintelligence Enhancement Act, which called for the creation of what is now the National Counterintelligence and Security Center (NCSC, established 2014; formerly the National Counterintelligence Executive, NCIX). The NCSC is the head of U.S. counterintelligence and is responsible for developing counterintelligence plans and policies. This includes an annual strategic CI plan, a national CI strategy, and the oversight and coordination of CI damage assessments. The intelligence law of 2004 puts the NCSC under the DNI. NCSC has no control, however, over the agencies or offices that conduct counterintelligence. Therefore, there is something of a disconnect between the office creating a fairly broad and general strategy and those offices responsible for actually conducting counterintelligence.

LEAKS

Leaks are a constant security concern. They may not be seen as dangerous as an espionage penetration, but they can have obvious counterintelligence concerns, because leaks often entail the unauthorized release of classified information. It is a generally held view that the leak problem is much worse now than it has ever been, but this perception was prevalent through much of the latter twentieth century. (President Franklin D. Roosevelt, decrying leaks during his tenure, wondered why the British had so many fewer leaks, even though Britain had freedom of speech and tea parties.)

Once a leak occurs, the agency whose information has been compromised can ask the Justice Department to open a criminal probe. However, there are two immediate impediments. The first is that, in many cases, too many people have had access to the information to be able to pin down the source of the leak. Agencies keep "**bigot lists**" of people with access to certain categories of intelligence, but these are often rather lengthy rather than exclusive. The second is the legal basis for prosecuting a leak. Several nations, including Britain, Canada, and India, have laws protecting classified information and creating legal penalties for unauthorized disclosure. But there is no single U.S. statute covering leaks. The Intelligence Identities Protection Act (1982) makes it a crime for someone who has access to classified information to knowingly reveal the identity of a clandestine agent. It is also a crime to engage in a "pattern of activities" intended to reveal the identity of a clandestine agent or agents. This law was passed in reaction to the 1975 assassination of Richard Welch, the CIA chief of station in Athens. The "pattern of activities" clause was aimed at individuals such as former CIA officer Philip Agee, who made a practice of revealing the identity of CIA case officers overseas after he quit the CIA. This act was also initially at issue in the 2003 revelation that Valerie Plame was a CIA officer, which was part of the larger Iraq weapons of mass destruction (WMD) controversy. However, Lewis Libby, then chief of staff to Vice President Richard Cheney, who became the focus of the leak investigation, was convicted in 2007 of obstruction of justice, perjury, and making false statements to federal investigators, and not of the leak itself. The Plame leak investigation also led to questions about the roles and responsibility of the press with regard to classified information. (See chap. 13.)

In 2011, President Obama signed an executive order (EO 13587) designed to make structural reforms to improve security on classified networks while also allowing for the sharing of classified information. This executive order included a mandate to create an Insider Threat Program to deter, detect, and mitigate **insider threats**. The details of this program came to light in 2013, after the Snowden leaks. According to press reports, this program covers not only classified material but any other leaks and includes many agencies beyond the intelligence community. The program is based, in part, on federal employees and contractors looking for and reporting "high-risk persons or behaviors"—many similar to the indicators for espionage—and also imposes penalties for failing to report them. The program also includes greater protection for whistle-blowers who use proper internal channels to report fraud, waste, and abuse. In late 2015, the Defense Insider Threat Management Analysis Center (DITMAC) was stood up under the Defense Security Service (DSS). DITMAC is the central clearinghouse for collecting and coordinating potentially "adverse" information about employees and other people with access to Defense facilities. DITMAC is not responsible for detecting and acting on threats. Critics of the program note the large number of people holding clearances and argue that the indicators for high-risk behaviors are set rather low and are also somewhat subjective, which may result in a plethora of false reports. Concern about insider threats again raises issues about the personnel security system and the need for more frequent, if not continuous, evaluations. This was one of the recommendations made by the National Insider Threat Task Force, created under the Obama executive order and part of the National Counterintelligence and Security Center. The task force published its *Insider Threat Program: Maturity Framework* in November 2018.

In 2012, DNI Clapper announced steps designed to deter unauthorized disclosures of national security information. A question related to unauthorized disclosures would be added to the counterintelligence polygraph for all agencies administering that examination (CIA, DIA, DOE, FBI, NGA, NRO, and NSA). Second, the inspector general for the intelligence community would be tasked with leading independent investigations of leaks that the Justice Department declined to prosecute. Parallel efforts to include anti-leak legislation in the intelligence authorization bill failed to pass.

There are technologies that can disable the use of removable storage devices, such as CDs and thumb drives. The Defense Department reportedly bought such a system, the Host Based Security System (HBSS), after the Manning leaks, but it is not clear that it was in place at NSA to prevent the Snowden leaks. The Espionage Act (1917) has been used as the legal basis for leak prosecutions. Enacted months prior to the United States's entry into World War I, this act covers traditional espionage but is also deemed broad enough to cover leaks, even of information that is not classified but is related to the national defense. During World War I, the act was used to jail antiwar protesters, such as U.S. socialist leader Eugene V. Debs, who was convicted of sedition for speaking out against the draft. The Espionage Act was used to convict Samuel L. Morison, a U.S. Navy intelligence officer who provided classified imagery to a British publication with whom he had a business relationship. Morison was convicted in 1985 of espionage and theft of government property.

Use of the Espionage Act became controversial in 2006 when it was used as the basis for prosecuting two officials of the lobbying group the American Israel Public Affairs Committee (commonly called AIPAC) who received classified information from a Defense Department official, Lawrence Franklin, and then passed it on to an Israeli official and a journalist. Franklin pleaded guilty and was sentenced to more than twelve years in prison, later reduced to ten months of house arrest and 100 hours of community service after the cases against the AIPAC lobbyists were dropped. But the cases of the AIPAC officials, Steven J. Rosen and Keith Weissman, were the first use of the Espionage Act to prosecute nongovernment officials for leaking. The FBI also conducted an investigation of AIPAC for connections to Israeli intelligence. The judge in the case refused to dismiss the charges on the claim made by the defendants' lawyers that the use of the Espionage Act infringed on their clients' right of free speech, but he also raised questions about the applicability of the statute during the trial. He also ruled that the defendants could use classified information in their defense, despite government opposition. In 2009, the Justice Department dropped the charges.

Another aspect of leaks that became controversial was an offshoot of the Plame/Libby case. In 2006, Libby reported that President George W. Bush authorized him in 2003 to discuss aspects of the then-classified 2002 national intelligence estimate (NIE) on Iraq WMD with a reporter. Although the president can decide to declassify information, Bush's action seemed to undercut his administration's complaints about leaking. It can be argued that the president cannot leak because the president also has the right to declassify intelligence, but the motives behind a revelation can be debated, as they were in this case. Similarly, President Obama and other senior officials clearly cooperated with a reporter writing a book about administration policy in Iraq and Afghanistan in Obama's first year in office. At the same time, the Obama administration was much more aggressive than past administrations in prosecuting individuals accused of leaking, with nine prosecutions in all. Some were successful, such as the prosecution of CIA officer John Kiriakou, who was found guilty of leaking information about the identity of CIA officials involved in the rendition and interrogation program. Kiriakou received a sentence of thirty months. However, the case against Thomas Drake, an NSA officer accused of leaking information related to a program that had run into trouble, proved to be problematic. The judge in this case questioned the delays involved in the investigation and ruled that the jury would have to be shown some of the reportedly classified material, which NSA refused to do. Drake pleaded guilty to a misdemeanor and not to felonies under the Espionage Act as originally charged. (Drake and several others charged with NSA leaks have sued several agencies and officials, charging violation of rights, illegal searches, retaliation for whistle-blowing, cancellation of clearances, and so on.) In 2018, Reality Winner, a contractor working for NSA, was sentenced to five years and three months in prison after pleading guilty to leaking information about Russian interference in the 2016 election.

In 2013, Pvt. Bradley Manning was found not guilty of aiding the enemy but was found guilty of other violations of the Espionage Act and sentenced to thirty-five years. The "aiding the enemy" charge in the Manning case disturbed some First Amendment authorities as it advances the legal argument that leaking to the press can be equated to the treason charge if the leaker knows the information may get to an enemy, even by indirect means. Commentators have noted that Manning was charged under military law, but this leaves open whether similar charges could be brought against nonmilitary personnel. Former State Department and FBI employees were also successfully prosecuted by the Obama administration for leaks.

In January 2017, President Obama commuted Manning's sentence to time served, seven years. Finally, the Manning case also raises the issue of what is a journalist under First Amendment protections. Does this include a website like WikiLeaks, whose sole purpose is to publish classified material? The Obama administration struggled with this issue but decided not to indict Julian Assange, the founder and operator of WikiLeaks. However, in November 2018, a federal court filing inadvertently revealed that Assange had been secretly indicted by the United States. In April 2019, Ecuador ended Assange's almost seven-year asylum status at their London embassy, and he was arrested and sentenced to fifty weeks in prison for jumping bail on a Swedish sex assault warrant. After his arrest, the initial U.S. indictment was revealed. Assange was charged with conspiracy to commit computer intrusion against a U.S. government computer, referring to his work with Manning. This charge, which carries a five-year sentence, avoided possible issues regarding Assange's claimed status as a journalist. In May 2019, the U.S. government released a second indictment against Assange, this time covering seventeen counts under the Espionage Act. This second indictment raised concerns among journalists and free press advocates, although some observers questioned whether Assange is a journalist. Snowden has also been indicted under the Espionage Act.

Some observers have argued that there may be a double standard when it comes to prosecuting government leakers, depending on their rank. In March 2015, former DCIA Gen. David Petraeus (2011–2012) pleaded guilty to one misdemeanor for the unauthorized removal and retention of classified material, having shared highly classified material with Paula Broadwell, who was Petraeus's biographer and mistress. Petraeus was sentenced to two years of probation and a $40,000 fine. Former Secretary of State Hillary Clinton (2009–2013) was severely criticized by the FBI for her use of a private, unsecured email server but was not indicted, which also may be seen by critics as a double standard. Finally, in 2016, General James Cartwright, former vice chairman of the Joint Chiefs of Staff, pleaded guilty to making false statements to the FBI concerning an investigation of a leak about supposed U.S.-Israeli operations against Iran. President Obama pardoned Cartwright in 2017, before he was sentenced, at the same time that Manning was pardoned.

All of the cases cited above involved government employees who had access to classified information. The Obama administration was also aggressive about journalists who receive such information. In 2012, the Justice Department secretly seized phone records for Associated Press editors and reporters to investigate a State Department leak. In July 2013, Attorney General Eric Holder announced new guidelines for obtaining journalists' records, including more advanced notice in most cases and a process for news organizations to challenge requests in court. A more complex case involves former CIA officer Jeffrey Sterling and *New York Times* reporter James Risen. Sterling was indicted under the Espionage Act in 2010 for alleged leaks, presumably to Risen. Risen received a subpoena ordering him to reveal some of his sources as part of the Sterling case. Risen lost every legal effort he made to have the subpoena quashed, including an appeal to the Supreme Court. However, at the outset of Sterling's trial in late 2014, Attorney General Holder decided not to call upon Risen to testify, convinced that the reporter would refuse to do so. Sterling was convicted and sentenced to three years and six months. Interestingly, Sterling's attorneys cited Petraeus's plea bargain in requesting a less severe sentence, which Sterling did not receive. In June 2018, James Wolfe, the former head of security for the Senate Intelligence Committee, was accused of lying to the FBI during a leak investigation. In making their case against Wolfe, prosecutors had obtained phone records, but not the actual content, of Ali Watkins, a reporter with whom Wolfe had had a personal relationship. Other journalists objected to this, but there was also the question of journalistic ethics, as Watkins's various employers allowed her to be assigned to a beat, the Senate committee, where she had a personal relationship. Wolfe pleaded guilty to one count of making a false statement to the FBI. He was sentenced to two months in prison.

Presidents, by definition, do not leak. If they say something publicly, it is declassified. For example, U.S. intelligence officials were caught off-guard by the first unclassified acknowledgment that the United States used imagery satellites, which came in a speech made by President Lyndon B. Johnson in 1967. In a June 2011 speech, President Obama acknowledged the U.S. role in the death of Anwar al-Awlaki, a U.S. citizen who was abetting terrorism. However, Obama avoided mentioning how Awlaki had been killed. As noted in chapter 5, President Trump was criticized for sharing foreign liaison intelligence, presumably Israeli, with Russian Foreign Minister Sergei Lavrov, violating the third party rule.

It is important to understand the status of classified information that is leaked. The fact that classified information is released to the public by unauthorized means does not mean that this information is now declassified. The information is still considered to be classified and remains so until declassified by someone with the authority to do so.

An underlying issue regarding leaks is the large amount of material that is classified, some of it incorrectly. As noted in chapter 5, there are rules and definitions by which material is properly classified. Also, as noted before, cases like that of David Petraeus and potentially Hillary Clinton make it more difficult to defend a system that apparently allows exceptions. In March 2016, the Obama administration began a Fundamental Classification Guidance Review to eliminate obsolete requirements and reduce the amount of classified material. The Obama administration created a category called "sensitive but unclassified" (SBU), meaning the information is unclassified but still must be controlled in its distribution. This strikes some security professionals as anomalous, arguing that material is either classified or not, but there is no middle case like SBU.

In April 2017, the ODNI published *Principles of Classification Management for the Intelligence Community*, which promulgates uniform guidelines for classifying and marking **Classified National Security Information (CNSI)**. These include a risk-management strategy for classification decisions to avoid automatic over-classification, and making declassification and downgrading an integral part of the strategy.

A new type of leak has arisen with the advent of sites like WikiLeaks, whose avowed purpose is to publish classified information. WikiLeaks publications to date have involved thousands of documents, underscoring the added security problem created by information technology, which enhances the ability to access, remove, and transfer large amounts of data easily. The leaks have exposed the names of foreigners who have cooperated with the United States and Democratic National Committee emails during the 2016 presidential election. Interestingly, the organizations Amnesty International and Doctors Without Borders have condemned WikiLeaks's activity, making for an unlikely coalition with the Defense Department. There has been a debate within and beyond U.S. intelligence as to whether or not WikiLeaks works for the Russian government. No conclusions have been reached publicly, but it is clear that Russian president Vladimir Putin's foreign policy goal of sowing discord in the West has benefited from WikiLeaks's activity.

In March 2017, WikiLeaks published thousands of pages detailing alleged CIA tools to hack into computers, cell phones, and other technology. The CIA, of course, refused to authenticate the leaks. In June 2018, a former CIA employee, Joshua Schulte, was charged with theft of classified material. A few months before this leak, a group calling itself Shadow Brokers began leaking what it said were tools used by NSA to hack into systems. Reactions to this leak appeared stronger and more concerned than to the CIA leak, especially as various groups began using the stolen NSA tools. According to some press accounts, Israel hacked into the system of Kaspersky, a Russian cyber security firm, and then alerted the United States to the presence of stolen tools. Both cases, involving the CIA and NSA losses, raised new concerns about the intelligence community's vulnerability to leaks and about lost capabilities. Also according to press accounts, the cyber firm Symantec reported that China had captured some NSA tools that were being used in an intrusion on Chinese systems.

A 2013 report by the RAND Corporation on leaks was fairly pessimistic on the likelihood of stemming what the authors called "a culture of leaking." In March 2014, DNI Clapper signed Intelligence Community Directive (ICD) 119, "Media Contacts," limiting such contacts by all intelligence community employees and requiring authorization for all such contacts. The ODNI later offered a clarification that appeared to indicate that a major concern was that intelligence community employees not use leaked material as sourcing when speaking to the press, although the underlying concern about trying to limit press contacts remained.

Leaks, like espionage cases, raise the issue of damage assessments. Both the Manning and Snowden leaks have entailed costs to U.S. diplomatic relations. Manning leaked the details of U.S. diplomatic traffic and assessments of various foreign officials. As noted, Snowden leaked details of intelligence collection in various nations, some of which are U.S. allies. The Snowden leaks also put the collection programs themselves in jeopardy by exposing their existence and how they function. Assessing the damage—or potential damage—done by Snowden may be difficult, as it may never be known with certainty the full extent of the files he copied and took with him.

The large number of leaks, particularly by contractors, also raises issues about relying on contractors for secure support and the insider threat issue. Contractors go through the same security review for clearances as all government employees, so they do not represent an inherently weak link in the security system. There are multiple efforts ongoing to identify insider threats as they develop and before they result in lost intelligence, but these do not appear to be very different from efforts to identify potential spies in advance. As noted, there are some behaviors that may be indicative of a willingness to spy or to leak, but they may also be no more than indicators of personal problems that many people face.

Leaks also raise the issue of the reliability of the United States as an intelligence partner. As noted in chapter 5, there are multiple foreign liaison relationships between U.S. intelligence agencies and their foreign counterparts. These relationships are built on shared interests and on trust regarding the security of shared intelligence. In the aftermath of Trump's remarks to the Russians concerning Israel, several press reports suggested that Israel would curtail is intelligence sharing with the United States. Officially, of course, Israel denied this. The British government was concerned about police intelligence related to the 2017 suicide bombing in Manchester that had been shared with the United States but appeared in the *New York Times*.

The Trump administration, like others before it, has tried to stop leaks. In September 2017, the Trump administration ordered every federal department and agency to hold one-hour training sessions on "unauthorized disclosures" and their consequences. The document mandating this program, although not classified, leaked. The FBI's counterintelligence division has created a unit devoted to countering leaks.

There is also the question of leaks and whistle-blowing. Snowden, for example, has claimed to be a whistle-blower, revealing programs that he believed were a threat to civil liberties, even though these had been created by a public law passed by Congress and signed by the president. Snowden also released a great deal of material wholly unrelated to the two NSA programs, which undercuts his assertion. But the question remains: What differentiates a leaker from a whistle-blower? Whistle-blowing is a recognized and legitimate action. There is a Whistleblower Protection Act (1989), defining the range of activities that can be reported and offering protections against retaliation. The intelligence community has the Intelligence Community Whistleblower Protection Act (1998), Presidential Policy Directive 19 (PPD-19, 2012), and ICD 120 (2014), all of which have similar purposes to the 1989 law. There is a formal Whistleblowing Program under the Office of the Intelligence Community Inspector General (IC IG), but the overall program seems small. The latest IC IG report, covering October 2017–March 2018, stated that there were fourteen whistle-blower reports to Congress and no external review requests of possible retaliation against whistle-blowers for the period. The previous semiannual report listed fifteen congressional disclosures and eleven external review requests. In 2018, NSA announced that it was taking steps to give higher priority to whistle-blower protection. There are always questions about the effectiveness of these various laws and policies, especially the ability to be heard and the protection from retaliation. The point remains that for an employee, there is a specific process to be followed in the event of suspected misfeasance, malfeasance, or illegality, in lieu of going to the press. This view is also undercut, however, by "official" leaks, which do occur and which, again, appear to create a double standard.

Finally, leaks also raise the issue of the responsibility of the press. Should members of the press publish any classified material that comes their way, or do they also have a responsibility, on occasion, to withhold information that has been classified but leaked? There are instances in which journalists have agreed not to publish classified information at the request of government officials. In a famous case, the *New York Times* became aware of preparations for the 1961 Bay of Pigs operation but agreed not to publish key details, a decision the editors regretted after the operation failed so disastrously. But would they have had the same regrets had the operation succeeded? Who in the press makes these decisions, and how, remains controversial. (See Gabriel Schoenfeld, *Necessary Secrets*, in this chapter's bibliography.)

ECONOMIC ESPIONAGE

Finally, there are issues surrounding cases that involve foreign economic espionage that does not come under the 1917 Espionage Act, as in the theft of information that may be proprietary but not classified. In recent years, the U.S. government had four cases collapse involving Chinese Americans accessing information of this sort. None of them had been charged as spies, meaning working for a foreign government. As a result of these failures, the Justice Department said that all cases affecting national security, even tangentially, would be coordinated with Justice's national security staff, rather than being treated exclusively as white-collar crime.

NATIONAL SECURITY LETTERS

One investigative technique that has been used in espionage cases, as well as counterterrorism, is **national security letters (NSLs)**. Although these have been authorized since 1978 as an exception to the law protecting personal financial data, their existence became widely known only in 2005. NSLs are a type of administrative subpoena—that is, they do not require a judicial order. NSLs are used most often by the FBI but are also used by the CIA. NSLs require the recipients to turn over records and data pertaining to individuals, with the added proviso of a gag order—the recipient of the NSL may not reveal its contents or even the fact of its existence.

Since their inception, NSLs have expanded beyond their original provisions to include electronic communications and credit information. The USA PATRIOT Act, passed after the 2001 attacks, expanded the authority to issue NSLs from FBI headquarters only to field offices, included terrorism as a target as well as espionage, and eliminated the requirement that the information being sought pertain to a foreign power or its agent.

Several controversies surround NSLs. First, and most obvious, is the fact that NSLs are not subject to judicial review and that they come under a gag order, which raises civil liberties concerns. Second, the use of NSLs expanded since 2001. According to the DNI's *Statistical Transparency Report* for 2017, 12,762 NSLs were issued in that year, resulting in 41,579 requests for information (one NSL can include multiple information requests). The number of NSLs has been fairly steady for the past several years, but the number of requests has varied. Third, subsequent internal FBI and Justice Department scrutiny also revealed that some NSLs were issued without the proper "exigent circumstances." FBI Director Robert Mueller (2001–2013) took responsibility for the lapses and apologized, but this was not the first time that the FBI's management had been called into question in the press and in Congress. In March 2013, a federal judge struck down the law authorizing NSLs and the statute prohibiting legal challenges by those receiving NSLs. However, the judge also stayed implementation of the ruling pending an appeal by the FBI. In 2017, the Ninth Circuit Court of Appeals held that NSLs are constitutional and that the nondisclosure provision does not violate the First Amendment (freedom of speech). Also in 2017, Twitter had a gag order lifted and published NSLs it had received in 2015 and 2016. The letters asked for details about various Twitter accounts (name, address, length of service, transaction records) but not the content of the accounts.

One of the recommendations in the December 2013 report of the President's Review Group on Intelligence and Communications Technologies, which was formed in the aftermath of the Snowden disclosures, was that NSLs should be granted under a court order. A month later, FBI Director James Comey (2013–2017) took issue with this recommendation, calling the NSLs "essential" and arguing that the recommended procedure would make it very difficult to obtain them. In his January 2014 speech, President Obama took a position similar to Comey's but said steps would be taken to make them less secret.

The USA FREEDOM Act (2015; see chap. 5) revised the NSL program. NSL requests must now identify the specific information being sought, rather than make a blanket request for information. Nondisclosure orders may be issued only if the recipients are informed of their right to judicial review. Issuing officials must also certify that disclosure could result in danger to national security, interference with certain operations, or the safety of the recipient. Finally, the act requires that the ODNI post on its website annual numbers of NSLs issued and the number of requests covered by these NSLs during the previous year. Recipients of NSLs, in this case meaning corporations, may also report publicly—within certain categories—on the number of NSLs and the number of customers covered by them.

CONCLUSION

As VENONA confirms, the espionage threat during the cold war was pointed and obvious, even though some cases of Soviet espionage—such as those of Rosenberg and

Hiss—still remain controversial to some people. But, as the Ames and Hanssen cases indicated, Russian espionage did not end with the cold war. Neither did U.S. activities against Russia, given the Russians arrested and killed by dint of Ames's spying or the source who led to Hanssen. (In 2003, Russia arrested Alexander Zaporozhsky, a former intelligence officer who had settled in the United States but had been lured back to Russia. Zaporozhsky was sentenced to eighteen years for spying for the United States. Some observers believed that Russia held Zaporozhsky responsible for helping identify Hanssen.) In 1999, the Cox Committee found that China had stolen U.S. nuclear weapons designs during the 1980s, when the two states were tacit allies against the Soviet Union.

Assessing the nature and scope of the espionage threat to the United States may be more difficult in the post–cold war world than it had been before the demise of the Soviet Union, not only because the ideological conflict is over but also because the sources and goals of penetrations may have changed. A 2002 report prepared for Congress listed China, France, India, Israel, Japan, and Taiwan as being among the most active collectors. The most commonly targeted types of intelligence are U.S. military capabilities, U.S. foreign policy, technological expertise, and business plans. Government officials need not be the sole targets. For certain types of intelligence, government contractors may be key. Several recent studies suggest that China has replaced Russia as the main counterintelligence concern of the United States. Also, just as the United States relies on liaison relationships to enhance its HUMINT, so do foreign nations. In 2001, Ana Belen Montes, a DIA analyst, was arrested for spying for Cuba. U.S. officials assume that much of the intelligence that Montes provided over seventeen years was shared by Cuba with Russia and possibly other nations. Reports in 2002 and 2008 prepared by the Defense Personnel Security Research Center noted changes in the demographics of U.S. citizens who spied against their country. Since the end of the cold war, spies have tended to be older, to have lower clearances, to be naturalized citizens instead of native born (although 65 percent of the spies since 1990 are still native born), and to include more women. Thus, it would be naïve to believe that the need for rigorous counterintelligence and counterespionage ceased with the end of the cold war.

KEY TERMS

big CI 214
bigot lists 216
Classified National Security Information (CNSI) 221
compartmented 205
counterespionage 202
counterintelligence 201
counterintelligence poly 204

damage assessment 215
double agents 212
graymail 215
insider threat 217
lifestyle poly 204
little CI 214
mole 213
national security letters (NSLs) 223

FURTHER READINGS

Reliable and comprehensible discussions of counterintelligence—apart from mere spy stories—are rare. What follows are among the most reliable sources.

Bearden, Milt, and James Risen. *The Main Enemy: The Inside Story of the CIA's Final Showdown With the KGB*. New York: Random House, 2003.

Benson, Robert Louis, and Michael Warner, eds. *VENONA: Soviet Espionage and the American Response, 1939–1957*. Washington, D.C.: NSA and CIA, 1996.

Bruce, James B., and W. George Jameson. *Fixing Leaks: Assessing the Department of Defense's Approach to Preventing and Deterring Unauthorized Disclosures*. Washington, D.C.: RAND Corporation, 2013.

Charney, David L. "True Psychology of the Insider Spy." *Intelligencer: Journal of U.S. Intelligence Studies* 18 (fall/winter, 2010): 47–54.

————. "NOIR: A White Paper. Part One: True Psychology of the Insider Spy." 2014. "Part Two: Proposing a New Policy for Improving National Security by Fixing the Problem of Insider Spies." 2014. "Part Three: Prevention: The Missing Link." 2017. (All available at noir4usa.org.)

Clark, Robert M., and William L. Mitchell. *Deception: Counterdeception and Counterintelligence*. Newbury Park, Calif.: CQ Press, 2018.

Doyle, Charles. *National Security Letters in Foreign Intelligence Investigations: Legal Background*. CRS Report RL33320. Washington, D.C.: Congressional Research Service, July 30, 2015. (Available at www.fas.org/sgp/crs/intel/RL3320.pdf.)

Ehrman, John. "What Are We Talking About When We Talk About Counterintelligence?" *Studies in Intelligence* 53 (June 2009): 5–20.

Elsea, Jennifer K. *The Protection of Classified Information: The Legal Framework*. CRS Report RS21900. Washington, D.C.: Congressional Research, Service, January 10, 2013. (Available at https://fas.org/sgp/crs/secrecy/RS21900.pdf.)

Finklea, Kristin, coordinator. *Cyber Intrusion Into U.S. Office of Personnel Management: In Brief*. CRS Report R44111. Washington, D.C.: Congressional Research Service, July 17, 2015. (Available at https://fas.org/sgp/crs/natsec/R44111.pdf.)

Godson, Roy S. *Dirty Tricks or Trump Cards: U.S. Covert Action and Counterintelligence*. Washington, D.C.: Brassey's, 1995.

Hitz, Frederick P. "Counterintelligence: The Broken Triad." *International Journal of Intelligence and Counterintelligence* 13 (fall 2000): 265–300.

Hood, William, James Nolan, and Samuel Halpern. *Myths Surrounding James Angleton: Lessons for American Counterintelligence*. Washington, D.C.: Consortium for the Study of Intelligence, Working Group on Intelligence Reform, 1994.

Jervis, Robert. "Counterintelligence, Perception, and Deception." In *Intelligence: The Secret World of Spies*. Ed. Loch K. Johnson and James J. Wirtz. New York: Oxford University Press, 2015.

Johnson, William R. *Thwarting Enemies at Home and Abroad: How to Be a Counterintelligence Officer.* Bethesda, Md.: Stone Trail Press, 1987.

Masterman, J. C. *The Double-Cross System.* New Haven, Conn.: Yale University Press, 1972.

Redmond, Paul J. "The Challenges of Counterintelligence." In *The Oxford Handbook of National Security Intelligence.* Ed. Loch Johnson. Oxford, U.K.: Oxford University Press, 2015.

Rosenzweig, Paul, Timothy J. McNulty, and Ellen Shearer, eds. *Whistleblowers, Leaks, and the Media: The First Amendment and National Security.* Washington, D.C.: ABA Book Publishing, 2014.

Schoenfeld, Gabriel. *Necessary Secrets: National Security, the Media, and the Rule of Law.* New York: W. W. Norton, 2010.

Shulsky, Abram N., and Gary J. Schmitt. *Silent Warfare: Understanding the World of Intelligence.* 2d rev. ed. Washington, D.C.: Brassey's, 1983.

Sims, Jennifer E., and Burton Gerber, eds. *Vaults, Mirrors and Masks: Rediscovering U.S. Counterintelligence.* Washington, D.C.: Georgetown University Press, 2009.

Sulick, Michael J. *American Spies: Espionage Against the United States From the Cold War to the Present.* Washington, D.C.: Georgetown University Press, 2013.

————. *Spying in America: Espionage From the Revolutionary War to the Dawn of the Cold War.* Washington, D.C.: Georgetown University Press, 2012.

Thompson, Terence. *Why Espionage Happens.* Florence, S.C.: Seaboard Press, 2009.

U.S. Department of Homeland Security. Classified National Security Information Program for State, Local, Tribal and Private Sector Entities. Washington, D.C., February 2012.

U.S. House Permanent Select Committee on Intelligence. *Report of Investigation: The Aldrich Ames Espionage Case.* 103d Cong., 2d sess., 1994.

————. United States Counterintelligence and Security Concerns—1986. 100th Cong., 1st sess., 1987.

————. Executive Summary of Review of the Unauthorized Disclosures of Former National Security Agency Contractor Edward Snowden. September 15, 2016. 114th Cong., 2nd sess., 2016. (Available from https://intelligence.house.gov/uploadedfiles/hpsci_snowden_review_-_unclass_summary_-_final.pdf.)

U.S. House Select Committee on U.S. National Security and Military/Commercial Concerns With the People's Republic of China (Cox Committee). *Report.* 106th Cong., 1st sess., 1999.

U.S. Information Security Oversight Office. *Report to the President. ISOO 2017 Annual Report.* Washington, D.C., 2018.

U.S. Library of Congress, Congressional Research Service. *National Security Letters in Foreign Intelligence Investigations: Legal Background and Recent Amendments.* CRS Report RL 33320. Washington, D.C., September 8, 2009. (Available at www.fas.org/sgp/crs/intel/RL33320.pdf.)

U.S. National Insider Threat Task Force. *Insider Threat Program: Maturity Framework.* Washington, D.C., 2018. (Available at https://www.dni.gov/files/NCSC/documents/nittf/20181024_NITTF_MaturityFramework_web.pdf.)

U.S. Office of the Director of National Intelligence. *2014 Report on Security Clearance Determinations.* Washington, D.C.: ODNI, 2015.

_____. National Counterintelligence and Security Center. *National Counterintelligence Strategy of the United States of America 2016*. Washington, D.C.: ODNI, 2015. (Available at http://www.ncsc.gov/publications/strategy/docs/National_CI_Strategy_2016.pdf.)

_____. *Principles of Classification Management for the Intelligence Community*. Washington, D.C.: ODNI, 2017. (Available at https://www.dni.gov/files/documents/Principles-of-Classification-Management-for-the-IC.pdf.)

_____. *Statistical Transparency Report Regarding Use of National Security Authorities, Calendar Year 2017*. Washington, D.C.: ODNI, April 2018. (Available at https://www.dni.gov/files/documents/icotr/2018-ASTR----CY2017----FINAL-for-Release–5.4.18.pdf.)

Zuehlke, Arthur A. "What Is Counterintelligence?" In *Intelligence Requirements for the 1980s: Counterintelligence*. Ed. Roy S. Godson. Washington, D.C.: National Strategy Information Center, 1980.

CHAPTER EIGHT

COVERT ACTION

Covert action, along with spying, is a mainstay of popular ideas about intelligence. Like spying, **covert action** is fraught with myths and misconceptions. Even when understood, it remains one of the most controversial intelligence topics.

Covert action is defined in the National Security Act as "[a]n activity or activities of the United States Government to influence political, economic or military conditions abroad, where it is intended that the role of the United States Government will not be apparent or acknowledged publicly." Consider the irony: An activity that the United States will deny having conducted is defined in U.S. law.

Some intelligence specialists have objected to the phrase "covert action," believing that the word "covert" emphasizes secrecy over policy. (The British had earlier referred to this activity as special political action—SPA.) The distinction is important, because even though these activities are secret, they are undertaken as one means to advance policy goals. This cannot be stressed enough. Proper covert actions are undertaken because policy makers have determined that they are the best way to achieve a desired end. These operations do not—or should not—proceed on the initiative of the intelligence agencies.

During the Jimmy Carter administration (1977–1981), which exhibited some qualms about force as a foreign policy tool, the innocuous and somewhat comical phrase "special activity" was crafted to replace "covert action." The administration thus substituted a euphemism with a euphemism. But when the Ronald Reagan administration came into office (1981–1989), with different views on intelligence policy, it continued to use "special activity" in its executive orders governing intelligence. (See the Congressional Research Service report by DeVine and Peters in "Further Readings" for a discussion of various legal definitions.)

Ultimately, what covert activities are called should not matter that much. What is significant is that in making changes in appellation, the United States reveals a degree of official discomfort with the tool.

The classic rationale behind covert action is that policy makers need a **third option** (yet another euphemism) between doing nothing (the first option) in a situation in which vital interests may be threatened and sending in military force (the second option), which raises a host of difficult political issues. Not everyone would agree with this rationale, including those who would properly argue that diplomatic activity is more than doing nothing without resorting to force. Also, there are military operations, such as the killing of Osama bin Laden, that are conducted by the military (with strong intelligence community support) but are clandestine—that is, secret but attributable. Such operations begin to blur the line between classic military actions and intelligence covert actions.

As with counterintelligence, two pertinent questions are whether covert action was a product of the cold war and whether it remains relevant today. Under the leadership of Director of Central Intelligence (DCI) Allen Dulles during the Eisenhower administration (1953–1961), covert action became an increasingly attractive option. (See chap. 2.) It had both successes and failures but was seen as a useful tool in a broad-based struggle with the Soviet Union. In the post–cold war period, situations could arise—involving proliferators, terrorists, or narcotics traffickers—in which some sort of covert action can be the preferred means of action.

THE DECISION-MAKING PROCESS

Covert action makes sense—and should be undertaken—only when tasked by duly authorized policy makers in pursuit of specific policy goals that cannot be achieved by any other means. Covert action cannot substitute or compensate for a poorly conceived policy. The planning process for covert action must begin with policy makers justifying the policy, defining clearly the national security interests and goals that are at stake, and believing that covert action is a viable means as well as the best means for achieving specified ends.

Maintaining a capability for covert action entails expenses, for the operation itself and for the infrastructure involved in mounting the action. Even though covert actions are not planned and executed overnight, a certain level of preparedness (such as having on hand equipment, transportation, false documents and other support items, and trained personnel, including foreign assets) must exist at all times. The operational support structure—which also includes prearranged meeting places, surveillance agents, letter drops, and technical support—is sometimes referred to as **plumbing**. Forming and maintaining such a standby capability takes time and costs money. But the key question at this point in the decision-making process is whether the cost—both monetary and political—of carrying out a covert action is justified. Both types of cost become especially important when looking at actions that may last for months or longer.

Alternatives to covert action need to be considered. If overt means of producing a similar outcome are available, they are almost certainly preferable. Using overt means does not preclude either covert action if overt means fail or covert action employed in conjunction with overt means, but the overt means should usually be tried first.

Policy makers and intelligence officials examine at least two levels of risk before approving a covert action. The first is the risk of exposure. William E. Colby, perhaps reflecting on the large-scale investigations of intelligence that dominated his tenure as DCI (1973–1976), said a director should always assume that an operation will become public knowledge at some point. A difference clearly exists between an operation that is exposed while under way or shortly after its conclusion and one that is revealed years later. Nonetheless, even a long-delayed exposure may still prove to be embarrassing or politically costly.

The second risk to be weighed is failure of the operation. Failure of this nature may be costly on several levels: in human lives and as a political crisis for the nation carrying out the operation, as well as for those it may be trying to help. Decision makers must weigh the relative level of risk against the interests that are at stake. An extremely risky operation may still be worth undertaking if the stakes are high enough and no alternatives are available. In other words, the ends may justify the means, or at least the risks. For example, in the 1980s the United States was looking for ways to aid the mujahideen rebels in Afghanistan who were fighting Soviet invaders. One option was to arm the rebels with Stinger antiaircraft missiles, which would counter the successful Soviet use of helicopters. But policy makers were concerned that some Stingers would fall into the wrong hands or be captured by the Soviets. Ultimately, the Reagan administration decided to send the Stingers, which helped alter the course of the war. It also left Stingers in the hands of the mujahideen after their victory, but policy makers deemed that a smaller risk than Soviet victory in Afghanistan.

Even though intelligence analysis and operations exist only to serve policy, intelligence officers may be eager to demonstrate their covert action capabilities. Several factors may drive officers to do so: a belief that they can deliver the desired outcome, a bureaucratic imperative to prove their value, and their professional pride in doing this type of work. However, unless the operation is closely tied to agreed-upon policy goals and is supported as a viable option by the policy community, it starts off severely hampered. Covert action planners must therefore closely coordinate their plans and actions with policy offices.

Covert actions are extraordinary steps, something between the states of peace and war. That alone is enough to raise broad ethical questions, although the policy makers' willingness to maintain a covert action capability indicates some agreement among them on the propriety of its use. The specific details of an operation are likely to raise ethical issues as well. Should assistance be given to foreign political parties facing a close but democratic election against communist parties (e.g., France and Italy in the 1940s)? Should a democratically elected but procommunist government be subverted and overthrown (e.g., Guatemala, 1954)? Should a nation's economy be disrupted—with attendant suffering for the populace—to overthrow the government (e.g., Cuba, 1960s)? Should a group opposed to a hostile government be armed, with a view toward fomenting an insurgency (e.g., Nicaragua, 1980s)? The issues these questions raise are important not only intrinsically but also because of the risk of exposure. How do covert actions fit with the causes, standards, and principles that the United States supports?

The decision making that went into the operation to kill bin Laden is again instructive, even though it was not strictly a covert action. Once the policy makers were fairly convinced that bin Laden was in the house in Abbottabad, Pakistan, Obama administration officials considered several means to kill him: unmanned aerial vehicle (UAV, or drone) strikes, conventional bombs, or a special operations team. Key factors that weighed in favor of the special operations team were the large number of bombs that would be needed to be certain of killing bin Laden, the likelihood of innocent casualties in a large bombing raid, and the importance of being certain that bin Laden was dead, which would be unlikely if the house was obliterated by bombing. At the same time, policy makers had no more than a 60 to 80 percent certainty that bin Laden was in the house but decided to launch the operation anyway.

It is also important to note the very important role played by various lawyers when a covert action is being considered. First, does the action violate either U.S. laws or U.S. treaty obligations? Second, is it something deemed permissible for the United States to be doing? Are there precedents? The officers responsible for the covert action are especially interested in the lawyers' views because the operators do not want to be put in potential legal jeopardy for conducting an illegal operation. So, despite the bravado usually associated with covert action, there is an inherent legal caution during the planning stage. Again, the planning for the bin Laden raid is instructive. According to press reports, attorneys from the National Security Council (NSC), Central Intelligence Agency (CIA), Department of Defense (DOD), and Joint Chiefs of Staff (JCS) were involved in reviewing all aspects of the operation, including the permissibility of burying bin Laden at sea. (See the article by Charlie Savage in Further Readings.)

In evaluating proposed covert actions, policy makers should examine analogous past operations. Have they been tried in this same nation or region? What were the results? Are the risk factors different? Has this type of operation been tried elsewhere? Again, with what results? Although these are commonsense questions, they run up against a governmental phenomenon: the inability to use historical examples. Decision makers are so accustomed to concentrating on near-term issues that they tend not to remember accurately past analogous situations in which they have been involved. They move from issue to issue in rapid succession, with little respite and even less reflection. Or, as Richard E. Neustadt and Ernest R. May pointed out in *Thinking in Time: The Uses of History for Decision Makers* (1988), they learn somewhat false lessons from the past, which are then misapplied to new circumstances.

Legislative reaction to covert actions is a bigger issue for the United States than it is for other democracies. The congressional committees that oversee the intelligence community are an integral part of the process, as providers of funding and as decision makers who need to be apprised of planned operations. Although congressional support is important, it is not mandatory. The long lead times required for the operations also mean that they can be put into the budget process in advance so that funds can be allocated for them. Assuming that appropriated funds exist and that there are no specific bars to the covert action in question, Congress must be informed but has no approval role. Again, a limited number of congressional leaders were informed about the bin Laden mission prior to its execution.

Covert action does require formal approval in the executive branch. The president must sign an order approving the operation, based on the president's finding that covert action is "necessary to support identifiable foreign policy objectives of the United States, and is important to the national security of the United States." In intelligence parlance, this document is called a **presidential finding**. Congress and the American public did not know that the president signed off on each operation until Secretary of State Henry A. Kissinger (1973–1977) was forced to reveal as much before a congressional committee in the mid-1970s. Presidential findings are now required by law and must be in writing (except for emergencies, in which case a written record must be kept and a finding produced within forty-eight hours). The president may not delegate this responsibility. Covert actions are therefore somewhat personal in nature for the president, as each president will have different thresholds of willingness to take risks, inflict casualties, and so on.

The finding is transmitted to those responsible for carrying out the operation and to the members of the House and Senate Intelligence Committees or a more limited congressional leadership group in a **memo of notification (MON)**. Often, because of the long time lines involved, the congressional committees will already have learned about the operation via the budget process, which includes a review of the year's covert action plan. Congress may wish to be briefed on the specifics of the finding and the operation. The briefings are advisory in nature. Other than denying funding during the budget process, Congress has no basis for approving or disapproving an operation, unless specific laws or executive orders ban them—such as the acts passed by Congress in the 1980s limiting aid to the contras in Nicaragua or the executive order banning assassination (discussed later in this chapter).

However, should committee members or the staffers raise serious questions, a prudent covert action briefing team reports that fact to the executive branch. This should be enough to cause the operation to be reviewed. The executive branch may still decide to go ahead, or it may make changes in the operation to respond to congressional concerns. According to press accounts, the George W. Bush administration considered a covert action to support certain parties and candidates in the Iraqi election in 2005 but rescinded the action because of congressional opposition.

The covert action policy system, for all of its rules, remains fragile because of its inherent secrecy. The Iran-contra scandal underscored some of its weaknesses. A Democratic majority in Congress, opposed to support for the contras in Nicaragua, cut off funding. President Reagan, in his usual broad manner, urged his NSC staff to help the contras "keep body and soul together." NSC staffer Lt. Col. Oliver L. North did this by soliciting donations from private individuals and foreign governments, alleging that DCI William J. Casey (1981–1987), who died just as the scandal broke, had approved his actions. North also argued that Congress's restrictions applied to DOD and intelligence agencies, not to the NSC staff. In a parallel activity, the NSC staff pursued clandestine efforts to improve ties to Iran and free hostages in the Middle East, despite earlier objections to this policy by the secretaries of state (George P. Shultz) and defense (Caspar W. Weinberger). Israel shipped antitank missiles to Iran at the behest of the NSC staff, with the United States replacing them in Israel's inventory. North also became involved in the Iranian initiative and suggested diverting to the contras the money that Iran had paid for the missiles.

Iran-contra pointed up several problems in the covert action process:

- Questionable delegations of authority ordered and managed covert actions (the actions of North on the NSC staff).

- Presidential findings were postdated and signed *ex post facto* (the finding authorizing the sale of missiles to Iran).

- Disparate operations were merged (using the Iranian money to fund the contras).

- The executive branch failed to keep Congress properly informed (disregarding the laws restricting aid to the contras and not briefing on the finding to sell missiles to Iran).

Debates on the worthiness of the respective policies involved in Iran-contra notwithstanding, NSC staff and other executive branch officials violated the law banning aid to the contras, as well as a host of accepted norms and rules in managing the operations.

The 2013 debate on providing covert arms assistance to the Syrian rebels is also illustrative of many of these policy issues. Top decision makers in the Obama administration had been divided for several years on whether or not to give assistance to the rebels, deterred, in part, by reluctance to get involved in yet another conflict in the Middle East. However, once the Bashar al-Assad government had apparently used chemical weapons against the rebels, President Obama was forced to act, owing to this crossing of his self-proclaimed "red line" on chemical weapons use. According to press accounts, the CIA had already been providing intelligence assistance to the rebels. Administration lawyers held the view that overt arms support was precluded by international law, which forbids aiding rebels to overthrow an established government. Covert aid circumvented this problem. However, some members of Congress questioned whether this very limited program would make any difference on the battlefield and also raised concerns about U.S.-provided weapons possibly falling into the hands of rebels linked to al Qaeda. The Syrian operation thus became—like Afghanistan and Nicaragua in the 1980s—an overtly debated covert action.

The creation of the position of director of national intelligence (DNI) in 2004 raised new questions for the supervision of covert action. The DNI is now the president's senior intelligence adviser, which presumably includes covert action, one of the most important types of intelligence activities. Operational responsibility for conducting covert action remains within the CIA. The law states that the director of the CIA (DCIA) reports to the DNI, but it does not specify how extensive this reporting requirement is. The law is clear that the DNI does not have operational control over the CIA. Thus, the DNI needs means to gain insight into covert action capabilities and the status of ongoing operations. This became an issue between DNI Dennis Blair (2009–2010) and DCIA Leon Panetta (2009–2011), which the NSC decided largely in favor of the CIA. The CIA remains in charge of covert action and the right to select chiefs of station. The DNI was given a role in assessing and evaluating covert action when requested by the president or the NSC, which was much less than Blair apparently sought.

THE RANGE OF COVERT ACTIONS

Covert actions encompass many types of activities.

Propaganda is the old political technique of disseminating information that has been created with a specific political outcome in mind. Propaganda can be used to support individuals or groups friendly to one's own side or to undermine one's opponents. It can also be used to create false rumors of political unrest, economic shortages, or direct attacks on individuals, to name a few techniques. The creation of "fake news" via websites, blogs, and other social media, as Russia apparently did during the 2016 U.S. presidential election, probably falls into this category, although the World Wide Web makes doing so much easier in terms of both means and deniability. For example, there is growing concern about "**deep fakes**," which are digitally altered audio or video clips that are very difficult to detect as having been altered. Artificial intelligence techniques, specifically deep learning algorithms, appear to be the means by which deep fakes are produced.

These activities all come under the heading of "**disinformation**," which is a synonym for propaganda. According to press reports, the Senate Intelligence Committee has written a draft report detailing the use of social media by Russia to create disinformation during the 2016 U.S. presidential election. Among their tactics was the targeting of African Americans, which also fed into the goal of suppressing Democratic voter turnout. Unfortunately, the firms that own and manage the main social media platforms—Facebook, Twitter, Google (YouTube)—have been slow to admit the ways in which their platforms have been misused and to take corrective measures.

Political activity is a step above propaganda, although they may be used together. Political activity enables an intelligence operation to intervene more directly in the political process of the targeted nation. As with propaganda, political activity can be used to help friends or to impede foes. For example, in the late 1940s the United States supplied scarce newsprint to centrist, anticommunist political parties in Italy and France during closely contested elections. The United States has also funneled money to political parties overseas to help during elections. Alternatively, a state can use political activity more directly against its foes in other nations, such as disrupting rallies or interfering with their publications.

The United States has tended to use economic activity against governments deemed to be hostile. Every political leadership—democratic or totalitarian—worries about the state of its economy because this has the greatest daily effect on the population: the availability of food and commodities, the stability of prices, the relative ease or difficulty with which basic needs can be met. Economic unrest often leads to political unrest. Again, other techniques may be used in conjunction with economic activity, such as propaganda to create false fears about shortages. Or the economic techniques may be more direct, such as attempts to destroy vital crops or to flood a state with counterfeit currency to destroy faith in the monetary system. For years, the United States attacked Cuba's economy directly as well as indirectly via a trade embargo. Economic unrest was also a key factor in U.S. efforts to undermine the government of Salvador Allende in Chile in the early 1970s. Economic destabilization may be more effective against a more democratic state, as in Chile, than against a dictatorship, as in Cuba, which has fewer qualms about inflicting want or privation on its people and is much less responsive to (or tolerant of) popular protests.

Sabotage, the deliberate destruction of property or facilities, has reentered the covert action tool bag in the past several years. There can be aspects of sabotage in economic activity (destroying crops, industrial facilities, etc.), but the current focus of sabotage relates to efforts to stem proliferation. Sabotage can be a straightforward effort to subvert ongoing activities or can be used to sow distrust between a supplier and a would-be proliferator—for example, by sabotaging shipped parts but allowing them to go through. Sabotage requires some detailed knowledge about an activity and its location, as well as access. There have been several press accounts of efforts to slow down Iran's nuclear program, including the introduction of computer programs, such as Stuxnet. (See chap. 12.) According to press reports, a similar effort was made against the North Korean nuclear program, which did not succeed, although efforts to impede North Korea's missile progress had some success. Thus, sabotage and cyberspace can go hand in hand.

Indeed, it is likely that cyberspace will increasingly be seen as one means of conducting several types of covert actions, including propaganda, political activity, economic activity, and sabotage. For the United States, at least, this raises several issues about legal authorities and oversight. Cyber capabilities reside largely in the National Security Agency (NSA), which is both an intelligence agency and a combat support agency, and in several military components, including Cyber Command. For a cyber activity to be considered a covert action, as opposed to a military action, it would have to be conducted by an intelligence agency. As discussed below, covert actions and military actions are subject to different types of congressional oversight. Gen. Keith Alexander, who served as both the director of NSA (usually called the DIRNSA; 2005–2014) and as the commander of Cyber Command (2010–2014), said that cyberattacks on enemy computer systems should be authorized by the president and secretary of defense and not be undertaken at the discretion of military commanders.

Coups, the overthrow of a government, either directly or through surrogates, are another step up the covert action ladder. (See Figure 8.1.) Again, a coup may be the culmination of many other techniques—propaganda, political activity, or economic unrest. The United States used coups successfully in Iran in 1953 and in Guatemala in 1954 and was involved in undermining the Allende government in Chile, although the coup that brought down his government was indigenous.

Figure 8.1 The Covert Action Ladder

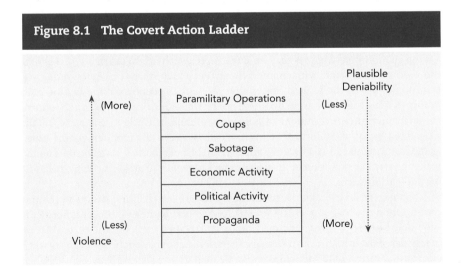

Paramilitary operations are the largest, most violent, and most dangerous covert actions, involving the equipping and training of large armed groups for a direct assault on one's enemies. They do not involve the use of a state's own military personnel in combatant units, which technically would be an act of war. The United States was successful in this type of operation in Afghanistan in the 1980s but failed abysmally at the Bay of Pigs in 1961. The contra war against the Sandinistas in Nicaragua was neither won nor lost, but the Sandinistas were defeated at the polls when they held a free election in the midst of a deteriorating economy. (They regained power in a subsequent election.)

Some nations have also practiced a higher level of covert military activity—secret participation in combat. For example, Soviet pilots flew combat missions during the Korean War against United Nations (primarily U.S.) aircraft, and Russian "volunteers" have been active against Ukraine. This type of activity raises several issues: military action without an act of war, possible retaliation, and the rights of combatants if captured. The United States has largely eschewed the practice of direct covert military intervention because of such complications, preferring to allow intelligence officers to take part in paramilitary activities with indigenous forces.

Paramilitary operations run the risk that the forces being trained and supported will have agendas of their own and may not conduct themselves according to one's own rules. Given that many paramilitary operations are either insurrections or civil wars, the chances of higher levels of animosity are always present. (A French diplomat in the 1920s cynically observed that civil wars were bloodier than wars between nations because "it was more fun killing people you know.") Most recently, press accounts have raised concerns about the conduct of Afghan paramilitary units that had reportedly been trained by the CIA.

Paramilitary operations need to be distinguished from special operations forces. The most fundamental and important distinction is that special forces are uniformed military personnel conducting a variety of combat tasks not performed by traditional military arms. The United States has a Special Operations Command (SOCOM). Other such forces are the British Special Air and Special Boat Services (SAS and SBS). Paramilitary operations do not involve the use of one's own uniformed military personnel as combatants. In the war in Afghanistan (2001–), the role of paramilitary personnel appears to be closer to actual combat than was primarily the case in Nicaragua, but their main role remains training, helping supply, and offering leadership assistance to indigenous forces. The CIA's paramilitary forces in Afghanistan are part of the CIA Directorate of Operations Special Activities Division. According to press accounts, CIA paramilitary personnel were the first U.S. forces in Afghanistan, establishing contact with members of the Northern Alliance and preparing them for the offensive against the Taliban.

The war on terrorists has focused attention on a covert activity that does not fall neatly into the customary range of actions—**renditions**. Renditions are the seizure of individuals wanted by the United States. These individuals are living abroad and are not in countries where the United States either can or wants to use legal means to take them into custody. The operations are called renditions because the individual in question is rendered (that is, formally delivered) to U.S. custody. Renditions predate the war on terrorists, although the scale clearly increased after 9/11. U.S. officials have justified renditions as part of the United States's right to self-defense against people plotting to attack it.

Renditions are controversial for several reasons. First, they are extraterritorial actions. In some instances, the foreign government in whose territory the rendition occurred was aware of the operation and looked the other way, allowing the rendition to proceed but preserving its own **plausible deniability**. In the case of terrorists, some renditions have been controversial because the United States did not retain custody of the suspects but sent them on to their home nations, most often in the Middle East. Rules about custody, civil rights, and limits on interrogation tend to be different in most of these states, with the effect that some rendered suspects have likely been subjected to harsh treatment if not outright torture. Although the United States has sought pledges from these states about how they would conduct interrogations, U.S. officials cannot be present at all times in these countries. Critics charge that the United States is therefore knowingly complicit in torture. Others argue that the United States cannot hold all suspects, that it is doing as much as it can to prevent torture, and that the importance of breaking up terrorist networks and gleaning information about them requires such use of foreign nations. (See chap. 13.)

Since 2005, in both Italy and Germany, judges issued indictments against U.S. intelligence officers for renditions, one in Milan and one in Macedonia. Although the U.S. government made no official response, CIA officials stated unofficially that any rendition would have been known to the governments. The Italian government denied any such knowledge. However, in 2013 Niccolo Pollari, former head of SISMI—Italian Military Intelligence and Security Service—was sentenced to ten years in prison for his role in the Milan rendition. In 2014, Pollari's sentence and those of four other Italian intelligence officers were vacated on the grounds that they should not have been prosecuted because the case involved classified information. One person sought by Italy, reportedly a CIA officer, was Sabrina de Sousa, who was arrested in Portugal in 2017 on an Italian extradition warrant. After official U.S. intervention, Italy granted de Sousa a partial pardon. The German case ended after the United States made it clear that it would not cooperate in the case and would not hand over U.S. citizens to be prosecuted. According to press accounts, in March 2007, CIA director Michael Hayden (2006–2009) complained to European diplomats about the inaccurate and negative information being generated in Europe about CIA activities. Hayden also said that fewer than 100 people had been held in secret sites and fewer than half of these had been subjected to more intensive interrogation procedures. Referring to a report by the European Parliament on secret rendition flights, Hayden said that fewer than 100 flights concerned renditions to third countries and that these were undertaken with the knowledge and assistance of the countries involved, a point also made by the European report.

It is unlikely that even the number of flights claimed by Hayden could have been conducted without the knowledge of European countries. It is also possible that the leaders of the governments involved, or their intelligence services, would rather not admit their cooperation and perhaps see judicial proceedings as a way of quieting domestic opinion.

The actual techniques used to interrogate terrorists or suspected terrorists have been controversial for some time. These are sometimes referred to as **enhanced interrogation techniques (EITs)**. In the period immediately following the 9/11 attacks, various executive-branch legal counsels approved a variety of EITs, arguing that these did not constitute torture, which is banned under the United Nations Convention Against Torture (1984), to which the United States is a signatory. The Eighth Amendment to the Constitution bans "cruel and unusual punishment." The legal opinions also found that the captured terrorists were enemy combatants, not criminal defendants. The most controversial of the EITs was waterboarding, which was banned by President George W. Bush in 2006. This was confirmed by President Obama in 2009, when he also banned some other EITs.

The controversy over EITs resumed when the majority (Democratic) staff of the Senate Intelligence Committee undertook a study of the CIA's detention and interrogation program in 2009. (For the various controversies surrounding this study, see chap. 10.) Portions of the study were released in December 2014. The staff report found that the EITs, some of which were seen as being overly brutal, were not effective in obtaining useful intelligence and that the CIA made unjustified claims about their effectiveness in order to keep the program going. The report also faulted the overall management and oversight of the program. DCIA John Brennan rebutted these findings, as did former DCIs and DCIAs Tenet, Porter J. Goss, and Hayden and several other former senior CIA officials, asserting that the EITs provided intelligence that thwarted terrorist attacks.

The involvement of psychologists in designing the EIT program was also controversial. The American Psychological Association (APA) commissioned an external review of its role in the EIT program. Press reports in July 2015 said that the review concluded that APA members had cooperated with the program and had issued "loose" ethical guidelines to support it. Several APA executives resigned as a result. In January 2016, the Defense Department asked the APA to revisit its ban on the use of psychologists in national security investigations, arguing that a code of conduct that allowed participation under certain conditions was more in the national interest than a blanket prohibition. In 2017, two psychologists who helped design the CIA program reached an out-of-court settlement with three former detainees.

EITs came up again during Gina Haspel's confirmation hearings to be DCIA in 2018. Haspel declined to condemn the use of some of the EITs outright but said that the CIA should not have been part of the rendition and interrogation program and would not do so in the future.

The use of armed UAVs falls somewhere beyond the usual use of force but not quite into covert action. Such flights are sometimes conducted by intelligence personnel, as opposed to military operators, but they are not entirely covert. That is, there is little question about which country is responsible for the air strikes, even though the United States does not acknowledge each attack. A United Nations report found this to be problematic, suggesting that it could lead to a future in which many states felt free to use UAVs in this manner. (See chap. 13.)

ISSUES IN COVERT ACTION

Covert action, both in concept and in practice, raises a host of issues. The most fundamental is whether such a policy option is legitimate. Like most questions of this sort, there is no correct answer. The prevailing opinions can be divided into two schools—idealists and pragmatists. Idealists argue that covert intervention by one state in the internal affairs of another violates acceptable norms of international behavior. They argue that the very concept of a third option is illegitimate. Pragmatists may accept the arguments of the idealists but contend that the self-interest of a state occasionally makes covert action necessary and legitimate. Historical practice over several centuries would tend to favor the pragmatists. Idealists would respond that the historical record does not justify covert intervention. (This debate took a curious turn with passage of the 1998 Iraq Liberation Act, in which Congress and President Bill Clinton agreed to spend $97 million to replace the regime of Saddam Hussein—an overt commitment to interfere in Iraq's internal affairs.)

In several instances during the nineteenth and twentieth centuries, the United States intervened in other nations, primarily in the Western Hemisphere, but these activities were largely overt and usually military in nature. The United States began to use covert action in the context of the cold war. Did the nature of the Soviet threat make covert action legitimate? Did the use of this option—not only directly against the Soviet Union but also in developing nations that were often the battlegrounds of the cold war—lessen the moral differences between the United States and the Soviet Union? Again, there are broad differences of opinion. To U.S. policy makers during the administrations of Harry S. Truman (1945–1953) and Dwight D. Eisenhower (1953–1961), the Soviet threat was so large and multifaceted that the question of the legitimacy of covert action never arose. In any event, both administrations preferred covert action to the possibility of a general war in Europe or Asia. However, some people believe that the use of the covert option blurred important distinctions between the two nations.

Assuming that covert action is an acceptable option, is it circumscribed by the nature of the state against which it is being carried out? Or does this question become irrelevant if one accepts the legitimacy of covert action? For example, the United States used covert economic destabilization against Fidel Castro's Cuba and Allende's Chile. Both were communists, but Castro had seized power after a guerrilla war; Allende never commanded an electoral majority, but he had been elected according to the Chilean constitution. Castro turned Cuba into a hostile Soviet base; Allende showed only disturbing signs of friendliness to Castro and to other Soviet allies. Instead of having a second Soviet satellite in the Western Hemisphere, the United States opted to destabilize Allende in the hope of fomenting a coup against him. Should the fact that Allende had been elected according to Chilean law have been sufficient to preclude covert action by the United States? Or were U.S. national security concerns of sufficient primacy to make the covert option legitimate? This was not the first time the United States had intervened in democratic processes. As noted, the United States gave covert assistance in a variety of forms to centrist parties in Europe in the late 1940s to preclude communist victories.

Central to the U.S. concept of covert action is plausible deniability—that U.S. denials of a role in the events stemming from a covert action appear plausible. The need to mask its participation stems directly from the idea that the action has to be covert. If the situation could be addressed overtly, the role of the United States would not be an issue. DCI Richard Helms (1966–1973) held that plausible deniability was an absolute requirement for a covert action but also conceded that it was becoming an outmoded concept because of the expanded requirements for oversight and notification.

Plausible deniability depends almost entirely on having the origin of the action remain covert. Once that is lost, deniability is barely plausible. Deniability may have been sustainable during the 1950s and 1960s, but this has become more difficult since the revelation that the president signs each finding to order a covert action.

The scale of the activity also matters. For example, in the aftermath of the Bay of Pigs debacle, President John F. Kennedy (1961–1963) sought counsel from his predecessor, President Eisenhower. Kennedy defended his decision not to commit air power to assist the invasion on the grounds of maintaining deniability of a U.S. role. Eisenhower scoffed, asking how—given the scale and nature of the operation—the United States could plausibly deny having taken part.

Plausible deniability also raises concerns about accountability. If one of the premises of covert action policy is the ability to deny a U.S. role, does this also allow officials to avoid responsibility for an operation that is controversial or perhaps even a failure? Or does the fact that the president must sign a finding put the responsibility on him or her?

The main controversy raised by propaganda activities is that of **blowback**. The CIA is precluded from undertaking any intelligence activities within the United States. However, a story could be planted in a media outlet overseas that will also be reported in the United States. That is blowback. This risk is probably higher today with global twenty-four-hour news agencies and the World Wide Web than it was during the early days of the cold war. Thus, inadvertently, a CIA-planted story that is false can be reported in a U.S. media outlet. In such a case, does the CIA have a responsibility to inform the U.S. media outlet of the true nature of the story? Would doing so compromise the original operation? If such notification should not be given at the time, should it be given afterward? The proliferation of social media has also made propaganda easier to create and spread but much more difficult to counter or to stop. Very few voices are seen as being authoritative any longer and there is a large amount of skepticism about official pronouncements and explanations. In 2018, DOD transferred $40 million to the State Department's Global Engagement Center to counter foreign propaganda and disinformation overtly.

Not all covert actions remain covert. One of the key determinants seems to be the scale of the operation. The smaller and more discreet the operation, the easier it is to keep secret. But as operations become larger, especially paramilitary operations, the ability to keep them covert declines rapidly. Two operations undertaken during the Reagan administration—aid to the contras in Nicaragua and to the mujahideen in Afghanistan—illustrate the problem. Should the possibility of public disclosure affect decision makers when they are considering paramilitary operations? Or should disclosure be accepted as a cost of undertaking this type of effort, with the understanding that it is likely to be something less than covert and not plausibly deniable?

Despite the desired separation of intelligence and policy, covert action blurs the distinction in ways that analysis does not. Instead of providing intelligence to assist in the making of decisions, through covert action the intelligence community is being asked to help execute policy. Of necessity, it has a role in determining the scale and scope of an operation, about which it has the greatest knowledge. The intelligence community also has a day-to-day part to play in managing an operation.

The distinction blurs further because the intelligence community has a vested interest in the outcome of a covert action in ways that are vastly different from its interest in the outcome of a policy for which it has provided analysis. Covert action is not just an alternative means of achieving a policy end; it is also a way for the intelligence community to demonstrate its capabilities and value that may be more concrete than analysis.

Thus, covert action makes the policy and intelligence communities closer collaborators, as the separation between them diminishes. Conversely, the intelligence community takes on additional responsibilities in the eyes of the policy community. The intelligence community usually bears a greater burden for a less-than-successful covert action than it does for less-than-perfect intelligence analysis.

Paramilitary operations raise numerous issues. In addition to the problem of keeping them covert and the strains they put on plausible deniability, paramilitary operations raise serious questions about the amount of time available to achieve their stated goals. Unless these operations appear to have a reasonable chance of success in a well-defined period of time, policy makers find their ensuing options limited. On the one hand, they can decide to continue the operation even if the chances of success—usually defined as some sort of military victory—appear slim. It may be that the paramilitary force is unlikely to be defeated but unlikely to win, offering the prospect of an open-ended operation. On the other hand, policy makers can decide to terminate the operation. U.S. abandonment of the Kurds in Iraq in the 1970s is a case in point. The United States had been supporting the Kurds in their struggle against Iraq to create an independent homeland. Covert aid was given to the Kurds via Iran, which also had an interest in weakening its neighbor. However, the Kurdish effort was inconclusive. In the mid-1970s, the shah decided to resolve his differences with Iraq and ordered the operation to cease. The United States complied, abruptly leaving the Kurds to fend for themselves. But when an operation such as this is shut down, extricating all of the combatants may not be possible. In such a case, what is the obligation of the power backing the operation to the combatants? Do the combatants understand the risks they have undertaken, or are they simply assets of the power backing the covert action?

Within the United States, a long-standing debate has taken place about which agency should be responsible for paramilitary operations: the CIA or DOD. The CIA has traditionally run paramilitary operations because, initially, DOD wanted no involvement in them. If covert action is an alternative to military operations, DOD might find it difficult to keep the two options separate. International law poses another difficulty. Although no international acceptance has been given to covert action, the target may consider the use of military personnel (in or out of uniform) in such an activity to be an act of war. Ironically enough, the covert nature of the action also allows the target to ignore or downplay the fact of the intervention, lest relations deteriorate further as they likely would under an overt attack. Finally, the involvement of DOD may undercut the effort to achieve plausible deniability.

However, DOD has greater expertise than the CIA in the conduct of military operations as well as a greater infrastructure to carry them out, which might save money. Removing paramilitary operations from the CIA might spare the intelligence community some internal strains caused by having responsibility for both analysis and operations. New strains might subsequently appear in DOD. The May 2011 attack on bin Laden was a special operations mission, not a paramilitary operation supporting non-U.S. forces in the field.

The war in Afghanistan and the war against terrorists renewed the debate. Secretary of Defense Donald Rumsfeld (2001–2006) pushed for a greater role for SOCOM, including recruiting and maintaining spies in enemy forces. At the same time, the CIA had increased its own paramilitary capability, both as part of DCI Tenet's overall effort to enhance the Directorate of Operations and to respond to the war on terrorists. In its 2004 report, the 9/11 Commission (National Commission on Terrorist Attacks Upon the United States) recommended that SOCOM take over paramilitary operations from the CIA, based on the view that the two organizations had redundant capabilities and responsibilities. The commission envisaged the CIA organizing paramilitary units while SOCOM was responsible for final planning and execution.

A January 2004 study by the Army War College pointed out some fundamental differences in how the two groups operate, suggesting that even a collaborative effort would be difficult. For example, in jointly conducted operations, would military personnel be covered by the Geneva Convention? Would the necessary secrecy create chain of command problems and make it more difficult to communicate with or to identify friendly units? How would Congress oversee such operations? In February 2005, a study requested by President George W. Bush came out against the recommendations of the 9/11 Commission and argued that the CIA should retain its paramilitary capabilities. In June 2005, the Bush administration confirmed the CIA's role in covert action. Still, SOCOM can be expected to continue to play a larger part in this area than was the case in the past, probably necessitating some clarification of duties in the future. The war in Afghanistan continued to raise issues of this sort. The House Intelligence Committee, in 2009, said that certain military operations, called Operational Preparation of the Environment (OPE), which appear to be a combination of intelligence collection, covert action, and unconventional warfare, evade intelligence oversight because they are conducted by the military. Press accounts state that the CIA has trained Afghan paramilitary units, and DOD has confirmed that U.S. military personnel have been training Pakistani troops in counterinsurgency warfare. Press accounts have also described a major expansion of military clandestine bases and activities in the Central Command (CENTCOM) area of operations.

Efforts by SOCOM to expand its ability to deploy units overseas more quickly and more independently have raised questions about the relationship of SOCOM and the regional commanders as well as the effect such authority would have on the role of the State Department in decisions about increased overseas deployments. SOCOM's budget has continued to grow, but some members of Congress have raised concerns about the degree of secrecy in SOCOM budget requests—some of which Congress had sanctioned in the past—which makes congressional oversight of the budget more difficult. A SOCOM program to assess the effectiveness of propaganda was put on hold in 2014 because of congressional concerns.

Other factors of importance in this discussion of special operations versus covert intelligence teams are legal authorities, funding, and congressional notification.

The U.S. military operates under Title 10 (Armed Forces) of the U.S. Code; intelligence comes under Title 50 (War and National Defense). The legal authorities for their missions are therefore different and can lead to some difficult, if not comical, debates. A senior former intelligence official described how a cross-border operation involved both special operations and intelligence personnel, so it was not clear if it came under Title 10 or Title 50. The Solomonic decision in this case was as follows: If the operation took place during the day, it would be an intelligence lead and a covert action so as to be able to deny responsibility. However, if it took place at night, it would be a special operations mission, as plausible deniability would be less of an issue. There are also issues of who funds the operation and requirements for congressional notification, which are more stringent for covert action than they are for small-scale military operations—although the May 2011 bin Laden operation was briefed to a small number of congressional leaders because of the risk involved. Recent press accounts suggest an increase in joint intelligence–special forces operations against various terrorist targets.

A related issue has been the relative expertise of the cadre in the CIA responsible for covert action. Like the rest of the intelligence community, this staff, which has always been quite small, suffered losses in the budget cuts of the 1990s. Like the analytic cadre, it underwent fairly rapid growth after the 2001 attacks. President George W. Bush ordered a 50 percent increase in the Directorate of Operations at the time. As with the analysts, this has meant a larger but more inexperienced workforce. This relative inexperience was seen as one of the factors in the attack at a CIA base in Khost, Afghanistan, in December 2009, when a Jordanian agent who had been a source blew himself up and killed seven CIA officers. A review commissioned by DCIA Panetta concluded that the Jordanian had not been sufficiently vetted and that security precautions were insufficient. Several of the post-Khost actions that Panetta announced underscored the need for greater involvement in operations by more veteran officers.

According to press accounts, a CIA study commissioned in 2012 or 2013 found that covertly arming rebels seldom worked, the mujahideen in Afghanistan being a major exception. Efforts by both the CIA and Defense to arm "moderates" among the Syrian rebels fighting the regime of Bashar al-Assad underscore the difficulties of paramilitary operations. The Defense program was abandoned in 2015 as a near total failure, very few Syrians having been trained. The CIA program, another overt covert operation, was hampered by limited funding and by the complexity of the Syrian conflict. Determining which of the many rebel groups was "moderate" was difficult, and each group was so small as to likely make little difference to the overall outcome even if they did receive more arms. The Trump administration ended the Syria program in June 2017, apparently based on the view that it had little success of toppling al-Assad.

As with human intelligence (HUMINT), some covert actions rely on working with foreign liaison services. The issues relating to HUMINT raised earlier remain the same: motivation, reliability, and the ability to keep matters secret, as well as their standards of conduct. In the war against terrorists in Afghanistan and neighboring Pakistan, these issues have been of particular concern with Pakistan's Directorate of Inter-Service Intelligence (ISI), which had been a sponsor and patron of the Taliban prior to 2001. Saudi intelligence appears to have been instrumental in stopping the printer cartridge bombs that were being sent from Yemen as air freight to the United States but were intercepted in Dubai in October 2010. (See chap. 15 for a more complete discussion of foreign intelligence services.)

One concern raised by the conduct of covert actions is their possible effect on intelligence analysis, which is carried out, in part, by the same agency conducting the operation. If the CIA is conducting an operation—particularly a paramilitary operation—is it reasonable to expect analysts of the CIA to produce objective reports on the situation and the progress of the paramilitary operation? Or will there be a certain impetus, perhaps unstated, to be supportive of the operation? DCI Dulles kept the Directorate of Intelligence—the CIA's analytical arm— ignorant of operations in Indonesia (1957–1958) and at the Bay of Pigs (1961) so as not to contaminate it with knowledge of these operations. This potential problem can be addressed by the creation of mission centers in the CIA, staffed by operations officers and analysts.

In seventeenth- and (to a lesser extent) eighteenth-century Europe, statesmen occasionally used assassination as a foreign policy tool. Heads of state, who were royalty at this time, were exempt from this officially sanctioned act, but their ministers and generals were not. Soviet intelligence occasionally undertook "wet affairs," as it referred to assassinations. Israeli intelligence has allegedly killed individuals outside of Israel. In 2006, a former KGB officer, Alexander Litvinenko, was assassinated in London via radioactive polonium. A British public inquiry said Litvinenko's death was a Russian intelligence operation and was probably ordered by President Vladimir Putin. In 2018, another former Russian intelligence officer and spy for Britain, Sergei Skripal, along with his daughter, were hospitalized after exposure to a nerve agent, Novichok. The British government blamed Russia and expelled twenty-three Russian diplomats. One Briton died and another became seriously ill after coming into contact with the bottle apparently used by two Russian agents who had been identified as the ones who carried out the attempt. (See chap. 15 for a fuller discussion of the Russian role.)

The Church Committee (Senate Select Committee to Study Governmental Operations with Respect to Intelligence Activities), chaired by Frank Church, D-ID, was formed in 1975 to investigate allegations that the CIA had exceeded its charter. The panel found in 1976 that the United States was involved in several assassination plots in the 1960s and 1970s—the most famous being that against Fidel Castro— although none succeeded. (*See box, "Assassination: The Hitler Argument."*)

Since 1976, the United States has formally banned the use of assassination, either directly by the United States or through a third party. The ban has been written into three successive executive orders, the most recent signed by President Reagan in 1981, and updated in 2008, which remains in effect.

Still, the policy continues to be controversial. Although support for the ban was fairly widespread when instituted by President Gerald R. Ford (1974–1977), debate over the policy has grown. Opponents continue to hold that it is morally wrong for a state to target specific individuals. But proponents have argued that assassination might be the best option in some instances and might be morally acceptable, depending on the nature of the target. Drawing up such guidelines still appears to

ASSASSINATION:
THE HITLER ARGUMENT

Adolf Hitler is often cited as a good argument in favor of assassination as an occasional but highly exceptional policy option. But when would a policy maker have made the decision to have him killed? Hitler assumed power legally in 1933. Throughout the 1930s, he was not the only dictator in Europe who repressed civil liberties or arrested and killed large numbers of his own population. Josef Stalin probably killed more Soviet citizens during collectivization and the great purges than the number of people sent by the Nazis to death camps. Deciding to kill Hitler prior to his attacks on the Jews or the onset of World War II would have required a fair amount of foresight as to his ultimate purposes. Little about Hitler was extraordinary until he invaded Poland in 1939 and approved the "final solution" against the Jews in 1942.

Britain revealed in 1998 that its intelligence service considered assassinating Hitler during the war, even as late as 1945. The British abandoned the plan not because of moral qualms or concerns about success but because they decided that Hitler was so erratic as a military commander that he was an asset for the Allies.

be so difficult as to preclude a return to the previous policy. In the aftermath of the September 11, 2001, terrorist attacks, debate over the assassination ban was renewed. (*See box, "The Assassination Ban: A Modern Interpretation."*) The issue had changed somewhat, however, in that the United States now considered itself to be at war with terrorists, which altered the nature of the target and the legitimacy of using violent force. (See chap. 13 for a more detailed discussion of the ethical and moral issues raised by assassination.)

The use of UAVs to kill terrorists is not strictly a covert action, although it does involve acts that the United States does not always acknowledge. However, there is little deniability at present as the United States has been the only nation using armed drones in the areas where these attacks occur—although Britain used drones in September 2015 to kill two Britons fighting for the Islamic State. Prime Minister David Cameron cited self-defense, saying the two Britons had been planning attacks in the United Kingdom. If more states begin using drones unilaterally, there may be a need to reach some sort of international consensus on what types of operations are allowed or not—similar to other rules of war—although this could be difficult to achieve.

According to press accounts, the United States began using armed drones over Pakistan around 2002. The use of armed UAVs continued and increased significantly during the Obama administration. Some strikes targeted specific individuals; others have been "signature strikes" based on observed activities, such as men of military age gathering in groups—the "pattern of life" discussed in chapter 5. The use of

THE ASSASSINATION BAN: A MODERN INTERPRETATION

In August 1998, the United States launched a cruise missile attack on targets in Afghanistan associated with al Qaeda leader Osama bin Laden. The United States believed that bin Laden was behind the terrorist attacks earlier that month on two U.S. embassies in East Africa.

The Clinton administration later stated that one goal of the raid was to kill bin Laden and his lieutenants. Administration officials also argued that their targeting of bin Laden did not violate the long-standing ban on assassinations. Their view was based on an opinion written by National Security Council lawyers that the United States could legally target terrorist infrastructures and that bin Laden's main infrastructure was human.

After the September 2001 attacks, bin Laden and other terrorists were seen as legitimate combatant targets, as the United States was at war against them in self-defense, as described by Attorney General Eric Holder after bin Laden's death in 2011.

armed UAVs became more controversial in 2012–2013 for several reasons. Some—including former DNI Dennis Blair and former Afghan commander Gen. Stanley McChrystal—argued that the number of high-value terrorist targets was decreasing and that the continued heavy reliance on drones was having a negative effect on U.S. relations with Pakistan and other states and was negatively affecting "hearts and minds" in areas where terrorists sought support. Pakistan has protested UAV attacks flown from inside Pakistan but may have used the U.S. presence as cover for Pakistani-flown attacks against terrorists. The United States has offered some concessions in UAV operations to mollify Pakistan but has not been willing to end the flights.

Another area of controversy in UAV operations has been civilian casualties. Although steps are taken to avoid or minimize these casualties, the fact that terrorists live within local populations makes these casualties inevitable given the number of UAV missions. There is a certain odd aspect to some of the protests over the use of drones and civilian casualties given the near certainty that using conventional munitions from airplanes or cruise missiles would put many more civilians at risk. This issue became more controversial in April 2015, when President Obama announced that a UAV strike on al Qaeda in Pakistan in January had also killed two Western hostages, Warren Weinstein and Giovanni Lo Porto; the United States subsequently gave Lo Porto's family 1.185 million euros "in his memory." On July 1, 2016, the Office of the DNI (ODNI) acknowledged that 64 to 116 noncombatants had been killed in 473 drone strikes in nonactive combat areas over the course of the Obama administration. Critics and private groups that track drone strikes questioned the official figures for noncombatant deaths. President Obama also signed Executive Order 13732 listing steps to minimize civilian casualties and calling for an annual report similar to the one released in July 2016.

The greatest controversy about UAVs stemmed from the killing of Anwar al-Awlaki in a drone attack in Yemen in September 2011. Awlaki was born in the United States in 1971 and had dual U.S.-Yemeni citizenship. He apparently became radicalized in the 1990s—in part as a reaction to FBI surveillance that revealed Awlaki's use of prostitutes—and, after leaving the United States in 2002, served as a recruiter for al Qaeda and encouraged terrorist attacks against Americans and American targets. Awlaki had been linked to Maj. Nidal Hasan, who attacked fellow soldiers at Fort Hood, Texas, in November 2009, and to Umar Abdulmutallab, who tried to set off explosives on an airliner in December 2009. The Fifth Amendment to the Constitution states that "[no] person [shall] . . . be deprived of life, liberty, or property without due process of law." Thus, a question arose concerning the legality of the decision to kill Awlaki, which was a targeted strike. This debate became more pointed during the hearings over John Brennan's nomination to be director of the CIA in early 2013.

Brennan, as President Obama's counterterrorism adviser, had given a speech in April 2011 in which he acknowledged the targeted strike policy in Pakistan and alluded to it in Yemen and Somalia. In February 2013, the Justice Department released a white paper that offered a legal justification for using lethal force against a U.S. citizen operating abroad who was a senior operational leader of al Qaeda or an associated force. The main criteria are (1) that the individual poses an "imminent threat of violent attack" against the United States, (2) that "capture is infeasible," and (3) that "the operation would be conducted in a manner consistent with applicable law of war principles." According to press reports, President Obama reviewed the names of possible terrorist targets in a weekly "kill list," as it was popularly called, but did not approve specific strikes. The Obama administration criteria included verifying the identity of a proposed target. There were two different types of drones strikes: (1) against specifically identified **"high-value targets,"** and (2) **"signature strikes"** based on observed activities—such as large groups of armed individuals or groups of vehicles—in areas where terrorists operate and that tend to indicate possible terrorist activity. According to press accounts, the CIA had been conducting drone strikes in Pakistan, but Obama shifted responsibility for the actual strikes from the CIA to the Defense Department. Again according to press accounts, DCIA Mike Pompeo (2017–2018) argued successfully to President Trump that CIA authority to conduct drone strikes should be broadened to include Afghanistan, Yemen, and Somalia. Critics held that this decision would erode the greater transparency into drone operations that had been part of Obama's order. The reported change in the CIA role regarding drones was consistent with other press reports that Pompeo had also been told to expand the role of CIA teams in Afghanistan, in conjunction with Afghan forces, to locate and kill Taliban militants.

In a May 2013 speech, President Obama admitted that four U.S. citizens had been killed in drone strikes, one alongside Awlaki and two others—including Awlaki's son—in strikes on larger groups. In June 2014, a federal appeals court released portions of a 2010 Justice Department memo that gave the legal justification for the attack on Awlaki, laying out the arguments that were later embodied in the 2013 white paper. In November 2015, a federal appeals court ruled that internal documents concerning targeted operations against noncitizens could be kept classified.

Despite the Justice Department white paper, the policy of targeting certain U.S. citizens remains controversial. Former DCIA Michael Hayden pointed out an interesting irony when he observed that it takes a court order to tap the telephone of a U.S. citizen who is a terrorist, but not to kill him under certain conditions. Having previously fought successfully in court to maintain the secrecy of drone-related memos, in his May 2013 speech Obama announced the release of material that was briefed to Congress. He also announced new restrictions on the use of drones. As noted above, in July 2016, the Obama administration released figures for drone strikes and combatant and noncombatant deaths.

In November 2013, three Democratic members of the Senate Intelligence Committee supported the attack against Awlaki but called for a better understanding of the "evidentiary threshold" for conducting attacks on U.S. citizens. As of early 2014, the Senate and House Intelligence Committees were at odds on this issue, with the Senate favoring an additional review process for such attacks and the House opposing this. The Senate committee also supported an annual public report on the casualties resulting from drone strikes, which the House committee opposed.

Several other issues also arose regarding the use of armed UAVs. One was the issue of congressional oversight, often expressed in the new buzzword, "transparency." Although the intelligence committees are briefed on covert action findings, this may not be the case for UAV policy, which—as noted—is not necessarily a covert action as currently used. Members wanted more insight into the basis of the use of drones, leading to the release of the Justice Department memo. Some members also suggested establishing a secret court, similar to the Foreign Intelligence Surveillance Court (FISC), to review potential UAV attacks. Critics of this proposal pointed out that courts review legal cases but are not intended to make wartime decisions and that such a court could, in effect, become superior to decisions made by the president as commander-in-chief. Also, federal judges are not elected; the president is. Such a court would also not necessarily improve the due process rights of a proposed target as the target would have no representation in or chance to appeal the proceedings. In April 2016, a federal appeals court dismissed a suit seeking more access to how decisions are made to use drones.

Another issue was the question of which government agency or agencies should conduct drone strikes. They have been conducted by both the CIA and the Defense Department, although President Obama and DCIA Brennan both expressed the view that these flights should be shifted to Defense, in large part if not entirely. Such a shift would make the policy more transparent but would add other complications. The chain of command is shorter and more immediate in the CIA than it is in the military. Also, given that UAVs fly from bases in foreign countries, there is the issue of keeping the host government informed of operations, which is usual for U.S. military forces but not for CIA activities.

Despite this stated goal of shifting UAV-based attacks from the CIA to Defense, the transition apparently did not occur. In January 2014, the omnibus appropriations bill reportedly included language barring such a shift. Various senators complained that they were unaware of the language, which is contained in a classified annex. According to aides, Sen. Dianne Feinstein, D-CA, then chair of the Senate Intelligence Committee, and other legislators had concerns about how Defense would manage the UAV program and whether Defense would take steps to prevent collateral damage. Supporters of the current program also argue that the CIA has, by now, developed much greater expertise in these operations. Those who favor a shift to Defense argue that the emphasis on UAV operations is harming the core CIA roles of espionage and analysis.

ASSESSING COVERT ACTION

In addition to raising ethical and moral issues, the utility of covert action is difficult to assess. When examining a covert action, what constitutes success? Is it just achieving the aims of the operation? Should human costs, if any, be factored into the equation? Is the covert action still a success if its origin has been exposed?

Some people question the degree to which covert actions produce useful outcomes. For example, critics point to the 1953 coup against Iranian premier Mohammad Mossadegh and argue that it helped lead to the Khomeini regime in 1979. Proponents argue that an operation that put in place a regime friendly to the United States for twenty-six years, in a region as volatile as the Middle East, was successful. If no covert action is likely to create permanent positive change given the volatility of politics in all nations, is there some period of time that should be used to determine the relative success of a covert action?

As with all other policies, the record of covert action is mixed, and no hard-and-fast rules have been devised for assessing them. Assistance to anticommunist parties in Western Europe in the 1940s was successful; the Bay of Pigs was a fiasco. The view here is that the Mossadegh coup was a success, for the reasons noted earlier. But covert action is also subject to the law of unintended consequences. Abetting the fall of Allende helped lead to the regime of Gen. Augusto Pinochet. Average Chileans were probably better off than they would have been under an evolving Marxist regime, but many people suffered repression and terror. Aid to the mujahideen in Afghanistan was highly successful and played an important role in the collapse of the Soviet Union. At the same time, Afghanistan remained mired in a civil war ten years after the last Soviet troops withdrew and was eventually ruled by the Taliban, which hosted the al Qaeda terrorists.

This is sometimes seen as a "law of unintended consequences" effect. The fictional vaccination program created in Pakistan as a means to obtain DNA on the individuals in the bin Laden compound in Abbottabad is another example, given the subsequent Muslim militant attacks killing dozens of Pakistani public health workers, claiming they were spies (see chap. 5). Try as policy makers and covert actions planners might to foresee all of the possible outcomes and effects of an operation, this clearly is not possible. Indeed, it may become more problematic the further one gets from the covert action itself.

Covert action tends to be successful the more closely it is tied to specific policy goals and the more carefully defined the operation is.

KEY TERMS

blowback 241
covert action 229
deep fakes 235
disinformation 235
enhanced interrogation
    techniques (EITs) 238
high-value targets 248
memo of notification (MON) 233

paramilitary operations 237
plausible deniability 238
plumbing 230
presidential finding 232
propaganda 234
renditions 237
signature strikes 248
third option 229

FURTHER READINGS

The works listed do not go into the details of specific operations, with a few exceptions. Instead, they focus on the major policy issues discussed in this chapter.

Barry, James A. "Covert Action Can Be Just." *Orbis* 37 (summer 1993): 375–390.

Berkowitz, Bruce D., and Allan E. Goodman. "The Logic of Covert Action." *National Interest* 51 (spring 1998): 38–46.

Chesney, Robert. "Military-Intelligence Convergence and the Law of the Title 10/Title 50 Debate." *Journal of National Security Law and Policy* 5 (February 2012): 539–629.

Chomeau, John B. "Covert Action's Proper Role in U.S. Policy." *International Journal of Intelligence and Counterintelligence* 2 (fall 1988): 407–413.

Coll, Steve. *Directorate S: The CIA and America's Secret Wars in Afghanistan and Pakistan.* New York: Penguin Press, 2018.

Cormac, Rory, and Richard J. Aldrich, "Grey Is the New Black: Covert Action and Implausible Deniability." *International Affairs* 94 (May 2018): 477–494. (Available at https://academic.oup.com/ia/article/94/3/477/4992414.)

Daugherty, William J. "Approval and Review of Covert Action Programs Since Reagan." *International Journal of Intelligence and Counterintelligence* 17 (spring 2004): 62–80.

DeVine, Michael E., and Heidi M. Peters. *Covert Action and Clandestine Activities of the Intelligence Community: Selected Definitions in Brief.* CRS Report R45175. Washington, D.C.: Congressional Research Service, April 25, 2018.

Feickart, Andrew. *U.S. Special Operations Forces (SOF): Background and Issues for Congress.* CRS Report RS21048. Washington, D.C.: Congressional Research Service, January 3, 2013.

Gilligan, Tom. *10,000 Days With the Agency.* Boston, Mass.: Intelligence Books Division, 2003.

Godson, Roy S. *Dirty Tricks or Trump Cards: U.S. Covert Action and Counterintelligence.* Washington, D.C.: Brassey's, 1996.

Harlow, Bill, et al. *Rebuttal: The CIA Responds to the Senate Intelligence Committee's Study of Its Detention and Interrogation Program.* Annapolis, Md.: Naval Institute Press, 2015.

Johnson, Loch K. "Covert Action and Accountability: Decision-Making for America's Secret Foreign Policy." *International Studies Quarterly* 33 (March 1989): 81–109.

Knott, Stephen F. *Secret and Sanctioned: Covert Operations and the American Presidency*. New York: Oxford University Press, 1996.

Mazzetti, Mark. *The Way of the Knife: The CIA, a Secret Army, and a War at the Ends of the Earth*. New York: Penguin Press, 2013.

Neustadt, Richard E., and Ernest R. May. *Thinking in Time: The Uses of History for Decision Makers*. New York: Free Press, 1988.

Prados, John. *Presidents' Secret Wars: CIA and Pentagon Covert Operations Since World War II*. New York: William Morrow, 1986.

Reisman, W. Michael, and James E. Baker. *Regulating Covert Action: Practices, Contexts, and Policies of Covert Coercion Abroad in International and American Law*. New Haven, Conn.: Yale University Press, 1992.

Rositzke, Harry. *The CIA's Secret Operations: Espionage, Counterespionage, and Covert Action*. New York: Reader's Digest Press, 1977.

Savage, Charlie. "How 4 Federal Lawyers Paved the Way to Kill Osama bin Laden." *New York Times*, October 28, 2015. (Available at http://www.nytimes.com/2015/10/29/us/politics/obama-legal-authorization-osama-bin-laden-raid.html.)

Schulman, Loren De Jonge. *Behind the Magical Thinking: Lessons From Policymaker Relationships With Drones*. Washington, D.C.: Center for New American Security, 2018. (Available at https://www.cnas.org/publications/reports/behind-the-magical-thinking.)

Shane, Scott. *Objective Troy: A Terrorist, a President, and the Rise of the Drone*. New York: Tim Duggan Books, 2015.

Shulsky, Abram N., and Gary J. Schmitt. *Silent Warfare: Understanding the World of Intelligence*. 2d rev. ed. Washington, D.C.: Brassey's, 1993.

Stiefler, Todd. "CIA's Leadership and Major Covert Operations: Rogue Elephants or Risk-Averse Bureaucrats?" *Intelligence and National Security* 19 (winter 2004): 632–654.

Treverton, Gregory F. *Covert Action: The Limits of Intervention in the Postwar World*. New York: Basic Books, 1987.

U.S. Department of Justice. "Memorandum for the Attorney General. Re: Applicability of Federal Criminal Laws and the Constitution to the Contemplated Lethal Operations Against Shaykh Anwar al-Aulaqi." Washington, D.C., July 16, 2010. (Available at https://www.aclu.org/legal-document/aclu-v-doj-foia-request-olc-memo?redirect=national-security/anwar-al-aulaqi-foia-request-olc-memo.)

———. "Lawfulness of a Lethal Operation Directed Against a U.S. Citizen Who Is a Senior Operational Leader of Al-Qa'ida or an Associated Force." Washington, D.C., draft November 8, 2011. (Available at www.justice.gov/oip/docs/dept-white-paper.pdf.)

U.S. Office of the Director of National Intelligence. *Summary of Information Regarding U.S. Counterterrorism Strikes Outside Areas of Active Hostilities*. ODNI News Release No. 17–16, July 1, 2016. (Available from https://www.dni.gov/files/documents/Newsroom/Press%20Releases/DNI+Release+on+CT+Strikes+Outside+Areas+of+Active+Hostilities.PDF.)

U.S. President. Executive Order 13732, United States Policy on Pre- and Post-Strike Measures to Address Civilian Casualties in U.S. Operations Involving the Use of Force. July 1, 2016. (Available at https://www.federalregister.gov/articles/2016/07/07/2016-16295/united-states-policy-on-pre-and-post-strike-measures-to-address-civilian-casualties-in-us.)

U.S. Senate Select Committee on Intelligence. *Committee Study of the Central Intelligence Agency's Detention and Interrogation Program*. Washington, D.C., December 9, 2014. (Available at http://www.intelligence.senate.gov/press/committee-releases-study-cias-detention-and-interrogation-program.)

Wall, Andru E. "Demystifying the Title 10–Title 50 Debate: Distinguishing Military Operations, Intelligence Activities & Covert Action." *Harvard National Security Journal* 3 (2011): 85–141. (Available at http://harvardnsj.org/wp-content/uploads/2012/01/Vol-3-Wall.pdf.)

CHAPTER NINE

THE ROLE OF THE POLICY MAKER

M any authors and experts in the area of intelligence do not consider the policy maker to be part of the intelligence process. In their opinion, once the intelligence has been given to the policy client, the intelligence process is complete. The view in this book is that policy makers play such a central role at all stages of the process that it would be a mistake to omit them. Policy makers do more than receive intelligence; they shape it. Without a constant reference to policy, intelligence is rendered meaningless. Moreover, policy makers can play a determining role at every phase of the intelligence process.

THE U.S. NATIONAL SECURITY POLICY PROCESS

Although much of this book is intended to be a generic discussion of intelligence, the main reference point is the U.S. government. Therefore, a brief discussion of how national security policy is formed in the United States is appropriate.

Structure and Interests. The five main loci of the U.S. national security policy process are

1. The president, as an individual;

2. The departments, the State Department and the Department of Defense (DOD), which has two major components: the civilian (the Office of the Secretary of Defense) and the military (the Joint Chiefs of Staff, or JCS, the Joint Staff, and the four military services), and on certain issues, other departments will also be involved, including Justice, Commerce, Treasury, Energy, Agriculture, Health and Human Services, and, after the September 2001 attacks, the newly created Department of Homeland Security (DHS);

3. The National Security Council (NSC) staff, which is the hub of the system;

4. The intelligence community; and

5. Congress, which controls all expenditures, makes policy in its own right, and performs oversight.

The main national security structure was remarkably stable from its inception in the National Security Act of 1947 until the Intelligence Reform and Terrorism Prevention Act of 2004 (IRTPA), which radically changed the top management structure of the intelligence community.

The five groups that carry out the intelligence process have varying interests. Presidents are transient, mainly concerned about broad policy initiatives and, eventually, their place in history. Richard M. Nixon (1969–1974), who was intensely suspicious of the permanent bureaucracy, argued—correctly—that a gulf exists between the president's interests and those of the bureaucracy. Sometimes they work together; at other times they are at odds. The bureaucracy tends to be more jaded and, on occasion, to take the view that it can outlast the president, presidential appointees, and their preferred policies.

The principal interest of the State Department is maintaining diplomatic relations as a means of furthering U.S. policy interests. Critics of the State Department argue that Foreign Service officers sometimes forget which nation they represent, becoming advocates for the nations on which they have expertise instead of for the United States.

DOD is concerned primarily with having a military capability sufficient to deter hostile nations from using force or, if that fails, being able to bring to bear an overwhelming preponderance of force so as to terminate the conflict quickly and on favorable terms. Critics of DOD hold that the department overestimates its needs and threats and requires too large a margin against any potential foe. In response to the Vietnam War, the unofficial but influential rules for the use of force promulgated by Secretary of Defense Caspar W. Weinberger (1981–1987) and JCS chairman Gen. Colin L. Powell (1989–1993) set high requirements for domestic political support and force preponderance before any troops are committed. The protracted struggles in Afghanistan (2001–) and Iraq (2003–2011) will probably result in a renewed debate over the Weinberger and Powell requirements. Disagreements over how and when to use force were also reflected in the debate between Secretary of Defense Donald Rumsfeld (2001–2006) and Army Chief of Staff Gen. Eric Shinseki (1999–2003). Shinseki argued that more troops would be needed to occupy Iraq than had been allocated; Rumsfeld ignored Shinseki.

DHS is responsible for coordinating the activities of many long-standing agencies, including the Coast Guard, Immigration and Naturalization, the Border Patrol, the Secret Service, and the Federal Emergency Management Agency (FEMA). It has also established new components, such as the Transportation Security Administration (TSA). DHS seeks to prevent new terrorist attacks in the United States and serves as a bridge between the federal government and state and local law enforcement agencies on domestic security issues. It is also responsible for critical infrastructure protection, most of which belongs to the private sector, and for much of the cyber policy enunciated by the Obama administration. DHS has had to deal with a difficult structure, as it tries to meld together the activities of several former independent agencies or offices taken from other departments, as well as the issue of determining what it is that DHS is responsible for. (See chap. 12 for a broader discussion of the intelligence implications of this doctrinal issue.)

The NSC, as constituted by law, consists of the president, the vice president, the secretaries of state and defense, and, more recently, the secretary of energy. The chairman of the JCS serves as the military adviser; the director of national intelligence (DNI) is subordinate to the NSC and serves as the intelligence adviser. That said, it has been the practice since the first DNI in 2005 to have both the DNI and the director of the Central Intelligence Agency (DCIA) present at NSC meetings. This may seem redundant given that the DNI is the senior intelligence adviser, but it must be recalled that the DCIA controls most of the all-source analysts in the intelligence community and has direct day-to-day responsibility for the two most politically dangerous intelligence activities, espionage and covert actions. This underscores, once again, an inherent weakness in the DNI's position and the importance for the DNI to have good relations with the DCIA. As noted in chap. 3, the Trump administration initially wanted to limit the attendance of the DNI and chairman of the Joint Chiefs to NSC meetings in which issues relevant to their expertise were being discussed. There may be issues that have no military component, but it is difficult to conceive of issues where some intelligence input would not be useful, if not necessary. What made this decision more unusual was the inclusion of Trump's chief strategist, Stephen Bannon, as an NSC member. All of these decisions were later reversed; Bannon was fired a few months later.

As a corporate group, the full NSC meets irregularly. The Principals Committee (called the PC) is made up of the NSC members (less the president) and is presided over by the national security adviser. The Deputies Committee (DC) meets more often. Below the DC are Interagency Policy Committees (IPCs) and Sub-Interagency Policy Committees (Sub-IPCs), dealing with specific issues at a lower level. According to press accounts, National Security Adviser John Bolton (2018–) has replaced some PCs with "paper PCs," where options and views are circulated among members but there is no actual meeting. This reduces the number of meetings but also makes it more difficult to have vigorous debates. In addition, it enhances the role of the national security adviser in controlling policy discussions.

Day-to-day, the National Security Council staff (NSC staff) reports to the national security adviser. This is a key position, as the national security adviser sets much of the tone for the overall process of policy deliberation. This position does not exist in law and is not subject to Senate confirmation. The national security adviser can be either civil or military. There are two major models for conducting this job. One might be called the Brent Scowcroft model. Scowcroft was national security adviser twice, under President Gerald Ford from 1975 to 1977 and under President George H. W. Bush from 1989 to 1993. Scowcroft operated as an "honest broker," making sure that all points of view were brought before the president but not acting as a policy advocate. The other model might be called the Henry Kissinger model. Kissinger was national security adviser under Presidents Nixon and Ford, from 1969 to 1975. Kissinger operated as a policy maker in his own right and came to dominate nearly all aspects of national security policy. For two years, Kissinger served simultaneously as secretary of state and national security adviser. Regardless of the model, the national security adviser serves at the pleasure of the president and it can be a volatile relationship. Ronald Reagan had six national security advisers in his eight-year tenure. Donald Trump was on his third national security adviser after fifteen months as president.

The NSC staff consists of career civil servants, military officers, and political appointees who have day-to-day responsibility for conveying the wishes of the president to the policy and intelligence communities and for coordinating among the departments and agencies. The NSC staff consists of regional and functional offices. The NSC staff is interested primarily in the execution of policy as defined by the president and senior presidential appointees. The size of the NSC staff has been an increasing point of concern as it has continued to grow—going from 20 staffers under President John F. Kennedy to more than 40 under President George H. W. Bush to roughly 100 under President Bill Clinton to more than 400 under President Barack Obama. This expansion has not only made the NSC staff unwieldy, but it has also meant that more and more policy development has been concentrated in the NSC staff rather than in the departments. For example, under previous administrations, IPCs and Sub-IPCs had been chaired by lead departments or agencies. In the Obama administration, these were brought under the NSC. Although it is usual for departments to complain about "White House micromanagement" in each administration, there now seems to be genuine concern, to the point where the Obama administration recognized the problem and said that it would reduce the size of the NSC staff. The FY2017 National Defense Authorization Act (P.L. 114-328, December 23, 2016) limits the professional staff of the NSC to 200, a substantial reduction but still a large staff.

The intelligence community has no policy interests per se, although it wants to be kept informed about the course of policy to make a contribution to it.

Policy Dynamics. Policy makers often refer to the "interagency process" or "the interagency." The term reflects the involvement of any and all necessary agencies and players in the process. The ultimate goal of the U.S. policy process is to arrive at a consensus that all parties can support. But consensus in the U.S. bureaucratic system means agreement down to the last detail of any paper being considered.

The process has no override mechanism, that is, no way of forcing agreement, of isolating an agency that refuses to go along. This safeguards the rights and interests of all agencies, because the agency that does not agree with the others on an issue today may not be the one that objects tomorrow. To ensure that an agency is not coerced, the interagency process emphasizes bargaining and negotiation, steering away from dictating from above or by majority rule. Bargaining has three immediate effects. First, it can require a great deal of time to arrive at positions that everyone can accept. Second, the system gives leverage to any agency that refuses to reach an agreement. In the absence of any override process, the agency that "just says 'no'" can wield enormous power. Third, the necessity of reaching agreement generates substantial pressure in favor of lowest common denominator decisions.

On controversial issues, the system can suffer inertia, as agencies constantly redraft papers that never achieve consensus or that one agency refuses to support, effectively bringing the system to a halt. The only way to break such logjams is for the NSC staff or someone higher—meaning the president and senior appointees—to apply pressure. Without their intervention, the system would spin endlessly if an agency continues to hold out. Senior pressure renews the impetus to reach a conclusion or raises the prospect that officials in the holdout agency will be told to support what the president wants or to resign. But without pressure from above, holdouts suffer no penalty.

Neither the policy community nor the intelligence community is a monolith. Each has multiple players with multiple interests, which do not always coincide with one another. It is important to remember that executive departments are also not monolithic. DOD is clearly divided between the Office of the Secretary of Defense (OSD) and the JCS. Even though the concept of civilian control of the military is a deeply ingrained value, the two parts may not agree. As noted, in the period just before the invasion of Iraq, Army chief of staff General Shinseki held the view that the number of troops that would be needed to occupy Iraq was far larger than what Secretary of Defense Rumsfeld had planned. Under the doctrine of civilian control of the military, the secretary prevailed. But Shinseki's effectiveness as Army chief of staff was at an end. Also, within Defense each of the four military services has distinct interests. The State Department is famously divided between the regional bureaus and the functional bureaus, with the regional bureaus tending to dominate. The Foreign Service, that is, the career diplomats, also see themselves apart from the political appointees with whom they work or to whom they report. DHS has yet to forge the agencies that were placed together into a coherent whole; many seem to acknowledge that they are part of DHS only by sufferance. A similar internal dichotomy can be described for virtually all other departments.

The Role of the Intelligence Community. Policy makers accept the intelligence community as an important part of the system. But the role of intelligence varies with each administration and sometimes with each issue within an administration. The way in which an administration treats intelligence is the key determinant of the role it plays.

Everyone accepts the utility of intelligence as part of the basis on which decisions are made. Again, translating this generality into practice is the important issue. Policy makers have many reasons to find fault with or even to ignore intelligence. They do not necessarily view intelligence in the same way as those who are producing it.

Policy makers also understand that the intelligence community can be called on to carry out certain types of operations. Again, the willingness to use this capacity and the specific types of operations that are deemed acceptable vary with the political leadership. These elected or presidentially appointed leaders must make the final decisions on operations and are held accountable, in a political sense, if the operations fail. To be sure, intelligence officers can and do get their share of the blame, but policy makers perceive that their own costs are much greater. But the nature of the relationship is captured in a rueful saying among intelligence officers: "There are only policy successes and intelligence failures. There are no policy failures and intelligence successes."

Finally, the intelligence relationship with most new administrations begins somewhat tentatively. Richard Kerr, a former deputy DCI and acting DCI, noted, "We sometimes know more about foreign governments than we do about our own government. We sometimes know more about foreign leaders than we do about an incoming administration." Even though the mechanics of presidential transitions are well-established, there will always be some uncertainty, driven to a greater or lesser

extent by personalities and expertise, or lack thereof, on the part of the new administration's senior officials.

WHO WANTS WHAT?

The fact that the government is not a monolithic organization helps explain why
policy makers and intelligence officers have different interests. At a high macro level,
everyone wants the same thing—successful national security policy—but this statement is so general that it is misleading. Success can mean different things to policy
makers and intelligence officials.

The president and an administration's senior political appointees define success
as the advancement of their agenda. Even though a broad continuity had existed in
U.S. foreign policy until the Trump administration, each administration interprets
goals individually and fosters initiatives that are uniquely its own. The success of an
administration's agenda must be demonstrable in ways that are easily comprehended,
because its successes are expected to have a political dividend. This is not as crass as it
sounds. National security policy is created within a political system and process, the
ultimate rewards of which are election and reelection to national office. Finally, policy
makers expect support for their policies from the permanent bureaucracy.

The intelligence community defines its goals differently. Recall the three wishes
posed by Sherman Kent. (See chap. 6.) The intelligence community also wants to
maintain its objectivity regarding policy. Intelligence officials do not want to become,
or even to be seen as becoming, advocates for policies other than those that directly
affect their activities. Only by maintaining their distance from policy can they hope to
produce intelligence that is objective. But objectivity is not always easily achieved. To
cite one example, Director of Central Intelligence (DCI) George J. Tenet (1997–2004)
was intimately involved in the Israeli-Palestinian negotiations in October 1998. The
Central Intelligence Agency (CIA) took responsibility for creating a security relationship between the two sides. As a result, the CIA had a vested interest in the outcome
of the agreement, not because of any intelligence it had produced but because it had
become a participant. In this sort of case, legitimate questions can be raised about the
potential effect on subsequent analyses of the implementation of the agreement. Will
analysts feel free to report that security arrangements are failing, if that is the case,
knowing that their own agency is charged with implementing these same arrangements? The answer may be yes, but it is subject to serious question.

In 2008, DNI Mike McConnell (2007–2009), in *Vision 2015*, stated that the intelligence community's mission was to provide policy makers with "**decision advantage**."
This concept, first developed by Jennifer Sims, a professional intelligence officer and
scholar, seeks to provide policy makers with intelligence that will give them an advantage over adversaries, allowing them to act with greater confidence and greater likelihood of success. In many respects, decision advantage is a variation on opportunity
analysis discussed earlier. (See chap. 6.) Like opportunity analysis, decision advantage
runs the risk of getting too close to the policy-intelligence line. The inherent risk for
intelligence officers is that the action will not play out advantageously and much of the
onus for failure will then fall on the intelligence officers.

The policy maker–intelligence community relationship changes the longer the policy makers stay in office. At the outset of their relationship, most policy makers tend to be more impressed and more accepting of the intelligence they receive. Even for policy makers who are returning to government service, albeit in different and usually more senior positions, this tends to be true. However, as the policy makers become more familiar with the issues for which they are responsible and with the available intelligence, they tend to have higher expectations and to become more demanding. There is also an interesting dichotomy between the attitudes of most incoming presidents and their immediate subordinates in terms of how they view intelligence. Very few incoming presidents have any working familiarity with national intelligence. If we look at the presidents since World War II, only three (Dwight Eisenhower, Richard Nixon, and George H. W. Bush) had any significant exposure to national intelligence before taking office. But many of their subordinates will have worked with intelligence agencies earlier in their careers, as they moved up the policy ladder. Thus, senior and mid-level political appointees are likely to be more familiar and more comfortable with intelligence than their presidents—and perhaps more jaded about it as well.

The Trump administration transition was something of an exception. Resentful that allegations of Russian interference during the 2016 election undermined the legitimacy of his victory, Trump compared U.S. intelligence agencies to Nazis and accused them of being part of a "deep state," a phrase more often used to describe authoritarian or semiauthoritarian governments where the security services have a largely independent existence and can dictate the course of policy and even change governments. (The details of the investigations into Russian interference are beyond the scope of this book. Russia's actions are discussed in chaps. 8, 12, and 15.) These comments did little to start relations between the new administration and the intelligence agencies on a sound footing.

After taking office, Trump continued to take public exception to intelligence community positions. He repeatedly questioned the view that Russia had interfered in the 2016 election. In a joint appearance with Russian president Vladimir Putin in Helsinki, Finland, in July 2018, Trump said he accepted Putin's claim that Russia had not interfered. In October 2018, Trump refused to accept the intelligence community assessment that dissident Saudi journalist Jamal Khashoggi was killed on orders of the Saudi government in the Saudi consulate in Istanbul and not by accident. The April 2019 report of special counsel Robert Mueller found no collusion between the Trump presidential campaign and Russia but reaffirmed that Russia took steps to influence the outcome of the election. Again, there is nothing wrong or novel about policy makers disagreeing with or rejecting intelligence. Presidents Kennedy, Lyndon Johnson, Nixon, and George W. Bush all took issue at various points with the support they received from intelligence agencies.

In February 2019, after DNI Dan Coats (2017–2019) and other leaders in the intelligence community had delivered their annual *Worldwide Threat Assessment* testimony, Trump publicly took issue with some of their views, in particular those on North Korea and Iran (see chaps. 11 and 12). Trump called the intelligence community leadership "naïve" and said "perhaps they should go back to school." After a meeting and photo opportunity in the Oval Office with Coats, DCIA Gina Haspel, and FBI director Christopher Wray, Trump claimed that the intelligence chiefs said they had been misquoted and taken out of context. However, news reports of their testimony were accurate. Trump could not distinguish between differences of opinion on how other states might behave versus opposing policy, which would be out of bounds. This type of disagreement very rarely happens in public or repeatedly.

In May 2019, Trump gave Attorney General William Barr authority to declassify intelligence agency documents as part of Barr's examination of how U.S. intelligence agencies investigated relations between the Trump campaign and Russia during the 2016 election. Some observers argued that Barr could "cherry pick" among classified intelligence and that he might put intelligence sources and methods at risk, depending on which documents he chose to release. The DNI is responsible in law for protecting intelligence sources and methods, and typically agency heads decide which documents can be declassified. These various incidents suggest that there is little trust between Trump and the intelligence community, which is extremely problematic.

To some, the nature of the relationship between the DCI or DNI and the president also is a factor. George Tenet enjoyed what was probably the closest relationship of any DCI to a president, usually seeing George W. Bush at least five or six days a week, and sometimes several times a day. This began on the president's taking office in 2001, when he said he wanted daily briefings from the DCI. This was a dramatic change from the situation under Clinton, when the DCI saw the president much less often. Clinton's first DCI, R. James Woolsey (1993–1995), left office in frustration over his lack of access. As DCI Richard Helms (1966–1973) observed, a great deal of the DCI's authority derived from the perception that he had access to the president when he needed it. So, for Tenet, the increased access to President Bush was a great gain. But some observers questioned whether such increased access had an effect on the DCI's objectivity. Critics cited Tenet's enthusiastic report on the likelihood of weapons of mass destruction (WMD) in Iraq. However, the report by the Senate Select Committee on Intelligence said no evidence existed that the intelligence had been politicized.

The same questions are relevant for the DNI. Like the DCI, the DNI needs to have access to the president. In some respects, this may be even more important for the DNI because, unlike the DCI, the DNI has no large institutional base (the CIA) on which to fall back. The DNI may have to put more effort into keeping abreast of what the intelligence community is doing and which parts of it are also communicating with the president. This was one of the issues, with specific reference to covert action and espionage, that created a rift between DNI Dennis Blair and DCIA Leon Panetta in 2009–2010. There is no definitive answer. Frequent contact between the DNI and the president is bound to run risks, but no DNI would be likely to choose the alternative relationship. The DNI should trust his or her instincts and rely on professionalism to maintain the proper bounds on the relationship. Once the Trump administration understood that it had to appoint a DNI, despite its preference not to do so, it was not clear how much access to Trump DNI Coats had, as opposed to DCIA Mike Pompeo (2017–2018). Pompeo clearly had great influence as DCIA, as shown when he, rather than Secretary of State Rex Tillerson or Coats, was sent to Pyongyang to feel out the North Koreans on possible talks. Pompeo replaced Tillerson at State in 2018, and it has been reported that Coats attends Trump's intelligence briefings.

Proximity to the president can also have a cost within the ranks of the intelligence community, especially if the DNI is not a professional intelligence officer. Like any other group of professionals, intelligence officers prefer to be directed by one of their own, someone who understands them, who shares their values and cultures, and who shares some of their experiences. Remember that only three DCIs were professional intelligence officers (Richard Helms, William E. Colby, and Robert M. Gates) and two had wartime intelligence experience (Allen Dulles and William Casey). (Since then, three DCIAs have had intelligence experience. Porter J. Goss served in the Clandestine Service, as has Gina Haspel; John Brennan was an analyst and manager for many years.) The other DCIs tended to be treated skeptically at first by the intelligence community or, more specifically, by the CIA, with some gaining acceptance and others not. Therefore, a DCI who was seen as being too close to the policy makers and was also not a career intelligence officer could be seen as perhaps being more suspect by the rank and file. The same may run true for the DNIs, whose only legal requirement for the job is "extensive national security experience." The added liability for the DNI is separation from all intelligence agencies, including the CIA. Again, much will depend on the nature of the DNI's relationship with the president and how DNIs conduct themselves vis-à-vis the rest of the intelligence community. To date, two of the five DNIs, McConnell and James Clapper, have been professional intelligence officers, in both cases serving in the military and eventually heading major defense intelligence agencies—the National Security Agency (NSA) for McConnell, and the Defense Intelligence Agency (DIA) and National Geospatial-Intelligence Agency (NGA) for Clapper. Clapper was also the under secretary of defense for intelligence before becoming DNI.

The intelligence community also wants to be kept informed about policy directions and preferences. Although this would seem obligatory if the intelligence community is expected to provide relevant analysis, it does not always happen. All too often, policy makers do not keep intelligence abreast below the most senior levels, either by design or by omission. Such behavior not only makes the role of intelligence more difficult but also can lead to resentment that may be played out in other ways.

Another difference between the two groups is that of outlook. As a senior intelligence officer observed, policy makers tend to be optimists. They approach problems with the belief that they can solve them. After all, this is the reason many of them have gone into government. Intelligence officers are skeptics. Their training teaches them to question and to doubt. Although they may see an optimistic outcome to a given situation, they also see the potential pessimistic outcomes and likely feel compelled to analyze them as possible outcomes.

A revealing indication of the potential costs of the difference in outlook emerged in 2004, when relations between the Bush administration and the CIA deteriorated seriously. Differences over the progress being made in containing the insurgency in Iraq appear to have been the main stimulus. Leaks of intelligence analyses, which some White House officials characterized as being written by "pessimists, naysayers, and handwringers," exacerbated the problem. At one point, President Bush said the CIA "was just guessing" about potential outcomes in Iraq, a remark that some intelligence officers found demeaning. It became customary to say that the CIA and the White House were "at war." The fact that the exchange took place in the middle of a presidential election undoubtedly added to the tension. Indeed, the relationship deteriorated to the point where the acting DCI, John McLaughlin, felt it necessary to go to President Bush and assure him that the CIA was not covertly supporting Democratic nominee Sen. John Kerry of Massachusetts in the election.

Similarly, in March 2011, early on during the Libyan civil war and before either the United Nations (UN) or the North Atlantic Treaty Organization (NATO) decided to intervene, DNI Clapper assessed the military situation in Libya as a stalemate but with the Muammar Qaddafi regime prevailing over the longer term. Later that same day, President Obama's national security adviser made a conference call to reporters, stating that the president continued to have confidence in the DNI but also expressing the view that Clapper's analysis was "static and uni-dimensional" when it should be "dynamic and . . . multi-dimensional," a polite way of saying the policy makers disagreed publicly with the DNI's assessment.

Several lessons are derived from this byplay. First, war or warlike situations—especially those that may be inconclusive—tend to increase the overall tension, as can be easily understood. Second, in such circumstances both parties can forget the nature of their relationship, although this is probably more likely for the policy makers. The combination of uncertainty and casualties, with the attendant political costs, raises the policy makers' anxiety. Third, the leadership of the intelligence community understands that it can never win this sort of struggle with policy makers and therefore will seek to avoid such confrontations. The professional ethos and training of senior intelligence officials work to preclude such an outcome. Even if their analyses prove to be correct, the costs to their relationship with senior policy officials would be so great as to result in a Pyrrhic victory. This does not mean that analysts should temper their views or hedge what they write but that intelligence officers are unlikely to engage in gratuitous and overt hostility to policy makers.

Finally, the policy makers' expectation of support from the permanent bureaucracy extends to the intelligence community. But policy makers may be seeking intelligence that supports known policy preferences, thus running the risk of politicization. Politicization can also work in the other direction. The intelligence officer's desire to be listened to (Kent's second wish) may lead to analysis that is meant to please the policy makers, either consciously or unwittingly. In either case, the desire for a good working relationship can directly undermine the desired objectivity of intelligence. This aspect of the relationship was exacerbated by Congress's increasing practice of levying requests for national intelligence estimates (NIEs) that were essentially progress reports on the war on terrorists or the situation in Iraq and then also insisting that the Key Judgments (KJs) of these NIEs be declassified and published. Congress is entirely within its right to request NIEs, although these progress report estimates appear to have had political agendas behind them. Publication of the KJs certainly increases the likelihood that the estimates will be used by one or both sides in the political debate. It also increases the likelihood that either the president or Congress or both will assume that unpalatable judgments were written to please opponents in the debate. In October 2007, DNI McConnell decided that NIEs would not be made public any longer because of his concerns about the effect this had on the quality of the analysis. However, as noted, he reversed this decision seven weeks later in the case of the Iran nuclear NIE and allowed the KJs to be published in declassified form. Interestingly, in his memoirs, President George W. Bush argues that the Iran estimate limited his options for dealing with Iran and said that the NIE made him "angry." The requirement to publish the KJs from certain NIEs receded after President Obama took office in 2009 and as the United States ended its military involvement in Iraq. This again suggests that much of the motivation for requesting that KJs be published was political in nature.

THE INTELLIGENCE PROCESS: POLICY AND INTELLIGENCE

The differences between the policy and intelligence communities—and the potential for tension—appear at each stage of the intelligence process.

One of the ways in which the difficulties of the policy-intelligence relationship surface is through terminology. Policy makers refer to the intelligence community as such. But intelligence officers use an interesting range of words to describe the policy makers: consumers, clients, customers. Of the three, "consumer" may be the most accurate and least charged. A consumer is someone who uses some commodity, in this case, intelligence. The word says nothing about how the consumer obtains the commodity or any relationship to the provider of the commodity. But "client" and "customer" both suggest some economic relationship with the provider of the service or commodity, with varying degrees of volition on the part of the client or customer. (For example, someone with serious injuries has little choice but to engage a doctor but a decision about cosmetic surgery is more volitional.) The words "client" and "customer" also suggest more mutual interdependence than exists between policy makers and intelligence officers. Although most intelligence officers use the various terms interchangeably and mostly as a means of occasionally saying something shorter and other than "policy maker," they do convey a degree of uncertainty about the exact nature of the relationship.

Requirements. Requirements are not abstract concepts. They are the policy makers' agenda. All policy makers have certain areas or issues on which they must concentrate as well as others on which they would like to concentrate. Some issues are of little or no interest to them but require their attention either occasionally or regularly. This mixture of preferences is important in forming the agenda and thus the requirements. For example, Secretary of State James A. Baker III (1989–1992) was clear, on taking office, that he was not going to spend a lot of time on the Middle East. His decision was based not on a view that the region was unimportant but that he was unlikely to achieve much in the Middle East and therefore his time would be better spent elsewhere. Senior subordinates could handle the Middle East. Iraq's 1990 invasion of Kuwait undermined his choice. Ironically, the war also helped lead to the 1991 Madrid conference—presided over by Secretary Baker—at which Israel and its Arab foes met together openly for the first time.

The intelligence community wants guidance on the priorities of the agenda so that its collection and reporting can be as helpful as possible. At the same time, the community tends to understand that it rarely has the luxury of ignoring a region or issue entirely, even if it is not high on the agenda because of the global coverage requirement. Sooner or later, one region or issue is likely to blow up. That said, the intelligence community regularly makes resource choices that lead to some regions or issues receiving little attention.

The degree to which each administration formally communicates its requirements—versus relying on the intelligence community to know which issues matter—also varies. President Clinton was willing to go through a formal require-ments exercise only once in eight years. Under the National Intelligence Priori-ties Framework (NIPF) instituted under President George W. Bush and continued under Presidents Obama and Trump, the requirements are reviewed annually by the president and the NSC and then quarterly by the intelligence community, with ad hoc adjustments made when dictated by events. Regardless of which method is used or the frequency of formal requirements, the intelligence community is held responsible for ensuring that it has collection and analytical resources on the most important issues. Policy makers also tend to expect that the intelligence community anticipates the emergence of new issues. After all, isn't this one of the main functions of intelligence? The answer is not a firm yes if you take into account the fact that surprises occur: assassinations, coups, elections, reversals of policy. Not everything can be anticipated.

The difference in the approaches of policy makers and intelligence officials to requirements is not played out entirely in formulating the requirements themselves but in the ensuing phases of the intelligence process.

Collection. Policy makers tend to be divorced from the details of collection unless they involve political sensitivities. In such cases, policy makers can have direct and dramatic effects. (*See box, "Policy Makers and Intelligence Collection."*) Their practical concerns lie, first, in the budget, as collection is one of the major intelligence costs, particularly technical intelligence. "Large-ticket items" are always attractive targets during budget-cutting exercises, but policy makers tend to understand that there is not a surplus of collection systems on which to rely. However, the policy makers are often being asked to approve the initiation of programs for very expensive collection systems that will not be of any use to them, given how long it takes to build large overhead systems. Therefore, the normal political calculus that is used to evaluate programs may not work.

Policy makers also tend to assume, incorrectly, that everything is being cov-ered, at least at some minimal level. Thus, when one of the low-priority issues explodes, they expect that a certain low level of collection and on-the-shelf intel-ligence already exists and that collection can be quickly increased. Both assump-tions may be strikingly false. Collection priority decisions tend to be zero-sum games—collect more here and less there, and not all collection assets are easily fungible.

The intelligence community would rather collect more than less, although intelligence officials recognize that they cannot cover everything and hope to get policy makers to concur in the areas to which few resources are devoted. That is the entire purpose of a requirements or priority system. Still, collection is the bedrock of intelligence. But when policy makers place limits on collection, the intelligence community obeys, even if its preference is to collect. Like the policy makers, intelligence officials are aware of the costs of collection, but they cannot spend more on collection than the policy makers (the president and Congress) are willing to allocate. The customary practice is for the policy community to set budgetary limits on collection resources that are lower than the intelligence community would like, although there have been cases in which Congress mandated collection that the executive branch did not believe was necessary. In 1988, President Reagan was about to conclude the Intermediate-Range Nuclear Forces (INF) Treaty with the Soviet Union and was still negotiating the Strategic Arms Reduction Treaty (START). Sen. David Boren, D-OK, chairman of the Senate Intelligence Committee, insisted on the acquisition of new satellites to help monitor these treaties, which the Reagan administration—which otherwise was not averse to spending on intelligence—did not believe was necessary. Agreement on the new satellites was one of the political requirements to get the INF Treaty through the Senate.

The intelligence community has a greater understanding, as would be expected, of the limits of collection at any given time. Intelligence officials know that they are not collecting everything. They make decisions on a regular basis to omit certain regions or issues in favor of more pressing ones. In their own budget requests, intelligence officials also determine how much of the collection to process and exploit, which is always far less than is collected. The intelligence community sees no reason to convey these facts to the policy makers. At one level, doing so is unnecessary. A region not receiving much collection allocation may stay quiet, which is the bet that the intelligence managers are making. At another level, it may undermine their relationship with policy makers. Why arouse concerns about collection coverage over an issue that is not expected to be a significant priority? Their choices can lead to even worse relations should one of the regions suddenly become a concern and collection be found wanting.

Finally, policy makers may have preferences for or against certain types of collection. For example, it has been reported that Trump does not trust human intelligence (HUMINT) because these are people, in his view, who have betrayed their country and therefore are unreliable.

Analysis. Policy makers want information that enables them to make an informed decision, but they do not come to this part of the process as blank slates or wholly objective observers. Already in favor of certain policies and outcomes, they would like to see intelligence that supports their preferences. Again, this is not necessarily as crass as it sounds. Policy makers naturally prefer intelligence that enables them to go where they want. This attitude becomes problematic only when they ignore intelligence that is compelling but contrary to their preferences or if they attempt to prescribe certain "supportive" analysis.

Some policy makers also want to keep their options open for as long as possible. They may resist making important decisions. Intelligence can occasionally serve to limit options by indicating that some options are either insupportable or may have

POLICY MAKERS AND INTELLIGENCE COLLECTION

In several instances, policy makers have intervened in intelligence collection for political reasons.

In Cuba, at the onset of the missile crisis in 1962, Secretary of State Dean Rusk opposed sending U-2s over the island because a Chinese Nationalist U-2 had recently been shot down over China and an Air Force U-2 had accidentally violated Soviet air space in Siberia. The need for imagery of possible Soviet missile sites in Cuba was great, but Rusk had other—also legitimate—concerns about avoiding further provocation.

In Iran, several successive U.S. administrations imposed limits on intelligence collection. Basically, intelligence officers were not allowed to have contact with those in the souks (markets and bazaars) who were opposed to the shah, because the shah's regime would be offended. Instead, U.S. intelligence had to rely on the shah's secret police, SAVAK, which had an institutional interest in denying that any opposition existed. Thus, as the shah's regime unraveled in 1978–1979, policy makers denied U.S. intelligence the sources and contacts it needed to better analyze the situation or to influence the opposition.

Again, regarding Cuba, President Jimmy Carter unilaterally suspended U-2 flights as a gesture to improve bilateral relations. Carter came to regret his decision in 1980, when he faced the possibility that a Soviet combat brigade was in Cuba and he required better intelligence on the issue.

dangerous consequences. The imposition of such limitations serves as yet another area of friction.

Intelligence often deals in ambiguities and uncertainties. If a situation were known with certainty, intelligence would not be needed. (*See box, "Intelligence Uncertainties and Policy."*) Honestly reported intelligence highlights uncertainties and ambiguities, which may prove to be discomforting to policy makers for several reasons. First, if their desire is intelligence that helps them make decisions, anything that is uncertain and ambiguous is going to be less helpful or perhaps even a hindrance. Second, some policy makers cannot appreciate why the multi-billion-dollar intelligence community cannot resolve issues. Many of them assume that important issues are ultimately "knowable," when in fact many are not. This attitude on the part of policy makers can serve as an impetus for intelligence analysts to reach internal agreements or to try to play down disagreements.

Policy makers may also be suspicious of intelligence that supports their rivals in the interagency policy process. They may suspect that rivals have consorted with the intelligence community to produce intelligence that undercuts their position. Again, the increased political use of NIEs was a case in point. Finally, policy makers are free to ignore, disagree with, or even rebut intelligence and offer their own analyses. Such

INTELLIGENCE UNCERTAINTIES AND POLICY

In 1987 U.S.-Soviet negotiations were drawing to a close on the Intermediate-Range Nuclear Forces (INF) Treaty. The U.S. intelligence community had three methods for estimating the number of Soviet INF missiles that had been produced—all of which had to be accounted for and destroyed. Meanwhile, any final number given by the Soviets would be suspect.

Each of the three major analytic intelligence agencies advocated its methodology and its number as the one that should go forward. But the senior intelligence officer responsible for the issue decided, correctly, that all three numbers had to go to President Reagan. Some agency representatives argued that this was simply pusillanimous hedging. But the intelligence officer argued that the president had to be aware of the intelligence uncertainties and the possible range of missile numbers before he signed the treaty. That was the right answer, instead of choosing, perhaps arbitrarily, among the methodologies.

actions are inherent to a system that is dominated by the policy makers. (*See box, "The Limits of Intelligence and Policy: Hurricane Katrina."*)

This behavior on the part of policy makers can become controversial. Although policy makers are free to disagree with or to ignore intelligence, it is not seen as legitimate for them to set up what appears to be intelligence offices of their own and separate from the intelligence community. In the period before the onset of the war in Iraq (2003–2011), Under Secretary of Defense for Policy Douglas Feith (2001–2005) set up an office that he claimed was a permissible analytic cell. Critics argued that it was charged with coming up with intelligence analysis that was more supportive of preferred policies than was being

THE LIMITS OF INTELLIGENCE AND POLICY: HURRICANE KATRINA

Hurricane Katrina is an excellent example of the limits of intelligence and the role of policy makers, even though it was not a foreign intelligence issue. The intelligence on Katrina was nearly perfect: The size and strength of the storm, the likely track of the storm, and the unique nature of the threat that it posed to New Orleans in particular because of that city's topography were all known. In fact, these were known for days before the storm hit New Orleans. However, policy makers in New Orleans and at the state level in Louisiana reacted much too late, thereby increasing the effect of the storm on an unprepared population. The lesson is that even perfect intelligence is useless unless someone acts on it.

written by the intelligence community. Without admitting any fault, the office ultimately was disbanded. In February 2007, DOD's inspector general (IG) released a report on the role played by this DOD policy office, an investigation requested by Sen. Carl Levin, D-M. The IG found that the office had developed and disseminated "alternative intelligence assessments" on al Qaeda's relationship with Iraq that disagreed with the assessments of the intelligence community. The IG found this to be inappropriate (although not illegal) because the DOD-produced assessments were intelligence assessments but they failed to highlight for policy makers the disagreements with the intelligence community. In some cases, DOD-produced papers were presented as intelligence products. According to the IG, a version of the assessment shown to DCI Tenet and DIA director Vice Adm. Lowell Jacoby also purposely omitted material that was used when the briefing was given to senior officials in the White House. Feith disagreed with the IG's findings.

A similar issue arose during the Senate hearings over John Bolton's 2005 nomination to be ambassador to the United Nations. Critics, including Carl Ford, the former assistant secretary of state for intelligence and research, charged that Bolton objected to intelligence analyses that ran counter to his policy preferences and that he substituted intelligence analysis with views of his own without making clear what he had done. During his confirmation hearings, Bolton told the Senate Foreign Relations Committee that a policy maker should be allowed "to state his own reading of the intelligence" but agreed that policy makers should not purport that their views are those of the intelligence community.

The intelligence community tries to maintain its objectivity. Some policy makers raise questions that can undermine the ability of the intelligence community to fulfill Kent's wishes to be listened to and to influence policy for the good as well as to be objective. Some conflicts or disconnects can be avoided or ameliorated if the intelligence community makes an effort to convey to policy makers as early as possible the limits of intelligence analysis. The goal should be to establish realistic expectations and rules of engagement. (*See box*, "*Setting the Right Expectations.*")

SETTING THE RIGHT EXPECTATIONS

During the briefings that each new administration receives, an incoming under secretary of state was meeting with one of his senior intelligence officers on the issue of narcotics. The intelligence officer laid out in detail all the intelligence that could be known about narcotics: amounts grown, shipping routes, street prices, and so forth. "That said," the intelligence officer concluded, "there is very little you will be able to do with this intelligence."

The under secretary asked why the briefing had ended in that manner.

"Because," the intelligence officer replied, "this is an issue where the intelligence outruns policy's ability to come up with solutions. You are likely to grow frustrated by all of this intelligence while you have no policy levers with which to react. I want to prepare you for this at the outset of our relationship so as to avoid problems later on."

The under secretary understood.

Policy makers are the main driver behind the emphasis on current intelligence. Their days and inboxes are filled with near-term issues and concerns. Despite their occasionally stated desire to read longer term intelligence, in reality they have little time—and sometimes little inclination—to do so. The intelligence they receive reflects the reality of the majority of their days.

Finally, policy makers can and do act as their own intelligence analysts. There are several reasons for this. First, they tend to have confidence in their ability and their judgment. Second, the longer they are in office, the more facile they become with certain problems, and their perceived need for intelligence—especially background information—decreases. Third, at a certain point, senior policy makers may actually have more experience dealing with their opposite numbers in various countries and certainly more direct contact than the intelligence officers writing about that nation or about that foreign policy maker. Indeed, policy makers have sometimes expressed frustration with the intelligence they have received on foreign leaders, believing that it did not accurately reflect or capture the people they had gotten to know. One secretary of state said to his advisers, "I have met the Soviet foreign minister twenty times. Can anyone else say that?" He knew the answer and later said that the biographical briefs he read on his Soviet counterpart were not particularly useful even after the secretary had sat down with intelligence analysts to share with them his impressions and experience.

Covert Action. Covert action can be attractive to policy makers because it increases available options and theoretically decreases direct political costs because of plausible deniability. Policy makers may assume that an extensive on-the-shelf operational capability exists and that the intelligence community can mount an operation on fairly short notice. The assumptions are, in effect, the operational counterpart to the assumption that all areas of the world are receiving some minimal level of collection and analytical attention.

Policy makers of course want covert actions that are successful. Success is easier to define for short-term operations, but it may be elusive for those of longer duration. As a result, tension may arise between the intelligence and policy-making communities. Most senior policy makers tend to think in blocks of time no longer than four years—the tenure of a single administration. The intelligence community, as part of the permanent bureaucracy, can afford to think in longer stretches. It does not face the deadline that elections impose on an administration. Indeed, there can be risks involved in operations that overlap a change in administrations. Planning for what became the Bay of Pigs operation began in the last months of the Eisenhower administration (1953–1961). When Kennedy took office, the plans already had a fair degree of bureaucratic momentum behind them. Also, Kennedy was a novice in national security, unlike his predecessor, so he relied more heavily on the advice he received from CIA and the Joint Chiefs. Still, Kennedy made some changes in the plans that were detrimental to their ultimate success—although the overall likelihood of success remained questionable, relying as it did on a popular anti-Castro uprising that was extremely unlikely.

The intelligence community harbors a certain ambivalence about covert action. A covert action gives the intelligence community an opportunity to display its capabilities in an area that is of extreme importance to policy makers. Covert action is also an area in which the intelligence community's skills are unique and are less subject to rebuttal or alternatives than is the community's analysis. However, disagreement over covert action is highly probable if policy makers request an operation that intelligence officials believe to be unlikely to succeed or inappropriate. Once the intelligence community is committed to an operation, it does not want to be left in the lurch by the policy makers. For example, in a paramilitary operation, the intelligence community likely feels a greater obligation to the forces it has enlisted, trained, and armed than the policy makers do. The two communities do not view in similar ways a decision to end the operation.

Policy Maker Behaviors. Just as certain intelligence analyst behaviors matter, so do certain policy maker behaviors. Not every policy maker consumes intelligence in the same way. Some like to read, for example, while others prefer being briefed. Policy makers are better served if they convey their preferences early on instead of leaving them to guesswork.

Policy makers do not always appreciate the limits of what can be collected and known with certainty, the reasons behind ambiguity, and, occasionally, the propriety of intelligence. They sometimes confuse the lack of a firm estimate with pusillanimity when that may not be the case. Intelligence officers sometimes liken this problem to the difference between puzzles and mysteries. Puzzles have solutions; these may be difficult but they can be found. Mysteries, on the other hand, may not have a knowable solution. This distinction may be lost on policy makers, but it is very real in the minds of intelligence officers. They expect to be asked to solve puzzles; they know they may not be able to solve mysteries.

Given the range of issues on which they must work, senior policy makers probably are not fully conversant with every issue. The best policy makers know what they do not know and take steps to learn more. Some are less self-aware and either learn as they go along or fake it.

The most dreaded reaction to bad news is killing the messenger, referring to the practice of kings who would kill the herald who brought bad news. Messengers—including intelligence officers—are no longer killed for bringing bad news, but bureaucratic deaths do occur. An intelligence official can lose access to a policy maker or be cut out of important meetings.

Policy makers can also be a source of politicization in a variety of ways (see chap. 6): overtly—by telling intelligence officers the outcome the policy maker prefers or expects; covertly—by giving strong signals that have the same result; or inadvertently—by not understanding that questions are being interpreted as a request for a certain outcome. Again, the repeated briefings requested by Vice President Richard Cheney in the period before the start of the war in Iraq were seen by some, mostly outside the intelligence community, as a covert pressure on the intelligence community for a certain outcome—agreement that Iraq was a threat based on its possession of weapons of mass destruction. Even though this was the ultimate analytic conclusion, an investigation by the Senate Select Committee on Intelligence that was highly critical of the analytic process found no evidence of politicization.

The Uses of Intelligence. One of the divides between policy makers and intelligence officers is the use to which the intelligence is put. Policy makers want to take action; intelligence officers, although sympathetic and sometimes supportive, are concerned about safeguarding sources and methods and maintaining the community's ability to collect intelligence.

For example, suppose intelligence suggests that officials in a ministry in Country A have decided to arrange a clandestine sale of high-technology components to Country B, whose activities are a proliferation concern. The intelligence community has intelligence strongly indicating that the sale is going forward, although it is not clear whether Country A's leadership is fully aware of the sale. The State Department, or other executive agencies, believes that the situation is important to U.S. national interests and wants to issue a démarche to Country A to stop the sale. The intelligence community, however, argues that this will alert Country A—and perhaps Country B as well—to the fact that the United States has some good intelligence sources. At a minimum, the intelligence community insists on having a hand in drafting the démarche so as to obscure its basis. This can result in a new bureaucratic tug of war, because the State Department wants the démarche to be as strong as possible to get the preferred response—cessation of the sale.

Similarly, talking points—internally agreed-upon official statements used to explain a policy, decision, or event—are often sources of tension between policy officials and intelligence officers. Talking points can be issued by either. The tension comes in clearing the talking points, that is, vetting them and coming up with an agreed text before they are used. Remember the necessity within the policy process of getting complete agreement on everything in the text. The policy maker wants to be able to show that a policy or decision is correct or well handled and wants intelligence that is supportive or that does not call into question the policy or decision. The intelligence officer wants to show that useful intelligence was provided, regardless of the policy outcome. There may be several points of contention. The policy maker may want more intelligence or more precise intelligence than the intelligence officer believes can be provided safely. Or the policy maker may prefer not to use intelligence if it calls into question the decision. Now the intelligence officer may want to use the intelligence to show that he or she gave good support despite the outcome. The result in each case is a negotiation seeking to meet all concerns and needs to the extent possible. However, as always, the policy makers remain in charge and determine the final outcome.

This type of situation arises so frequently that it is accepted by both sides—policy and intelligence—as one of the normal aspects of national security. The struggle is analogous to the divide between intelligence officers and law enforcement officials: Intelligence officers want to collect more intelligence, whereas law enforcement officials seek to prosecute malefactors and may need to use the intelligence to support an indictment and prosecution. On occasion, policy officials cite a piece of open-source intelligence that makes the same case that the classified intelligence does, and they then argue that it can be used as the basis of a specific course of action. However, the intelligence officers may not agree, contending that the open-source intelligence is validated only because the same information is known via classified sources. Thus, the intelligence officers may argue that even using open-source intelligence can serve to reveal classified intelligence sources and methods. In the case of imagery, at least, the greater availability of high-quality commercial imagery may obviate the entire debate.

However, there can be occasions when the specifics of the situation reveal deeper policy-intelligence tensions. The events surrounding the attack on the U.S. mission in Benghazi, Libya, on September 11, 2012, which resulted in the deaths of U.S. ambassador J. Christopher Stevens and three other Americans, is illustrative. Two issues were at stake: the intelligence warnings prior to the attack and the drafting of talking points that UN Ambassador Susan Rice later used on television to explain how the attacks happened and whether they were spontaneous or planned, which also went back to the issue of warnings. Coming as the attacks did during a presidential election campaign, the issue also took on a partisan tinge.

Within a very short time, there were multiple investigations of the Benghazi incident. There was general agreement in several of these that the threat environment in Benghazi was high, although this was not acknowledged in all quarters, and that security was not robust. However, as the State Department's Accountability Board noted, Ambassador Stevens was the leading State Department expert on Libya and as such his own decisions on travel times and arrangements carried additional weight.

The issue of Ambassador Rice's talking points is more complex. Rice said in several television interviews that the attacks were spontaneous. The trail of released e-mails remains difficult to follow, but it would appear that several parties were involved in editing the talking points. The draft originated at CIA. State Department officials objected to references to CIA warnings about extremist activities at Benghazi as it might put the State Department in a bad light. It appears that after much fairly typical bureaucratic back and forth, CIA deputy director Michael Morrell edited the talking points and took out the more controversial points about warnings and extremists. This then became the position of the Obama administration, including White House press spokesman Jay Carney: that the CIA provided the draft, even though, in the end, it was a negotiated document.

The Benghazi incident is instructive for several insights into the policy maker–intelligence relationship:

- First, this all came up in the aftermath of the event, not during it.

- Although CIA did provide the final draft, there was a great deal of back-and-forth between policy makers and the CIA as to what should or should not be said.

- The goals of the two groups, in terms of the language, were not identical. Policy makers did not want to contradict past versions of events and also did not want to be too far in front of investigations. CIA, in the early drafts, provided more information than the policy makers wanted or with which they felt comfortable.

- Finally, at a certain point, the policy-making community closed ranks and blamed the CIA for the final talking points, which is fair at the drafting level but not necessarily at the negotiating level.

In January 2014, the Senate Intelligence Committee released a report on the Benghazi attack. The report did not address the issue of the talking points but did find that the attacks were avoidable, placing most of the blame on the State Department for failing to increase security after intelligence warnings about potential threats.

There is no correct answer to this debate. The intelligence exists solely to support policy. If it cannot be used, it begins to lose its purpose. However, policy and intelligence officials must balance the gain to be made by a specific course of action versus the gains that may be available by not revealing intelligence sources and methods, thus allowing continued collection. Usable intelligence is a constant general goal, but which intelligence gets used when and how is open to debate.

Tensions. The relationship between policy makers and the intelligence community should be symbiotic: Policy makers should rely on the intelligence community for advice, which is a major rationale for the existence of the intelligence community. For the community to produce good advice, policy makers should keep intelligence officers informed about the major directions of policy and their specific areas of interest and priority. That said, the relationship is not one of equals. Policy and policy makers can exist and function without the intelligence community, but the opposite is not true.

The line that divides policy and intelligence—and the fact that policy makers can cross it but intelligence officers cannot—also affects the relationship. Policy makers tend to be vigilant in seeing that intelligence does not come too close to the line. However, they may ask intelligence officers for advice in choosing among policy options—or for some action—that would take intelligence over the line. If intelligence officers decline, as they should to preserve their objectivity regardless of the outcome, policy makers may become resentful. The line also can blur at the highest levels of the intelligence community, and the DNI may be asked for advice that is, in reality, policy.

In the United States, partisan politics has also become a factor in the policy-intelligence relationship. Although differences in emphasis developed from one administration to another (such as the greater emphasis on political covert action in the Eisenhower administration and even more so during the Kennedy administration), general continuity has existed in intelligence policy. Moreover, until 1976, intelligence was not seen as part of the spoils of an election victory. DCIs were not automatically replaced with each new administration, as were the heads of virtually all other agencies and departments. President Nixon (1969–1974) tried to use the CIA for political ends in an attempt to curtail the Watergate investigations. But it was the Carter administration (1977–1981) that ended the political separateness of the intelligence community. Jimmy Carter, in his 1976 campaign, lumped together Vietnam, Watergate, and the recent investigations of U.S. intelligence. When Carter won the presidency, DCI George H. W. Bush (1976–1977) offered to stay on and eschew all partisan politics, saying that the CIA needed some continuity after the investigations and four DCIs in as many years. President-elect Carter said he wanted a DCI of his own choosing. This was the first time a serving DCI had been asked to step down by a new administration and a change of partisan control. Similarly, Reagan made "strengthening the CIA" part of his 1980 campaign and replaced Carter's DCI, Stansfield Turner (1977–1981), with William Casey (1981–1987). In a presidential transition within the same party, President George H. W. Bush kept on DCI William H. Webster (1987–1991) for most of his term, but Clinton took office and replaced DCI Robert M. Gates (1991–1993) with James Woolsey. Thus, a partisan change in the White House came to mean a change in DCIs as well. However, in 2001, President George W. Bush retained DCI Tenet, who had been appointed by Clinton, despite some advice from within Bush's own party to remove him. Tenet thus became the first DCI since Helms to survive a party change in the presidency. Many observers have wondered if President George W. Bush's decision to retain Tenet was influenced by what happened to his father and President Carter. The 2001 retention of Tenet notwithstanding, it is not clear that a new practice has been established. DNI Mike McConnell stepped down at the end of the George W. Bush administration but did so for reasons of his own. DCIA Michael Hayden's tenure ended at the same time, but he apparently was willing to stay on and was replaced. A new DNI and DCIA came in after Trump's inauguration. Thus, it is not clear that senior intelligence posts are once again seen as being separate from other political appointments, as was the case through 1977.

The argument made in favor of changing DCIs (now DNIs) when a new administration takes office is that presidents must have an intelligence community leader with whom they are comfortable. But back in the days of a nonpartisan DCI, many people in Washington, D.C., emphasized the professional nature of the DCI (even for DCIs who were not career intelligence officers) and had the sense that intelligence is in some way different from the rest of the structure that each president inherits and fills with political appointees. An objective intelligence community was not to be part of the partisan spoils of elections. The shift since 1977 has affected the policy-intelligence relationship by tagging DCIs—and now, presumably, DNIs—with a partisan coloration. The shift also meant a movement, at least for the period 1977 through 2001 and now with the Trump administration, away from professional intelligence officers serving as DCIs. As noted, two of the five DNIs have been intelligence officers; the other three— Ambassador John Negroponte, Admiral Blair, and former senator and ambassador Dan Coats—clearly had the "extensive national security expertise" required in legislation.

Finally, external intrusions, particularly that of the electronic news media, can have an effect on the relationship. Contrary to popular belief, television news does not foster major changes in policy. It does serve as a means of communication for states and their leaders, and it competes with the intelligence community as an alternative source of information. The media do occasionally scoop the intelligence community. This is not because they know things that the intelligence community does not. Instead, the electronic media—especially the twenty-four-hour news networks—put a premium on speed and have the capacity and willingness to provide updates and corrections as necessary. The intelligence community does not have the same luxury and tends to take more time in preparing its initial report. Being scooped by the media can lead policy makers to believe, mistakenly, that the media offer much the same coverage as the intelligence community—and at greater speed and less cost.

Although a number of issues are likely to create tension between policy makers and the intelligence community, conflict has not been the mainstay of the policy-intelligence relationship. Again, this changed to a certain degree between Trump and the intelligence community. But continued close and trusting working relationships prevail between policy makers and intelligence officers at working levels. A good working relationship is not a given, and it cannot be fully appreciated without understanding all of the potential sources of friction.

KEY TERM

decision advantage 258

FURTHER READINGS

Despite its centrality to the intelligence process, the policy maker–intelligence relationship has not received as much attention as other parts of the process.

Best, Richard A., Jr. "Intelligence and U.S. National Security Policy." *International Journal of Intelligence and Counterintelligence* 28 (fall 2015): 449–467.

Betts, Richard K. "Policy Makers and Intelligence Analysts: Love, Hate, or Indifference?" *Intelligence and National Security* 3 (January 1988): 184–189.

Blackwill, Robert D., and Jack Davis. "A Policymaker's Perspective on Intelligence Analysis." In *Intelligence: The Secret World of Spies*. Ed. Loch K. Johnson and James J. Wirtz. New York: Oxford University Press, 2015.

Brimley, Shawn, et al. *Enabling Decision: Shaping the National Security Council for the Next President*. Washington, D.C.: Center for a New American Security, 2015. (Available at http://www.cnas.org/shaping-the-national-security-council#.VjwIHCsnqKI.)

Central Intelligence Agency, Center for the Study of Intelligence. *Intelligence and Policy: The Evolving Relationship*. Washington, D.C.: CIA, June 2004.

Davis, Jack. *Analytic Professionalism and the Policymaking Process: Q&A on a Challenging Relationship*. Vol. 2, no. 4. Washington, D.C.: CIA, Sherman Kent School for Intelligence Analysis, October 2003.

Ford, Carl. "My Perspective on Intelligence Support of Foreign Policy." *The Intelligencer* 21 (winter 2014–2015): 61–65.

George, Roger Z., and Harvey Rishikof, eds. *The National Security Enterprise: Navigating the Labyrinth*. Washington, D.C.: Georgetown University Press, 2011.

Heymann, Hans. "Intelligence/Policy Relationships." In *Intelligence: Policy and Process*. Ed. Alfred C. Maurer and others. Boulder, Colo.: Westview Press, 1985.

Hughes, Thomas L. *The Fate of Facts in a World of Men: Foreign Policy and Intelligence Making*. New York: Foreign Policy Association, 1976.

Hulnick, Arthur S. "The Intelligence Producer–Policy Consumer Linkage: A Theoretical Approach." *Intelligence and National Security* 1 (May 1986): 212–233.

Kerbel, Josh, and Anthony Olcott. "Synthesizing With Clients, Not Analyzing for Customers." *Studies in Intelligence* 54 (December 2010): 11–27.

Kovacs, Amos. "Using Intelligence." *Intelligence and National Security* 12 (October 1997): 145–164.

Lowenthal, Mark M. "The Policymaker–Intelligence Relationship." In *The Oxford Handbook of National Security Intelligence*. Ed. Loch Johnson. Oxford, U.K.: Oxford University Press, 2010.

———. "Tribal Tongues: Intelligence Consumers and Intelligence Producers." *Washington Quarterly* 15 (winter 1992): 157–168.

Marrin, Stephen. "At Arm's Length or at the Elbow? Explaining the Distance Between Analysts and Decisionmakers." *International Journal of Intelligence and Counterintelligence* 20 (fall 2007): 401–414.

_____. "Why Strategic Intelligence Analysis Has Limited Influence on American Foreign Policy." *Intelligence and National Security* 32 (October 2017): 725–742.

Miller, Paul D. "Lessons for Intelligence Support to Policymaking During Crises." *Studies in Intelligence* 54 (June 2010): 49–56.

Poteat, Eugene. "The Use and Abuse of Intelligence: An Intelligence Provider's Perspective." *Diplomacy and Statecraft* 11 (2000): 1–16.

Sims, Jennifer E. "Decision Advantage and the Nature of Intelligence Analysis." In *The Oxford Handbook of National Security Intelligence*. Ed. Loch Johnson. Oxford, U.K.: Oxford University Press, 2010.

Steiner, James E. *Challenging the Red Line Between Intelligence and Policy*. Washington, D.C.: Institute for the Study of Diplomacy, Georgetown University, 2004.

Thomas, Stafford T. "Intelligence Production and Consumption: A Framework of Analysis." In *Intelligence: Policy and Process*. Ed. Alfred C. Maurer and others. Boulder, Colo.: Westview Press, 1985.

U.S. Department of Defense. Deputy Inspector General for Intelligence. *Review of the Pre-War Iraqi Activities of the Office of the Under Secretary of Defense for Policy*. Report No. 07-INTEL-04. Washington, D.C.: Department of Defense, February 9, 2007.

U.S. Office of the Director of National Intelligence. *Vision 2015*. Washington, D.C.: U.S. Office of the Director of National Intelligence, 2010. (Available at http://www.dni.gov/files/documents/Newsroom/Reports%20and%20Pubs/Vision_2015.pdf.)

Wilder, Dennis. "Improving Policymaker Understanding of Intelligence: An Educated Consumer Is Our Best Customer." *Studies in Intelligence* 55 (June 2011): 15–23.

Wirtz, James J. "The Intelligence–Policy Nexus." In *Intelligence: The Secret World of Spies*. Ed Loch K. Johnson and James J. Wirtz. New York: Oxford University Press, 2015.

CHAPTER TEN

OVERSIGHT AND ACCOUNTABILITY

Sed quis custodiet ipsos custodes? ("But who will guard the guards?"), the Roman poet and satirist Juvenal asked. The **oversight** of intelligence has always been a problem. The ability to control information is an important power in any state, whether democratic or despotic. Information that is unavailable by any other means and whose dissemination is often restricted is the mainstay of intelligence. By controlling information; by having expertise in surveillance, eavesdropping, and other operations; and by operating behind a cloak of secrecy, an intelligence apparatus has the potential to threaten heads of government. Thus, government leaders' ability to oversee intelligence effectively is vital.

In democracies, oversight tends to be a responsibility shared by the executive and legislative powers. The oversight issues are generic: budget, responsiveness to policy needs, the quality of analysis, control of operations, propriety of activities. The United States is unique in giving extensive oversight responsibilities and powers to the legislative branch. The parliaments of other nations have committees devoted to intelligence oversight, but none has the same broad oversight powers as Congress. (*See box, "A Linguistic Aside: The Two Meanings of Oversight."*)

A LINGUISTIC ASIDE: THE TWO MEANINGS OF OVERSIGHT

Oversight has two definitions that are distinct, if not opposites:

- Supervision; watchful care (as in "We have oversight of that activity.")

- Failure to notice or consider (as in "We missed that. It was an oversight.")

In overseeing intelligence, Congress and the executive branch try to carry out the first definition and to avoid the second.

EXECUTIVE OVERSIGHT ISSUES

The core oversight issue is whether the intelligence community is properly carrying out its functions, that is, whether the community is asking the right questions, responding to policy makers' needs, being rigorous in its analysis, and having on hand the right operational capabilities (collection and covert action). Policy makers cannot trust the intelligence community alone to answer for itself. At the same time, senior policy officials (the national security adviser, the secretaries of state and defense, the president) cannot maintain a constant vigil over the intelligence community. Outside the intelligence community, the National Security Council (NSC) Office of Intelligence Programs is the highest level organization within the executive branch that provides day-to-day oversight of intelligence as well as policy direction. Of course, as was discussed in the previous chapter, policy makers may have strong views about the quality of intelligence based on their own policy preferences, so they may not always be objective either.

Although the 2004 intelligence reform law created a Joint Intelligence Community Council (JICC) to improve oversight, Director of National Intelligence (DNI) Mike McConnell (2007–2009) found that the JICC did not meet his needs. He created the Executive Committee (EXCOM). The EXCOM is, like the JICC, a mixed policy/intelligence body, comprising both the heads of intelligence components and senior policy officials, usually at the under secretary level. This slightly lower representation by policy departments is probably an advantage, because under secretaries have (slightly) more time to devote to these issues and will undoubtedly have greater working familiarity, in most cases, with intelligence. A major feature of the EXCOM is the fact that the under secretary of defense for intelligence (USDI) sits on the EXCOM in that capacity and as director of defense intelligence, making clear his or her position over the heads of the defense intelligence agencies—the Defense Intelligence Agency (DIA), the National Geospatial-Intelligence Agency (NGA), the National Security Agency (NSA), and the National Reconnaissance Program (NRO)—but acting as part of the Office of the DNI (ODNI). This is a significant step in allowing better coordination between the DNI and the Department of Defense (DOD), which is both the largest aggregation of intelligence agencies and the largest consumer of intelligence. But this added function for the USDI has not been formally institutionalized and thus will depend on the preferences of future DNIs and secretaries of defense.

Since the administration of Dwight D. Eisenhower (1953–1961), with two brief lapses, presidents have relied on what was originally called the **President's Foreign Intelligence Advisory Board (PFIAB)** to carry out higher level and more objective oversight than the NSC Office of Intelligence Programs does. With the advent of the more all-encompassing term "national intelligence" in the Intelligence Reform and Terrorism Prevention Act (IRTPA, 2004), as opposed to "foreign intelligence," the PFIAB became the **President's Intelligence Advisory Board (PIAB)**. PIAB members are appointed by the president and usually include some former senior intelligence and policy officials and individuals with relevant commercial backgrounds. (In the 1990s, some people were appointed to the then-PFIAB largely as political favors.) PIAB can respond to problems (such as the investigation of alleged Chinese spying at

Los Alamos National Laboratory) or can initiate activities (such as the Team A–Team B competitive analysis on Soviet strategic capabilities and intentions).

The PIAB's relationship to policy makers can be subject to the same strains that are seen in the relationship between policy makers and intelligence agencies. From 2001 to 2005, PFIAB was chaired by Brent Scowcroft, who had served as national security adviser under President Gerald R. Ford from 1975 to 1977 and President George H. W. Bush from 1989 to 1993. Scowcroft spoke out against the decision to invade Iraq in 2003, which surprised some people given his previous close working relationship with George H. W. Bush. In 2005, President George W. Bush replaced Scowcroft, apparently displeased over his remarks. This was the first time that the chairman of PFIAB was replaced because of a policy disagreement with the White House.

The executive branch has tended to focus its oversight on issues related to espionage and covert action, although analytical issues (Team A–Team B; the September 11, 2001, terrorist attacks) and organizational issues are occasionally investigated. Espionage oversight is inclined to concentrate on lapses, such as the Aldrich Ames spy case or allegations of Chinese espionage. For example, in 1999 PFIAB issued a scathing report on Department of Energy security practices related to Chinese espionage. As with all other activities, executive branch organizations divide responsibility for overseeing covert action. The president is responsible for approving all covert actions, but the day-to-day responsibility for managing them resides with the director of the Central Intelligence Agency (DCIA) and the Directorate of Operations (DO). As noted, DNI Dennis Blair (2009–2010) did win authority to evaluate the effectiveness of specific covert actions when requested by the White House during his struggle with DCIA Leon Panetta (2009–2011). This same authority presumably now resides with the current DNI but it may not be an often-used role and is dependent on executive office officials asking the DNI to undertake an evaluation. The DNI cannot do so on his or her own. The FY2010 Intelligence Authorization Act (Public Law 111–259) gives the DNI authority to conduct an "accountability review" of an intelligence community element. The DNI can also be requested to do so by Congress.

One oversight issue relating to covert action centers on the operating concept of plausible deniability. In the case of large-scale paramilitary operations—such as the Bay of Pigs or the contras in Nicaragua—deniability is somewhat implausible. But many covert actions are much smaller in scale, making it possible to deny plausibly any U.S. role. Some critics of covert action argue that plausible deniability undermines accountability by giving operators an increased sense of license. Because the president will deny any connection to their activities, they operate under less constraint. The critics raise a point worth considering but overlook the professionalism of most officers.

Another oversight issue relating to covert action has to do with broad presidential findings, sometimes called **global findings**, versus narrow ones. Global findings tend to be drafted to deal with transnational issues, such as terrorism or narcotics. The broader the finding, and thus the less specificity it contains, the greater is the scope for the intelligence community to define the operations involved. Although not suggesting that the president must always precisely define covert actions, a broad finding does run a greater risk of disconnecting policy preferences from operations.

Policy makers must also be concerned about the objectivity of the intelligence community when it is asked to assess or draw up a covert action. Once again, intelligence officers who feel a need to demonstrate their capabilities may not be able to assess in a cold-eyed manner the feasibility or utility of a proposed action.

Similar concerns may arise when assessing the relative success of an ongoing covert action. Have policy makers and intelligence officials agreed on the signs of success? Are these signs evident? If not, what are the accepted timelines for terminating the action? What are the plans for terminating it?

Finally, can intelligence analysts offer objective assessments of the situation in a country where their colleagues are carrying out a major covert action, particularly a paramilitary one? This issue may be of heightened concern in view of the merger of Directorate of Analysis and DO officers in CIA mission centers.

The PIAB under the Barack Obama administration (2009–2017) looked into the effectiveness of the DNI, which was undertaken at the request of Congress. This report stressed the importance of the DNI being the acknowledged leader of the intelligence community. Ironically, Obama received the report shortly before he asked DNI Blair to step down. As noted earlier, one of the issues that undercut Blair was his turf fights with the Central Intelligence Agency (CIA), which failed when the NSC supported the CIA over the DNI.

The propriety of intelligence activities is also an aspect of oversight. Are the actions being conducted in accordance with law and **executive orders** (EOs)? All intelligence agencies have inspectors general and general counsels. In addition, the **President's Intelligence Oversight Board (PIOB)**, a subset of PIAB, can investigate. However, the PIOB is a reactive body, with no power to initiate probes or to subpoena. It is dependent on referrals from executive branch officials. Nonetheless, the PIOB has carried out some useful classified investigations. However, the PIOB fell into disuse during the George W. Bush administration (2001–2009). Members were not appointed until 2003, two years after Bush took office. According to press accounts, the PIOB did not take any actions on various potential violations that were reported to it—mostly in connection with the war on terrorists—until 2006. President Bush curtailed the purview of the PIOB and ordered that it report to the president, not the Justice Department. However, President Obama restored the practice of having the PIOB report potential instances of law breaking to the Justice Department.

A recent addition to executive oversight has been the **Privacy and Civil Liberties Oversight Board (PCLOB)**, which had been recommended by the 9/11 Commission (National Commission on Terrorist Attacks upon the United States) report and was created legislatively in 2004. The board, more popularly known as the Civil Liberties Protection Board, is chartered to ensure that concerns about privacy and civil liberties are considered when laws, regulations, and policies to combat terrorism are developed. The board has both advisory and oversight functions. The board is part of the Executive Office of the President, which selects its members. The chairman and vice chairman are subject to Senate approval. The Bush administration's commitment to the board came into question because members were not selected until March 2006. A change in legislation terminated all board appointees in January 2008. President Bush did not nominate new members; President Obama began nominating members in December 2010, nearly two years into his term. The PCLOB is required to have three board members from both parties to conduct business. In the Trump administration, nominees were not confirmed until October 2018, 22 months after the term began. There is also a civil liberties protection officer in the ODNI.

The PCLOB had its first official meeting in July 2013, when it conducted a series of public hearings on the role of the **Foreign Intelligence Surveillance Court (FISC)** (discussed later) and the NSA programs leaked by Edward Snowden. In two separate reports in 2014, the PCLOB questioned both the utility and the legal basis for the bulk-collection program but found that the USA PATRIOT Act Section 702 program collecting data on foreigners' use of the Internet within the United States was legal. In August 2013, DNI James Clapper (2010–2017) announced the creation of a Review Group on Intelligence and Communications Technologies. This group was formed at President Obama's direction to assess whether, given the advances in communications technology, U.S. technical collection was conducted so as to protect national security and advance foreign policy while also accounting for the risk of unauthorized disclosure and the need to maintain public trust. The review group made forty-six specific recommendations to the president in its December 2013 report, but few of them were adopted specifically in his January 2014 order. In October 2018, the PCLOB issued a report on the implementation of President Obama's policy directive (PPD-28) on signals intelligence activities.

The controversies that engulfed intelligence after 2001, primarily the September 11 attacks and Iraq's alleged possession of weapons of mass destruction (WMD), led to an increased use of outside commissions to provide assessments of intelligence. In the United States, great political pressure was brought to bear on President George W. Bush to appoint a commission to investigate intelligence performance before September 11, after Congress's joint inquiry reported to little satisfaction on anyone's part. Similarly, after the Iraq controversy, Bush appointed the WMD Commission. The prime ministers of Britain and Australia also appointed commissions to look into intelligence on Iraq. Britain's Butler Report concluded that few reliable sources were available on Iraq WMD programs, especially human resources. Lord Butler and his colleagues found that the intelligence assessments made good use of the intelligence they did have, although much of it was inferential. As was the case in the United States, analysts did not have complete knowledge of the background of key human resources. The report also found that there was no politicization of intelligence. Australia's Flood Report made similar findings, noting the paucity of information—much of which came to Australia from the United States or Britain—and the failure to examine the political context in Iraq as well as the technical issue of WMD, a criticism that some have made regarding U.S. intelligence, including DCIA Michael Hayden during his 2006 confirmation hearings. The Flood Report doubted, however, that better intelligence processes would have led to the correct conclusion about the state of Iraq WMD. The report also noted that there was no evidence of politicized intelligence.

A fitting conclusion to this issue, which will likely haunt the intelligence agencies in all three countries for years to come, is the report of Charles A. Duelfer, who headed the Iraq Survey Group (ISG) for Director of Central Intelligence (DCI) George J. Tenet (1997–2004). The ISG spent two years in Iraq examining the state of Iraq WMD after the occupation of Baghdad. Duelfer had been a senior member of the United Nations Special Commission (UNSCOM), charged with overseeing the disarmament of Iraq after the 1991 Persian Gulf War, until it was ejected by Iraqi leader Saddam Hussein in 1998. Duelfer concluded that Saddam was determined to obtain WMD but would have waited until United Nations sanctions had been lifted. But to achieve that goal, Saddam wanted to preserve the capacity to reconstitute WMD, especially missiles and chemical weapons, as quickly as possible once the sanctions were gone. Finally, Saddam sought to create a state of strategic ambiguity, seeking to convince Iran that Iraq had WMD as a means of deterring Iran while Iraq remained weak. If Duelfer's assessments are correct, then one could argue that the intelligence agencies were accurate in their assessment of Saddam's intentions but not the state of his inventory (capabilities) and that they correctly picked up the signs that he was transmitting that he had WMD. They were not able to see through them, however.

The increased use of these commissions raises several issues. First, the commissions are, almost by definition, political in nature. A government is either trying to gain some political advantage or bowing to political pressure in creating a commission. Second, given that commissions are created by a sitting government, the issue of a commission's objectivity always arises. This is usually addressed by appointing a range of commissioners whose political views or backgrounds are diverse. But this raises a third issue: How much expertise do they bring to the subject? Intelligence, like any other profession, has its own vocabulary and its own practices, some of which are difficult for an outsider to comprehend or to learn with much facility over the course of an investigation. If too many former intelligence professionals are appointed, the commission will appear to be biased. But if most of the commissioners have little or no intelligence experience, their ability to investigate in a meaningful and perceptive manner may suffer. Finally, the political circumstances that create the commission increase the likelihood that a significant group in the body politic will be dissatisfied with the result, charging either a whitewash or a lynching.

One area of executive branch oversight has become more controversial in recent years. This is the role played by inspectors general (IGs), particularly the CIA IG. Every cabinet department, every major agency, and several small ones have an IG. All IGs essentially have the same function: to ensure that his or her department or agency is operating within legal guidelines, effectively carrying out its mission and not engaging in activities that are unlawful, wasteful, or criminal. The CIA has had an IG since 1952; the position was given a statutory basis in 1989. The CIA IG must be confirmed by the Senate, making this IG one of the few intelligence officials below the level of agency director who requires Senate confirmation. The CIA IG reports to the director of the CIA, but the director has limited authority to constrain or limit the IG. If the director acts to limit the IG's activities, for reasons of national security, the director must inform the Senate and House Intelligence Committees of his or her reasons. Only the president can remove the CIA IG and, again, the president must also inform the intelligence committees of the reasons for doing so. Thus, to the extent possible, Congress tried to give the CIA IG a fair amount of independence.

An intelligence community IG, part of the ODNI, was created in legislation in 2010. The intelligence community IG is also confirmed by the Senate and is responsible to the DNI and to Congress. Its functions are similar to other IGs. This position also leads and coordinates the activities of other intelligence agency IGs through the intelligence community IG Forum, which was established in the same legislation.

The DNI may prevent an IG inspection or audit in order "to protect vital national security interests of the United States." In such cases, the DNI must inform the congressional intelligence committees of the reasons for this action.

All IG investigations come after the fact, which can lead to a certain amount of dissonance for officers who are told by the general counsel that a program is legal and then find themselves being investigated for conducting that program, as former CIA general counsel Jeffrey Smith noted. Smith also noted the difference between operational decisions made under pressure and the hindsight of an IG review. Smith's comments summarize the problem with IG and other ex post facto reviews, especially on fast-moving or highly important and sensitive issues. It can also be difficult for IG investigations to capture correctly the analytical process that may have led to an errant conclusion or a larger intelligence failure, unless glaring pieces of intelligence were overlooked or omitted. All of these issues came to a head in 2007, when DCIA Hayden released, under congressional direction, a CIA IG report on the agency's performance before 9/11; the report found systemic problems and specifically criticized the performance of several senior officials, including then-DCI Tenet. Hayden ordered a review of the IG, citing concerns about its impartiality and fairness. Eventually, Hayden and the IG agreed to the appointment of an ombudsman and a quality control officer who would ensure that "exculpatory and relevant mitigating information" was also included in IG reports, as well as more rapidly conducted investigations.

In 2015, the Obama administration ruled that inspectors general need permission for access to wiretaps, grand jury information, and some other data. Critics believed this undercut the ability of the IGs to do their job, especially in agencies like the Federal Bureau of Investigation (FBI) and the Drug Enforcement Administration (DEA).

The Office of Management and Budget (OMB), although not strictly an oversight entity, should be mentioned because of its central and pervasive role. First, OMB assembles the president's annual budget. OMB takes the submissions from the various departments and agencies, including the National Intelligence Program (NIP) and Military Intelligence Program (MIP), and makes a final decision as to how much each will be requesting in the president's budget. Heads of departments and agencies can appeal OMB decisions to the president. Second, OMB keeps track of all agency and department spending rates. OMB's goal is to ensure that allocated funds are spent at an even pace through the fiscal year, trying to combat the bureaucratic urge to hoard money in the early part of the year and then spend all of it in the latter part of the year, leading to more difficult program management. All of this budget oversight, plus some management oversight, is performed by OMB program managers. In the case of defense and intelligence, the program managers are integrated throughout the budget development cycle because the defense budget, which includes intelligence, is too large to be reviewed at the end of the process each autumn as is the case with most program submissions. OMB is also responsible for issuing "Statement(s) of Administration Policy," which state the administration's support for or opposition to pending legislation, including threats to veto by the president. Finally, OMB serves as the political guardian of all testimony given by administration officials, including senior intelligence officials. OMB seeks to ensure that all statements adhere to official administration policy and that officials do not recommend programs or initiatives that are not part of the president's policies.

CONGRESSIONAL OVERSIGHT

Congress approaches intelligence oversight—and all oversight issues, whether national security or domestic—from a different but equally legitimate perspective as that of the executive branch.

The concept of congressional oversight is established in the Constitution. Article I, Section 8, paragraph 18, states, "Congress shall have Power . . . To make all Laws which shall be necessary and proper for carrying into Execution the foregoing Powers, and all other Powers vested by this Constitution in the Government of the United States, or in any Department or Officer thereof." Courts have found that the Necessary and Proper Clause includes the power to require reports from the executive branch on any subject that can be legislated. It is important to recall that most agencies have been created by Congress with specific goals in mind. (The major exceptions in intelligence are the NRO and NSA, which were created by presidential order.) Therefore, Congress has the right to examine whether these agencies are performing as intended. Second, Congress funds all agencies, again with specific programs or purposes in mind, which again provides a basis for oversight. The essence of congressional oversight is the ability to gain access to information, usually held by the executive branch, that is relevant to the functioning of the government.

Apart from its constitutional mandate, a major factor driving Congress in all matters of oversight is the desire to be treated by the executive as an equal branch of government. This is not always easy to achieve, as the executive branch ultimately speaks with one voice, that of the president, whereas Congress has 535 members. This significant difference leads some people to question whether Congress's constitutional authority works in reality.

Moreover, in the area of national security, Congress has often given presidents a fair amount of leeway to carry out their responsibilities as commander-in-chief. This is not to suggest that partisan debates do not arise over national security or even intelligence issues, such as the 1960 allegations about a missile gap or the 1970s allegations about a strategic window of vulnerability. (See chap. 2.) To the contrary, debate has become more partisan in the post–cold war period. Effective or forthcoming oversight can also help forge more united policies between the branches, especially during times of crisis. As Sen. Arthur Vandenberg, R-MI, then-chairman of the Senate Foreign Relations Committee (1947–1949) famously told President Harry S. Truman at the outset of the cold war: "If you want us there for the landings, we have to be there for the take-offs."

Beyond the constitutional mandate, intelligence oversight is also established in the Intelligence Oversight Act (1980), which requires that the two intelligence committees be kept "fully and currently informed of all intelligence activities carried out by or on behalf of the United States including any significant anticipated activity." The act also states that notification is not a necessary precondition for beginning an activity. Finally, the act requires "timely" reports on "any illegal activity or significant intelligence failure." This is a fairly broad mandate but also a somewhat vague one, hinging on the definition of the words "currently" and "significant." In 2011, DNI Clapper issued guidelines (Intelligence Community Directive 112, November 16, 2011) as to what constitutes "significant anticipated intelligence activities," including those that (1) entail significant risk of exposure, compromise, and loss of human life; (2) will have a major impact of foreign policy or national security interests; (3) entail deployment of new collection techniques that are a significant departure from previous ones; (4) are related to certain specific budget-related events; and (5) others. "Significant failures" include (1) large-scale and likely systematic loss or disclosure of classified intelligence; (2) major interruptions in or loss of collection capabilities; (3) major analytical errors that can have a significant effect on U.S. policies; and (4) others. Clapper's directive does add specificity, but there will still be instances in which certain events are at issue as to whether or not they should be or should have been reported under the "significant" standard.

Congress has several levers that it can use to carry out its oversight functions.

Budget. Control over the budget for the entire federal government is the most fundamental lever of congressional oversight. Article I, Section 9, paragraph 7, of the Constitution states, "No Money shall be drawn from the Treasury, but in Consequence of Appropriations made by Law; and a regular Statement and Account of the Receipts and Expenditures of all public Money shall be published from time to time."

The congressional budget process is complex and duplicative. It comprises two major activities: **authorization** and **appropriation**. Authorization consists of approving specific programs and activities. (See chap. 3 for the programs that make up the National Intelligence Program [NIP] and Military Intelligence Program [MIP].) Authorizing committees also suggest dollar amounts for the programs. The House Permanent Select Committee on Intelligence and the Senate Select Committee on Intelligence are the primary authorizers of the intelligence budget. The House and Senate Armed Services Committees authorize some defense-related intelligence programs. Appropriation consists of allocating specific dollar amounts to authorized programs. The defense subcommittees of the House and Senate Appropriations Committees perform this function for intelligence.

Technically, Congress may not appropriate money for a program that it has not first authorized. If authorizing legislation does not pass before a congressional session ends, the appropriations bills contain language stating that they also serve as authorizing legislation until such legislation is passed. This can be very important if Congress fails to pass an authorization bill, as was the case for intelligence for fiscal years 2006 through 2009. (The FY2010 bill was actually passed in FY2011.) President George H. W. Bush (1989–1993) once vetoed an intelligence authorization bill because Congress had included a requirement that the president give Congress forty-eight hours' prior notice of covert actions. Congress subsequently passed a refashioned authorization bill omitting that language. Ironically, the congressional staffer responsible for managing this piece of legislation was George Tenet, who was the staff director of the Senate Intelligence Committee and later served as DCI.

Some tension usually can be felt between the authorizers and the appropriators. Authorization and appropriations bills sometimes vary widely. For example, authorizers may approve a program but find that it is not given significant funds—or any funds—by the appropriators. This is called **hollow budget authority**. Or appropriators may vote money for programs or activities that have not been authorized. These funds are called **appropriated but not authorized** (or "A not A"). In both cases, the appropriators are calling the tune and taking action that disregards the authorizers. (*See box, "Congressional Humor: Authorizers Versus Appropriators."*)

CONGRESSIONAL HUMOR: AUTHORIZERS VERSUS APPROPRIATORS

The tension between those who sit on authorizing committees and those who sit on appropriations committees is pithily characterized by a joke often heard on Capitol Hill:

"Authorizers think they are gods; appropriators know they are gods."

When funds are appropriated but not authorized, the agency receives the money but may not spend it until Congress passes a bill to authorize spending. Sometimes, however, an agency submits a reprogramming request to Congress, asking permission to spend the money, and Congress can informally approve it. If Congress does not pass a new authorization bill or approve a reprogramming request, the money reverts to the Treasury at the end of the fiscal year.

Some congressional staff believe that several factors have begun to give the authorizers more clout. These include the increased difficulty for members of Congress to create **earmarks** (legislative provisions directing funds to be spent on specific projects); increased member resistance to "appropriated but not authorized" spending; and the general reduction of the budget since sequestration in 2013, where the greater programmatic expertise and insight of the authorizers comes more into play.

After the 9/11 Commission issued its report, some discussion emerged about combining intelligence authorization and appropriations into one committee in each chamber. Such a change would end some of the potential budget disconnects. It also would remove intelligence budgets from the defense appropriations process. Congress did not act on the proposal, but in 2007, the House created the Special Intelligence Oversight Panel (SIOP) as an improved link between the authorizers, the House Intelligence Committee, and the appropriators. However, the Republican majority abolished the SIOP in January 2011 at the beginning of the 112th Congress. Instead, the House Intelligence Committee includes three members from Appropriations in some of its hearings and briefings, not as voting members but to give Appropriations insight into the committee's deliberations and, it is hoped, avoid the legislative disconnects noted earlier.

Congress has debated the issue of making all or part of the intelligence budget public since the 1970s. (See later discussion.) Beginning with FY2007, Congress mandated that the president release the NIP figure for the previous fiscal year. As noted in chapter 3, in October 2010, DNI Clapper released the NIP figure for the previous year—$53.1 billion—and, for the first time, the Defense Department released the MIP figure—$27 billion. The declassification of the aggregate intelligence budget has some implications for Congress. It had been the practice, when the intelligence budget was classified, to "hide" the numbers in the defense authorization and appropriations bills. This is no longer necessary; it is theoretically possible to have a freestanding intelligence budget, the aggregate of which would be public, although the details would remain classified. This would not affect the jurisdictions of the various authorizing committees to work on their respective portions of the intelligence budget, but it does raise the question of which appropriations committee then has jurisdiction, because there is no intelligence appropriations subcommittee. The easiest solution would be to leave the appropriations bills with the defense subcommittees, but there may be some sentiment to create intelligence subcommittees that would be less likely to make trades between defense programs and intelligence programs. Past efforts to create an intelligence appropriations subcommittee have not been successful. DNI Clapper spoke out in favor of separating the NIP from the defense budget. In 2013, the House again voted against such a provision.

The centrality of the budget to oversight should be obvious. In reviewing the president's budget submission and crafting alternatives or variations, Congress gets to examine the size and shape of each agency, the details of each program, and the plans for spending money over the next year. No other activity offers the same degree of access or insight. Moreover, given the constitutional requirement for congressional approval of all expenditures, in no other place does Congress have as much leverage as in the budget process.

Critics of the annual budget process argue that it not only gives Congress insights and power but also subjects the executive branch to frequent fluctuations in funding levels, given that they can vary widely from year to year. Every executive agency dreams of having multiyear appropriations or **no-year appropriations**—that is, money that does not have to be spent by the end of the fiscal year. Although some funds are allocated in these ways, Congress resists doing so on a large scale, because such a move would fundamentally undercut its power of the purse. Appropriated funds that are not spent at the end of a fiscal year are returned to the U.S. Treasury. Each agency keeps careful watch over its spending to ensure that it spends all allocated funds by the end of the fiscal year. OMB also monitors agencies' spending rates throughout the fiscal year to ensure that they are not spending either too quickly or too slowly.

Congress has, in recent years, used **supplemental appropriations** bills with increasing frequency for intelligence. Basically, supplemental appropriations make available to agencies funds over and above the amount originally planned. In the case of an unforeseen emergency, the requirement for a supplemental bill is easily understood. This is often true for ongoing military or intelligence operations. But when supplementals are used on a recurring basis—perhaps annually—they become problematic. Supplemental appropriations are single-year infusions of money. Although no guarantee is made for the size of any appropriation from year to year, supplementals are seen as being riskier in terms of the uncertainty that they will be used again. Thus, if a crucial activity is being funded by supplemental appropriations, it may be necessary in the following year either to terminate the activity for lack of funds or to curtail some other activity in the budget (called "taking it out of hide"). Clearly, agencies would prefer to have the supplemental funds included in the base—that is, added to their regular budget, so that they can plan more effectively for the ensuing years. Congress has been unwilling to do this, largely as a means of controlling growth, despite the effect that repeatedly passing supplementals has had on programs. The use of supplementals has become so regular that both Congress and executive agencies often plan for them at the beginning of a budget cycle. This became a significant issue for intelligence in 2013 as operational funds tied to the wars in Iraq and Afghanistan—called OCO, or overseas contingency operations—began to be cut back and were not put into the budget base.

The budget gives Congress power over intelligence. In the 1980s, for example, Congress used the intelligence budget to restrict the Ronald Reagan administration (1981–1989) policy in Nicaragua, passing a series of amendments, sponsored by the chairman of the House Permanent Select Committee on Intelligence, Edward P. Boland, D-MA, that denied combat-support funds for the contras. Efforts to circumvent these restrictions led to the Iran-contra scandal. But this budget power only works if the House and Senate are in agreement. For the past several years, the two houses have been divided over the future of imagery satellites, especially in the aftermath of the Future Imagery Architecture (FIA) debacle. (See chap. 5.) The House supported the DNI/Defense compromise to build new "large" satellites, but the Senate was adamant about also building some smaller imagery satellites. The result was deadlock and was one of the reasons why no intelligence authorization bill passed for five years.

As noted in chapter 8, the 2014 omnibus appropriations bill included language in the classified annex preventing the shift of responsibility for unmanned aerial vehicle (UAV)-based attacks from CIA to Defense because of the qualms of some members over how Defense would conduct these operations.

Hearings. Hearings are essential to the oversight process as a means of requesting information from responsible executive branch officials and obtaining alternative views from outside experts. Hearings can be open to the public or closed, depending on the subject under discussion. Given the nature of intelligence, a majority of the hearings of the two intelligence committees are closed.

Hearings are not necessarily hostile, but they are adversarial; they are not objective discussions of policy. Each administration uses hearings as a forum for advancing its specific policy choices and as opportunities to sell policy to Congress and to interested segments of the public. Congress understands this and is a skeptical recipient of information from the executive branch, regardless of party affiliation. Intelligence officials are somewhat exempt from selling policy in that they often give Congress the intelligence community's views on an issue without supporting or attacking a given policy. They gain some protection from congressional recriminations because of the line separating policy and intelligence, unless they are perceived as having crossed that line. Again, this was a concern for some members of Congress in the case of Iraq WMD. (Executive branch policy makers may also perceive the intelligence community's congressional testimony as unsupportive or as undermining policy, even if that was not the intelligence community's intent.) However, when intelligence officials testify about intelligence policies—capabilities, budgets, programs, or intelligence-related controversies—they are also in a sales mode vis-à-vis Congress.

Hearings are often followed by questions for the record (QFRs or "kew-fers") submitted to the witnesses and their agencies by members or their staffs to follow up on issues that surfaced during the hearings. Although QFRs give the executive branch an opportunity to make its case again or to add new supportive information, the requests are often viewed as punitive homework assignments. QFRs can also be used by Congress as a tool (or weapon) in a struggle with an agency that seems unwilling to offer information or is stubborn about certain policies.

Nominations. The ability to confirm or reject nominations is a profound political power, which resides in the Senate. Nominations for the DCI were not controversial until 1977, when President Jimmy Carter's first nominee, Theodore Sorensen, withdrew his nomination after appearing before the Senate Select Committee on Intelligence and responding to a number of issues that had been discussed publicly about him. The issues included Sorensen's World War II status as a conscientious objector, which raised questions about his willingness to use covert action; the possible misuse of classified documents in his memoirs; and his defense of Daniel Ellsberg, who leaked to the press the classified Pentagon Papers (a DOD study of the Vietnam War), which raised concerns about his ability to protect intelligence sources and methods.

Since 1977, the Senate has held several other controversial DCI nominee hearings. Robert M. Gates withdrew his first nomination in 1987 as the Iran-contra scandal unfolded. His second nomination, in 1991, featured a detailed investigation of charges that Gates had politicized intelligence to please policy makers. In 1997, Anthony Lake withdrew his nomination at the onset of what promised to be a grueling and perhaps unsuccessful series of hearings. In 2009, John Brennan hoped to be named DCIA by President Obama but withdrew from consideration when liberal critics questioned Brennan's role in the rendition and interrogation programs. Brennan was nominated and confirmed as DCIA in 2013.

Critics of the nomination process—not just of intelligence positions but across the board—charge that it has become increasingly political and personal, delving into issues that are not germane to a nominee's fitness for office. Defenders of the process respond that it is a political process, that the Senate is not supposed to be a rubber stamp, and that careful scrutiny of a nominee may preclude embarrassments later on. Regardless of which view is correct, the nomination process has become so formidable that it has convinced some potential nominees to decline office.

One of the tools available to senators that some find objectionable is the ability to put a "hold" on any pending Senate matter, effectively suspending action until the hold is lifted. Since all Senate business requires unanimous consent (or a UCR, a unanimous consent request), a hold undercuts this requirement. One aspect of the senatorial hold that some find objectionable is the fact that a hold can be placed anonymously, although the Senate rules now require that this anonymity be lifted after two days. Holds are usually lifted after the senator's specific concerns are met. Holds can be placed on nominations. In 2007, Sen. Ron Wyden, D-OR, put an indefinite hold on the nomination of John Rizzo to be CIA general counsel. At issue was the advice that Rizzo, a career-long CIA attorney who had served as acting general counsel for long periods, had given concerning interrogation techniques for terrorist suspects. Facing strong Democratic opposition, Rizzo requested that his nomination be withdrawn. In 2017, Wyden put a hold on the nomination of CIA officer Isabel Patelunas to be assistant secretary of the Treasury for intelligence and analysis until the Trump administration provided the Senate Finance Committee with Treasury documents related to Russia. This hold remained in place until the summer of 2018, at which point Patelunas was confirmed.

Treaties. Advising and consenting to an act of treaty ratification is also a power of the Senate. Unlike nominations, which require a majority vote of the senators present, treaties require a two-thirds vote of those present. Intelligence became a significant issue in treaties during the era of U.S.-Soviet arms control in the 1970s. The ability to monitor adherence to treaty provisions was and is an intelligence function. U.S. policy makers also called on the intelligence community to give monitoring judgments on treaty provisions—that is, to adjudge the likelihood that significant cheating would be detected. The Senate Select Committee on Intelligence, created in 1976, was later given responsibility for evaluating the intelligence community's ability to monitor arms control treaties. The committee gave the Senate another lever with which to influence intelligence policy. As noted in chapter 9, in 1988 the Senate Select Committee on Intelligence, on evaluating the Intermediate-Range Nuclear Forces (INF) Treaty and concerned about the upcoming Strategic Arms Reduction Treaty (START), demanded the purchase of additional imagery satellites, which the Reagan administration did not want but agreed to nonetheless. Similar issues resurfaced in 2010 when some Republican senators questioned the New START treaty that President Obama had signed with Russia in April 2010. Although the main objections centered on the ability to modernize the U.S. nuclear arsenal, issues concerning the ability to verify were also raised. Treaty proponents, as they have in the past, argued that an arms control treaty offers greater transparency and insight into Russian forces given the treaty's verification requirements, a position also taken by the Joint Chiefs of Staff.

In 2013, when President Obama expressed willingness to consider Russia's offer that Syria hand over its entire chemical weapons arsenal, many experts noted the difficulty of monitoring and verifying such an agreement, assuming it could be negotiated. This agreement was not to be a treaty, but the same intelligence concerns would arise. Similarly, the Obama administration resisted calls for the 2015 nuclear agreement negotiated with Iran to be a treaty, in large part because he did not believe the Senate would advise and consent to ratification. Regardless of how it was brought into force, Iranian compliance and U.S. intelligence community capabilities to monitor the agreement remained important areas of congressional oversight until President Trump abandoned the agreement in May 2018 (see chap. 12).

Reporting Requirements. The separation of powers between the executive branch and the legislative branch puts a premium on information. The executive branch tends to forward information that is supportive of its policies; Congress tends to seek fuller information to make decisions based on more than just the views that the executive branch volunteers. One of the ways Congress has sought to institutionalize its broad access to information is by levying reporting requirements on the executive branch. Congress often mandates that the executive branch report on a regular basis (often annually) on specific issues, such as human rights practices in foreign nations, the arms control impact of new weapons systems, or, during the cold war, Soviet compliance with arms control and other treaties.

Reporting requirements, which grew dramatically in the aftermath of the Vietnam War, raise several issues. Does Congress require so many reports that it cannot make effective use of them? Do the reports place an unnecessary burden on the executive branch? Would the executive branch forward the same information if there were no reporting requirements? To give some sense of the scope of activity involved, in 2002 the House Intelligence Committee said it had asked for eighty-four reports in the past year, most of which were either late or incomplete. The House Intelligence Committee's May 2012 report accompanying the FY2013 intelligence authorization bill noted that it had voted to repeal or modify six reporting requirements "so as to alleviate the burden on the IC" (intelligence community). The committee took cognizance of the many reporting requirements but also defended the concept as "a critical part of Congressional oversight." The DNI had nominated thirty reports for repeal; the House Intelligence Committee had agreed that half of those nominated might be repealed but also took into account the views of other congressional committees. In each year's intelligence authorization bill, there are new reporting requirements levied on the intelligence community. Some are one-time requests; others are more permanent. Many reflect a genuine desire to improve oversight. But there is also a cost in terms of where and how the intelligence community expends resources, and the question of the ultimate utility and effect of so many reports remains open.

An important but less visible adjunct to reporting requirements is congressionally directed actions, or CDAs. CDAs are usually studies that the intelligence community (or other executive agencies) is tasked to conduct by Congress, most often via the Intelligence Authorization Act. CDAs are but one more opportunity for Congress to get the information it desires from the executive branch. As a rule, the offices responsible for producing the CDAs find them bothersome and intrusive. CDAs can be a dangerous tool in that they are cost-free for members of Congress and their staff. They have to do no more than levy the requirement. But CDAs do impose time-consuming costs on the executive agencies to which they are sent. In some years, the number of CDAs has been onerous. CDAs, like other reporting requirements, also raise questions about their utility and the degree to which Congress uses them for substantive reasons.

Investigations and Reports. One of Congress's functions is to investigate, which it may do on virtually any issue. The modern intelligence oversight system evolved from the congressional investigations of intelligence in the 1970s. Investigations tend to result in reports that summarize findings and offer recommendations for change, thus serving as effective tools in exposing shortcomings or abuses and in helping craft new policy directions. The two intelligence committees regularly report publicly on issues that have come before them. These reports may be brief because of security concerns, but they assure the rest of Congress and the public that effective oversight is being carried out, and they create policy documents that the executive branch must consider.

Just as the executive branch has come to rely more on outside commissions for intelligence issues, Congress has increasingly created investigations of its own.

After the September 11, 2001, terrorist attacks, Congress conducted a joint inquiry, which consisted of the House and Senate Intelligence Committees. The Senate committee also undertook a long study of intelligence on Iraq WMD. The Democratic majority staff of the Senate Intelligence Committee investigated the CIA's detention and interrogation program. Both intelligence committees have undertaken investigations of Russian activity during the 2016 presidential election. The dynamics of these investigations are different from those created in the executive branch. First, by definition, Congress is a partisan place, made up of a party that supports the president on most issues and one that opposes the president. This can always affect an investigation and puts a certain premium on making investigations as bipartisan as possible. Second, Congress has some responsibility for the performance of intelligence by virtue of its control of the budget and its oversight. Thus, Congress's ability to be objective about its own role comes into question.

The Senate Intelligence staff inquiry into the CIA's detention and interrogation programs is instructive as to the difficulties of conducting intelligence investigations. The initial vote to conduct the inquiry was bipartisan, but the Republican staff then withdrew because they believed that an ongoing criminal investigation of the program by the attorney general would make some participants unwilling to cooperate with the Senate inquiry. Partisan reports—or reports that are perceived to be more partisan—will always be more contentious and seen by some as less authoritative. The investigative methodology used in this report, only reviewing documents but conducting no interviews, was questionable. Documents may be incomplete or self-serving; not all documents may be available. Although the staff held that their approach was more objective ("letting the documents speak for themselves"), it was likely less complete. By comparison, the investigation of the Senate Armed Services Committee in the Abu Ghraib prison scandal included seventy interviews, and two hundred people were asked to fill out questionnaires. This latter approach does not preclude false statements, but it does serve to round out and give context to documentary findings.

In March 2014, Dianne Feinstein, D-CA, then chair of the Senate Intelligence Committee, admitted that staffers had, without CIA permission, removed certain documents from CIA computers to which they had access and stored copies in safes in the committee's offices. Senator Feinstein said this was necessary to prevent their possible destruction by CIA, citing the 2005 destruction of videotapes of interrogations ordered by then–deputy director of operations Jose Rodriguez. Feinstein said the CIA had then unlawfully searched committee computers to determine how the documents were removed. The CIA referred the removal of the material to the FBI for a criminal investigation, which Feinstein saw as intimidation. DCIA John Brennan initially denied the hacking but later admitted that it had occurred. The Justice Department declined to investigate the CIA on this point. Brennan appointed an internal review panel that found the intrusion into the SSCI computers to be lawful. In some cases, DCIA Brennan had ordered the intrusion.

Finally, in April 2014, the committee voted to send a revised version of the report to CIA for classification review. This led to eight months of contentious debate between the committee versus the CIA and the White House staff over the redactions being requested in the finally released executive summary.

One could argue that this entire episode was somewhat extraordinary given the highly charged issue being investigated. However, it does point out many of the potential pitfalls of congressional investigations into intelligence activities.

Each of these levers—hearings, reports, QFRs, CDAs, investigations—is part of the larger struggle over information that is central both to oversight and to friction between Congress and the executive branch. Essentially, Congress needs and wants information and the executive branch wants to limit the information that it provides, especially information that may not be supportive of preferred executive-branch policies. As with so much else, beyond barebones agreements on information that must be shared (budget justifications, treaty texts, background information on nominees), the remainder falls into a gray zone of debate. Therefore, struggles over information are constant in the oversight relationship. For example, in the 109th and 110th Congresses (2005–2008), issues related to policies to combat terrorism became regular information battlegrounds. Members of Congress sought information (usually internal administration papers) on wiretapping and interrogation techniques. These struggles for information become especially important when the issue at hand is vague or may be breaking new ground, perhaps apart from legislation, as was the case in these two issues. Congress can issue subpoenas, but both branches usually seek to avoid taking the matter to court, in part because this involves yet a third branch of government in the decision. Congress can also deny funding or hold up action on legislation or nominees. Similarly, the degree to which Congress had been apprised of the details and scope of the various NSA programs that had been leaked in 2013 also became oversight issues. (See below for a fuller discussion.) Finally, the conduct of the Senate Intelligence staff investigation into the CIA's detention and interrogation programs became mired in controversy, as noted earlier.

Hostages. If the executive branch disagrees with Congress about some issue, Congress may seek means of forcing it to agree. One way is to take hostages—that is, to withhold action on issues that are important to the executive branch until the desired response by the executive branch is given. This type of behavior is not unique to Congress; intelligence agencies use it as a bargaining tactic in formulating national intelligence estimates (NIEs) and other interagency products.

During the debate on the INF Treaty, the demands of the Senate Select Committee on Intelligence for new imagery satellites was one case of hostage taking. In 1993, Congress threatened to withhold action on the intelligence authorization bill until the CIA provided information on a Bill Clinton administration DOD nominee, Morton H. Halperin. Halperin, who had publicly criticized U.S. covert actions in the 1970s and 1980s, eventually withdrew his nomination for the newly created post of assistant secretary of defense for democracy and peacekeeping. In 2001, the intelligence committees "fenced" (put a hold on) certain funds for intelligence to prod the George W. Bush administration into nominating a new CIA inspector general. Critics argue that hostage taking is a blunt and unwieldy tool; supporters argue that it is used only when other means of reaching agreement with the executive branch have failed.

Prior Notice of Covert Action. One of Congress's main concerns is that it receive prior or timely notice of presidential actions. Most members understand that prior notice is not the same as prior congressional approval, which is required for few executive decisions other than the spending of money. Covert action is one of the areas that have been contentious. As a rule, Congress receives advance notice of covert action in a process that has been largely institutionalized, but successive administrations have refused to make prior notice a legal requirement. A congressional demand for at least forty-eight hours' notice led to the first veto of an intelligence authorization bill, by President George H. W. Bush in 1990. In 2008, the House Intelligence Committee threatened to fence money for all covert actions unless it was briefed on each of them. In May 2013, President Obama said that Congress would be briefed on all UAV strikes beyond the Iraq and Afghan theaters—with an exception made in the case of the attack on Anwar al-Awlaki in Yemen.

The Senate Intelligence Committee's 2013 summary of its activities in the 112th Congress (2011–2012) stated that during each quarter Congress receives a written report on each covert action being carried out under a presidential finding.

As noted in chapter 8, some covert actions are debated openly by officials in the executive branch and by members of Congress. This does not violate any laws but does undercut the plausible deniability of the action. Most recently, this had been the case with the Obama administration's overt and covert plans to send arms to the Syrian rebels.

ISSUES IN CONGRESSIONAL OVERSIGHT

Oversight of intelligence raises a number of issues that are part of the "invitation to struggle," as the separation of powers has often been called.

How Much Oversight Is Enough? From 1947 to 1975—the first twenty-eight years of the modern intelligence community's existence—the atmosphere of the cold war promoted fairly lax, distant, and trusting congressional oversight. A remark by Sen. Leverett Saltonstall, R-MA (1945–1967), a member of the Senate Armed Services Committee, characterized that viewpoint: "There are things that my government does that I would rather not know about." This attitude was partly responsible for some of the intelligence agency abuses that investigations uncovered in the 1970s.

Working out the parameters of the intelligence oversight system has not been easy. Successive administrations, regardless of party affiliation, have tended to resist what they have seen as unwarranted intrusions.

There is no objective way to determine the proper level of oversight. Committees review each line item on the budget. They do so to make informed judgments on how to allocate funds, which is Congress's responsibility. Reviewing specific covert actions may seem intrusive to some, but it represents an important political step. If Congress allows the operation to proceed unquestioned, the executive branch can claim that it had political support should problems arise later. Similarly, serious questions raised by Congress are a signal to rethink the operation, even if the ultimate decision is to go ahead as planned.

Does rigorous oversight require just detailed knowledge of intelligence programs, or does it require something more, such as information on alternative intelligence policies and programs? Congress has, on occasion, taken issue with the direction of intelligence policy and acted either to block the administration, such as with the Boland amendments that prohibited military support to the contras in Nicaragua, or to demand changes, such as with the purchase of the arms control–related satellites.

Recently, the buzzword "transparency" has gained currency in congressional discussions of intelligence programs. It may strike some as odd to use the word transparency when talking about activities that are usually secret, but the word is simply another way of Congress asking for more insight into and information about certain activities. The activities that have been most often cited as requiring more transparency have been the use of armed drones and the NSA surveillance programs.

Interestingly, in October 2015, the ODNI released an implementation plan for "Principles of Intelligence Transparency for the Intelligence Community." The paper was clearly in response to the various leaks and accusations made against U.S. intelligence in recent years, with the stated goal of giving the American public greater understanding of what intelligence does so as to maintain their confidence. The general goal is to make more information about intelligence publicly available while also protecting intelligence sources, methods, and activities.

Secrecy and the Oversight Process. The high level of security that intelligence requires imposes costs on congressional oversight. Members of Congress have security clearances (through top secret) by virtue of having been elected to office. Members must have clearances to carry out their duties. Only the executive branch can grant security clearances, but there is no basis for its granting or denying clearances to certain members of Congress, as this would violate the separation of powers. At the same time, member clearances do not mean full access to the entire range of intelligence activities. Congressional staff members who require clearances receive them from the executive branch after meeting the usual background checks and demonstrating a need to know. Congressional staffers are not polygraphed as a prerequisite for clearances, as are employees in most (but not all) intelligence agencies and national security–related agencies.

All members are deemed to be cleared, but both the House and Senate limit the dissemination of intelligence among members who are not on the intelligence committees. Although this limitation replicates the acceptance of responsibility that all congressional committees have, in the case of intelligence it entails additional burdens for the panels, as their information cannot be easily shared. Thus, the intelligence committees require special offices for the storage of sensitive material and must hold many of their hearings in closed session. Both houses have also created different levels of notification for members about intelligence activities, depending on the sensitivity of the information. Intelligence officials may brief only the House and Senate leadership (known as the **Gang of 4**), the leaders plus the chairs and ranking members of the intelligence committees (known as the **Gang of 8**), some additional committee chairs as well, or the full intelligence committees. These more limited briefings have no basis in statute, but the practice of the executive branch providing limited briefings predates the intelligence committees.

This issue became extremely controversial in 2009–2010. At issue was whether Congress had been briefed on enhanced interrogation techniques (EITs) being used against terrorists, including waterboarding. House Speaker Nancy Pelosi, D-CA, insisted that she had never been briefed on the use of such EITs, only on the fact that these techniques might be used. DCIA Panetta, himself a former member of Congress (1977–1993), insisted that members had been briefed correctly. The discussion quickly descended into a shrill and highly partisan debate in both houses and included the issue of CIA's veracity when briefing Congress, which Pelosi and others questioned, and the issue of who decides which members get briefed, with Pelosi advocating larger groups and less frequent use of the Gang of 8 or Gang of 4. President Obama then threatened to veto the intelligence authorization bill, which included new provisions largely eliminating the Gang of 8 briefings. He also threatened to veto a less onerous Senate version of the bill and a redrafted House version. As often happens in Congress, other issues merged into the briefing issue. Because Pelosi would not allow a bill to reach the House floor that she did not believe was strong enough, senators threatened to stall on the nomination of Clapper to be the DNI, replacing DNI Blair, who had departed in May 2010. Some nineteen months after the controversy began, the House and Senate agreed on a slightly altered briefing procedure. Under the new agreement, Gang of 8 briefings continue; the full committees are to be notified of covert action findings 180 days after a briefing unless the president states in writing that the issue remains sensitive. All intelligence committee members are given a general description of the briefing but no details.

Despite these precautions that limit access and the internal rules intended to punish members or staff who give out information surreptitiously, Congress as an institution has the undeserved reputation of being a fount of leaks. This image is propagated mainly by the executive branch, which believes that it is much more rigorous in handling classified information. In reality, most leaks of intelligence and other national security information come from the executive branch, not from Congress. (In 1999, DCI Tenet admitted before a congressional committee that the number of leaks from executive officials was higher than at any time in his memory.) This is not to suggest that Congress has a perfect record on safeguarding intelligence material, but it is far better than that of the CIA, State Department, DOD, or the staff of the NSC. The reason is not superior behavior on the part of Congress so much as it is relative levers of power. Leaks occur for a variety of reasons: to show off some special knowledge, to settle scores, or to promote or stop a policy. Other than showing off, members of Congress and their staffs have much better means than leaks to settle scores or affect policy. They control spending, which is the easiest and most effective way to create or terminate a policy or program. Even minority members and staff can use the legislative process, hearings, and the press to dissent from policies or attempt to slow them down. Officials in the executive branch do not have the same leverage and therefore resort to leaks more frequently. However, the misperception of Congress as a major leaker persists. (The reputation of the Senate Intelligence Committee suffered when its former longtime head of security, James Wolfe, pleaded guilty in October 2018 to lying to the FBI during an investigation of leaks. Wolfe had lied about his contacts with reporters. He was not accused of leaking. Wolfe pleaded guilty and was sentenced to two months in prison.)

The other issue raised by secrecy is Congress's effectiveness in acting as a surrogate for the public. The U.S. government ostensibly operates on the principle of openness: Its operations and decisions should be known to the public. (The Constitution does not mention the public's right to know, however. The Constitution safeguards freedom of speech and freedom of the press, which are not the same as a right to all information relating to government activities.) In the case of intelligence, the principle of openness does not apply. Some people accept the reasons for secrecy and the limitations that it imposes on public accountability. Others have concerns about the role of Congress as the public's surrogate in executive oversight. Their reasons vary, from doubts about the executive branch's willingness to be forthcoming with Congress to concerns about Congress's readiness to air disquieting information.

Another oversight access issue that arose at the same time as the Gang of 8 issue was the desire by some members to give the Government Accountability Office (GAO) greater access to intelligence programs. The GAO was created in 1921 (as the General Accounting Office) with broad authority to support Congress by investigating how federal money is spent and how federal programs are managed. This usually involves audits or performance reviews of ongoing programs. Although the GAO had some access to intelligence programs, such as some defense **special access programs** (called **SAPs**), the GAO was largely excluded from intelligence for many decades, much to its chagrin. Obama threatened to veto the intelligence authorization bill over the provision granting the GAO more access. The compromise language added to the legislation left it to the DNI to prepare a directive concerning GAO access to intelligence. DNI Clapper's directive, issued in 2011, mandated intelligence community cooperation with the GAO with certain limitations on information that would not be shared: intelligence on sources and methods, information related to covert action, and "information that falls within the purview of the congressional intelligence oversight committees." Supporters of GAO access found this last phrase problematic because it is so broad, but it was generally agreed that the directive improved GAO access overall.

Congress and the Intelligence Budget. A recurring issue for Congress has been whether to reveal some aspects of the intelligence budget. Article I, Section 9, paragraph 7, of the Constitution requires that accounts of all public money be published "from time to time." This phrase is vague, which allowed each successive administration to argue that its refusal to disclose the details of intelligence spending was permissible. Critics contended that this interpretation vitiated the constitutional requirement to publish some account at some point. Most advocates of publication were not asking for a detailed publication of the entire budget but wanted to know at least the total spent on intelligence annually. (*See box, "Intelligence Budget Disclosure: Top or Bottom?"*)

The argument over publishing some part of intelligence spending came to a head in 1997, when DCI Tenet revealed that overall intelligence spending for FY1998 was $26.6 billion. He provided the number in response to a Freedom of Information Act suit, acting to end the suit and to limit the information that the intelligence community revealed. Tenet later refused to divulge the amount requested or appropriated for FY1999, arguing that to do so would harm national security interests and intelligence sources and methods. Various attempts to make publishing the overall intelligence budget mandatory failed over disagreements between the House and Senate until

INTELLIGENCE BUDGET DISCLOSURE: TOP OR BOTTOM?

One of the curiosities of the debate over intelligence budget disclosure was the term used for the number most at issue. The overall spending total for intelligence was alternatively described as the "top line number" or the "bottom line number." It sometimes sounded as if people on the same side—those in favor of or opposed to disclosure—were at odds with themselves.

July 2007, when Congress passed a requirement to do so as part of a bill implementing the recommendations of the 9/11 Commission. The law requires the DNI to disclose the aggregate amount appropriated in the NIP, beginning one month after the end of the previous fiscal year. (In the federal budget process, fiscal years end on September 30 and begin on October 1.) The law requiring the disclosures allows the president to delay or waive release of the NIP figure if the president informs the intelligence committees that disclosure would damage national security. To date, this has not happened and is increasingly unlikely because, since October 2010, the DNI and DOD have released both the NIP and MIP figures for the previous year. Moreover, the amount being requested for the NIP in FY2012 was revealed in early 2011, the first time that a NIP request (as opposed to the previous year's appropriation) had been declassified. The release of NIP and MIP requests and final appropriations has now become the normal practice.

There is no inclination on the part of DNI or DOD to give more public detail on how intelligence dollars are spent, either by activity or by agency. Does this limited disclosure satisfy the constitutional requirement? The basic lines in the debate remain as they were before. Proponents of disclosure cite, first and foremost, the constitutional requirement for publication. They also argue that disclosure of this one number poses no threat to national security, because it reveals nothing about spending choices within the intelligence community.

Proponents of continued secrecy tend not to cite the "time to time" language of the Constitution, which is a weak argument at best. Instead, they argue that Congress is privy to the information and acts on behalf of the public. They also say that disclosure of the overall amount could be the beginning of demands for more detailed disclosure. Noting how little this one number reveals (and implicitly accepting their opponents' argument that its disclosure would not jeopardize security), proponents of continued secrecy contend that the initial disclosure would inexorably lead to pressure for more detailed disclosures about specific agency budgets or programs and that these disclosures would have security implications. Four members of Congress introduced a bill in March 2018 requiring the president to release budget figures for each intelligence agency. No action was taken on the bill in the House or the Senate.

Disclosing the overall number entails political risks for U.S. intelligence. Relating spending to outputs is more difficult for intelligence than it is for virtually any other government activity. How much intelligence should $78.4 billion (or any other figure) buy? Should output be assessed by the number of reports produced? The number of covert actions undertaken? The number of spies recruited? Moreover, the overall number—which does not strike many as a small sum—leads some people to question intelligence community performance. Statements along the lines of "How could they miss that coup (or lose that spy) when they have $78.4 billion?" would ensue. Such sentiments would add little to a meaningful debate about intelligence because these types of questions reveal a lack of appreciation for how intelligence functions. The budget is not neatly divided into specific issues (for example, terrorism or China). Rather, it funds activities (collection, analysis, systems administration, and so on), which are then allocated by senior managers into the areas where they are deemed to be most needed. Moreover, the intelligence community does not have the luxury of concentrating on just a few issues and disregarding the others or putting them on hold until resources are available or the issues grow critical. The intelligence agencies devote resources to a very large array of issues at any one time. Therefore, the overall budget figure offers virtually no insight into how well intelligence should be able to perform on any given issue or across the board.

Exactly this type of discussion followed after the release of details of the NIP in 2013 as part of the Snowden leaks. Journalists tended to focus on a few numbers and then made fairly broad and often inaccurate assumptions about what these said about U.S. intelligence priorities or activities. (As noted earlier, these numbers remain classified despite their having been published and therefore cannot be discussed further.)

The general trajectory of the budget also affects how Congress deals with it. As would be expected, it is easier dealing with a growing budget than with a static or declining budget. But even in a growing budget, there will be differences between the branches and among members of Congress as to where the additional dollars should be spent. Also, Congress will always be on the lookout for waste, which tends to happen more in times of plenty than of want. Static or declining budgets are more difficult as choices have to be made between what is maintained and what is cut. One of the agreed "lessons" of the 1990s intelligence budget reductions is that across-the-board cuts are the wrong way to deal with the problem and are more harmful. Indeed, DNI Clapper, when faced with the decline of the intelligence budget, said that he would not repeat that mistake and that he would select "winners and losers." However, the DNI lost some of that ability once sequestration began, as Congress mandated equal percentage cuts across all intelligence budget program elements. As shown in Table 10.1, the intelligence budget peaked in FY2010 at $80.1 billion ($53.1 billion NIP; $27 billion MIP) and then declined steadily to $66.8 billion in FY2015. However, the budget has been increasing again since then and the 2019 request, if fully funded, would be a new high total. The MIP, however, would still be $5.8 billion below its high in FY2010, a decrease of just over 21 percent.

Table 10.1 U.S. Intelligence Budget, 2007–2020

(All figures are $billions)			
Fiscal Year	Total	NIP	MIP
2007	63.5	43.5	20
2008	70.4	47.5	22.9
2009	76.2	49.8	26.4
2010	80.1	53.1	27
2011	78.6	54.6	24
2012	75.4	53.9	21.5
2013	71.9	52.7	19.2
2013 (after sequester)	67.6	49.0	18.6
2014	67.7	50.3	17.4
2015	66.8	50.3	16.5
2016	70.7	53.0	17.7
2017	73.4	54.9	18.5
2018 (request)	78.4	57.7	20.7
2019 (request)	81.2	59.9	21.2
2020 (request)	85.75	62.8	22.95

Finally, just as the budget is Congress's main means of control over the intelligence community, it is also the locus of Congress's responsibility for how well intelligence performs. Congress ultimately decides which satellites are built, how many are built, and how many analysts and clandestine officers the intelligence community can afford to have on its payroll. Although this was self-evident, it did not become an issue until after the 2001 terrorist attacks. Some people observed that Congress bore some responsibility for intelligence performance because of the steep decline in resources devoted to intelligence after the fall of the Soviet Union in 1991. Budgets were cut and, according to DCI Tenet, the equivalent of 23,000 positions were lost over the decade of the 1990s, affecting performance and capabilities. As one senior official observed, the decision at the time was "to cut people not programs." This congressional responsibility apparently became a controversial issue within the joint inquiry, as some members wanted to take note of this responsibility and others refused. Ultimately, the joint inquiry's report did not address the issue. Given that the joint inquiry was a combination of the House and Senate Intelligence Committees, some critics felt they had not been forthright in addressing their own responsibilities.

Regulating the Intelligence Community. Since the end of World War II, Congress has passed only two major pieces of structural intelligence legislation: the National Security Act of 1947 and the Intelligence Reform and Terrorism Prevention Act of 2004. Thus, the structure of the intelligence community was remarkably stable throughout the cold war and the immediate post–cold war period. Only as a result of the terrorist attacks and the issue of WMD in Iraq was there sufficient political impetus to foster major changes. (See chap. 14.) Four presidents issued extensive EOs on intelligence—Gerald R. Ford in 1976, Jimmy Carter in 1978, Ronald Reagan in 1981, and George W. Bush in 2004 and 2008—the latter of which updated President Reagan's 1981 executive order, EO 12333, which remains one of the fundamental documents in U.S. intelligence.

President George Washington issued the first executive order under his presumed authority, setting a precedent. Each president since also has done so. No specific constitutional power grants a president this authority. The authority to write EOs stems from the president's obligation, under Article II, Section 3, to "take Care that the Laws be faithfully executed." EOs are legal documents but may not conflict with a law or a judicial decision. Thus, they sometimes tend to operate in areas where there is neither legislation nor judicial decisions. The major advantage of EOs is that they give presidents the flexibility to make changes in the intelligence community to meet changing needs or to reflect their own preferences about how the intelligence community should be managed or its functions limited. The major disadvantages of EOs are that they are impermanent, subject to change by each president (or even by the same president); they are not statutes and therefore are more difficult to enforce; and they give Congress a limited role. (The executive branch usually provides Congress with drafts of executive orders in advance of their promulgation and has given Congress opportunities to comment on them.)

Despite the difficulty that Congress and the executive branch have experienced in making legislative changes, they offer the advantages of being permanent, of being statutes in law and therefore more enforceable, and of allowing Congress a major and proper role. However, legislation is more likely to raise major disputes between Congress and the executive branch and thus is more difficult to enact. Congress is also more likely to harbor several points of view on major intelligence issues than is the executive branch, where the major issues tend to be agency-parochial in nature. This divergence of views within Congress was evident during the debate on the 2004 intelligence reform bill.

The split between the House and Senate Intelligence Committees over attacks on U.S. citizens, an outgrowth of the Anwar al-Awlaki case, is instructive. As of early 2014, the Senate favored an additional review process for such attacks, and the House opposed this. The Senate committee also supported an annual public report on the casualties resulting from drone strikes, which the House committee also opposed. As noted, the DNI released such a report in July 2016.

Similarly, the NSA programs that became controversial after the Snowden leaks also underscored the problem. The two most controversial programs were based on Sections 215 and 702 of the USA PATRIOT Act. The legislation provided authorization for certain activities but not specifics about how they would be conducted. Some members expressed the view that the actual conduct of the collection exceeded what they thought they had approved. In his January 2014 speech, President Obama defended the legality and the conduct of the collection.

Given the more permanent nature of legislation, some people question whether certain regulations should not be made statutory largely because the actions they cover are embarrassing or inappropriate. However, if legislation lists proscribed activities, does it implicitly permit those activities that are not listed? No one wants to or is likely able to come up with a comprehensive list of activities that should either be explicitly permitted or banned. Moreover, some activities will likely enter into a gray zone of interpretation. The debate over torture or—more correctly—what constitutes torture, is a good example. Few people would advocate the use of torture. Moreover, torture is specifically banned in the Constitution. The Eighth Amendment bans "cruel and unusual punishment." But few people would be comfortable going over a list of techniques and then choosing which ones should be specifically permitted in legislation.

The parameters of congressional oversight are usually not dealt with in legislation. All congressional committees are created as part of the rules of the House and the Senate. The same is true for jurisdiction and membership. The National Security Act does specify types of intelligence information that have to be shared with Congress, such as that relating to covert action, but the law is written as a requirement levied on the executive branch. During the debate over the 2004 IRTPA legislation, some suggested combining the two intelligence committees into one joint committee, an old issue, for reasons of security and to reduce the time executive officials have to spend testifying, often on the same subject, before more than one committee. As has been the case in the past, congressional organization was not legislated and was left to the respective chambers.

The Issue of Co-option. As eager as Congress is to be kept informed about all aspects of policy, a cost is incurred when it accepts information. Unless members raise questions about what they are told, they are, in effect, co-opted. Their silence betokens consent, as the maxim of English law says. They are free to dissent later on, but the administration will be quick to point out that they did not raise any questions at the time they were briefed. Having been informed before the fact tends to undercut Congress's freedom of action after the fact.

This dynamic is not unique to intelligence, but intelligence makes it somewhat more pointed. The nature of the information, which is both secret and usually limited to certain members, makes co-option more easily accomplished and has more serious consequences. It also puts additional pressure on the members of the intelligence committees, who are privy to the information and are acting on behalf of their entire body.

Congress has no easy way to avoid the inherent exchange of foreknowledge and consent. It is unlikely to revert to the trusting attitude expressed by Senator

Saltonstall. Nor can Congress be expected to raise serious questions about every issue just to establish a record that allows it to dissent later on.

This became an issue after the Snowden leaks revealed the NSA collection programs in 2013. The leadership of both intelligence committees defended the programs and noted that they had been briefed on them. According to press reports, briefings to Congress about this type of collection dated to 2001. Most of the members who raised concerns over the NSA programs were not on the intelligence committees, creating a divide based in large part on access. Congress is part of a delegated system: Members stand in for their constituents in terms of knowing about certain government activities, and certain committees stand in for the broader membership of both houses. This tends to be generally accepted except when highly classified and controversial programs are revealed. In July 2013, a coalition of conservative and liberal members in the House attempted to curtail the NSA program via an amendment to the Defense appropriations bill. The debate pitted the House leadership and the intelligence committee against the amendment's supporters. The amendment was defeated in a close vote, 217–205.

The Snowden leaks also raised once again the issue of how forthcoming executive branch witnesses should be when testifying on intelligence matters, especially in unclassified sessions. In a case that was very reminiscent of the Richard Helms testimony controversy in 1973 (see chap. 13), Sen. Ron Wyden, D-OR, a longtime critic of many collection programs, asked DNI Clapper in an unclassified hearing for a "yes or no" response as to whether NSA collects "any type of data at all on millions or hundreds of millions of Americans?" Clapper answered that NSA did not, at least "not wittingly." When confronted with this answer after the Snowden leaks, Clapper said he was trying to give the "least untruthful" answer possible, a response that raised obvious criticism. Clapper sent a letter to Senate Intelligence Chairman Dianne Feinstein, D-CA, explaining why he had given the answer he did, stating that he had misunderstood Wyden's question, which had begun with the use of the term "dossiers," which was what Clapper said he had focused on. Clapper also said that he had clarified the matter with Wyden as soon as he realized his error.

What Price Oversight Failures? Even when the intelligence oversight system is working well, most members and congressional staff have difficulty running the system so as to avoid all lapses. Most members and staff involved in the process understand the difference between small lapses and large ones. Some of the larger lapses for which Congress has taken the intelligence community to task are these:

- Failure to inform the Senate Intelligence Committee that CIA operatives were directly involved in mining Corinto, a Nicaraguan port, in 1984, during the contra war. The CIA let it appear that the contras had carried this out on their own. When the truth became known, not only did Vice Chairman Daniel Patrick Moynihan, D-NY, resign—although he later changed his mind—but Chairman Barry Goldwater, R-AZ, also reprimanded DCI William J. Casey (1981–1987) in harsh and public terms.

- Failure to inform Congress on a timely basis when agents in Moscow began to disappear, which was later presumed to be the result of the espionage of CIA officer Aldrich Ames. (The assessment as to who caused the losses may have changed as a result of the damage assessment from the Robert Hanssen spy case.) The House Intelligence Committee issued a public report critical of the CIA in 1995, with which the CIA agreed.

- The revelation in 2007 of the existence and subsequent destruction, in 2005, of tapes made in 2002 during the interrogation of two senior al Qaeda members. The CIA insisted that some members had been briefed about the existence of the tapes but none knew about their destruction, which was ordered by the then-head of the National Clandestine Service (now the DO), Jose Rodriguez and carried out by Gina Haspel, who became DCIA in 2018. Rodriguez was subpoenaed to testify before Congress but excused at the request of his attorney, Robert S. Bennett, who had asked for immunity for Rodriguez given the possibility of criminal charges. In November 2010, the Justice Department dropped criminal charges related to the tapes' destruction, citing a lack of evidence.

Congress does have at hand some levers to enforce its oversight. It can reduce the intelligence budget, delay nominations, or, in the case of a serious lapse, demand the resignation of the official involved, although that decision is ultimately up to the official and the president. If the lapse is serious enough and can be traced back to the president, impeachment might be an option. In the cases cited above, Congress did not impose any of these penalties.

But even without inflicting concrete penalties, Congress can enforce its oversight. The loss of officials' credibility before their major committees is serious in and of itself. As hackneyed as it sounds, much of Washington runs on the basis of trust and the value of one's word. Once credibility and trust are lost, as happened to Casey in the Corinto affair, they are difficult to regain.

INTERNAL DYNAMICS OF CONGRESSIONAL OVERSIGHT

Even though oversight is inherent in the entire congressional process, the way Congress organizes itself to handle intelligence oversight is somewhat peculiar.

Why Serve on an Intelligence Oversight Committee? Members of Congress take office with specific areas of interest, derived from either the nature of their district or state or their personal interests. Most members, at least early in their legislative careers, tend to focus on issues that are most likely to enhance their careers. For most members, intelligence is unlikely to fit any of these criteria. Therefore, why would members spend a portion of their limited time on intelligence?

At first blush, the disadvantages are more apparent than the advantages. Intelligence is, for most members, a distraction from their other duties and from those issues likely to be of greatest interest to their constituents. Few districts have a direct interest in intelligence. The main ones are those in the immediate Washington, D.C., area, where the major agencies are located, and those districts where major collection systems are manufactured. But these are a small fraction of the 435 House districts in the fifty states.

Once involved in intelligence issues, members cannot discuss much of what they are doing or what they have accomplished. Co-option is also a danger. Should something go wrong in intelligence, committee members will be asked why they did not know about it in advance. If they did know in advance, they will be asked why they did not do something about it. If they did not know, they will be asked why not. These are all difficult questions to answer.

Finally, the intelligence budget is remarkably free of pork, that is, projects to benefit a member's district or state that are earmarked for funding. Therefore, members on the committees have few opportunities to help their constituents.

With all of those disadvantages, why serve on an intelligence oversight committee? Because some advantages accrue from membership. First, service on the intelligence committees allows members to perform public service within Congress, to serve on a committee where they have few, if any, direct interests. Second, their service gives members a rare opportunity to have access to a closed and often interesting body of information. Third, it gives members a role in shaping intelligence policy and, because of the relatively small size of the two committees (in the 116th Congress—2019–2020—twenty-two members on the House Intelligence Committee and fifteen on the Senate Intelligence Committee), perhaps a greater role than they would have on many of the other, larger oversight committees. (The House Armed Services Committee, for example, has fifty-seven members.) Fourth, membership on the intelligence committee may offer opportunities for national press coverage on high-profile issues about which few people are conversant. Fifth, because members of the two intelligence committees are selected by the majority and minority leadership of the House and the Senate, being chosen is a sign of favor that can be important to a member's career. (Select committees usually have limited life spans, especially in the House. The House Intelligence Committee is called "permanent select" to denote its continued existence, even though it remains "select.")

There are also some different sensitivities involved in selecting members for the intelligence committees because of the issues they oversee. The party leadership in both houses wants to be sure that members are selected who not only will take their oversight role seriously and will be careful not to disclose classified information but also reflect that Congress is a serious steward when it handles intelligence. This sensitivity became apparent in late 2006, as then-representative Pelosi, who would be the speaker of the House in the 110th Congress in January 2007, considered whom to select to chair the House Intelligence Committee. The ranking Democrat on the committee was Rep. Jane Harman, D-CA, with whom Pelosi had a strained relationship. If Pelosi bypassed Harman, next in line was Rep. Alcee Hastings, D-FL. Pelosi found herself caught between the fact that Hastings is an African American, an important constituency in the Democratic caucus and party, and the fact that Hastings had been impeached by the House in 1988 (when it was controlled by Democrats) and removed from office by the Democrat-controlled Senate the following year because of alleged bribery when he served as a federal district court judge. (Pelosi had been among the 413 representatives who voted to impeach Hastings. Hastings was removed from office but acquitted in a federal criminal trial because his alleged co-conspirator refused to testify.) Pelosi eventually decided to bypass Hastings as chairman as well, finally selecting Rep. Silvestre Reyes, D-TX, instead. Hastings was designated as vice chairman.

The Issue of Term Limits. Service on the House and Senate Intelligence Committees, unlike other committees, was initially limited. Congress adopted term limits for committee membership based on the view that the pre-1975 oversight system had failed, in part, because the few members involved became too cozy with the agencies they were overseeing.

The major advantage of term limits is the distance that they promote between the overseers and the overseen. Limited terms also make it possible for more members of the House and the Senate to serve on the intelligence committees, thus adding to the knowledgeable body necessary for informed debate.

Term limits also carry disadvantages. Few members come to Congress with much knowledge of, and virtually no experience with, intelligence activities. Because the subject can be arcane and complex, requiring some time to master, members are likely to spend some portion of their tenure on the committee simply learning about intelligence. Once they have become knowledgeable and effective, they are nearing the end of their term. Term limits also make service on the intelligence committees less attractive, because they reduce the likelihood that a member can become chairman through seniority.

In 1996, Larry Combest, R-TX, who was then chairman of the House Intelligence Committee, testified that he thought it was time to consider longer tenure on the committee, which would be to Congress's advantage. Members on the House committee, however, are still limited to eight years' service; the chairman and ranking minority member can serve for up to ten years. In 2004, the leaders of the Senate Intelligence Committee, Pat Roberts, R-KS, and John D. Rockefeller IV, D-WV, also spoke out in favor of revising the limits, which had been dropped for the Senate panel.

Bipartisan or Partisan Committees? The Senate and House Intelligence Committees are distinctly different in composition. Typically, the ratio of seats between the parties on committees in both chambers roughly reflects the ratio of seats in each chamber as a whole. The Senate Intelligence Committee has always been exempt from this practice, with the majority party having just one more seat than the minority. Moreover, the ranking minority member is always the vice chairman of the Senate committee. The Senate leadership took these steps in 1976 to minimize the role of partisanship in intelligence. When the House Intelligence Committee was formed in 1977, the House Democratic leadership rejected the Senate model, insisting that membership on the committee be determined by the parties' ratio in the House, which reflected the will of the people as expressed in the last election.

A bipartisan committee offers opportunities for a more coherent policy, because the committee is removed—as far as is possible—from partisanship. A committee united on policy and not divided by party may also have more influence with the executive branch. In the case of the Corinto mining, Chairman Goldwater and Vice Chairman Moynihan agreed that the intelligence community was guilty of a significant and unacceptable breach. Thus, DCI Casey had no political refuge for not keeping the committee informed. Despite the continuation of this bipartisan structure on the Senate committee, the Democratic minority showed signs of restiveness in the 108th Congress (2003–2005) and the 109th Congress (2005–2007). A formal division of the committee's budget was made in 2004 (60 percent for the Republican majority; 40 percent for the Democratic minority). In early 2005, Democratic members sought ways to limit the powers of the committee's staff director in the areas of hiring and staff assignments. Although their goal was greater bipartisan control, the issue was discussed and decided on partisan terms. As noted, the Senate report on the CIA's detention and interrogation program was undertaken by only the majority Democratic staff.

Partisanship runs counter to the preferred myth that U.S. national security policy is bipartisan or nonpartisan. A partisan committee has the potential to be more dynamic than a bipartisan committee, where political compromise is more at a premium. In many ways, the compromise that a bipartisan committee engenders is equivalent to the lowest common denominator dynamic that one sees in intelligence community estimates.

The different structures of the two committees are not necessarily an indicator of the degree of partisanship. In the 114th Congress (2015–2016), the House committee exhibited a high degree of bipartisanship on key issues, under the highly effective leadership of chairman Mike Rogers, R-MI, and ranking Democrat Dutch Ruppersberger, D-MD. At the same time, the Senate committee was deeply divided over the Democratic staff report on interrogation techniques. In the 115th Congress, Senate committee chairman Richard Burr, R-NC, and vice chairman Mark Warner, D-VA, were able to work together on the Russia investigation, while the House committee became highly dysfunctional because of that same issue, with chairman Devin Nunes, R-CA, having to recuse himself from the investigation because of his efforts to work with White House staff to exonerate President Trump. In the 116th Congress, the Senate committee structure was unchanged. Democrats took control of the House committee, but the tension apparently remained, when Republicans delayed naming their members to slow down chairman Adam Schiff, D-CA, in his attempts to investigate issues related to Donald Trump and Russia.

In its own accidental way, Congress may have achieved the right balance, with a bipartisan intelligence committee in one chamber and a partisan committee in the other. Still, the political issues themselves and the personalities involved also matter a great deal in how the two committees function.

Committee Turf. All congressional committees guard their areas of jurisdiction jealously. For example, in 1976, when the Senate was considering the creation of an intelligence committee, the Senate Armed Services Committee resisted, seeking to preserve its jurisdiction over the DCI and the CIA. Dividing issues or agencies cleanly and clearly between or among committees is not always possible, in which case the jurisdiction is shared and certain bills get referred to more than one committee. But jurisdiction equates to power.

There is also a more subtle aspect to congressional jurisdiction. Committees tend to become protectors of the agencies they oversee, at least when the jurisdiction or authority of these agencies is under question or attack. There is no inconsistency or hypocrisy involved in the committees serving as agencies' "best friends and severest critics." Committee members believe that they have a better and more complete understanding of the agencies they oversee. Also, if the agencies they oversee lose power, then the committees also lose power.

This dynamic, which is inherent in the committee system that dominates Congress, was in evidence during the drafting of, and debate over, the 2004 intelligence legislation. The Senate was initially more responsive to calls to accept the recommendations of the 9/11 Commission, but jurisdiction over the legislation went to the Senate Governmental Affairs Committee (SGAC), not the Senate Intelligence Committee. This could be rationalized in terms of jurisdiction, as the SGAC as it then was (now the Senate Committee on Homeland Security & Governmental Affairs) oversees government organization. However, in the past, bills of this sort had gone to the intelligence committee. Thus, the Senate leadership did not display much confidence in the intelligence committee for reasons that are not entirely clear. (Some believe the Senate leadership and perhaps the George W. Bush administration were concerned about the possible outcome as the Senate Intelligence Committee chairman, Pat Roberts [R-KS], had independently issued his own plan for intelligence reorganization that was widely seen as too radical.) In the House, the intelligence committee was given jurisdiction. But friction arose with the House Armed Services Committee when Chairman Duncan Hunter, R-CA, raised questions about the military's access to intelligence and the chain of command. There was a certain disingenuous aspect to this debate. Hunter made public a letter from Gen. Richard Meyers, chairman of the Joint Chiefs of Staff, stating concerns of the type that Hunter voiced, but Secretary of Defense Donald H. Rumsfeld (2001–2006) said he had no advance knowledge of the general's action. John W. Warner, R-VA, chairman of the Senate Armed Services Committee, was supportive of Hunter but let him do most of the arguing. In the end, a DNI was created, but the secretary of defense lost little if any authority over the intelligence budget or over defense intelligence agencies. As a result, the two armed services committees had not lost any jurisdiction, either.

The jurisdictions of the two intelligence committees are not the same. The Senate Intelligence Committee has exclusive jurisdiction over the DNI and the CIA but shares all other jurisdiction, primarily with the Senate Armed Services Committee, which guards its oversight of NGA, NSA, NRO, and DIA very jealously. The House Intelligence Committee has jurisdiction over all NIP agencies and shares jurisdiction with the House Armed Services Committee over MIP agencies.

How Does Congress Judge Intelligence? An important but little discussed issue is how Congress views and judges intelligence, as opposed to the criteria used by the executive branch. No matter how much access Congress has to intelligence, it is not a client of the intelligence community in the same way that the executive branch is, even as congressional requests for specific analytic products have increased. Congress never achieves the same level of intimacy in this area and does not have the same requirements or demands for intelligence.

The budget is one major divide. No pattern has been set as to which branch wants to spend more or less. The Reagan administration favored spending more on intelligence than Congress did and was allowed to, up to a point, after which Congress began to resist. However, the Reagan administration did not want to buy the additional imagery satellites demanded by the Senate Intelligence Committee. During the Clinton administration, it was Congress, after the Republican takeover in 1995, that was willing to spend more than was requested. Congress takes the firm view that all budget requests from the executive branch are just that—requests. They are nonbinding suggestions for how much money should be spent. To put it succinctly, the executive branch has programs; Congress has money.

The second major divide is the intimacy of the relationship that each branch has with intelligence. Executive officials may have unrealistic expectations of intelligence, but over time they have far greater familiarity with it than do the majority of members of Congress. Thus, the possibility of even larger false expectations looms in Congress. Moreover, having provided the money, members may have higher expectations of intelligence performance. At the same time, members of Congress may be more suspicious of intelligence analysis, fearing that it has been written largely to support administration policies. Members and staff have rarely heard of intelligence that questions administration policies, even when such intelligence exists. Thus, the Congress-intelligence relationship is fertile ground for doubts, whether justified or not. The statements in the FY2016 authorization report by the Senate Intelligence Committee concerning analytic "redundancy" cited in chapter 6 may also be a reflection of this difference of views. Although the report says that the committee values competitive analysis, its request to reduce "duplication" can also be read as a desire for a more uniform, if not homogenized, intelligence product.

The relationship between Congress and the intelligence community has undergone a change in recent years. Both before and after the modern oversight system was created in 1976–1977, the main requests Congress made of the intelligence community, other than for testimony at hearings, were for briefings. Congress has had access to some intelligence products on a regular basis, but they were written for the executive branch. In the mid-1990s, Congress began to take a greater interest in the substance of intelligence analysis. Dissatisfaction among some members with a 1995 NIE about missile threats to the United States led Congress to create a commission headed by Donald Rumsfeld, which came to different conclusions about the nature of the threat.

More significant, in October 2002, prior to the onset of the war in Iraq (2003–2011), members of the Senate Intelligence Committee requested that an updated national intelligence estimate on Iraq's WMD programs be written so that senators could have the benefit of reading it before they considered voting on a resolution authorizing the president to use force against Iraq. This took the intelligence relationship with Congress into a new and difficult area. Although the National Security Act states that the National Intelligence Council "shall prepare national intelligence estimates for the Government," it is also understood that the intelligence community is part of, and works for, the executive branch. Meanwhile, the intelligence community finds it difficult to refuse such a request for both professional and political reasons. The resulting NIE became controversial after the war started, when surveys of

Iraq did not discover the WMD programs that were assessed to exist. Many senators questioned the quality of the analysis and the underlying reasons for the apparently incorrect conclusions. A criticism lodged against the intelligence community was that it had rushed the NIE, although the Senate had imposed a three-week deadline. (This particular criticism was somewhat ironic, as NIEs are usually criticized for how long they take, from several months to a year in some cases.) Although the conclusions of the NIE were not borne out, the estimate probably had little effect on the Senate as, according to press accounts, only six senators read the NIE before voting. (This was known because Senators had to sign for the NIE given its high classification. The Senate voted 77–23 to "[a]uthorize the President to use the U.S. armed forces to . . . defend U.S. national security against the continuing threat posed by Iraq." Senate staffers note that several senators were briefed on the NIE by their staffs, although these senators did not read the NIE.) The Senate Select Committee on Intelligence investigated the intelligence community's performance on Iraq WMD. Among its major findings were that many of the NIE's key judgments were overstated or not supported by the underlying intelligence; that the uncertainties for some judgments were not explained; that some of these judgments were then used as the analytic basis for further judgments ("layering" of assumptions; see chapter 6); that an excessive reliance was placed on foreign liaison reporting; and, most significant, that a groupthink dynamic had led to a presumption that Iraq had an ongoing WMD program.

Congress continued to make further requests for intelligence analysis crafted for its needs, which entailed the same risks evidenced in the Iraq NIE experience. The intelligence community is part of the executive branch and works for the president or the president's senior cabinet officers. Intelligence managers will be hard put, however, to make choices between serving their usual policy makers and Congress. Although there may be grounds to respond to Congress only as time allows or after executive branch demands have been met, the consequences of such a course may be harsh. Congress's most obvious retaliation would be the budget. There is also the question of priorities. In 2007, the House Intelligence Committee strongly requested that an NIE on global warming be written. DNI McConnell resisted initially and then agreed, even as he noted that this NIE would not take away resources from terrorism. McConnell was saying, in effect, that the intelligence community would respond to the committee's request but that it was clearly not at the same level of priority as other issues.

Another major divide is partisanship. Whether it is the majority or the minority, a substantial group in Congress always opposes the administration on the basis of party affiliation as well as policy. Partisanship inevitably spills over into intelligence, often in the form of concerns that the executive branch has cooked intelligence to support policy. This has been evident to an extreme in the handling of the investigation of Russian activity during the 2016 election, primarily in the House. Dissent about intelligence policy could arise within the executive branch, but it would not be based on partisanship.

External Factors. The intelligence oversight system does not take place in a vacuum. Among the many factors that come into play to affect oversight, the press is a major one. The lingering effects of Watergate, including the search for scoops and major scandals, have influenced reporting on intelligence. The press, as an institution, gets more mileage out of reporting things that have gone wrong than it does from bestowing kudos for those that are going right. The fact that intelligence correctly analyzes some major event is hardly news; after all, that is its job. Moreover, in the aftermath of the 1975–1976 investigations, the intelligence community found it impossible to return to its previous state of being largely ignored by the press. The greater coverage given to intelligence and the press's emphasis on flaws and failures influence how some members of Congress approach oversight. (The issue of the press's responsibilities when it gets access to classified information is touched on in chapter 13.)

Finally, even intelligence has partisans who appear in the guise of lobbyists. Some groups are made up of former intelligence community employees, and some advocate strong stances and spending on national security. Groups have been formed that oppose certain aspects of intelligence, usually covert action, as well as some aspects of intelligence collection; that are concerned about U.S. policy in every region of the world; and that would prefer to see some portion of the funds devoted to intelligence spent elsewhere. In the aftermath of 9/11, a faction of families who lost relatives in that attack became a powerful lobby in favor of the legislation creating a DNI, an issue in which their inputs were understandably more emotional than analytical and substantive. Finally, there is a group made up of firms that derive large portions of their income from the work they do for the intelligence community. All of these groups are legitimate within the U.S. political system and must be taken into account when considering how Congress oversees intelligence.

Competition Within the Congressional Agenda. A series of debates influencing intelligence oversight recur in every Congress, with varying degrees of strength. One is the debate between domestic and national security concerns, which is especially important when dealing with the budget. During the cold war, national security rarely suffered. In the post–cold war period, with national security concerns more difficult to define, the intelligence community had difficulty—until the terrorist attacks in 2001—maintaining level spending, let alone winning increases.

Another debate is that between civil liberties and national security. The debate is almost as old as the republic, dating back to the Alien and Sedition Acts of 1798. Other instances of civil liberties clashing with national security concerns predate the advent of the intelligence community: President Abraham Lincoln's suspension of *habeas corpus* in Maryland during the Civil War, the arrest of antiwar dissidents during World War I, the mass arrests and detention of Japanese Americans during World War II, and acts aimed at rooting out communist subversion during the cold war. In each case, political leaders cited national emergencies to place temporary limitations on civil liberties. This debate resumed in 2001 in the aftermath of the terrorist attacks, as the George W. Bush administration sought increased powers for surveillance, nonjudicial trials (the proposed use of military tribunals), and other types of authority. President Obama also focused on the balance between civil liberty and security in his January 2014 speech about the NSA collection programs.

The precedents notwithstanding, the intelligence investigations of the mid-1970s revealed several instances in which intelligence agencies violated constitutional guarantees, laws, and their own charters. The violations included surveillance of dissident groups, illegal mail openings, illegal wiretaps of U.S. citizens, and improper use of the Internal Revenue Service. Some of these actions were known by presidents at the time; some were not. The revelation of these activities underscored concerns about the ability of secret agencies to act without safeguards and the need for strong executive and congressional oversight. As noted, this is the area in which the Civil Liberties Protection Board is supposed to be active.

A third perennial congressional debate focuses on the level and range of U.S. activism abroad. From World War I through the first twenty years of the cold war, the Democrats were largely the interventionist party; and the Republicans, the noninterventionist party. During World War II and the cold war, an interventionist consensus formed, although a Republican faction remained noninterventionist. The damage that the Vietnam War inflicted on the cold war consensus fostered a shift in the positions of the two parties. The Democrats largely became the noninterventionist party and the Republicans became the interventionist party. In the post–cold war period, a renascent noninterventionist faction grew within the Republican Party. After September 2001, wide support emerged for both military and intelligence operations abroad, although this unraveled, largely as a result of Iraq and Afghanistan. Iraq and Afghanistan, like Vietnam, will likely engender a set of "lessons" that will be applied—rightly or wrongly—to the next foreign policy debate. Partisan politics have shifted again, with an apparent meeting of minds between liberal Democrats and conservative Republicans, both of whom are much more skeptical about future interventions and about intelligence community programs. The Trump administration appears to have a policy stance that seeks to limit or curtail some of the United States's foreign obligations and commitments if not relations. Finally, the immigrant basis of the U.S. population is reflected in foreign policy debates. Every region of the world and virtually every nation is represented within the U.S. population. U.S. policies or actions around the world— real, planned, or rumored—are likely to stir reactions from some segment of the population and perhaps even different reactions. Members of Congress having ethnic ties to a region or representing constituents who do are also likely to voice opinions.

THE COURTS

As noted earlier, the courts have had a role in intelligence oversight—beyond their normal judicial function—since the passage of the Foreign Intelligence Surveillance Act (FISA) in 1978, which mandated court orders for surveillance and established the Foreign Intelligence Surveillance Court (FISC) for this purpose. The chief justice of the United States selects FISC members from among sitting federal judges. The eleven FISC judges must be drawn from at least seven judicial circuits, and at least three must reside within twenty miles of the District of Columbia. One judge must be a member of the U.S. District Court for the District of Columbia to deal with time-urgent warrants. The FISC judges serve overlapping terms of no more than seven years. There is also a Foreign Intelligence Surveillance Court of Review, made up of three district or appeals court judges also appointed by the chief justice. The Review Court hears government appeals of a FISC decision. According to the official website of the federal judiciary, it was not necessary for the Review Court to meet until 2002, given the "almost perfect record" of requests for warrants.

There had been some criticism of the FISC over the years, particularly about the secrecy with which it operates and the fact that only one party, the U.S. government, is represented at FISC proceedings. Two former FISC judges have recommended creating a security-cleared public advocate to argue against government applications. In August 2013, President Obama said he would support such a change. However, in January 2014, U.S. District Judge John D. Bates, a former chief judge of the FISC, sent a letter to the Senate Intelligence Committee on behalf of past and current FISC members saying that the judges opposed a permanent public advocate, arguing that it would be too disruptive; that it might be of questionable value given that the advocate could not consult with the intended target; and that given the secrecy, the advocate would not be able to conduct his or her own investigation of the case at hand. Bates did endorse the use of an advocate appointed at the discretion of the FISC. Bates's letter also opposed court approval for each national security letter, given that some 20,000 are issued annually. In its December 2013 report, the President's Review Group on Intelligence and Communications Technologies favored a FISC public advocate. However, in his January 2014 speech on the NSA programs, President Obama endorsed a panel of advocates in cases involving novel and important privacy issues and without the authority to review FISC cases and to decide when its presence would be warranted.

Also, the FISC has no investigative powers and is dependent on intelligence agencies to report noncompliance with its orders.

Former FISC judge James Robertson is among those who believe the FISC's role has changed and that, under the terms of the FISA Amendments Act (2008), the FISC now makes rules for the conduct of surveillance programs, making it "an administrative agency," rather than a law court, in Robertson's critique. For example, in April 2016, a FISC judge expressed concern about NSA's retention of some data beyond the agreed two to five years (depending on how it is collected) and for failing to keep the FISC informed. Some FBI practices were also cited. Some of these concerns about the FISC's administrative role were addressed in legislation passed in 2015 (discussed later).

Critics also note the extremely high percentage of warrants that are approved each year—well over 99 percent—although observers note that government attorneys rarely bring a request that they think will not pass judicial muster. In August 2013, the U.S. government said it would release annual totals for the different types of surveillance orders, including the number of people targeted. In October 2013, FISC member Judge Reggie Walton noted that although the court approves almost every request it receives, the court also demands substantial changes to nearly one-quarter of the applications before approving them. In 2017, the FISC denied 26 applications in full and 50 applications in part and granted 1,147 applications without modification.

There has also been criticism about how the members of the FISC are chosen, with critics contending that more conservative judges and those with former prosecutorial experience are being chosen more frequently, especially by U.S. Chief Justice John Roberts (2005–), thus making it more likely that they will approve warrant applications. Several suggestions have surfaced for alternative ways to select the FISC members, including having each appeals court select a judge, having the Review Court's decisions reviewed by six other Supreme Court judges, or having the president nominate the FISC members, subject to Senate confirmation.

The NSA leaks by Edward Snowden in 2013 focused new attention on the FISC, and many of the reform proposals noted above came after the Snowden leaks. The FISC had approved the Internet metadata collection in 2004 and the telephone metadata collection in 2006. Even though these programs did not collect the actual communications, they were widely seen as being much larger than any past court-approved surveillance programs. This created renewed pressure to declassify some of the FISC's rulings. As noted, some believed this was important as the FISC had, in effect, developed a body of law based on its administrative decisions, as Judge Robertson noted. In June 2013, Robert Litt, the general counsel for the DNI, spoke in favor of releasing as many of the rulings as could be done while safeguarding national security, and the government began doing so in September 2013.

According to press reports and documents released by DNI Clapper, the NSA programs exceeded their bounds on several occasions and were reprimanded by the FISC for doing so. These disclosures have been interpreted in two different ways: Critics of the NSA program argued that the programs lack sufficient oversight, even by the FISC, and violate their own boundaries. Supporters of the programs, including the leadership of the House Intelligence Committee, argued that NSA has been forthcoming to the FISC about problems encountered in managing the programs, indicating both good governance and good oversight. The opinion issued by FISC Judge Claire Eagan in September 2013 took note of past violations but stated that these issues had been resolved through the FISC's oversight. Judge Eagan also made the point that the court's job is to rule and oversee the legality of the program but that any decision about the future of the program is a political one.

The USA FREEDOM Act (June 2015), as noted in chapter 5, made some changes in how the FISC operates, several of which had been recommended by the PCLOB. The basis on which warrants are granted for certain investigations was made more specific. The law also allows for the appointment of up to five people as amici curiae (literally, "friends of the court") to assist in applications or reviews that represent novel or significant interpretations of law or, in other instances, to provide technical expertise. The FISC Review Court may certify questions of law to be reviewed by the Supreme Court, in which cases, amici curiae may be appointed as well. Finally, the DNI is required to conduct a declassification review and make publicly available (with some redactions permitted) all FISC decisions and opinions that include novel or significant interpretations of law. The DNI may waive declassification and publication to protect national security or intelligence sources and methods and if the attorney general makes publicly available a summary of the legal interpretation.

One legal result of the NSA leaks was a July 2013 Justice Department ruling that defendants in criminal cases need to be told when some of the evidence against them comes from broad surveillance programs.

As noted in chapter 8, the increased use of unmanned aerial vehicles (UAVs) and—in at least one case, that of Anwar al-Awlaki—the specific targeting of a U.S. citizen, led some to suggest creating a court similar to the FISC for drone attacks. During his Senate confirmation hearings to be DCIA, John Brennan said that the Obama administration had discussed the concept. In theory, this court would hear the intelligence presented to justify a given target and grant approval—or not—to the strike. Critics raised a number of issues. Some are similar to those raised with the FISC: the secrecy of proceedings; the absence of one party in the court, that is, the intended target; and the means by which judges would be selected. Another key issue is the role of the president as commander-in-chief and the possible intercession of nonelected officials—judges—in the chain of civilian command. If a president disagreed with a court decision, could he or she still order a UAV strike? Other issues include how judges would assess such issues as potential collateral damage and casualties, and the issue of timeliness if a legitimate terrorist target was suddenly discovered but the government first had to go to court. Again, the "drone court" is still a largely unformed notion, but it does reflect interest in an increased role for the courts in intelligence oversight.

The FISA process and the FISC became enmeshed in the partisan politics of the Russia investigations when Republican members of the House Intelligence Committee released a memo, declassified by the Trump administration, in February 2018, questioning why FISA warrants were approved in the case of Carter Page, a former Trump campaign adviser and ongoing adviser to President Trump. The Republican memo charged that the warrants were based on questionable sources with ties to the Democratic Party. In July 2018, the FBI, responding to various lawsuits, released redacted portions of the warrant application, the first time a FISA warrant application had been released. This release did nothing to end the partisan debate over the warrant on Page. In September 2018, Trump ordered the declassification of parts of the warrant applications, which met with resistance from intelligence community leaders and, according to press, British intelligence. Trump agreed, instead, to have the Justice Department review the documents.

It is important to understand that a warrant is not an indictment, that is, a formal accusation of having committed a crime. A FISA warrant is authorization to collect evidence, issued on the basis of "probable cause" of intelligence activity occurring. In Page's case, he had several contacts with Russians and the FBI believed he might be a target for Russian intelligence recruitment. This entire incident unfortunately politicized what had been a very successful intelligence/law enforcement process.

CONCLUSION

The nature of congressional oversight of intelligence changed dramatically in 1975–1976. Although Congress may go through periods of greater or lesser activism, it is unlikely to return to the laissez-faire style of intelligence oversight. Congress has become a consistent player in shaping intelligence policy.

This seems novel in the case of intelligence only because it is relatively recent. Congress has played the same activist role in all other areas of policy since adoption of the Constitution, and its role is inherent in the checks and balances system that the framers established. The willful division of power creates a system that is a constant "invitation to struggle."

The oversight system is, of necessity, adversarial but does not have to be hostile. Any system that divides power is bound to have debates and friction. But they do not have to be played out in an antagonistic manner. When antagonism arises, it is more often the effect of personalities, issues, and partisanship than of the oversight system per se.

KEY TERMS

appropriated but not authorized 285
appropriation 285
authorization 285
earmarks 286
executive orders 280
Foreign Intelligence Surveillance
  Court (FISC) 281
Gang of 4 295
Gang of 8 295
global findings 279
hollow budget authority 285
no-year appropriations 287

oversight 277
President's Foreign Intelligence Advisory
  Board (PFIAB) 278
President's Intelligence Advisory Board
  (PIAB) 278
President's Intelligence Oversight Board
  (PIOB) 280
Privacy and Civil Liberties Oversight
  Board (PCLOB) 280
special access programs (SAPs) 297
supplemental appropriations 287

FURTHER READINGS

The expansion of the role of Congress as an overseer has been matched by an increasing number of books and articles on the topic. Much less has been written about executive branch oversight issues.

Congressional Oversight

Barrett, David M. *The CIA and Congress: The Untold Story From Truman to Kennedy.* Lawrence: University of Kansas Press, 2005.

Best, Richard A., Jr. *Intelligence Estimates: How Useful to Congress?* CRS Report RL33733. Washington, D.C.: Congressional Research Service, November 21, 2006.

Central Intelligence Agency. *OIG Report on CIA Accountability With Respect to the 9/11 Attacks. Executive Summary.* June 2005. (Available at www.cia.gov/library/reports/Executive%20Summary_OIG%20Report.pdf.)

Cohen, William S. "Congressional Oversight of Covert Actions." *International Journal of Intelligence and Counterintelligence* 2 (summer 1988): 155–162.

Colton, David Everett. "Speaking Truth to Power: Intelligence Oversight in an Imperfect World." *University of Pennsylvania Law Review* 137 (December 1988): 571–613.

Conner, William E. *Intelligence Oversight: The Controversy Behind the FY1991 Intelligence Authorization Act.* McLean, Va.: Consortium for the Study of Intelligence, 1993.

Currie, James. "Iran-Contra and Congressional Oversight of the CIA." *International Journal of Intelligence and Counterintelligence* 11 (summer 1998): 185–210.

Davis, Christopher M. *9/11 Commission Recommendations: Joint Committee on Atomic Energy—A Model for Congressional Oversight?* Washington, D.C.: Congressional Research Service, August 20, 2004.

Erwin, Marshall Curtis. *Intelligence Authorization Legislation: Status and Challenges.* CRS Report R40240. Washington, D.C.: Congressional Research Service, March 25, 2013.

————. *Intelligence Issues for Congress.* CRS Report RL33539. Washington, D.C.: Congressional Research Service, April 23, 2013.

Goldman, Zachary K., and Samuel J. Rascoff, eds. *Global Intelligence Oversight: Governing Security in the Twenty-First Century.* New York: Oxford University Press, 2016.

Gumina, Paul. "Title VI of the Intelligence Authorization Act: Fiscal Year 1991: Effective Covert Action Reform or 'Business as Usual'?" *Hastings Constitutional Law Quarterly* (fall 1992): 149–205.

Jackson, William R. "Congressional Oversight of Intelligence: Search for a Framework." *Intelligence and National Security* 5 (July 1990): 113–147.

Johnson, Loch K. "The CIA and the Question of Accountability." *Intelligence and National Security* 12 (January 1997): 178–200.

————. "Controlling the Quiet Option." *Foreign Policy* 39 (summer 1980): 143–153.

————. *Spy Watching: Intelligence Accountability in the United States.* New York: Oxford University Press, 2018.

————. "The U.S. Congress and the CIA: Monitoring the Dark Side of Government." *Legislative Studies Quarterly* 5 (November 1980): 477–499.

Latimer, Thomas K. "United States Intelligence Activities: The Role of Congress." In *Intelligence Policy and National Security.* Ed. Robert L. Pfaltzgraff Jr., Uri Ra-anam, and Warren Milberg. Hamden, Conn.: Archon Books, 1981.

Light, Paul C. *Government by Investigation: Congress, Presidents, and the Search for Answers, 1945–2012.* Washington, D.C.: Brookings Institution Press, 2013.

Miles, Anne Daugherty. *Intelligence Spending: In Brief.* CRS Report 44381. Washington, D.C.: Congressional Research Service, February 26, 2016.

Pickett, George. "Congress, the Budget, and Intelligence." In *Intelligence: Policy and Process.* Ed. Alfred C. Maurer, James M. Keagle, and Marion D. Tunstall. Boulder, Colo.: Westview Press, 1985.

Rizzo, John. "The CIA-Congress War." *Defining Ideas.* The Hoover Institution, March 30, 2012. (Available at www.hoover.org/publications/defining-ideas/article/112491.)

Rollins, John, and Rebecca S. Lange. *"Gang of Four" Congressional Intelligence Notifications.* CRS Report R40698. Washington, D.C.: Congressional Research Service, November 19, 2012.

Simmons, Robert Ruhl. "Intelligence Performance in Reagan's First Term: A Good Record or Bad?" *International Journal of Intelligence and Counterintelligence* 4 (spring 1990): 1–22.

Smist, Frank J., Jr. *Congress Oversees the United States Intelligence Community.* 2d ed. Knoxville: University of Tennessee Press, 1994.

Snider, L. Britt. *The Agency and the Hill: CIA's Relationship With Congress, 1946–2004.* Washington, D.C.: Center for the Study of Intelligence, 2008.

————. *Sharing Secrets With Lawmakers: Congress as a User of Intelligence.* Washington, D.C.: CIA, Center for the Study of Intelligence, 1997.

Treverton, Gregory F. "Intelligence: Welcome to the American Government." In *A Question of Balance: The President, the Congress, and Foreign Policy.* Ed. Thomas E. Mann. Washington, D.C.: Brookings Institution, 1990.

U.S. Congressional Research Service. "Intelligence Community Spending: Trends and Issues." CRS Report R44381. Washington, D.C.: Author, June 18, 2018.

U.S. Privacy and Civil Liberties Oversight Board. First Annual Report, March 2006–March 2007. (Available at http://www.wired.com/images_blogs/threatlevel/files/pclob_congress2007.pdf.)

U.S. Senate Select Committee on Intelligence. *Legislative Oversight of Intelligence Activities: The U.S. Experience.* 103d Cong., 2d sess., 1994.

Executive Oversight

Absher, Kenneth M., Michael Desch, and Roman Popadiuk. "The President's Foreign Intelligence Advisory Board." In *The Oxford Handbook of National Security Intelligence.* Ed. Loch Johnson. Oxford, U.K.: Oxford University Press, 2010. This has been expanded into a book, *Privileged and Confidential: The Secret History of the President's Intelligence Advisory Board,* Lexington: University of Kentucky Press, 2012.

Adler, Emanuel. "Executive Command and Control in Foreign Policy: The CIA's Covert Activities." *Orbis* 23 (1959): 671–696.

Light, Paul C. *Monitoring Government: Inspectors General and the Search for Accountability.* Washington, D.C.: Brookings Institution Press, 1993.

Miles, Anne Daugherty. "'Taking a Footnote:' Budgetary Oversight of the Intelligence Community and the Role of OMB." Paper presented at the International Studies Association, April 2013.

Nolan, Cynthia M. "The PFIAB Personality: Presidents and Their Foreign Intelligence Boards." *International Journal of Intelligence and Counterintelligence* 23 (spring 2010): 27–60.

Tomkins, Shirley. *Inside OMB: Politics and Process in the President's Budget Office.* New York: M. E. Sharpe, 1998.

U.S. Office of the Director of National Intelligence. "Principles of Intelligence Transparency: Implementation Plan." Washington, D.C., October 27, 2015. (Available at http://www.dni.gov/files/documents/Newsroom/Reports%20and%20Pubs/Principles%20of%20Intelligence%20Transparency%20Implementation%20Plan.pdf.)

U.S. President's Civil Liberties Oversight Board. "Report to the President on the Implementation of Presidential Policy Directive 28: Signals Intelligence Activities." Washington, D.C., October 16, 2018. (Available at https://www.pclob.gov/library/PPD-28%20Report%20(for%20FOIA%20Release).pdf.)

Judicial Oversight

U.S. Foreign Intelligence Surveillance Court. "Rules of Procedure." Washington, D.C., November 10, 2010. (Available at http://www.fisc.uscourts.gov/sites/default/files/FISC%20Rules%20of%20Procedure.pdf.)

U.S. Foreign Intelligence Surveillance Court. Report of the Director of the Administrative Office of the U.S. Courts on activities of the Foreign Intelligence Surveillance Court for 2017. (Available at http://www.uscourts.gov/sites/default/files/ao_foreign_int_surveillance_court_annual_report_2017.pdf.)

CHAPTER ELEVEN

THE INTELLIGENCE AGENDA
Nation-States

To some extent, a distinction between nation-state targets and transnational issues is artificial: Nation-states are not of interest per se. They are of interest because of their activities. The nature of our interest in them varies with the state of our relations with them and by the nature of their activities. For example, the U.S. intelligence community is interested in Russia's political system, its military forces, its energy policy, and so forth because it is an important international player, a rival, and a potential threat. In the case of Britain, the United States does not have concerns about its political system, although we are deeply interested in who is prime minister and the policies he or she will follow. The United States is interested in the British military as an allied force rather than as a rival. There are also several small and remote countries in which the United States would have few, if any, intelligence interests at all.

Conversely, the transnational issues about which the United States is most concerned do not exist in the abstract. Weapons of mass destruction (WMD), terrorism, crime, narco-trafficking, and the like all occur in nation-states—either with or without the cooperation of the host government. Even when dealing with nongovernmental actors, such as terrorist cells, they have to exist someplace. James Clapper, the director of national intelligence (DNI, 2010–2017), put it succinctly when he said, "Intelligence is not just about things and not just about places. It is about things in places." This is why the National Intelligence Priorities Framework (NIPF) that has been in effect since 2003 was seen as such a breakthrough: It allowed policy makers and intelligence officers to identify the countries or non-state actors of interest and their activities that are of interest and then to give them relative levels of importance as intelligence priorities.

However, it is possible to make a distinction between the activities of interest that any state might undertake and those that only a few states would pursue. This rubric tends to divide into a set of "normal" state activities (political, economic, social, diplomatic, military) and activities that will tend to be clandestine or covert and will often fall into the transnational category (WMD, support for terrorism). Even though many aspects of the so-called normal activities will be secret—especially plans and intentions or military research and development—the demands of these issues on the intelligence community will be very different from those activities that are more likely to be covert. With these distinctions in mind, in this chapter we examine current intelligence issues observing this separation: normal state-based activities versus transnational issues, keeping in mind that the two sets are not truly separable.

As a matter of organization, most intelligence services divide at least their analytical offices into regional and subject matter or issue-oriented offices. Most observers will recognize that the division is somewhat artificial but intellectually necessary; the real goal is to bring together the two types of expertise.

Director of the Central Intelligence Agency (DCIA) Gina Haspel (2108–) said in a September 2018 speech that the CIA needed to focus more on nation-state adversaries. This is not to suggest that the intelligence community had not been working on nation-state issues, but after the terrorist attacks in 2001 there was a shift in emphasis to transnational issues. Haspel's remarks underscore a shift that has been underway for some time, back toward nation-state issues. This does not mean that transnational issues will be ignored. Rather, it is a recognition that collection and analytic resources are always limited and that priority choices have to be made, and rethought, on a continuing basis.

THE PRIMACY OF THE SOVIET ISSUE

To shed additional light on the distinctions raised in this chapter, it is instructive to understand how the United States addressed the Soviet Union as an intelligence issue. First, the scope of U.S. intelligence concerns about the Soviet Union was broad and far-reaching, embracing virtually every type of activity. Second, many of the forms and processes used to track activities in the Soviet Union continue to influence U.S. intelligence some three decades after the end of the cold war.

A series of related Soviet issues—including the Soviet Union, Soviet satellites and developing-world allies, and communist parties in some Western nations—dominated U.S. national security and foreign policy from 1946 to 1991, when the Soviet Union ceased to exist. During this period, the requirements for intelligence on the Soviet issue were never in doubt. Although other issues might occasionally and temporarily supplant the Soviet issue, it remained in the top tier of matters of interest to the policy and intelligence communities.

A great clarity and continuity also existed in the policy that intelligence was expected to support. Inspired by the career diplomat George Kennan, the United States developed a policy of **containment** vis-à-vis the Soviet Union. Kennan argued, first in his famous "long telegram" from Moscow in February 1946 and then in his "Mr. X" article in the July 1947 issue of *Foreign Affairs*, that the Soviet Union was, by its nature, an expansionist state. If the Soviet Union were contained within its own geographic limits, it would eventually be forced to deal with the inconsistencies and shortcomings of its communist system and either change or collapse. Kennan viewed the struggle between the United States and the Soviet Union as largely political and economic. But others responsible for shaping policy, particularly Paul Nitze, the director of policy planning at the State Department (1950–1953), who played a key role in drafting planning guidance document NSC-68 in early 1950, gave containment a more military dimension, as did the outbreak of the Korean War in June of that year. Still, this was a profound and extremely rare moment in any nation's national security policy, when a largely intellectual argument that could not be tested or proved to any great degree became the accepted basis for the future development of national security. It also was important as a policy model after the cold war when, as noted, successive administrations sought unsuccessfully to find a similarly coherent intellectual means of encapsulating their foreign policy.

The Intelligence Implications of Containment. The containment policy included a role for intelligence analysis and operations. Analytically, the intelligence community was expected to know or be able to estimate the following:

- Likely areas of Soviet probes or expansion

- Imminence and strength of the probes

- Overall Soviet strength—military, economic, and social

- Likely Soviet allies or surrogates

- Strength of U.S. allies or surrogates

- Signs of relative Soviet strength or weakness (signs of the contradictions predicted by Kennan)

This is a long list and an ironic reflection of Sherman Kent's desire to know everything. (See chap. 6.) In terms of intelligence operations, containment required the following:

- An ability to collect intelligence on the Soviet target to enable analysts to fulfill their requirements

- An operational ability to help blunt Soviet expansion

- An ability to weaken the Soviet Union and its allies and surrogates

- A counterintelligence capability to deal with Soviet espionage and possible subversion

- A wealth of information on Soviet military capabilities, both to support the development of appropriate U.S. and North Atlantic Treaty Organization (NATO) defenses and to help target Soviet forces and facilities in the event of war

Neither set of tasks, analytical nor operational, arrived full-blown with the acceptance of the containment policy. Both sets evolved over time as the United States dealt with the Soviet problem.

The Difficulty of the Soviet Target. The Soviet Union was a uniquely difficult target for intelligence collection and analysis. First, it was a very large nation (spread over two continents, spanning eleven time zones; the continental U.S. spans four) with a remote interior, providing Soviet leaders with a vast amount of space in which to hide capabilities they preferred to keep secret. Second, large portions of the Soviet Union were subject to adverse weather conditions that impeded overhead collection. Third, it was a closed and heavily policed society, which meant that large areas of the Soviet state—even in its more developed regions—were inaccessible to foreigners, even to legally posted diplomats, who were typically confined to Moscow and perhaps a few other major cities where they might be allowed consulates.

Long-standing Russian traditions compounded the geographic difficulties. Russians traditionally have been suspicious of foreigners. Before the reign of Peter the Great (1682–1725), foreigners were often sequestered in special areas of the Russian capital, where they could be watched easily and their contact with Russians kept limited and controlled. Russians also have a tradition of obscuring the physical realities of the Russian state, which came to be known as *maskirovka* (literally, masking, camouflaging, or deceiving), whose roots go back to the tsars. The most famous instance of obscuring reality occurred during the reign of Catherine the Great (1762–1796). Her minister of war, Grigory Potemkin, built what appeared to be villages but, in reality, were merely facades to impress Catherine with the success of his policies. These **Potemkin villages** presaged *maskirovka*.

As the scope of the cold war spread from the Soviet Union to Europe, Asia, and then all over the world, the field within which intelligence had to be collected and analyzed and within which operations might be required expanded as well. The bilateral cold war was, in intelligence terms, a global war.

For all of these reasons, but primarily because of the size and inaccessibility of the Soviet Union, the intelligence community developed technical means to collect the required intelligence remotely. The United States continued to pursue human intelligence operations, both in the Soviet Union and against Soviet diplomats posted around the world, but the technical collection disciplines (INTs) were relied upon most. The technical INTs can be applied to post–cold war issues with some adjustments, but they could not be replaced en masse. In effect, some aspects of the collection system were a legacy that could not simply be scrapped or easily modified but would eventually pass out of the system over time, perhaps after twenty years. Ironically, the relative longevity of U.S. space-borne systems—usually far beyond their estimated endurance—that had been one of these systems' major assets became something of a liability for the United States. For reasons of budget alone, no one would propose scrapping functioning but older systems in favor of more modern ones.

Again, the United States has important legacies with respect to the Soviet Union in terms of ongoing state-based issues. First, the states about which the United States is most concerned tend to be secretive or engage in political processes that are not transparent, such as China, Russia still, North Korea, Iran, Cuba, Syria, Saudi Arabia, and Pakistan. Second, these states pose the same dilemma in terms of the limits of technical collection and the difficulty of human collection. Third, some of the technical collection systems in orbit in 2018 were designed and launched either at the end of the cold war or in its immediate aftermath, when the nature of the post–cold war world left little guidance as to intelligence needs. So, to an extent, the United States has only recently emerged from a technical collection system built to some degree for the Soviet target, whose applicability to early-twenty-first-century problems may be somewhat limited.

THE EMPHASIS ON SOVIET MILITARY CAPABILITIES

The predominant question within the Soviet issue was that of the nation's military capabilities, which posed a threat to the United States and its allies.

Capabilities refer to the current forces or those being planned. The U.S. intelligence community sought information about the quantity and quality of Soviet armed forces across the board; the directions of Soviet military research and development, and new capabilities the Soviets might be pursuing; the degree to which current and planned capabilities posed a threat to U.S. and allied interests; and the Soviet doctrine, that is, how the Soviets planned to employ forces in combat.

With the right collection systems, much of a potentially hostile nation-state's capabilities can be known. This is particularly true of deployed conventional and strategic forces, which are difficult to conceal, as they tend to exist in identifiable garrisons and must exercise from time to time. They also tend to be garrisoned or deployed in large numbers, which makes hiding them or masking them impractical at best. The regularity and precision that govern each nation's military make it susceptible to intelligence collection. Forces tend to exercise in regular and predictable patterns, which also reveal how they are intended to be employed in combat. Research and development may be more difficult to track up to a point, but systems must be tested repeatedly before they are deployed, again exposing them to collection. In other words, these military activities in any state tend to **self-reveal**. Moreover, the large and interconnected international arms market provides many opportunities to collect weapons-related intelligence at trade shows or when weapons are deployed to other countries, where security may be more lax.

Although the U.S. intelligence community made mistakes during the cold war, such as overestimating Soviet intercontinental and underestimating theater missile forces in the 1960s, overall Soviet capabilities were fairly well known in detail. Some level of comfort may even have been derived from tracking these hard objects. As one senior military intelligence officer put it, "The Soviet Union was the enemy we came to know and love." Some people dismissed the so-called **bean counting**, arguing that tracking the military inventories was undertaken largely to justify bigger defense budgets. ("Bean counting" is a somewhat pejorative term that refers to intelligence products that tally up the number of forces, equipment, and manpower in foreign militaries. Although this work is demanding and necessary, critics do not see these products as insightful or analytical.) The logic of this view was difficult to follow, because the intelligence community had little institutional interest in larger military forces. Within the national security sector of the budget, every dollar that went to defense was one dollar less that was available for intelligence, which was always funded at significantly lower levels than defense, roughly on the order of 1:10.

Intentions—the plans and goals of the adversary—are a more amorphous subject and pose a much more difficult collection problem. Intentions need not be demonstrated, exercised, or exposed in advance, and they may not even be revealed by regular military exercises. It may be possible to derive intentions from capabilities—such as the Chinese decision to develop aircraft carriers—but this is very imprecise.

Standoff or remote collection systems, which may be useful for collecting against capabilities, may reveal nothing about intentions. Signals intelligence may reveal intentions, but this collection task may also require espionage. Moreover, intentions can be changed quickly and with few indicators, while capabilities are long-term investments that cannot be easily or rapidly changed.

The pitfalls of an overreliance on presumed capabilities were evident in the aftermath of the Iraq WMD estimate of October 2002. Director of Central Intelligence (DCI) George J. Tenet (1997–2004) commissioned a series of evaluations of the intelligence on Iraq WMD, which was undertaken by a group of retired senior analysts headed by former deputy DCI Richard Kerr. Among the Kerr Group's findings, presented in July 2004, was the wealth of presumed detail about Iraq WMD and the paucity of analysis about Iraq as a country, that is, what sort of government would make the decisions that had led to this crisis with the United States and the United Nations (UN). There was a certain abstract aspect to the Iraq WMD intelligence analysis, which focused on capabilities but not intentions or even the milieu in which these intentions would be made. This does not necessarily mean that had these other factors been taken into account the analysts might have reached a different conclusion. It does mean that the analysis and estimate, although responsive to the Senate's request for "a technical update," were too narrowly drafted.

During the mid-1970s, a **capabilities versus intentions** debate about the Soviet Union took place in the United States, largely among policy makers and influential individuals outside of government but involving the intelligence community as well. U.S. intelligence was fairly well informed about Soviet military capabilities but not about Soviet intentions. The question was whether these intentions mattered. U.S. officials engaged in long and sometimes heated debates about whether the Soviet Union planned to conduct large-scale offensive conventional operations preemptively or at the outset of a war with NATO; whether it could carry out such operations from a standing start—that is, with forces already deployed and supplied—without bringing up telltale reserves and additional supplies, thus with little or no warning; and whether the Soviet Union thought a nuclear conflict was winnable.

Those who believed that intentions mattered argued that simply keeping track of the number of military forces was not enough to gauge the threat they posed. Only intentions made it possible to gauge the true level of threat. For example, Britain has a substantial nuclear force but is of no concern to the United States because the two nations are close allies. By taking into account Soviet intentions, the United States would have a much clearer picture of the true nature of Soviet policy, which was central to U.S. and Western security concerns. Proponents of this view believed that the Soviet threat was being underestimated because intentions were not a factor in national estimates.

Those who were less concerned about intentions argued that if one were aware of a certain level of hostility and also knew the adversary's capabilities, then knowing specific intentions was not that important. They argued that a worst case based on capabilities could serve as a planning yardstick. Finally, as noted, intentions (that is, plans) may be changed at will, making them a highly elusive target. Differences over the importance of intentions led to the Team A–Team B competitive analysis. The Team A–Team B exercise arose from concerns by members of the President's

Foreign Intelligence Advisory Board (PFIAB) during the latter part of the Gerald Ford administration (1974–1977) about intelligence community estimates of Soviet programs. PFIAB members felt that the estimates emphasized the weapons programs and not the geopolitical strategy behind them. They convinced DCI George H. W. Bush (1976–1977) to conduct a competitive analysis, with a group of outside experts (Team B) looking at the same intelligence as the government analysts (Team A). Such a competitive exercise had promise, but the results were undercut by the fact that Team B was made up entirely of hawks, experts who were highly suspicious of Soviet motives and of intelligence community analysis. Not surprisingly, Team B's conclusions were much the same as the PFIAB concerns that prompted the study. The lack of balance in Team B diminished interest in doing this type of exercise in the future.

The intelligence track record for Soviet intentions is much less certain. The United States was never able to ascertain, for example, whether the Soviets subscribed to the nuclear doctrine of mutual assured destruction (MAD), which provided the basis for the size of U.S. strategic nuclear forces. Secretary of Defense Harold Brown (1977–1981) questioned the idea of a shared U.S.-Soviet strategic vision when he observed, "When we build, they build; when we cut, they build." The U.S. thinking behind MAD was that nuclear devastation was such an awesome prospect that it made nuclear forces almost unusable, the two forces holding each other in check. The United States spent many negotiating rounds of the early strategic arms control talks proselytizing the Soviets on the importance of MAD. Did the Soviets agree at last or give lip service to the idea of MAD merely as a way to get on to negotiations? Did it matter? Similarly, did the Soviets think that nuclear war was winnable? Did they plan to invade Western Europe? Soviet doctrine certainly emphasized keeping war away from the homeland, but this is true of most nations' doctrines.

Mirror imaging underlay some of the debate over Soviet intentions. Did U.S. analysts impose their own views of Soviet intentions in lieu of knowing them? Another question was the utility of **worst-case analysis**. Is it a useful analytical tool? For defense planners, the answer is yes. If they are going to commit forces to combat, they need to be able to gauge the worst level of threat they are likely to face. For other planners and analysts, the worst case may be an overestimate that is much less useful.

Finally, some people question whether the intelligence products themselves affected the intelligence process. Each year, the intelligence community completed a national estimate on Soviet strategic military capabilities (NIE 11–3-8). U.S. policy makers viewed this estimate as necessary for strategic planning, including preparation of forces and budgets. But did the preparation of an annual major estimate also affect intelligence? Did it lock intelligence into set patterns, making it more difficult for the community to effect major changes or shifts in analyses? In other words, once the community had produced an NIE 11–3-8 for several years, how easy was it for analysts to propose dissenting, iconoclastic, or wholly new views? One remedy for these possible flaws was competitive analysis, tried most prominently in the Team A–Team B exercise.

Direct comparison of forces, a legitimate intelligence activity, often took place in a politicized atmosphere. Policy makers in successive administrations and Congresses tended to have preconceptions about the nature of the Soviet threat and thus viewed intelligence as being either supportive or mistaken. They engaged in long debates about quality (a U.S. advantage) versus quantity (a Soviet advantage) of weapons systems. The inconclusive nature of the debates led many to seek other means of comparison. One means was defense spending, both in direct costs and in the percentage of gross domestic product devoted to defense, which were taken as signs of intentions as well as capabilities.

THE EMPHASIS ON STATISTICAL INTELLIGENCE

Much of the intelligence that was produced (as opposed to collected) about the Soviet Union was statistical, including the following:

- The size of Soviet and Soviet-satellite forces in terms of manpower and all levels of weaponry
- The size of the Soviet economy and its output
- The amount and percentage of the Soviet economy devoted to defense
- A variety of demographics about life in the Soviet Union

Not all areas of inquiry were equally successful. The capabilities of the Soviet military were tracked quite well. Analysis of the Soviet economy was less successful. Ultimately, the intelligence community both overestimated the size of the Soviet economy and underestimated the portion of it devoted to defense, which probably totaled 40 percent of gross domestic product annually—a staggering level. Demographic data in the late 1980s and early 1990s pointed to a steady decline in the quality of Soviet life. Much of the compelling Soviet quality-of-life data was produced from open sources outside the intelligence community, by Professor Murray Feshbach at Georgetown University.

As important as the data were, the overall effort to quantify aspects of the Soviet issue had an effect of its own. Although much about this issue remained intangible, the intelligence community emphasized its ability to track various attributes in detail.

Looking back, one finds some efforts a bit comical. For example, the U.S. intelligence community devoted a great deal of time and energy—perhaps too much—to various means of comparing Soviet defense spending with that of the United States. Some analysts converted the cost of U.S. defense into rubles; others converted assessed values for the Soviet defense establishment into dollars. Each of these methodologies was artificial, and their respective proponents usually ended up preaching to the converted or to the stubbornly unbelieving regarding the Soviet threat.

What was often missing in this wealth of detailed data were the intangibles: the solidity of the Soviet state, the depth of support for it in the general population, and the degree of restiveness among the satellite populations. Few analysts questioned the stability or viability of the Soviet Union in the near term. Discussions about the possible collapse of the Soviet Union tended to be mostly hypothetical in nature as opposed to a potential policy problem. Moreover, despite the goal of containment being a situation in which the Soviet Union would be forced to abandon foreign adventures in order to address severe internal problems or face the prospect of collapse, many analysts viewed the actual possibility of a Soviet collapse with alarm. After all, there were tens of thousands of nuclear weapons deployed across the fifteen Soviet republics. Successor regimes might not maintain control over them, or the Soviet Union might devolve into civil war among nuclear armed foes. This clearly was a concern of President George H. W. Bush in 1991, as the Soviet Union fell apart. Bush gave a speech in Kiev, Ukraine, urging the Ukrainians—and, by implication, the other Soviet republics—not to rush headlong to dissolve the Soviet Union. Bush's critics, who saw this as a retreat of U.S. support for freedom, caustically labeled this the "Chicken Kiev speech."

THE "COMFORT" OF
A BILATERAL RELATIONSHIP

In addition to the comfort drawn from the relative predictability of watching highly routinized Soviet military activities, there was another comfort drawn from the competitive bilateral relationship. There was a belief, probably in both capitals, that policy makers could influence one another's actions. "If we do X, they will do A or B. We'd prefer B, but they may do A." This belief, which was borne out fairly often in diplomacy and military activities, gave the relationship a certain rhythm and assurance and thus a certain assumed level of predictability. It was exactly this sense of comfort that began to bother more hawkish U.S. national security experts in the late 1970s, who felt that U.S. policies failed to be confrontational enough. They felt that the edge had gone out of containment—that the main goal now was to accept the Soviet Union and its advances and find ways to accommodate it. Ronald Reagan, when running for president in 1976 and 1980, made it clear that he would reverse this policy of accommodation. This sense of comfort implied a certain level of unstated agreement between the two sides on the acceptable boundaries of actions. There was an assumed sense of shared rationality, even if it did not necessarily extend to philosophical issues such as MAD.

This is akin to the "rational actor" model in social science, which requires a certain level of shared assumptions, values, and boundaries. This behavior may occasionally occur, but it is not an entirely useful premise for intelligence analysis on an ongoing basis. There will be times when a policy maker makes a decision that seems entirely rational and beneficial but still oversteps when seen by others. Unsurprisingly, individuals miscalculate. The Soviet decision to invade Afghanistan in December 1979 is a good example. In Moscow, the invasion seemed a logical next step after years of military advice and increased military presence in support of a friendly regime just over the Soviet border. In other words, the Soviets could feel confident that they were acting within their acknowledged sphere of influence. The high level of protest encountered worldwide must have come as a shock to the Soviet leadership. President Jimmy Carter's (1977–1981) reaction, however, also betrayed the sense of cold war comfort he had enjoyed. Having said at the outset of his administration that he did not want the Soviet Union to be the sole focus of his foreign policy, he now admitted that he had never understood the Soviet Union until then.

COLLAPSE OF THE SOVIET UNION

Much of the controversy surrounding the U.S. intelligence record on the Soviet Union stems from the sudden Soviet collapse. Critics of intelligence performance argue that the demise deeply surprised the intelligence community, which had overestimated the strength of the Soviet state and thus missed the biggest story in the community's history. Some people even contended that this intelligence failure was sufficient reason for a profound reorganization of U.S. intelligence. Defenders of intelligence performance argued that the community had long reported the inner rot of the Soviet system and its weak hold on its own people and the satellite states.

The defenders of U.S. intelligence performance are, in part, correct. Intelligence provided numerous stories about the gross inefficiencies of the Soviet system, many of them anecdotal but too many to ignore. Insights into the sad realities of the Soviet system grew with the beginning of on-site inspections of Soviet intermediate-range nuclear forces (INF) bases in 1988. But few, if any, analysts compiled the anecdotal accounts into a prediction that the Soviet state was nearing collapse. It was weak; it might even be tottering. But no one expected that the Soviet Union would suddenly—and, most important, peacefully—pass from the scene. At least two factors were at work. First, many U.S. analysts working on the Soviet Union could not bring themselves to admit that the center of their livelihood might disappear or that it was as weak politically as it turned out to be. Such a conclusion was literally inconceivable. They concentrated on the perils and pitfalls of reform but did not consider the possibility of collapse. Also, given the past brutality of Soviet (and Russian) governments, the idea of a peaceful collapse seemed impossible, leading to violent scenarios too horrific to contemplate. Second, analysts failed to factor into their calculations the role of personalities, particularly that of Mikhail S. Gorbachev, who became general secretary of the Soviet Communist Party (the most powerful position) in 1985.

The difficulty in assessing Gorbachev should not be underestimated. He came to power through the usual Politburo selection process. Like each new Soviet leader before him, Gorbachev was an orthodox Soviet communist, promising reforms to make the admittedly inefficient state work more effectively. Eduard A. Shevardnadze, Gorbachev's foreign minister, reveals that at a certain point they both admitted that fixing the economy would require something more basic than tweaking reforms. Even while accepting this fact, Gorbachev remained committed to the basic forms of the Soviet state, not understanding that any true reform was, by definition, revolutionary. Only over time did Gorbachev come to these conclusions, and he could not accept their ultimate implications. In other words, he did not know where his reforms would lead. Should the intelligence community have known better than Gorbachev himself?

Many intelligence analysts were also slow to pick up on Gorbachev's approach to most of his foreign policy problems—arms control, Angola, even Afghanistan—which was to liquidate them as quickly as possible to be free to concentrate on more pressing domestic problems. Nor did many correctly analyze that the Soviet Union would acquiesce in the collapse of its European satellite empire. The satellite empire dissolved peacefully in 1989, as a few satellite leaders made efforts to liberalize, which led to the dissolution of the old order in all of the satellites. Czechoslovakia, maybe. But

East Germany? Never. Again, the degree to which this was knowable remains uncertain. Ironically, Gorbachev succumbed to the premises of containment as described by George Kennan forty years earlier. Stymied abroad, Gorbachev had to face the manifold problems he had at home.

The factors that went into Gorbachev's thinking or into the sudden Soviet collapse remain unknown. Did the U.S. defense buildup under President Reagan convince Gorbachev that he needed to strike some deals with the United States or be outpaced and outspent and face even deeper economic ruin? Shevardnadze suggests that the answer is yes. Some observers believe that President Reagan's proposed Strategic Defense Initiative (SDI) was an important spur to arms control, not because of any near-term change that SDI might effect in the military balance but because it brought home to Soviet leaders their country's weaknesses in technology, in computers, and in wealth. One of the ways to avoid economic ruin was to strike arms control deals. (SDI was the catch-phrase for the effort promoted by President Reagan to find ways to defend against nuclear attacks. Reagan believed that such a defensive capacity, which he said the United States would share, would make all nuclear weapons obsolete.)

Whether the so-called **Reagan Doctrine**—a U.S. effort to aid anti-Soviet guerrillas—had any effect on Soviet thinking also remains unknown. The effort to aid the contras in Nicaragua became a political liability for the Reagan administration. But aid to the mujahideen in Afghanistan and the stalemate of that war shook the Soviet leaders. They were unable to win a war just over their border. Soviet military prowess was meaningless. Some analysts believe that a rift developed between the General Staff in Moscow and the "Afgantsy"—Soviet field commanders in the war, many of whom rallied to Boris N. Yeltsin in August 1991, when opponents of radical reform attempted to overthrow Gorbachev.

Gorbachev clearly thought that the price of empire was too high, overseas and even in Eastern Europe. What neither Western analysts nor Gorbachev himself understood was that piecemeal liquidation of these problems could not save the Soviet state.

INTELLIGENCE AND THE SOVIET PROBLEM

No U.S. intelligence estimate boldly predicted the peaceful collapse of the Soviet Union and its dissolution into several independent republics. (There were analysts who predicted a likely coup attempt against Gorbachev.) U.S. intelligence largely assumed that the Soviet state would go on, perhaps ever weaker but still intact. At the same time, the community produced numerous reports about how inefficient, weak, and unsustainable (over some unknown period of time) the Soviet Union was.

Two key questions need to be answered: Should intelligence have done better? Did intelligence matter for the United States in its final cold war victory?

Those who argue that intelligence should have done better do so on the grounds that the Soviet Union was the central focus of U.S. intelligence and that all of the expertise and spending over five decades should have provided greater insight into the true state of affairs. But a large gap exists between knowing that a state has fundamental weaknesses and foreseeing its collapse. To a large extent, the collapse of the Soviet Union was unprecedented. (In the past, some once-great empires, such as the Ottoman Empire, had suffered long, lingering demises. Other great empires had suffered sudden collapses, but usually in the context of war, as did the German, Austrian, and Russian empires after World War I.) Nor was there anything in Soviet behavior—which had shown its brutal side often enough—to lead analysts to expect that the nation's elite would acquiesce to its own fall from power without a struggle. An irony of history is that an attempt by the so-called power ministries of the Soviet state (the military, the defense industrial complex, the *Komitet Gosudarstvennoi Bezopasnosti* [KGB]—the State Security Committee) to derail Gorbachev revealed how little support the Soviet system had. (Rumors persist that Gorbachev knew about the coup or abetted it as a means of isolating his opposition.)

The debate about the performance of U.S. intelligence in the final stages of the cold war continues. Perhaps some analyst should have made the leap from the mountain of anecdotal evidence to a better picture of the true state of Soviet staying power. But much that happened from 1989 to 1991 was unknowable, both to U.S. analysts and to those taking part in the events in the Soviet Union.

How can the role of intelligence be assessed overall on the Soviet problem? In collection, U.S. intelligence performed some remarkable feats, finding sophisticated technical solutions to the problems posed by the remote and closed Soviet target. In analysis, U.S. intelligence accurately tracked Soviet military numbers and capabilities. This was important not only on a day-to-day basis but also during periods of intense confrontation, such as in Cuba in 1962, when President John F. Kennedy (1961–1963) acted confidently because he knew a great deal about the true state of the U.S.-Soviet military balance. Discussions of Soviet intentions veered quickly to the political realm, where equally adamant hawks and doves dominated the debate, often freed from the constraints of intelligence by its unavailability. Operationally, the record is much less clear. Early efforts to foment rebellion within Soviet domains were disasters. Attempts to limit Soviet expansion were uneven. U.S. intelligence operations were successful in Western Europe, Guatemala, and Iran but were failures in Cuba and Southeast Asia. The contra war in Nicaragua probably could have been dragged out inconclusively and indefinitely. But the intervention against Soviet forces in Afghanistan was a major and telling success. In espionage, U.S. intelligence scored important successes, including the handling of the walk-ins Col. Oleg Penkovsky and Col. Ryszard Kuklinski, and also suffered a number of Soviet penetrations, some of which, notably those conducted by Aldrich Ames and Robert Hanssen, bridged the Soviet and post-Soviet Russian states.

In short, the record of intelligence in the cold war is mixed. Perhaps a better way to pose the original question might be this: Would the United States have been better off, or more secure, without an intelligence community during the cold war?

THE CURRENT NATION-STATE ISSUE

As was noted in the introduction to this chapter, nation-states still form the basic unit of analysis for a great deal of intelligence. Even in the face of abundant transnational issues, the actions of state actors tend to dominate on a regular basis, as DCIA Haspel noted. And even though policy makers want opportunity analysis, the basic means for selecting which nations to focus on remain those that are seen as threatening or as rivals in a serious way. Therefore, opportunity analysis may often come within the context of dealing with a state that is a rival or a threat. Warning analysis and opportunity analysis are not antithetical; it is more a question of which one is best suited to the issues and problems at hand. Sometimes there may be a chance or a need to do both.

Levers of Power. This translates into capabilities and intentions, and, as was the case with the Soviet Union, capabilities remain the easier of the two to collect against and to assess. One of the striking changes in the immediate post–cold war period was the decreased emphasis on military power and the increased emphasis on economic power. But it is legitimate to ask whether this reflects an actual shift in the bases of power or the recognition by other states that militarily the United States is, for the foreseeable future, unassailable. Despite China's forays into the South China Sea and Russian intervention in Syria, economic leverage seems more important than before, up to a point. At the same time, economic power is inherently less pliable than military power because it depends on successful relations with others. China's economy requires trade, markets, and resources. Without a U.S. market, the Chinese economy will suffer greatly, as will, by extension, whatever internal legitimacy the Chinese Communist Party may still have. However, China's reaction to tariffs imposed by the Trump administration strongly suggests that China will absorb whatever pain is required rather than unilaterally submit—a reflection of China's eagerness to avoid the more acquiescent relations it had with European states in the nineteenth century. Russia serves as a cautionary example of an imbalanced economy. Russia's economic basis is largely that of a Third World state, exporting natural resources (oil, gas, timber, and gold) but not manufacturing anything with a significant market share except weapons. The abundance of oil and natural gas on the international market weakened Russia's position as prices fell far below what Russia needs to sustain its economy. Even though Russia's cooperation with OPEC (Organization of Petroleum Exporting Countries) helped increase oil prices, they still remain below Russia's (and Saudi Arabia's) preferred level. This, coupled with Western economic sanctions imposed after Russia seized the Crimea, continues to underscore Russia's inherent economic weakness.

Russian president Vladimir Putin clearly sees military weapons as an important lever, not only for their own sake but also as a way of competing with and claiming parity with the United States. But just as the Soviet Union did not have the long-term economic capability to sustain an arms race, it is fair to ask whether Russia is any better off today. Interestingly, in 2017, the Defense Intelligence Agency (DIA) revived an unclassified publication that was begun in 1981. Then called *Soviet Military Power*, it is now called *Russia Military Power* but its purpose remains the same: to examine "a resurgent Russia's military power to foster a deeper understanding of its core capabilities, goals, and aspirations. . . ." Cyber, by contrast, offers Russia—and all states—advantages in terms of lower cost and the ability to take action far short of direct military confrontation. (See chap. 12.)

Indeed, it can be argued that growing economic interdependency limits freedom of action in the ability to use force to settle regional disputes. For China, the primary regional issues had been Taiwan and North Korea. In neither case has Chinese economic interest helped. Taiwan remains opposed to reuniting with China despite a great deepening of economic ties. North Korea's near dependence on China has not translated into increased Chinese leverage. China's efforts to create sovereign positions in the South China Sea have alienated several nations that might otherwise come under China's economic sway. Instead, Vietnam, the Philippines, and other states look to the United States for military backing. What does all of this mean for intelligence analysts? They will continue to track military developments, but they must take into account economic developments as well and understand that these two areas may run athwart each other.

North Korea has only one lever, its nuclear weapons and missile programs. Beyond that, it is a dismal state, unable to feed its own people and with almost no friends or allies. This might suggest the inherent weakness of North Korea, but it also underscores the skepticism of those who doubt that North Korea will ever agree to denuclearization, regardless of the economic incentives that are offered, a position voiced by DCIA Haspel in September 2018. A similar view expressed in the 2019 *Worldwide Threat Assessment*, that North Korea "is unlikely to give up all of its WMD stockpiles, delivery systems, and production capabilities," was one of the views that prompted a strong negative reaction from President Trump.

Mirror Imaging. One of the intellectual traps in intelligence that tends to appear most often when assessing other nations is mirror imaging. It is very tempting to ascribe ambitions, goals, and drives similar to one's own to one's opposite numbers as well. This was evident during the cold war. Analysts and policy makers would often discuss Soviet "hawks and doves"—that is, hardliners and those with whom one could deal. After all, the United States has hawks and doves, so the Soviet Union must as well. There was little concrete intelligence upon which this conclusion was based, and it is difficult to describe any Soviet leader other than Gorbachev as someone who was willing truly to accommodate Western concerns. Mirror imaging tends to recur, however. For example, discussions about the internal politics of Iran often focus on radicals and moderates. This may be a valid distinction, but even if it is, does an "Iranian moderate" mean a "moderate" in the U.S. sense of the word or just someone who is less radical but still not moderate as we would understand it? Analytically, these types of global descriptions can be misleading and not particularly useful.

Internal Stability. Given our experience with the Soviet Union and its satellite empire, it is worth assessing the internal stability of China and Russia and other states. How likely are their publics to support more aggressive policies? One of the supposed advantages of authoritarian states is the absence of any need to renew one's legitimacy through a genuine competition at the ballot box, although events in the Middle East in 2011 (the Arab Spring) undermine this assumption. But it is also a disadvantage as there is then no accurate gauge of public sentiment beyond the internal security forces, whose main job is to stamp out dissent and who are most likely either to overestimate dissent as a means of safeguarding their role or underestimate it as a means of showing their prowess. Again, this was evident in the Middle East, as was the wholly unknown effect of social networking, which allowed relatively small numbers of protestors to communicate more widely and increase their numbers. But, as was noted with the Soviet Union, if the internal security forces cannot accurately gauge public sentiment in an authoritarian or politically limited state, such as Iran, how does an intelligence service do this from outside? China has shown a willingness in recent years to stir up nationalist sentiment, as in 2001 when a U.S. Navy EP-3 aircraft collided with a Chinese interceptor. The concern for any government that stirs up nationalism is the possibility that it will lose control of the crowd, which, for China, is a constant preoccupation.

Russia presents a case that is at once both familiar and new. Vladimir Putin's political supremacy is unquestioned, making him much like past Soviet leaders, who ruled with minimal opposition. But Putin exists beyond the political system, without any real political party or support group. In that sense, he represents a much more personalized type of rule that makes it difficult to understand who might succeed him or how. Indeed, Putin likely must prevent anyone from appearing to be a possible heir apparent, as this would undercut one of his major political appeals: the sheer necessity of there being no alternative to his being in office. This is a situation that is inherently unstable and shows little prospect for longevity after Putin.

North Korea, which is among those states about which the United States is currently most concerned, is also among the most difficult to judge from the outside, a quintessential intelligence "hard target." It is also one of the few states where so much rests on the thoughts and goals of only one individual, Kim Jong Un. Russia and China, by contrast, are authoritarian states (of different degrees) that might be described as translucent. They have government apparatuses, legislatures (with varying degrees of fairly minimal power), and internal factions that lead to a type of competitive political system. But it is entirely a struggle within accepted elites, much of which happens behind closed doors, after which a result is announced. During the last presidential transition in China, in 2012, Bo Xilai, a senior party official, was seen as making an overt play to be named to the Politburo Standing Committee, the Communist Party's highest decision-making body. An overt move like Bo's is highly unusual and is likely seen as unsettling in a system that prizes consensus. Bo was brought down by issues seemingly related to his tenure in Chongqing. Bo's wife was found guilty of murder; Bo was relieved of all of his posts, expelled from the party, and put on trial as well. The Bo Xilai affair underscores the inherent fragility of the Chinese political system, especially at its highest levels, something that analysts should keep in mind when looking at China. At the same time, one of the most striking aspects of China's transformation is that three successive generations of leaders, who either helped create or build or were raised in a communist state, have managed deftly to transform, if not wholly jettison, their economic ideology while maintaining political control. President Xi Jinping has done away with presidential term limits, which has two effects. It assures him, theoretically, of being able to stay in power for as long as he desires. However, it can also build up resentment in the Politburo among would-be contenders who see no opportunity for advancement.

Another factor in Chinese analysis is Xi's ongoing anticorruption campaign, aimed at both "tigers and flies," meaning high-level officials and relatively low ones as well. Among the "tigers" who have been given long prison sentences for corruption are Zhou Yongkang, a former member of the Politburo and minister of state security, and several very senior military officers. Zhou's arrest was particularly striking, as there was an assumption, at least among Western analysts, that Politburo members were beyond such punishment. The underlying question is whether the arrest of more "tigers" will build up a faction that opposes Xi, if only out of concerns for their own future safety.

Iran is an interesting case. Iran is not a liberal democracy in that there are restrictions on the media and on who can run for office, but within those bounds there is competition, regular elections, and the ability to throw out the incumbent government, albeit to be replaced by another candidate also approved by the theocratic rulers. It could be argued that Iran resembles, in some respects, the Soviet Politburo. Any individual who can rise to that rank and then aspire to power is unlikely to be willing to overhaul or liberalize the system radically. The outlook from Tehran is probably mixed. Iran's ally in Syria, Bashar al-Assad, appears to be in the final stages of winning the civil war that has been going on there since 2011. Iranian-backed rebels in Yemen have withstood Saudi attacks. But the United States has jettisoned the nuclear deal with Iran and imposed sanctions. Moreover, the economic benefits that were supposed to result from the nuclear accord were ephemeral even before the United States's action, buttressing those hardliners who opposed the agreement. (The nuclear accord remains in effect between Iran and the other signatories. The intelligence implications of the nuclear agreement are discussed in chap. 12.)

Failed States. The issue of **failed states** is complex and difficult to assess or even to categorize. It is clearly about states but in a more generic way, so that it almost resembles a transnational issue. There is an oxymoronic aspect to including failed states in a chapter on nation-states, as failed states have largely ceased to function as states.

A failed state is one in which there has been a breakdown of the legitimacy of the government and the ability of the government to maintain a minimal level of control over its own territory. The Fund for Peace offers a fairly broad list of attributes of a failed state:

- No longer deemed legitimate by the state's own people
- Faltering economy and collapse of public services
- Factionalization of the population or of significant groups
- Various social factors or crises that lead to displacement of the population
- Largely independent security apparatus and suspensions of basic rights

Different failed states will display different attributes in varying degrees. (Every year the Fund for Peace publishes a list of what it now calls "fragile" states worldwide and the degree to which different factors led to the ranking.) The policy issues raised by failed states are threefold. First, there is concern for the effects of the failure on the state's population. Second, the effects of the failure tend to spill over its borders. Among the most frequent manifestations of this is the shifting of populations from failed states to neighboring states that are deemed more secure. This puts additional demographic pressure on the neighboring state to house and feed the refugees. As we have seen with the Syrian refugee crisis, the spillover effect can now extend rather far, with several European nations trying to pass along the problem to their neighbors, resulting in a political crisis for Angela Merkel in Germany beginning in 2015. Third, the failed state becomes a magnet for groups that would prefer to operate in an area where there is little government control or law enforcement—terrorists, criminals, narcotics dealers, human traffickers, and even WMD proliferators. Thus, failed states become the loci for many of the transnational issues. Afghanistan is an excellent example, serving as a host for al Qaeda after Osama bin Laden left Sudan (another failed state) and then the site of combat between the Taliban and NATO. The fact that bin Laden then sought refuge in Pakistan and was able to hide there in a relatively open area, apparently for five years, raises questions about Pakistan's status as a failed or near-failed state, as do many other factors.

The first intelligence challenge posed by failed states is to identify which ones have either reached this nadir or appear to be approaching it. This is a difficult task as not everyone will agree on what constitutes a failed state; and some states will display some of the attributes but still function, albeit at a minimal level. This indication and warning function is made more difficult by the fact that policy makers often do not know what to do about a failed state. Indeed, in most cases the options are fairly limited. Unilateral intervention is rarely attractive (such as the U.S. intervention in Somalia in late 1992), and crafting a coherent multilateral approach is often difficult as the interests of states will differ when viewing the failed state. The crisis in Darfur that began in 2003 is an excellent example. Most people would agree that Sudan is a failed state. (The Fund for Peace assessed Sudan to be the seventh most fragile state in its 2018 list. South Sudan, whose independence was recognized in 2011, is listed as the most fragile state.) Few would disagree that the actions of the Sudanese military and associated militias in Darfur were horrific. However, meaningful international action was stymied because China, which has a veto on the UN Security Council, did not want to upset the Sudanese government and put at risk the oil that China imports from Sudan. The inability of the international community to deal with the Syrian civil war—as opposed to backing either the Assad regime or various rebel factions—is another example.

It is also important to correlate the failed state with our national security interests. For example, on the Fund for Peace list of the top twenty most fragile states in 2018, fourteen are in Africa. It would be difficult to define major U.S. national security interests in most of these nations beyond the fact that they are failed states. Afghanistan (ninth most fragile in 2018) is of concern as U.S. and allied troops are engaged there. Pakistan (twentieth) and North Korea (twenty-eighth) are not only important to U.S. national security interests but also have nuclear weapons. Finally, Nigeria (fourteenth) has significant oil deposits, and Haiti (twelfth) is a local concern for the United States. In short, all failed states are of concern if they become magnets for transnational issues, especially terrorism and its supporting issues, but some failed states are more problematic because of specific attributes.

The second intelligence challenge posed by failed states is then identifying which transnational issues may be growing or flourishing. Collection can be difficult because the groups in question tend to be covert and because the conditions in the states can be chaotic and dangerous. The internal security apparatus in these states may also be of questionable value. This has been one of the United States's concerns in dealing with the Nigerian government to combat the Boko Haram radical group. These states and the issues in which the United States has the most interest are also less likely to be susceptible to technical collection systems.

Leadership. A key component when assessing nation-states is the issue of leadership. One of the questions policy makers ask most frequently is about leadership intentions. Despite the intellectual objections of those who argue that systems and institutions are the major building blocks, leaders and their personalities matter in all states regardless of their political system. Gorbachev, again, stands out as an excellent example, as do Deng Xiaoping, Fidel Castro, Margaret Thatcher, and Reagan. Other than outright revolution, many "radical" or transformative leaders come to power through the accepted political forms of their nations and then decide to go off in an entirely new direction, often one that analysts have assumed is on the low end of probability. Gorbachev in the Soviet Union, Deng Xiaoping in China, F. W. de Klerk in South Africa, and Anwar Sadat in Egypt all exemplify this outcome. Few intelligence analysts would have predicted the directions these leaders chose.

Interestingly, one of the best sources of intelligence on these foreign leaders is the leaders or senior officials in one's own government who deal with them, as most intelligence analysts will have little opportunity to observe foreign leaders close up or to interact with them. As noted in chapter 6, at some point, policy makers may have a greater feel for their opposite numbers than do the intelligence analysts. To mine this source requires policy makers to be willing to set aside some time to be debriefed by their intelligence officers, which appears to happen quite rarely. And, even if it does, the intelligence officer must take into account the subjectivity of the source answering the questions. Still, the CIA, for example, has a branch that studies and produces "assessments of foreign leaders and other key decision-makers in the political, economic, science and technology, social and cultural fields," as a job posting on the CIA website advertised. Leadership analysis is a somewhat controversial endeavor, dividing those who believe it can be a successful activity from those who remain skeptical of doing this type of analysis from a fairly long distance and with little or no personal contacts. It is also important to remember that an actor can be rational by his or her own lights without sharing a common rationality. Then, too, there are those actors who are not entirely rational by anyone's standards.

Leadership analysis can also include psychological or personality profiles and medical assessments. Political leaders who are ill often try to mask the true state of their health. Although we tend to think of this as a feature of nondemocratic states—Kim Jong Il's stroke or Hugo Chavez's cancer—it can happen in democracies as well. An excellent example in U.S. history is the effort by Edith Wilson to disguise the state of President Woodrow Wilson's health after his stroke in 1919. Presidents Grover Cleveland, Franklin D. Roosevelt, and John F. Kennedy were all less than candid about health issues. Leadership personality and health assessments are issues where foreign liaison relationships can be helpful if the state of diplomatic relations precludes close-up observation.

Beyond current leaders, policy makers often want to know who is likely to succeed the people with whom they are currently dealing. This is difficult enough in a democracy, where sudden events may derail a likely successor—such as Dominique Strauss-Kahn's arrest for sexual assault in 2011 when he seemed to be on the verge of being the French Socialist Party's presidential candidate—or where political unknowns suddenly rise to prominence and become viable candidates—such as Jimmy Carter in 1976 and Barack Obama in 2008. The problem is obviously more pronounced in authoritarian systems, where the entire process is much more opaque and where leaders may often be loath to anoint successors lest they become challengers. Vladimir Putin's Russia is an excellent example of this type of problem. Putin manipulates his inner circle to suppress possible rivals. In the case of North Korea, where succession has been exclusively through the Kim family, there is no clear "heir apparent" to Kim Jong Un. He has siblings and a daughter.

The emphasis on leaders can also be a trap, especially in nondemocratic countries. In those countries, one tends to focus on the power elites and much less on the opposition. This was a problem in Iran in 1979, in large part responding to U.S. and Iranian policy maker preferences. In 2012, the deputy director of DIA, David Shedd, admitted that this missed focus had also occurred in the Middle East during the Arab Spring. In uprisings, it can be difficult to determine who the leaders of the rebellion are or which faction, if there are several, is most likely to win.

Regional Stability. It is also important to think about the core national security issues that may suggest which nations are important to watch more closely. As noted in chapter 2, the United States is a status quo power. This essentially requires the intelligence services to be alert to states that seek either violent or sudden alterations to the status quo, as well as states whose relative stability or instability can affect the international status quo. At present, those states that appear to seek a true change in the international status quo do not possess multiple levers of power: primarily Iran and North Korea. But each state controls at least one lever—weapons or oil—or in the case of Iran, possibly both, until it agreed to the nuclear agreement. There are also states that serve as platforms for these anti–status quo states, such as Venezuela, Cuba, and—to a much lesser degree—the Assad regime in Syria, none of which has many significant levers of power. Venezuela has oil, but that is likely to be a dwindling asset. All three have useful geographic positions and a willingness to exploit regional opportunities. Again, one must consider these states not only as potential threats to U.S. interests but also to broader regional interests. This suggests a number of flashpoints: Venezuela-Colombia; North Korea–South Korea; Iran in Syria, Iraq, Lebanon, or Israel.

The Islamic State (also known as ISIL, ISIS, or Daesh) posed an interesting problem as it was not quite a nation-state but had pretensions to be one. Indeed, ISIL may represent a new phenomenon, a "quasi-state," holding down territory and exploiting resources (oil, ancient artifacts, internal taxes) to create a revenue stream. ISIL also used social media to attract recruits from around the world. U.S. policy makers and intelligence officers admitted, in September 2014, that they had underestimated ISIL in terms of its fighting power and staying power. These factors suggest that ISIL was more difficult to analyze, as it combined the attributes of both a terrorist group (claiming responsibility for a series of attacks in 2015 and 2016: a bombing in Beirut, the downing of a Russian airliner, and attacks in Paris and Brussels) and a state in a way that has not been seen before. ISIL differed from terrorists, who tend to avoid holding fixed locations, although its geographic control became a vulnerability once a coalition formed to attack ISIL. The issue is made more complex by the internal politics of Islam, where there are various factions that are at war with one another for largely doctrinal reasons, a phenomenon that the West (broadly defined) has not experienced since 1648, with the exceptions of Northern Ireland and the former Yugoslavia. In the aftermath of the collapse of the Islamic State's territory, the return of foreign fighters to their home countries became a concern.

The most obvious role of intelligence in a regional crisis is warning, both for the immediate participants and for other states that may have interests in the outcome. But intelligence can also serve to defuse a regional crisis by allaying false perceptions of the other side's activities. This happened in the early 1990s, when India and Pakistan appeared to be moving inexorably toward another war. DCI Robert M. Gates (1991–1993) shared imagery with both sides, showing their actual troop dispositions. Gates was able to give an objective sense of assurance when none would have been possible on a bilateral basis.

Several states likely fall into the category of those whose sudden change in stability could be problematic, as the unrest in the Middle East has shown. This would include Saudi Arabia and Pakistan. The main issues here are internal stability and cohesion, but we once again run into the problems noted earlier in successfully collecting against and analyzing this problem. Tunisia, for example, had been quiescent for years and probably would not have been high on any intelligence priority list in late 2010, prior to the outbreak of the Arab Spring. So, this is not only a case of paying little attention, rationally, to a certain country but also not likely foreseeing the probably unpredictable effects that major instability in Tunisia could have for the rest of the region. This is also an issue where the intelligence is not likely to suggest many ways in which U.S. policy can influence the outcome successfully. For example, the United States has urged reform on many of its Arab and Muslim allies on a fairly constant basis. In most people's minds, reform should lead, inevitably, to some sort of democratic system. But elections in the Gaza Strip, Algeria, and Egypt might also suggest that any truly open election could result in the victory of those very forces that the United States does not want taking control: radical Muslims. Even worse, having now achieved power by democratic means, they arguably have greater legitimacy than the regimes they replaced. This remains the underlying concern in the Middle East even as the United States continues to support anti-authoritarian movements.

Vladimir Putin's more aggressive foreign policy suggests a willingness to challenge the status quo. The key issue is how far Putin is willing to go. The intervention in Ukraine and seizure of the Crimea occurred within what can be thought of as Russia's sphere, although these acts upset accepted norms of international behavior, especially in Europe. The decision to intervene in Syria, ostensibly to battle ISIL but more clearly to support the Assad regime, is more problematic. Several press accounts charged that U.S. intelligence "missed" the Russian move into Syria, which intelligence managers deny. Again, assuming that intelligence had warned about the Russian move, what might U.S. policy makers have done about it? No thought would have been given to trying to block the move, and there were few levers available to dissuade Putin. More important, if Putin perceives that he is successful both in his strategic goals and in his tactics ("volunteer forces" that can be easily disclaimed), might he push against the three Baltic republics that are now members of NATO?

Thus, one must give some intelligence attention to one's allies and friends. How will NATO react to a more aggressive Russia? Will the European Union (EU) survive as a coherent entity? Again, we are looking more at intentions than at capabilities.

Linearity Versus Discontinuity. A major concern when dealing with nation-states— or any international trend—is the nearly overwhelming temptation to succumb to linear analysis, that is, to assume that present conditions will largely prevail over the near term. There is a certain rationale to this approach in that our daily experience of the world suggests that one day is very much like the others. Linear thinking, however, tends to blind analysts to discontinuities that can quickly derail current conditions. Several recent events come to mind:

- The collapse of the Soviet Union
- The economic stagnation of Japan
- The global economic crisis that began in 2008
- The unrest in the Middle East

In each of these cases, one can find isolated analysts who questioned the durability of the status quo, but the majority view was for continuity. Thus, the challenge for intelligence analysts, and for policy makers, is to probe the status quo and ask which states or conditions are less firm than they might appear and what signs we might see if conditions were to begin to change. Some analysts call this "What if" thinking. For example, several states might be worth examining:

- China's economy slows, leading to political instability.
- The political transition process within the Saudi royal family falters, especially in light of the murder of journalist Jamal Khashoggi and the international reaction.
- Continued low energy prices and sanctions undermine the Russian government.
- Mexico becomes much less stable.
- Venezuela responds to profound internal problems by becoming more aggressive externally.

It is important to understand that these scenarios are meant not to predict disruption but rather to flag situations where linear thinking predominates and where discontinuities could be most problematic. Although this can be an interesting exercise for intelligence analysts, several factors militate against it. The first is the time to do this sort of speculative analysis in the face of ongoing demands. The second is the ability of analysts to think beyond current conditions and posit plausible scenarios for discontinuity. The third is the way in which policy makers might react to such an analysis, especially if there were not many signs of a change coming. Policy makers could be hard put to know what to do with such analysis or how to react to it. Still, there is an argument to be made that intelligence analysts have to be alert to these discontinuities even as they continue to analyze the more linear present and near-term future. The list earlier is by no means an exhaustive catalog of the nation-state issues that policy makers and intelligence officers face. It does suggest several problems for intelligence. First, there is no longer any ability or rationale for focusing on a single state as the United States did during the cold war. This means that priorities must be more finely drawn and that more difficult allocations of collection and analytical resources must be made. It also means that a more diverse workforce must be recruited, with broader regional knowledge, including languages. Again, the massive focus on the Soviet issue is a long-dead model. It is also important to look more critically at the levers of power that each state has. Some of these, such as the economic lever, have built-in dependencies, as was noted earlier, that serve to limit their use. It is also important to be alert to opportunities for influence and for change as well as to sudden shifts in alignments. As Lord Palmerston (prime minister of the United Kingdom, 1855–1858, 1859–1865) noted, "Nations have no permanent friends or allies, they only have permanent interests."

But even with the improvements suggested above, one has to appreciate the unpredictability of certain events. The self-immolation of a Tunisian fruit vendor would neither be forecast in and of itself nor seen as the catalyst for the toppling of several Middle Eastern regimes. At the same time, analysts could and should have written about the inherent brittleness of some of these long-standing nondemocratic regimes—although even then, the prevalent model likely would have been continuity because that has usually been the case in the past. Spotting significant discontinuities without constantly crying "wolf!" remains difficult.

KEY TERMS

bean counting 323
capabilities 323
capabilities versus intentions 324
containment 320
failed states 334
intentions 323

maskirovka 322
Potemkin villages 322
Reagan Doctrine 329
self-reveal 323
worst-case analysis 325

FURTHER READINGS

As might be expected, the literature on U.S. intelligence regarding the Soviet Union is rich. The readings listed here include some older pieces that are of historical value. There are also articles about other nation-state issues.

Berkowitz, Bruce D. "U.S. Intelligence Estimates of the Soviet Collapse: Reality and Perception." *International Journal of Intelligence and Counterintelligence* 21 (summer 2008): 237–250.

Berkowitz, Bruce D., and Jeffrey T. Richelson. "The CIA Vindicated: The Soviet Collapse Was Predicted." *National Interest* 41 (fall 1995): 36–47.

Brisard, Jean-Charles, and Damien Martinez. *Islamic State: The Economy-Based Terrorist Funding.* New York: Thomson Reuters, 2014. (Available at https://risk.thomsonreuters.com/sites/default/files/GRC01815.pdf.)

Burton, Donald F. "Estimating Soviet Defense Spending." *Problems of Communism* 32 (March–April 1983): 85–93.

Central Intelligence Agency, History Staff. *At Cold War's End: U.S. Intelligence on the Soviet Union and Eastern Europe, 1989–1991.* Washington, D.C.: CIA, 1999.

Firth, Noel E. *Soviet Defense Spending: A History of CIA Estimates, 1950–1990.* College Station: Texas A&M University Press, 1998.

Freedman, Lawrence. "The CIA and the Soviet Threat: The Politicization of Estimates, 1966–1977." *Intelligence and National Security* 12 (January 1997): 122–142.

———. *U.S. Intelligence and the Soviet Strategic Threat.* Boulder, Colo.: Westview Press, 1977.

Herman, Michael, and Gwilym Hughes. *Intelligence in the Cold War: What Difference Did It Make?* London: Routledge, 2013.

Kerr, Richard, Thomas Wolfe, Rebecca Donegan, and Aris Pappas. "Issues for the U.S. Intelligence Community: Collection and Analysis on Iraq." *Studies in Intelligence* 49 (2005). (Also available at www.cia.gov/library/center-for-the-study-of-intelligence/csi-publications/csi-studies/studies/vol49no3/html_files/Collection_Analysis_Iraq_5.htm.)

Koch, Scott A., ed. *Selected Estimates on the Soviet Union, 1950–1959.* Washington, D.C.: History Staff, CIA, 1993.

Lee, William T. *Understanding the Soviet Military Threat.* New York: National Strategy Information Center, 1977.

Lowenthal, Mark M. "Intelligence Epistemology: Dealing With the Unbelievable." *International Journal of Intelligence and Counterintelligence* 6 (1993): 319–325.

MacEachin, Douglas J. *CIA Assessments of the Soviet Union: The Record vs. the Charges.* Langley, Va.: Center for the Study of Intelligence, CIA, 1996.

Moynihan, Daniel Patrick. *Secrecy: The American Experience.* New Haven, Conn.: Yale University Press, 1998.

Pipes, Richard. "Team B: The Reality Behind the Myth." *Commentary* 82 (October 1986): 25–40.

Prados, John. *The Soviet Estimate: U.S. Intelligence and Russian Military Strength.* New York: Dial Press, 1982.

Reich, Robert C. "Re-examining the Team A–Team B Exercise." *International Journal of Intelligence and Counterintelligence* 3 (fall 1989): 387–403.

Steury, Donald P., ed. *CIA's Analysis of the Soviet Union, 1947–1991.* Washington, D.C.: History Staff, CIA, 2001.

———. *Intentions and Capabilities: Estimates on Soviet Strategic Forces, 1950–1983.* Washington, D.C.: History Staff, CIA, 1996.

U.S. Defense Intelligence Agency. *Russia Military Power: Building a Military to Support Great Power Aspirations.* Washington, D.C.: DIA, 2017. (Available at http://www.dia.mil/Portals/27/Documents/

News/Military%20Power%20Publications/Russia%20Military%20Power%20Report%202017
.pdf.)

U.S. General Accounting Office. *Soviet Economy: Assessment of How Well the CIA Has Estimated the Size of the Economy.* GAO/NSIAD-91-0274. Washington, D.C.: U.S. GAO, September 1991.

U.S. National Intelligence Council. *Tracking the Dragon: National Intelligence Estimates on China During the Era of Mao, 1948–1976.* Washington, D.C.: NIC, 2004.

U.S. Office of the Director of National Intelligence. *Worldwide Threat Assessment of the U.S. Intelligence Community.* February 26, 2015. (Available at http://www.dni.gov/files/documents/2015%20WWTA%20As%20Delivered%20DNI%20Oral%20Statement.pdf.)

U.S. Senate. Select Committee on Intelligence. *The National Intelligence Estimate A–B Team Episode Concerning Soviet Strategic Capability and Objectives.* 95th Cong., 2d sess., 1978.

CHAPTER TWELVE

THE INTELLIGENCE AGENDA
Transnational Issues

As noted in chapter 11, the division between nation-state issues and transnational issues is artificial if for no other reason than that the transnational issues, whether sanctioned or illicit, all have major centers of activity in nation-states. Nonetheless, these transnational issues tend to be addressed in somewhat different ways and raise additional issues for intelligence services.

U.S. NATIONAL SECURITY POLICY AND INTELLIGENCE AFTER THE COLD WAR

For the first forty-five years of the existence of the intelligence community, one issue dominated its work—the Soviet Union. Director of Central Intelligence (DCI) Robert M. Gates (1991–1993) estimated that 50 percent of the intelligence budget went to the Soviet target—meaning the Soviet Union itself; its Warsaw Pact satellites; other states closely aligned to the Soviet Union, such as Cuba; and Soviet activities worldwide. Other issues or regional crises arose from time to time, but the Soviet issue, as defined in chapter 11, remained the primary focus of U.S. intelligence. Also, given the global nature of the cold war, many of the other crises also had salience largely because they played a role in the bipolar rivalry.

With the dissolution of the Soviet Union on December 25, 1991, U.S. national security policy entered into a period of uncertainty in terms of focus and priorities. Several circumstances were important. First, there was a yearning within the United States for a "peace dividend," meaning a reallocation of resources with less going to national security and more to domestic needs. (Cold war spending on defense as a percentage of gross domestic product [GDP] actually peaked in 1953 at 14.2 percent. During the so-called Ronald Reagan buildup, defense spending never went higher than 6.2 percent of GDP. For 1991, the last year of the Soviet Union's existence, U.S. defense spending was at 4.6 percent of GDP. The Soviet Union had allocated roughly 40 percent of an admittedly smaller GDP to defense on a fairly consistent basis, showing the overemphasis they put on this issue.) Second, there was a widely held belief that the remaining issues that might challenge U.S. national security were of a much lower order than the nuclear-armed Soviet Union had been. Third, there were a few ultimately futile attempts to create a grand theme (much like containment) under which U.S. national security could be organized. The George H. W. Bush administration (1989–1993) tried "New World Order." The Bill Clinton administration (1993–2001) briefly tried "Preventive Diplomacy" and later the concepts of engagement and enlargement. These concepts failed because they were too vague, they did not seem to be tied to any specific national security issues, and the United States was content not to be faced with major foreign policy challenges after half a century of world war and then cold war, which included several smaller "hot wars." There was also an interesting intellectual discussion, prompted primarily by the work of political scientist Francis Fukuyama in *The End of History and the Last Man* (1992), who argued that the end of the cold war marked the end of ideological conflict and the triumph of Western democratic liberalism. At the same time, some assumed that there would be a new "ism" to confront the United States and other nations with shared values, but no one could define what it might be. No one predicted the return of extremist religious views as the next "ism."

An oft-repeated but misguided question about intelligence was whether the role of intelligence had changed. The question betrayed a certain lack of understanding about intelligence, implying that its role was somehow bound up directly with the fact of the cold war. However, the role of intelligence—to collect and analyze information that policy makers need and to carry out covert actions as lawful authorities direct—did not and does not change. This mission is—or should be—independent of any particular target, relationship, or crisis. It is the reason for having an intelligence community and should not be subject to the vagaries of international politics. U.S. intelligence targets and priorities have changed, but the community's mission has not.

This intellectual policy interregnum lasted for a decade, ending decisively with the terrorist attacks of September 11, 2001. (As discussed later, there had already been a series of terrorist attacks, beginning with the first attack on the World Trade Center in New York in February 1993. These did not have the same galvanizing or emotional effect as the 2001 attacks.) During this intervening decade, the intelligence community's responsibilities neither changed nor receded, but the leadership of the community found it more difficult to focus or to prioritize. They also received little help from the Clinton administration, which did not get actively involved in setting intelligence priorities other than one time in the middle of its eight years in office. The priority tier system introduced in the mid-1990s showed some initial promise but broke down as the priorities were never updated and revised and as policy makers and intelligence officers figured out how to manipulate the system to claim higher priorities for their favored issues.

The post–cold war interregnum created several strains for the intelligence community. The main one was budgetary. On a percentage basis, the intelligence community, rather than the much larger defense budget, bore the brunt of calls for a peace dividend. This had costs not only in real terms but also as an impediment to making a transition away from a cold war–based workforce, workforce skills, and the unexpected advent of the computer revolution. For example, some agencies found themselves with too many Soviet experts or Russian speakers, many of whom were rather senior. Was it worthwhile to invest in retraining them, knowing that their ongoing service would be short? It might seem wiser to let them go and invest in younger people with new skills and longer career prospects. But the more senior staff could not be fired, and many did not want to retire, thus creating a situation in which there was insufficient funding for new slots to bring on new people. DCI George J. Tenet (1997–2004) has stated that during the 1990s the intelligence community lost the equivalent of 23,000 positions—meaning either people never hired or positions actually lost.

The cost of this was twofold. First, there was a draining away of veteran talent and a resultant smaller workforce to handle a more complex and diverse set of policy issues. Second, as the intelligence workforce began to increase dramatically after 2001, it meant that the number of experienced analysts dropped steadily as a percentage of the workforce, until, by 2015, roughly half of the analysts had no more than six or seven years of experience, a figure that has remained somewhat stable. This was, arguably, the least experienced analytic workforce since the inception of the intelligence community in 1947.

Therefore, at the end of the second decade of the twenty-first century we find an intelligence community that needs to rebuild and refocus; with a workforce that is perhaps less experienced than at any time in its history since its inception; and facing a series of issues that are much more difficult, more interconnected, and among which there is no clear priority. It is necessary to rebalance the workforce, presumably deemphasizing terrorism and counterinsurgency to some degree, and reemphasizing nation-state issues, as director of the Central Intelligence Agency (DCIA) Gina Haspel (2018–) has stated.

INTELLIGENCE AND THE NEW PRIORITIES

An examination of several issues that have risen in priority in the post–cold war period reveals some of the difficulties that the intelligence community faces. A major problem is the fact that many of these issues are closely related to one another. Terrorism, for example, has a direct connection to weapons of mass destruction (WMD) as it is widely assumed that terrorist groups would like to have access to these weapons. Terrorism is also related to narcotics, which serves to fund many terrorist activities, as do some other international criminal transactions. For example, the Taliban, which suppressed narcotics traffic when it ruled Afghanistan, now uses that same traffic to finance its operations against the Afghan government and the North Atlantic Treaty Organization (NATO). Director of National Intelligence (DNI) James Clapper (2010–2017) noted this problem in his *Worldwide Threat Assessments* for 2011 and 2012, when he said, "It is virtually impossible to rank—in terms of long-term importance— the numerous, potential threats to US national security. . . . Rather, it is the multiplicity and interconnectedness of potential threats—and the actors behind them—that constitute our biggest challenge."

Many of these issues are related to the problem of failed (or "fragile") states, which provide safe havens for such activities. Thus, just as it is somewhat artificial to separate nation-states and transnational issues, it is also somewhat artificial to discuss each of those transnational issues in isolation when that is not how they occur. However, there is no coherent way to discuss them as a single entity. Therefore, they will be discussed individually and, where appropriate, their relationship to other issues will be acknowledged.

This difficulty is reflected in the question of intelligence priorities. How does one make resource allocations among issues that have interdependencies but may not have the same priority individually? It is important to make some distinctions, or one is left in the situation where there are, in effect, no priorities. When everything is important, nothing is important. For example, terrorism is a very high-priority issue. Should narcotics be given an equally high priority because of its relationship to terrorism, or can it be dealt with at a lower level and not lose the importance of the connection? This problem recurs across the spectrum of transnational issues.

CYBERSPACE

Like most other transnational issues, conflict in cyberspace is not entirely new, although it has undergone several transformations in the past twenty years. Indeed, even the name has gone through a series of changes—**information operations**, information warfare, net-centric warfare, and now cyber war—underscoring the still developing intellectual underpinnings of the issue.

It is somewhat difficult to give a precise starting point for cyberspace issues. Moore's Law about computing power and cost was first posited in 1965. Personal computers began to proliferate in the mid-1970s; the publicly accessible World Wide Web dates from 1989. Since then, computer-based technology has become pervasive in public and private activities. Jason Healey, a historian of cyberspace conflict, dates it from 1986, when German hackers searched through U.S. computers and sold the results to the Soviet KGB.

One of the most difficult aspects of the cyberspace issue is the great deal of hype, if not hysteria, that surrounds it—such as fears about a "cyber Pearl Harbor" (see below). Cyber has remained at the top of the DNI *Worldwide Threat Assessment* for several years. In 2015, DNI Clapper noted that the cyber threat was expanding but also said, "Rather than a 'Cyber Armageddon' scenario that debilitates the entire U.S. infrastructure . . . we foresee an ongoing series of low-to-moderate level cyber attacks from a variety of sources over time, which will impose cumulative costs on U.S. economic competitiveness and national security." DNI Clapper also said, "The cyber threat cannot be eliminated; rather, cyber risk must be managed." In 2016, the DNI added the **Internet of things**, or **IOT** (a host of devices all connected to the Internet) and artificial intelligence to the list of cyber concerns.

The issue is not cyberspace per se but the uses to which it may be put. Broadly speaking, there are four major areas of concern beyond the use of cyberspace to support military operations:

- Infrastructure attacks

- Cyber espionage (government and commercial targets)

- Denial-of-service attacks

- Cyber-based terrorism

The main U.S. national security concern with cyberspace is the vulnerability of the cyber world to intrusion, corruption, or disruption, with potentially catastrophic effects for government or commerce. In his 2010 annual threat assessment, DNI Dennis Blair (2009–2010) noted that "acting independently, neither the U.S. government nor the private sector can fully control or protect the country's information infrastructure." Cyberspace is also an important arena for intelligence activities and war fighting. That is, nations need both to defend their government and private sector from intrusion and to use cyberspace to conduct military or intelligence operations against potential or current adversaries.

A major problem in cyberspace is its relative newness and the still inchoate nature of policy and doctrine related to cyber conflict. One of the truisms for all weapons is that doctrine—the ways in which the capability can be used to maximum effect—always comes *after* the technology's invention and initial use in the field. The development of air warfare offers a useful analogy. The first powered flight was in 1903; the first use of airplanes in warfare came in the Italo-Turkish War (1911–1912), fought over control of what is now Libya. Italy pioneered the use of airplanes first for reconnaissance and then to drop hand-held explosives on Turkish positions. The use of airplanes evolved further in World War I (1914–1918) and saw the evolution of plane-to-plane combat (dogfights) and strategic bombing against enemy civilian populations. However, the first comprehensive examination of air power doctrine did not come until Giulio Douhet's *Command of the Air,* published in 1921. A similar course can be traced for armored warfare as well. Thus, it should not be surprising to find that the doctrine for the use of cyberspace is still very much unformed.

The stated premise of this book is that properly conceived and conducted intelligence derives from and serves policy. This helps explain a great deal of the problem in cyberspace, where there is much confusion about our policy goals—beyond the simplistic one of trying to prevent intrusions and attacks. To be fair, it is difficult to craft policy for technology that serves simultaneously as a means of communication, of industrial control, of intelligence collection, and, possibly, of warfare, among other roles, and that exists in the international public sector. For the United States, the problem is further complicated by the fact that most of the nation's infrastructure, broadly defined, belongs to the private sector. Among the concepts with which the U.S. government is grappling, each of which has intelligence implications, are the following:

- *Information sharing about cybersecurity.* In February 2015, President Obama signed Executive Order 13691, "Promoting Private Sector Cybersecurity Information Sharing." The goal is to encourage the private sector to share cyber threat information. Such sharing is seen as necessary to get a better sense of the cyber threat and to create better responses. However, as the executive order recognizes, this is a voluntary concept. Private-sector firms may be unwilling to admit they have had serious cyberattacks and may be wary of sharing information about their infrastructure and operations for reasons of security and competitiveness.

  Despite evidently shared interests, cyber cooperation between the government and the private sector has been contentious. Classification issues have limited sharing from the government to the private sector.

Government officials have noted that private-sector firms tend to turn to cybersecurity firms and not the government when they suffer a cyberattack. Also, a number of technology firms have declined to work with the government on various projects. Google employees successfully protested their firm's involvement in Project Maven, an artificial intelligence imagery project that could be used to guide drone strikes. Twitter cut off the Central Intelligence Agency (CIA), the National Security Agency (NSA), and other intelligence agencies from access to its Dataminr program.

- *Commercial encryption.* In large part as a reaction to the Edward Snowden leaks, several companies—including Apple and Google, among others— decided to go to an encryption standard that does not have a key that can be shared with the U.S. government and that would be extremely difficult to break. Previous government access was sometimes referred to as **backdoor encryption.** Obama administration officials considered but then dropped, in October 2015, the idea of pursuing legislation to mandate such access. Federal Bureau of Investigation (FBI) director James Comey (2013–2017) was especially vocal about the problems raised by the new encryption and the advantage that it gives to terrorists and criminals. Computer security specialists note that there are several other ways to get the data, besides directly through a device. They also note that any backdoor could possibly be exploited by others as well. As noted earlier, Comey and DCIA John Brennan (2013–2017) raised what they saw as grave national security implications of this new commercial practice in the aftermath of the November 2015 Paris attacks. Interestingly, European Union (EU) officials have also made the same request of various technology companies—again reacting to the Paris attacks. This represents a major shift, as many EU officials have been extremely critical of U.S. signals intelligence (SIGINT) activities in the aftermath of the Snowden leaks and had been zealous about the need to safeguard privacy.

  In September 2018, the Five Eyes intelligence partners (Australia, Canada, New Zealand, the United Kingdom, and the United States) issued a statement of principles on encryption essentially calling on the technology industry to provide "lawful access" to encrypted material or face the decision of these governments to "pursue technological, enforcement, legislative or other measures to achieve lawful access. . . ."

- *Hack back.* To date, the United States has opposed entities that have been hacked taking retaliatory action on their own, citing the difficulties of accurate attribution and the possible evolution into a "wild west" scenario of hacks and counterhacks without end, some of which would actually be misdirected. At the same time, firms in the private sector have bridled at what they see as a lack of action on the government's part. Several questions arise. If propriety data are stolen, what is the appropriate response? No hack back will retrieve the data, so is the goal revenge? There are also concerns about collateral damage from a hack back and the possibility of escalatory attacks. Finally, for U.S. firms, there are legal issues. The Computer Fraud and Abuse Act makes it illegal to access a computer network without permission. There is no exception if you have been attacked.

- *Deterrence.* There have been increasing calls for some sort of deterrence policy in cyberspace. The essential dynamics of deterrence are well known: holding something of value at risk as a means of preventing certain actions. Deterrence was one of the underlying concepts of the U.S.-Soviet relationship during the cold war: maintaining large nuclear forces on both sides that could not be wholly eliminated in a first strike, leaving open the likelihood of devastating retaliation. Deterrence is based in part on the reality of the deterrent force and in part on perception, the belief that you will use the force if necessary. However, there is also the problem that a deterrent may become a target if the other power decides not to be deterred any longer. This was the case for the U.S. fleet at Pearl Harbor. Indeed, one of the underlying problems in deterrence is the uncertainty that the deterrent is having the desired effect. Did the Soviets not attack because they were deterred, or did they never plan to attack anyway?

  All of these uncertainties are compounded in cyberspace. First, the fact of deterrence has to be declared, either overtly or by the creation and deployment of a deterrent force. In cyberspace, how would one distinguish current capabilities from a deterrent force? Second, what would be held at risk: opposing cyber forces or physical assets? This appears to run the risk of immediate escalation. Third, the use of a cyber deterrent would still depend on successful attribution. This might be an issue if a state decided to go to the United Nations to justify a defensive strike. Would there be sufficient intelligence to garner international support? Fourth, what threshold would differentiate current activities in cyberspace from an action that would require a counterstrike? Finally, deterrence relies on the assumed shared rationality of the parties involved. Assuming this works among most nation-states, does it extend to terrorists, hacktivists, and criminals? Likely not. Moreover, how would you hold these more ephemeral groups at risk to create deterrence?

- *Export control.* Initial international efforts to control the sale of software that could be used maliciously have run into difficulties. Much of the software in question—encryption, surveillance, and security—may have legitimate uses, depending on who is using it and for what reason. There is also the very strong possibility that groups will use fronts or cutouts to get access to the needed software and tools.

Another problem that relates to cyberspace for the United States has been organizational: deciding where responsibility for cyber activities should be located. To an observer, it would appear that there are too many players, none of whom has much authority in cyberspace. Much of the cyber infrastructure in the United States belongs to the private sector. The Department of Homeland Security (DHS) is responsible for the nation's cyber defense and protecting critical infrastructures, but as DNI Blair noted, this must be done in cooperation with the private sector. In 2009, DHS set up the National Cybersecurity and Communications Integration Center (NCCIC), which has an awareness-raising function, an operational role, and a cyber response role. Since 2016, the NCCIC has issued a series of reports on Russian cyber activity, called GRIZZLY STEPPE. There had been a cyber security coordinator in the National Security Council (NSC), but the Trump administration ended that position in May 2018. In November 2018, President Trump signed legislation creating the Cybersecurity and Infrastructure Security Agency (CISA) at DHS. CISA is the lead for protecting the critical infrastructure and managing the NCCIC. CISA is a coordination and situational awareness agency, not a policy or intelligence agency.

For the military, after much debate, the Obama administration set up Cyber Command (USCYBERCOM), with overall responsibility for all aspects of defending Department of Defense (DOD) cyber networks and for coordinating, planning, and conducting military cyber operations. CYBERCOM is headed by a four-star officer who is concurrently the director of NSA. This led some observers to conclude that CYBERCOM is part of NSA, but it is not. They are two separate organizations, and the only overlap is in the position of their leader. Moreover, each of the military services has retained its own organic cyber capabilities. In 2013, the Defense Science Board, an advisory group, criticized Defense's "fragmented" approach to cyberspace.

In the aftermath of the Snowden leaks, some commentators suggested that the positions of NSA director and cyber commander be split, especially given the impending retirement of Gen. Keith Alexander in 2014. Ultimately, the Obama administration decided to keep the current structure, with Adm. Michael Rogers succeeding to both positions. The Trump administration decided to maintain the current dual-hat status when Gen. Paul Nakasone succeeded Rogers in May 2018. However, CYBERCOM became an independent Unified Combatant Command at that time (it had formerly been subordinated to STRATCOM—Strategic Command).

The existence of CYBERCOM does not preclude the possibility of some cyber activities being carried out by intelligence agencies. This is not just a bureaucratic issue. There are distinct legal implications on the use of cyber capabilities as a weapon or an intelligence tool in terms of who controls the activity, the legal framework within which it operates, and the ways in which Congress should be informed, just as there is for special operations and intelligence, as discussed earlier. According to press accounts, in 2018 the Trump administration reversed an Obama policy (Presidential Policy Directive 20, PPD-20) on requirements to initiate a cyberattack. The Obama policy required fairly broad consultations across the government, which have now been streamlined or reduced. The FY2019 Defense Authorization Act defines clandestine cyberattacks conducted by CYBERCOM as a "traditional military activity" and not a covert action. However, this does not clarify the status of an operation conducted by NSA, which is both an intelligence agency and a Defense combat support agency. General Alexander had noted that no matter which hat he was wearing when conducting a cyberattack—NSA or CYBERCOM—he needed presidential authorization first.

As noted earlier, there was not much support in the intelligence community for the creation of CTIIC (the Cyber Threat Intelligence Integration Center) on the grounds that it was largely duplicative, but the Obama NSC staff insisted on it.

As part of his reorganization of CIA, DCIA Brennan created a Digital Innovation Directorate, which has three areas of emphasis: (1) improving CIA's ability to gather cyber-based intelligence; (2) improving CIA data management; and (3) making better use of the large amounts of data that the CIA collects, for both operations and analysis.

Finally, there has been a general recognition that the United States—both government and industry—does not have the trained workforce it needs to be successful in cyberspace. Although there is frequent reference to a generation of "digital natives," there is a very significant difference between being conversant or generally familiar with computer technology and being able to be effective in cyberspace. Former deputy director of NSA Chris Inglis (2006–2014) describes most of the young people as "apps users, not digital natives." Again, part of this stems from the lack of firm doctrine.

For the sake of discussion, cyber operations can be broadly divided into offensive and defensive activities. A third important activity is forensics, which in cyberspace means investigating what has happened either in an activity that you are conducting or in one that you are defending against. Thus, forensics is tied to both cyber offense and cyber defense and can be thought of as a major intelligence activity. The offensive activities include the use of cyber capabilities either as a military weapon or as an intelligence tool, either for collection or for operations. One of the key issues here is **computer network exploitation (CNE)** versus **computer network attack (CNA)**. Once one has achieved access to a target's computers, one can exploit that access, determining capabilities, collecting available data retrieved, and possibly taking control of all or part of the network for one's own ends. All of that is CNE. There may also be reasons to bring down the network, to disrupt command and control or vital services within the target nation. That is CNA. One can obviously carry out CNE and, at some point, move to CNA. Much will depend on goals and surrounding circumstances. But these can become stark choices, not unlike the counterintelligence choice of allowing a known spy to operate as a means of determining how he or she works and for whom, as well as feeding false intelligence to him or her, versus arresting the spy. An interesting case was reported in the press in which NSA and CIA disagreed about using cyber capabilities against an online jihadist magazine, *Inspire*. NSA saw the magazine as a legitimate counterterrorism target to be blocked and thus help protect U.S. troops deployed overseas. CIA argued that this would expose sources and methods and deprive them of an important intelligence source. CIA reportedly won the debate, but the magazine was then attacked by British cyber activity.

CNE had been considered an intelligence activity to be conducted by intelligence agencies, rather than a military operation. Because of the bureaucratic implications of such a division, DOD advocated the concept of the **cyber operational preparation of the environment (cyber OPE)** to cover military activities that intrude into adversary systems in advance of offensive operations. As noted, legislation now designates CYBERCOM as a "traditional military activity" and not a covert action.

An interesting intelligence issue for CNA is determining the degree to which an attack has been successful, again requiring forensics. In military operations, this is called **battle damage assessment (BDA)** and can usually be determined by geospatial intelligence (GEOINT) or SIGINT. The cyber "battlefield" is more difficult to assess. How could it be determined that an enemy's computer system has been successfully disrupted or that the enemy has just shut it down when it recognized that an attack was under way? How could it be determined if the enemy has backup systems? If a successful cyberattack is a precondition for some type of overt military operation, how can it be determined that the precondition has been satisfied? How much disruption should be caused? Disrupting enemy communications is useful, but should such action preclude, for example, the ability of an enemy headquarters to signal its troops authoritatively that hostilities are to cease? Or, having disrupted the enemy's ability to communicate, how can an enemy's offer to cease hostilities, to negotiate, and so on, be verified?

The interconnectedness of various systems worldwide also may serve to limit offensive activities as there can be unexpected and undesired consequences. For example, according to press accounts, in 2003 the United States considered crippling the Iraqi financial system via cyberspace before the actual invasion so that Saddam Hussein could not purchase war supplies. However, there was also concern that such an attack would affect the Middle Eastern and, then, potentially the global banking system, so the attack was not undertaken. Websites can also serve multiple purposes, creating conflicting opportunities and risks. Again, press accounts state that in 2008 the United States launched a cyberattack on a site that officials believed was being used by extremists planning attacks on U.S. forces in Iraq. The site had been sponsored by Saudi Arabia to lure extremists and would-be terrorists as a means of identifying them and tracking them. Even though the Saudis were told about U.S. plans, they were frustrated by the loss of an intelligence source. This is a classic case of competing and conflicting goals: the operational safety of U.S. forces versus luring in more terrorists. Finally, during the NATO air war against Muammar Qaddafi in 2011, the United States reportedly considered launching cyberattacks on Libya's air defense systems, which is always one of the first targets in an air campaign. However, these cyberattacks were not made, apparently out of concern for setting a precedent about the use of cyber in warfare. Decisions like those in Iraq in 2003 and Libya in 2011 underscore the relative novelty of cyber and uncertainties about how and when to use it. These uncertainties do not preclude the use of cyber by several states and by non-state actors for various types of intelligence operations, from collection to sabotage. Nor is U.S. restraint likely to be sufficient to preclude actions by others.

Much of the concern about cyberspace focuses on the problems of defense and the chance of an "electronic Pearl Harbor." Again, this is analogous to early concerns in air warfare about a devastating strategic bombing surprise attack and the mistaken belief, prevalent in Britain in the 1930s, that "the bomber will always get through." As DNI Clapper and some cyber analysts point out, however, the chance of a surprise cyberattack carried out by a nation-state would most likely come only after a serious deterioration of relations, thus providing a period to prepare to whatever extent was possible. This would not be the case for non-state actors (terrorists, narco-traffickers, criminals, hackers), but they are also likely to have less well-developed cyber capabilities. Thus, the issue of cyber indications and warnings depends, to some degree, on the nature of the attacker. Two of the most prominent cyberattacks followed varying periods of tension. In April 2007, Estonia was the target of widespread denial-of-service attacks, following a period of nationalist tension with Russia. Although independent Russian groups claimed responsibility for the attacks, many believed that these had to have been orchestrated by the Russian government. Before Russia's military attack on

Georgia in August 2008, there was a series of cyberattacks on Georgian sites. There has also been Russian activity, apparently related to its campaign against Ukraine, against Ukrainian and NATO targets. This has included the use of "trolls," either robots or human commentators, to sway social media.

There has been an overall increase in Russian cyber activity, which appears to be part of the more aggressive posture assumed by President Vladimir Putin. A major instance was Russian activity during the 2016 U.S. presidential election, which apparently had two goals: (1) to support Trump over Hillary Clinton and (2) to sow doubts about the credibility of the U.S. electoral process. The Obama administration has been criticized for how it dealt with intelligence about Russian activity during the 2016 election, particularly the lack of counter-activity and reluctance to "name and shame" Russia. Among the rationales offered for the Obama administration's low-level response were concerns about intelligence sources and methods, the belief that the Russian effort would fail and that Hillary Clinton would win, and Obama's not wanting to appear to be interfering in the election. This last point, while lofty, has no basis in law or tradition, as many presidents have done what they could to ensure the election of a preferred successor.

The election issue has become greatly politicized, as Trump repeatedly refused to believe the findings of the intelligence community, which issued an assessment in January 2017 that included the view that Putin personally ordered the operation (see Further Readings). Trump's allies in the 115th Congress did what they could to minimize the effects of House and Senate investigations, as well as the work of special counsel Robert Mueller, a former FBI director (2001–2013).

Finally, according to press reports, there has been increased Russian surface ship and submarine activity near the undersea cables that are the backbone of the international Internet, raising concerns about possible Russian efforts to tap the cables or to cut them during a crisis.

A key intelligence issue in cyberspace is that of **attribution**. Again, for a large-scale nation-state attack, this presumably would be relatively easy as the cyberattack would not likely come in isolation from a deterioration in relations or other actions. The problem becomes more difficult for non-state actors and for CNE. Any response to a CNA or CNE depends on the ability to determine with some certainty who is behind the hostile action. This is made more difficult by the nature of cyber, where the origin of attacks can be masked in terms of location or actor by having the attack travel through several points from origin to target or by attacking, either entirely or in part, by commandeering otherwise innocent computers. This becomes both an intelligence task and a policy decision: What level of certainty will policy makers need about attribution before ordering a response? This cannot be determined in advance and will depend, in part, on the nature of the intrusion or attack and the damage it has caused, which will lead to increased pressure for a response; the ramifications of a response, depending on who is believed to be the intruder; and the personality of the policy maker. In his 2015 assessment, DNI Clapper said attribution was improving and that most intruders will be detected and identified. Analysts note that the United States was able to identify the source of the November 2014 North Korean cyberattack against Sony Pictures. North Korea is seen as being less capable than China or Russia. (Some cyber analysts question this attribution.)

The barrier to entry for a cyberspace capability is clearly much lower than for WMD, although there are still varying degrees of capability. Cyber analysts view the United States as being the most capable and the most active nation in cyberspace. Britain, China, and Russia likely have cyber capabilities roughly comparable to those of the United States, followed, at a slightly lower level, by Israel and then France and India. Most of these nations, including the United States, have been cited as cyberspace attackers in the past several years. In January 2017, U.S. intelligence leaders said that thirty nations were developing offensive cyberattack capabilities. The capabilities of non-state groups are likely lower than those of the most sophisticated nation-state cyber programs.

A great deal of attention in the United States has focused on the cyberspace activities of China. Chinese cyber activities can be divided into four major groups: (1) economic espionage against U.S. high-technology firms, (2) military espionage against new U.S. weapons systems, (3) reconnaissance in control systems for U.S. critical infrastructure, and (4) retaliation against groups publishing adverse information about China. Given the nature of the Chinese state, it is widely assumed that the vast majority of this activity is directed by the Chinese government, although some smaller fraction of it likely comes from Chinese nationalists or hackers. Mandiant, a U.S. computer security firm, identified People's Liberation Army (PLA) Unit 61398, based in Shanghai, as a major source of cyber activity against the United States.

It is interesting to look at each of these motives in turn. DNI Clapper said in his 2013 *Worldwide Threat Assessment* that it is difficult to quantify the economic losses of cyber espionage. That same year, the FBI put total U.S. losses at $13 billion, without breaking down what portion is due to China. However, some analysts point out that although there are gains to be made in economic espionage, true economic success comes from innovation and marketing, not copying. Economic espionage and espionage against weapons systems are hardly new; cyberspace simply provides another means of accomplishing them. Reconnaissance against critical infrastructure can be either economic espionage or preparation for a possible attack should this eventually become desirable or necessary. Some examples of retaliatory Chinese cyberattacks include those against Mandiant after its report was published and against *The New York Times* after it published detailed articles alleging official corruption in the family of then-premier Wen Jiabao. Therefore, it can be argued that Chinese cyber activity represents traditional ends through new means.

Interestingly, DNI Clapper refused to characterize the 2015 Office of Personnel Management (OPM) data loss as a cyberattack, saying that it was "passive intelligence collection," similar to what the United States does. In December 2015, China stated that the OPM intrusion was the work of criminal hackers and not the government, which some observers doubted for obvious reasons. Three months earlier, NSA director Admiral Rogers had said that there were no signs that the OPM data were being used for fraud or financial crimes, which is typical of criminals, again calling into question the Chinese assertion.

There are other China-based cyber threats as well. Many, if not most of the computers purchased worldwide are assembled in China, presenting opportunities for both CNE and CNA. In 2013, U.S., British, and Australian intelligence agencies banned the use of highly classified networks of computers manufactured by Lenovo, a Chinese firm that acquired IBM's personal computer business in 2005. "Backdoors," that is, means for allowing remote unauthorized access, were found on Lenovo products. Possible backdoors have also been the main source of U.S. concerns over the use of Huawei products.

Early press accounts indicated a decrease in cyber intrusions by China's People's Liberation Army after five PLA officers were indicted by the United States in May 2014, although observers questioned whether this was a tactical or more meaningful change. In September 2015, President Obama and Chinese president Xi Jinping agreed to a "common understanding" that neither nation would engage in cyber intrusions to steal intellectual property. It is not clear how this agreement will be enforced. Notably, DNI Clapper questioned whether Chinese behavior would change. In November 2015, William Evanina, head of the National Counterintelligence and Security Center (NCSC), said he had not seen any indication of a decrease in Chinese economic espionage. U.S. concerns about China's and other nations' cyberspace activities were severely undercut by the exposure of NSA programs by Edward Snowden in 2013. Although these were intelligence collection programs rather than efforts to manipulate cyber systems, the extent of the alleged activity has made it difficult for the United States to appear as an injured party. The reality, of course, is that cyber activities—like espionage—are practiced by virtually every nation that can do so. According to press accounts, the agreement with China fell into abeyance as a result of U.S.-China trade tensions, as evidenced by an increase in Chinese cyberattacks on U.S. commercial enterprises.

The Stuxnet virus that received a great deal of press attention and speculation in 2010 is a useful example of many of the issues noted above. Stuxnet was malware (malicious software) designed to attack a specific target, control systems for nuclear plants, especially those systems produced by Siemens, the German engineering firm. Although Stuxnet has reportedly affected systems in ten countries, the greatest interest was in Iran, where the largest number of systems was affected. Many press reports state that the virus caused damage among the centrifuges needed to create enriched uranium by altering their operating speeds. Iran, although admitting to some problems, downplayed any setbacks. Less attention was paid to the Flame virus, apparently created by the same people as Stuxnet. Flame, instead of sabotaging computers, apparently turns them into captive information retrieval devices.

Several germane points stand out. First, Stuxnet was apparently introduced via a thumb drive. Thus, we have human-enabled cyber (as opposed to an attack over the World Wide Web), just as there was human-enabled SIGINT in collection. Second, although it is assumed that the main target was Iran, several other countries also had Stuxnet intrusions. Third, the source of the attack remains unknown. Several countries were opposed to Iran's ongoing nuclear activities, many of whom could have produced the malware. It is unlikely that the actual source would voluntarily reveal itself. Fourth, Stuxnet is a case of using one transnational issue, cyberspace, to create a result in another one, WMD proliferation. Finally, whoever created Stuxnet and for whatever purpose, it was an advanced piece of malware designed for effect not in cyberspace but in the physical world of industrial systems. As such, Stuxnet has been seen as a harbinger of more dangerous attacks to come against other such systems—whether dams, power plants, electrical grids, factories, or water treatment plants.

Unfortunately, cyberspace provides a medium by which nations—or non-state actors—can carry out campaigns and retaliation against one another during peacetime and presumably without the risks of more overt military acts. For example, in 2012–2013, Iran apparently launched a series of cyberattacks on U.S. banks, U.S. and foreign energy firms, and the Saudi oil fields. These attacks were seen as being twofold in nature: as retaliation for the Stuxnet attack and as a means of retaliating for the economic sanctions imposed as a result of Iran's nuclear program. In 2012, Iran announced that certain ministries would be off the World Wide Web for a month in what was seen as way of avoiding further hostile cyberattacks. In December 2014, the firm Cylance published a detailed report on the breadth of Iran's cyber activities, which it called Operation Cleaver. According to press reports, the Obama administration ordered cyberattacks on Iran's nuclear program and offered cyber defensive support to friendly states in the Middle East and in East Asia that might be cyber targets of Iran and North Korea, respectively. Should attacks and counterattacks like these rise to a level where one state or another decided to move to conventional weapons, that state would once again face the problem of attribution. Press accounts in late 2015 stated that there was an increase in "sophisticated" Iranian cyber espionage attacks against State Department employees working on Iran and the Middle East. Some observers thought this might be a reaction by Iranian hardliners opposed to the nuclear agreement, either to undermine the agreement or to find ways to continue hostile action against the United States.

Both nation-states and international bodies have been working on rules of engagement and rules of conduct for cyberspace. U.S. officials have said that a U.S. offensive cyberattack on foreign computers would require presidential authorization but defensive action against cyberspace attacks could be conducted by commanders on their own. The degree and intensity of that response would have to be defined further, especially if commanders acted on their own authority. According to press reports, an Obama administration policy review concluded that the president has the authority to launch a preemptive cyberattack if there is credible intelligence of an imminent major cyberattack. President Obama reportedly signed PPD-20 in 2012 to establish principles and processes for the use of cyber operations.

Internationally, NATO sponsored the drafting of the *Tallinn Manual on International Law Applicable to Cyber Warfare* (usually referred to as the Tallinn Manual). The manual sets forth definitions of various legal issues regarding cyberspace, such as sovereignty, and attempts to create rules for the conduct of cyber operations or reaction to these operations. Although only suggestions at this point, the Tallinn Manual may be the starting point for an international discussion of conduct in cyberspace, which may then affect related intelligence operations. For example, the Tallinn Manual says that hackers are legitimate military targets but also states that Stuxnet constituted "an act of force" against Iran and therefore was illegal according to international law, but the drafters were divided on whether this constituted an "armed attack." Critics of the Tallinn Manual point out that the Russian cyberattack on Estonia in 2007 was not seen by NATO as an act of force on a member nation and the alliance therefore did not invoke Article V, which calls upon NATO members to come to an ally's defense.

The cyberspace issue now also embraces several new technology concepts. The first is the Internet of things, or IOT, as DNI Clapper noted in his 2016 assessment. The IOT refers to the interconnection of all sorts of disparate machines and devices that have electronics, sensors, software, WiFi capability, and so on, allowing them all to be connected and accessed. Any device that is part of the IOT represents either a vulnerability to intrusion, manipulation, or espionage or an opportunity to conduct those same activities. An example is pacemakers, which are typically read out remotely over telephone lines. In 2013, doctors removed the wireless capability of Vice President Richard Cheney's pacemaker to preclude assassination attempts.

The second concept is **artificial intelligence (AI)**, which is closely related to the third term, **machine learning**. Artificial intelligence refers to the ability of machines to do tasks or solve problems as humans do. Machine learning refers to computers being able to learn without being programmed to do so. The victory of a computer over a champion at Go in 2015 is a frequently cited instance of both concepts. AI and machine learning depend on a great deal of data and are obviously dependent on the algorithms written for them. Advances have been made, but they are not near operational capability. Still, most of the major powers are investing heavily in AI in the hopes of making breakthroughs and not being at a disadvantage.

NSA has been criticized for its unwillingness or slowness in revealing **zero-day vulnerabilities**. These refer to flaws in hardware or software that can be exploited by an attacker. NSA exploits some of these as part of its operations, hence its reluctance to publicize all of the vulnerabilities it discovers. Some critics believe the public should be apprised of these vulnerabilities for their own safety.

In conclusion, the continuing evolution of cyberspace and cyber operations takes both policy and intelligence into relatively new areas, where issues of policy, goals, doctrine, and roles and responsibilities are still being debated and formed.

TERRORISM

The September 2001 attacks led to a greatly increased U.S. focus on terrorism, which became the primary national security issue, although not dominating intelligence activities as did the Soviet issue during the cold war.

Historical Context. The intelligence community's interest in terrorism predates the 2001 attacks. First, there had been a series of earlier attacks by al Qaeda on U.S. interests, beginning with the first attack on the World Trade Center in New York in February 1993. Second, it is also important to remember that terrorism is a recurring phenomenon in international politics. In the late nineteenth century, there was a series of anarchist assassinations, killing President Sadi Carnot of France (1894), Empress Elisabeth of Austria-Hungary (1898), and President William McKinley of the United States (1901). In the United States from 1917 to 1920, there was the Red Scare, largely a series of bombings by anarchists, labor radicals, and pro-Soviet individuals. In the 1970s and 1980s, there were several strands of terrorism: European and Japanese radicals (West Germany's Baader Meinhof Gang or Red Army Faction, Italy's Red Brigades, Japan's Japanese Red Army); various Middle East terrorist groups (Black September, the Abu Nidal Organization, and others); and state-based terrorism (including Libya, Iran, and North Korea). These strands sometimes came together in cooperative terrorist attacks. Thus, one can argue that the U.S. intelligence community has had more than forty years of experience with terrorism.

However, unlike the consistency of the Soviet target, terrorism has been a shifting target as groups rise and fall or are defeated and as the locus of terrorism changes. Therefore, it may be fair to say that there is more generic experience with terrorism than specific experience as terrorist threats continue to morph. Moreover, the earlier terrorist campaigns all were political in nature. The current terrorist threat has a self-selected religious basis, which makes it much more difficult to discuss as a policy issue because of our concerns about religious freedom and our understandable desire not to blame an entire religion for the acts of a faction within that religion. The religious aspect of modern terrorism also poses an analytic challenge in that Western states (with the exception of Northern Ireland and the former Yugoslavia, if we include the Balkans) largely stopped fighting about religion in the seventeenth or early eighteenth centuries. Ironically, the next "ism" that some assumed would come about to replace communism as a foe—religious fanaticism—may actually be a historical throwback, at least in terms of Western experience.

Lessons From the Cold War. To understand the difficulties inherent in tracking and forestalling terrorism, one must recall the intelligence legacies of the cold war. Terrorist groups, unlike the Soviet Union, typically do not operate from large, easily identifiable infrastructures and do not rely on extensive communications networks. As more becomes known publicly about U.S. intelligence sources and methods, terrorists have made greater efforts to avoid detection. For example, al Qaeda leader Osama bin Laden reportedly gave up the use of cell phones and fax machines to avoid being located by the United States. Ironically, it was bin Laden's reliance on human couriers to communicate that helped lead to his safe house in Pakistan. Also, terrorist groups do not conduct large-scale repetitive exercises, as do organized military forces. Thus, the visible signature of terrorists is much smaller than that of the Soviet Union or any nation-state. This calls for collection systems different from those used to track nation-states, yet the nation-state collection approach is needed as well. Another major distinction between the Soviet target and the terrorist target has been noted by John McLaughlin, former deputy DCI: In the case of the Soviets we had a good sense of their capabilities but not their intentions. In the case of the terrorists, we know their intentions but not their capabilities.

As noted in chapter 11, the Islamic State (ISIL, ISIS, or Daesh) may be seen as an exception to some of the above observations since ISIL had pretensions to be a state and behaved like a "quasi-state," in that it occupied territory and conducted both military operations and terrorist attacks. ISIL also recruited much more widely than typical terrorist groups, which have tended to be small and rather insular. ISIL used social media very effectively to draw recruits from several Western countries. This is a complicating factor, making it more difficult to find the right way to analyze ISIL. Nick Rasmussen, director of the National Counterterrorism Center (NCTC) from 2014 to 2017, said in congressional testimony in October 2015 that the ISIL threat was viewed as a spectrum, from the implications of its quasi-state status to its role in inspiring individuals to act. Several press accounts suggest that the intelligence community and policy makers took some time before they fully understood the threat represented by ISIL and how it differed from other terrorist problems. The rise of ISIL has also raised the question of which group is the greatest terrorist threat, which is an important question in terms of resource allocation. In that same testimony, Rasmussen stated that al Qaeda and its affiliates were still "a principal counterterrorism priority," but that was before the series of attacks in November 2015 for which ISIL claimed responsibility: a major bombing in Beirut, the downing of a Russian airliner over the Sinai, and the series of attacks in Paris. (In 2014, Boko Haram accounted for more victims than any other terrorist group.) The December 2015 shootings in San Bernardino, California, also appeared to have an ISIL nexus, if only as an inspiration to the two people who committed the attack.

Determining relative success against terrorist groups is often difficult. In the case of ISIL, it has been somewhat easier in that they held fixed positions, many of which they have now lost. In 2016, the Obama administration said that its use of cyber countermessaging had reduced ISIL recruitment from 2,000 a month to 500. Others argued that the reduction was simply a result of ISIL's loss of territory and resources, making them less appealing to potential recruits. A new concern was ISIL veterans returning home, mostly to Western Europe, and conducting operations there. Intelligence assessments held that 43,000 fighters from 120 countries had joined ISIL from 2011 to 2016. Of these, 7,400 were Westerners—mostly from Europe but including 250 Americans.

Analysts sometimes refer to **chatter** when they describe intelligence on terrorism. "Chatter" is a difficult term to define. It refers less to precise intelligence than to patterns of intelligence: communications and movements of known or suspected terrorists. As chatter increases—more messages, even those that may not contain direct references to attacks—or as suspects suddenly drop from sight, an increased urgency is felt about the possibility of an attack. In that sense, chatter is much like indications and warnings (I&W)—anything that represents a change in observed patterns is the subject of increased attention. But chatter is also imprecise and, as terrorists learn more about how the United States collects intelligence, chatter can decrease for reasons other than pending operations. According to press accounts, the August 2013 U.S. alert that closed embassies in the Muslim world was based on fairly persuasive chatter.

In the aftermath of the September 2001 attacks, familiar claims were made that the United States was overly reliant on technical intelligence (TECHINT) and needed more human intelligence (HUMINT). Although HUMINT can, theoretically, collect terrorist-related intelligence that TECHINT cannot, the realities of terrorism must again be examined. Terrorist groups, and certainly their leadership cells, tend to be small and well known to one another. They have tended to operate in parts of the world where the United States does not have ready access. Even if trained agents were available who knew the required language and could be provided with a plausible cover story for their presence in one of these areas, penetrating the terrorist organization would remain problematic at best. One does not simply show up in Kabul, ask for the local al Qaeda or ISIL recruiting office, and then request to see the person in charge. (The press made much in this regard of the activities of the American John Walker Lindh in Afghanistan. Lindh was captured fighting for the Taliban, not for al Qaeda, in 2001. Recruitment into the Taliban was fairly simple.

One had to be a self-professed Muslim willing to carry a gun—a far easier task than joining al Qaeda.) Finally, if HUMINT penetration were to be achieved, the new recruit would likely be asked to take part in some operation to prove his or her commitment to the cause. This raises important moral and ethical issues for intelligence. How far would the United States be willing to go to sustain a HUMINT penetration—putting an agent's life at risk by taking part in a terrorist operation, possibly directed against U.S. personnel?

Some advocacy for more HUMINT was odd in that it seemed to treat HUMINT as a numbers issue: That is, if enough agents were sent, penetrating the target would prove inevitable. Such a scenario shows a fundamental misunderstanding of how HUMINT operates and the nature of the terrorist target. HUMINT is not an en masse activity. It relies on precision.

Finally, much of U.S. HUMINT against the Soviet Union was carried out in foreign diplomatic posts outside the Soviet Union, where Soviet officials were present and more accessible. Terrorists do not have this same overt overseas presence and thus present a smaller accessible target.

This does not mean that human penetrations of terrorist cells are impossible. As with the Soviet Union, a walk-in may occur. This apparently was the case with Ilich Ramirez Sánchez, a Venezuelan-born terrorist better known as Carlos the Jackal. He apparently was betrayed either by someone in his organization or by his Sudanese hosts. Walk-ins remain fortuitous, although, as discussed later, they can come as a result of ongoing successes against terrorists.

Beyond HUMINT, the terrorist target puts a premium on several types of intelligence:

- Signals intelligence (SIGINT): Very broadly defined, to include a wide variety of communications, including a presumed extensive presence on the World Wide Web and the Dark Web

- Open-source intelligence (OSINT): To collect and dissect the many public statements made by terrorist leaders and factions and, now, tracking their various social media sites

- Measurement and signatures intelligence (MASINT): To collect against acquisition of various types of WMD

- Geospatial intelligence (GEOINT): To collect against ISIL when it held territory but also against other groups that may have camps or staging areas

Media exploitation is also an important part of the campaign against terrorists. For example, the operation that killed bin Laden also retrieved computers and associated materials that have been exploited for links to other terrorists, plans for operations, and so on. Finally, terrorism is an intelligence issue in which foreign liaison is important, as is true for all transnational issues.

State Sponsorship of Terrorism. State sponsorship of, or at least acquiescence to, terrorism makes the intelligence issue more complicated. The intelligence community must collect not only against the terrorists but also against other governments and their intelligence services. At one level, this is easier than is the terrorist collection itself, as it falls within more common intelligence practice. However, it also puts an additional strain on intelligence resources. Liaison relationships may be questionable in such cases. For example, the government of Pakistan had been relatively supportive of U.S. operations in Afghanistan up to a point, but the Pakistani Inter-Services Intelligence (ISI) was also a longtime sponsor of the Taliban. As noted earlier, bin Laden's longtime presence in a relatively open area of Pakistan raised questions about Pakistan's ultimate support of U.S. efforts. State sponsorship also raises the issue of the failed states. Here it is useful to know if the terrorists are actually being hosted by the government, as was the case in Sudan and Afghanistan for bin Laden, or whether the lack of internal order simply provides an atmosphere where terrorists can work relatively freely, perhaps without official sanction. The lack of Pakistani authority over its western border region with Afghanistan, known as the Federally Administered Tribal Areas (FATA) until its 2018 merger with an adjacent province, was one of the reasons analysts presumed this to be where bin Laden was hiding rather than in what was assumed to be the more exposed area of Pakistan not far from the capital. Again, bin Laden's five-year residence in Abbottabad raised questions about Pakistani complicity at some level in the government. A Pakistani commission that investigated this issue found "gross incompetence . . . collective failures . . . [and] culpable negligence" on the part of the Pakistani military and security services but did not charge anyone with colluding with bin Laden. In March 2015, DCIA John Brennan noted that Iran was a state sponsor of terrorism and would likely continue to be, regardless of the nuclear agreement. Finally, ISIL again represented a hybrid situation, a terrorist group that took on some aspects of a state, including holding territory and trading in some commodities.

Closely related to state sponsorship is the even murkier question of relations between and among terrorist groups. For example, Libya had contact with factions of the Irish Republican Army. The Japanese Red Army worked with the Popular Front for the Liberation of Palestine (PFLP). Members of an Irish Republican Army faction were arrested after spending time with the armed rebels in Colombia (Fuerzas Armadas Revolucionarias de Colombia, or FARC). Such ties are both important and difficult to track or disrupt. The issue of ties among terrorist groups is important in the current campaign against terrorists as a means of assessing both threat and success. For example, most of the al Qaeda members who planned the September 11 attack are either captured or dead; al Qaeda's safe haven in Afghanistan has been overrun. One of the concerns raised by these successes has been the effect on al Qaeda's command and control. Is it still a unitary group, planning and ordering attacks from wherever its leaders are, or has it, in effect, become a franchised activity, with like-minded cells inspiring one another and occasionally working together but not necessarily in direct command and control? This morphing of al Qaeda into more regionally focused groups was evident in Mali in 2013, for example. The Tuaregs in northeastern Mali are a Berber people who felt oppressed by the African rulers who are based largely in the west. Allying with African-based al Qaeda cells was less an expression of a Tuareg commitment to terrorism or to jihad than a search for convenient allies. Boko Haram in Nigeria has ties to al Qaeda but has also pledged loyalty to ISIL. Thus, as the campaign against terrorists continues, it will be necessary to discern distinctions between local grievances and alliances of convenience as opposed to actual terrorists. It is also necessary to understand which groups may be in conflict with one another as potential opportunities to combat them. But as NCTC director Rasmussen has noted, this can also serve to create more uncertainty in terrorism analysis as well.

Some of the materials captured in May 2011 after bin Laden's death suggest that he was more involved in ongoing attack planning than had previously been the assumption. Similarly, once an attack has occurred, it is important to know if it was planned or ordered by an external group or was carried out by indigenous individuals. The September 11 attack clearly was carried out by terrorists who entered the United States. However, the attacks in Madrid (2004) appear to have been directed by terrorists in Morocco, for whom a direct connection to al Qaeda has not been proved. The 2005 attack in London also appears not to be connected directly to al Qaeda, although some of the bombers had been in madrassas (religious schools) in Pakistan. Similarly, Maj. Nidal Hasan, convicted in the 2009 Fort Hood shootings, was inspired by and in communication with Anwar al-Awlaki, but it has not been established that Awlaki ordered the attack. A conclusion of this sort may be more troubling because it indicates an indigenous problem that will be much more difficult to identify: radicalized, home-grown terrorists. The November 2015 attacks in Paris had a nexus in Belgium, leading to questions about security and intelligence cooperation within the free-travel Schengen Area. Also, on a per-capita basis, more ISIL foreign recruits have come from Belgium than any other European country. It is widely thought that the arrest of one of the Paris terrorists in Brussels precipitated the Brussels attack in March 2016—not the decision on whether or not to attack but the decision to attack then, lest other conspirators be arrested. This question of connections among various terrorist groups also indicates why so much emphasis is put on **link analysis**, that is, establishing connections between various people to get a sense of their broader social networks. This is also one of the major types of information gleaned by phone and social media surveillance, connections between people, in addition to the actual content of their conversations.

War on Terrorists. The intelligence services have two roles in the campaign against terrorists: defense and offense. Defense consists of preventing future attacks by disrupting terrorists or deterring them. This means, in turn, trying to obtain both detailed intelligence about any attacks that are being planned as well as ongoing intelligence about terrorist organizations and their intentions and capabilities. One of the most difficult aspects of defense is learning to think like a terrorist. This means not only being able to conceive of attacks that many analysts would consider too horrific to contemplate for long but also appreciating the importance of randomness, which is a key ingredient of terror. It has been suggested that terrorist analysts focus too much on specific dates and events (holiday travel periods, major sporting events, national holidays). Although these dates have symbolic value or indicate periods when large numbers of people are either traveling or gathering in one place, they also may be easier to defend against. Of the major terrorist attacks that have occurred to date, only two—the failed millennium attack at the beginning of 2000 and the attempted on-board bombing of an airliner on Christmas Day 2000—were tied to an iconic date. In other words, this may be another case of mirror imaging. How successful are analysts at thinking like terrorists versus thinking like Westerners thinking like terrorists?

Offense consists of identifying, locating, and then attacking terrorists. These activities are important not only for eliminating terrorists but also for introducing uncertainty into their activities and making it more difficult for the terrorists to organize, plan, and train. Offensive activities go from analysis into operations and raise questions about assassinations, renditions, detentions, and the continued use of unmanned aerial vehicles (UAVs, or drones). As with all other intelligence operations, decisions on these types of activities, or their limits, properly belong to policy makers, not intelligence officers. The war on terrorists adds another intelligence task: support to military operations. This requirement encompasses both the usual military-related support and new activities. For example, the press has reported that the CIA has a Special Activities Division in the Directorate of Operations (DO) that was engaged in operations against the Taliban and al Qaeda. Although little is known publicly about the division, it would appear to occupy a niche between Special Forces and the DO's paramilitary activities in support of indigenous groups, such as the contras or the mujahideen. Also, important developments have been made in geospatial intelligence with the use of UAVs and commercial imagery. All of these issues came into play in the May 2011 operation in which bin Laden was killed. There have been press reports stating that one consequence of the Arab Spring has been the loss of some useful intelligence sources in the security services of the affected states.

One of the most difficult aspects of the campaign against terrorists is trying to gauge the relative degree of success. Unlike conventional wars, there are no battle fronts moving one way or another. Nor is it clear that the absence of another attack entirely means success. Again, it is possible that the nature of al Qaeda has changed under the pressure of the U.S. response since 2001, going from a more centrally controlled structure to a looser one in which there may be many small centers of activity rather than a central one. If this is so, then the intelligence agencies face uncertainty about what this means for the future of terrorist attacks and for the best way to counter terrorists, both defensively and offensively. It is known that al Qaeda has fairly long planning cycles. Therefore, a quiescent period may simply be somewhere in this cycle. Also, it matters how one thinks about the terrorist issue. Although the United States has not been successfully attacked by al Qaeda since 2001, the other attacks—Bali (2002 and 2005), Madrid (2004), London (2005 and attempted 2007), Algeria (2007), and several others—all suggest that it is better to look at the terror issue on a global basis. This certainly appears to be the case after the spate of attacks claimed by ISIL in November 2015. Moreover, in a global and clandestine war, it is difficult for intelligence or security agencies to meet the apparent political requirement of stopping any and all attacks. One of the truisms of warfare is that "the enemy has a will of his own." Although no one wants to be cavalier about future attacks and casualties, a standard of stopping all future attacks is doomed to failure. Terrorists, like any other group, need successes. President Obama said as much in his May 23, 2013, speech at the National Defense University: "Neither I, nor any President, can promise the total defeat of terror." Thus, long periods of no attacks or thwarted attacks can be seen as counterterrorist successes, but they cannot go on indefinitely. Controlling the frequency and nature of successful attacks is a more realistic approach than a standard of no future attacks at all.

The death of bin Laden is an important psychological victory, but it is unlikely to mean an end to al Qaeda or other terrorist groups. Whether he is replaceable as an inspirational leader remains to be seen.

For several years, U.S. officials had claimed that al Qaeda was on the verge of defeat. This was based, in part, on the fact that almost all the original core al Qaeda leaders involved in planning the 2001 attacks were either dead or captured. It was also based on analysis, since proved incorrect, that the Arab Spring would undermine the appeal of al Qaeda and similar groups. Instead, the ensuing political unrest offered opportunities for extremists to exploit, particularly in Libya but also in Egypt. The U.S. alert in 2013 that closed nineteen embassies or consulates in the Muslim world appeared to undercut claims of success, as the threats were al Qaeda–based, centering on al Qaeda in the Arabian Peninsula (AQAP), which operates out of Yemen. There is broad agreement that al Qaeda has morphed into more regionally based pockets, as noted above, although in the case of the 2013 alert there were apparently communications between Ayman al-Zawahiri, who succeeded bin Laden as the head of al Qaeda, and Nasser al-Wuhayshi, the head of AQAP. (Some commentators also thought that the Obama administration wanted to avoid another assault like that in Benghazi in 2012. See chap. 9.) It is probably necessary to draw a distinction between the ability of these groups to conduct terrorism in their regions and their ability to conduct large-scale operations against the United States or Europe similar to 2001 and 2015. This does not mean that U.S.-targeted operations are no longer possible, but they have likely become much more difficult to conduct. It is also important to recognize that a group (or military) can be losing but still be capable of some offensive action.

There has also been a change in the terrorist threat with the rise of so-called lone wolves, terrorists acting on their own who may be motivated by various radical ideas but who are not controlled by terrorist groups. The Tsarnaev brothers, who attacked the Boston Marathon in 2013, fall into this group, as may Maj. Hasan. Lone wolves are, by definition, more difficult to spot in advance of their acts and again raise difficult questions about civil liberties and surveillance. The December 2015 San Bernardino, California, attack can be characterized as a lone wolf, albeit possibly inspired by ISIL. The possibility of ISIL volunteers returning to the United States or other countries, possibly to commit terrorism, has increased the lone-wolf concern.

Lessons Learned. For each of the nations that have been attacked, the degree to which they have learned the lessons that led to their earlier vulnerability is an important question. For the United States, however, the "lessons" of September 11 are not necessarily clear or agreed upon. There does seem to be agreement that information sharing, especially between the CIA and the FBI, was highly flawed, although it does not necessarily follow that the numerous improvements made in information sharing will foil the next attack. Better sharing techniques and technologies are hollow if the necessary information or intelligence is not available. The 9/11 Commission and some other analysts have catalogued several missed opportunities in the period before the September 11 attack that they believe might have disrupted the plot. The problem, analytically, is that almost all of these missed opportunities would have had to fall into place, and even then the outcome would be uncertain. We know, for example, that the attackers had substitutes in case some were denied entry into the United States, as did happen. No critic, including the 9/11 Commission, has shown how the missed opportunities would have led to the tactical intelligence necessary to identify the specific four flights on September 11. Also, many of the security practices that we now take for granted did not exist on the day of the attack. Part of the problem in assessing the causes of the attack is also political. It is more comforting for the public and for officials to believe that we can identify and remedy the several factors that made us vulnerable in 2001 because then we can return to some greater sense of safety. But if the flaws are more subtle than some believe or if the remedies appear to be more difficult to implement, then we must live with a continuing sense of vulnerability.

Moreover, the repeated emphasis on information sharing and on checking "all of the databases" runs the risk of creating analytical paralysis. Analysts may become so concerned about sharing and about checking all available data that they cannot bring themselves to act on the information or to set others into action out of fear that something may have been missed. Neither extreme is correct and much depends on the nature of the situation, but it can be argued that the emphasis on information sharing has reached a point of minimal further returns. The reaction to the failed December 2009 attempt to set off a bomb on an airplane landing in Detroit is instructive. One of the U.S. reactions to Umar Abdulmutallab's ability to come as close as he did to a successful attack was to expand the watch list of people either suspected of being threats or banned from flights. Although an expanded watch list may make it less likely that a would-be terrorist can board a plane, it also increases the amount of searching that has to be done to make the watch list system effective. For example, according to press reports in 2012, the "no fly" list doubled to more than 21,000 names in one year.

The access to fairly broad amounts of intelligence given to and exploited by Bradley Manning and Edward Snowden is likely to have the effect of setting greater limits on access and intelligence sharing, thus undoing some of the changes made after 2001.

The September 2001 attacks raised new questions about intelligence–law enforcement organization, coordination, and cooperation. DHS, the NCTC, and the FBI's National Security Branch are all efforts to deal with this issue. The 2004 intelligence reform law puts a major emphasis on information sharing, which is an important aspect of all intelligence. There have been recurrent discussions about whether the United States needs to create an MI5, referring to Britain's Security Service, which is responsible for domestic security and is part of the Home Office. (See chap. 15 for details.) The FBI is not quite analogous to MI5 and has limits on what it can do beyond those activities that are considered federal crimes. The FBI had difficulty making the transition to greater emphasis on terrorism and also had difficulty making the shift from a largely law enforcement agency to more of an intelligence agency. The legal difficulty encountered in the United States is inherent in the federal system, which places responsibility for local law enforcement on the states and their cities or counties. As a means of improving liaison between the federal and local levels, a series of fusion centers, called **Joint Terrorism Task Forces (JTTFs)**, have been formed, although the majority of them tend to be staffed by state law enforcement personnel. Their ability to provide the desired liaison and integration and future remains uncertain.

The rather large and rapid proliferation of federal, state, and local offices to deal with terrorism has also attracted criticism—from the DHS inspector general, the Government Accountability Office (GAO), and a Senate subcommittee—about unnecessary overlapping, lack of communication, useless reporting, and the inevitable reorientation of some state and local resources back to traditional police issues. GAO also found that DHS helped the fusion centers create "baseline capabilities" but questioned whether these had any effect on homeland security—in other words, the ability to relate outcomes to expenditures. The fusion centers have been a particular source of concern. Some of this may be unavoidable in a complex and large federal republic, but these critiques also suggest that it may be useful to review the structure, number, and role of these various centers. Part of the problem is political. These various centers are sources of federal funds for localities. Second, no one wants to scale back or shut down a fusion center and then have an attack take place, with the inevitable questions that will follow. In January 2017, DNI Clapper issued a paper describing how national intelligence was working with domestic agencies, as well as some of the difficulties involved, including protecting privacy and civil liberties, information sharing, and security clearance reform.

Once one gets beyond the traditional national security community, the issue of clearances comes up. Very few officials at the state, local, and tribal levels have clearances. Very few seem to want them. So an immediate issue is how to pass along terrorist information without revealing sources and methods. This issue first arose as DHS was being formed in 2002. Sen. Richard Shelby, R-AL, insisted that DHS have access to all raw intelligence. DCI Tenet refused to go along with this and was supported by the incoming DHS secretary, Tom Ridge. Ridge said that if the DCI passed threat information, then he (Ridge) would assume it was well-sourced and needed to be acted upon. This rather commonsense approach is preferable to either withholding information from first responders because they are not cleared or requiring that they obtain clearances.

A more serious problem is doctrinal. More than a decade after 2001, U.S. policy makers and intelligence officers are still working out what homeland security intelligence (sometimes called HSINT—pronounced "hiz-int") means. Doctrine matters because it helps determine what intelligence needs to be shared with whom and how quickly. This discussion is still under way, but some commentators have advocated that DHS serve as a bridge between federal intelligence agencies of all sorts and first responders, helping translate national intelligence down to the first responders and helping pass along detailed local knowledge from the first responders to the intelligence agencies. This means that DHS would take on responsibility for deciding which threats were passed and which were not, undoubtedly in consultation with other intelligence agencies. Some criteria for selectivity are crucial. Otherwise, DHS becomes a pass through for all threats, flooding the first responders, who recognize they cannot protect everything all the time and want, most of all, vectoring information to help them safeguard targets that are most threatened. It is important to recognize that the intelligence agencies and the first responders are working in a relatively new field and still working out the parameters of their actions and their interactions. DHS's Office of Intelligence and Analysis (I&A) is its main—but not only—counterterrorism locus, but I&A has struggled to come up with a meaningful doctrine and role, despite having had a succession of highly skilled veteran intelligence officers as under secretary. This would seem to suggest that the problems are institutional rather than in leadership.

The FBI has also experienced some difficulties in responding to the terror-ist threat, particularly in making the transition from being almost exclusively a law enforcement agency (albeit with some intelligence tasks, particularly counterintel-ligence) to an agency with a greater intelligence analytic role. Congress mandated the creation of a Review Commission to look at the FBI's role in homeland security. The March 2015 report noted areas where the FBI had made improvements and also noted the need to improve the FBI's intelligence capabilities, particularly in elevating the status of intelligence analysts.

But even information sharing is dependent, first, on information collection. For example, none of the investigations of September 11 found evidence that the one or two pieces of intelligence that might have led to the plot were somehow misdirected or not shared. Such evidence was never collected and may not have been collectible. Officials have also raised concerns about cyberattacks on the United States as part of a terrorist campaign. The main fear is that such actions could affect vital parts of the United States's infrastructure. Such an attack would likely have even fewer indicators, and the perpetrators might never be known after the attack.

It has been suggested that more time be spent on studying past terrorist efforts, virtually all of which failed to achieve their objectives despite rather lengthy periods of activity. Certain features begin to emerge. First, like all other activities, terrorist oper-ations need success to maintain momentum and to recruit new adherents. This can prove to be a vulnerability for terrorists, as any disruption or deterrence is the equiva-lent of a defeat. This was apparently the case for ISIL, which had very rapid early successes and was able to attract many recruits from the West, which then declined as ISIL was rolled back. At the same time, it takes only one spectacular attack to regain momentum. Second, it appears that later generations of terrorists are somewhat less fanatical and more susceptible to negotiation—assuming there is something about which to negotiate. Again, the religious aspect of early twenty-first-century terrorism makes this very difficult. Third, the current campaign against terrorists has created a series of operational and ethical dilemmas not only for intelligence officers but also for the policy makers who direct them. Much of this stems from the sheer novelty of conducting operations against terrorists on the scale that evolved after 2001. As noted, terrorism has been an issue for U.S. intelligence since the 1970s, but previously it involved specific groups or individuals. Those terrorists who were apprehended could be tried for specific acts. Post-2001, the scope has widened. In addition to seek-ing individuals who can be brought to trial, there is a need to destroy terrorist cells and networks by apprehending or killing participants. But these individuals fall into a somewhat uncertain legal status, being neither enemy combatants in the way in which uniformed soldiers of nations are nor indicted criminal suspects.

Operations and intelligence collection against known or possible terrorist threats have also raised legal and ethical issues for intelligence. As noted, the United States has conducted renditions (that is, extraterritorial arrests) that have become issues between the United States and some of its allies, although there was likely knowledge of the United States's activities at some level in most of these governments. Once captured, some terrorists have been transferred to other nations for interrogation. Critics, including the Senate Intelligence Committee majority staff report, charged that this allowed U.S. intelligence officers to use extraordinary interrogation techniques beyond U.S. territory or to have terrorist suspects be interrogated in nations where harsher methods are sanctioned. This, in turn, led to a debate within the United States about the use of techniques that might be deemed torture. According to press reports, there have been renditions in the Obama administration as well as the George W. Bush administration.

As noted, there has also been a debate about the efficacy of harsher techniques. The Senate Intelligence majority staff report and other critics argue that information obtained under these circumstances cannot be reliable. Several former CIA directors have disagreed.

In addition to these controversies, there have been issues raised about several means by which intelligence agencies have collected terrorist-related intelligence. The NSA Internet and telephone programs leaked by Edward Snowden are prime examples. The Treasury Department used a tracking program to trace financial transactions within SWIFT (Society for Worldwide Interbank Financial Telecommunications). Tracking and, where possible, preventing the transfer of funds to terrorists is an essential part of the counterterror strategy. Access to SWIFT allows analysts to know who is transferring funds, the amounts, and the accounts. Press revelations raised the usual concern about privacy. Interestingly, Congress was supportive of the effort to glean useful intelligence from SWIFT. After some European opposition in 2010 to continuing this cooperation, it was renewed, allowing the sharing of bank transfer data presumed to be connected to terrorism. Again, civil liberties groups in Europe and the United States have raised concerns. The FBI came under criticism for its use of national security letters (NSLs), as was discussed in chapter 7.

Several points stand out across these various efforts. First, as stated earlier, the campaign against terrorists has forced the intelligence agencies to reexamine how they operate and the types of information that may be useful. Second, these efforts underscore the multifaceted aspects of countering terrorism and the difficulties inherent in combating it. The terrorism target is, in many ways, much more complex than was the old Soviet foe. Third, even with a well-conceived collection plan, it will be very difficult to coordinate all of these efforts and to use the collected data in ways that produce meaningful results, as opposed to overwhelming analysts with huge databases. Fourth, these efforts will increase the demands for oversight of intelligence, both internally and externally.

The use of drones against terrorists raises several issues. First, the drones are key intelligence collectors, especially in areas where there is not much other access, such as the Afghanistan-Pakistan border, Yemen, and Somalia. Second, armed drones have proved to be effective tools in killing known or suspected terrorists; their use increased as much as fourfold under the Obama administration. As will be discussed later (see chap. 13), the United Nations (UN) has raised objections about how the United States uses drones for attacks. Targeted killings of terrorists also became an issue in the case of U.S.-born Anwar al-Awlaki, who had promoted terrorist attacks against the United States and appeared to be connected to several attacks, including that of Maj. Nidal Hasan. The Obama administration approved placing al-Awlaki on the target list, raising constitutional issues about the deprivation "of life . . . without due process of law" under the Fourth Amendment. The Obama administration argued that international law allows the use of lethal force against persons deemed to be an imminent threat.

Finally, there is the issue of the overall operational tempo at which the counterterrorist campaign has been conducted since 2001. This has been difficult to sustain for the armed forces as well as for intelligence operators and analysts.

PROLIFERATION

Preventing the proliferation of WMD has been a long-standing goal of U.S. policy, but it is now a more important issue with added dimensions. The United States has always given primary emphasis to nuclear weapons, given their lethal capability and the fact that they were central to the U.S.-Soviet relationship. But even during the cold war, the United States also worked to contain the spread of chemical and biological weapons (CBW or CW and BW). The nexus between terrorism and WMD has given added importance to the issue. Since the Iraq WMD estimate in 2002, intelligence efforts regarding proliferation have been an ongoing source of controversy and of political and sometimes partisan debate.

There are two major strands in proliferation, which are not entirely separate. The first is the requirement to keep track of the WMD activities of nation-states, both for their own sake as factors in regional stability and as possible sources of material to terrorists. Then there is the terrorist nexus itself. Al Qaeda has stated bluntly that one of its goals is to obtain WMD—again, simplifying the intentions question but not the capabilities question. The primary concern in state-based activity is nuclear weapons, although some attention is paid to the CW and BW programs of various states as well. There clearly has been an unwelcome shift in nuclear proliferation since 1998, when India and then Pakistan tested nuclear weapons. North Korea conducted six nuclear tests between 2006 and 2017. The February 2004 admissions by Pakistani scientist A. Q. Khan also made public the details of a web of private firms and experts trading in nuclear expertise and technology. In April 2011, the International Atomic Energy Agency (IAEA) confirmed that the Syrian site destroyed by Israeli bombers in September 2007 had been a covert nuclear reactor. The agreement between Iran and the P5+1 (the five permanent members of the UN Security Council—the United States, Britain, France, China, and Russia—plus Germany) was seen by many as a success in countering proliferation, at least for a specific period, but opinion was divided in the United States. In May 2018, President Trump abandoned the agreement. In his 2019 *Worldwide Threat Assessment*, DNI Dan Coats (2017–2019) noted that Iran was not undertaking the key activities necessary to produce nuclear weapons, another view that incurred the wrath of President Trump. In the summer of 2019, Iran announced various activities that appear to have breached some of the limits set by the agreement.

Role of Intelligence. The task for intelligence agencies is to identify which nations may be pursuing any or all WMD and then try to determine the state of their programs, as well as connections to other programs, sources of material, expertise, and so forth. This also represents a shift, as a *sub rosa* network of technology and expertise has developed, complicating efforts to isolate and understand programs. The most obvious problem is that these programs all operate covertly and often rely on facilities that can be difficult to find. In September 2009, the United States, Britain, and France briefed the IAEA on a hitherto secret Iranian nuclear facility near Qom. Press articles stated that Western intelligence had been tracking the site since 2006 but it had not yet received public attention. In November 2010, North Korea revealed a new uranium processing facility at its Yongbyon complex, where major facilities had been disabled in 2007 and 2008. Despite Yongbyon's importance as a proliferation intelligence target, the extent and sophistication of these new facilities came as a surprise to many North Korea "watchers." Even when suspect sites are discovered, some of them may have perfectly legal, nonlethal applications as well. This is certainly true of nuclear programs, which can have connections to peaceful uses of nuclear material, such as power plants. At the same time, peaceful nuclear programs can serve as cover for clandestine weapons development.

Intelligence on North Korea's proliferation activities has been the subject of many news reports. An initial set of reports described an Obama administration program that used cyber and electronics to sabotage North Korean missile tests, although it was also noted that failures in developing missile programs are not that unusual. Some reports stated that the repeated failures moved North Korea to abandon the Musudan missile program for another that has proved more reliable, which may raise questions about the ultimate success of the reported Obama program.

A second set of reports called into question the ability of U.S. intelligence to keep track of North Korean progress, arguing that the nuclear and missile programs had moved faster than expected. This view misunderstands the role of intelligence in proliferation, which is, above all, to report the fact of a program and to characterize its nature. Beginning with the first Soviet atomic test in 1949, there has been a tendency to underestimate the rate of progress, which is much more difficult to discern. It can be argued that once the "fact of" a proliferation program has been established, policy makers can begin making necessary preparations and taking whatever actions are available to stop the program. Proliferation programs are by their nature clandestine and usually difficult to penetrate or to collect against in detail. Tests of weapons or systems may be the first indication of progress. It can be assumed that with enough time and enough money, most programs will achieve their end goal if not stopped. (Commenting in 1965 on the possibility of an Indian nuclear weapon, Pakistan's then-foreign minister Zulfikar Ali Bhutto said, "We will eat grass, even go hungry, but we will get one of our own. . . . We have no other choice!")

Finally, in 2018, there were several reports that North Korea continued to work on nuclear weapons and missiles. The 2019 *Worldwide Threat Assessment* said the same thing. This should not be surprising, given the huge leverage that Kim Jong Un has gotten to date from this program. Also, given Trump's abandonment of the Joint Comprehensive Plan of Action (JCPOA) with Iran, North Korea may see a need to hedge against any deal negotiated with the United States. In the end, North Korea remains a very difficult intelligence target, perhaps the most difficult nation-state target.

Assuming that the U.S. goal is the complete denuclearization of North Korea, "going to zero," a key intelligence issue is establishing and confirming the exact size of the North Korean nuclear arsenal. This underscores the importance of an initial data exchange, which the intelligence community would have to confirm as best it could. The precise number may not be determined with absolute certainty. Press accounts say that North Korea has between forty and sixty nuclear weapons. Indeed, being able to have some weapons that go uncounted could be a motivation for the ongoing activity that has been reported.

U.S. intelligence efforts on proliferation continue to be seen through the prism of the October 2002 NIE on Iraq WMD. The absence of WMD in Iraq was a major factor in the impetus behind the 2004 intelligence legislation, which ostensibly addresses the issue of combating terrorism. Of the two issues—September 11 and Iraq WMD—the Iraq issue is far more serious in terms of the future of the intelligence community. For all of the pre–September 11 warnings about al Qaeda hostility, including the possibility of the use of aircraft, insufficient intelligence existed to act upon and disrupt the plot. Nor, in the preattack atmosphere, would it have been possible to implement the types of security steps in place now. The Iraq WMD issue, however, raised serious questions about analytic tradecraft, not only in WMD issues but also across the board. The Senate Intelligence Committee focused on the problem of groupthink, but more serious issues may have been at play:

- The effect of not allowing analysts better insight into the nature of HUMINT sources

- The proper way to pose alternative analytic questions that yield true alternative hypotheses instead of supporting or simply refuting the current one

- The need to rethink the prevalence of denial and deception (see chap. 6)

- The larger estimative process (see chap. 6)

The proliferation issue was then made even more contentious politically by the release in December 2007 of the unclassified Key Judgments (KJs) of a new NIE on Iran's nuclear program, which concluded that Iran had halted its nuclear weapons program in 2003, a reversal of the judgments made in a 2005 estimate. As noted earlier, this NIE was also controversial, with some observers questioning whether analysts had political motives in writing these judgments. Again, as noted earlier, a 2015 analysis by the IAEA, based on partial Iranian responses to questions about its past activities, reported that Iran was actively designing a nuclear weapon until 2009 but that coordinated efforts to create weapons stopped after 2003, largely agreeing with the NIE.

Iraq WMD, like the Cuban Missile Crisis and a few other intelligence experiences, will probably be a touchstone for years to come in debates over intelligence analysis. (Iraq may also have an ironic and dangerous effect on other would-be proliferators. The lesson they may take away from Iraq's fate could be this: Get a nuclear weapon. Iraq, without a weapon, was overrun with impunity, whereas North Korea, which has tested nuclear weapons as well as intercontinental missiles, was able to achieve a high level of recognition and attention in the various Trump-Kim meetings in 2018 and 2019. The very fact of the meetings represented a diplomatic gain for

North Korea. Libya may offer a similar "lesson," having given up its WMD programs in 2003 and then being attacked by NATO in 2011.)

The role of intelligence in the WMD policy area is fairly obvious: Identify proliferation programs early enough to stop them before they are completed. As former DCI Tenet noted in his memoirs, for proliferation policy to be successful, intelligence must identify and discern the nature of a program before a test occurs, not record the fact of a test, as was the usual case in tracking Soviet weapons developments. Intelligence also targets the clandestine international commerce in some of the specialty items required to manufacture WMD. Again, proliferation programs are, by their very nature, covert. Thus, the types of collection that the United States must undertake tend to come from the clandestine side of the intelligence community. The evidence of nascent programs—as well as mature programs—that U.S. intelligence might obtain may be ambiguous. Fuzzy information complicates the ability of policy makers to confront potential proliferators with confidence or to convince other nations that a problem exists. As the exposure of Khan's nuclear proliferation network shows, however, doing so is not an impossible task. But it is time consuming (the effort against Khan went on for years) and sensitive diplomatically. In the case of the Khan network, the sensitivities of Pakistan had to be taken into account, first, given its logistical support for the anti-Soviet effort in Afghanistan and then its stated support for the war on terrorists. Khan's activities also confirmed the international nature of nuclear proliferation. His enterprises spanned three continents and may have been involved in more than just the Pakistan and Libyan programs. This points up another intelligence challenge: determining how vast the interconnections are between would-be proliferators and would-be providers. Although the disruption of the Khan network was a major intelligence success, parts of the program could continue to operate without Khan's guidance.

A January 2014 report by the Defense Science Board was rather pessimistic about the future of nuclear proliferation, suggesting that there would be more potential actors and states that needed to be watched and that current capabilities for verification, inspection, and monitoring (see below) are inadequate to meet future needs.

The completion of the JCPOA between Iran and the P5+1 that went into effect in October 2015 brought intelligence back to the familiar field of arms control **monitoring** and **verification**. As noted earlier (chap. 1), it is important to understand the difference between these two activities. Monitoring is an intelligence activity, keeping track of activities in foreign countries. U.S. intelligence conducts monitoring because the activities in certain countries are of importance to U.S. national security. Monitoring occurs whether or not there are arms control agreements. During the course of monitoring, activities may be observed that call into question compliance with agreements. These activities are reported to the policy community, which then makes a policy judgment on verification—that is, whether or not the activity in question is a possible violation and what should be done about it.

Although the distinction between the intelligence and policy functions in arms control seems clear, politics intrudes and tends to drag intelligence into policy debates. The first order of questioning is the adequacy of the monitoring provisions in the agreement itself. These cannot be ironclad between sovereign states and usually assume some level of cooperation, as well as some level of resistance. Assuming these provisions are adequate—a judgment that the intelligence community is asked to reach—the U.S. military and intelligence community tend to be supportive of such agreements, as they offer some transparency and predictability into weapons programs that are seen as potential threats.

The monitoring provisions of the Iranian agreement were a combination of data disclosures about past activities, monitoring, and inspections. DNI Clapper said that he was confident that this combination would "make it nearly impossible for Iran to develop a covert enrichment effort without detection." Critics of the agreement raised questions about the decision to allow Iran to collect samples from the Parchin military base, suspected of being a nuclear experimentation site, and to give these samples to the IAEA, rather than have the IAEA collect them. The collection was done, according to the IAEA, where it could be seen by surveillance devices.

Some observers also raised questions about the completeness of the data disclosures. The initial position of the P5+1 was that Iran had to be completely forthcoming about its past activities. Arms control agreements often rest on data exchanges, and this was seen, initially, as a necessary part of the negotiation. However, the United States decided that an agreement that dismantled Iran's capability for fifteen years was of greater importance and that the past activity was not entirely relevant given the completion of the agreement. Some question this approach, arguing that it goes to the issue of Iran's honesty and also its overall level of knowledge and expertise once the agreement ends in fifteen years. The December 2015 IAEA report on Iran's past activities was based on Iran's answers to about three-quarters of the questions asked.

The major critique of the JCPOA and the main reason for Trump's decision to leave the agreement had little to do with the nuclear proliferation aspects, although some commentators noted that the agreement represented a fifteen-year halt and not necessarily complete abandonment of Iran's nuclear ambitions. Critics tended to focus on the fact that the agreement did not also limit Iran's missile capabilities or its destabilizing activities in the Middle East. However, in his February 2018 *Worldwide Threat Assessment*, DNI Coats said the JCPOA "has extended the amount of time Iran would need to produce enough fissile material for a nuclear weapon from a few months to about one year, provided Iran continues to adhere to the deal's major provisions. The JCPOA has also enhanced the transparency of Iran's nuclear activities, mainly by fostering improved access to Iranian nuclear facilities. . . ." The other parties to the JCPOA have stayed with the agreement, so there will be continuing interest in whether Iran is in compliance. It is not clear if the other parties will be willing to share their intelligence on this issue with the United States now that it has left the JCPOA.

Debates over compliance with arms control agreements have tended to break down into two opposing views: (1) those who see any signs of noncompliance as indicators of bad faith and therefore want to abandon the agreement, and (2) those who will argue that the overall agreement is more important than minor transgressions. Decisions on the meaning of activity and resulting actions are political ones and are not made by intelligence agencies, but these agencies will inevitably be drawn into the political debate. In the case of the Iranian agreement, these decisions would be more complex because it is a multilateral agreement and not a bilateral one. Had the United States discovered Iranian actions that appear to be violations, it would be necessary to share sensitive intelligence with other powers—including Russia and China—in order to convince them as well. Sharing this intelligence, however, is no guarantee that other powers will agree as to a violation, as they may have diverging interests in terms of the agreement.

It should also be noted that Russian compliance with arms control agreements returned as an issue in 2014, when the United States accused Russia of violating the 1987 Intermediate-Range Nuclear Forces (INF) Treaty by testing a ground-launched cruise missile (GLCM) banned by the treaty. Russia has refused to address U.S. concerns. This issue—and any possible violations of arms control agreements— take us back to the arms control policy question first raised by Fred Ikle in 1961: "After detection—what?" In October 2018, the Trump administration announced its intention to withdraw from the INF Treaty because of Russian violations. Putin has denied this and accused the United States of violations, which reminded veteran arms control officials of a characterization of past Soviet responses to accusations of arms control violations: "No, we're not; so are you." Unable to resolve the GLCM issue through negations, the United States withdrew from INF in February 2019. Again, withdrawal does not end the core intelligence task of monitoring Russian arms activities.

Stopping Proliferation. Beyond the problem of amassing convincing intelligence lies this policy question: How can a would-be proliferator be stopped? The preferred means is diplomacy, but the track record in this area is unimpressive. To date, no nation has been talked out of developing nuclear weapons by diplomacy alone.

The United States has used its influence, and its leverage as the guarantor of a state's national security, to pressure a state into desisting from nuclear weapons development. Press accounts allege that the United States used this method with Taiwan in the 1980s. Some other nations—for reasons of their own—decided to abandon nuclear programs. Japan and Sweden chose not to develop programs. Argentina and Brazil agreed bilaterally to abandon their fledgling efforts. The white South African government gave up its nuclear weapons and its capabilities on the eve of the black majority's advent to power. Libya's admission in 2003 that it had a range of covert WMD programs that it had formerly denied was largely a result of two factors: successful HUMINT that caught shipments going to Libya and Libya's concerns about potential U.S. actions after the invasion of Iraq. The Libya case was an intelligence and policy success but not a result of diplomacy. Given the minimal success of moral suasion, some people have argued that the only workable solution is an active nonproliferation policy—intervening to destroy the capability, as both Israel and the 1991 Persian Gulf War allies did with Iraq and as Israel did with Syria. (*See box, "Iraq's Nuclear Program: A Cautionary Tale."*)

The September 2007 Israeli air strike against a presumed nuclear site in Syria underscores these concerns as well as the inherent ambiguities involved. After the raid, Syria denied that it had occurred, although subsequent commercial imagery revealed considerable Syrian efforts to clean up and mask the site by extensive bulldozing. In April 2008, the United States released its conclusion that North Korea had been assisting Syria in building a plutonium-processing plant, and not a peaceful nuclear use plant, at the site. As noted, the IAEA confirmed that it was a covert nuclear site in April 2011. There are several issues at play in this incident. First, once again there is the circumstance of unilateral military action being taken as a means of ensuring that the program will be stopped. Second, if there was North Korean assistance to Syria,

IRAQ'S NUCLEAR PROGRAM: A CAUTIONARY TALE

During the 1980s, Iraq was one of the nations whose nuclear weapons program was closely watched by U.S. experts. The existence of a program was not in question; its status was.

On the eve of the 1991 Persian Gulf War, the considered analytical judgment, according to subsequent accounts, was that Iraq was at least five years away from a nuclear capability. After Iraq's defeat in the war, analysts learned that Iraq had been much closer to success, even though Israel had attacked and destroyed some of its facilities years earlier.

What had gone wrong with U.S. estimates?

Iraq was a closed target, one of the most repressive and heavily policed states in the world. The state's nature makes collection more difficult, but that is not the answer to the question.

The answer lies in an analytical flaw, namely, mirror imaging. To manufacture the fissionable material it required, Iraq chose a method abandoned by the United States in the early days of its own nuclear program after World War II. The method works, but it is a very slow and tedious way to produce fissionable material.

For Iraq, however, it was the perfect method, not because it was slow, but because foreign analysts disregarded it. The method allowed Iraq to procure materials that were more difficult to associate with a nuclear weapons program, to mask its status. A program of this sort was also more difficult for Western analysts to spot because they largely dismissed the approach out of hand, assuming that Iraq would want—just as the United States and others had—to find the fastest way to produce fissionable material.

In the course of U.S. military action in Iraq that commenced in 2003, expected Iraq WMD programs were not found. Some observers wondered if analysts had compensated for their earlier error by overinterpreting evidence of a possible program without considering alternative interpretations. The analysts themselves denied this assessment, and none of the postwar investigations of the intelligence community's performance found overinterpretation to have been a factor.

did this indicate a possible violation of North Korea's agreement with the United States (and China, Russia, and Japan) to cease nuclear weapons activity or, at a minimum, an effort to circumvent that agreement by exporting part of its program? Third, it raises the specter of yet another clandestine nuclear relationship to be tracked. Concerns about Syria per se have likely abated given the Assad regime's preoccupation with the civil war, but the role of North Korea and the broader implications of the event remain problematic.

Pakistan's nuclear weaponry has increased concerns about the stability of the Pakistani government. Two factors are at issue: the fractious internal politics of Pakistan and the internal political effects of Pakistan's cooperation with the United States against Muslim terrorists, including the presumed presence of other al Qaeda leaders in Pakistan. According to press accounts, the United States has given Pakistan technical equipment and assistance designed to help safeguard the security of Pakistan's nuclear arsenal, although this effort has been made more difficult by Pakistan's reluctance to provide details about the nature and location of its weapons. The concern is that Muslim extremists or officials sympathetic to them will get control of a Pakistani bomb or of the fissile material. The May 2011 operation that killed bin Laden affected the Pakistan nuclear issue in two ways. First, given Pakistani claims that they did not know about bin Laden's presence in Abbottabad, it raised U.S. concerns about Pakistan's ability to detect threats and safeguard its nuclear arsenal. Second, the success of the U.S. raid raised Pakistani concerns about a future U.S. operation intended to take over some part of that nuclear arsenal. Press accounts characterize Pakistan's nuclear arsenal as "the fastest growing" today, perhaps in the range of 80–120 weapons, with the ability to have 200 or more within several years. Immediate U.S. concerns focus on the development and possible deployment of tactical nuclear weapons, which would be much smaller, much more difficult to track, and much easier to steal.

The loose nukes aspect of the issue adds a new and more difficult complication. The Soviet Union agreed with the goal of nuclear nonproliferation, recognizing that it could be a target of would-be proliferators. The prospect of tracking unknown quantities of weapons-grade material (which even Russian and other authorities have been unable to account for with accuracy) and the international movement of experts from former Soviet states is an even more difficult and more troubling issue. The collapse of the post-Soviet economy and the end of the privileged status that scientists once enjoyed were seen as incentives to would-be proliferators.

CW and BW proliferation require much less expertise and technical capability than nuclear proliferation does. CW and BW weapons are far less accurate than nuclear weapons, but the random terror they portend is part of their appeal to nations and terrorists. Such programs are more difficult than nuclear programs to identify and track. The anthrax scare in the United States in late 2001 underscores these points and also indicates how difficult it is to detect this type of attack in advance or to stop it once under way.

The use of CW in the Syrian civil war is also illustrative. The initial question was whether or not CW had been used, especially in a Damascus neighborhood in March 2013. Various states claimed that they had intelligence of the attack, but it was not until the UN inspectors reported in September 2013 that this was confirmed, although the UN report did not place blame for the attack. The Syrian government and its backer Russia continued to claim that the attacks were conducted by the rebels. However, the imminent prospect of a U.S. air attack led to a U.S.-Russian agreement on the elimination of Syria's CW arsenal, which Syria now admitted to possessing, after decades of denial.

The intelligence experience in WMD is mixed. In Iraq, the analysis did not bear out. The exposure of Khan's network points out the importance of years of determined analysis and highly successful operations to penetrate the network until enough intelligence had been established to make the case incontrovertible. The Libyan surrender also owes much to years of collection, analysis, and some highly successful operations. There was also an important benefit years later, when NATO confronted Muammar Qaddafi over his efforts to suppress a revolt, knowing that a large part of his WMD had been removed. Reactions to the 2007 Iran nuclear NIE indicate the continuing controversial nature of proliferation intelligence.

In short, intelligence can bring important assets to bear on WMD proliferation, but it will always be a shadowy area and one liable to analytic missteps. It has become increasingly difficult for the intelligence community to produce analysis on proliferation without its being received in a highly politicized manner. This is the sort of distraction that analysts are taught to rise above or to ignore, but this makes it increasingly difficult to write objectively about proliferation.

NARCOTICS

Narcotics policy is a difficult area in which to work. The main social policy goal is to prevent individuals, by a variety of means, from using drugs that the government deems addictive and harmful. Almost everyone who has ever worked on narcotics policy has said that it is a domestic issue, not a foreign policy issue. Also, given that individuals use drugs for numerous reasons, preventing their use is a difficult goal to attain. For both practical and political reasons, narcotics has become, in part, a foreign policy problem, because the United States attempts to reduce the overseas production of illegal drugs and to intercept them before or just as they arrive in the country.

The intelligence community is capable of collecting and analyzing intelligence related to the illicit trade in narcotics. The plants from which certain narcotics are derived can be grown in large quantities only in certain parts of the world. Coca is produced in the Andean region of South America. Poppies, from which heroin is made, are grown predominantly in two parts of southern Asia, centering roughly on Afghanistan and Myanmar (formerly Burma). Areas where these plants are processed into narcotics are also fairly well known, as are the routes customarily used to ship the finished products to customer areas. Drugs like methamphetamines, which can be made in small laboratories, and opioids, which are prescription drugs, present more difficult policing problems.

The real problem lies in converting this intelligence about foreign sources into successful policy. Efforts at crop eradication and substitution stumble on the simple economic choices facing local farmers. Narcotics crops pay more to growers than do food crops. Processing facilities, although U.S. intelligence can locate them, tend to be small and numerous. Drugs are so profitable that small amounts, which are easily shipped, are economically attractive. Shippers can use any number of routes, which they can change in response to pressure and efforts at interdiction. Finally, narcotics activities yield money in sufficient amounts to subvert the local authorities—civil, military, and police. This has been a persistent problem in Mexico, where competition among narcotics traffickers has also led to increasing violence across the country and just across the border from the United States. Thus, narcotics becomes an issue in the possible destabilization of the southwestern border of the United States. As noted, the

Obama administration agreed to support Mexican counternarcotics efforts with the use of UAVs over the shared border.

All experienced policy makers point to the importance of a domestic answer. If people do not have an interest in using illegal drugs, then everything else—growth, processing, shipping, and even price—becomes irrelevant. The drugs become value-less commodities. But the elusiveness of a successful domestic response leads policy makers back to foreign policy. (Legalizing drugs might not have the same effect on production and distribution as eliminating demand, because a black market might arise to compete with government-approved providers.)

The conjunction of the narcotics trade with international crime and with terror-ism adds a further dimension to the intelligence-gathering and policy-making prob-lem. The profits from sales of narcotics, instead of being an end in themselves, now become the means to fund a different end. Also, new and more difficult demands are put on intelligence, because terrorists and criminals operate clandestinely. The United States must be able to establish intelligence about networks, contacts, relationships among individuals and groups, flows of capital, and so forth. For example, guerrilla and right-wing paramilitary groups in Colombia used cocaine to finance their opera-tions. It therefore becomes necessary to draw distinctions between various narcotics producers in terms of their relative importance as an intelligence and policy priority. During the crack cocaine epidemic in the United States in the 1980s, the key areas of concern were Peru and Colombia. However, with the rise of terrorism as a priority, much greater attention was put on the opium crop in Afghanistan.

Finally, narcotics crosses the line between foreign and domestic intelligence and between intelligence and law enforcement. The point at which an issue is handed from one agency to another is not always clear but is important, raising both practical and legal questions, some of which can impede prosecution. The status of the Drug Enforcement Administration (DEA) is an interesting bellwether. Formally part of the Justice Department, the DEA has moved in and out of the intelligence community. The DEA was considered to be part of the intelligence community in the late 1970s and early 1980s but then reverted to its former position as a law enforcement agency. In 2006, however, the DEA's Office of National Security Intelligence was formally made part of the intelligence community specifically because of the link between drugs and terrorism.

ECONOMICS

Economics can be subdivided into several issues: U.S. economic competitiveness overseas, U.S. trading relations, **foreign economic espionage** and possible coun-termeasures, and the intelligence community's ability to forecast major international economic shifts that may have serious consequences for the U.S. economy.

During the late 1980s, some people maintained that several of these issues (over-seas competitiveness, trading relations, foreign economic espionage, **industrial espi-onage** undertaken by businesses, and possible countermeasures) could be addressed, in part, through a closer connection between intelligence and U.S. businesses. Few advocates of closer intelligence-business collaboration, however, had substantial answers for some of the more compelling questions that it raised (which is one reason this approach was quickly rejected):

- If the intelligence community were to share intelligence with businesses, how would they safeguard the sources and methods used in obtaining the information? If the underlying sources and methods could not be shared, would businesses accept the intelligence?

- With whom would the intelligence be shared, or, in other words, what constitutes a "U.S. company"? In an age of multinational corporations, the concept is not easy to define.

- Given that every business sector has many competitive businesses, which ones would the community provide with intelligence? What would be the basis for selecting recipients and nonrecipients of the intelligence?

- Would providing intelligence be part of an implicit quid pro quo on the part of the government—that some action should or should not be taken by industry in exchange for access to intelligence?

Foreign Economic Espionage. The collection of foreign economic intelligence by other nations was also controversial. An aggressive collection policy was central to those proposing greater intelligence support to business. Supporters of the policy cited cases in which supposed friends of the United States, such as France, were caught engaging in such activity. Advocates saw similar activity by the United States as fighting fire with fire. Critics argued that to do so would justify the initial hostile action. They also raised some of the arguments about the limits on how such information might be used. But then-DCI Gates put it best when he said that no U.S. intelligence officer was "willing to die for General Motors."

Allegations of U.S. economic espionage arose in the late 1990s concerning a government program called **ECHELON**. In simplest terms, ECHELON searches through collected SIGINT, using key words via a computer. Key-word searching allows more material to be processed and exploited. Some European officials claimed that ECHELON was being used to steal advanced technology secrets, which were then being passed to U.S. firms to enhance their competitiveness. Former DCI R. James Woolsey (1993–1995), in a stinging article in 2000, held that ECHELON was used to detect attempts by European firms to bribe foreign officials to make sales and to uncover the illicit transfer of dual-use technologies—technologies that have both commercial and WMD applications, such as supercomputers and some chemicals. Cyber intrusions have now become the major focus of concern in safeguarding competitive economic information. China has been the main center of U.S. attention, although this has been blunted somewhat by the Snowden revelations, which undercut some of the U.S. position. As noted above, presidents Obama and Xi reached "common understanding" in September 2015 not to use cyber intrusions to steal intellectual property. Press accounts suggest that Chinese economic espionage has continued and even escalated despite the agreement, leading the intelligence community to share more information with the Justice Department not only to result in indictments but also to expose Chinese activities and methods.

U.S. policy makers viewed foreign economic counterintelligence as largely noncontroversial. Most of them considered it a proper response to foreign economic intelligence, although questions were raised about the extent of the problem. Press accounts of the issue often cited the same shopworn cases, creating echo—the impression of a larger problem through repetition. But the problem may be underreported, given that many businesses do not want to admit that they have been the victims of successful foreign intelligence operations or of major cyber intrusions unless they have no choice, as in the case of the loss of customer data. Some people also argue that foreign economic counterintelligence, although necessary, treats the symptom but not the cause. They acknowledge that blunting attempts at economic intelligence collection may be important but contend that the issue should be addressed at a political level—perhaps by negotiations that offer nations the choice of cessation or countermeasures.

Legislation passed during the 105th Congress (1997–1999) extended the role of FBI counterintelligence in the business information area, which has been controversial. The legislation reflects a continuing expansion of FBI authority in the gray areas between foreign and domestic intelligence and between intelligence and law enforcement.

Much attention has been given to the use of cyber for economic espionage. The theft of economic proprietary information was noted above, in the discussion of cyber. There are also concerns about threats to the **supply chain**, meaning the organizations, people, resources, information, and activities required to move products or services from the producer to the consumer. Threatening activities include theft of goods or data and sabotage of equipment or products. Again, China is most often cited as a threat to the supply chain. In 2018, press reporting stated that China had been able to insert microchips on the servers of major firms, including Apple and Amazon, which would allow China to modify those servers covertly. Russia and Iran are also among the major, but not the only, concerns. In 2016, the National Counterintelligence and Security Center announced a classified cyber information sharing initiative to assist economic sectors where the supply chain is being targeted. In 2018, the NCSC issued a report on foreign economic espionage in cyberspace, describing and assessing the current threat.

Forecasting Major Economic Shifts. Beyond the counterintelligence aspects of economics is the day-to-day tracking of trends and events. At least four serious currency-related crises have occurred since the end of the cold war. In 1995, Mexico experienced a peso meltdown, which the intelligence community apparently handled well, giving policy makers significant advance warning. In 1998, the two-year Thai economic crisis turned into a full Asian economic debacle, encompassing Indonesia, Malaysia, the Philippines, and South Korea. Little has been said about intelligence performance in this crisis. The 2000–2001 Argentine financial collapse was long evident. The global recession that began in 2007 with the collapse of the housing bubble in the United States, which many had foreseen, then played out internationally to a depth that was largely unexpected. The ensuing crisis in the euro zone was perhaps the primary example of unforeseen consequences. The likelihood that other such crises will occur in years to come underscores the importance of economic intelligence in this area, especially given the greater interrelatedness of the global financial market.

Competition for Materials. Trends in international trade are of obvious national interest. There is a growing international competition for raw materials, primarily between China and India—which are still industrial (as opposed to postindustrial) states—but involving other nations as well. This competition includes oil, iron ore, and other minerals. The China-India rivalry is important because it affects world commodity prices and it has political ramifications. For example, China was reluctant to press Sudan's government to allow foreign peacekeepers into the Darfur region, where the Sudanese government conducted a genocidal ethnic war against local tribes, in part because Sudan is an increasingly important source of oil for China. This competition also reveals a dependency in terms of China, in particular, sustaining its economic growth, which can become useful in developing opportunity analysis.

China's predominant control of rare earth metals, estimated by some to be 95 percent, became a concern. These elements are crucial for a variety of advanced technologies, including computers and cell phones. China's manipulation of rare earth metal exports has serious industrial and trade implications, but it also must be examined as a possible insight into how China views its role internationally.

Energy. Oil and natural gas are also important economic intelligence issues for several reasons. The most obvious is their effect on the domestic economy. In addition, control of energy supplies translates into both a source of income and political power. What is interesting is the sheer volatility of this sector and its effects. Beginning with the Arab oil embargo of 1973, the general consensus was that the oil-producing states, concentrated in OPEC (Organization of Petroleum Exporting Countries), would have continuing streams of wealth and great power given Western dependency. However, OPEC proved to be a fractious bloc, with various members violating production quotas for reasons of their own. At a certain point, politics trumped energy, with Saudi Arabia making up for shortfalls caused by embargoes on Iraq or Iran. In the first decade of the twenty-first century, the high international energy prices became important factors in the reemergence of a more powerful Russia, whose economics are wholly dependent on the export of commodities (oil, gas, gold, timber) and in the less compelling power of problematic states like Venezuela and Iran—although Iran was limited by sanctions tied to its nuclear program. There is also another nexus to terrorism, as the Saudi oil fields are both a target for terrorists as a means of disrupting Western economies, one of al Qaeda's stated goals, and an economic opportunity, should al Qaeda succeed in taking over the Saudi kingdom.

However, by the second decade of the century, energy power had shifted again. New methods for extracting oil and natural gas have led to new estimates that suggest energy independence for the United States in about two decades and a worldwide glut of natural gas. After OPEC and Russia curtailed production in 2017, prices rose again but remained about one-third below their previous high. Several intelligence questions are pertinent. The first is the accuracy of any oil market prognostications. The second is the likely geopolitical effect of markedly lower prices on key players. How long can Saudi Arabia afford to produce oil below its necessary price level? How will

Putin react to a declining Russian economy? Will this make him seek foreign adventures to divert Russian public opinion? There are also the effects to be considered in other oil states, such as Venezuela, whose economy is in free fall as a result of low oil prices and destructive economic policies.

Finally, economics are always important as a possible precipitating cause of political instability. This can range from the stresses felt in the European Union to the recurring concerns in the Chinese government about its ability to hold onto power should the growing but still nascent economy stall or experience a recession.

Financial Intelligence. An increasingly important part of economic intelligence is financial intelligence (sometimes called **FININT**)—in simplest terms, following money flows, especially those related to illicit or illegal activities. Today, it is no longer necessary (or practical) to move large sums of money physically. Most major transactions, either domestic or international, take place electronically, over the World Wide Web. Therefore, financial intelligence quickly shades into cyber intelligence as well.

Several activities are of interest in financial intelligence. Some are rather obvious, such as terrorism and narcotics trafficking. Others include proliferation; international sanctions regimes; and corrupt practices, such as bribery or money laundering. As noted above, the SWIFT system tracks movements of money in the international banking system. But now there is the advent of "crypto-currencies," such as Bitcoin and others, a peer-to-peer payment system that relies on a block chain, a continuously updated database that acts as a ledger for all transactions. Bitcoin and other similar products have been variously characterized as a financial service or a virtual currency, according to the U.S. Treasury. The value of Bitcoins has been highly volatile. Because there is no banking intermediary, Bitcoin and other crypto-currencies have an obvious appeal for illegal transactions or even for licit transactions involving large sums that might attract unwanted attention.

There is also a law enforcement aspect to financial intelligence, providing information used to ensure the enforcement of various banking and securities laws.

In terms of collection, financial intelligence will be primarily SIGINT or HUMINT and some OSINT as well. The analytic burden falls primarily on the Treasury Department, which has had an Office of Intelligence and Analysis (OIA) since 2004. (There had been an Office of National Security at Treasury since 1961.) OIA is part of the intelligence community and focuses on the financial aspects of the various issues noted above. There are several other offices at Treasury dealing with aspects of financial intelligence, and they all (including OIA) come under an under secretary for terrorism and financial intelligence.

DEMOGRAPHICS

Demographics, the characteristics of population in terms of age and sex distribution, is not usually thought of as an intelligence issue, but may become one over the next several years. The often used, and often disagreed with, characterization is that "demographics are destiny."

The issue for the intelligence community is how certain demographic trends will affect the stability and behavior of various states or regions. There are two major concerns, both of which focus on divergences from the normal distribution of age groups within a population. Simply put, there should be fewer old people and more young people because of birth rates, death rates, and life expectancy. The numbers should be in some rough proportion, often ideally portrayed as a pyramid, with the younger groups at the bottom and the older at the top. A key part of the pyramid is the middle band, those people who can work to support the young and the old.

However, there are a number of nations where the ratios are skewed. In Africa, South Asia, and the Middle East there is a "youth bulge," that is, a disproportionately young population, leading to fewer opportunities for employment, let alone advancement. Some, but not all, analysts believe that youth bulges lead to instability because of a view, especially among males, that they have no opportunities, making them more susceptible to involvement with narcotics or to disaffected behaviors like terrorism.

In several developed nations, there is the opposite problem, a rapidly aging population in which there are low death rates but also low birth rates. This creates a different economic problem, as the working population needed to support the elderly shrinks while the elderly grow. This is of particular concern in Japan. Japan's population is expected to decline from 127 million in 2010 to 90 million in 2055, some 41 percent of whom will be over sixty-five. Russia will experience a similar decline, with roughly similar numbers. Russia's population is shrinking by about 750,000 people annually as deaths exceed births. Alarmingly, for Russian leaders, the Muslim part of the Russian population has very high birth rates. Italy and Germany are also experiencing population declines, albeit less severe, which is why some people in Europe saw the refugee flow from the Middle East as a positive thing. Finally, by 2040, China will begin to feel the effects of the one-child-per-family policy, instituted in 1979 and abandoned in 2015, as its population also shows signs of decline and aging with too few workers to support them. Despite the end of the one-child policy, there are early indications that many couples will continue to adhere to it because of the economic costs of raising more children. China also faces a severe male-female imbalance in many regions, as males are most often the preferred offspring for Chinese couples if they are limited to only one child. This sex imbalance may have destabilizing political results.

Interestingly, demographers argue that programs urging couples to have more children, as seen in China, or incentivizing them via economic benefits, as seen in Russia, tend not to have much effect on the birth rate, while greater gender equality does appear to improve the number of births.

Other than through pandemic or war, the world has never experienced this sort of demographic shift. Although there is little need for sensitive intelligence collection on this issue, there is a need to begin to explore the possible political and economic ramifications.

HEALTH AND THE ENVIRONMENT

Health and environmental issues are relatively new to the intelligence agenda. They have sometimes been treated as one issue but are now more often treated separately.

The health issue gained increasing prominence because of the AIDS (acquired immune deficiency syndrome) pandemic and smaller outbreaks of deadly diseases, such as the Ebola virus and SARS (severe acute respiratory syndrome) in East Asia and the Zika virus in the Western hemisphere. The intelligence task with respect to health is largely one of tracking patterns of infection, but a large gap exists between intelligence and policy. Take AIDS as an example. The causes, means of infection, and results of AIDS are well known. Although the disease strikes people worldwide, some areas, notably eastern and central Africa, have extremely high concentrations of AIDS cases. The intelligence community's ability to track rates of infection and mortality has little effect on any useful international policy. Many of the African governments that face the highest rates of AIDS infection have chosen, for a variety of reasons, to ignore or even to deny their health crisis. The same had been true of the government of China, although it now admits the seriousness of the AIDS problem. In the case of Africa, local culture is a major factor in the spread of AIDS: toleration of polygamous relationships and low literacy rates, thus making even minimal efforts at education about prevention more difficult, and minimal use of prophylactics. Nor is it clear what these nations or the international community should be doing in the absence of any cure for the disease. Outsiders' attempts to change the cultural factors that facilitate the spread of AIDS not only would be difficult to make but also would probably be resisted as interference.

A major issue surrounding health-related crises is tracking official foreign government statements against other intelligence to determine both the extent of the health problem and the openness of the government involved. This has been a point of contention with China over SARS. For the United States, two issues are involved. One is the duty to warn, as in terrorism, that is, to alert U.S. citizens and others about potential health risks overseas. The other is an insight into the behavior of another government. Tracking an issue of this sort is a combination of clandestine intelligence (such as SIGINT between foreign officials) and open sources (such as reports by travelers, hospital admissions, larger than normal requests for drugs, and so on).

Again, there is a nexus to terrorism. Outbreaks of certain diseases (such as anthrax, smallpox) must be studied to determine if they are natural occurrences or terrorist attacks. Even if it can be proved that an attack is **bioterror**, determining the point of origin can prove to be extremely difficult, as was the case with the anthrax mail attacks in the United States in 2001. In such instances, there will also be tremendous political pressure (governmental and public) to provide an answer as quickly as possible.

Health issue concerns now encompass aspects of advanced biological research such as the genome project and gene splicing and editing, which could lead to new organisms that might prove to be dangerous to human health, either inherently or if misused.

The environment issue is also somewhat amorphous. The basic goal—preserving a healthier global ecology—stumbles when it comes down to practicalities. As has been the case with international efforts to deal with AIDS, the nations at the center of the issue have different interests and preferences. The international community may believe that it has a vested interest in the preservation of some local ecological habitat, such as a rain forest. However, the nation whose land it is may be more interested in its own economic development than in the stewardship of a world ecological resource.

The basic intelligence tasks are identifying major threats to the environment, identifying states whose policies may be harmful to the environment, and tracking major changes in the environment. Again, a gap separates intelligence from what policy makers are supposed to do with it. Substantial intelligence community involvement in environmental policy dates back only to the late stages of the cold war. A longer-range intelligence concern that has begun to receive more attention is the possible economic and political consequences of global climate change, including droughts, flooding, more violent weather, resulting shifts of population, and the potential for either political or military intervention.

Unfortunately, climate change has become a political issue in the United States. In September 2016, President Obama issued a memorandum ordering most of the departments and several other agencies to form a Climate and National Security Working Group to address the national security implications of climate change. The intelligence community released a study, *Implications for U.S. National Security of Anticipated Climate Change*, at the same time. Observers noted that President Trump's 2017 national security strategy did not list climate change as a national security threat. However, DNI Coats, in his 2018 and 2019 *Worldwide Threat Assessments*, highlighted the security implications of climate change, again taking a position at variance with the Trump administration. In November 2018, the U.S. government released its fourth National Climate Assessment, highlighting a series of environmental and economic risks if climate change issues are not addressed.

If nations enter into treaties to limit certain emissions, such as greenhouse gases, then the intelligence community may be asked to assist in monitoring compliance with these treaties. This will be more complex and likely more ambiguous than monitoring compliance with arms control treaties.

Much of the intelligence about health and environmental issues can be carried out by means of open sources. Commercial infrared satellites can track environmental changes. The spread of disease also can be tracked overtly. Intelligence on these issues has tended to suffer from the inattention of policy makers and from the fact that overt means of collecting intelligence have been less fully developed than the clandestine means. The fact that much intelligence for health and environmental issues can be drawn from OSINT tends also to make these less compelling issues for intelligence officers, who revert to their professional ethos that their job is to steal secrets. There is debate about the degree to which the intelligence community should devote resources to the climate issue. In 2011, the Defense Science Board—an expert advisory group—recommended that the DNI establish a group to study the economic and political effects of climate change. But a year later, the CIA closed its Center on Climate Change and National Security, which had been created in 2009. The CIA also had a program called MEDEA (Measurements of Earth Data for Environmental Analysis), which allowed the sharing of sensitive environmental data with scientists. MEDEA began in the 1990s but was curtailed early in the George W. Bush administration (2001–2009). DCIA Leon Panetta (2009–2011) revived MEDEA in 2010, but it was closed again in 2015 as a result of opposition in Congress, where some members do not see environmental issues as an area on which the intelligence community should be focusing. At the same time, the Defense Department issued a *2014 Climate Change Adaptation Roadmap*, to begin planning for operations in a changing environment. During the Ebola epidemic in West Africa, the National Geospatial-Intelligence Agency (NGA) created a publicly accessible website showing where the outbreaks were, transportation networks, and so on, to help governments and nongovernmental organizations put their efforts where they were most needed.

Access to water is an important issue in its own right and in relationship to global climate change. The issue is driven, in part, by the growth in global population, which puts increasing demands on all water sources, both surface and aquifers. Building dams, to control flooding and to create reservoirs, has political and environmental consequences. For example, China's population and its continued economic growth is outpacing available water resources; and water, unlike oil or minerals, cannot be shipped in sufficient quantities to make any appreciable difference. The growing need for water worldwide has serious policy implications and is an area in which more intelligence analysis may be required over the next few years. In February 2012, the intelligence community released an assessment on global water security, drafted at the request of then–secretary of state Hillary Clinton. Looking out ten years, the assessment concluded that water problems would "contribute to instability in states important to the U.S." but that "a water-related state-on-state conflict is unlikely."

In a related area, in September 2015, the intelligence community released an assessment on global food security, an issue mentioned in DNI Clapper's 2015 *Worldwide Threat Assessment*. Concerns were raised about the adequacy of future food supplies in regions deemed to be important to U.S. national security, including the Middle East, South Asia, and Latin America.

PEACEKEEPING OPERATIONS

Since the end of the cold war, international peacekeeping operations have expanded dramatically. Regional outbursts of violence, most of them within the borders of one country (or former country), have required the imposition of external troops to restore and then maintain peace. Peacekeeping operations are a direct reflection of the failed-states issue discussed in chapter 11. The external troops have customarily been formed into multinational units. Although many of these nations have experience in allied operations—at least training operations—the participants tend to cross the boundaries of old alliances. UN-mandated forces in Bosnia, for example, included NATO allies (Britain, France, Italy, Spain, and the United States) and their former Warsaw Pact foes (Russia, Ukraine), along with other nations. A similar array has been formed in Afghanistan. Successful military operations require strong intelligence support; multinational operations require intelligence sharing. But even in the aftermath of the cold war, some U.S. policy makers and intelligence officials have been reluctant to share intelligence with former foes, nonallies, and even some allies. Responsible civil and military officials may find themselves torn between the need to keep peacekeeping partners well informed to carry out successful operations and the recognition that sources and methods may be compromised even beyond the limited peacekeeping theater of operations.

The use of peacekeeping or other internationally sanctioned operations for unilateral intelligence purposes became an issue in 1999. A former member of the UN Special

Commission (UNSCOM)—which was responsible for monitoring Iraqi destruction of its WMD—alleged that the United States used a UNSCOM inspection team to plant intelligence collection devices. Some observers saw the U.S. action as a necessary precaution against a hostile state; others believed it violated the basis of the UNSCOM mission.

SUPPORT TO THE MILITARY

Supporting military forces engaged in combat operations, sometimes called support to military operations (SMO), is one of the highest intelligence demands. A key aspect of SMO is the concept of **dominant battlefield awareness (DBA)**. At the National Defense University in June 1995, then-DCI John M. Deutch (1995–1997) defined DBA as the integration of imagery intelligence (IMINT), SIGINT, and HUMINT to give "commanders real-time, or near real-time, all-weather, comprehensive, continuous surveillance and information about the battlespace in which they operate. . . . Dominant battlefield awareness, if achieved, will reduce—never totally eliminate—the 'fog of war,' and provide you, the military commanders, with an unprecedented combat advantage." DBA refers to the totality of information that is available to all commanders at all levels. It is not a single type of report or activity. DBA is closely tied to the **revolution in military affairs (RMA)**. RMA is an ongoing broad doctrinal evolution and debate about the likely nature of future warfare, encompassing technology, strategy, tactics, and the use of intelligence.

DBA reflects at least two trends. The first is the great strides that U.S. intelligence has made in collecting and disseminating intelligence to military commanders in the field. Commanders believe that this superiority allows them to use forces more effectively so as to achieve ends more quickly and with fewer casualties. The second is the so-called lessons learned from the first Gulf War about the problems in bringing intelligence to the field and getting the right intelligence to the right military user.

Although Deutch cautioned that the "fog of war" (a term coined by nineteenth-century Prussian general and military theorist Karl von Clausewitz for the confusion and uncertainty that are inevitable in any combat) will never be eliminated, many advocates of DBA seem not to have heard him. DBA is often oversold as the ability to bring near-total intelligence to commanders. This hyperbole puts intelligence on the spot for capabilities it does not have. Unrealistically high expectations may lead commanders to place greater reliance on intelligence (which may not be forthcoming) and less on their own instincts when dealing with the fog of war, which is the ultimate skill of a combat commander. (Gen. William T. Sherman observed that Gen. Ulysses S. Grant was the superior commander because he was unconcerned about what the enemy was doing when out of sight.)

DOD official statements on the topic are somewhat confusing. The two key documents are *Joint Vision 2010* and *Joint Vision 2020*. Both emphasize the importance of DBA and the role of intelligence but tend to use "intelligence" and "information technology" interchangeably. However, information technology is a means to, but is not the same thing as, intelligence.

Another problem with DBA is that delivering on its promise could require the intelligence community to allocate a large percentage of collection assets to the task, to the detriment of other priorities elsewhere in the world. As with SMO, the question "How much is enough?" is pertinent. Finally, an essential ingredient in successful DBA is getting the right type and amount of information to the right user. An army commander's intelligence needs differ from those of an infantry squad leader or a combat pilot. Some critics are concerned that too much information is pushed down to users who have no need for it, flooding them with irrelevant intelligence simply because the means are available to do so. As a result, their jobs are made more difficult.

The military campaign in Iraq that began in 2003 illustrated both the promise and the problems involved in DBA and RMA. The vastly superior strategic and tactical intelligence of the United States and its allied forces enhanced both the general campaign plan—including the decision to make a dash for Baghdad with a fairly small number of forces—and the ability to locate, identify, and attack in detail regular Iraqi forces. But the war also pointed out that the evolution of U.S. military doctrine continues to put pressure on intelligence for increasing degrees of support. Given the likelihood that the size of U.S. forces (as opposed to their mobility and lethality) will decrease under budget pressure, intelligence will increasingly be seen as one of the factors that allows these relatively small forces to achieve both dominance and victory. How much support is entailed and what it means for the shape and practice of intelligence are not entirely clear. Also, it remains uncertain how the DNI fits into the relationship between intelligence agencies—especially those such as NGA and NSA, which are national but are also designated in law as combat support agencies—and DOD. The situation is especially murky because the DNI does not control any of the agencies upon which the military relies for intelligence support. The DNI could be bypassed by DOD as it seeks intelligence support from national and defense agencies.

The strike against bin Laden, by contrast, showed how intelligence and the military could produce a nearly flawless outcome in a very well-defined operation of high risk but limited scope.

Intelligence is a key component of the Defense Department's "Third Offset Strategy," which refers to the use of technology to compensate for potential adversaries' advantages. Intelligence is responsible for monitoring the current and future capabilities of potential adversaries. However, some of the areas of concern include aspects of artificial intelligence, machine learning, and the uses of big data, which will be more difficult to discern and to determine levels of proficiency as these do not necessarily have to be tested in the overt way that conventional weapons do.

A major issue for intelligence support to military operations is the nature of the likely engagement. The United States is less likely to be involved in a major nation-state conflict than it is in unconventional conflicts such as counterinsurgency (COIN). As noted above, the intelligence requirements of these types of conflicts are more difficult as the enemy forces are smaller, more covert targets.

CONCLUSION

In the first decade after the end of the cold war (using as a benchmark the breaching of the Berlin Wall in 1989), the U.S. national security agenda remained largely unformed, not in terms of which issues mattered but which of them mattered the most, which would receive the highest priority over time (as opposed to immediate reactions to events), and what the United States would be willing to do to achieve its preferred ends. In the absence of clear definition, the intelligence community found it difficult to perform. Intelligence officials have a broad understanding of policy makers' preferences and immediate interests, but these do not provide the basis for making a coherent set of plans for investments, collection systems, personnel recruitment, and training. The war on terrorists offered some clarity in that it has given one issue priority over all the others, although not to the same extent as the old Soviet issue. Moreover, the terrorism issue is different from the Soviet issue in many important respects, thus emphasizing the importance of the cold war legacy for the intelligence community, as well as the need to transcend this legacy. As noted, after more than a decade, President Obama signaled a change in the relative emphasis on the terrorism issue.

Many issues in the new U.S. intelligence agenda share an important hallmark: the gap between the intelligence community's ability to provide intelligence and the policy makers' ability to craft policies to address the issues and to use the intelligence. This gap may even be seen in the war against terrorists. If the disparity persists, the intelligence community and its policy clients may become disaffected. Clients want to be more than just informed; they want to act (that is, to receive opportunity analysis). And intelligence is not meant to be collected and then filed away. It is intended to assist people in making decisions or taking action. This is not to suggest that the intelligence community will suddenly disappear. But it may come to be seen as less central and necessary—a provider of information that is interesting but not as useful as it has been in the past because of the changed nature of the issues and the rapidity with which overall policy emphasis shifts—shifts that are difficult for intelligence to match, especially at the analytical level.

KEY TERMS

artificial intelligence (AI) 357
attribution 353
backdoor encryption 348
battle damage assessment (BDA) 351
bioterror 384
chatter 359
computer network attack (CNA) 351
computer network exploitation
    (CNE) 351
cyber operational preparation of the
    environment (cyber OPE) 351
dominant battlefield awareness
    (DBA) 387
ECHELON 379

financial intelligence (FININT) 382
foreign economic espionage 378
industrial espionage 378
information operations 346
Internet of things (IOT) 346
Joint Terrorism Task Forces
    (JTTFs) 365
link analysis 362
machine learning 357
monitoring 372
revolution in military affairs (RMA) 387
supply chain 380
verification 372
zero-day vulnerabilities 357

FURTHER READINGS

Writings on the post–cold war intelligence agenda remain somewhat scattered across issue areas, reflecting the nature of the debate itself.

General

Colby, William. "The Changing Role of Intelligence." *World Outlook* 13 (summer 1991): 77–90.

Goodman, Allan E. "The Future of U.S. Intelligence." *Intelligence and National Security* 11 (October 1996): 645–656.

Goodman, Allan E., and Bruce D. Berkowitz. *The Need to Know: Report of the Twentieth Century Fund Task Force on Covert Action and American Democracy*. New York: Twentieth Century Fund, 1992.

Goodman, Allan E., Gregory F. Treverton, and Philip Zelikow. *In From the Cold: Report of the Twentieth Century Fund Task Force on the Future of U.S. Intelligence*. New York: Twentieth Century Fund, 1996.

Johnson, Loch K. *Bombs, Bugs, Drugs, and Thugs: Intelligence and America's Quest for Security*. New York: New York University Press, 2000.

Johnson, Loch K., and Kevin J. Scheid. "Spending for Spies: Intelligence Budgeting in the Aftermath of the Cold War." *Public Budgeting and Finance* 17 (winter 1997): 7–27.

U.S. Director of National Intelligence. *Worldwide Threat Assessment of the U.S. Intelligence Community*. Washington, DC, January19, 2019. (Available at https://www.dni.gov/files/ODNI/documents/2019-ATA-SFR---SSCI.pdf)

U.S. National Intelligence Council. *Global Trends 2030: Alternative Worlds*. Washington, D.C.: National Intelligence Council, 2012.

Cyberspace

Aldrich, Richard W. *The International Legal Implications of Information Warfare*. Colorado Springs, Colo.: U.S. Air Force Institute for National Security Studies, 1996.

Chang, Amy. *Warring State: China's Cybersecurity Strategy*. Washington, D.C.: Center for a New American Strategy, 2014. (Available at http://www.cnas.org/chinas-cybersecurity-strategy#.VkPNbL8nqNI.)

Cheng, Dean. *Cyber Dragon: Inside China's Information Warfare and Cyber Operations*. Santa Barbara, CA: Praeger Publishers, 2016.

Healey, Jason, ed. *A Fierce Domain: Conflict in Cyberspace, 1986–2012*. Washington, D.C.: The Atlantic Council and the Cyber Conflict Studies Association, 2013.

———. "A Short History of Cyber Conflict in the United States." Washington, D.C.: Cyber Conflict Studies Association, September 13, 2010.

Intelligence and National Security Alliance. *A Framework for Cyber Indications and Warning*. Arlington, Va., October 2018. (Available at https://www.insaonline.org/wp-content/uploads/2018/10/INSA-Framework-For-Cyber-Indications-and-Warning.pdf.)

_____. *Cyber Intelligence: Preparing Today's Talent for Tomorrow's Threats*. Arlington, Va., September 2015. (Available at http://www.insaonline.org/i/d/a/b/CyberIntel_PrepTalent.aspx.)

————. *Operational Cyber Intelligence*. Arlington, Va., October 2014. (Available at http://www.insaonline.org/i/d/a/b/OCI_whitepaper.aspx.)

————. *Strategic Cyber Intelligence*. Arlington, Va., March 2014. (Available at http://www.insaonline.org/i/d/a/b/StrategicCyberWP.aspx.)

Kerr, Paul K., John Rollins, and Catherine A. Theohary. *The Stuxnet Computer Worm: Harbinger of an Emerging Warfare Capability*. CRS Report R41524. Washington, D.C.: Congressional Research Service, December 9, 2010.

Lindsay, Jon R., Tai Ming Cheung, and Derek S. Reveron. *China and Cybersecurity: Espionage, Strategy, and Politics in the Digital Age*. New York: Oxford University Press, 2015.

Mandiant. *APT1: Exposing One of China's Cyber Espionage Units*. 2013. (Available at http://intelreport.mandiant.com/Mandiant_APT1_Report.pdf.)

Robertson, Jordan, and Michael Riley. "The Big Hack: How China Used a Tiny Chip to Infiltrate U.S. Companies." *Bloomberg Business*, October 4, 2018. (Available at https://www.bloomberg.com/news/features/2018-10-04/the-big-hack-how-china-used-a-tiny-chip-to-infiltrate-america-s-top-companies.)

Schmitt, Michael N., general ed. *Tallinn Manual on International Law Applicable to Cyber Warfare*. Cambridge, U.K.: Cambridge University Press, 2013. (Available at http://www.nowandfutures.com/large/Tallinn-Manual-on-the-International-Law-Applicable-to-Cyber-Warfare-Draft-.pdf.)

Stokes, Mark A., and L. C. Russell Hsiao. *Countering Chinese Cyber Operations: Opportunities and Challenges for U.S. Interests*. Arlington, Va: Project 2049 Institute, October 29, 2012. (Available at http://www2.gwu.edu/~nsarchiv/NSAEBB/NSAEBB424/docs/Cyber-079.pdf.)

U.S. Computer Readiness Team (US-CERT). *GRIZZLY STEPPE: Russian Malicious Cyber Activity*. (Available at https://www.us-cert.gov/GRIZZLY-STEPPE-Russian-Malicious-Cyber-Activity.)

U.S. Department of Defense. *Department of Defense Strategy for Operating in Cyberspace*. Washington, D.C.: DOD, July 2011. (Available at www.defense.gov/news/d20110714cyber.pdf.)

U.S. Office of the Director of National Intelligence. *Background to "Assessing Russian Activities and Intentions in Recent US Elections": The Analytic Process and Cyber Incident Attribution*. Washington, D.C.: ODNI, January 6, 2017. (Available at https://www.dni.gov/files/documents/ICA_2017_01.pdf.)

————. Statement for the Record. *Worldwide Cyber Threats. House Permanent Select Committee on Intelligence*. Washington, D.C.: ODNI, September 10, 2015. (Available at http://www.dni.gov/files/documents/HPSCI%2010%20Sept%20Cyber%20Hearing%20SFR.pdf.)

Dominant Battlefield Awareness

Nolte, William. "Keeping Pace With the Revolution in Military Affairs." *Studies in Intelligence* 48 (2004): 1–10.

Economics

Fort, Randall M. *Economic Espionage: Problems and Prospects*. Washington, D.C.: Consortium for the Study of Intelligence, 1993.

Hulnick, Arthur S. "The Uneasy Relationship Between Intelligence and Private Industry." *International Journal of Intelligence and Counterintelligence* 9 (spring 1996): 17–31.

Lowenthal, Mark M. "Keep James Bond out of GM." *International Economy* (July–August 1992): 52–54.

U.S. National Counterintelligence Executive. *Annual Report to Congress on Foreign Economic Collection and Industrial Espionage, 2008*. Washington, D.C., July 23, 2009.

U.S. National Counterintelligence and Security Center. *Foreign Economic Espionage in Cyberspace*. Washington, DC, July 24, 2018. (Available at https://www.dni.gov/files/NCSC/documents/news/20180724-economic-espionage-pub.pdf)

Woolsey, R. James. "Why We Spy on Our Allies." *Wall Street Journal*, March 17, 2000, A18.

Zarate, Juan C. *Treasury's War: The Unleashing of a New Era of Financial Warfare*. New York: PublicAffairs Books, 2013.

Zelikow, Philip. "American Economic Intelligence: Past Practice and Future Principles." *Intelligence and National Security* 12 (January 1997): 164–177.

Health and Environment

CNA Corporation. "National Security and the Threat of Climate Change." Alexandria, Va., 2007.

U.S. Department of Defense. *2014 Climate Change Adaptation Roadmap*. Washington, D.C.: DOD, June 2014. (Available at http://www.acq.osd.mil/ie/download/CCARprint_wForeword_c.pdf.)

U.S. Global Change Research Program. *Fourth National Climate Assessment*. Washington, D.C., November 2018. (Available at https://nca2018.globalchange.gov/downloads/NCA4_Report-in-Brief.pdf.)

U.S. Office of the Director of National Intelligence. *Global Food Security*. Intelligence Community Assessment 2015-04. Washington, D.C.: ODNI, September 22, 2015. (Available at http://www.dni.gov/files/documents/Newsroom/Reports%20and%20Pubs/Global_Food_Security_ICA.pdf.)

———. *Global Water Security*. Intelligence Community Assessment 2012-08. Washington, D.C.: ODNI, February 2, 2012. (Available at http://www.dni.gov/files/documents/Newsroom/Press%20Releases/ICA_Global%20Water%20Security.pdf.)

U.S. National Intelligence Council. *Implications for US National Security of Anticipated Climate Change*. NIC WP 2016-01. Washington, D.C.: NIC, September 21, 2018. (Available at https://www.dni.gov/files/documents/Newsroom/Reports%20and%20Pubs/Implications_for_US_National_Security_of_Anticipated_Climate_Change.pdf.)

Law Enforcement

Hulnick, Arthur S. "Intelligence and Law Enforcement." *International Journal of Intelligence and Counterintelligence* 10 (fall 1997): 269–286.

Snider, L. Britt, with Elizabeth Rindskopf and John Coleman. *Relating Intelligence and Law Enforcement: Problems and Prospects*. Washington, D.C.: Consortium for the Study of Intelligence, 1994.

Narcotics

Best, Richard A., Jr., and Mark M. Lowenthal. *The U.S. Intelligence Community and the Counternarcotics Effort*. Washington, D.C.: Congressional Research Service, 1992.

Peacekeeping

Best, Richard A., Jr. *Peacekeeping: Intelligence Requirements.* CRS Report 92–74F. Washington, D.C.: Congressional Research Service, 1994.

Johnston, Paul. "No Cloak and Dagger Required: Intelligence Support to UN Peacekeeping." *Intelligence and National Security* 12 (October 1997): 102–112.

Pickert, Perry L. *Intelligence for Multilateral Decision and Action.* Ed. Russell G. Swenson. Washington, D.C.: Joint Military Intelligence College, 1997.

Proliferation

Hansen, Keith A. *Intelligence and Nuclear Proliferation: Lesson Learned.* Paris, France: Institut Francais des Relations Internationales (IFRI), Summer 2011. (Available at http://www.ifri.org/downloads/pp38hansen.pdf.)

Ikle, Fred Charles. "After Detection—What?" *Foreign Affairs* 39 (January 1961): 208–220.

International Atomic Energy Agency. *Final Assessment on Past and Present Outstanding Issues Regarding Iran's Nuclear Programme.* GOV/2015/68. Vienna, Austria: IAEA, December 2, 2015. (Available at http://isis-online.org/uploads/isis-reports/documents/IAEA_PMD_Assessment_2Dec2015.pdf.)

Kerr, Paul K. *Iran's Nuclear Program: Tehran's Compliance With International Obligations.* CRS Report R40094. Washington, D.C.: Congressional Research Service, September 18, 2012.

Nikitin, Mary Beth. *North Korea's Nuclear Weapons: Technical Issues.* CRS Report RL34256. Washington, D.C.: Congressional Research Service, April 3, 2013.

U.S. Department of Defense, Defense Science Board. *Task Force Report: Assessment of Nuclear Monitoring and Verification Technologies.* Washington. D.C.: DOD, January 2014. (Available at http://www.acq.osd.mil/dsb/reports/NuclearMonitoringAndVerificationTechnologies.pdf.)

U.S. National Intelligence Council. *National Intelligence Estimate: Iran: Nuclear Intentions and Capabilities.* Washington, D.C.: NIC, December 2007. (Available at http://www.dni.gov/files/documents/Newsroom/Reports%20and%20Pubs/20071203_release.pdf.)

Support to the Military

Deutch, John M. Speech at National Defense University, Washington, D.C., June 14, 1995. (Available at http://www.defense.gov/speeches/speech.aspx?speechid=922.)

Terrorism

Best, Richard A., Jr. *The National Counterterrorism Center (NCTC)—Responsibilities and Potential Congressional Concerns.* CRS Report R41022. Washington, D.C.: Congressional Research Service, January 15, 2010.

Byman, Daniel. "The Intelligence War on Terrorism." *Intelligence and National Security* 29 (December 2014): 837–863.

Cilluffo, Frank J., Ronald A. Marks, and George C. Salmoiraghi. "The Use and Limits of U.S. Intelligence." *Washington Quarterly* 25 (winter 2002): 61–74.

Grimmett, Richard F. *Terrorism: Key Recommendations of the 9/11 Commission and Recent Major Commissions and Inquiries.* CRS Report RL32519. Washington, D.C.: Congressional Research Service, August 11, 2004.

Jameson, W. George. "Intelligence and the Law: Introduction to the Legal and Policy Framework Governing Intelligence Community Counterterrorism Efforts." In *The Law of Counterterrorism*. Ed. Lynne K. Zusman. Washington, D.C.: American Bar Association, September 2011.

Marks, Ronald A. *Spying in America in the Post 9/11 World*. Santa Barbara, CA: Praeger, 2010.

Masse, Todd, and John Rollins. *A Summary of Fusion Centers: Core Issues and Options for Congress*. CRS Report RL34177. Washington, D.C.: Congressional Research Service, September 19, 2007.

Randol, Mark A. *Homeland Security Intelligence: Perceptions, Statutory Definitions, and Approaches*. CRS Report RL33616. Washington, D.C.: Congressional Research Service, January 14, 2009.

————. *The Department of Homeland Security Intelligence Enterprise: Operational Overview and Oversight Challenges for Congress*. CRS Report R40602. Washington, D.C.: Congressional Research Service, March 19, 2010.

Steiner, James E. "Needed: State-level, Integrated Intelligence Enterprises." *Studies in Intelligence* 53 (September 2009): 1–10.

————. *Homeland Security Intelligence*. Thousand Oaks, CA: CQ Press, 2015.

Treverton, Gregory F. *Intelligence in an Age of Terror*. New York: Cambridge University Press, 2009.

Treverton, Gregory F., et al. *State and Local Intelligence in the War on Terrorism*. Washington, D.C.: RAND Corporation, 2005.

U.S. Department of Homeland Security, Office of the Inspector General. *Major Management and Performance Challenges Facing the Department of Homeland Security*. Report OIG-16-07. Washington, D.C.: DHS, November 13, 2015. (Available at https://www.oig.dhs.gov/assets/Mgmt/2016/OIG-16-07-Nov15.pdf.)

U.S. Office of the Director of National Intelligence. *Domestic Approach to National Intelligence*. Washington, D.C.: ODNI, January 19, 2017. (Available at https://www.dni.gov/index.php/newsroom/reports-publications/reports-publications-2017/item/1739-domestic-approach-to-national-intelligence.)

CHAPTER THIRTEEN

ETHICAL AND MORAL ISSUES IN INTELLIGENCE

The phrase "ethical and moral issues in intelligence" is not as much of an oxymoron as some people consider it. Important ethical standards and moral dilemmas challenge intelligence officers and policy officials and must be dealt with. As with most discussions of ethics and morality, some of the questions have no firm or agreed-upon answers.

GENERAL MORAL QUESTIONS

The nature of intelligence operations and issues and the basis upon which they are created raise a number of broad moral questions.

Secrecy. Much intelligence work is done in secret, although the definition of intelligence set out in chapter 1 does not include secrecy as a necessary precondition. The question remains: Is secrecy necessary in intelligence? If so, how much secrecy? And at what cost?

If secrecy is necessary, what drives the need? Governments have intelligence services because they seek information that others would deny them. Thus, secrecy is inherent not only in what your intelligence service is doing (collection, analysis, and covert action) but also in the information that others withhold from you. You also do not want the other state to know your areas of interest. Is this second level of secrecy necessary? After all, those keeping information from you often know—or at least presume—that you want it. That is one reason for hiding it from you (although many authoritarian states attempt to control *all* information, understanding that it poses a threat to their regime). Or is secrecy driven primarily by your attempts to gain access to hidden information? Is it based on not allowing those who are attempting to deny you information to know the degree to which they have succeeded or failed? How necessary is that? After all, you will act on the intelligence collected, although you will attempt to mask the reasons for your actions. Won't your opponents at least guess, based on your decisions and actions, that you have gained some access to the information they were safeguarding?

Beyond the motivations for secrecy are the costs it imposes. This does not refer to the monetary costs—for background checks, control systems for access, and so forth—which are substantial. The issue is how operating in a secret milieu affects people. Does secrecy inherently lead to a temptation or willingness to cut corners or take steps that might be deemed unacceptable if they were not cloaked in secrecy? This is not to suggest that thousands of people are morally compromised because they work in organizations that prize secrecy. Many businesses operate on and safeguard proprietary information. But the nature of some aspects of intelligence—primarily collection and covert action—combined with the fact that they are undertaken in secret, might conceivably lower an intelligence official's inhibitions to commit questionable actions. These factors put a premium on the careful selection and training of officers and on vigorous oversight.

The other cost of secrecy in intelligence, at least for democracies, is the limit secrecy imposes in building public support for intelligence. As David Omand and Mark Phythian (see Further Readings) point out, "Democratic legitimacy is required for the safe conduct of secret intelligence." The U.S. intelligence community has recognized this in its relatively recent (2015) emphasis on transparency. The first of the director of national intelligence's (DNI's) "Principles of Intelligence Transparency" is to "Provide appropriate transparency to enhance public understanding about" the intelligence community (IC). The Office of the DNI (ODNI) now issues an annual *Transparency Report*, detailing the number of Foreign Intelligence Surveillance Act (FISA) warrants, U.S. persons queries, national security letters, and so on.

War and Peace. Moral philosophers and states have long presumed that the conditions of war and peace are different and allow different types of activity. The most obvious wartime activity is organized violence against the territory and citizens of other states. During peacetime, overt conflict is precluded. Does this division between acceptable peacetime and wartime norms extend to intelligence activities? Are efforts to subvert and overthrow the governments of enemy states acceptable in peacetime, as they are in wartime? One of the issues confronting U.S. policy makers in 2013 with regard to possible intervention in Syria was that international law precludes aiding rebels. (The 2011 intervention in Libya had United Nations [UN] approval.)

Even during periods of peace, the United States has relations with states that are hostile. The cold war between the United States and the Soviet Union may have been the epitome of such relationships: hostile at virtually all levels but never reaching the point of overt conflict between the two primary antagonists (as opposed to some of their surrogates).

A relationship such as that between the two cold war antagonists occupies a gray middle ground between peace and war. Intelligence activities—both collection and covert action—became one of the principal means by which the two countries could combat each other. Even in this unique situation, however, the United States and the Soviet Union accepted some limits. The two sides did not kill each other's nationals who were caught spying. Instead, they jailed the spies and sometimes exchanged them, as was the case with Col. Rudolf Abel, a Soviet spy imprisoned in the United States in 1957, and U-2 pilot Francis Gary Powers. (One's own national caught spying for the other side could be executed, as were Julius Rosenberg in the United States and Col. Oleg Penkovsky in the Soviet Union.) The national leadership of each side was safe from physical attacks. But did these unwritten rules create necessary boundaries, or did they serve to allow a great many other activities, including propaganda and subversion? As noted in chapter 12, cyberspace offers both the means and the venue for states to act against one another, including attacks with physical results, without— thus far—risking open conflict. As noted, there are very few agreed rules about what can or cannot be done in cyberspace.

Military operations like the North Atlantic Treaty Organization's (NATO's) 1999 bombing of Serbia over Kosovo or its 2011 operation in Libya to protect anti-Qaddafi rebels also blur the line between war and peace. These are certainly military operations, although limited in scope and means, but at the same time, NATO and the states being attacked maintained diplomatic relations and communicated about the issues at hand. In 2011, the United States conducted a clandestine military operation in Pakistan, ostensibly an ally, to kill Osama bin Laden, without informing the Pakistani government.

If a country threatens to make war or if war seems imminent, does the concept of self-defense allow states to engage preemptively in certain activities, including intelligence operations? In an age of cyberspace operations, this question is increasingly important, as noted in chapter 12 with the concept of cyber operational preparation of the environment. The George W. Bush administration (2001–2009) advocated a preemptive strategy in 2003 as part of its rationale for the war against Iraq, but it is not clear that this will have future support in that war's aftermath, given that the expected weapons of mass destruction (WMD)—the presumed reason for preemption—were not found.

The campaign against terrorists occupies a still undefined middle ground between war and peace. In part, it is a military campaign, being conducted largely in Afghanistan and Pakistan but also in Yemen and Somalia against pro–al Qaeda elements and in Syria against the Islamic State. In part, it is a law enforcement activity, within the United States and overseas as well. But there are also aspects of the effort against terrorists that fall in between these two positions. The implications of this issue are discussed later in the chapter.

Ends Versus Means. The usual answer to the question, "Do the ends justify the means?" is "No." But if the ends do not justify the means, what does? Policy makers face difficult choices when means and ends are in conflict. For example, during the cold war, was it proper for the United States, which advocated free elections, to interfere in Western European elections in the late 1940s to preclude communist victories? Which choice was preferable: upholding moral principles or allowing a politically unpalatable and perhaps threatening outcome? How does U.S. interference in postwar European elections compare with the subversion of the Chilean economy as a means of undermining the government of Salvador Allende, or with Russian interference in the 2016 U.S. presidential election?

Within the U.S. political experience, such questions represent two deeply rooted concepts: realpolitik and idealism. In the milieu of the cold war, realpolitik predominated. The moral aspect of the cold war (Western democratic ideals versus Soviet dictatorship) made choices such as those described earlier easier for policy makers. Would they make the same choices in the post–cold war world in the absence of such a moral imperative?

Again, these concerns are at issue in the campaign against terrorists and the constant struggle to balance civil liberties and national security. Some of those who believe that it is necessary to make adjustments to civil liberties in order to preserve the larger framework of our government use the phrase "the Constitution is not a suicide pact." Federal appellate court judge Richard Posner is a leading proponent of this view, which has its roots in the similar dilemma faced by President Abraham Lincoln and the suspension of *habeas corpus* in Maryland during the Civil War. Lincoln argued that it was necessary to suspend one law in one state, *habeas corpus*, in order to preserve the Union and enforce all laws in the seceding states. In a July 1861 message to Congress, Lincoln posed the question this way: "To state the question more directly, are all the laws, but one [*habeas corpus*], to go unexecuted, and the government itself go to pieces, lest that one be violated? Even in such a case, would not the official oath be broken, if the government should be overthrown, when it was believed that disregarding the single law would tend to preserve it?" Again, the issue is one of balance.

The Nature of the Opponent. For nearly half a century the United States faced successive totalitarian threats: the Axis and then the Soviet Union and its satellite states. A vast gulf existed between the accepted values and behavioral norms of the United States and its allies and their opponents. Do the actions of your opponents affect the actions you may undertake? Are they a useful guide to action?

"All's fair in . . ." is one response. On the one hand, a state would be foolish to deny itself weapons or tactics that are being used by an opponent bent on the state's destruction. On the other hand, does a state not lose something important when it sinks to the level of an opponent who is amoral or immoral? John le Carré, in his novels featuring the spy George Smiley, argued that little difference can be found between the intelligence actions of the United States and the Soviet Union during the cold war, that a certain moral equivalence existed. Was le Carré correct, or did the moral distinctions between the two states remain strong and important, even if similarities existed in some types of intelligence operations?

National Interest. The concept of national interest is not new. In the period that historians refer to as "early modern Europe," roughly the seventeenth century, all statesmen agreed that *raison d'état*—literally "reason of state"—guided their actions. *Raison d'état* implied two tenets: first, that the state embodied its own ends and, second, that the interests of the state were the only guides for actions—not resentments, emotions, or other subjective impulses. *Raison d'état*, as practiced in early modern Europe, also implied the use of intrigue by one state against another and the ultimate sanction: the use of force.

In the late seventeenth and eighteenth centuries, international relations were, beneath a refined veneer, brutal. One could argue that even the creation of an international body, the United Nations, has done little to modify the behavior of states in the late twentieth and early twenty-first centuries. For example, witness the brutality of many parties in the dismemberment of Yugoslavia or of the Khmer Rouge in Cambodia. A direct line follows from seventeenth-century *raison d'état* to twentieth-first-century national interest.

Is national interest a sufficient guide to the ethics and morality of intelligence? On the one hand, it is the only guide. If intelligence activities are not undertaken in support of the policies of the legitimate government, then they are meaningless at best or dangerous rogue operations at worst. On the other hand, legitimate governments—even those that adhere to democratic ideals and principles—can sometimes reach decisions and take actions that are morally or ethically questionable.

Thus, national interest is a difficult guideline, both indispensable and insufficient at the same time.

Changes in Ethics and Morals. Ethics and morals change over time. For example, slavery was accepted in Britain as late as the 1830s, in some parts of the United States as late as the 1860s, in Brazil as late as the 1880s, and in Saudi Arabia until 1962. Slavery reportedly continued in Sudan in the late 1990s. One hundred years ago, in the 1910s, the issue of women's suffrage was still being vigorously debated in Britain and the United States; in Switzerland, the debate continued into the 1960s.

Assuming that intelligence activities are undertaken on lawful authority, should they keep abreast of changes in ethics and morality? Citizens should want to say yes. But who decides when these changes have come? How quickly do changes in ethics and morals get translated into policies and actions? For example, political intervention of the sort undertaken in Europe during the cold war is probably insupportable today (with the 1998 Iraq Liberation Act, which publicly appropriated money to foster a change in the regime in Iraq, a notable exception). But when did that change come? When the Soviet Union collapsed, or earlier? In 1975, the United States faced the prospect of seeing one of its NATO allies, Portugal, elect a communist government. After a strenuous debate between U.S. ambassador Frank Carlucci (who opposed covert intervention in the Portuguese elections) and national security adviser Henry Kissinger (who advocated it), the United States opted not to intervene, and the Communists lost the election. The decision was based not on a new morality but on the view that the United States had more to lose by intervening and possibly being exposed than by allowing the elections to take their course. The outcome proved favorable from the U.S. perspective, as Carlucci believed it would. The same debate arose in 1990, when the Sandinista government in Nicaragua agreed to open elections (much to the chagrin of their patron, Fidel Castro). Again, some in the United States urged covert intervention. Costa Rican president Oscar Arias Sanchez argued against the intervention, saying that, given what they had done to the Nicaraguan economy, the Sandinistas could not win an open election. The United States listened and the Sandinistas lost, although they did later return to power via elections.

Another important question prompted by changes in values is whether new standards should be imposed after the fact. For example, during the cold war the United States often supported regimes that were undemocratic and sometimes brutal, but they were anticommunist. Although some people in the United States found these relationships objectionable, many accepted their apparent necessity. In the mid-1990s, Director of Central Intelligence (DCI) John M. Deutch (1995–1997) ordered the Central Intelligence Agency (CIA) to review all of its contacts and operations to see if any involved links to human rights abuses. Many in the CIA felt that this review, and some of the disciplinary actions that the CIA leadership took against some officers, was an unfair ex post facto imposition of standards. (The Constitution bars laws that are ex post facto in nature.) Was Deutch's action a necessary cleaning up of past errors or an unfair imposition of new standards on officers who had acted in good faith under old standards? In the aftermath of the September 2001 attacks, many people felt that the so-called Deutch rules had placed hobbling limits on human intelligence (HUMINT). The CIA claimed that no useful contact had been turned away because of the rules, but critics argued that their mere existence and the threat of some later punishment bred extreme caution in the Directorate of Operations. At any rate, the Deutch rules were abandoned after the terrorist attacks.

Markus Wolf ran East German intelligence operations for years, successfully penetrating many levels of the West German government, including the chancellor's office. When East Germany collapsed and was absorbed by West Germany, the now-unified German government put Wolf on trial for treason. Its rationale for doing so ran as follows: According to the constitution of West Germany, it was the one legitimate government of all Germany, and Wolf had carried out espionage against that government. (Despite its constitutional claims, West Germany had granted East Germany diplomatic recognition, and the two states had exchanged ambassadors.) Wolf argued that he had been the citizen of a separate state and therefore could not be guilty of treason. In 1993, he was convicted of espionage, but in 1995 the highest German court voided the verdict, accepting Wolf's argument that the charge should not have been made in the first place because he had not broken the laws of the state he had served, East Germany. After receiving a suspended sentence for kidnappings carried out by agents under his authority, Wolf, in 1998, was jailed for refusing to identify an agent he had referred to in his memoirs.

A case similar to Wolf's—but with an odd twist—is that of Col. Ryszard Kuklinski, a Polish general staff officer. Kuklinski provided the United States with crucial intelligence on the Warsaw Pact during the late 1970s and early 1980s, including a December 1980 warning that the Soviets were preparing to invade Poland to end the protests of the labor movement Solidarity. The intelligence allowed the United States to use diplomatic means to forestall the Soviet invasion. Kuklinski was brought out of Poland just before martial law was declared. Kuklinski was sentenced to death in absentia. But even after the fall of the communist regime in Warsaw, many Poles were ambivalent about what Kuklinski had done. He had been motivated by his dislike of the Soviet Union and the regime it had imposed on Poland. Some Poles, however, felt that Kuklinski had spied on Poland, regardless of the Soviet issue. Many of his fellow officers argued that if Kuklinski was now a hero for what he had done, what did that say about all of the officers who had not acted against the Soviets and their puppets? Even Lech Walesa, as president of Poland, refused to pardon Kuklinski. The charges were finally dropped in 1998, after much U.S. pressure.

The issue of changing moral standards arises again with the interrogation of known or suspected terrorists. As was noted earlier, the various interrogation techniques that were used were vetted by the Justice Department and others in the executive branch and were briefed to a limited number of senators and representatives, who were also supportive, according to press accounts. But between these decisions in 2002 and 2006, there had been a shift in political opinion, with many members of Congress expressing more qualms about the types of techniques that could be used.

Director of the CIA (DCIA) Gen. Michael Hayden (2006–2009) said in February 2008 that waterboarding—a form of interrogation—was undertaken based on this Justice Department ruling, was used only in a few cases, and, in his opinion, would no longer be allowed under the rules now in force. If the standards for interrogation do change, should officers who conducted interrogations based on former standards be held liable for their actions? This issue arose again in reference to the Senate Intelligence Committee's Democratic majority staff report on enhanced interrogation techniques (EITs). Some observers who were convinced by the published findings were supportive of Justice Department action against the CIA officers involved.

ISSUES RELATED TO COLLECTION AND COVERT ACTION

Many ethical and moral issues arise from collection and covert action. As with the broad moral issues, there are many questions and little consensus on answers.

HUMINT. HUMINT collection involves the manipulation of other human beings as potential sources of information. The skills required to be a successful HUMINT collector are acquired over time with training and experience. They basically involve psychological techniques to gain trust, including empathy, flattery, and sympathy. The more direct methods of gaining cooperation can include in some services bribery, blackmail, and sex. (Directorate of Operations officers note that they do not use blackmail or sex as a means of recruiting spies, if for no other reasons than that these spies are not reliable.)

Two issues predominate. The first is the morality of the manipulation itself. One might argue that psychological techniques are used on someone who is already susceptible to manipulation. An unwilling subject will likely terminate the relationship. (Walk-ins are different by virtue of the fact that they volunteer their services.) Are these legitimate activities to be undertaken by a government against the citizens of another country, whether an enemy or not? Friendly states do spy against one another: the U.S. and France; Israel against the United States; and the various collections identified in recent leaks.

The second issue is the responsibility of the government doing the recruiting to the source:

- How far does the government's responsibility go?

- How deep an obligation, if any, does the government incur in the recruitment?

- If the HUMINT asset is compromised, how far should the recruiter go to maintain the asset's safety? Does this obligation extend to his or her family as well?

- What if the asset has not been productive for some time? For how long a period is the government obliged to protect the asset once the relationship ended its usefulness?

- What if the asset proves to be unproductive? Perhaps the asset has misrepresented his or her access and capabilities. Is there still an obligation?

One of the most compelling arguments in favor of strong and continued responsibility for recruited sources has little to do with morality and ethics. It is the more practical concern that recruitment of new sources becomes more difficult if word gets out that current or former sources are not given the support and protection they need. In other words, failing to protect a source is bad for business.

Another issue tends to be specific to certain areas, such as terrorism and narcotics, that depend heavily on HUMINT for good intelligence. To collect that intelligence, U.S. officials must develop contacts with—and usually pay money to—members of terrorist or narcotics-trafficking organizations. These people have the needed intelligence. Such a case arose in 1995, when the press reported that a CIA-paid asset was instrumental in the arrest of the terrorist known as Carlos (born Ilich Ramirez Sánchez in Venezuela). The asset was also a terrorist, a member of Carlos's group. (Carlos, the "Jackal," was an international terrorist during the 1970s and 1980s, usually working closely with radical Arab groups. Carlos was captured in Sudan in 1994 and was sentenced to life imprisonment in France.) Penetration of a terrorist group may require the agent to prove himself or herself by taking part in a terrorist activity. This probably approaches a line that many would find impossible to cross. Thus, for understandable reasons, reviewing the assumptions about the efficacy of HUMINT against terrorism is necessary.

Some people find it morally objectionable that relationships are forged with those who may have engaged in activities directed against U.S. interests. Policy and intelligence officials must make a difficult choice between access to useful information that cannot be obtained through other means and the distasteful prospect of paying money to a terrorist or narcotics trafficker.

Collection. Beyond the recruiting of human assets, intelligence officials use a number of techniques to collect intelligence, including the theft of material and various types of eavesdropping, which are deemed unlawful in everyday life. What legitimizes these activities as intelligence operations of the state? Within the United States, intelligence and law enforcement officials are required to have court orders for eavesdropping and other techniques, and procedures are in place to prevent intelligence collections from including information about U.S. citizens, a category that includes legally resident aliens. However, as the Edward Snowden leaks about the National Security Agency (NSA) revealed, the Foreign Intelligence Surveillance Court (FISC) authorized blanket surveillance activities as well as specifically targeted ones and, in some cases, collection rules were violated, albeit inadvertently. The 2007–2008 debate about reforming FISA touched on these safeguards versus the need to adjust collection techniques in response to changing technology. The problems that have occurred in the NSA program raise a further question: Is it acceptable to conduct such a large program with the knowledge that there will likely be some violations of rules? Or is it better not to run that risk? Advocates of the program would note that statistically the number of reported violations was minuscule—roughly 2,800 out of millions of calls that were tracked. Is there an acceptable level of errors? Does it matter that the errors were largely inadvertent as opposed to willful?

The same issues arise in counterintelligence when a potential suspect has been identified. In the United States, unlike many other countries, the law requires intelligence officials to obtain a court order before performing collection activities against a possible spy.

Collection also raises the moral question of responsibility for the knowledge that has been gained. Do intelligence officials or policy makers incur any obligations by discovering some piece of intelligence? For example, during World War II, British and U.S. intelligence became aware, via signals intelligence, of the mass killing of Jews by the Germans. The Allies did not carry out military action (bombing rail lines and camps) for two reasons. One was the belief that attacking purely military targets would end the war sooner and thus save more people in the concentration camps than would direct attacks on the camps. Another reason was concern over safeguarding the sources and methods by which the Allies had learned about the camps. What are the ethical and moral implications of the decision to desist?

In 2004, a former minister in the British government alleged that Britain and the United States had conducted espionage at the UN in the period prior to the 2003 Security Council vote on Iraq WMD. By international treaty, the UN is supposed to be inviolate from any espionage activities, although it is widely known that many states ignore this agreement. For example, for years U.S. officials assumed that Soviet members of the UN Secretariat engaged in espionage for their home country even though they were supposed to be international civil servants. In 1978, Arkady Shevchenko, a Russian UN under secretary, defected to the United States after having passed information to the CIA for several years. Shevchenko confirmed that the Soviet Union used the UN to gather intelligence. Separate allegations also were made that the United States had conducted intelligence collection against the International Agency for Atomic Energy (IAEA), arising from concerns over Iran's nuclear program. The IAEA, like the UN, is supposed to be inviolate from members' intelligence activities. The attraction of the UN, or other international bodies, as an intelligence collection target for any nation is obvious. Almost every nation in the world has a diplomatic presence at the UN, affording a breadth of access that is likely unavailable in many other capitals. The arrangement may be especially important for collecting against nations with which a state does not have diplomatic relations or whose diplomatic presence worldwide is limited.

One could argue that the treaty status of the UN is no different from the sovereignty of any nation. After all, no nation permits hostile intelligence collection in its territory. This is another instance in which the *raison d'état* takes precedence over treaty obligations.

Covert Action. Covert actions are interventions by one state in the affairs of another. The basic ethical issue is the legitimacy of such operations. Concepts of national interest, national security, and national defense are most commonly used to support covert operations. But, taken to the extreme, every nation could be both a perpetrator and a target, creating Hobbesian anarchy. In reality, many states do not have the capability, the need, or the will to carry out covert actions against other states. But those states that do have the need and the ability believe their covert actions to be legitimate in terms of self-interest, if not in international law.

Covert actions also may conflict with personal goals or beliefs. Across the range of covert actions, from purely political (electoral aid, propaganda) to economic subversion and coups, innocent citizens in the targeted state can be affected and perhaps put in jeopardy. Military attacks on civilians in wartime have long been accepted as a legitimate activity, such as the large-scale bombings of cities. Are peacetime covert actions different? What about a cyberattack that damages critical infrastructure, putting lives at risk?

Propaganda operations raise concern in the United States over blowback—the danger that a false story planted in the foreign press by U.S. intelligence might be picked up by U.S. media outlets. (See chap. 8.) If U.S. intelligence informs these outlets of the true nature of the story, it runs the risk of a leak, thus undoing the entire operation. How serious a concern should blowback be? Is it a major threat to the independence of the press?

What are the moral limits of operations? During the Soviet invasion of Afghanistan, some Soviet troops, dispirited by the interminable war, succumbed to the ready availability of narcotics, as had U.S. troops in Vietnam. The United States supplied arms to the anti-Soviet mujahideen, including sophisticated Stinger missiles. Would it have been legitimate and acceptable to take steps to increase drug use by the Soviet troops as a means of undermining their military efforts?

Paramilitary operations—the waging of war via surrogate forces, placing them somewhat beyond the norms of accepted international law—raise a number of ethical and moral issues. Are they legitimate? They raise the prospect of innocent civilians being put in jeopardy. Are there limits to paramilitary operations? For example, does the nature of the regime that is being fought matter? Are such operations legitimate against oppressive, undemocratic regimes but illegitimate against those with more acceptable forms of government? If there are differences, who determines which governments are legitimate targets and which are not? As noted, international law precludes assisting rebels fighting a recognized government, regardless of the nature of that government.

As with HUMINT, paramilitary operations raise questions about the sponsoring power's obligations to the combatants. This is a problem particularly for operations that are unsuccessful or appear to be inconclusive. In the case of a failed operation, does the supporting power have an obligation to help extricate its surrogate combatants and move them to a safe haven? In the case of an inconclusive operation, the choices are even more difficult. The supporting state may be able to continue the paramilitary operations indefinitely, perhaps knowing that there is little chance of success, but also little prospect of defeat. Should the supporting power continue the operation despite its near pointlessness? Or does it have a responsibility to terminate the operation? If it decides to terminate, does it have an obligation to extricate the fighters it has supported?

Even a successful operation can raise ethical and moral issues. In the aftermath of the Soviet withdrawal from Afghanistan, one faction, the Taliban, eventually took over much of the country. The Taliban imposed a strict Muslim regime on Afghanistan, much at odds with Western notions of civil liberties and the rights of women. Did the

United States and its anti-Soviet partners in Afghanistan (China, Pakistan, and Saudi Arabia) bear some responsibility to attempt to moderate the rule imposed by the Taliban? Eventually, the Taliban played host to al Qaeda leader Osama bin Laden, raising further questions about the results of the earlier policy.

Assassination. Most people would, and official U.S. policy does, draw a distinction between casualties inflicted as a result of military operations and the targeted assassination of a specific individual. (See chap. 8 for further discussion of assassination and the U.S. ban on it.) At the same time and even before the 2001 terrorist attacks, the formerly broad support for the assassination ban had eroded among the general public and to some extent in the press. The change in attitude perhaps reflected some of the difficulties the United States encountered in imposing its will since the end of the cold war.

Even if the ban were to be lifted selectively, it is difficult to imagine how useful criteria for implementing assassination could be drawn up. What level of crime or hostile activity would make someone a legitimate target? As with Britain's interest in assassinating Adolf Hitler, it is not easy to identify a potential target at the right time. Also, some possible targets are former partners. Saddam Hussein, for example, received U.S. backing in his war with Iran (1980–1988), which was then seen as the bigger problem. His behavior became problematic only after Iraq invaded Kuwait in 1990.

In the case of Osama bin Laden and other terrorist leaders, the debate over assassination became irrelevant. The United States recognized the attacks of 2001 as an act of war, making these individuals legitimate military targets. As noted earlier, Attorney General Eric Holder characterized the killing of bin Laden in 2011 as a legitimate act of self-defense. There is a distinction, at least in U.S. practice, between assassination, meaning a political murder, and killing enemy combatants. Assassination is also a remarkably sloppy tool. Without absolute assurances about who will follow the victim into power and how the successor will behave, assassination provides no guarantee of solving the problem at hand. The political unrest in Lebanon following the assassination of former prime minister Rafik Hariri in 2005 is instructive. It is widely assumed that Hariri was killed by Syria as he opposed Syria's continued military presence in Lebanon. The result of Hariri's death was widespread protests in Lebanon and international condemnation of Syria, resulting in the beginning of the long-delayed Syrian withdrawal of military forces and intelligence officers. NATO attacks on Qaddafi family compounds in 2011, resulting in the death of one of Qaddafi's sons and several relatives, were denounced by the Libyan government as assassination attempts. NATO insisted it was a legitimate military command-and-control target.

The leaders who would be considered assassination targets are not in democracies; they are in states where the mechanisms for political succession are ill defined or subject to contest. One thug could replace another. Thus, the gain would be little, while the risk to international reputation would be great.

Assassination also raises the specter of reprisal. An absence of rules cuts both ways.

The Use of Armed UAVs to Carry Out Attacks Has Raised Other Issues. As noted in chapter 12, placing a U.S. citizen, Anwar al-Awlaki, on the target list, raised legal questions about the due process of law. Also, the increased use of drone-based attacks incurred civilian casualties in Afghanistan and Pakistan while killing known or suspected terrorists. This raises another question about acceptable costs and the unintended consequences of certain actions. In June 2010, the UN Human Rights Council received a report from its "special rapporteur on extrajudicial, summary and arbitrary executions," who argued that the use of these weapons might violate international law and might also establish a precedent for their use beyond their territories by other states. The report especially took issue with unmanned aerial vehicles (UAVs) operated by the CIA, versus those operated by the military, where the rules of engagement were less clear. The UN report discounted the "law of 9/11" rationale for UAV use. The Obama administration (2009–2017) stated that the use of armed UAVs comports with international law and the right of a state to defend itself. As noted (see chap. 8), in February 2013, the Justice Department released a white paper giving the legal basis for lethal operations against a U.S. citizen. The three main criteria are (1) imminent threat of violent attack against the United States, (2) infeasibility of capture, and (3) conducting the operation consistent with applicable war of law principles. Again, as noted, in January 2014, Congress delayed the transfer of armed UAV strikes from the CIA to the Defense Department reportedly because of concerns that the military might be less discriminate in their use.

At the same time, some weapons specialists and ethicists have looked at the use of drones and have concluded that they may be more ethical weapons as they are more precise. Although drone strikes do result in civilian casualties, these tend to be far lower than the use of bombs, missiles, or ground attacks also aimed at terrorists. The contrary argument is that this may also make drones too attractive as the costs appear to be lower.

Renditions and Torture. The war on terrorists has seen an increase in renditions, the seizure of foreign nationals overseas and, in many cases, transportation to their country of origin for incarceration and interrogation. (See chap. 5.) Although the United States has obtained pledges from these countries about the manner in which rendered suspects are treated, allegations have been made that some suspects have been tortured and that the United States is at least complicit in this torture.

Most countries have a legal sanction against torture, whether it is enforced or not. Within U.S. law, at least, torture is specifically forbidden by the Eighth Amendment to the Constitution, which bans "cruel and unusual punishment." But the war on terrorists has given rise to a debate over what constitutes torture (as opposed to harsh and even degrading treatment) and whether or not this is acceptable. The debate is also colored by the treatment of Iraqi prisoners held by the U.S. military at Abu Ghraib, where U.S. military personnel did mistreat prisoners, although Abu Ghraib was an issue of the breakdown of military discipline and command and not an agreed U.S. policy on how to treat detainees. Several moral and ethical questions arise. First, if one were convinced that a detainee had knowledge of a proximate terrorist attack, what limits should be imposed—if any— to obtain the information he or she has? Does the possibility of preventing the attack and saving many lives make a harsher interrogation permissible? Second, how much transparency is desired into how these terrorist suspects are treated? The question raises an ends-and-means issue. Some commentators have argued that there is a vast difference between discussing these first two questions in the abstract and facing the reality of capturing a terrorist who one knows is likely to have been involved in future attacks. Third, what effect does harsh treatment or torture have on the United States and the ethical purposes for which it says it is fighting terrorism?

The development of U.S. policy in this area has been extremely difficult. There has been much debate and legal dispute about the status of captured terrorists and whether they have combatant rights under the Geneva Convention, which would preclude torture and humiliating treatment. By mid-2008, there were several official and conflicting views, including a Supreme Court decision ruling that detainees had Geneva Convention rights and a new executive order that would allow the resumption of detention and interrogation as defined by the DCIA and compliant with the convention. The nature of these aspects of the U.S. campaign against terrorists is likely to remain controversial and subject to both redefinition and litigation as long as the campaign persists.

A related issue is the ultimate fate of the senior terrorists who have been captured by the United States, including some of al Qaeda's senior planners for the 2001 attacks. Although concern is voiced about releasing them, questions arise about how long they can be held, especially without some sort of judicial proceedings. After a certain point, they have no intelligence value as they have either told what they know or their information is dated. These terrorists are currently being treated as enemy combatants and therefore can be held for the duration of the conflict. But in a conflict that may have no definite end, does a time come when they have to be put on trial or released?

A Final Look at Operational Ethics. James Barry (see "Covert Action Can Be Just" in Further Readings) has argued that criteria can be established for making morally guided decisions about intelligence operations. Barry suggests the following:

- Just cause
- Just intention
- Proper authority
- Last resort
- Probability of success
- Proportionality
- Discrimination and control

In the abstract, this is a compelling list of checkpoints for policy makers to consider before launching an operation. But policy makers do not act in the abstract. And once they have decided upon the necessity for an operation, they can find ways to rationalize each of the succeeding steps.

ANALYSIS-RELATED ISSUES

The ethical and moral issues surrounding analysis center largely on the many compromises that analysts may make as they prepare their product and deal with policy makers.

Is Analysis "Truth-Telling"? One of the most common descriptions of intelligence is that it is the job of "telling truth to power." (This sounds fairly noble, although it is important to recall that court jesters once had the same function.) Intelligence, however, is not about truth. If something is known to be true, then we do not need intelligence services to find it. Yet the image persists and carries with it some important ethical implications. If truth were the objective of intelligence, does that raise the stakes for analysis? Are analysts working on a more well-informed and, they hope, successful policy than their policy customers? Moreover, does a goal of truth allow analysts greater latitude to pursue and defend their views of likely outcomes?

A problem with setting truth as a goal is that it has a relentless quality. Most individuals understand the importance of being honest most of the time (and acknowledge the occasional need to at least shade the truth). But if an analyst's goal is to tell the truth—especially to those in power who might not want to hear it—then there is no room for compromise, no possible admission of alternative views. After all, if one has the truth, those who disagree must have falsehood. Thus, an analyst cannot compromise with other analysts whose views may differ, even slightly. Moreover, what should a truth-teller do if the powerful reject his or her analysis, as they are free to do? Once the powerful have failed to accept the truth, is their legitimacy at stake? Underlying all of this is the more important question: Who determines what is truth in a situation in which the answer is, at the outset, uncertain?

These questions may seem far-fetched, but they underscore the problems raised by truth-telling as a job description. As noble as it may be as a goal, as a practical matter, truth-telling raises many problems in an already complex intelligence and policy process.

Analytic Pressures. Assume that the role of intelligence is not to tell the truth but to provide informed analysis to policy makers to aid their decision making.

Even with this less demanding role, analysts can reach judgments that are based on deep and strongly held beliefs. They may be convinced not only of the conclusions they have reached but also of the importance of the issue for the nation. What should they do if their views are rejected, disregarded, or ignored by their policy clients?

- Accept the situation as the policy maker's prerogative and move on to the next issue?

- Attempt to raise the issue again with the policy maker, based on the possibility that the policy maker misunderstood the importance of the issue and the analysis? How often can analysts do this, either on one particular issue or as a regular practice? How does this behavior affect their credibility?

- Try to take their analysis to other policy makers, either going over the head of their original client or elsewhere in the policy process? Even if this ploy is successful, what is the cost to the analysts' relationship with the original client and all other policy clients?

- Threaten to quit? Is the issue that important? Are the analysts willing to carry out the threat or risk the loss of credibility? What does quitting accomplish beyond a protest?

The multioffice or multiagency nature of intelligence analysis raises many issues of group dynamics. (See chap. 6.) Analyses are often the products of negotiation and compromise among several analysts with differing views. An analyst needs to consider a number of questions:

- To what extent should an analyst be willing to compromise with other analysts? Which types of trades are acceptable and which are not?

- At what point do the compromises affect the integrity of the document? If the compromises appear to have jeopardized the document's utility or integrity, can an analyst go back on previous compromises?

- Can an analyst warn policy makers that, in his or her view, the analysis has been overly compromised? In other words, at what point should an analyst feel obligated to break free of the procedural constraints of the multiagency process and venture out as a lone wolf? What types of issues merit this behavior? What is the likelihood of efficacy? What are the costs in terms of future working relationships within this process, even if one wins his or her point? Will there be an inevitable and irreplaceable loss of trust that makes all future interactions difficult at best?

Finally, the nature of the relationship between the intelligence officer and the policy maker is an issue. When Sherman Kent stated that the analyst wants to be believed or listened to (see chap. 6), he was mainly referring to the quality of the analysis. However, an analyst's access also depends on the nature of the relationship itself.

- How great a concern, if any, should the relationship be for an analyst? Should an analyst avoid stands that would alienate policy makers to keep open the best lines of communication?

- What if the analyst strongly believes that he or she must take a stand? Again, should the stand be tempered for the sake of the long-term relationship with policy makers?

- Alternatively, what should an analyst do in the face of pressure to produce intelligence that is perhaps more supportive of policy? Such a request may be subtle, not overt. Can, and should, the intelligence officer resist outright? How many small compromises add up to large ones that politicize the product? What if the analyst knows that the policy maker will write a memo with contrary views and will ultimately prevail? Is it still worth resisting blandishments, knowing he or she will lose both the argument and perhaps access to a key policy client as well?

Many games are being played simultaneously: the intelligence process itself, the policy process, and the desire of the intelligence officers to have access to policy makers and to keep their funding levels safe and preferably growing. It is easy, in the abstract, to declare that the integrity of the intelligence process is primary. In the trenches, however, such a declaration is not always so obvious or so appealing.

Analysts' Options. An intelligence analyst may believe that something fundamental is at stake, that neither compromise nor silence is possible. What are the analyst's options, then? They boil down to two: continue the struggle from within the system or quit. (*See box, "Analysts' Options: A Cultural Difference."*) Continuing the struggle from within is appealing in that one's professional standards are preserved. But is it a realistic choice or a rationalization? Are there real prospects of continuing to fight for that viewpoint from within the bureaucratic system? For whatever reason, the viewpoint did not prevail either in the intelligence community or with policy makers. Short of capitulation, the analyst is now tagged with a certain view that has been found wanting. How influential will he or she be on this issue in the future? Or is the analyst, not wishing to abandon a chosen career, simply putting the best gloss on having lost? If such choices must be made, the analyst can only hope to make them over an issue of some significance. Not every issue is worth engaging at this level.

Alternatively, the analyst can quit. Honor and professional standards are preserved intact. But by quitting, the analyst abandons all hope of further influencing the process. Yes, one can attempt to influence policy from outside the government, but such attempts are rarely effective. The analyst who quits has, in effect, conceded the field to those with a different viewpoint.

ANALYSTS' OPTIONS: A CULTURAL DIFFERENCE

The two options for analysts who find they cannot compromise—fighting from within or quitting—tend to play out differently in the bureaucracies of Britain and the United States. In Britain, a strong tradition exists of quitting in protest. To cite a high-level example, Foreign Secretary Anthony Eden resigned in February 1938 when he disagreed with Neville Chamberlain's policy of appeasement toward Nazi Germany. In the United States, resignation is rarer, with individuals opting instead to fight from within. Nothing definitive accounts for the difference. Several U.S. civil servants did resign, however, during the early stages of the civil war in Bosnia to protest the lack of action by the United States.

OVERSIGHT-RELATED ISSUES

The demands of oversight raise ethical issues for witnesses before Congress and for the members and staff as well.

The Helms Dilemma.   In 1973, while testifying first before the Senate Foreign Relations Committee in executive session and then before the Senate Foreign Relations Subcommittee on Multinational Corporations in an open session, DCI Richard Helms (1966–1973) was asked if the CIA had been involved in operations to overthrow the Allende government in Chile. Helms said that the CIA had not been involved. In 1977, the Justice Department considered a charge of perjury against Helms for his false testimony before Congress. After negotiations, Helms agreed to plead guilty to a misdemeanor and was fined $2,000 and given a suspended two-year prison sentence.

Helms believed that the extreme limits that President Richard M. Nixon (1969–1974) had put on who was allowed to know about this effort (the secretaries of state and defense were excluded) precluded his answering. Helms also believed that his testimony was accurate, in that the CIA had tried to prevent Allende's election but had not been part of the plot to overthrow him once he was in office. This fine line notwithstanding, what options did Helms have when he was asked about CIA activity in Chile?

Under the National Security Act at that time, the DCI was personally responsible for protecting the sources and methods of U.S. intelligence. (This responsibility has now passed to the DNI.) Helms found himself caught between that obligation and his obligation to testify fully and honestly before Congress. If he had stated that the CIA was involved in some way, he would have revealed operations in an open, public hearing. Alternatively, had he expressed the wish to answer that question in private or in a closed session (although he had also not answered when in a closed session), it would have been tantamount to admitting CIA involvement. After all, if the CIA had not been involved, why not answer in public? Helms opted for a third choice: to view the question within narrow bounds, preserve secrecy, and deny CIA involvement. There may have been a fourth choice: to respond as he did in public and then visit the senators privately to discuss the realities of CIA activity in Chile. Helms apparently did not consider this choice. In 1973, oversight of CIA activity was the prerogative of a small group of members of the Senate Armed Services Committee, not those on Foreign Relations. Thus, Helms also construed his oversight responsibilities within a narrow spectrum.

Did Helms make the right choice? Should he have been prosecuted for false testimony under these circumstances? How responsible were the senators for asking such questions in an open session (particularly Sen. Stuart Symington, D-MO, who knew the facts of the matter because he was also a member of the Senate Armed Services Committee, which then had oversight of the CIA)?

The Clapper Corollary.   A similar case arose as a result of the Snowden NSA leaks. DNI James Clapper (2010–2017), at a March 2013 unclassified Senate Intelligence hearing, was asked by Sen. Ron Wyden, D-OR, a somewhat lengthy question, the crux of which was this: "Does the NSA collect any type of data at all on millions or hundreds of millions of Americans?" Clapper answered that they did not do so "wittingly" but might have done so "inadvertently." Once the Snowden-leaked material came out, it became apparent that Clapper's answer was incorrect. Clapper's immediate response was to say that he had answered in "the most truthful, or least untruthful manner, by saying, 'no.'" This comment created a predictable firestorm and brought to mind the Helms dilemma.

In June 2013, Clapper sent a letter to Sen. Dianne Feinstein, D-CA, who chaired the Senate Select Committee on Intelligence, explaining why he answered as he had. He said his answer focused on the Sec. 702 program, which collected content but not on Americans, rather than on the Sec. 215 program, which did collect metadata on Americans. He also said that when he realized his mistake, he clarified his response with Wyden but now was doing so publicly. Clapper's letter appeared to resolve the issue, which again suggests that Helms might have been better off doing the same, despite the narrow construction Helms put on congressional oversight prerogatives.

But the Clapper case also resurfaces the issue of the responsibilities of members of Congress. Although there are no constitutional or legal bars on their doing so, should they ask questions about classified programs in open hearings? And, if they do, is it fair to expect executive officials to answer forthrightly, given the responsibilities for safeguarding classified information?

The Torricelli Case. In 1995, Rep. Robert G. Torricelli, D-NJ, a member of the House Permanent Select Committee on Intelligence, wrote a letter to President Bill Clinton accusing the CIA of having misled Congress about its activities in Guatemala and having had on its payroll a Guatemalan officer involved in human rights violations. Torricelli also made his letter available to *The New York Times.* He admitted having leaked the information to the press but argued that his duty as a member of Congress to preserve the integrity of government was greater than the two oaths to preserve secret information that he had taken as a member of the House and the House Intelligence Committee. Torricelli also argued that he had not violated committee rules, because he had received the information in his personal office from a State Department officer—that is, not within the House Intelligence Committee— and it was not clear to him that the information had been properly classified.

The chairman of the House Intelligence Committee, Larry Combest, R-TX, filed ethics charges against Torricelli, which were adjudicated by the House Committee on Standards of Official Conduct (popularly known at the Ethics Committee). The committee decided that House rules concerning the handling of classified information were vague and ordered that, in the future, members would have a positive obligation to ascertain the true classification of information before releasing it. The committee went on to say that had this ambiguity been resolved at the time Torricelli released the information, he would have been guilty of violating House rules.

Torricelli believed that the information provided by the State officer, a former employee on his House staff, revealed CIA duplicity. Having written to the president, was it necessary to release the information to *The New York Times* as well? Should he first have expressed his concerns to the committee leadership or his party's leadership?

The only person in the affair who was punished was the State Department officer, Richard Nuccio, who gave the information to Torricelli. A panel appointed by DCI Deutch decided that Nuccio had provided the information without proper authorization. Nuccio lost his clearances and resigned from the State Department, eventually returning to work on Torricelli's staff. Torricelli could have saved Nuccio by saying that he had asked Nuccio for the information. But, by doing so, Torricelli would have undercut his argument that he had been the innocent recipient.

WHISTLE-BLOWERS

As a result of the Torricelli case, in 1998, the Intelligence Community Whistleblower Protection Act became law, after much debate in Congress and the executive branch. The law established procedures by which intelligence community employees may report a complaint or urgent concern. They must first do so through channels in the intelligence community but are free to inform the intelligence committees if the community has taken no action by a specific time. Even then, the employees must inform executive branch officials that they are going to Congress and must handle their information in accordance with proper security procedures. Reflecting the Torricelli case, the whistle-blower law states, "A member or employee of one of the intelligence committees who receives a complaint or information . . . does so in that member or employee's official capacity as a member or employee of that committee."

This law raises questions about the actions of individuals like Edward Snowden. Snowden said that he had serious qualms about the NSA programs and wanted to foster public debate. However, he did so by fleeing, first to China and then to Russia, and releasing a great deal of classified information that goes far beyond the NSA collection programs. Are his claims to being a whistle-blower legitimate given that he refused to avail himself of a process that might still have led to a broader discussion within Congress?

This, in turn, raises a series of questions. How serious does an issue have to be for someone to choose to become a whistle-blower? How persistent should he or she be within the system before invoking the rules regarding whistle-blowing? For certain types of misfeasance or malfeasance, the answer may be fairly obvious, but what about lesser cases? For example, if an analyst is on the losing side of an analytic debate and believes quite deeply that the outcome is wrong, is that a proper whistle-blowing issue? For lesser cases, the best remedy may be a system in which complaints are heard and addressed, with the goal of finding some interim solution before going to that last step—not with the goal of forestalling but with the goal of giving the aggrieved party a forum in which to be heard. For most people and for lesser cases, that will usually suffice. But for the whistle-blowing system to work, it also has to be honest, open-minded, and free from punitive action.

THE MEDIA

Reporters and their media outlets exist to publish stories. The First Amendment to the Constitution offers the press broad freedom: "Congress shall make no law . . . abridging the freedom . . . of the press."

The government has no way to prevent the media from reporting information that it has obtained, even if it has been classified. But freedom to publish is not the same as "the people's right to know," which is an enticing catchphrase but does not appear anywhere in the Constitution. The press's right to report also does not obligate government officials to provide information, especially classified information.

But what, if any, obligations does the press have when it obtains information with national security implications? Should press limits be self-imposed, or should the press operate on the premise of "finders keepers, losers weepers"? Just as ethics and morals change in other areas, so, too, they change in the media.

In the past, the press has come upon intelligence activities and agreed not to write about them for the sake of national security. For example, reporters discovered Cuban exile training camps in Florida prior to the Bay of Pigs and also learned about the construction of the *Glomar Explorer*, built by the Hughes Corporation for the CIA to retrieve a sunken Soviet submarine. More recently, in 2007, *The New York Times* said that it had initially refrained from publishing information it had obtained about U.S. efforts to help safeguard Pakistan's nuclear weapons. This issue resurfaced in November 2010 when WikiLeaks provided more than 250,000 State Department cables to media outlets around the world. *The New York Times*, for example, which received the cables in a leak from another news source, felt the cables were newsworthy but made redactions to safeguard "confidential informants" and made some other redactions requested by the State Department. Other news outlets were less scrupulous, and in January 2011, the State Department warned "hundreds" of its sources (human rights organizations, nongovernmental organizations, foreign officials, businesspeople) of potential threats to their safety because of their exposure in WikiLeaks. Similar questions can be raised by the degree and detail of the material printed by newspapers, but especially the *Washington Post*, in the aftermath of the Snowden leaks.

In the post-Watergate era of investigative journalism (a wonderful redundancy, as all journalism is investigative), it is more difficult to imagine that many reporters or media outlets would be willing to suspend publication or drop a story entirely. One has only to think about such scenes as U.S. television camera crews waiting onshore as the first U.S. troops landed in Somalia in 1993 to question the premise. It is more likely that, at some point, the story will be published.

The November 2018 leak, ironically, about the federal indictment of Julian Assange, founder and editor of WikiLeaks, raised the freedom of press issue again. Some observers contend that WikiLeaks is not a journalism site and therefore not protected. Assange was initially indicted for conspiracy to commit computer intrusion, related to his abetting Bradley Manning's leak of classified material. This indictment did not address press-related issues. Assange was subsequently indicted under the Espionage Act for publishing the material Manning provided. This second indictment is seen by some as a threat to freedom of the press, although—as noted—there is not broad agreement as to whether Assange can be considered a journalist.

Still, the questions remain: At what point, if any, should reporters put aside their professional and career interests for the sake of preserving the secrecy of some intelligence activity or information? What responsibilities, if any, does the press have for the results of a story it publishes?

CONCLUSION

Intelligence is not without its ethical and moral dilemmas, some of which can be excruciating. That these intelligence dilemmas exist also means that policy makers have choices to make that can have ethical and moral dimensions. Intelligence, perhaps more than any other government activity, operates on the edge of acceptable morality, occasionally dealing in techniques that would not be acceptable elsewhere in government or in private life. For most citizens, the trade-off between ethics and increased security is acceptable, provided that the intelligence community operates with rules, oversight, and accountability.

FURTHER READINGS

Bar-Joseph, Uri. "The Professional Ethics of Intelligence Analysis." *International Journal of Intelligence and Counterintelligence* 24 (spring 2011): 22–43.

Barry, James A. "Covert Action Can Be Just." *Orbis* 37 (summer 1993): 375–390.

———. *The Sword of Justice: Ethics and Coercion in International Politics.* New York: Praeger, 1998.

Diderichsen, Adam and Kira Vrist Rønn. "Intelligence by Consent: On the Inadequacy of Just War Theory as a Framework for Intelligence Ethics." *Intelligence and National Security* 32 (June 2017): 479–93.

Erskine, Tom. "'As Rays of Light to the Human Soul'? Moral Agents and Intelligence Gathering." *Intelligence and National Security* 19 (summer 2004): 359–381.

Gendron, Angela. "Just, War, Just Intelligence: An Ethical Framework for Foreign Espionage." *International Journal of Intelligence and Counterintelligence* 18 (fall 2005): 398–434.

Godfrey, E. Drexel. "Ethics and Intelligence." *Foreign Affairs* 56 (April 1978): 624–642. (See also the response by Art Jacobs in the following issue.)

Helms, Richard, with William Hood. *A Look Over My Shoulder: A Life in the Central Intelligence Agency.* New York: Random House, 2003.

Herman, Michael. "Ethics and Intelligence After September 2001." *Intelligence and National Security* 19 (summer 2004): 342–358.

Lauren, Paul Gordon. "Ethics and Intelligence." In *Intelligence: Policy and Process.* Ed. Alfred C. Maurer and others. Boulder, Colo.: Westview Press, 1985.

Levinson, Sanford, ed. *Torture: A Collection.* New York: Oxford University Press, 2004.

Masters, Barrie P. *The Ethics of Intelligence Activities.* Washington, D.C.: National War College, National Security Affairs Forum, spring–summer 1976.

Olson, James M. *Fair Play: The Moral Dilemmas of Spying.* Dulles, Va.: Potomac Books, 2007.

Omand, Sir David, and Mark Phythian. "Ethics and Intelligence: A Debate." *International Journal of Intelligence and Counterintelligence* 26 (spring 2013): 38–63.

_____. *Principled Spying: The Ethics of Secret Intelligence*. Washington, D.C.: Georgetown University Press, 2018.

Perry, David. *Partly Cloudy: Ethics in War, Espionage, Covert Action and Interrogation*. Lanham, Md.: Scarecrow Press, 2009.

Posner, Richard A. *Not a Suicide Pact: The Constitution in a Time of National Emergency*. New York: Oxford University Press, 2006.

Powers, Thomas. *The Man Who Kept the Secrets: Richard Helms and the CIA*. New York: Knopf, 1979.

Rosenzweig, Paul, Timothy J. McNulty, and Ellen Shearer, eds. *Whistleblowers, Leaks, and the Media: The First Amendment and National Security*. Washington, D.C.: ABA Book Publishing, 2014.

Schoenfeld, Gabriel. *Necessary Secrets: National Security, the Media, and the Rule of Law*. New York: W. W. Norton, 2010.

Shane, Scott. "The Moral Case for Drones." *New York Times*, July 15, 2012, SR4. (Available at http://www.nytimes.com/2012/07/15/sunday-review/the-moral-case-for-drones.html.)

Sorel, Albert. *Europe Under the Old Regime*. Trans. Francis H. Herrick. New York: Harper and Row, 1947.

United Nations Human Rights Council. *Report of the Special Rapporteur on Extrajudicial, Summary or Arbitrary Executions, Philip Alston*. A/HRC/14/24/Add.6. May 28, 2010. (Available at http://www2.ohchr.org/english/bodies/hrcouncil/docs/14session/A.HRC.14.24.Add6.pdf.)

CHAPTER FOURTEEN

INTELLIGENCE REFORM

Efforts to improve, alter, or reorganize the intelligence community are as old as the community itself. Richard A. Best Jr., in a Congressional Research Service (CRS) study prepared for the House Intelligence Committee as part of its review of intelligence community functions (*IC21: The Intelligence Community in the 21st Century*), examined nineteen major studies, reviews, and proposals, covering the period 1949 to 1996, for change in the intelligence community. For devotees and critics of the community, reform is something of a cottage industry. Like the caucus race in *Alice in Wonderland*, debates over intelligence reform seem to have neither a beginning nor an end.

"Intelligence reform" is a catchall phrase, used to connote any and all efforts to make significant changes in the intelligence community. However, in the mid-1970s, in the aftermath of the Church and Pike Committees' investigations, "reform" took on a more specific meaning. It referred to efforts to prevent the recurrence of abuses of authority or illegal acts that had been uncovered by the committees and the earlier "family jewels" report, written at the direction of Director of Central Intelligence (DCI) James Schlesinger (1973), describing illegal Central Intelligence Agency (CIA) activities. This usage reappeared among critics of the National Security Agency (NSA) programs in the aftermath of the Edward Snowden leaks.

The use of the word "reform" remains problematic in that it can imply that something needs fixing, as opposed to simply being improved. In this chapter, "reform" should be read in the broader, more benign sense of the word—improvement, not necessarily the correction of abuses.

THE PURPOSE OF REFORM

When one sifts through the reform proposals, a key question must be asked: What is the purpose of the reforms? In his CRS study, Best delineated three broad chronological categories of proposals:

1. To improve the efficiency of the intelligence community in the context of the cold war

2. To respond to specific intelligence failures or improprieties, including the Bay of Pigs, the "family jewels," the Iran-contra affair, and others

3. To refocus intelligence community requirements and structure in the post–cold war era

The third category, post–cold war efforts to update the community's structure, reached a culmination with the passage of the Intelligence Reform and Terrorism Prevention Act (IRTPA) in 2004, although this legislation was a reaction to both the 2001 terrorist attacks and the Iraq weapons of mass destruction (WMD) estimate and not a result of any of the post–cold war studies. This is not to suggest that the issue of intelligence reform is closed. It is not. The intelligence community will never reach an end state but will be subject to periodic reviews and organizational changes.

Efforts to redress glaring failures or misdeeds are easy to understand. Efforts to improve intelligence per se are more difficult to assess. Few reliable guidelines are available for measuring intelligence, which makes it difficult to determine what constitutes an acceptable level of regular success or how to achieve it. The problem may be more difficult for analysis than it is for collection or operations. Assessing the latter two activities is more straightforward. Either the capability to collect against a target exists or it does not, and if it does, then the collection has either been accomplished or it has not. Extenuating circumstances may arise, but the evaluation process for collection is simple. Similarly, for operations, the goals are either achieved or unmet. Some operations may go on without resolution, such as U.S. support to the Nicaraguan contras in the 1980s, but the lack of resolution itself may be an important indicator of the likelihood of ultimate success. Analysis remains more elusive. Few metrics are to be had in what is essentially an intellectual process. Volumes of reports or batting averages are not useful measurements. One of the customarily offered standards is "efficiency," which is also likely incorrect. Collection activities can sometimes be efficient, but satellites operate in response to the laws of physics, which create severe limitations on where they are and what they collect. Analysis is even less likely to be efficient, given that it is an intellectual activity. We can hardly urge analysts to think faster or more efficiently. As Director of National Intelligence (DNI) James Clapper (2010–2017) has pointed out, efficiency is perhaps the wrong measure; it should be effectiveness.

The terrorist attacks in 2001 brought renewed calls for intelligence reform, with some of the most persistent advocates arguing, "If not now, when?" Even so, the purposes of reform have not been entirely clear. Several different purposes, not all of which are mutually exclusive, can be discerned:

- To improve the intelligence community's ability to deal with terrorism overall

- To prevent further terrorist attacks against the United States

- To determine if the attacks occurred because of specific intelligence lapses and, if so, who was responsible for them

- To use the attacks as an opportunity to push intelligence reform concepts, whether or not related to the attacks or the war on terrorists

However, the issue that provided the ultimate impetus for the intelligence legislation of 2004 was not the investigations into the September 11 attacks but the flawed analysis of Iraq WMD. The gap between prewar estimates and what was found (or not found) in Iraq once military action commenced in 2003 helped push many who had been undecided into the camp of intelligence reform. This factor also helps explain why the legislation focused so heavily on the management and oversight of analysis, with less attention given to the perceived problems that led to the September 11 attacks.

One final factor that must be taken into account is the misperception that the advent of multiple round-the-clock news media makes the intelligence community redundant. Those who hold this view believe that the community must transform itself to be more competitive.

Journalism and intelligence have some interesting similarities: the need for reliable sources, the need to make complex stories comprehensible, and the tyranny of deadlines. But there are also important differences. Deadlines may be even more tyrannical for the news media—both print and broadcast, but especially the latter—than they are for the intelligence community. News broadcasts must go on the air as scheduled, regardless of the day's events. Journalists accept this operating necessity and use updates, corrections, or retractions as necessary. Whenever possible, intelligence managers and analysts seek to delay reporting (sometimes too long) until they have the story correct, or as correct as collection will allow. Indeed, Gen. Michael Hayden, when he was the director of the NSA, urged his staff "to get the intelligence out" as soon as it was useful to someone—in other words, to publish intelligence as soon as it informs someone, even if it can be refined further, at which point it still can be published for yet another audience. Also, the average noncrisis news broadcast contains a great deal of filler and repetition over a twenty-four-hour period. The intelligence community also needs to report, but not around the clock. This is a saving grace. Moreover, the intelligence community seeks to do more than report; value-added analysis is an essential part of what it produces. Such analysis happens much less frequently in the news media, particularly the broadcast media. When it does occur, analysis can spill over into opinion. Squabbles among the twenty-four-hour news networks about which of them has a liberal or a conservative bias, or which is "fake" and which is not, underscore the problem.

Still, the misperception persists, even among some policy makers, that round-the-clock news sources upstage the work of the intelligence community. The misperception that the two are in competition may reveal a less than firm understanding of their fundamental differences, although the news media may employ concepts, technologies, and approaches that would be of use to intelligence. Interestingly, just as some in the intelligence community believe they must compete with twenty-four-hour news sources, those same sources now see themselves in competition with various types of social media, which can report even faster, albeit with fewer strictures as to sourcing or accuracy. This problem became evident in the aftermath of the April 2013 Boston Marathon bombing, when CNN issued several reports based on Twitter feeds, which proved to be erroneous. In intelligence and in journalism, there is a trade-off between speed and accuracy.

ISSUES IN INTELLIGENCE REFORM

Discussions about intelligence reform tend to fall into two broad areas: structure—or reorganization—and process. Both approaches have their advocates. Ideally, the issues should be approached together. Altered structure and unaltered process can become little more than moving boxes on the bureaucratic organization chart. Changing the process without changing structure would likely end in few, if any, meaningful results, as the old structure would probably resist the new processes. The sections that follow address some of the more frequently discussed issues in intelligence reform, some of which have been mentioned in preceding chapters. Some issues have been settled by the 2004 legislation, but they are likely to be touchstones of future debate as the new intelligence structure functions but remains under scrutiny.

The Role of the DCI and the DNI. The most central issue in the management and functioning of the U.S. intelligence community was the gap between the responsibilities (extensive) and the authority (limited) of the DCI. Under Executive Order 12333 (signed by President Reagan in 1981), the DCI was "the primary adviser to the President and the NSC [National Security Council] on national foreign intelligence." The designation included "full responsibility for [the] production and dissemination of national foreign intelligence," which included the authority to task agencies beyond the CIA. These responsibilities have passed to the DNI, although it is not clear that the problem of the DNI's authorities has been resolved.

The DNI's authority remains limited and may be subject to even more stress than was the case for the DCI. Some 75 to 80 percent of intelligence agencies and their budgets remain under the direct control of the secretary of defense. Any additional power granted to the DNI can come only from the secretary of defense. Initially, the secretary of defense and the under secretary for intelligence (USDI) had a more fractious relationship with the DNI. Since 2006, senior defense officials have taken a much more cooperative approach to their relationship with the DNI, although the secretary of defense will always be the more powerful position. It still remains unlikely that there will be major shifts of actual power or control over the two collection agencies, the National Geospatial-Intelligence Agency (NGA) and NSA, which are also defense intelligence agencies and combat support agencies. Much depends on personalities and on the issues of the day, but the secretary of defense will always have a superior position bureaucratically. This is also true for the defense intelligence agencies vis-à-vis the DNI. If these agencies have a significant issue with the DNI, they can always go to the secretary of defense for support. The DNI can, theoretically, go the president, but this is not something one would do except for the most important issues. Therefore, bureaucratically, the DNI is largely left to his or her own devices.

Congress also is a factor in any redistribution of power, with the House and Senate Armed Services Committees jealously guarding the turf of the Department of Defense (DOD) that they oversee. The argument over power is a zero-sum game. Although few, if any, secretaries of defense believed that the DCI threatened their authority, DOD was clear about preserving all of its authority during the congressional debate in 2004. Defense officials worry about two fronts: the authority of the secretary (often referred to as "Title 10 prerogatives," as spelled out in the U.S. Code, and discussed in chapter 8) and intelligence support for military operations. The latter became the main point argued by DOD supporters in the 2004 debate.

The other main concern for the DNI (beyond that of his or her relationship to the president) is the DNI's relationship with the director of the CIA (DCIA). The most obvious areas of contention are control of covert action and human intelligence (HUMINT). Both of these are conducted by the Directorate of Operations (DO), and the DCIA is the HUMINT manager. These are also the two most sensitive activities undertaken by intelligence, so of course they are of concern to the DNI. As has been noted, these became issues, along with the naming of chiefs of station, between DNI Dennis Blair (2009–2010) and DCIA Leon Panetta (2009–2011). Panetta was widely perceived to have won this struggle. The other DNI-CIA issue is analysis. Simply put, the DNI has very few analysts working directly for him or her, essentially the national intelligence officers (NIOs) and their small staff. The CIA, by contrast, has the largest number of all-source analysts in the intelligence community. Thus, when intelligence analyses may be driving policy discussions, the DNI is less likely to have the same familiarity with the analysts who produced it. There are also analysts who come under the DNI at the National Counterterrorism Center (NCTC), which is important for that one issue. But the director of the NCTC can be problematic for the DNI when the NCTC director is engaged in strategic operational planning, a function for which the NCTC director is allowed direct access to the president.

Much of the problem with the DCI's authority stemmed from the origins of the office and how the intelligence community developed. The designation DCI predates the creation of the CIA. The first DCIs ran the Central Intelligence Group (CIG), which became the CIA in the National Security Act of 1947. President Harry S. Truman's goal in creating the CIA under the DCI was to have a central organization that could coordinate the disparate analyses coming from the State Department and the military. No one envisioned the CIA's producing finished intelligence in its own right or conducting operations. Thus, the limited authority granted to the DCI was consistent with the role as coordinator. The CIA was seen as the agency that supported this coordinating role.

As the CIA moved to fill both analytical and operational voids in the early 1950s, the DCI's power base grew, but it also diverted the DCI's attention from the community-wide role. This is the issue that the 2004 legislation sought to correct, freeing the DNI from running any agency and thus allowing the DNI to concentrate on the larger community role. What remains at issue is the degree to which this larger role can be accomplished without the strong institutional base that the CIA afforded the DCI. As former acting DCI John McLaughlin (2004) noted in his testimony on the proposed legislation, the reason DCIs have relied on the CIA is that it was the only agency they could command. The DNI does not have this base on which to fall back.

The DCI's role could have been significantly enhanced if the office had been given budget execution authority over the National Intelligence Program (NIP; in 2004 it was still called the National Foreign Intelligence Program, or NFIP)—that is, determining how the money is spent. The ability to direct the allocation and spending of money is a major source of power and control, which is why DOD fought to keep this power from the DNI. But a political issue also was involved in choosing this course: It was too bureaucratic and not dramatic enough to suit those seeking major changes. Furthermore, some of the September 11 families proved an effective and difficult-to-refute lobbying force in favor of the DNI legislation. Although some commentators have questioned the propriety of allowing the grieving families to dictate national security structure, they had tremendous political clout.

DOD's arguments against ceding spending control to either the DCI or DNI are based on the view that such a change runs the risk of limiting intelligence support to military operations and that, without direct DOD control, this intelligence support may be wanting. The likelihood of this happening seems small. It is difficult to believe that any DCI or DNI would run the political risk inherent in not giving full support to the military in peacetime or in war, if for no other reason than self-protection, to avoid being blamed for military setbacks or casualties. Nothing in past practice over the more than sixty years of the modern intelligence community's existence would suggest that any substance can be found behind DOD's argument.

The declassification of both the NIP and the Military Intelligence Program (MIP) top-line numbers may give the DNI greater budgetary freedom. As long as the NIP figure was classified, it was necessary to hide the money elsewhere in an appropriations bill. The Defense Appropriations bill became that vehicle for fairly logical reasons. However, this meant that a large enough "wedge" had to be put in defense appropriations to cover the intelligence amount. This led to bargaining between intelligence authorizers and defense authorizers and appropriators in Congress over the size of the intelligence budget; it also gave the Defense Department a certain control over intelligence budgets if DOD felt that the wedge was too large, especially if it came at the expense of weapons or personnel. With the two budgets now unclassified, this hide-and-seek system is less necessary, in effect, giving the DNI more budget latitude. The congressional part of the system would now make more sense if there was a separate intelligence appropriations bill, as well as an intelligence appropriations subcommittee, but these do not seem to be likely. Again, the issues are power and control, in this case, for the House and Senate Defense Appropriations subcommittees.

The DNI position had a difficult beginning. First, there was the opposition from Defense to anything that was perceived as impinging on its authorities or needs in intelligence, which limited the DNI's authority within the intelligence community. Second, this new position was being placed over 16 agencies that had been up and running for decades in some cases. The first DNI, John Negroponte (2005–2007), was criticized by his congressional overseers for not being firm enough in establishing and using his authority. Negroponte deserves credit for getting what many perceived to be an unwieldy structure up and functioning, but he did not exercise much guiding authority over the intelligence community. His successor, Mike McConnell (2007–2009), put more emphasis on the problem areas that he saw as being the main inhibitors to a more collaborative and integrated intelligence community, but he ended up spending a great deal of his time in legislative debates, especially over the revision of the Foreign Intelligence Surveillance Act (FISA). Dennis Blair ran into the problems noted above, as well as a series of bureaucratic arguments in the aftermath of the December 2009 terrorist attempt on the airliner in Detroit. James Clapper made efforts to reduce the Office of the DNI (ODNI) and shift many of its functions to other agencies that would act as executive agents on his behalf while he focused on actions that enabled the agencies to do their jobs and especially for the community to act in a more unified manner, promoting **intelligence integration** toward common goals. Dan Coats (2017–2019) has continued to emphasize the importance of intelligence integration. This may prove to be a more successful approach, although in times of crisis the DNI will inevitably be drawn into becoming an action officer and will be held responsible for any shortcomings even though he or she has little control over the actual intelligence activities. It is also important to note, once again, the volatility of the DNI job thus far. There were four DNIs in the first five years; Clapper's longer tenure offered much needed stability, but it is not likely that many DNIs will serve for seven years.

The main locus for intelligence integration is the **national intelligence managers (NIMs)**, who have regional or functional portfolios. The NIMs are responsible for intelligence integration—meaning collection and analysis—in their portfolios and are also responsible for crafting **unifying intelligence strategies (UIS)** for their portfolios. Some of the NIMs also manage DNI centers (NCTC, National Counterintelligence and Security Center [NCSC], National Counterproliferation Center [NCPC]), which gives them more of an institutional base. This NIM system is still a work in progress and depends on the various intelligence agencies actually cooperating with the DNI and the NIMs.

Much also still depends on the DNI having sufficient authority to force compliance or to mete out consequences for obstruction. As DCI Richard Helms (1966–1973) observed about the DCI's position, much of the DNI's authority stems from both the real and the perceived support the DNI has from the president. The initial signals from President George W. Bush (2001–2009) were ambiguous: granting authority to the DNI, as in the case of the morning briefing, but assuring CIA that its role was not diminished. As was the case when the secretary of defense position was created in 1947, the legislation may have to be revised once the flaws have been revealed. The DNI is also supposed to improve the overall coherence of the intelligence community—hence, the NIMs and the UIS. The issue remains whether the legislation provides the levers necessary to do these jobs. The DNI will also come under tremendous political pressure should another major terrorist attack occur in the United States. Supporters of the IRTPA argued that the creation of a DNI freed from any agency and the emphasis on information sharing and integration would lessen the likelihood of an attack. Many intelligence officers and some outside observers fail to see any connection between the new structures and what is needed to prevent a terrorist attack, as the law seems largely to have created another layer without making any marked changes in how terrorism is addressed.

McConnell, after leaving office, recommended creating a Cabinet-level Department of Intelligence as a means of improving the DNI's ability to manage the community. It is not clear how such a department would function or what it would contain. Defense, for example, is unlikely to give up its control over signals intelligence (SIGINT) or geospatial intelligence (GEOINT). Nor would any Cabinet secretary likely be willing to give up his or her in-house analytical support. Thus, the new Intelligence Department might become a super-office of the DNI, which many observers feel is already too large and too unwieldy. Clapper did not support this idea when he became DNI.

How do we know if the DNI is working? This is one of the great uncertainties in the role of the DNI—the absence of any agreed set of hallmarks that will help determine whether or not the new structure is working and whether it is making a positive contribution to the management of U.S. intelligence. Most of the "doing" functions of intelligence—collection, analysis, and operations—take place within the agencies and not at the DNI level. Improvements in any of these functions may not be directly attributable to initiatives from the DNI. Thus, we are left with either few useful hallmarks by which to judge the DNI function or one very stark hallmark—another foreign terrorist attack (as opposed to further lone-wolf attacks)—which most observers judge to be likely regardless of which structure is chosen. Indeed, at his 2010 confirmation hearings, Clapper noted that if this is the one hallmark of success, then he was not likely to succeed, noting the likelihood of another attack at some point in the future. However, judging by the reaction of members of Congress and the press after the December 2009 terrorist attempt, there does seem to be a real underlying belief that the creation of the DNI should somehow have made these attempts less likely.

Stovepipes. As discussed in earlier chapters, the term "stovepipes" refers to agencies in similar or analogous lines of work (collection or analysis) that tend to compete with one another, sometimes to a wasteful and perhaps harmful extent.

The stovepipe issue is most often discussed in reference to the big three collection disciplines (INTs)—SIGINT, GEOINT, and HUMINT—and particularly the technical INTs (especially SIGINT and GEOINT). Some have proposed putting at least the technical INTs (SIGINT, GEOINT, and measures and signatures intelligence, or MASINT) under a single agency with the authority to decide which INTs should respond to which requirements, thus limiting some collection that may not be optimal or necessary. This solution raises questions of its own:

- Who would run such an agency? Would it matter if that person were civilian or military?

- Would this new agency be manageable?

- Given that DOD currently controls all the technical INTs, would this remain true? What are the implications either way?

The main goal is some modicum of collection efficiency and improved resource management. However, the suggested solution would create a large entity, the inherent power of which might rival that of the DNI. Cooperation has grown significantly between NGA and NSA, although still far from the point of a merger of any sort.

Some commentators have suggested that the two HUMINT components—the CIA's Directorate of Operations, or DO, and the Defense Clandestine Service of the Defense Intelligence Agency (DCS)—be unified, also to avoid duplication. Changes made to DCS by Under Secretary of Defense for Intelligence Michael Vickers, both to expand DCS and to realign it more closely with the DO, ran into opposition in Congress in 2013 precisely because it looked duplicative, as noted in chapter 5.

Recognition of the need to improve coordination among the various HUMINT collectors—which include the Federal Bureau of Investigation (FBI), Drug Enforcement Administration (DEA), and the military services as well as the CIA and Defense Intelligence Agency (DIA)—was the impetus behind DCI/DCIA Porter J. Goss's (2004–2006) creation of the National Clandestine Service (replacing the Directorate of Operations until DCIA John Brennan's 2015 restructuring), which includes a deputy to coordinate HUMINT across the intelligence community. Once again, we face the competing goals of greater efficiency in terms of overall management but also the utility of separate HUMINT efforts, which permits a broader and more diverse HUMINT collection effort. Along similar lines, some have proposed that the clandestine services (HUMINT and covert action) be a separate agency, either to improve management responsibility or to avoid contaminating analysis or both. Sen. Pat Roberts, R-KS, made such a proposal in 2004, at the outset of the debate over the new intelligence structure. Judging by the reaction Roberts received, it is fair to say that very few support this concept, although it is not as radical as it is often portrayed, replicating, as it does, the British structure.

In the area of collection, open-source intelligence (OSINT) is a specific and fairly constant reform issue. OSINT was long underutilized and had no strong organizational locus. Reformers have advanced several ideas to improve the role of OSINT, including creating an OSINT agency or office or contracting out stronger OSINT services. The common goal is to elevate OSINT to a full-standing INT that is readily available to all analysts, as opposed to the more random situation that currently exists. One of the DNI's first responsibilities was to report to Congress on the future of OSINT and the possibility of creating a separate OSINT agency. The WMD Commission (Commission on the Intelligence Capabilities of the United States Regarding Weapons of Mass Destruction) recommended creating an Open Source Directorate at the CIA. DNI Negroponte created an Open Source Center (OSC), which was largely a renaming of the old Foreign Broadcast Information Service (FBIS), which had long been the leading OSINT producer. Negroponte gave management responsibility for the OSC to the CIA, which made sense given that FBIS had long been part of the CIA's Directorate of Science and Technology (DS&T). However, this left the OSC open to criticism that it was old wine in new bottles. The ODNI and OSC went to great pains to show that there is now an increased reliance on and better utility of OSINT in intelligence products, including the President's Daily Brief (PDB) and National Intelligence Estimates (NIEs), such as the Iran WMD NIE. Today, OSINT probably has greater visibility than has been the case for many years, but its bureaucratic status remains uncertain. In 2015, as part of his overall restructuring, DCIA Brennan renamed the OSC the Open Source Enterprise and made it part of the new Digital Innovation Directorate. It is not clear if this represents a changed status (either better or worse) or simply a reshuffling.

A final aspect of OSINT to be considered is the greater portion of required intelligence that is open. This has a benefit, in that this intelligence is easier to obtain, but it also has a downside. It means that the intelligence community has less control over its sources than it did before and that many other nations can have access to the same open intelligence. In effect, the collection playing field has been leveled to some degree. Does this shift make intelligence less valuable overall, or does it put an even greater premium on the classified collection sources, as these then become the major discriminators in the collection arena writ large?

Two other collection issues that are part of the reform debate have already been discussed: the balance between HUMINT and technical intelligence (TECHINT) and the need for improved TPEDs (tasking, processing, exploitation, and dissemination).

The TPEDs discussion has several dimensions. The first is the applicability of this process to the age of largely digital intelligence. Critics argue that the TPEDs process is outdated and slow, although few question the necessity of the various steps in the process. Given that most of the process is already digital in nature, where and how could it be improved? The nature of the term "improved" in the context of TPEDs is also interesting. Does it mean a faster processing of the collected data or processing more intelligence? This has always been one of the shortcomings of the system: the disparity between what is collected and what is processed and disseminated. Another issue is the accessibility of the process, which focuses on collection, to analysts. Should they have more input and insight into the process? If so, how would that be managed and controlled without overwhelming the system with analyst requests?

The TPEDs issue also leads to a discussion of the intelligence process. As noted in chapter 3, the intelligence process is less a step-by-step program that must be followed precisely than an overarching guide to the way in which intelligence is collected, processed, and turned into something that policy makers can use. Still, the process is worth examining, or reexamining, from time to time to determine if it needs to be updated or changed as technology and issues change. These issues are discussed below.

Finally, as suggested in chapter 5, there is nothing sacred about five INTs or any other number. It may be worthwhile to consider both social media and data as separate INTs if we are to reap the full benefit of these intelligence sources. This, of course, would lead to issues of ownership and placement within the intelligence community, not unlike the fate of open source.

Analysis. Turning to analysis, the main issues highlighted in the 2004 legislation were ways to improve the oversight of intelligence at the DNI level in terms of timeliness, objectivity, and quality of analysis as well as to foster more alternative analysis. Similar issues were discussed in the 2005 WMD Commission report. Although the goals are worthy, the idea of legislating analytical standards strikes some as unrealistic, or divorced from the reality of analysis.

Underlying the provisions may be a changing view about the acceptable tolerances within which intelligence analysis exists. Coming up with reliable standards for assessing the quality of analysis is difficult. (See chap. 6.) An obvious but stark one would be "right or wrong." The problem with this standard is that most analytical issues play out over time, during which some analytical judgments are right and some are wrong. The analytical standards promulgated by the office of the then-deputy DNI for analysis recognized this time lag problem. In the end, creating a balance sheet could be possible, but doing so would be secondary in importance to whether policy goals were met over that period. The intelligence community's experience with the Soviet Union is instructive. Over the forty-four years that the intelligence community spent analyzing the Soviet Union, it made numerous analytical judgments. Again, some were right and some were wrong. The wrong judgments, although problematic, never put U.S. security at risk, although one could argue about the intelligence community's analytic performance during the early phases of the Cuban Missile Crisis. More important, however, is that U.S. policy vis-à-vis the Soviet Union, supported by intelligence, succeeded, and the Soviet Union collapsed. Part of the problem is perceptual. By virtue of the issues they address and the highly charged political atmosphere in which they now exist, much attention goes to NIEs. These are high-value analytical products, although they have not tended to be influential in terms of policy making. A great deal of the intelligence community's analytical effort takes place at a lower, more constant level, providing daily intelligence support to a broad range of policy makers.

But September 11 and Iraq WMD, for example, reflect a starker situation. Despite multiple warnings about al Qaeda hostility and intentions, no specific intelligence warning—as opposed to a more general one—was possible about the terrorist attacks. Many observers have noted that the threads of intelligence make sense only in hindsight, but a body of opinion sees September 11 as a right or wrong issue. The discussion may be on firmer ground with Iraq WMD. The situation on the ground in Iraq did not reflect prewar estimates. Although, as DCI George J. Tenet (1997–2004) pointed out in his 2004 speech at Georgetown University, parts of the estimate were borne out, both over- and under-estimative judgments were made, and overall the analysis was not correct. But does this argue for the acceptability or the wider utility of a right or wrong standard? The fear among some in the intelligence community is that little tolerance now exists for anything other than absolutely correct intelligence judgments and that the legislative provisions regarding analysis reflect this view. If so, then the intelligence community is doomed to fail, as it will never achieve success in a right or wrong system. It is also difficult, although probably necessary, to have a discussion about how right analysis can or should be. The answer is "right as often as possible." But the key to that answer is the word "possible." A level of reasonable expectations of intelligence analysis may have been lost and will be difficult to regain. (There is also an interesting and somewhat humorous legal question. If analysis turns out to be wrong, and not all of the strictures in the legislation were followed, is the intelligence community guilty of violating the law?)

Former deputy DCI Richard Kerr offers a more nuanced approach in an article he wrote in 2008 (see Further Readings). After reviewing roughly fifty years of intelligence analysis, Kerr concluded that the intelligence community deserved high marks for keeping a diverse set of policy makers reasonably well informed so that they could make difficult decisions with a greater sense of confidence. This does not mean that all of the analysis was correct, but Kerr's paradigm represents a considerable and useful service, albeit one that may seem mundane to some observers.

Since 2007, the NIP total has been declassified, which inevitably leads to questions as to why, given that sum of expenditure, the intelligence community cannot do better. Again, intelligence is among the most difficult government activities when it comes to trying to relate expenditures to results. The relationship between expenditures and better analytic outcomes is very difficult to prove.

The reports of the 9/11 Commission (National Commission on Terrorist Attacks upon the United States) and the WMD Commission also focused attention on how best to organize analysts across the community. The 9/11 Commission recommended organizing all analysts by regional or functional national intelligence centers. In the commission's concept, the centers would carry out all-source analysis and plan intelligence operations and "would be housed in whatever department or agency is best suited for them." The center concept arose during the late 1980s and early 1990s as the community put increased emphasis on transnational issues that—by definition—crossed national borders. The centers allowed analysts from various agencies to be brought together to focus on an issue, although the centers tended to be dominated by the CIA. The 2004 reform law mandated only one center, the NCTC, but also stipulated that the DNI report to Congress on creating a center for nonproliferation, which has been done. A clear expectation is presented in the legislation that other centers will be created as well. As noted, in 2015, DCIA Brennan reorganized the DO and the DA (Directorate of Analysis, formerly the Directorate of Intelligence, DI) into regional and functional centers, not unlike the 9/11 Commission recommendation. The main advantage of the centers is, in theory, the ability to get cross-cutting analysis on an issue, assuming that they are true community centers and not dominated by one agency. In the case of the new CIA centers, the goal is to have analysts work more closely with collectors/operators. But centers also have disadvantages:

- To date, centers have been primarily functional in nature, although in the case of the CIA, there are also regional ones. Analysts in functional centers consult with their regional colleagues, but this requires some effort. Organizing by centers—either regional or functional—can exacerbate the tendency to view the issue in a more unidimensional aspect. Also, some of the issues handled by centers have close relationships, such as terrorism and narcotics. Sharing analyses across these boundaries can also be difficult. In other words, centers may create analytical stovepipes of their own.

- Getting resources out of or away from centers has proved difficult once they are established. Although a DNI should be able to effect changes, past performance indicates that centers can run counter to the desire for greater analytic agility.

- Centers have tended to focus on the most pressing issues. In a center-based community, devoting some level of resources to those issues or regions that have lower priorities may prove even more difficult than it has been. Again, the CIA structure may obviate this to some extent, although it is safe to assume that resource allocations will be based on perceived levels of importance from center to center.

The WMD Commission recommended the creation of one new center, the National Counterproliferation Center, although it would not function like the other intelligence centers. As established by the DNI in 2005, the NCPC serves "to identify critical intelligence gaps or shortfalls in collection, analysis or exploitation, and develop solutions to ameliorate or close these gaps." Thus, it is not an intelligence production center. Its ability to carry out its mandate depends on knowing exactly what the intelligence community is doing concerning proliferation and the DNI's ability to then make changes.

Closely related to the center issue is the older issue of the flexibility and agility of the analytical corps. The analytical agencies have no reserve or surge capacity. Analysis is still organized around the two basic structures: regional and topical offices. These are not mutually exclusive, but no intelligence service around the world has discovered a third organizing principle.

The problem stems, in part, from the fact that analysts have to be expert in something, which necessarily defines and limits the issues on which they can work. Creating a corps of intelligence generalists is impractical and dangerous. They will likely know a little about many issues but not much about any single issue. Successful intelligence analysis requires expertise, and long-term expertise is one of the major value-adds of the intelligence community. Thus, the problem is to maintain some level of flexibility or surge within this body of experts. As noted earlier, one of the issues facing the analytic components is that many of the analysts hired since 2001 have worked mostly on tactical issues—counterterrorism and counterinsurgency (CT and COIN). Now there are growing needs to work on nation-state issues—such as Russia and China— that have tactical aspects but are much more strategic in nature. DCIA Gina Haspel (2018–) highlighted this in 2018.

Surge is most important during crises, especially in areas that previously had a low priority. However, in giving a low priority to a particular issue or nation, the policy and intelligence communities have already decided not to allocate many resources to it. Short of either finding someone already on staff who has some working knowledge of the issue or dragooning others into working on it, not much can be done internally. A frequently suggested reform proposal is the creation and use of an intelligence reserve—a body of experts, either former intelligence analysts or outside experts, who can augment analytical ranks during a crisis.

Congress created such a reserve in 1996, but the intelligence community has never fully implemented it. Several issues are involved, one of which is security. Many outside experts do not have security clearances and may be unwilling to accept the restrictions they impose. Thus, either they are eliminated as sources, or the intelligence community is required to find ways to tap their expertise without revealing classified information. Although the latter is not impossible, those responsible for security are likely to raise some objections. The irony is that these outside experts are useful because of what they know and not because they need access to classified material. It should be possible to tap their expertise and avoid the clearance issue entirely. Another issue is cost. The intelligence community does not budget for such contingencies— just as DOD does not budget for wartime operations during peacetime. As with the military, budget mechanisms—reallocations, supplemental appropriations—are available. The main impediment appears to be attitudes within the intelligence community.

Then there is the issue of redundancy in the three all-source agencies—the CIA, the DIA, and the State Department Bureau of Intelligence and Research (INR). The intentional duplication stems from two fundamental operating principles of the intelligence community: the distinct intelligence needs of different senior policy makers and the concept of competitive analysis. Unless one is willing to give up either or both operating principles, one must accept the cost of the redundancy. Neither the executive branch nor Congress is likely to abandon the concepts or to accept the idea of having a single analytical agency, which has been among the more radical proposed alternatives. In times of budget reductions, however, reducing some level of competitive analysis may appear to be attractive—assuming you can foretell which areas are likely to remain less important.

A more recent issue is the effect of the analytical standards promulgated by the ODNI in a series of intelligence community directives (ICDs). As noted in chapter 6, some managers and analysts see these as draconian rules as opposed to guidelines, which can have a self-limiting effect on analysis that certainly was not the intended result.

As also noted in chapter 6, there is concern about the difference between multi-INT products (primarily SIGINT and GEOINT) and all-source products. Part of this is a struggle over turf, but it also goes to a more fundamental issue—the level of analysis required by policy makers and who should be producing this analysis. As discussed, multi-INT products have a definite place in intelligence production. The problems created by these products are twofold. First, the analysts who write multi-INT are strong on the technical aspects of their intelligence but weak on the "softer" issues—politics, economics, and so on. Therefore, these analysts may be writing beyond their capabilities or expertise. Second, and closely related to the first issue, policy makers who read multi-INT products often cannot distinguish multi-INT analysis from all-source analysis and may therefore presume that it is true all-source analysis and that the "softer" judgments have the analytical authority that they have come to expect.

Finally, there is the intellectual aspect of analysis, which often seems to get lost in the discussion. One of the most striking aspects of the intelligence community is its very limited "lessons learned" capacity. There are several reasons for this. First, there is the issue of time. Analysts and their managers are very busy and do not have much time for reflection. As soon as one issue subsides, another rises to take its place. Second, no one likes to be reviewed. They would rather move on to the next issue. Although steps have been taken to improve the "lessons learned" capacity of intelligence within the ODNI, it remains very small and without much clout. There are useful examples of how to conduct such a function. The best may be the U.S. Army, which has such a center and an extensive process for conducting such studies. It is also important to recognize that one learns not only from one's mistakes but also from one's successes. What if the success ran counter to doctrine? Was it a fluke, or should the doctrine be revised? Most of the reforms most frequently mentioned for analysis, such as information sharing, address the apparatus of analysis but not its core: experts making difficult judgments with only partial information. In truth, it is much easier to make recommendations about the apparatus, but they are also less likely to affect this core activity. The core activity, at the same time, remains more elusive and less responsive to any bureaucratic or legislative fixes.

There is also the issue of building knowledge. The intelligence community once prided itself on having depth of expertise. This declined in the 1990s as people retired and budgets contracted. The influx of young analysts obviously creates a less expert workforce. Thought should therefore be given to the career choices and skills required to recreate a workforce that is not only agile and facile but is also expert on key issues.

Intelligence and the IT Revolution. A major and continuing source of reform ideas stems from the ongoing information technology (IT) revolution. Some ideas concern technology; others focus on process.

The IT revolution had an interesting effect on the intelligence community. For years, its homegrown technology—that is, technology developed entirely internally or with trusted contractors—was much more advanced than that available on the open market. However, the advent of the computer revolution allowed the open market to leapfrog over the intelligence community, through no fault of its own. The community's first reaction was to resist the externally developed technology in a classic case of the "not invented here" syndrome. Various reasons were cited, including special needs or security requirements.

The resistance phase passed, although the intelligence community (and the rest of the government) still has problems in bringing new technologies on board quickly. Note that the word "technology" is being used broadly here, including computer technology, analytical tools and other software, and new information sources. The issue has become more difficult as the marketplace fills with many technologies and tools, all making competing claims about their capabilities. The intelligence community, like every other modern enterprise, seeks technologies that are best suited to its specific needs. A good scouting force is required that can sample as many technologies as possible and make purchasing decisions quickly. In 1995, an IT industry expert noted that computer technology was changing every eighteen months but that the intelligence community (and the rest of the government) took from two to five years to purchase a computer. Thus, at best, an analyst was getting a computer that was already six months out of date. The situation today may be better, but the rapid absorption of modern technology remains an issue.

Process is a more difficult issue. Some reform advocates suggest that advances in IT would allow a looser intelligence structure, with a community of networks and more flexible organizations. Again, agility becomes a key goal.

The applicability to intelligence is uncertain. Greater flexibility in the analytical corps would be a tremendous improvement, but the intelligence community is unlikely to become completely free-form, relying on shifting networks of analysts to provide its structure. Much can be said for having the ability to bring together disparate and even physically distant analysts to work on pressing issues and then to disband them or to allow new groups to form as the issues change. However, such a scenario will not eliminate the need for some bureaucratic apparatus: supervisors who can relay requirements and oversee the meeting of deadlines, reviewers of analysis, and so on. The key is to find a way to provide the necessary structure without stifling analytical fluidity. Some will bridle at what seems to be a half-hearted solution, although it may prove to be more practical in the end.

The new technologies and concepts should not be overburdened with more promise than they can deliver. The dot-com meltdown of 2001–2002 is instructive in this regard. Many prognosticators had proclaimed a new economic age and the victory of virtual enterprises over bricks-and-mortar firms. However, a rapid and somewhat savage winnowing of the dot-coms occurred, while the bricks-and-mortar firms go on. The problem has been a confusion of means and ends. The IT revolution is not an end in itself, at least for intelligence. Instead, it is—or should be—a means by which the intelligence community can perform certain tasks more efficiently.

The terrorist attacks and the joint inquiry and 9/11 Commission investigations brought renewed focus on IT issues. An increased emphasis has been placed on the need to share information better. The ODNI produced a lengthy report on information sharing, which emphasized technology rather than policies and cultures, both of which are major impediments to improved sharing. Technology is the means to this end, but it cannot make sharing happen on its own. That depends on policies that mandate sharing and penalize those who do not. Such policies have not been implemented in the past and would be difficult to enforce, but it is necessary before questioning why the technology does not work. One example of the types of policies that are needed is the concept promoted by General Hayden, noted earlier, about getting the intelligence out sooner. Underlying the emphasis on technology may be the unstated belief that IT improvements can affect analysis. Although Americans have had a historical belief in the power of technology, no substantive cases serve as examples in which technology precluded either sharing or better analysis. Abundant stories can be told about incompatible IT systems from agency to agency, but that is not the same issue. This belief is, in some respects, the technological counterpart to the right or wrong analysis belief. To date, the search for improved analytical tools has not been particularly successful, and for some it has taken on the aspect of a hunt for the Holy Grail. Part of the problem is that intelligence analysis remains an intellectual process, not a mechanical one. IT can be helpful in amassing data, collating it, sifting it, creating relationships among databases, and so on, but it cannot replace an insightful and experienced analyst.

The ODNI has been pursuing a program call ICITE (Intelligence Community Information Technology Enterprise, pronounced "eyesight"). ICITE originated, in part, from the realization that the intelligence community had on hand billions of dollars' worth of legacy computer systems, dated computer systems, and incompatible computer systems. At a public forum, DNI Clapper put the value of these legacy systems at some $2.5 billion. This reflects, in part, the problem with a largely federated intelligence community. Another impetus behind ICITE related to Clapper's goal of intelligence integration by creating a common enterprise architecture across the intelligence community. According to a 2013 study, the intelligence community spends three times more of their budget on IT than do other government agencies. It would be difficult to argue that intelligence is more IT-dependent than all other government sectors given the ubiquity of the technology. But it does represent a major cost center.

ICITE relies on the IC Cloud but has discovered that as flexible as that is, the growth of data still creates problems. Also, despite the agreed need to work together, various intelligence agencies have distinct needs, applications, and tools that are not common to one another. The goal of creating a common desktop environment has not been practicable. Therefore, ICITE has shifted to being a "common reference architecture," meaning that it will serve as a common template for future IT efforts but will allow agencies a greater degree of individuality.

Again, the Manning and Snowden leaks also revealed one of the dangers of more intelligence sharing—putting a great deal of material in places where it can be easily accessed by individuals who have no need whatsoever and who may, in at least these two cases, use this access for their own ends. For example, in the case of Pvt. Manning, most of the cables had very low levels of classification. They had been placed on a Defense system called SIPRNET (Secret Internet Protocol Router Network), which has more than 500,000 users. The systems apparently had no internal safeguards or gateways, thus allowing the large-scale downloading. In the aftermath of the leaks, the State Department took steps to remove its materials from SIPRNET, which seems to be very much after the fact but also goes against the concept of information sharing.

The 2003 capture of Iraqi leader Saddam Hussein may be instructive in terms of IT and analysis. U.S. military officials and intelligence analysts assumed that Saddam had to be depending on someone for support while he was in hiding. They began by focusing attention on his innermost circle, but the search proved fruitless. So they began to widen the group of people in whom they were interested to more relatives, tribal allies, and lower level functionaries. More raids, more arrests, and more interrogations resulted, all of which served to expand the lists further. Eventually, they located Saddam's hideout. Although IT could have played a role—amassing names, comparing them, creating relationship maps—the key was analysis. A similar process was used to identify Osama bin Laden's key courier and use him to locate bin Laden's hideout.

The other argument in favor of improved IT tools is the commonly held perception that analysts are drowning in information. No substantive studies are available to compare the amount of data available to analysts twenty years ago, when everything was in hard copy, and today. The perception may be based, in part, on confusing the means by which the intelligence is delivered, IT, and the amount that is delivered. IT has not greatly expanded the working day of the French Foreign Ministry or the Chinese army. People can still work on and produce only so much information in a given day, whether or not there is IT. Technical collectors are struggling to put out as much finished GEOINT and SIGINT as they have in the past so that they are not sources of a major flood of information. IT certainly creates unnecessary redundancies of information, as the same data come in from separate sources. But this is not the same as a flood of new information. The irony is that people are looking to IT to solve the problems largely created by IT. As noted, one of the reactions to the attempted airplane bombing in December 2009 was to expand the number of names on the watchlists, thus increasing the amount of data that has to be screened.

The more recent emphasis on big data is also an issue within U.S. intelligence. Big data advocates tend to be IT specialists, not analysts. Nothing captures this better than the statement made by some big data advocates: "Collect now, analyze later." Intelligence cannot just keep collecting and not analyze quickly. To date, big data—beyond the hype—offers more vague promise than actual results, at least in intelligence. There may be some analytical answers to be had in some types of big data, but there is likely little to be gained from inundating analysts with data in the hope that something useful might emerge. One of the goals behind DCIA Brennan's creation of a Digital Innovation Directorate is to use its capabilities to create intelligence by mining the vast amounts of data the CIA receives. The assumption appears to be that there should be something useful in all of these data that was not seen before. Databases or data holdings have to be queried with specific goals in mind; data are inert and useless otherwise. At some point, it may become necessary to evaluate the time spent on this activity versus the return in additionally useful intelligence.

As noted in several chapters, both artificial intelligence and machine learning, which are closely interconnected, are being examined as potential opportunities for intelligence. This usually means assisting with big data, or freeing analysts from more mundane tasks. Both technologies remain far from substantive contributions, which does not mean they should be ignored. But it is also important to remember that human dependencies will remain in choosing and entering data and algorithms. Also, very few analysts or policy makers would be comfortable making major decisions based solely on "what the machine said."

Administrative Reform. An important although seemingly minor issue is administrative reform. Because the intelligence community comprises separate agencies, it has many distinct processes for security, personnel policies, training, and so on. To many observers, these seem wasteful and duplicative. Although significant differences exist in training a cryptanalyst, an imagery analyst, and a case officer, personnel procedures and some training are to a certain extent generic. The disparate infrastructure systems impose unnecessary costs. For example, if a terrorism analyst at the DIA seeks a better job at the CIA, also covering terrorism, more is involved than a simple transfer. The analyst must apply to the CIA, be vetted again for security, and resign from the DIA. Managing analysts as some larger integrated corps would be an improvement. This may be a seemingly minor area where the DNI can make real progress.

Personnel security is a key component of intelligence community administration. Edward Snowden's activities raise several broader issues. The first is the system of vetting all personnel, not just contractors, and how this can be done both effectively and efficiently. As noted, preferences in this area tend to be politically driven rather than based on a serious discussion of which means is best. Closely related to this is the insider threat issue. The IT revolution plays a twofold role here, both of them negative in nature. The first is the ease with which a would-be leaker or spy can access and remove large amounts of classified data. Solutions here appear to lie in the area of more controls over access, which can run athwart the desire to share more intelligence. The more problematic issue is the effect of social media, which promotes the self-proclaimed importance of the user. Blogs, tweets, and selfie pictures can be completely innocent, or they can be ways of establishing one's presence and one's significance, if not importance. Snowden may represent an exemplar of this behavior: His own personal views of the NSA programs were so much clearer and more accurate than those of the majority of Congress who voted for them and the president who signed them into law. Snowden's supporters would likely endorse this view, but most people would hesitate before making this assertion and taking those actions on their own. Thus, how do agencies—and especially their security officials—distinguish between innocent postings to social media and signs of an insider threat?

Transparency. As noted above, the intelligence community has embraced the necessity for greater transparency, in effect responding to some criticism it had received. The call for transparency arose, first, regarding the use of armed unmanned aerial vehicles (UAVs), driven by two concerns: (1) the killing of Anwar al-Awlaki and the rules for attacking a U.S. citizen and (2) the number of civilian casualties resulting from UAV attacks. Calls for transparency arose again in reaction to the Snowden leaks. The idea of transparency runs counter to intelligence activities that are designed to be kept secret but is also an important means of building and maintaining public support, which is crucial in a democracy. The concepts of transparency and secrecy are, to a great degree, antithetical. That said, the Obama administration released its criteria for attacks on U.S. citizens. The degrees of required transparency may also vary, depending on who is being informed for what purpose. In the case of the NSA programs, for example, their existence was in public law; the details and management were known to the president, to the intelligence oversight committees in Congress, and to the Foreign Intelligence Surveillance Court. To some, this would appear to be sufficient levels of transparency and oversight within a system of delegated responsibility. Widening this group becomes problematic. Should all members of Congress be briefed? Should the details of the programs have been made known to the public? In both cases, and in the issue of transparency overall, we are back to the issue of whether the "public's right to know" discussed in chapter 8 exists and, if so, whether it applies to classified intelligence activities.

DNI Clapper's "Principles of Intelligence Transparency" are seen as a means of assuring the American public regarding intelligence activities and as a means of building greater support for U.S. intelligence. This is a somewhat different concept of transparency than that noted above, which focuses on controversial operational activities. Clapper's transparency principles are a good indicator as to how far the political atmosphere surrounding intelligence has come since the days of the cold war, when there was a great deal of trust and much less political pressure to divulge secrets or the perceived need to assure the public.

The Intelligence Process. Some practitioners and some observers have raised questions about the intelligence process (requirements, collection, processing and evaluation, analysis, dissemination, consumption, and feedback). They argue that this is a twentieth-century century "industrial age" process in a twenty-first-century digital age. (This process provides much of the organizational framework for this book.) To some extent, the critiques misunderstand or misstate the nature of the intelligence process. It is not a strict set of steps, each of which must be followed to the fullest, to produce useful intelligence. Rather, it can be seen as a means of organizing disparate but interrelated activities in an orderly manner. Some steps will get more or less emphasis in each iteration, but there is a logical progression. Several of the steps are "twenty-first century," in that they are largely computer based and automated. But no one has suggested which steps might be eliminated or streamlined or proposed a wholly alternative process. The key part of the process, analysis, remains a cerebral human activity, various analytic tools notwithstanding.

Other Reform Concepts. Among the many other proposals for intelligence reform, a market-based intelligence community has been advocated. Proponents argue that intelligence currently exists as an essentially free benefit for policy makers, which undercuts its value to them. In part, this view may stem from the intelligence community's habit of referring to policy makers as clients or customers, as noted earlier. Such usage represents an effort to indicate the closeness of the relationship, but it also implies a type of relationship that may not be apt. Policy makers could be more of a captive audience than they are customers. Market advocates take the term "customer" literally. They believe that if policy makers had a better understanding of the true costs of intelligence—in terms of collection, analysis, and so on—they could make more informed decisions about the specific intelligence they wanted, for which they would then be charged. Presumably, policy agencies would have intelligence expense budgets that could be spent as they saw fit. In a variant of this proposal, a mixed economy has been suggested: Policy makers would receive a certain amount of intelligence without charge but would have to supply resources if greater intelligence support was desired.

Advocates of the idea have not yet fully developed it, so considering all the questions it raises may be unfair. The underlying premise—market competition will make intelligence more efficient and more competitive—might work in some respects for issues that are currently high on the policy agenda. However, how one would handle the sudden unexpected crisis or maintain some level of expertise on less pressing issues is not clear.

The market concept also flies in the face of some generic aspects of intelligence, especially for collection. Determining the cost of collecting against specific issues is difficult, if not impossible. For example, a SIGINT or GEOINT satellite over Iran may be collecting intelligence on terrorism or proliferation or regional stability. Similarly, over Afghanistan, one might collect intelligence for support to military operations or on terrorism or narcotics. How does one then determine the fair cost for any one issue?

A Last Thought: The "Lessons" of September 11 and Iraq WMD. Most would agree that the creation of the DNI and the other attendant changes in the intelligence community were the result of two successive events: September 11 and Iraq WMD. Both of these events have entered into popular legend as to the mistakes that were made and the necessary fixes. However, a critical examination of the "received" lessons of these two events (that is, those that are broadly agreed to in the press and among those individuals who pay attention to intelligence) reveals that they are almost diametrically opposed:

- Warning: The lesson of September 11 is to warn as stridently as possible to make sure that policy makers comprehend the gravity of the situation. But the lesson of Iraq WMD is to warn only when you are absolutely certain that the situation is real. You can warn extravagantly or cautiously but not both.

- Information sharing: The lesson of September 11 is that intelligence must be shared broadly across the intelligence community so that necessary connections can be made. But the lesson of Iraq WMD is to be careful and not share information that is dubious, such as the discredited reporting of the human source known as CURVE BALL.

- "Connect the dots": If we overlook the inappropriate relationship of this phrase to the work of intelligence, for the moment, we see that the lesson of September 11 is the need to connect the dots. But the lesson of Iraq WMD is not to connect too many dots and create a false picture.

These lessons assume that the intelligence analysts or managers know with a fair degree of certainty which intelligence is reliable and which is not. As has been stated throughout this book, this is often not the case. There is much hindsight in both sets of lessons. But the fact that the creation of the DNI is the result of these largely opposed impressionistic sets of lessons underscores the nature of many of the problems inherent in the DNI structure. There seems to have been a fairly uncritical assumption that September 11 and Iraq WMD represented similar types of lapses and, therefore, a uniform set of fixes could be applied. In reality, they were very different lapses calling for very different changes in how intelligence is structured and how it functions.

CONCLUSION

The intelligence reform debate has an inconclusive aspect, which reflects both the difficulty of the issues and choices involved and the boundless enthusiasm of reform advocates, particularly those outside the intelligence community.

Although improvements undoubtedly can be made in intelligence, determining how effective an inherently inefficient and intellectual process can be remains elusive. A wide gulf exists between government-based reviews of the intelligence community, which largely tend to accept the status quo and thus suggest modest changes, and the more acerbic critiques offered by those wholly outside the system, some of whom are intelligence community veterans. Are these differences real, or do they reflect, to some extent, parochial prejudices? The executive branch has rarely shown enthusiasm for major reforms. At least three factors explain this: First, many, if not most, policy makers believe that their most important needs are usually met, so they are not deeply dissatisfied. Second, many proposals for reform would require greater involvement of policy makers, which they would prefer to avoid if only because they already have more than enough to do. Third, many policy makers understand some of the fragility of the intelligence community and fear the possibility of making things worse.

Furthermore, remember that intelligence is a government activity. Revolutionary proposals tend to be ignored or, at best, to be severely moderated before they are enacted.

What is certain is that the debate over intelligence reform will go on, largely on its own momentum, with heightened attention during crises or after incidents deemed to be intelligence failures.

KEY TERMS

FURTHER READINGS

Literature on intelligence reform is extensive but uneven. Many opinions and proposals are on offer, not all of which are practical, with a few hobbyhorses among them. The following readings include some of the more recent studies and some of the more thoughtful and practical works by knowledgeable observers.

Berkowitz, Bruce, and Allan Goodman. *Best Truth: Intelligence in the Information Age.* New Haven, Conn.: Yale University Press, 2000.

Best, Richard A., Jr. *Proposals for Intelligence Reorganization, 1949–1996.* Washington, D.C.: Congressional Research Service, 1996. (Appendix to *IC21: The Intelligence Community in the 21st Century*; see below.)

Betts, Richard K. "Fixing Intelligence." *Foreign Affairs* 81 (January–February 2002): 43–59.

Carter, Ashton, B. "The Architecture of Government in the Face of Terrorism." *International Security* 26 (winter 2001–2002): 5–23.

Commission on the Intelligence Capabilities of the United States Regarding Weapons of Mass Destruction [WMD Commission]. *Report to the President of the United States.* Washington, D.C., March 31, 2005.

Council on Foreign Relations. *Making Intelligence Smarter: The Future of U.S. Intelligence.* New York: Council on Foreign Relations, 1996.

Eberstadt, Ferdinand. *Unification of the War and Navy Departments and Postwar Organization for National Security.* Report to James Forrestal, secretary of the Navy. Washington, D.C., 1945.

Gentry, John A. "Has the ODNI Improved U.S. Intelligence Analysis?" *International Journal of Intelligence and Counterintelligence* 28 (winter 2015–2016): 637–661.

Gomez, Gary. "Intelligence Reform Commissions and the Producer-Consumer Relationship." *Intelligence and National Security* 33 (October 2018): 894–903.

Hansen, James. "U.S. Intelligence Confronts the Future." *International Journal of Intelligence and Counterintelligence* 17 (winter 2004–2005): 674–709.

Hulnick, Arthur S. "Does the U.S. Intelligence Community Need a DNI?" *International Journal of Intelligence and Counterintelligence* 17 (winter 2004–2005): 710–730.

Johnson, Loch. "Spies." *Foreign Policy* 120 (September–October 2000): 18–26.

Kerbel, Josh. "The U.S. Intelligence Community's Kodak Moment." *National Interest*, May 15, 2014. (Available at http://nationalinterest.org/feature/the-us-intelligence-communitys-kodak-moment-10463.)

Kerr, Richard J. "The Track Record: CIA Analysis from 1950 to 2000." In *Analyzing Intelligence: Origins, Obstacles, and Innovations*. Eds. Roger Z. George and James B. Bruce. Washington, D.C.: Georgetown University Press, 2008.

Lahneman, William J. "The Need for a New Intelligence Paradigm." *International Journal of Intelligence and Counterintelligence* 23 (summer 2010): 201–224.

Lowenthal, Mark M. "A Disputation on Intelligence Reform and Analysis: My 18 Theses." *International Journal of Intelligence and Counterintelligence* 26 (spring 2013): 31–37.

_____. *The Future of Intelligence*. Cambridge, UK: Polity Press, 2018.

Lowenthal, Mark M., and Ronald A. Marks. "Intelligence Analysis: Is It as Good as It Gets?" *International Journal of Intelligence and Counterintelligence* 28 (winter 2015–2016): 662–665.

National Commission on Terrorist Attacks upon the United States [9/11 Commission]. *The 9/11 Commission Report*. New York: W.W. Norton, 2004.

Neary, Patrick C. "Intelligence Reform, 2001–2009: *Requiescat in Pace?*" *Studies in Intelligence* 54 (March 2010): 1–16.

Quinn, James L., Jr. "Staffing the Intelligence Community: The Pros and Cons of Intelligence Reserve." *International Journal of Intelligence and Counterintelligence* 13 (2000): 160–170.

Treverton, Gregory F. *Intelligence for an Age of Terror*. New York: Cambridge University Press, 2009.

———. *Reshaping National Intelligence for an Age of Information*. New York: Cambridge University Press, 2001.

U.S. Commission on National Security/21st Century. *Road Map for National Security: Imperative for Change*. Phase III Report. Washington, D.C., 2001.

U.S. Commission on the Roles and Responsibilities of the United States Intelligence Community. *Preparing for the 21st Century: An Appraisal of U.S. Intelligence*. Washington, D.C., 1996.

U.S. House Permanent Select Committee on Intelligence. *IC21: The Intelligence Community in the 21st Century*. 104th Cong., 2d sess., 1996. (Available at https://www.gpo.gov/fdsys/pkg/GPO-IC21/content-detail.html.)

U.S. Office of the Director of National Intelligence. *ICITE Strategy, 2016–2020*. Washington, D.C.: ODNI, 2015. (Available at http://www.dni.gov/files/documents/CIO/IC%20ITE%20Strategy%202016-2020.pdf.)

CHAPTER FIFTEEN

FOREIGN INTELLIGENCE SERVICES

Although this book focuses on the U.S. intelligence community, examining how intelligence in foreign countries operates is instructive, both as a means of investigating alternative intelligence choices and as a way to shed light on the U.S. intelligence community. However, a problem with sources arises. No intelligence service, even those in other democracies, has undergone the same detailed scrutiny as has the U.S. intelligence community. The reliable literature on foreign intelligence services derives mostly from the press and from some more popular, as opposed to scholarly, histories. As is often the case, the accounts tend to emphasize organization and the more sensational activities. No other intelligence service is as transparent as that of the United States.

Although virtually every nation has some type of intelligence service—if not both civilian and military, and at least the latter—the services of five nations are worthy of close examination based on their importance and breadth of activity: Britain, China, France, Israel, and Russia. In addition, the status of several other services is worth examining, although there is a distinct paucity of authoritative and current information on some of these. As is the case with the United States, each nation's intelligence services are unique expressions of its history, needs, and preferred governmental structures. A final observation: One of the differentiators between democracies and authoritarian states is the organization of their intelligence services. In most democracies, the foreign and domestic services are kept separate; this is less typical in authoritarian cases, where internal dissent is the major concern.

BRITAIN

Despite their similarities and historical connections, the British and the U.S. governmental structures and civil liberties have significant differences, which are important in understanding their intelligence practices.

First, the Cabinet, which embodies Britain's executive, enjoys supremacy beyond that of the U.S. president. The Cabinet has the right to make appointments and to take major actions (declare war, make peace, sign treaties) without conferring with Parliament, where, by definition, the Cabinet usually enjoys a majority in the House of Commons. Minority governments are possible but very rare, the last being the Labour government of 1977–1979. (In recent years, the prime minister has asked Parliament for support before committing to use force, which is a change in practice.) Second, the division between foreign and domestic intelligence is less stark in Britain than it is in the United States. Third, Britain does not have a written bill of rights protecting specific civil liberties (although Prime Minister Tony Blair, 1997–2007, talked about creating one). In 1998, Parliament enacted the Human Rights Act, which does offer many individual and political liberties. The act was passed to bring Britain into compliance with the European Convention on Human Rights. This may change given the British decision to leave the European Union (EU), known as Brexit. However, this British act does not grant these rights in absolute terms, as does the U.S. Constitution. For example, in dealing with leaks to the press, the British government can issue a defence advisory (DA) notice (in one of five categories) to request officially that news media not publish or broadcast certain items. The request is not legally enforceable, but British media tend to be more compliant than their U.S. counterparts.

The three major intelligence components—MI5, MI6, and Government Communications Headquarters (GCHQ)—operate under statutory bases. MI5, whose formal name is the Security Service, is a domestic intelligence service of some 4,000 people, responsible for providing security against a range of threats—including terrorism, espionage, weapons of mass destruction (WMD) proliferation, threats to the economy, and cyberspace—and for giving support to law enforcement agencies. MI5 focuses on covertly organized threats. A major preoccupation had been combating Irish Republican Army (IRA) terrorism in Northern Ireland and Great Britain. According to the MI5 website, this is still a concern, focusing on dissident groups who have rejected the 1998 peace accords. MI5 devotes 65 percent of its resources to international terrorism and 15 percent to Northern Ireland–related terrorism. Subversion was a very large concern during the cold war but is no longer seen as a threat and has been dropped as an issue, although the MI5 website states that they could resume counter-subversion activity if necessary. As part of its efforts against terrorists, MI5 has begun sharing some intelligence with local councils (local government bodies) and police departments. In 2018, MI5 took the lead in combating extreme right-wing terrorism, which had been a police concern until then; right-wing terrorism is now classified as a major threat to national security.

MI5 has no police powers (such as arrest or detention) and is empowered to protect British interests overseas. MI5 uses human agents, communications intercepts, and eavesdropping to collect intelligence. MI5 apparently had success in recruiting senior IRA officials as informants, much to the embarrassment of the IRA's political arm, Sinn Fein, when these were revealed in 2005 and 2008.

In the 1990s, MI5 won Parliament's approval to expand its mandate to include organized crime, narcotics, immigration, and benefits fraud. The law provides authority to monitor telephones and mail (both of which require warrants from the home secretary) and to enter homes and offices of organized-crime suspects. However, the MI5 website now lists organized crime and subversion as "former issues" that are now inactive, as responsibility was transferred to the Serious Organized Crime Agency, established in 2006 as part of the Home Office. MI5 operates under the authority of the home secretary, for whom there is no precise U.S. equivalent. (The Home Office is responsible for police, immigration, drug enforcement, and other matters.)

The Security Service Acts of 1989 and 1996 govern MI5. In 2004, the home secretary announced a planned 50 percent increase in MI5 with the addition of 1,000 new analysts to respond to increasing concerns about terrorism. One area of emphasis is Arabic and South Asian languages. In 2006, MI5 came under criticism for its performance prior to the July 7, 2005, attacks on the London Underground. MI5 apparently had the leader of the attack and one other bomber under surveillance in 2003 but dropped it after coming to the conclusion that they were not immediate security threats. An investigation by Parliament's Intelligence and Security Committee released in May 2006 upheld this decision. This report also noted that the number of "primary investigative targets" in the United Kingdom had gone from 250 in 2001, to 500 in 2004, and to 800 in 2005, and increases of this magnitude meant that only a fraction of these individuals could be investigated. In November 2006, Dame Eliza Manningham-Buller, who had recently stepped down as the head of MI5, said 1,600 known active militants were being tracked.

The director general of the Security Service also oversees the Joint Terrorism Analysis Centre (JTAC). JTAC is staffed by officers from MI5, MI6, GCHQ, and the Defence Intelligence Staff and is responsible for counterterrorism intelligence, much like the National Counterterrorism Center (NCTC) in the United States.

MI6 is also known as the Secret Intelligence Service (SIS). Its activities are governed by the Intelligence Services Act of 1994, which also directs GCHQ. MI6 is charged with the collection (by means of human intelligence [HUMINT] and technical intelligence [TECHINT]) and production of "information relating to the activities or intentions of persons outside the British Islands." It also performs other related tasks—a legal echo of the vague U.S. Central Intelligence Agency (CIA) charter in the National Security Act. MI6 comes under the authority of the foreign secretary (equivalent to the U.S. secretary of state), who appoints the chief of the service. Like MI5, MI6 has grown, particularly in response to terrorism and WMD. According to British press estimates, MI6 shrank by some 25 percent during the 1990s in the aftermath of the cold war. As of 2008, MI6 has a website to explain its role and to broaden its recruiting base. Interestingly, the website is available in French, Spanish, Russian, Arabic, and Chinese. According to the Intelligence and Security Committee, MI6 had 2,594 officers in 2016.

GCHQ is the British signals intelligence (SIGINT) agency, also operating under the foreign secretary. It is the British equivalent of the National Security Agency (NSA), with which it enjoys a close working relationship. GCHQ's historical heritage goes back to the Tudor dynasty (1485–1603) code breakers. Like NSA, GCHQ has facilities at home and overseas. GCHQ, again like NSA, has both a SIGINT and an information assurance function. GCHQ has a staff of about 5,800. In 2017, several units were merged to create the National Cyber Security Centre (NCSC), under GCHQ. The NCSC says that it deals with at least ten cyberattacks weekly. Its role appears to be entirely defensive. GCHQ participates in the Centre for Protection of the National Infrastructure (CPNI), which is part of MI5 and works with government departments and the private sector to reduce vulnerabilities. This is akin to the Department of Homeland Security's responsibility for critical infrastructure protection. Like other intelligence agencies, GCHQ is concerned about competing with commercial firms for cyber-related staff, as it is estimated that cyber accounts for about half of GCHQ's activity. GCHQ, like its U.S. counterpart, has had to address how it deals with zero-day vulnerabilities. Former GCHQ director Robert Hannigan estimated that some 90 percent of these vulnerabilities could be released but that the other 10 percent could not. According to press accounts, the NCSC disagrees with the U.S. campaign against nations buying Huawei's fifth-generation (5G) mobile networks, which the U.S. sees as a security threat. The NCSC reportedly believes these risks can be limited.

The Defence Intelligence Staff (DIS), under the chief of defence intelligence, reports to the defense secretary. The DIS controls the Defence Geographic and Imagery Intelligence Agency, which, like the National Geospatial-Intelligence Agency (NGA), produces both geographic and imagery products. Emblematic of the close relationship between British and U.S. intelligence (and the other Five Eyes members as well), the U.S. Defense Intelligence Agency announced in October 2015 that a British flag officer would serve as the agency's first deputy director for Commonwealth intelligence, a position that rotates among the Five Eyes nations. The second incumbent is a New Zealand major general.

According to press reports, several of the British intelligence agencies have suffered from attrition. There was a large exodus of military intelligence officers from 2004 to 2007, lured away by better offers in the private sector; more recently, employees from GCHQ left to join a variety of Internet-related firms. GCHQ was given permission to offer retention bonuses. In 2012, Sir John Sawers, the head of MI6, said that poor pay and poor working conditions were also affecting his ranks.

Executive control of British intelligence is based on the Cabinet structure and its supporting Cabinet Office. In May 2010, incoming Prime Minister David Cameron (2010–2016) created a National Security Council (NSC) to oversee all aspects of British security and to "consider national security in the round and in a strategic way." Its organization resembles that of the U.S. NSC, although it has four committees rather than the U.S. structure of interagency working groups. One of the four committees is devoted to intelligence. The prime minister chairs the NSC. Other members are the chancellor of the exchequer (akin to the U.S. secretary of the treasury) and the secretaries for foreign and commonwealth affairs, home office, defence, international development, and energy and climate change. Other cabinet members, the chief of the defence staff, and the heads of intelligence agencies attend as well, depending on the issue. The prime minister now has a national security adviser, who also oversees the Single Intelligence Account (SIA), or the intelligence budget. For the fiscal year ending in March 2017, the SIA was 2.67 billion pounds ($3.47 billion).

In March 2015, a joint parliamentary committee, looking toward Britain's next national security strategy paper (the last one was published in 2010), said that the NSC was more reactive than forward looking and should take a greater role in guiding national security strategy.

The Joint Intelligence Committee (JIC) is part of the Cabinet Office, providing interdepartmental intelligence assessments to the government. Members of the JIC are detailed from other government agencies. The JIC, like all other British intelligence agencies, maintains its own set of liaison relationships with foreign services. The JIC's Assessments Staff produces intelligence assessments on key issues, both immediate and long range, which are roughly equivalent to U.S. national intelligence estimates. The chairman of the JIC is chosen by the prime minister and is also designated as the professional head of intelligence analysis (PHIA), responsible for the quality and objectivity of intelligence. The PHIA is an outgrowth of the Butler Report (an investigation led by Lord Butler into intelligence on Iraq's WMD in 2004) to separate the intelligence policy advice and analytical roles at the top of British intelligence.

The advent of the NSC raised questions about the role of the JIC. A series of steps were taken to ensure that the JIC remains "relevant . . . respected . . . and right." These steps include creating more products tailored to the needs of the prime minister; closer cooperation between the NSC staff and the JIC; reducing the JIC product line to three types of papers—JIC Assessments, Joint Intelligence Organisation (JIO) Briefs, and JIO Summaries; clearer presentation in all JIC products; and a pilot exercise to review JIC Key Judgments retrospectively to see whether they proved to be right. Unlike the U.S. intelligence community, the JIC does not produce a daily brief for the prime minister. British intelligence officers have held that a President's Daily Brief–like paper is tactical in nature and the political leadership should be working at the strategic level. They also note, however, that the prime minister is not the commander-in-chief of British armed forces as is the president for U.S. forces. However, during crises, the JIC will publish daily or twice daily updates.

In 2016, Parliament passed the Investigatory Powers Act, revising the law regulating the interception and collection, including bulk collection, of communications data. Warrants for interception are authorized by ministers, with a judicial commissioner (there are several) having veto powers. "Urgent cases" can be allowed by exemption for up to three days. The system is overseen by the investigatory powers commissioner, who is appointed by the prime minister. All of the commissioners must have held "high judicial office." The security services are authorized to conduct bulk collection and can also hack into or place collection devices in computers. Companies are obligated to assist in these operations to by-pass encryption. Also, Internet service providers and telecommunications firms are required to store records of all websites visited by citizens for up to twelve months, for possible official access. In December 2014, the Investigatory Powers Tribunal, a judicial body with oversight over surveillance, found that GCHQ's access to NSA's bulk-collection data had been illegal until 2014. The Home Office published a code of practice for "equipment interference," which the Investigatory Powers Tribunal found to be legal in February 2016.

Parliament's Intelligence and Security Committee (ISC), established in 1994, oversees all three intelligence components. The committee considers the budget, administration, and policy of MI5, MI6, and GCHQ, but its oversight function is not as powerful as that exercised by U.S. congressional committees. The ISC submits an annual report to the prime minister. The report is publicly released after sensitive portions have been deleted. The government then issues a response to the report. The prime minister appoints the members of the ISC, in consultation with the leader of the opposition, again reflecting the parliamentary system in which the executive is also part of the legislature. The ISC has not been able to range as wide or as freely as its counterparts in the U.S. Congress. However, as of 2013, the ISC could demand sensitive material from the three agencies and investigate operations more freely. Previously, the ISC's operational oversight was limited to those issues referred by the prime minister. Agency heads now testify in public on some occasions. In March 2015, the ISC issued a report calling for an overhaul of the legal framework by which intelligence agencies conduct mass surveillance in order to bring these up to date and to make them more comprehensible and transparent. In 2018, the ISC ran into some controversy over allegations that it had censored its report on the detentions and renditions for the years 2001 through 2010 at the request of the U.S. government. ISC chairman Dominic Grieve stated that one word in the more than 300 pages of the report had been redacted to meet U.S. security concerns. This report found that the British abetted the U.S. rendition and interrogation program. In an interesting reversal from the U.S. Senate staff report on these programs, which decided not to conduct interviews, the ISC wanted to interview but was prevented by the government, which expressed concerns about security and possible exposure of agents to legal action.

The close intelligence relationship between Britain and the United States is most evident in the dealings between GCHQ and NSA, but it exists elsewhere. The United States and Britain are two of the partners in the Five Eyes relationship, the others being Australia, Canada, and New Zealand. Britain's independent imagery intelligence (IMINT) capability had been restricted to airborne platforms, while receiving satellite imagery from the United States. In May 2018, Britain launched the Carbonite-2 satellite, on an Indian rocket. This experimental imagery satellite can take high-resolution color full-motion video. Carbonite-2 is seen as adding to Five Eyes capabilities rather than competing with the United States. Britain, like many others, is expanding its unmanned aerial vehicle (UAV) capability. A range of intelligence products, both collection and analytical, also is shared. British HUMINT does not completely overlap that of the United States, with Britain having some advantages in Commonwealth countries. The 2005 WMD Commission (Commission on the Intelligence Capabilities of the United States Regarding Weapons of Mass Destruction) report gives some indication of how the two HUMINT enterprises work together.

The revelations by Edward Snowden about NSA surveillance, which appeared in Britain's *Guardian* newspaper, also caused controversy in Britain, as might be expected. According to press accounts, GCHQ was active at G-20 (Group of 20) summits in London, which offered a wide range of high-value leadership targets. An ISC review of GCHQ's cooperation with NSA concluded that GCHQ had not violated the law and that all collection requests were accompanied by the requisite warrants. The British government demanded that the *Guardian* return or destroy all of the Snowden material and threatened legal action, eventually being given access to and destroying hard drives at the newspaper. The British also briefly detained David Miranda, the companion of *Guardian* reporter Glenn Greenwald, the main reporter on the Snowden material, who was transiting Britain. All of Miranda's electronic media were confiscated on the grounds that the materials put British agents at risk.

Britain also vetoed efforts by the EU to create working groups to meet with U.S. officials about the NSA program. Sweden joined Britain. Britain argued, and the EU eventually agreed, that intelligence and national security issues are beyond the EU's writ. Britain also refused to cooperate with a German parliamentary inquiry into the programs revealed by Snowden and threatened to end intelligence cooperation with Germany, much of which seems to be SIGINT related, if the inquiry revealed information about their cooperation.

During the cold war, British intelligence suffered several Soviet espionage penetrations. The most famous was Kim Philby, who, with four other Cambridge University associates, began spying for the Soviet Union in the 1930s. Philby became MI6's liaison to CIA, an invaluable position for a Soviet spy. Other Soviet spies included George Blake, an SIS officer, and Geoffrey Prime, a GCHQ employee. Most known British spies were motivated by ideological, not monetary, reasons. Allegations were made that Sir Roger Hollis, a director general of MI5, was a spy, but he was cleared after an investigation in 1974. Russia remains the main counterintelligence concern to Britain, followed by China, Syria, and North Korea. According to press accounts citing security service documents, Germany and France also conduct political and industrial espionage in Britain.

The British services do not conduct assassinations. However, British special forces units, the Special Air Service (SAS) and Special Boat Service (SBS), have taken part in antiterrorist activities against the IRA that some people have charged were assassinations. The most famous case occurred in March 1988, when the SAS killed three IRA members in Gibraltar. The British government claimed that the IRA members were on active service, planning a series of bomb attacks. The SAS has conducted special operations for MI6.

The British intelligence services, like those in the United States (and in Australia), came under scrutiny after the start of the Iraq war in 2003, when the expected WMD were not found. The Butler Report did not find substantial flaws in how the British intelligence on Iraq was produced. However, the report noted that the intelligence sources on Iraq had grown weaker and less reliable over time and that this fact was not properly conveyed. The report also said that no evidence existed that intelligence had been politicized, which was as serious an issue in Britain as it was in the United States. In response to the concerns raised about intelligence sources, MI6 created the position of a senior quality control officer to review collected intelligence for its credibility and veracity. The new officer is known as "R," for reports officer. (The head of MI6 has traditionally been known as "C," in honor of the first head of MI6, Sir Mansfield Cumming.) As in the United States, the effects of the Iraq WMD are still being felt.

A second report on Iraq was released in 2016. Formally called the Iraq Inquiry (known informally as the Chilcot report, after its chairman, Sir John Chilcot), the report questioned the case that Prime Minister Tony Blair had made for the war, although it stated that he did not invent or distort intelligence. However, the Joint Intelligence Committee and the then-director of MI6, Sir Richard Dearlove, were criticized for their handling of intelligence on Iraq.

According to press accounts, the JIC assessment on the possible use of chemical weapons in Syria was "highly likely," which was seen as much less definitive than U.S. views as stated by Secretary of State John Kerry. Some observers thought this JIC position was one of the reasons Parliament failed to support Prime Minister David Cameron on joining the United States in the use of force against Syria in 2013. Parliament reversed this decision in December 2015, after the terror attacks in Paris.

In August 2015, a Reaper UAV flown by British personnel, as part of a joint British-U.S. mission against the Islamic State (ISIL) in Iraq, killed two British subjects in a targeted attack. This raised questions similar to those regarding the U.S. action against Anwar al-Awlaki. It also raised questions about the legality of conducting strikes in Syria, even as part of the Iraqi mission. Prime Minister Cameron defended the strikes as self-defense, as the two British subjects were plotting to conduct terrorist attacks in the United Kingdom and could not be apprehended. In March 2015, the Counter-Terrorism and Security Act went into effect, allowing the government to seize and retain the passport of someone suspected of leaving for terrorism-related activity and also allowing the "temporary" exclusion of a British passport holder who is believed to have taken part in such activities. This is clearly aimed at the Islamic State foreign fighter problem. In 2015, it was estimated that some 600 Britons had joined ISIL.

British intelligence performance has been the target of earlier investigations. In the aftermath of the Falklands War (1982), a review by Lord Oliver Shewell Franks held that the changes in Argentina's policy regarding the Falkland Islands should have been obvious through diplomatic and open sources. However, no basis existed to conclude that the Argentine invasion could have been prevented, although the Franks report criticized Prime Minister Margaret Thatcher's government (1979–1990) for not paying enough attention to the issue prior to the war.

The main concern of the British intelligence apparatus today is terrorism. Given that there have been several attacks or attempted attacks since July 2005, a great deal of effort must be given to discerning the depth of the threat within the indigenous Muslim population. Indeed, one of the main concerns in the aftermath of the July 7, 2005, attack was whether or not there were connections between the four bombers and al Qaeda. There is evidence that some of the bombers traveled to Pakistan but none about the plot being directed by al Qaeda. The review by the Intelligence and Security Committee urged that greater attention be paid to causes of radicalization within the British population and the "homegrown" terrorism threat. According to press accounts, GCHQ has been providing intelligence to Syrian rebels about Syrian military movements. There have been several "lone-wolf" attacks in Britain.

British security services have also been more public in their concerns about foreign espionage against the United Kingdom. Russia and China are of concern. Intelligence relations with Russia center, first, on the 2006 death of Alexander Litvinenko, a former officer of the KGB (*Komitet Gosudarstvennoi Bezopasnosti*—Committee for State Security), as well as the successor FSB (see below), who was fatally poisoned by exposure to polonium, a radioactive element. British authorities formally charged Andrei Lugovoi, another KGB officer, with the murder, but Russia refused to allow his extradition. A formal inquest into Litvinenko's death began late in 2012, but the British government sought to limit the information it would disclose. The government relented, and an inquiry was conducted in 2015, ending in January 2016 with a conclusion by the presiding judge that there is "strong circumstantial evidence of Russian state responsibility" and that the operation was probably approved by the head of the FSB (Russian counterintelligence service, discussed later) and President Vladimir Putin. In 2012, MI5 disclosed a plot to assassinate dissident Chechen politician Akhmed Zakayev, who was living in Britain. In December 2007, Jonathan Evans, the director general of MI5 (2007–2013), sent a letter to the leaders of the British banking industry, warning of China's efforts to conduct espionage via computers. In 2013, Oleg Gordievsky, a onetime KGB officer who worked for Britain, said that Russia had as many spies in Britain now as it had during the cold war. In early 2016,

British intelligence warned its allies to look out for increased use of assassination by Russia against dissidents.

In March 2018, former GRU (*Glavnoye Razvedyvatelnoye Upravlenie*—Main Intelligence Administration) officer Sergei Skripal and his daughter were poisoned by Novichok nerve agent. They both recovered but a woman who came into contact with the bottle used to spray the agent later died. Skripal had been a British agent and had been arrested and imprisoned in Russia but was among those traded in 2010 for the Russian sleeper agents arrested in the United States. The British government accused Russia for the attack and expelled twenty-three Russian diplomats. Britain shared its intelligence on the attack widely, leading several other nations to expel Russians as well. The United States expelled sixty Russian diplomats and closed the Russian consulate in Seattle. Two Russian intelligence officers were subsequently identified as having introduced the nerve agent, publicly identified by a private website called Bellingcat. Facial recognition specialists also worked on this case. The two Russians later appeared on Russian television and denied involvement. (See Russia section below.)

As in other nations, cyberspace is of growing concern in Britain. MI5 and GCHQ reported seventy sophisticated cyberattacks monthly against government and industry. MI5 director Evans also noted large economic losses due to cyberattacks. The ISC also took note of the cyber threat but said that cyberspace also offered "significant opportunities for our intelligence and security services." In December 2018, Alex Younger, head of MI6, said that the blurring lines among physical, biological, and digital domains could pose a "potentially existential challenge" to liberal democracies.

In October 2015, the British government announced increased spending on security, some of which will go to intelligence. The UAV fleet is being doubled and upgraded, intelligence agencies will get 1,900 new positions, and spending on cyber defense will double. Cyber offense, run jointly by GCHQ and the Defence Ministry, will also increase.

The United States and Britain have had an extraordinarily close intelligence relationship since World War II. Each nation is off-limits to clandestine collection by the other, although both can assess each other's politics and policies. Occasional problems do arise, such as that in 2009, when a British court wanted to reveal the specifics of how a detainee was treated in Guantanamo, to which the United States objected, going so far as to say that this could hurt intelligence cooperation. Some of the information was released over the objection of the British services as well. According to press accounts, the Donald Trump administration's handling of intelligence has created friction with Britain. In March 2017, Trump's then–press secretary, Sean Spicer, repeated allegations that British intelligence had wiretapped Trump Tower; Trump had made the same charges about U.S. intelligence—none of which proved to be true. In a rare public statement, GCHQ termed the report "nonsense," and later press reports said that Spicer and then-national security adviser Lt. Gen. H. R. McMaster both apologized to British officials. British intelligence officers were later concerned that if Trump released the memo written by Devin Nunes, chairman of the House Intelligence Committee, on the Foreign Intelligence Surveillance Act (FISA) warrant for surveillance of Trump campaign adviser Carter Page (see chap. 10), it would reveal some British intelligence methods. After a terrorist attack in Manchester, Trump claimed that British police had knowledge of the terrorists, raising objections from Prime Minister Theresa May (2016–2019). The British also raised concerns over leaks from U.S. intelligence about the ongoing Manchester investigation.

In June 2016, the British public voted in a referendum to leave the EU. Known as Brexit, the split was scheduled to occur at the end of March 2019, though the deadline was extended. Brexit has several intelligence implications. The most obvious is the fate of British intelligence liaison with European services. Although none of these is as close as the "special relationship" with the United States, these are still valuable ties. Some EU representatives have suggested Brexit would affect that cooperation. This would also represent a loss for the United States as British and U.S. intelligence are often in accord and the U.S. derives benefit from Britain's access in Europe.

CHINA

In the past few years, the press has written much about Chinese intelligence, stemming largely from allegations of espionage and cyberspace activities against the United States and several other states. Intelligence in China, as in all authoritarian states, has a twofold purpose: internal security activities against dissidents and foreign intelligence operations. As was the case with the Soviet KGB, the internal suppressive function is an important distinction between the Chinese intelligence service and those of the United States or Britain.

Chinese intelligence is run by the Ministry of State Security. As with all other security issues in China, however, the most powerful body in the state is the Central Military Commission (CMC) of the Communist Party, which has much greater influence than its title would imply. Control over the commission was a sore point between outgoing president Jiang Zemin (1993–2003) and his successor, Hu Jintao (2003–2013). Although Hu became party leader in 2002, Jiang did not give up his chairmanship of the CMC until 2004. Their struggle underscores the importance of the commission as a key lever of control in the Chinese government. (President Xi Jinping, who succeeded Hu in 2013, took over the CMC upon becoming president.) Many Ministry of State Security bureaus are of importance in intelligence:

- First Bureau: secret intelligence collection (Europe, Central Asia)
- Second Bureau: open-resource intelligence collection (from overseas reporting sources)
- Third Bureau: Hong Kong and Macau
- Fourth Bureau: Taiwan
- Fifth Bureau: analysis and evaluation
- Eighth Bureau: counterintelligence
- Ninth Bureau: technology support
- Tenth Bureau: security of party and government leaders
- Eleventh Bureau: China Institute of Contemporary International Relations

- Sixteenth Bureau: possibly imagery analysis

- Eighteenth Bureau: United States (separate from First Bureau in 2009 or 2010)

In addition, several sections of the People's Liberation Army's (PLA) General Security Directorate (GSD) have intelligence functions. The Second Department manages clandestine and overt HUMINT, including defense attachés. The Third Department is China's cryptologic service and, like NSA, has become more involved in a variety of cyber operations. It also has at least some responsibilities for satellite imagery. The Fourth Department has electronic intelligence and electronic warfare duties. China is revamping its military structure, creating a headquarters for PLA ground forces, which apparently will also have some intelligence functions. It is not clear how this new structure will affect the GSD. Cyberspace and electronic warfare functions have been consolidated in a Strategic Support Force.

The Chinese government has passed new laws dealing with intelligence issues. In November 2014, President Xi signed a new Counterespionage Law, replacing the 1993 National Security Law. Analysts believed the change in title underscored the new emphasis of the law and China's increasing concern about being a target of foreign espionage. In July 2015, a new National Security Law to defend China's "core interests" affirmed the primacy of the Communist Party in all aspects of national security, which is defined as the "relative absence of threats." A 2017 law aims specifically at foreign spies operating in China, which the government claims is a rampant problem, but also allows investigations about foreign espionage to take place outside China. The Beijing bureau of the Ministry of State Security offers cash rewards ranging from $1,450 to $72,000 for citizens who help identify foreign espionage agents. There is also a National Security Education Day, April 15.

China apparently scored a major counterintelligence success starting in 2010. According to press reports, a web-based communications system used by CIA was penetrated, first by Iran and then China, allowing China to identify, arrest, and, in some cases, execute more than a dozen intelligence sources.

As noted in chapter 11, several senior Chinese intelligence officials have been arrested as part of President Xi's anti-corruption campaign against "tigers and flies," meaning both powerful and lesser figures. Zhou Yongkang, former minister of public security (internal security) and a member of the Politburo, was arrested and sentenced to life imprisonment for taking bribes and leaking secrets. Ma Jian, former executive deputy minister in the Ministry of State Security, was also arrested as part of this campaign, as was Major General Xing Yunming, who had run overseas espionage operations. Although certainly much less than a purge of the senior ranks of Chinese intelligence, these arrests are unusual in China and can be risky for Xi. (Then again, each of the leaders of the Soviet NKVD [precursor to the KGB] was arrested and shot in turn—Genrikh Yagoda and Nikolai Yezhov on Stalin's orders and Lavrenti Beria by his Politburo colleagues after Stalin's death.)

Part of Xi's anti-corruption campaign has included pressuring expatriates wanted for corruption charges to return home. In August 2015, the Obama administration warned China about covert agents operating in the United States as part of this campaign and demanded a halt to the activity.

Although much controversy surrounds allegations of Chinese espionage, its existence is not in doubt. China has a well-developed HUMINT program that relies on the large overseas Chinese population. For example, Larry Wu-tai Chin was a Chinese spy who worked for the CIA for decades before being arrested in 1985, the "year of the spy." A more controversial, and ultimately inconclusive case was that of Wen Ho Lee, a Los Alamos National Laboratory scientist who downloaded thousands of pages of sensitive material in 1999. Chinese espionage puts special emphasis on scientific and technology targets, both civil and military. These activities were the major focus of the 1999 report of the Cox Committee (U.S. House Select Committee on U.S. National Security and Military/Commercial Concerns with the People's Republic of China), especially allegations that China had stolen an array of information about nuclear weapons and satellite-related technology. Some observers have also expressed concern about the large number of Chinese students enrolled in U.S. colleges and graduate schools, many of them in technical areas (physics, computing) that might indicate national security concerns in terms of both the education these students receive and the likelihood that at least some of these students are intelligence officers who are either actively recruiting now or may intend to become sleeper agents. There have been many prosecutions of individuals on charges of spying for China since the Wen Ho Lee case, in government but also an increasing number in industry going after high-technology information. In a unique case, a Chinese intelligence officer, Yanjun Xu, a deputy director at the Ministry of State Security, was extradited from Belgium to the United States in October 2018, for his efforts to obtain military technology information. This was the first time a Chinese intelligence official was brought to the United States for prosecution in open court.

It is difficult to draw any conclusion other than that China is engaged in a "full court press" in espionage. Some of their intelligence activities rely on cyber, as discussed in chapter 12. Recruited agents include expatriate Chinese, current and former government employees, military personnel, academics, and business people. The Chinese use academia, social media, and false-front research and headhunter firms to contact potential spies. The Federal Bureau of Investigation (FBI) has said that 70 percent of the Chinese effort against the United States is aimed at the private sector, rather than the government.

The fact that so many people spying for China have been caught suggests either poor espionage tradecraft or a certain level of unconcern because there are so many recruited agents. However, it is also uncertain whether this Chinese espionage assault has any real focus or is simply omnivorous.

The United States is not the only Chinese intelligence target. The Five Eyes intelligence partners have begun sharing intelligence on Chinese activities with other nations, such as Germany and Japan, that are also concerned about China's intelligence operations.

In addition to HUMINT, China has an array of Earth-based SIGINT platforms, some of which are located in Cuba, where China began operating in the mid 1990s. China also has a space-borne imagery capability. More problematic, from the standpoint of the United States, was the Chinese ASAT (anti-satellite weapon) tests in 2007, 2014, 2017, and 2018. Not only do U.S. military and intelligence activities depend on satellites, but so do large portions of the economy, beyond that of telecommunications itself. In August 2007, Lt. Gen. Kevin Campbell, head of the U.S. Army's Space and Missile Defense Command, warned about Chinese jamming and computer attack capabilities as a threat to U.S. space-borne systems. China, like so many other countries, is investing more in UAVs. The Chinese satellite program has also become of greater concern as the Chinese begin to fly satellites in formation. This maneuver can serve many purposes. It can be part of the ongoing Chinese manned space program, which will require multi–space capsule flights for activities such as space walks or an eventual lunar landing. But it can also be used to practice moving intelligence collection satellites near other satellites in order to undertake collection. Again, it is the opaque nature of the Chinese program that is most bothersome. In 2016, China launched the first quantum satellite, meaning using quantum physics for communications that the Chinese hope will be unbreakable. According to Chinese scientists involved in the project, any attempt to intercept the message will change its quantum state and the message will self-destruct.

Allegations of Chinese computer intrusions have become the other main concern, alongside classic espionage. As noted, the head of Britain's MI5 warned British firms about this specific threat. There have been many press reports over the past few years about computer hacking attacks and intrusions alleged to have emanated from China, including against defense and national laboratory sites. The FBI, in its counterintelligence role, has put increased emphasis on Chinese economic espionage, which the FBI says focuses on ways to gain access to Western technology and then use China's cheaper labor market to "leapfrog" foreign rivals in that sector. In 2015, the FBI's chief of counterintelligence characterized China's activities as "the predominant threat." In 2007, Geng Huichang became the minister of state security. (Geng stepped down in 2016.) According to press accounts, Geng has expertise on the United States and Japan, as well as in commercial intelligence. (The head of the Canadian Security Intelligence Service [CSIS] told a Canadian Senate committee that China was Canada's top intelligence concern, with half of Canada's counterespionage effort devoted to Chinese spies. Technology and corporate secrets were again seen as the main targets.) In 2009, researchers at the University of Toronto said they found an extensive program of Chinese computer infiltration, covering 1,295 computers in 103 nations. In 2010, Google and several other major U.S. cyber and defense firms claimed that they had been under a concerted Chinese intrusion effort. As noted, in 2013, the computer security firm Mandiant identified what it said was the locus of most Chinese cyber activity, Army Unit 61398. The Chinese, of course, deny all of this.

In May 2014, the United States issued indictments against five members of the PLA for hacking activities that the United States said were commercially based and had nothing to do with national security. China protested the indictments and denied their basis, of course, although press reports suggested a decrease in PLA cyber intrusions after the indictments. Assuming this is true, it is not known if this represents a significant change or a tactical withdrawal. Not every nation draws the same distinction between national security and commercial activities. As noted, in September 2015, Presidents Obama and Xi agreed not to steal intellectual property via computer activities, although some observers now question China's adherence to this agreement.

In December 2015, China acknowledged that the cyber breach of U.S. Office of Personnel Management (OPM) files came from China but attributed it to criminal hackers and not a government-sponsored activity. Observers have said that the sophistication and duration of the attack looked more like a state-sponsored operation. NSA director Adm. Michael Rogers said in September 2015 that there had been no signs that the OPM materials had been used for financial gain or fraud, which are the usual motives of criminal hackers. Director of National Intelligence (DNI) James Clapper (2010–2017) had earlier characterized the breach as an intelligence collection operation, which again argues against a criminal, as opposed to national, origin.

In November 2007, the U.S.-China Economic and Security Review Commission, a bipartisan congressional group formed in 2000 to monitor the national security implications of U.S.-China economic relations, said that Chinese espionage was the largest threat to U.S. technological secrets. (In December 2007, Chinese foreign minister Yang Jiechi said that China opposes hacking attacks, that China itself had been the victim of such attacks; a spokesperson said that the MI5 warning was "slanderous.") As noted, the NSA programs leaked by Edward Snowden have given China counterarguments about U.S. cyber activity. China apparently created local access nodes (called "points of presence" or PoPs) to access the Internet backbone in North America and gain access to commercial message traffic.

As noted in chapter 12, Chinese espionage—meaning via cyberspace, technical intelligence, and HUMINT—appears to have four major targets:

- Economic data

- Military equipment

- Reconnaissance of critical infrastructure

- Attacks on critics and dissidents

None of these is particularly surprising in and of itself. But the Chinese do appear to have taken a mass assault approach to their collection as a means of gathering up as much intelligence as possible and also perhaps as a means of diverting the attention of security forces trying to stop them. The mass aspect of this collection raises questions about its ultimate utility to China as the Chinese can be overwhelmed by the amount they collect without making good use of it. China does have the ability to throw a lot of people at the problem, but at some point good analysis is a question of skill, not mass.

The U.S.-Chinese intelligence relationship serves as a barometer of the larger political relationship. The United States and China were hostile until President Richard M. Nixon's visit to China in 1972. That event, plus the shared fear of growing Soviet power, led to some level of intelligence cooperation. Gaining access to sites in far western China, the United States was able to recover monitoring capabilities it had lost in Iran, after the fall of the shah's government in 1979, to track Soviet missile tests. China and the United States also cooperated on the operational level, both supporting the mujahideen against the Soviet Union in Afghanistan in the 1980s. The collapse of the Soviet Union led to new fears on the part of China about U.S. hegemony, leading to a deterioration in relations. Chinese assertiveness prompted the prolonged captivity of a U.S. reconnaissance plane crew, which was forced to land in

China after colliding with a Chinese military jet in 2001. The incident occurred after the bombing of China's embassy in Belgrade, Serbia, in May 1999—a mistake caused by the use of outdated information on that city, which did not record the embassy's new location. In January 2002, news reports alleged that the United States had planted multiple listening devices in a plane being outfitted in the United States before delivery to China's president. China downplayed the reports, bolstering the view that such intelligence incidents were largely a means of expressing official attitudes about the relationship with the United States. According to subsequent press reports, some U.S. analysts believed that the listening devices were Chinese in origin, part of an internal power struggle.

Former president Hu emphasized China's "peaceful rise," meaning that China will become more powerful without threatening any other powers. At the same time, China's economic growth, its increased international economic influence—which also translates into increased political power—suggests the more natural occurrence of friction between China and other powerful states. President Xi is more assertive than his predecessor. An aggressive intelligence effort would be a natural adjunct to this.

The possibility of tension with the United States over the future of Taiwan also puts a premium on knowledge of U.S. deployments, strategy, and tactics in the western Pacific. China regards Taiwan as a rebellious breakaway province. The United States treats Taiwan as something like an independent state, although full, formal diplomatic relations no longer exist. However, the United States does have a formal obligation to defend Taiwan and sells arms to maintain Taiwan's defense, which always draws a stiff Chinese reaction. China has created several military bases on enlarged atolls and islands in the South China Sea. These run the risk of becoming flash points between the United States and China over freedom of the sea versus territorial claims. The islands can also serve intelligence functions. At the same time, some analysts believe that the Chinese government is also concerned that its own increasingly nationalistic population could become a factor in policy deliberations should there be more direct confrontations with the United States or its allies.

FRANCE

Since 2008, France has had a national intelligence coordinator (CNR—*coordonnateur national du renseignement*). (The complete title is *coordonnateur national du renseignement et de la lutte contre le terrorisme*: "national coordinator of intelligence and the struggle against terrorism".) The CNR is responsible for coordinating the six agencies that make up the French intelligence community. The CNR is part of the president's office and provides the president with a daily intelligence summary. The CNR oversees the National Intelligence Council (confusingly, also CNR—*conseil national du renseignement*), which defines strategic priorities and direction for intelligence.

The main French intelligence organization is the *Direction Générale de la Sécurité Extérieure* (DGSE)—the General Directorate for External Security—which reports to the minister of defense. The DGSE, created in 1982, is the latest in a series of French intelligence organizations.

The four major directorates largely define the DGSE mission:

- Strategic: responsible for establishing intelligence requirements with policy makers, especially the Foreign Ministry, and also conducting intelligence studies

- Intelligence: responsible for intelligence collection, particularly HUMINT, as well as its analysis and the dissemination of this intelligence

- Technical: collects SIGINT, largely through a number of ground sites

- Operations: responsible for clandestine operations

Thus, the DGSE has a much broader role than that of agencies in the United States or Britain, combining as it does analysis, operations, and several types of collection. DGSE's motto is *"Partout où nécessité fait loi"*—"Wherever necessity makes law." The *Direction Générale de la Sécurité Intérieure* (DGSI—General Directorate for Internal Security) was created in 2014, succeeding the *Direction Centrale du Renseignement Intérieur* (DCRI—Central Directorate of Internal Intelligence), which was created in 2008, merging the *Direction de Surveillance du Territoire* (DST—Directorate of Territorial Surveillance), which had been responsible for counterintelligence, and *Renseignements Généraux* (RG—General Intelligence). DGSI comes under the minister of the interior and is responsible for counterintelligence; combating terrorism and violent extremism; protection of French science, economics, and technology, which also includes combating the proliferation of WMD; and control of the special judiciary police. France maintains "S files" (*SÛreté de l'Etat*—Safety of the State) of people who are considered possible threats to the state. The utility or proper use of these files has come into question since the November 2015 terror attacks in Paris. According to press accounts, there are some 11,000 names in the S files, making them difficult to use. The *Direction du Renseignement Militaire* (DRM—Directorate of Military Intelligence) was organized in 1992, combining a number of TECHINT entities. As its name indicates, the DRM is responsible for military intelligence and imagery analysis. France has an independent satellite imagery capability. According to some reports, DRM has branched out into political and strategic intelligence areas where DGSE has been responsible. These are seen as areas of "intelligence of military interest."

The *Direction de la Protection et de la Sécurité de la Défense* (DPSD—Directorate for Defense Protection and Security) handles military counterintelligence and maintains, in a uniquely French function, political surveillance of the military, with a view to its political reliability. This function goes back to the French Revolution, when "representatives on mission" served as political commissars, looking over the shoulders of French commanders. It also reflects the occasional intrusion—or threatened intrusion—of the military into French political life, although this has not happened since the Algerian revolt against French rule (1954–1962), when dissident French officers rebelled against the decision to grant Algeria independence. DPSD is also responsible for the security of the national defense industrial and technology base.

In July 2017, President Emmanuel Macron created the National Center for Counter Terrorism, in response to a terrorist incident at Notre Dame in Paris, as well as several other attacks. This is essentially a watch-and-response center, as opposed to an analytical unit, initially focusing on French citizens who joined the Islamic State, the problem of radicalization, and the spread of jihadist information.

All of these intelligence agencies were created by decree rather than by legislation, although a 2011 law recognized the authority of the premier to appoint the heads of the services.

In addition to these major organizations, the official website for French intelligence notes several other offices in the Ministry of Defense, the Ministry of the Interior, and the Ministry of Economics and Finance that are dedicated to tracking terrorist-related activities.

France has independent IMINT and SIGINT capabilities, which led France to disagree with U.S. assertions about Iraqi troop movements in 1996. The Iraqi movements led the Bill Clinton administration (1993–2001) to send a warning to Iraq by means of a cruise missile attack. France has also played a central role in European efforts to build an independent imagery capability. In 2018, the French defense minister announced that France would spend 3.6 billion euros (just over $5 billion) to upgrade its military satellites and shield them from spying by rival states.

The Operations Division of the DGSE has had much greater latitude in its activities than do the clandestine services of the United States and Britain. This includes the use of violence against certain targets. The most famous case was the sinking, in July 1985, of the *Rainbow Warrior*, a boat being used by the Greenpeace organization to protest ongoing French nuclear tests in the South Pacific. French agents planted a bomb on the *Rainbow Warrior* while it was in the harbor at Auckland, New Zealand, which resulted in the death of one person on board. France initially denied responsibility but then admitted it, leading to the resignation of the defense minister and the firing of the head of the DGSE. In 2005, the head of DGSE at the time, Admiral Pierre Lacoste, said that French president François Mitterrand had approved sinking the boat.

France maintains a military presence in many of its former colonies in western and central Africa. It is presumed that French intelligence officers have a presence there, often in advisory capacities to the local governments. A growing al Qaeda presence in some of these states, particularly in West Africa, has led to French military involvement, as in Mali in 2013 against Tuareg rebels and radical Muslims from an al Qaeda offshoot and other groups. Presumably, France will have to devote more intelligence assets to monitoring those Francophone states where Muslim radicals pose a potential threat. France has also taken part in air operations against the Islamic State, which increased in intensity and scope after the terror attacks of November 2015.

The DGSE was also active in economic espionage, including activities against U.S. firms, but some observers believe this activity has been dropped. The targets appear to be companies that compete with major French firms, reflecting the semi-statist nature of parts of the French economy. In a response to apparent French economic espionage, the Hughes Aircraft Company announced in 1993 that it would not take part in the prestigious Paris Air Show. In 2009, France reorganized those offices involved in economic intelligence to improve the collection of open commercial data and help improve French competitiveness. Even though the French insisted this new office, which comes under the Ministry for Economy, Industry and

Employment, is not involved in espionage, its first director was a DGSE veteran. As noted in chapter 12, passing economic intelligence can be extremely problematic, at least for an economy like that of the United States. This is likely less of a problem in France, with its long history of *dirigisme*, that is, an economy in which the state plays a strong directing role without necessarily owning large sectors of the economy.

In the late 1990s, according to press accounts, a U.S. nonofficial cover (NOC) agent in Paris was discovered. The agent's area of concentration was economics. French press accounts in 2003 argued that one of the NOC agent's paid sources, a French government official, became a double agent at the request of the DST. As Director of Central Intelligence (DCI) R. James Woolsey (1993–1995) noted in a 2000 article on the SIGINT key-word search system known as ECHELON, the United States had two main economic intelligence concerns: foreign bribery intended to give firms unfair economic advantages and economic counterintelligence.

Two French intelligence components focus on economic issues. In the Ministry of Economy and Finance, there is the *Direction Nationale du Renseignement et des Enquêtes Douanières* (DNRED—National Directorate of Intelligence and Customs Investigations), responsible for preventing customs fraud. In the Ministry of Finance and Public Accounts, there is Tracfin, which focuses on illegal finance, money laundering, and terrorist finance.

As the member states of the EU work to foster a clearer and distinct European identity and role, the issue of intelligence cooperation becomes more complex. An EU foreign policy and security "high representative" has been designated, and nascent efforts have been made to build a European military capability that would be separate from the North Atlantic Treaty Organization (NATO). This includes the EU Situation Centre (SitCen), established in 2001 and renamed the Intelligence Center in 2011. The center has an integrated intelligence analytic capability. Judging from the U.S. experience, however, sharing intelligence with allies is a less straightforward proposition. Not all allies are equal. In 2004, the justice and interior ministers of EU nations rejected an Austrian proposal to create a European Intelligence Agency that would be an analytic and monitoring center focusing only on terrorism and proliferation. In the aftermath of the Snowden NSA revelations, European privacy advocates appealed to the EU's minister of justice, asking that inquiries be made about the extent of U.S. surveillance in Europe.

France, like many other Western services, now puts increased emphasis on counterterrorism and WMD intelligence. One French official stated that these two issues represent half of all French intelligence activities. After a lone-wolf attack in 2012 killed seven people, the General Inspectorate of the National Police found that the police and the domestic intelligence agencies had not properly coordinated their work. In January 2015, terrorists attacked the satirical magazine *Charlie Hebdo* and a Jewish grocery. In November 2015, terrorists carried out multiple attacks in Paris, killing 130 and injuring over 350. ISIL claimed responsibility for the November attacks. France has between one and two thousand citizens who have returned after fighting in Syria or Iraq, although the November 2015 attack appears to have had a nexus in Belgium as well, which has the highest per-capita number of foreign fighters who joined ISIL. French authorities have noted the difficulties involved in keeping large numbers of suspects under constant surveillance. The Belgian connection also called into question the continued viability of the Schengen Area in Europe, which allows passport-free movement between signatory nations, as did the March 2016 terror attacks in Brussels. In the aftermath of the November 2015 attacks, president François Hollande asked for a law that would strip the citizenship of French terrorists and include provisions to make it easier to deport suspected terrorists, which has proved to be extremely controversial.

Similarly, the January 2015 *Charlie Hebdo* and Jewish grocery attacks prompted a revision of the laws regarding surveillance. The July 2015 law updating the legal framework for intelligence gathering is the first text approved by Parliament on intelligence activities and procedures. Surveillance may be used for the preservation of national security; foreign policy interests and preventing foreign interference; safeguarding industrial and scientific economic interests; preventing terrorism; safeguarding republican institutions and preventing collective violence; preventing crime and organized delinquency; and preventing WMD. With some exceptions, surveillance must be authorized in advance by the premier. Depending on the type of data, they may be retained from between thirty days and four years. The law allows bulk collection and metadata analysis, as well as more direct surveillance in suspects' homes, cars, and computers and surveillance of their associates. The law covers both French citizens and foreigners. Oversight of surveillance is provided by the *Commission Nationale de Contrôle des Techniques de Renseignement* (CNCTR—National Commission for the Control of Intelligence Techniques). Requests to surveil individuals must be brought to the commission, although its decisions are not binding. Commission members are chosen from among members of the judicial and administrative offices. The CNTCR includes members of the Senate and the National Assembly and provides an opinion to the premier on whether or not to authorize the intercept. In emergencies, the CNCTR can be omitted. If the premier disagrees with a CNTCR recommendation and approves an operation, he or she must provide an explanation. There are intelligence oversight committees in the Senate and the National Assembly, but the constitution gives a great deal of power and discretion to the president and the premier.

Some observers questioned if there was sufficient capacity to process and use all of the data that might now be collected. The premier sets a limit on how many communications interceptions may be conducted simultaneously. As of 2015, the number was 2,700. Some observers thought the passage of the new surveillance law somewhat ironic, given French protests over the NSA programs leaked by Snowden.

Although there have been reports over the past several years of closer U.S.-French intelligence cooperation, particularly in counterterrorism, this liaison relationship is still less than that carried out by the United States with some of its Five Eyes partners. DNI Dennis Blair (2009–2010) apparently sought to increase the relationship with France unilaterally; the lack of success in this effort being another factor in his eventual departure. In the aftermath of the November 2015 terrorist attacks, the United States announced increased sharing of intelligence and military operational planning information to counter ISIL. However, U.S. officials said France would not be made part of what has been the Five Eyes group, so it would appear that the new intelligence cooperation will still be less intimate than that between the United States and its Commonwealth partners.

France, like some other nations, has had difficulty deciding how to organize for the cyberspace issue. In early 2011, the French government decided to give the army responsibility for cyberspace defense and to give the DGSE responsibility for cyberspace offense, therefore making the decision to treat offensive cyberspace activities as an intelligence task rather than a military one.

Finally, the French intelligence community, like so many others, occasionally has problems working in harmony. To address this problem, President Nicolas Sarkozy ordered the creation of a new intelligence academy (*Académie du Renseignement*— Intelligence Academy) in 2010. One of the academy's main goals is to forge a single culture and sense of community spirit among its students, who are in the junior and senior ranks of their respective agencies.

France, perhaps more than any nation friendly to the United States, raised strenuous protests in the aftermath of the Snowden NSA revelations. Then–president Hollande demanded that the U.S. cease surveillance of the EU, the French Foreign ministry, and French embassies, which reportedly had been targets. Hollande tried to use the reports as a means of delaying the opening of free-trade negotiations between the EU and the United States, which France opposed. However, the newspaper *Le Monde* then stated that DGSE conducted similar metadata surveillance in France on telephone calls, emails, and text messages, which then went into a large database. *Le Monde* said that DGSE also collected data from large U.S. networks like Google, Facebook, and Microsoft, as well as Orange, the French telecommunications company. According to news sources, France had cooperated with NSA in collection outside of France. Subsequent French comments on the U.S. surveillance were in a markedly lower tone. In March 2016, French legislators approved a bill, opposed by the Hollande administration, that would penalize technology firms that refused to provide encrypted data to an investigatory authority.

ISRAEL

Israeli intelligence proceeds from the premise that the state is, essentially, under siege. Israel has two major intelligence services: Mossad and Shin Bet. Mossad (*Ha-Mossad Le-Modiin Ule-Tafkidim Meyuhadim*—Institute for Intelligence and Special Tasks) is responsible for HUMINT, covert action, foreign liaison, and counterterrorism, as well as for producing a series of intelligence reports. Shin Bet (*Sherut ha-Bitachon ha-Klali*—General Security Service) has both counterintelligence and internal security functions, including a SIGINT Cyber Division. A third component, Aman (*Agaf ha-Modi'in*—Military Intelligence), is distinct from the intelligence components of each of the services, producing a series of intelligence reports, including national estimates. The Foreign Affairs and Security Committee of the Knesset (Parliament) oversees Israeli intelligence. The issue of creating a legal basis for the Mossad, other than the broad Basic Law on the government, has been debated since 1998 but has never been enacted. Mossad therefore comes under the direct control of the prime minister. A law defining the responsibilities of Shin Bet was passed in 2002, after twelve years of debate. There is also a Military Intelligence Directorate in the Israel Defense Forces (IDF). Within this directorate is the Research Department, which has both a military intelligence function and a national intelligence function to provide national strategic assessments. The Ministry of Foreign Affairs Research Center also conducts strategic intelligence estimates.

At a basic level, the intelligence requirements of Israel are simple. It is located in the midst of other nations, a few of which maintain proper diplomatic relations while the rest remain hostile. Israel must watch both kinds of neighboring states, the Israeli-occupied territories on the West Bank and the Palestinian enclave at Gaza harbor populations at least some sections of which are overtly hostile to Israel and unwilling to countenance its existence. Finally, Israel sees Iran as an "existential threat," given that nation's overt hostility and potential military capabilities. This allows a fair amount of focus but also demands a constant state of readiness. It is difficult to think of another state whose intelligence services face a similar challenge. Shin Bet claimed to have thwarted over 400 terror attacks in 2016.

Given this milieu, Israeli intelligence activities have always been given a fair amount of latitude and have become both legendary and controversial. Over the years, a number of successful HUMINT penetrations into Egypt and Syria have been conducted. However, one operation against Egypt in the early 1950s was discovered, resulting in the deaths of four Israeli agents and the prolonged incarceration of several others. It became known as the Lavon affair, after the defense minister at the time, Pinhas Lavon.

A more recent controversy involved a U.S. naval intelligence analyst, Jonathan Pollard. He appears to have been a walk-in, motivated by concerns that the United States was not sharing vital intelligence with Israel. However, Pollard also accepted cash and gifts in exchange for the intelligence he provided, including intelligence reports, imagery, and information about weapons systems. In 1985, he was arrested outside the Israeli Embassy, and in 1987, he was sentenced to life imprisonment. Under the sentencing guidelines then in effect, Pollard was eligible for parole after thirty years. The Obama administration considered releasing Pollard a few years before his sentence ended as a means of gaining concessions from Israel in the negotiations with the Palestinians. However, this idea was dropped. Pollard was released in November 2015. Some people felt that the sentence was too harsh, although successive reviews of Pollard's case have upheld the initial concerns that prompted the sentence. Pollard must remain in the United States under supervision (GPS tracker, limited Internet access) for five years because the intelligence he tried to pass is still considered top secret. Again, some observers have argued that Pollard should be allowed to emigrate to Israel upon release (he was granted Israeli citizenship in 1995) and that there is no point to this further sentence.

Israel initially attempted to pass off the case as a rogue operation but, in early 1998, admitted that Pollard had been working as a regular agent. In 2006, Rafi Eitan, who had been Pollard's handler, said that the information that Pollard provided was too good to resist and that Eitan could not put a stop to the operation. As noted, Pollard had also been granted Israeli citizenship. The Pollard case became a constant irritant in U.S.-Israeli relations, not only because of the ill will it engendered on the U.S. side but also because of constant Israeli attempts to get Pollard released. Most significant, Israeli prime minister Benjamin Netanyahu raised the Pollard issue during the 1998 peace talks at Wye River, where President Clinton brought together the Israelis and Palestinians. Clinton appeared to be receptive to releasing him. DCI George J. Tenet (1997–2004) reportedly threatened to resign if Pollard was pardoned and released to Israel, whereupon Clinton dropped the issue. (Pollard supporters argue that the United States traded Soviet spy Rudolf Abel for U-2 pilot Francis Gary Powers in the 1960s, thus creating a precedent. However, although the United States has proved willing to repatriate a foreign spy in exchange for a U.S. intelligence officer, it does not trade U.S. citizens convicted of espionage to the state for whom they spied.) In 2010, there were press reports that Netanyahu was willing to freeze the building of new Israeli settlements on the West Bank, a major irritant in Israel's relations with the United States, in exchange for Pollard's release. Israeli requests for a commutation of Pollard's sentence became a regular irritant in the bilateral relationship. The Pollard case is a classic example of a successful penetration whose political costs may far outweigh any intelligence that was obtained.

In 2014, officials from the Office of the DNI (ODNI) briefed Congress on continuing to exclude Israel from the Visa Waiver Program, which allows entry into the United States and a ninety-day stay without obtaining a visa. Thirty-eight nations are in the program. U.S. officials have previously stated that Israel does not meet the requirements—meaning the number of citizens refused entry and a reciprocal program with the United States. However, the exclusion is apparently also based on U.S. concerns about Israel using the program to insert spies into the United States more easily.

In 2015, there were several press reports alleging that Israel had used "spyware" to spy on the UN-Iran nuclear talks, which Israel had opposed. Stories vary as to how this alleged activity was discovered: by a cybersecurity firm or by U.S. SIGINT collection against Israel. Israeli defense minister Moshe Yaalon denied the allegations. There have also been press reports alleging that Israel eavesdropped on U.S. secretary of state John Kerry's talks with the Palestinians.

The United States is Israel's most important foreign intelligence liaison, but there have been periods of tension, most notably the Pollard case but also during periods when U.S. and Israeli policy appear at odds. In March 2015, the U.S. Defense Department published a 1987 report that gave details on Israel's nuclear program. There had been a long-standing "gentleman's agreement" that Israel never formally acknowledged its nuclear capability, and the United States said nothing formally as well. The release of the 1987 document was seen by many as a sign of Obama administration frustration over Israel's opposition to the Iran nuclear agreement and, in particular, Prime Minister Netanyahu's speech to Congress on that issue that same month. In May 2017, President Trump, meeting with Russian foreign minister Sergei Lavrov and Russian ambassador Sergei Kislyak, discussed intelligence the United States had received concerning the Islamic State. The intelligence apparently came from Israel, which was obvious given the way in which Trump discussed it. Although Trump asserted his right to share intelligence with Russia, the disclosure violated the third party rule of foreign intelligence liaison: A nation that receives intelligence from another nation does not share it further without asking permission. Publicly, Israeli officials expressed confidence in the relationship with the United States, but press reporting stated they were "furious." Israeli defense minister Avigdor Lieberman later said that

Israel "did a spot repair" and made some changes in the intelligence-sharing relationship, without offering any details.

But the relationship with the United States is not exclusive. In October 2015, Israeli news services reported that Israel was providing Russia with information about anti-Assad forces in Syria to facilitate Russia's military intervention. A similar meeting occurred in July 2016. Israel also reportedly paid some Syrian rebel groups to keep Iranian-backed group and ISIL militants away from Israel's borders.

Less controversial, and far less costly politically, have been Israel's penetrations in other hostile Arab targets. In Lebanon, there are recurring arrests of individuals accused of spying for Israel. An interesting insight into the convoluted world of espionage is the number of press reports concerning how Lebanon uncovered one espionage case. According to Israeli press, the Lebanese had received training and equipment provided by the United States. Other accounts state that the Russian service, the *Federal'naya Sluzba Besnopasnoti* (FSB; see below), had a unit that provided intelligence to Hezbollah, the radical Lebanese Shiite faction. There have also been press reports of successful Israeli penetrations of Hamas. In 2011, Russia expelled Israel's military attaché, charging that he had tried to obtain information concerning Russia's military relations with Arab states.

Some of the losses in Lebanon may be tied to an Israeli espionage controversy, the imprisonment and death of "Prisoner X." Much of this case remains murky, with few agreed facts. Prisoner X was Ben Zygier, an Australian who emigrated to Israel and worked for Mossad. He was released from Mossad for marginal performance. Apparently in an attempt to revive his intelligence career, Zygier tried to recruit sources in Hezbollah, in part by sharing with them the names of Israeli operatives in Lebanon, who were then arrested. Zygier was arrested by Israel and placed in a highly restrictive prison environment under a false name. Despite the fact that he was under constant surveillance in his cell, Zygier is said to have committed suicide. There have also been reports that Zygier divulged Israel's use of passports from other nations to move operatives around the world. The circumstances of Zygier's arrest, captivity, and death remain controversial, and the Israeli government has released few details.

Like any other intelligence service, Israel's record is mixed. Israel succeeded in penetrating an agent into Hezbollah, an anti-Israeli Islamic Shiite militant group based in Lebanon but heavily supported by Iran. The Israeli agent was able to thwart some Hezbollah operations against Israel. However, in 2014, Israel apparently was surprised by the extensive tunnel network dug by Hamas, the Palestinian Authority faction that controls Gaza and that has been characterized as a terrorist organization by several nations. In June 2018, Israel accused former minister of energy and infrastructure Gonen Segev of spying for Iran, apparently providing information concerning energy. Segev had served an earlier sentence for drug smuggling. Iran acknowledged the penetration.

Concerns about Israeli intelligence collection overseas continue to be problematic. In 2004, the FBI said that Israel had been overly aggressive in collecting information at military equipment exhibitions. The information involved appeared not to be classified, but the persistence of Israelis in asking questions about certain equipment raised concerns. The FBI also had under investigation a U.S. Defense Department official who might have passed information to Israel. New Zealand jailed and then expelled two Israelis for attempting to obtain New Zealand passports illegally. The New Zealand government accused them of being Mossad agents. They denied the allegation but admitted having committed criminal activity. Israel's Foreign Ministry issued an official apology in 2005. Access to foreign passports is essential to all intelligence agencies, which use them to mask the identities of agents sent overseas. The issue of Israel's use of foreign passports arose again in 2010, when Israeli agents killed a senior Hamas commander in Dubai, having used Australian, French, British, Irish, and German passports as cover. Several countries raised the issue in diplomatic protests with Israel; Britain expelled an Israeli diplomat over the issue.

In 2007, Ashraf Marwan, a wealthy Egyptian businessman living in London, fell from his fourth-floor apartment to his death. Marwan's death became the subject of much speculation, centering on allegations that he had been a longtime spy for Mossad or that he was a double agent. Marwan had been a son-in-law of Egyptian president Gamal Abdel Nasser (1956–1970). Egyptian president Hosni Mubarak (1981–2011) issued a statement denying that Marwan had spied for Israel. Also in 2007, Muhammad Sayyid Saber Ali, an Egyptian nuclear engineer, was sentenced to life in prison for spying for Israel. Ali admitted delivering reports taken from Egypt's atomic agency but said they were not secret and were available online.

In addition to its emphasis on HUMINT, Israel has developed an independent satellite imagery and radar capability and is at the forefront of imagery cooperation between nations. According to press reports, Israel has five intelligence satellites in orbit, including electro-optical and synthetic aperture radar. Press reports cite India and Turkey as two of its partners. Israel also has been a leader in developing small satellites, driven in part by its limited options for space-launching tracks, essentially westward over the Mediterranean Sea. Israel also makes extensive use of UAVs, beginning with the Yom Kippur War in 1973. Israeli UAVs span both the tactical and strategic reconnaissance roles and are bought by other states as well, including Russia.

Israeli intelligence has conducted a variety of covert operations abroad, including both kidnapping and assassination. The most famous kidnapping was of the Nazi official Adolf Eichmann, who was abducted in Argentina in 1960. Eichmann had been responsible for the implementation of Hitler's "final solution," the extermination of the Jews. He was brought to Israel, where he was tried and executed. In 1986, Israeli intelligence abducted Mordechai Vanunu, who had worked at Israel's secret nuclear installation at Dimona. A year after leaving Dimona, Vanunu published details about Israel's nuclear weapons program in the *London Sunday Times*. Lured from London to Rome, Vanunu was abducted and returned to Israel, where he was sentenced to eighteen years in prison.

Israeli assassinations have targeted terrorists outside of Israel or the occupied territories. Targets have included the terrorists responsible for the capture, torture, and death of Israeli athletes at the 1972 Munich Olympics, although one innocent Arab in Norway was misidentified and also killed by Israeli agents. More recently, Israel has killed a number of terrorists during the unrest in both occupied and Palestinian-controlled areas. Israel refers to these as targeted killings, or interceptions, not assassinations or military reprisals. They appear to have been carried out by either intelligence or military forces. As noted, in January 2010, Israeli agents killed a Hamas commander in Dubai. Various press accounts have alleged that Israel was also responsible for the deaths of Iranian nuclear scientists and a Syrian rocket scientist. Israel has successfully targeted Hezbollah and Hamas leaders. According to press accounts, assassinations are carried out by a highly compartmented unit in the Mossad, called Kidon ("Bayonet"). Israel is able to take advantage of the fact that it has a large number of citizens with Arabic or Iranian background, giving them the requisite language skills and physical appearance to operate in likely target countries.

Like the United States and the Soviet Union, Israel has suffered a major strategic intelligence failure. In 1973, Egypt and Syria achieved strategic surprise in the opening phase of the Yom Kippur War. In a still-controversial postwar investigation, the Agranat Commission primarily faulted the military leadership and Aman for the surprise. The commission found that, although many signs pointed to an impending attack, the military was overly committed to an indications and warnings (I&W) concept that led them to downplay what they were seeing because not all of the conceptual indicators had been observed. In other words, they had created an I&W model and refused to react to the indications they were seeing because the Arab actions did not fit the I&W concept. Thus, even with an I&W model, the threshold had been set too high. This experience provided a valuable lesson on the possibility of surprise. Commenting on it nine years after the war, the staff director of the Knesset committee responsible for oversight of intelligence said, "The United States [during the cold war] has to watch every part of the globe. We know who our enemies are. We only have to watch six or seven countries—and still we were surprised."

A more recent intelligence issue that raised concern in Israel was the 2011 political unrest in Egypt during the Arab Spring, which apparently caught Israel by surprise, along with many other states. Peace with Egypt is central to Israeli national security policy. Egypt was the first Arab nation to sign a peace treaty with Israel and to grant diplomatic recognition. Peace with Egypt also removes the threat of another two-front war. As the most populous and a very influential Arab nation, Egypt is seen as a necessary participant for any successful Arab attack on Israel. Israel, caught by surprise like everyone else, including the Egyptian government, therefore went back to review its political intelligence on one of its two most important diplomatic relationships, the other being the United States. The unrest in Egypt in 2013 following the overthrow of President Mohamed Morsi (2012–2013) renewed Israeli concerns. Multiple press reports stated that Israel, along with the Arab monarchies of Saudi Arabia and the United Arab Emirates (UAE), supported the initial military regime of Gen. Abdel Fattah el-Sisi and urged the United States to do so as well. In 2018, the Israeli government reportedly urged the Trump administration not to be too hard on Saudi Arabia in the aftermath of the murder of journalist Jamal Khashoggi in the Saudi consulate in Istanbul, Turkey. Israel's motivation is that Saudi Arabia opposes Iran, as does Israel.

Israel has long faced a terrorist problem and is also deeply concerned about WMD proliferation, for which it has an active and independent collection effort. Israel has also shown a willingness to act unilaterally against suspected WMD threats. In 1981, Israeli jets attacked the Osirak reactor near Baghdad. In 2007, as noted earlier, Israel conducted an air strike against a covert nuclear site in Syria, perhaps being supported by North Korea. Iran's nuclear program is an obvious concern, especially given the hostility expressed by Iran to Israel's existence. Interestingly, Israeli officials disagreed with the published conclusions of the 2007 national intelligence estimate (NIE) on Iranian WMD. Israeli defense minister Ehud Barak agreed that the program had probably stopped in 2003 but said that the program had since been restarted. This would appear to be in line with the December 2015 IAEA (International Atomic Energy Agency) report based on partial Iranian responses to a series of questions. Such public disagreements about intelligence estimates are rare, but the 2007 NIE was released in an unclassified form.

In 2011, Meir Dagan, the outgoing Mossad director, said he did not think Iran would have nuclear weapons before 2015. This was widely interpreted as a reassessment based on the damage to the Iranian nuclear program caused by the Stuxnet malware. Many observers believe Israel is a prime candidate for having created and distributed Stuxnet; some press accounts hold that the United States cooperated in testing the malware. As noted, many also believe that Israel was behind the fatal attacks on several Iranian scientists involved in the nuclear program. According to press reports, Iran's Quds Force, a special unit of the Revolutionary Guard, was given the assignment of retaliating against Israel for these attacks. However, the Quds Force, working with its ally, Hezbollah, had twenty attacks thwarted during 2011–2012. Israel opposed the Joint Comprehensive Plan of Action (JCPOA) with Iran, which became a point of friction with the Obama administration, and has devoted significant intelligence resources to Iranian military programs. In April 2018, Israel revealed that it had stolen a mass of material from Iran (55,000 pages, 183 compact discs) and had shared these with the United States. Prime Minister Netanyahu said the documents revealed Iran had been deceptive about the program but did not cite any violations of the JCPOA. The release came as President Trump was nearing his decision on whether or not to stay with the JCPOA, which he ultimately decided to leave.

As the Stuxnet operation would suggest, Israel is very active in cyberspace and is seen as being one of the more sophisticated practitioners. According to the *Financial Times*, Israel has 10 percent of the global cybersecurity market. According to press accounts, an Israeli cyber firm, Cellebrite, broke into the locked cell phone of the San Bernardino killer, assisting the FBI when Apple refused. Cellebrite has apparently assisted the FBI at other times. Several press reports identify Unit 8200 as Israel's cybersecurity unit, performing offensive and defensive operations, as well as SIGINT and big-data mining. (In September 2014, some reservists assigned to Unit 8200 said they would no longer spy on Palestinian civilians.) Unit 8200 also serves as a developer and feeder of talent for the Israeli cyber industry. In addition to the Iranian target, press reports note Israeli cyberattacks against Syria in conjunction with the eventual attack on the nuclear site being built there by North Korea and possible eavesdropping on the Iran nuclear talks. Israel, like most other nations, also worries about the growing cyber problem. In Israel's case, this is exacerbated by individuals or groups opposed to Israeli policies, such as the hacktivist group Anonymous, which targeted the websites of Mossad and the IDF. According to press reports, Israeli government sites were subjected to 44 million organized hacking attempts during a five-day period in late 2012. Finally, there are press reports about Unit 9900, which does geospatial intelligence.

Israel reportedly hacked into the network of Kaspersky Lab, a Russian software firm founded by Eugene (Yevgeny) Kaspersky, a former KGB technical officer. Kaspersky Lab sells a range of cybersecurity produces, including a popular antivirus software. Israel discovered that Russian hackers used the antivirus software to search computers at U.S. government agencies and informed the U.S. about the problem. In July 2017, the U.S. government removed Kaspersky Lab as a firm authorized to do business with the U.S. government. In June 2018, the U.S. blacklisted the Israeli firm Embedi because of its ties to Russian cyber firms.

In June 2017, Netanyahu stood up the National Cyber Directorate, as part of the prime minister's office. This directorate is "responsible for protecting civilian cyberspace, including critical infrastructure." The heads of Israeli intelligence reportedly had opposed creating this office, arguing that it was granted extensive powers but had a vague role. That same month, Mossad announced the creation of an investment fund, called Libertad, to support start-up firms investigating new techniques, including robotics, facial recognition, miniaturization, and encryption.

RUSSIA

More has been written about Russian intelligence than about any other intelligence service except for that of the United States. Russian intelligence capabilities probably most closely parallel those of the United States, although the KGB and the CIA were not directly comparable during the cold war.

The now-defunct KGB was the last in a long line of Russian and Soviet intelligence services whose primary responsibility was to combat internal dissent. The following KGB directorates had foreign intelligence roles:

- First Chief Directorate (Foreign): responsible for all nonmilitary intelligence, foreign counterintelligence, HUMINT, foreign propaganda, and disinformation

- Eighth Chief Directorate (Communication): SIGINT, both offensive and defensive, the latter role shared with the Sixteenth Directorate (Communications Security)

One can question the KGB's effectiveness in its broader and more important internal security role. KGB leadership was involved in the abortive 1991 coup against Communist Party general secretary Mikhail S. Gorbachev that led to the demise of the Soviet Union. Moreover, the KGB clearly misread—or failed to report—the depth of anticommunist discontent in both the satellite states and the Soviet Union itself.

The *Glavnoye Upravlenie* (GU—Main Directorate) was and remains the military intelligence organization charged with the collection of a large array of intelligence related to military issues. (Until 2010, it was known as the GRU—*Glavnoye Razvedyvatelnoye Upravlenie*, Main Intelligence Directorate.) The GU has HUMINT, SIGINT, and IMINT capabilities. During the cold war, the Western services viewed the GU as an occasional rival of the KGB. (Col. Oleg Penkovsky, who spied for the United States and Britain, was a GU officer.)

As with any other HUMINT enterprise, the records of the KGB and GU are mixed. Successful penetrations of U.S. and British services include the cases of walk-ins CIA agent Aldrich Ames and FBI agent Robert Hanssen, from the former, and Philby, Blake, and Prime, from the latter. At the same time, however, Western services recruited spies in the Soviet Union and, apparently, the post-Soviet state. Penkovsky is among the best known. It should also be noted that the damage done by Ames—and perhaps Hanssen simultaneously—involved at least twelve other U.S. sources. Moreover, Hanssen's arrest apparently came as a result of information supplied by a U.S. intelligence source in Russia. There continue to be regular press accounts about various individuals arrested, primarily in Europe, for spying for Russia, as well as articles in the Russian press about Russians accused of spying for the West. As noted in chapter 5, in 2013 a U.S. diplomat, Ryan Fogle, was arrested in Moscow for attempted espionage and was declared persona non grata. Unlike some other services, Soviet/Russian intelligence has long used "kompromat," or compromise as a means of recruiting or coercing agents. This refers to the use of compromising material that the individual would find highly embarrassing—in short, blackmail.

President Vladimir Putin has referred to the collapse of the Soviet Union as the "greatest political catastrophe" of the twentieth century. He appears to harbor a great deal of resentment over how the Soviet Union and then Russia were treated during and after the Soviet collapse. He cannot re-create the Soviet system or the larger Soviet state, but he has successfully returned to several themes that are important to intelligence operations, especially the view that Russia is essentially besieged and under attack from the West.

Like so much else in what was the Soviet Union, the intelligence services had to undergo an unplanned transition when the U.S.S.R. dissolved. The KGB's First Chief Directorate emerged as the *Sluzhba Vneshnei Razvedki* (SVR—External Intelligence Service). It is responsible for intelligence liaison, industrial espionage, and HUMINT and for the handling of Ames and Hanssen, carryover assets from the KGB period. The SVR has made much of the fact that it has reduced its overseas presence, attempting to portray itself as a more benign organization than its predecessor. Some observers believe this may have been largely cosmetic, especially given the high numbers of Russian agents now found abroad. Russia is now more open and accessible than was the Soviet Union, making it easier for the SVR to have contacts with agents in Russia instead of overseas. However, both Britain and Germany have reported the presence of large numbers of Russian spies. MI5 director Jonathan Evans said in 2007 that there had been no decrease in "undeclared Russian intelligence officers in the UK" and that their activities and those of the Chinese diverted resources from efforts against al Qaeda. Similarly, the head of Germany's domestic intelligence service BfV (*Bundesamt für Verfassungsschutz*—Federal Office for the Protection of the Constitution) said that one-third of all Russian diplomats in Germany (120 out of 360) were part of the SVR, working against a broad range of topics. Finally, in July 2007, Putin said that the SVR would have to increase its intelligence gathering and analytic efforts because of "growing imbalances" in the "international situation and [because of] internal political interests." Based on press reports, there appears to be an increase in Russian espionage in former eastern bloc countries, the United States, and Scandinavia. The Czech service has said that Russian espionage exceeds the levels of the cold war; Sweden estimates that one-third of Russian diplomats are spies. In May 2015, NATO ordered a reduction in the nonmember delegations. This was seen as a reaction to the Russian invasion of Ukraine and concerns about the presence of intelligence officers in the delegations. In June 2014, the head of the FSB (*Federalnaya Sluzhba Bezopasnosti*—Federal Security Service) and other Russian security officials were placed on sanctions and visa ban lists in reaction to Russia's intervention in Ukraine. There are also reports of Russian espionage activity in Portugal and Ireland.

The KGB's counterintelligence function reemerged as the FSB, which is responsible for internal counterintelligence, civil counterespionage, and internal security. Putin was a former KGB officer and headed the FSB from July 1998 until his elevation to the position of acting prime minister in August 1999. In 2003, Putin gave the FSB control over the border guards and *Federalnoe Agenstvo Pravitelstvennoi Svyazi I Informatsii* (FAPSI—Federal Agency for Government Communications and Information), which was the successor to the KGB's Eighth Chief Directorate, responsible for cryptography, SIGINT, and the Communications Troops. These functions are parallel to those of NSA, but FAPSI also controls internal electronic communications, again making comparisons imprecise. This consolidation under the FSB had led some observers to be concerned that the old powers of the KGB were being reconstituted. In 2013, Putin gave the FSB responsibility for the "detection, prevention and liquidation" of cyberattacks.

The GU has attracted much more attention in recent years as people have come to understand its larger and more aggressive role in Russian operations against Ukraine and in the attempted poisoning of Sergei Skripal. The Obama administration levied sanctions against some GU officers; and special counsel Robert Mueller, investigating Russia's role in the 2016 U.S. presidential election, issued indictments against twelve GU officers. The GU may have had something of a comeback after years in which press reports said the GU was out of favor with Putin.

Many observers of Russian intelligence believe that there is a high degree of competition among the intelligence agencies, largely as a means of vying for favor, budgets, and so on. Although competition can foster improved performance, in the case of Russia it tends to drive the agencies toward operations with quick results to bolster one's record. Also, these agencies do not produce refined analysis. Experts believe much of their analysis consists of either passing along raw intelligence or rather superficial analysis written with an eye to the views of the policy maker. That said, the Russian services remain important, powerful, and successful in many of their operations, and they have apparently entered a more aggressive phase of espionage worldwide.

The World Wide Web has also become a source of increasing concern as the Putin regime clamps down on protests. The SVR has invested in programs to monitor blog postings and social networks in order to determine where information originates and how it spreads. Another system is designed to spread information through the blogosphere. A senior FSB official cited the uncontrolled use of Skype, Gmail, and Hotmail as potential security threats. Kremlin officials later disavowed these comments but also expressed understanding for the FSB's position. There are two sources of concern. These providers are on servers based outside of Russia and use foreign encryption technology and therefore cannot be easily accessed. Second, they may be used by extremists.

Russian activity in cyberspace has become a major concern for several nations. Cyber is an almost ideal venue for Putin's goal of being treated as a great power and, preferably, the equal of the United States, again harking back to the cold war. Cyber has a fairly low technical barrier to entry, is relatively cheap, and offers deniability. Computer capabilities were a large differentiator between the United States and the Soviet Union, but the computer revolution has essentially leveled that playing field.

There is a substantial record of Russian cyber activity. According to press accounts, foreign heads of state and their staffs attending the G-20 summit in St. Petersburg in October 2013 received as gifts USB sticks and smartphone rechargers that gave Russian intelligence access to various communications, which the Russians denied. It is widely assumed that Russia was behind the massive denial-of-service (DoS) attack against Estonia in the spring of 2007, to protest the moving of a Soviet war memorial. Cyberattacks also preceded Russian intervention in Georgia in July 2008 and Russia's intervention in Ukraine in 2014. Russia uses "troll armies," meaning individuals who undertake a range of vigilante actions on targeted sites. According to press accounts, the Internet Research Agency in St. Petersburg is the center for this activity. This allows Russia to deny any involvement in the incidents. A Russian hacking group was said to hijack commercial satellite connections to gain access to U.S. and European military and diplomatic data.

The most prominent Russian cyber exploit was actions taken during the 2016 U.S. presidential election. As noted, U.S. intelligence has concluded, with "high confidence," that Putin sought to undermine faith in the election and to assist the campaign of Donald Trump. DHS Secretary Kirstjen Nielsen also confirmed: "It was the Russians." However, in his joint appearance with Putin in Helsinki, Finland, in July 2018, Trump again questioned these findings, saying he believed Putin's disavowals. Putin said that Russia does not hack but that "patriotic" individuals may have done so.

Russian cyber activity related to the 2016 election appears to have included the hacking noted above, and the extensive use of U.S.-based social media, especially on sites like Facebook—including buying some 3,300 advertisements and creating 470 fake pages and accounts—to stir up controversies, support certain positions, and inflame the political debate. Russian-bought ads were also found on Google.

In May 2017, Robert Mueller, former FBI director, was named special counsel to investigate "any links and/or coordination between the Russian government" and the Trump campaign. Seven individuals have pleaded guilty to various charges (six Americans, one Dutch), twelve Russians have been indicted for computer crimes and money laundering, and thirteen Russians have been indicted for interfering in the election. They apparently used the Bitcoin cryptocurrency to buy websites but mask their identity. In addition, the computers of the Democratic National Committee (DNC) were hacked by "Guccifer 2.0," who has been identified as a GU officer. The DNC documents ended up on the WikiLeaks site, as had the leaks provided by Pvt. Bradley Manning. Many observers suspect that a working relationship exists between WikiLeaks and Russian intelligence.

In 2017, the FBI created the Foreign Influence Task Force to identify and combat foreign influence operations against the United States. In December 2018, DNI Dan Coats (2017–2019) said that Russia, as well as China and Iran, ran influence operations aimed at the 2018 midterm elections.

Several other nations—including Lithuania, Sweden, the Netherlands, Norway, and Switzerland—have said they were targets of Russian cyber operations. Russians have also been implicated in many infrastructure intrusions in the West, in hacking routers and switches that control the Internet, and potentially in targeting underwater communications cables.

It would have been unreasonable and impossible for Russia to scrap the old Soviet intelligence apparatus entirely and start anew. Inevitably some of the same officers would have had to be retained. The key question for Russian intelligence is part of the larger question of the degree to which Russia is a country in which laws and rights are respected by the government and its agencies. Certainly, the political conditions prevailing under Putin since his return to the presidency in 2012 do not suggest an open or tolerant political system but, rather, one in which laws and institutions are used to stifle dissent or opposition. Putin has called the Internet originally "a special CIA project." A 2014 law requires any site with more than three thousand visitors to be responsible for the accuracy of information posted to it, which directly affects chat rooms and blogs. Bloggers can no longer be anonymous. Russian historical experience offers little basis upon which to create such democratic practices, in either the intelligence services or the wider society. Also, Russia faces some internal problems—typified by ongoing internal Muslim unrest, which has led to terrorist attacks in Moscow and elsewhere—that create pressure against more restrained intelligence functions. Russian intelligence services clearly have prospered both economically and in terms of power under Putin, being major recipients of the firms controlled by many of the oligarchs in the aftermath of the Soviet Union's dissolution.

Muslim unrest, which for Russia is an internal problem as much as, if not more than, an external problem, given the restive populations in the Caucasus region, has provided a locus of interest with the United States. The Tsarnaev brothers, who carried out the April 2013 Boston Marathon bombing, were originally from that region, and the older brother, Tamerlan, returned for a long visit in 2012. Apparently, the FSB shared concerns with the FBI in 2011 about Tamerlan having been radicalized but withheld the actual text messages that were the basis of the Russian alert, a step that U.S. officials later faulted. Efforts by the FSB and the FBI to cooperate since the Boston attack have been hampered by long-standing distrust and by the overall deterioration in U.S.-Russian relations. In November 2015, a Russian airliner was destroyed midair over the Sinai. The Islamic State claimed responsibility. This attack is assumed to be connected to Russia's decision, in late September 2015, to intervene in Syria, which was stated to be against ISIL but had mainly targeted rebel groups fighting the Assad regime, a Russian client.

Edward Snowden's flight to Russia after leaking the NSA programs, after first staying in China, and Russia's subsequent decision to grant Snowden temporary asylum became another irritant in relations in 2013. Snowden claimed that he had not shared his information with either China or Russia, but it is reasonable to assume that both countries targeted Snowden's computers remotely. Although he has continued to support Snowden, Putin also has said that the leaked U.S. programs were a "necessity."

Russian intelligence officers sometimes refer to themselves as Chekists, harking back to the Cheka, the first intelligence service under the Bolsheviks. Putin is fond of using the quote: "There is no such thing as a former Chekist." Putin has relied very heavily on KGB veterans to staff key regional positions across Russia and, perhaps more significantly, to take over the various economic enterprises that have been wrested from the oligarchs who took control of them after the Soviet collapse. These include banks, media, and the immensely important energy sector, which had been the basis of Russia's rebounding economic and political power. As Russian author Yevgenia Albats said, "The FSB is no longer just a police organization, it is a business." According to *The Economist*, three out of four senior Russian officials have ties to former or current intelligence organizations. According to Russian sources, 40 percent of the total Russian bureaucracy and 60 percent of the presidential administration have intelligence or security service backgrounds. They are referred to as *siloviki*, roughly meaning "strongmen." In 2012, for example, Putin named the head of the SVR and the minister of the interior to a new presidential commission dealing with the energy sector. The commission's executive secretary is a Putin ally and also a former KGB officer. Thus, there has been a definite resurgence in the power of the intelligence services, whose future thus became closely tied to that of Putin.

This mutual dependence decreases the likelihood of there being significant political challenges to Putin within the political system. In 2010, a law was enacted giving the FSB the power to warn citizens about "creating the conditions" for crimes, as well as penalties for refusing to obey a legal request from an FSB officer. Critics saw this as another threat to political rights of expression. A more recent Russian critique of the FSB, published in 2010, argues that it has more power and more freedom of action now than did the KGB in the Soviet system. In the Soviet system, all government entities came under the Communist Party. With the party defunct and the legislature, the Duma, largely neutered, the FSB comes under the direction of the president, thus enhancing the FSB's power and independence. Some Russian journalists claim that the FSB has been especially active in the former Soviet republics in Central Asia, allowing Russia to exert continued influence in these states.

Russia's TECHINT capabilities come closest to those of the United States, although reports of deterioration in these capabilities had been persistent in the period after the collapse of the Soviet Union. Numerous press reports noted financial constraints affecting these collection assets, in terms of both the number of satellites in orbit and problems affecting ground facilities. It is reasonable to assume that, just as Putin put resources into reviving Russia's long-range strategic forces (such as resumed strategic bomber patrols far into the North Atlantic), he probably did the same for Russia's technical intelligence capabilities. In 2013, the Russian Ministry of Defense asked Germany for permission to purchase two radar reconnaissance satellites, something that would have been unthinkable during the cold war. In June 2014, the Russian Defense Ministry said that its last geosynchronous satellite had ceased functioning. As with U.S. geo-orbit satellites, the Russian satellite served an early warning function, which Russia can sustain only for a few hours a day.

In November 2018, the FSB cancelled a contract between Roscosmos, the Russian space agency, and a U.S. firm, OneWeb, to launch an array of microsatellites over two years to enable remote parts of the Earth to have broadband Internet access. The FSB was concerned satellite-based Internet access would be difficult to monitor and to filter and also that the satellites might be used to spy on Russia. Russia has also considered legislation to limit the amount of personal information that personnel in the security services can post on social media. Such limits already exist for military personnel, enacted after the incursion in Ukraine when such information was used to identify some of the Russian troops who were involved.

Russia and the United States are among the signatories to the 1992 Open Skies Treaty, which allows unarmed observation flights over one another's territory. Flight plans are filed in advance and can be amended by the host nation, which also has several personnel on the overflight. The host nation also receives copies of all photos taken. In February 2016, Russia asked permission to put high-powered digital cameras on its flights over the United States, suggesting problems or gaps in Russia's satellite system. The request, which raised concerns in U.S. intelligence and Congress, may also be a way to improve targeting of critical infrastructure in the United States. In September 2018, the United States certified the plane and camera that the Russians planned on using for upcoming open skies flights.

In October 2001, President Putin announced that Russia would close its major SIGINT facility at Lourdes, Cuba. Located within 100 miles of U.S. territory, the Lourdes complex reportedly could intercept telephone, microwave, and communications satellite traffic and was also reportedly used to manage Russian spy satellites. It was a major irritant in U.S.-Russian relations and an added difficult aspect of the U.S.-Cuban relationship. The closing appears to have been motivated primarily by economics. Russia paid Cuba $200 million annually for the use of the site—a sum that one Russian general said could be better used to buy "twenty communications and intelligence satellites and 100 modern radars." Two other factors that may have prompted the decision were the deterioration of the Russian spy satellite fleet, limiting the importance of Lourdes, and the steady shifting of U.S. communications from microwave to fiber-optic cable. Some Russian officials expressed the hope that the United States would reciprocate by closing some ground-based SIGINT facilities on the Russian periphery, particularly the one at Vardo, Norway. At the same time, Russia announced the closing of its base at Cam Ranh Bay, Vietnam, which had been a major U.S. base during the Vietnam War. Soviet and Russian forces used it as a base for reconnaissance aircraft and a SIGINT facility targeting China. In July 2014, the press reported that Russia had decided to reopen the Lourdes site, but this apparently did not happen. However, in 2016, Russia began work on an intelligence collection site in Nicaragua, although Russia claimed the site was for its GPS-type satellites.

The Soviet intelligence apparatus conducted assassinations, or what they termed "wet affairs." The most famous was the assassination of Josef Stalin's former rival, Leon Trotsky, in Mexico City in 1940. Some analysts believed that the Soviet Union was behind the attempted assassination of Pope John Paul II in 1981, but no conclusive proof has been uncovered. Alexander Litvinenko, a former KGB/FSB officer living in London was poisoned in 2006 via radioactive polonium. It 2016, a public inquiry named two Russians in the case and found that Litvinenko's murder was probably ordered by the head of the FSB and Putin. In August 2007, ten persons, including former intelligence and police officers, were arrested for the murder of Anna Politkovskaya, a journalist who had been very critical of corruption and brutality under Putin. Interestingly, the Russian prosecutor argued the murder was motivated by a desire not to silence Ms. Politkovskaya but to embarrass the Russian government by suggesting its involvement—a double-think motivation that harkens back to the cold war. No convictions resulted from these arrests. In 2011, a senior police officer was arrested and convicted for organizing the murder, but the motives behind Politkovskaya's murder have never been officially investigated.

As noted above, in March 2018, former GU officer Sergei Skripal and his daughter were poisoned via the nerve agent Novichok in Salisbury, Britain. They recovered, but a woman who handled the bottle in which the agent was transported died. Two Russians, who had come to Britain under aliases, were identified as the would-be assassins in a combination of closed-circuit television footage (there are between 4 and 5.9 million CCTV cameras in Britain), the work of online investigators at a site called Bellingcat, and police employees whose specialty is facial recognition. They were also identified as GU officers. Although Putin claimed the two men were innocent, he urged them to appear on Russian television, which they did, to almost universal derision. Prime Minister May all but made the same claim about Putin's involvement.

Skripal had spied for Britain and was among those traded in 2010 for the Russian sleeper agents ("illegals" in Russian espionage parlance) arrested in the United States. Once free, Skripal continued to work with various intelligence services (Czech, Estonia, Spain) on Russian intelligence techniques.

The Skripal affair has led to two widely different assessments of Russian intelligence capabilities. One view holds that this attempt was laughably amateurish and incompetent, given the ease with which the two suspects were identified, as well as their unsuccessful television appearance. The other view holds that the Russian intelligence services, and Putin in particular, have little regard for world reaction and that what may appear as "incompetence" was an attempt to display a callous disregard. Also, the attempt, whether successful or not, sent a message to other former Russian intelligence officers who had defected not to go public or risk assassination. According to the press, the U.S. government has increased concerns about the safety of former Russian intelligence officers now in the United States

The Russian services have lost important former liaison partners. The intelligence services of former Soviet satellites served, in effect, as subcontractors. The East German and Czechoslovakian services both had contacts with guerrilla and terrorist groups. The Polish service was used for industrial espionage in the West. The Bulgarian service was occasionally used for assassinations. Bulgaria also assassinated one of its own dissidents, Georgi Markov, in London in 1978, under Russian guidance. The East German state no longer exists; Poland, the Czech Republic, and Bulgaria are now part of NATO.

Despite the losses incurred in the aftermath of the fall of the Soviet Union, there is reason to believe, based on press accounts, that Russian intelligence has become increasingly active in the past several years. The number of governments warning about increased Russian intelligence activity—Britain, Germany, Sweden, the Czech Republic, Denmark, and Canada—is one indicator. Another is the number of individuals who have been arrested for conducting espionage on behalf of Russia, including nationals from Austria (in Germany), Spain, Poland, the Netherlands, and Estonia. The latter case, an Estonian in charge of all classified communications and documents in Estonia, now a NATO ally, was especially disturbing. As mentioned above, the United States also arrested ten Russian sleeper agents in 2010, in a case that had been under development for many years. The ten, and later two others, were accused of working for the SVR. Some observers characterized the Russian operation as inept, given the places where some of the agents were living—suburban New Jersey, New York, and Massachusetts—and their apparent lack of any recruiting to date. However, this was also a classic Russian operation, placing sleepers, some of whom had children with them in the United States, and then allowing them to lead "normal" lives for long periods of time, building up seemingly innocent contacts, and then being activated. The sleepers were exchanged for four Russians, three of whom had been sentenced for espionage and one of whom was under suspicion. Russia was embarrassed by the arrest, but Putin personally welcomed them home. In May 2011, the Russian government charged Aleksandr Poteyev, a former FSB officer, with treason and desertion. Observers believe this is related to the uncovering of the sleepers. Some Russian news sources report that Poteyev had overseen the sleeper operation.

Russian law has treated espionage committed by Russians or assistance to a foreign state that damages Russia's external security as treason. In later 2012, the Russian Parliament began considering a law drafted by the FSB that would drop the word "external" and would include giving help or advice to a foreign state or giving information to an international or foreign organization. Critics see this as a means of dealing with internal dissent.

The renewed Russian intelligence services are unlikely to allow their power to be threatened as it was during the days of the Soviet collapse. At the same time, their role in suppressing dissent is less formidable than it was during the Soviet era, although it still exists. Instead, they have a huge interest in the economic status quo but then also bear a responsibility if the economy falters, an area in which most of the intelligence services have little practical experience.

OTHER SERVICES

The services of several other countries are worth noting, although the literature available on them is more limited than for those discussed above.

Australia. Australia's intelligence community reflects its membership as one of the Five Eyes partners referred to previously. Australia is a relatively small nation in terms of population and is geographically remote, but Australia is seen by many as "playing above its weight" in intelligence. Australia's primary security concerns are in its immediate region, but it has long taken part in activities farther away, including UN peacekeeping operations, the two Gulf Wars, and Afghanistan. Australian intelligence expanded after the 2001 attacks on the United States. In October 2002, 202 people, including eighty-eight Australians, were killed by a suicide bomber in Bali; four Australians were killed in the 2005 Bali bombing.

Australia has the Westminster form of government and, like Britain, ensures that the prime minister has close-in intelligence support. In 2017, Australia conducted its third independent intelligence review (the previous ones were in 2004 and 2011). Largely positive, the review recommended changes to enhance integration and cooperation among agencies, including the creation of an Office of National Intelligence

(ONI) under a director-general as part of the prime minister's office. ONI stood up in July 2018, absorbing the Office of National Assessments (ONA) and some intelligence functions within the prime minister's office. The Director General of ONI (DGNI) is designated head of the National Intelligence Community and the prime minister's principal intelligence adviser. ONI has a staff of about 300 and has three main functions: "(1) intelligence enterprise management, aiming to bring a more integrated and strategic focus to the NIC and its activities; (2) the production of all-source intelligence assessments; and, (3) through the Open Source Centre, the provision of open source tradecraft, analysis and training for the NIC and whole of government." Thus, ONI is modeled somewhat on the U.S. DNI.

The Office of National Assessments had also worked directly for the prime minister and was responsible for producing assessments on "international political, strategic and economic developments" for the prime minister and other national security officials. ONA had no collection capabilities of its own, drawing on a range of government and nongovernment sources.

The Australian Secret Intelligence Organisation (ASIO) was created in 1949 at the behest of the United States and Britain, which were concerned about Soviet espionage penetrations. ASIO is responsible for defending Australia from a range of threats: protection of territorial and border integrity, espionage, sabotage, politically motivated violence, the promotion of communal violence, attacks on Australia's defense system, and acts of foreign interference. ASIO's duties are codified in the Intelligence Services Act of 2001. ASIO is allowed to intercept communications, under a warrant. It can detain or question individuals, also under a warrant, but it does not have the power to arrest individuals. ASIO can operate both within and beyond Australia. The director-general of ASIO reports to the attorney general, whose role is roughly analogous to that in the United States. ASIO contains the National Threat Assessment Centre (NTAC), which assesses the likelihood of terrorist or protest violence in Australia or against Australian interests overseas. In 2013, Director-General David Irvine signaled a shifting of emphasis for ASIO, to give more attention to counterespionage and "foreign interference capabilities" after a decade of emphasis on terrorism, which is still seen as a threat. Australian law enforcement and intelligence agencies had requested that Internet service providers be required to store all data for up to two years.

The Australian Secret Intelligence Service (ASIS) was created in 1952 by executive order. Its existence was not acknowledged until 1972. ASIS's duties are also spelled out now in the 2001 legislation. ASIS is responsible for the clandestine collection of intelligence, foreign liaison, and, in words reminiscent of the CIA's duties in the U.S. National Security Act, "to undertake such other activities as the responsible Minister directs relating to the capabilities, intentions or activities of people or organisations outside Australia." A 2004 amendment to the law also allows ASIS to take part in paramilitary activities planned or undertaken by other intelligence services. According to press accounts, squadrons of Australia's Special Air Service (SAS, a special operations force), conducted intelligence-gathering missions in Africa but without ASIS officers accompanying them, which is the usual process. ASIS is part of the Department of Foreign Affairs and Trade. The director-general of ASIS is appointed by the prime minister in consultation with the leader of the opposition.

The Defence Intelligence Organisation (DIO) focuses on defense-related intelligence issues, including terrorism, defense economics, military capabilities, and science and technology with military applications. It also provides intelligence assessments in support of deployed Australian forces.

The Australian Geospatial-Intelligence Organisation's (AGO; prior to 2013, the Defence Imagery and Geospatial Organisation, DIGO) responsibilities are self-evident from its name. It was created in 2000, amalgamating the functions of three predecessor offices. According to press reports, AGO has access to U.S. and commercial imagery, and Australia has begun building an independent capability. Finally, the Australian Signals Directorate (ASD; prior to 2013, the Defence Signals Directorate, DSD) was created in 1949, a direct outgrowth of Allied SIGINT Cooperation in the Pacific in World War II. Like NSA, ASD has both a SIGINT and an information security role. ASD contains the Australian Cyber Security Centre (ACSC), co-locating all of Australia's cyber activities. Both AGO and ASD are part of the Intelligence Services Act. In 2018, ASD was made a statutory agency as a means of enhancing its capabilities. Like all others nations, Australia has become increasingly concerned about cyberattacks, particularly from China and Russia. Also in 2018, Australia passed legislation that would require, under certain circumstances, that computer and telecommunications firms cooperate with and provide technical assistance to the government. This reflects the view of the Five Eyes that they need means to get access to encrypted systems and communications on occasion. In 2008, the U.S. National Reconnaissance Office (NRO) acknowledged its presence at the Joint Defence Facility at Pine Gap, Australia.

As of 2017, the Australian intelligence agencies employed 7,000 and had a combined budget of AU$2 billion ($1.44 billion).

In 2008, Australia revamped its national security structure, creating the following offices:

- National Security Committee (NSC) of the Cabinet: Like other NSCs, it has a core membership of the key political and national security officials, with others attending as necessary. The directors-general of ONA, ASIO, and ASIS attend. The NSC creates the National Security Policy Framework and the National Intelligence Priorities (NIPs).

- Secretaries Committee on National Security (SCNS): This committee supports the NSC and is chaired by the secretary (the senior civil servant) of the prime minister's office and attended by the secretaries of other key departments, senior officers for domestic law enforcement (police, border protection, and crimes commission), and the directors-general of ONA, ASIO, and ASIS.

- National Intelligence Coordination Committee (NICC): This committee ensures that "foreign, security and law enforcement intelligence activities are closely aligned and consistent with national security priorities." In addition to the agencies noted above, DIO, ASD, and AGO also are members. ONI coordinates an annual all-hazards National Assessment that is used to help develop the NIPs.

- The NICC is also viewed as the National Intelligence Community. The NICC oversees two subcommittees:
  - National Intelligence Collection Management Committee (NICMC), which is chaired by ONA and sets requirements for collection and evaluates collection against the National Intelligence Priorities.
  - National Intelligence Open Source Committee, which is chaired by ONA and is responsible for enhancing open-source capabilities and efforts.

The Heads of Intelligence Agencies Meeting (HIAM) consists of the foreign intelligence components and is also chaired by ONA. The HIAM is considered the Australian Intelligence Community (AIC), as opposed to the National Intelligence Community as represented in the NICC. Unlike in the United States, the structure for parliamentary oversight of intelligence is laid out in law in Australia, again in the 2001 act. There is a Joint Committee on Intelligence and Security ("joint" meaning members of the Senate and the House of Representatives) with administrative and budget oversight over all of the agencies noted above. However, the law specifically exempts the following areas from the committee's purview: intelligence gathering, assessment priorities, operations, source and methods or intelligence acquired through foreign liaison, and ONA's evaluation and coordination activities. The law does require that the director-general of ASIS "consult regularly" with the leader of the opposition to keep the leader informed about "matters relating to ASIS." There is also an inspector general of intelligence and security, who is appointed by the governor general (the head of state), who reviews intelligence activities for legality and propriety.

Within the Prime Minister's Department is the Australia–New Zealand Counter-Terrorism Committee (ANZCTC), comprising federal and state officials from Australia and New Zealand, which had been an observer until 2012. The NCTC was created in 2002 to coordinate intelligence and counterterrorist capabilities and is responsible for effective intelligence sharing between all agencies and jurisdictions. The ANZCTC writes the National Counter-Terrorist Plan (NCTP).

Australian intelligence analysts, like their counterparts in the United States and Britain, concluded in 2002 that Iraq had WMD. The absence of WMD also led to an inquiry in Australia, headed by Philip Flood, a former director of ONA. Flood looked at both the specific issue of the Iraq analysis, as well as two other case studies, and the overall functioning of Australian intelligence. On the issue of Iraq WMD, Flood noted the inherent difficulty of intelligence collection in Saddam Hussein's Iraq, the general difficulty of leadership intentions, and the fact that Australian intelligence was almost completely dependent on others for intelligence collection and some assessments. Flood noted that it would have been very difficult to sustain a judgment that Iraq did not have WMD but also noted little rigorous challenging of assumptions or of intelligence reports, failure to mask clearer the confidence behind analytic judgments, and viewing the Iraq WMD issue in isolation. But Flood did not find any evidence of politicization of intelligence.

In April 2015, Australia announced an intelligence-sharing agreement with Iran to track Islamic State foreign fighters in Iraq. It was estimated that 100 Australians had gone to Syria and Iraq to fight.

In 2018, Australia enacted legislation banning foreign interference in elections, broadening the definition of espionage and making theft of trade secrets on behalf of a foreign government a crime. China was seen as the specific target of much of this legislation, and the Chinese government reacted negatively. China is seen as conducting "extensive" espionage against Australia. Two Chinese firms, Huawei and ZTE, have been banned from providing 5G equipment to the Australian government.

Canada. Canada's intelligence has been shaped by its history as a British dominion and by its proximity to and close relationship with the United States. However, its intelligence community is not as closely parallel to that of the United States as is Australia's. Canada is another member of the Five Eyes. Canada's security concerns include classic espionage; terrorism, including unwittingly serving as a base for an attack on the United States; and economic espionage against high-technology and corporate targets. Canada is attractive to these attacks both on its own merits and because of the close intertwining between the U.S. and Canadian economies, making Canada a potential "back door" to U.S. economic secrets. Canada has considered but rejected the idea of creating a foreign intelligence agency akin to the CIA or ASIS as being alien to how Canada sees itself and out of concern that all Canadians abroad would be seen as possible spies, putting them at greater risk. In the most recent review of this issue, by the Security Intelligence Review Committee in February 2011, chairman Arthur T. Porter noted the expense involved and also said, "You have to recognize that [by spying] you are probably breaking [some other country's] law by just the definition of what you are doing." (In 2013, Porter and his wife were arrested in Panama for extradition to Canada to face charges of accepting bribes and corruption.)

Canada also has the Westminster form of government, again giving the prime minister the chief responsibility for national security. The prime minister is supported by the Privy Council Office (PCO), which is made up of secretariats. Two of these have intelligence functions. The International Assessment Staff provides assessments on foreign developments. It is headed by an executive director who reports to the prime minister's national security advisor through the foreign and defence policy advisor. This secretariat also staffs the Intelligence Assessment Coordinating Committee. The Security and Intelligence Secretariat has both advisory and coordination roles on national security and intelligence issues. Its reporting chain is the same as the other secretariat. The PCO is seen as a nonpartisan organization. The PCO is headed by a clerk who chairs the Interdepartmental Committee on Security and Intelligence (ICSI), a deputy minister–level group that looks at strategic policy and resourcing issues, investigates sensitive national security matters, and recommends the annual intelligence priorities for the Meeting of Ministers on Security and Intelligence. There is a deputy clerk, who is the counsel and security and intelligence coordinator and who coordinates all security and intelligence activities. The deputy clerk is also accountable to the minister of national defence for the policy and operations of the Communications Security Establishment (CSE, see below). The PCO associate secretary responsible for security and intelligence also serves as national security advisor to the prime minister, providing advice and overseeing security and intelligence issues.

The Canadian Security Intelligence Service (CSIS) was created by statute in 1984 from the security intelligence service that traditionally had been part of the Royal Canadian Mounted Police (RCMP). Its role is similar to that of Australia's ASIO, the protection of the nation from threats. In the case of CSIS, the priorities are terrorism, WMD proliferation, espionage and foreign interference, information security threats, and providing security clearances for all government employees except the RCMP. CSIS collects intelligence from domestic and foreign sources; it can task foreign collection. It provides intelligence assessments on current threats and tactical assessments on specific cases. CSIS also conducts foreign liaison and, since 2008, has had an Academic Outreach Program to enhance understanding of current and emerging issues. CSIS has no law enforcement powers; those remain with the RCMP. CSIS operations are overseen by the Security Intelligence Review Committee (SIRC), which reports to Parliament annually. SIRC members are appointed by the governor-general, the head of state, in consultation with the prime minister and the leader of the opposition. The Canadian Parliament established the SIRC in 1984 to review the operations of the CSIS. The SIRC issues an annual report.

CSIS is divided into the following branches:

- Counter-Intelligence, which is further divided into Economic Security, Security Information Operations, Trans-national Crime, and Foreign Influenced Activity.

- Counter-Proliferation, which was created in 2002 and also watches for attempts to procure Canadian technology for WMD use.

- Counterterrorism.

- Research, Analysis, and Production, made up of Counterintelligence, Foreign Intelligence, Counterterrorism, and Distribution. This branch supports the PCO Intelligence Assessments Secretariat.

In 2012, the head of CSIS, Richard Fadden, gave a speech in which he said CSIS's mandate was no longer just about informants and communications intercepts but was more analytic in nature, including the importance of understanding social media. Also in 2012, the Court of Appeal struck down the blanket legal protection (formally, "class privilege") that CSIS had been able to provide to informants. The case arose from the legal proceedings to deport Mohamed Harkat, an Algerian-born permanent resident suspected of being a member of al Qaeda. Harkat's lawyers wanted to cross-examine CSIS informants, which under Canadian law could be conducted by security-cleared special advocates. CSIS's effort to deny this was overturned. In 2016, SIRC raised concerns about CSIS using paid al Qaeda or Taliban informants, saying this conflicted with UN rules prohibiting association with or funding of these two groups.

Canada has had two lone-wolf attacks to date and, like other nations, is concerned about returning foreign fighters and possible terrorist cells being created in Canada. In June 2015, in reaction to the lone-wolf attacks, Canada passed a new Anti-Terrorism Act, which authorizes CSIS to take measures (canceling travel, closing bank accounts, gaining access to buildings to plant surveillance devices) to reduce threats to Canadian security; improves information sharing; and makes promoting or advocating terrorism a crime. Detention is allowed for up to seven days; previously the limit was three days.

In 2018, a Canadian federal judge ruled that CSIS has no legal authority to spy outside of Canada because the law permitting foreign intelligence collection means activities within Canada against foreigners who may be a threat but not overseas collection.

The CSE (Communications Security Establishment) was established in 1946. As noted earlier, it is part of the Ministry of National Defence. Like many of its Five Eyes partners, among which there is a burden-sharing arrangement, CSE is responsible for providing SIGINT and for the security of information technology. CSE can collect domestically under certain circumstances, but the intercept has to be targeted against foreign entities operating outside of Canada. Since 1996, there has been a CSE commissioner who ensures compliance with the law. In January 2016, CSE suspended sharing metadata with its Five Eyes partners because metadata about Canadians had been unintentionally collected in foreign communications. The suspension would remain in effect until the software problems were resolved. In 2018, the Centre for Cyber Security was created within CSE. Like many of its counterparts around the world, the center seeks to work with the government, the private sector and the public to enhance cybersecurity. Its responsibilities include "incident management, situational awareness, and technical advice and guidance." The center is expected to reach full operational capability in 2020.

Canada's armed forces have intelligence capabilities of their own, but these have come under severe budget pressure as the Afghan war ends and, with that, pressure to reduce military spending. Canadian troops encountered intelligence shortfalls when they began deploying to Afghanistan in 2005, and Canadian forces now want to preserve the capabilities they built up in eight years of war.

There has been an increase in espionage cases in Canada. One of the most damaging ones involved Sub-Lieutenant Jeffrey Delisle, who sold to the Russians ship-tracking SIGINT data shared within the Five Eyes. Delisle received a twenty-year sentence. According to press reports, the United States requested that more rigorous intelligence-sharing protocols be put in place as a result of the Delisle case. At least six Russian diplomats returned home, several of whom were likely connected to the Delisle case. Canada has also been concerned about Russia's use of Canadian passports for Russian spies, including four of the sleepers expelled in 2010.

CSIS has also raised concerns about firms in strategic sectors of the economy being controlled by "hostile" governments. State-owned Chinese companies have been buying firms in Canada.

In 2017, Prime Minister Justin Trudeau created a National Security and Intelligence Committee of Parliamentarians to oversee Canadian intelligence.

Germany. German intelligence operates under a series of limitations, as does the German military, reflecting efforts to shun the history of the Nazi period and to avoid repeating the conditions and actions that brought the Nazis to power. There is also the history of the pervasive East German intelligence service, the Stasi, whose employees and full-time collaborators made up 2 percent of the East German population. Also, as Wolfgang Krieger has pointed out, there is no word in German for "intelligence" meaning secret information and operations.

The problem of nomenclature is evident in the *Bundesnachrichtendienst* (BND), which is typically translated as the Federal Intelligence Service but literally means the Federal News or Federal Information Service. The BND is responsible for the collection and analysis of foreign intelligence. As the only foreign intelligence agency in Germany, the BND has broad responsibilities: imagery analysis, OSINT collection, HUMINT collection, foreign liaison, SIGINT collection, and intelligence analysis. The BND is part of the chancellor's office and is overseen by the minister for special affairs. The BND was formally created in 1956 from the so-called Gehlen Organization, named for Gen. Reinhard Gehlen, who was in charge of the Foreign Armies East intelligence office (primarily the Soviet Union) on the wartime general staff. With the advent of the cold war, the United States found Gehlen's knowledge about the Soviet military extremely valuable. So the first controversy surrounding the BND's predecessor was its roots in wartime German intelligence and its use of former Nazis on its staff. The organization also suffered penetrations by the East Germans.

The BND and Bundeswehr (armed forces) intelligence apparently fought over control of military intelligence as Germany began to take part in NATO missions, beginning in 1999. The BND appears to have emerged the victor, with Bundeswehr intelligence limited to a Strategic Reconnaissance Command, which controls Germany's five radar imaging satellites. The Bundeswehr also gets some imagery reports from French and Italian satellites. The BND website lists "informational support of the armed forces in their operations abroad" as one of its tasks. However, in 2017, the BND had received funding for its own high-resolution satellite. This would be the first satellite controlled by a German intelligence agency.

The German press reported in 2013 that the BND planned to expand its surveillance of the Internet in order to go from monitoring 5 percent of all Internet and telephone communications to 20 percent, the maximum that the BND is allowed by law. Unlike NSA, the BND does not store the communications it monitors but filters them down to provide terrorist leads. In a rather odd development, in December 2015, the German government disavowed a BND assessment on Saudi Arabia that had been leaked to the press. The memo had said that Saudi Arabia was playing an increasingly destabilizing role in the Middle East. A German government spokesman said that the BND did not speak for the German foreign policy—not that BND had asserted such a role. The spokesman also said that the role of the BND was to supply information "and to deliver hopefully clever analysis."

In 2016, the Bundestag (Parliament) passed legislation giving the BND explicit authority for certain intelligence activities under certain conditions or threat, including espionage operations against certain EU institutions, and cooperation with foreign intelligence services for specific purposes. The law specifies different classes of targets, and authorization requirements and restrictions, and allows a range of intrusive activities. The law also strengthens government oversight. The German news magazine *Der Spiegel* reported that German intelligence had spied on foreign journalists. In 2018, press groups lodged a legal complaint stating that the law allowed "virtually unrestricted" monitoring of foreign journalists, which meant they could no longer protect their sources.

The *Bundesamt für Verfassungsschutz* (BfV), Federal Office for the Protection of the Constitution, is the domestic intelligence agency. Created in 1950, BfV is responsible for the collection and analysis of intelligence related to acts that may threaten German security, its democratic system, its foreign interests, and, more vaguely, Germany's commitment to international understanding, which is enshrined in the constitution. This latter task refers primarily to extremist groups. The BfV is also responsible for counterintelligence and countersabotage. BfV collection includes overt sources, attending extremist meetings and rallies, agents recruited from extremist groups, covert surveillance, and mail and telephone interception. BfV also cooperates with similar offices in each of the German states. BfV's main offices are as follows:

- German right-wing and left-wing extremism and terrorism

- Counterespionage, protective security, and countersabotage

- Threats to security and foreign extremists (less Islamists)

- Islamist extremism and terrorism

The BfV is part of the Ministry of the Interior. There are two offices that perform executive oversight, as does a control commission selected by the Bundestag. Penetration of the (West) German government by East Germany was a major concern throughout the cold war. The highest level penetration was that of Gunter Guillaume, who ended up on the staff of Chancellor Willy Brandt. Guillaume's arrest led to Brandt's resignation, which was not in East Germany's interest. More recently, Germany—like many other European countries—has seen an increase in Russian espionage activities.

During the late 1970s and 1980s, (West) Germany suffered through a series of kidnappings, bombings, murders, and airplane hijackings carried out by the Red Army Faction, also known as the Baader-Meinhof Gang. It also experienced two cases of international terrorism, in the 1972 Munich Olympics, when Arab terrorists took Israeli athletes hostage, several of whom were killed, and in 1986, when Libyan agents—with the possible connivance of East Germany—blew up a West Berlin disco frequented by U.S. personnel. Germany's main security concerns now relate to terrorism and Muslim extremism. Muslims make up about 5 percent of the German population, and the government is concerned about the degree to which they are integrated into German society and accept German values. Several of the 9/11 hijackers lived in Germany and apparently used a mosque in Hamburg, now closed, as a recruitment base. This concern will likely grow as Germany takes in tens of thousands of refugees from the Middle East, some of whom—as in the November 2015 Paris attacks—may be terrorists. The BND and the BfV have asked refugees to help identify potential terrorists and security risks.

In 2012, the head of the BfV resigned after it was revealed that the agency had failed to uncover a neo-Nazi group that was believed to be responsible for the deaths of nine immigrants over a decade. A 2013 investigation by the Bundestag said that the police and security services had prejudices and lacked cultural diversity, which led them to assume that the murders were internal immigrant group affairs rather than investigating the possibility of racism as a motive. The BfV also admitted to having shredded files on the neo-Nazi group.

The rise of the anti-immigrant group PEGIDA (the acronym translates as Patriotic Europeans against the Islamization of the West) and the right-wing political party AfD (Alternative for Germany) have created problems for the BfV as to whether these are extremist groups that should be monitored. PEGIDA has been associated with some violent demonstrations; the AfD, which has had some electoral success at the state level and won many seats in the 2017 elections, has attracted interest from more radical right-wing groups, including neo-Nazis. In September 2018, some Bundestag members said that Hans-Georg Maassen, the head of the BfV, had downplayed the right-wing problem; some called for his dismissal. This created tension within Chancellor Merkel's coalition. Eventually, Maassen was moved from the BfV to another post in the Interior Ministry, reportedly at higher pay; he was then given an advisory post without a pay raise. Maassen was forced to retire in November 2018, when his departure speech from BfV leaked, in which he blamed "radical-left forces" in the governing coalition for his downfall. It was later revealed that Maassen had met with AfD leaders and reportedly advised them on how to evade surveillance.

In January 2019, the BfV said it was placing the youth wing and some leaders of the AfD under surveillance as a threat to democracy. This was the first time in post-war German history that a party represented in the Bundestag had been placed under surveillance. The BfV could decide to place the AfD under a broader and more systematic surveillance.

Finally, the German government has had to deal with revelations about NSA surveillance programs, which have included surveillance with Europe, which became an issue in the ongoing federal elections in Germany. Unlike French President Hollande, Chancellor Merkel defended Germany's cooperation with NSA as being legal and refuted charges that this activity was reminiscent of East Germany's secret police, the Stasi. Merkel's chief of staff said that Germany and the United States would hold talks on an agreement not to spy on one another; U.S. officials refused to comment. President Obama said that the United States would no longer monitor the communications of heads of state or heads of government of nations with close ties to the United States. Although French comments on the NSA program ceased, political and popular outrage in Germany continued. It also appears that Merkel took the alleged U.S. surveillance much more personally than did other world leaders, with the possible exception of President Dilma Rousseff of Brazil. In 2014, Germany's top prosecutor opened a case concerning the tapping of Merkel's cell phone. This case was dropped in June 2015 for lack of evidence. Germany expelled the senior U.S. intelligence officer. In bilateral talks, the United States rejected a German demand to ban all espionage activities on German soil. The United States refused, saying it would set a precedent with all other U.S. allies. In August 2014, the German Foreign Ministry asked all foreign diplomatic missions to submit the names of all active secret service agents working in Germany.

Official German comments became less strident for two reasons. First, the demands of other events—Ukraine and terrorism, in particular—took precedence.

Second, and more to the point, were revelations about German intelligence activities. According to press reports, the BfV traded intelligence on German citizens in exchange for access to NSA programs. Other reports alleged that the BND gathered information on European firms at the behest of the United States. Merkel defended German intelligence cooperation with the United States, citing the terrorist threat. At the same time, Germany decided to limit ongoing intelligence cooperation with the United States and had dropped some joint projects. There were also press reports about German spying on Turkey, which appeared to violate Germany's belief in "no spying on friends," as Turkey is a NATO ally. In November 2015, press reports alleged that BND spied on several European states, the United States, the Vatican, and several nongovernmental organizations. Austria and Belgium had announced investigations into German spying on their territory. In April 2016, Gerhard Schindler, the head of the BND, was fired. The Merkel government said this was because of an impending reorganization of the BND, but many observers felt it was related to revelations about BND's cooperation with NSA.

Germany shares some intelligence with its EU partners, but German intelligence leaders have rejected the idea of an EU intelligence service, saying it would be duplicative and bureaucratic. They recognize that intelligence is, essentially, a national activity.

The arrest of a BND employee on charges of spying for the CIA served as another irritant. The spy sold to the United States lists of current and former German agents, including their aliases. There were also reports that he might have been working for the Russians as well. He confessed to spying for the CIA in court in November 2015. He received an eight-year sentence.

In August 2015, the top prosecutor opened a case against two bloggers who, it was alleged, had published details about German domestic intelligence plans to expand their online surveillance and to form a group to monitor social media. The bloggers were charged with treason for actions that harmed Germany or benefited another power. The Merkel government immediately distanced itself from the case and the minister of justice, citing support from Merkel, called for the prosecutor to be fired. A few days later the case was dropped.

Espionage has been an ongoing issue for Germany. There are press accounts of spying by Turkey, Iran and Jordan, and an Islamic State penetration of a German intelligence agency. Germany has also accused China of trying to penetrate the government via social media. Germany reportedly spied on Swiss firms in Austria, which led Austria to protest that and other reported German espionage activities. It has also been reported that Swiss intelligence conducted espionage in Germany against German tax collectors seeking financial data from Switzerland. In 2017, the two nations signed an agreement to preclude future collection operations.

In 2017, the Interior Ministry opened the Central Office for Information Technology in the Security Sphere (the German acronym is ZITiS). This office will address cybersecurity and digital espionage. ZITiS is neither an intelligence nor a police agency, but it does have cyber surveillance authority, which has been criticized by civil libertarians. As an independent agency within the ministry, ZITiS is exempt from some German laws. Germany has experienced hacking of government agencies that is presumed to be Russian in origin.

India. For decades, India's security concerns revolved around two states, Pakistan and China. India has fought three major wars and one limited conflict with Pakistan. China invaded India in 1962, less a war than a month-long punitive expedition. These two relationships still matter, but India, like China, now has significant interests much farther afield.

From independence in 1947, the Intelligence Bureau (IB) handled both internal and external intelligence. The IB's poor performance in the period prior to the Chinese invasion, whose buildup went unnoticed, led to a reorganization. In 1968, the IB was relegated to internal intelligence, and the Research and Analysis Wing (RAW) was created for external intelligence, with the China and Pakistan issues predominating. The IB reports to the Home Secretary and has units throughout India. It is heavily dominated by the Indian Police Service (IPS), and one senior IB official said it has a "police culture." Although the IB is the internal service, it is allowed to conduct "transborder operations" to collect tactical intelligence. For India, this means primarily Pakistan, not as a military threat but as a hostile base for and instigator of terrorist attacks in India, the most important of which was probably the attacks in Mumbai in 2008 in which Pakistani-based terrorists killed 164 people. Attacks in the disputed state of Kashmir are also a concern, as is the overall volatility of the multiethnic, multireligious Indian population. Communal violence is a recurring problem. The IB is also responsible for India's communications security and has an independent communications intelligence (COMINT) capability.

RAW is part of the Cabinet Secretariat and reports to the prime minister. RAW is responsible for the collection, analysis, and assessment of foreign intelligence; special operations abroad, including psychological warfare; foreign intelligence liaison (IB can conduct foreign liaison on counterterrorism); and counterintelligence outside of India. RAW appears to be completely free from parliamentary oversight. RAW posts its officers in Indian embassies. RAW's Aviation Research Centre controls aircraft involved in imagery collection; its Telecom Division has a COMINT role. In a somewhat confused structure, there is also—besides IB and RAW—the National Technical Research Organization (NTRO), which also has a role in controlling technical intelligence collection resources, including cryptanalysis, satellite monitoring, and remote sensing. NTRO also has a technical monitoring role and appears to have made attempts to monitor some Internet service providers, a function that will now be part of the Centralised Monitoring System. (See below.) In 2012, the Indian press reported that NTRO monitoring equipment seemed to be heavily focused in the capital area as opposed to the international border where NTRO was supposed to be intercepting communications. IB and RAW have also sought to limit NTRO's activities. The Joint Cipher Bureau is responsible for cryptography and signals interception and supports RAW and IB.

RAW has had its share of intelligence failures. For a while, India, in part through RAW, supported the Liberation Tigers of Tamil Eelam (LTTE) in Sri Lanka's civil war, which backfired, leading to an unsuccessful Indian military intervention and the assassination of former prime minister Rajiv Gandhi by the LTTE in 1991. In 1999, RAW failed to detect the movement of Pakistani troops into the Kargil region of Kashmir, which resulted in a brief military conflict. A review of intelligence performance by the Kargil Review Committee led to the creation of a Defence Intelligence

Agency (DIA) in 2002. DIA was given responsibility for military-related intelligence as well as control of the Signals Intelligence Directorate and the Defence Image Processing and Analysis Centre, which control India's imagery satellites. DIA can also conduct "transborder operations."

In the aftermath of the Mumbai attack, India created the National Intelligence Grid (NATGRID) that connects the databases of various ministries and agencies. The data include financial data, immigration, travel, credit cards, and so on. NATGRID collates these data and makes them available to eleven agencies that work in intelligence, crime, and finance. As could be expected, there are civil liberties concerns. Some critics also note that the data do not get passed to state police forces, which raises questions about how this will help prevent future terror attacks.

India has a growing cyberspace capability, which, like that of many other nations, appears to have been used against potential foes, such as China and Pakistan, and more friendly states, like the United States. India deployed a Centralised (or Central) Monitoring System (CMS) that is designed to track all communications within India—telephone, computer, landline, mobile, and so on. Unlike the NSA program, CMS does not have to ask providers' permission for access but has that built into the technology of the telecom and data service providers. CMS provides intelligence to foreign and domestic intelligence agencies, the police, and tax collectors—a list that some observers believe is too broad. Like the NSA program, CMS appears to focus on metadata. CMS is run by a government technology development center that is not part of the intelligence complex. The Ministry for Home Affairs has the power to determine who is monitored.

India's intelligence relationship with the United States remains a work in progress. The two nations have some shared interests: China, Pakistan, and Muslim extremist terrorism. There have been meetings, for example, between U.S. and Indian counterterrorist officials, but the Indian government has also sought to limit intelligence contacts between the two nations, fearing espionage recruitments or "defections." The Indian press has reported CIA penetrations of RAW.

In 2017, India opened the National Cybersecurity Coordination Centre (NCCC), which will screen communications metadata to identify threats and raise general awareness and to coordinate with intelligence agencies.

New Zealand. New Zealand is the final member of the Five Eyes relationship, although its history within that group has been troubled. In the mid-1980s, Prime Minister David Lange, who was opposed to nuclear weapons, instituted a policy requiring all ships visiting New Zealand to declare whether they carried any such weapons and to ban those that did. This conflicted with long-standing U.S. naval policy never to discuss whether or not nuclear weapons are present. As a result, the United States, with strong Australian backing, suspended New Zealand as a member of the Australia–New Zealand–United States (ANZUS) alliance, formed in 1951. Also, the United States essentially suspended intelligence cooperation with New Zealand. In the years following the 2001 terrorist attacks, intelligence ties resumed.

Another Westminster system government, New Zealand has a prime minister supported by the Department of the Prime Minister and Cabinet (DPMC), under which is the Security and Intelligence Group (S&I Group), which was created in 2014 and oversees national security policy and coordination, including intelligence coordination. The S&I Group has five directorates:

- National Security Policy: policy coordination and the lead for intelligence priorities.

- National Cyber Policy Office: cybersecurity policy.

- National Security Communications: internal and external communications and "reputation issues" for DPMC and the intelligence agencies.

- National Security Systems: supports the national security leadership in times of crisis; coordinates risk assessments, exercises and system testing, and contingency plans; coordinates joint planning and performance monitoring for the New Zealand Intelligence Community; operates joint arrangements for the governance, coordination, and support of New Zealand's national security and intelligence system.

- Intelligence & Assessment: production and quality assurance of intelligence assessments; operates a customer requirements process; leads the national intelligence and assessments community; chairs the National Assessments Committee; contains the National Assessments Bureau (NAB), which is New Zealand's central agency for assessments that draw on all forms of information available to the government. It provides analysis and reporting on issues of national security and foreign policy interest. NAB draws on classified and nonclassified government information and also private-sector information. As with many other intelligence analysis offices, NAB does not provide policy recommendations.

The Officials Committee for Domestic and External Security Coordination (ODESC), which is made up of cabinet ministers and the heads of the military, exercises policy oversight of the New Zealand intelligence community regarding foreign intelligence issues. The ODESC is supported by an intelligence coordinator. Below the ODESC is the Foreign Intelligence Requirements Committee (FIRC), which, as its name suggests, prepares and disseminates detailed foreign intelligence requirements.

The Security Intelligence Service was created (as the Security Service) in 1956, becoming SIS under legislation in 1969. Its role is to protect New Zealand from threats of espionage, sabotage, and subversion. SIS also collects foreign intelligence and provides "security advice and services" to the government. SIS includes the Combined Threat Assessment Group (CTAG), which advises the government on risk management. SIS has 200 employees.

The Government Communications Security Bureau (GCSB) was established in 1977, although there were many predecessor groups going back for many decades. It was originally part of the Ministry of Defence but became a separate organization in 1998 and received a legislative charter in 2003. GCSB is responsible for SIGINT and for information assurance. Since 2011, the GCSB has within it the National Cyber

Security Centre, initially responsible for government cybersecurity. There is also, within the DPMC, a National Cyber Policy Office. In November 2018, GCSB recommended and the government agreed to ban participation of the Chinese telecom firm Huawei in the rollout of the 5G infrastructure, just as Australia had done a few months earlier.

In the aftermath of the Snowden NSA leaks, Prime Minister John Key declined to give specifics on the relationship with NSA but stated that foreign intelligence agencies are not used to circumvent the law and spy illegally on citizens. Two months later, in August 2013, Parliament passed a bill expanding the role of the GCSB after a series of revelations that the bureau had spied illegally on New Zealanders. Under the new law, GCSB continues in its foreign intelligence function, in which it cannot collect intelligence on New Zealanders. The law also gives sanction to GCSB support to SIS, the police, and Defence in conducting warranted interceptions of New Zealanders. Finally, GCSB's cyber protection function is expanded from government systems to private ones as well if deemed important to New Zealand. This function can include surveillance on New Zealanders. Parliamentary oversight is provided by the Intelligence and Security Committee, created by legislation in 1996. This committee oversees the SIS and the GCSB. The prime minister and the leader of the opposition are both members of the committee; the prime minister chooses two more members and the leader of the opposition chooses one more. Parliament must approve all of the selections. There is also an inspector general of intelligence and security who oversees SIS and GCSB and a commissioner of security warrants, who issues interception warrants, jointly with the prime minister, for New Zealand citizens or residents. As noted, New Zealand is a member of the Australia–New Zealand Counter-Terrorism Committee (ANZCTC).

As noted, New Zealand was the site of the attack on the *Rainbow Warrior* by France's DGSE in 1985, in Auckland harbor. France made a payment to New Zealand and apologized; two French agents who had been arrested were both released early. New Zealand's issue with Israel's use of false New Zealand passports in 2004 also has been noted.

Pakistan. An eighteenth-century Prussian minister observed, "Prussia is not a country with an army; it is an army with a country." In many respects, it can also be said that Pakistan is not a country with an intelligence service; it is an intelligence service with a country.

Pakistan's Inter-Services Intelligence Directorate (ISID, usually called ISI) is mainly preoccupied with India and, secondarily, with the war in Afghanistan, which overlaps the Pakistan-Afghan border area. Pakistan has a tenuous strategic position vis-à-vis India. Islamabad is about 60 miles (100 kilometers) from the border, and the Pakistan "neck" is about 200 miles (320 kilometers) wide. Afghanistan is seen as giving Pakistan strategic depth. Pakistan also needs to keep Afghanistan from Indian or western control, in effect trapping Pakistan between Afghanistan and India. As ISI's name implies, it is a military intelligence organization, and some observers question whether it is ever under the control of any civilian Pakistani government. ISI is responsible for collection, including technical and human intelligence; analysis; counterintelligence; and intelligence operations.

ISI has seven main divisions:

- Joint Intelligence X (JIX): coordinates all other ISI departments; produces reports and assessments; and has administrative functions

- Joint Intelligence Bureau (JIB): collects intelligence inside Pakistan and has a division for operations in India

- Joint Counterintelligence Bureau (JCB): conducts surveillance of Pakistani diplomats abroad and is responsible for intelligence operations in the Middle East, South and Central Asia, including Afghanistan, China, and Russia

- Joint Intelligence North (JIN): collects intelligence in Kashmir and Jammu

- Joint Intelligence Miscellaneous (JIM): covert operations and espionage

- Joint Signal Intelligence Bureau (JSIB): SIGINT collection and communications support along the border with India and Kashmir

- Joint Intelligence Technical (JIT): technology research and development

Pakistan was a major conduit for arms to the mujahideen in Afghanistan in their war against the Soviet Union (1979–1989); ISI subsequently supported the Taliban when it took over Afghanistan in 1996. These ties and Pakistan's own strategic outlook have led some observers to question the depth of ISI's support for the U.S. effort to defeat the Taliban and to capture al Qaeda leaders who have sought refuge in Pakistan. As noted earlier, the killing of Osama bin Laden not far from the Pakistani capital and especially close to the Pakistani military academy raised questions in the United States about the depth of Pakistan's antiterrorist support and the possibility that some individuals in the Pakistani government were complicit with bin Laden. Again, the Pakistani Abbottabad Commission investigating both bin Laden's presence and the failure to detect the U.S. raid found there to be incompetence, negligence, and failure. The report stated it could not rule out direct or indirect support for bin Laden during the years he lived in Pakistan. Similarly, when Mullah Omar, the head of the Taliban, died in Karachi in 2013 (his death was not officially revealed until 2015), it was assumed that some Pakistani officials had to have known of his presence.

U.S. UAV strikes in Pakistan's tribal regions have also been a sore point, raising issues of sovereignty and of intelligence liaison. Pakistan has requested, unsuccessfully, more information about and access to UAV operations. There is also the question of ISI's support for terrorist operations in India. Both nations have practiced "transborder" operations, primarily in Kashmir. India has accused Pakistan's services of complicity in the 2008 Mumbai attack. U.S. officials also suspect that ISI revealed the name of the CIA chief of station in Pakistan in 2010, forcing him to return to the United States. In short, the prolonged antiterrorist campaign and Pakistan's own tenuous strategic position continue to strain its relationship with the United States.

ISI is not the only Pakistani intelligence agency, but it is the predominant one. Some press accounts estimate that there may be as many as thirty military and civilian intelligence agencies, including those in law enforcement. In March 2014, Prime Minister Nawaz Sharif established a National Intelligence Directorate (NID) to improve intelligence sharing. ISI, military intelligence, and federal and provincial law enforcement agencies are supposed to be part of the NID. The NID comes under the National Counter-Terrorism Authority (NACTA). There is no reason to suppose that the NID will in any way impinge on the authority or independence of ISI.

Pakistan has a certain dependence on China. The two reportedly exchange intelligence, essentially Pakistani HUMINT for Chinese TECHINT. China has also launched satellites for Pakistan, including a Chinese-built day/night remote-sensing satellite used to watch India.

In 2018, Asad Durrani, a former director-general of ISI, coauthored a book, *The Spy Chronicles*, with one of his Indian counterparts, A. S. Dulat. Durrani was barred from leaving Pakistan and was told he would face a court of inquiry.

OTHER SERVICES IN BRIEF

The services discussed below are worthy of note, but not much reliable literature is available about them.

Cuba. As is the case with other communist regimes, Cuba's main intelligence concerns are internal. The second concern is the United States, as both a threat and a target. Cuban intelligence has had a longtime deep association with Soviet and now Russian intelligence, and observers assume that this continues. The Directorate of Intelligence (DI, *Direccion de Inteligencia*, formerly the DGI, *Direccion General de Inteligencia*) is part of the Ministry of the Interior. Brian Latell, a former intelligence analyst and longtime scholar of Cuban intelligence, thinks that the DI may have been subject to budget cuts in the past several years. Cuban intelligence has been an active component of Cuban foreign policy, seeking to assist friendly movements and governments, such as Chile under Salvador Allende, Nicaragua under the Sandinistas, and Hugo Chavez and his successor, Nicolas Maduro, in Venezuela. Cuban intelligence has been successful in thwarting a number of attempted U.S. penetrations and has successfully managed U.S. citizens who volunteered to spy, most notably Ana Montes (DIA) and Kendall Myers (State) and his wife Gwendolyn, all of whom were caught. Montes received a twenty-five-year sentence, Myers received life without parole, and his wife received a sentence of six to seven-and-a-half years. As noted earlier, Russia appears to have renewed interest in using Cuba as an intelligence collection site. A major concern for Cuba, assuming that the normalization of relations with the United States continues, will be the influx of more U.S. visitors, increasing Cuban concerns about unauthorized foreign contacts, subversion, and espionage.

Beginning in 2016, U.S. diplomats stationed in Cuba began to complain about a variety of ailments. It is now thought that these were the result of high-intensity beams of microwaves, although it is not clear who—Cuba, Russia, others—is responsible.

Satellite images from 2018 indicate an expanded SIGINT facility at Bejucal, Cuba. It is uncertain if this is a Russian or Chinese facility.

South Korea. South Korea's National Intelligence Service (NIS) was founded in 1962 as the Korean CIA (KCIA). From 1981 to 1999, it was called the Agency for National Security Planning. NIS is responsible for collection, analysis, and the safeguarding of classified information and facilities. The main concern is obviously North Korea in several areas: nuclear and missile proliferation; the possibility of a large-scale overt attack; smaller incidents like the sinking of the corvette *Cheonan* and the shelling of Yeonpyeong Island (both in 2010); persistent North Korean efforts to infiltrate agents into South Korea; and terrorist attacks elsewhere, such as the attack on the South Korean cabinet delegation in Rangoon (now Yangon) in 1983.

South Korean intelligence controversies have included its role under the dictatorship of Park Chung-hee (1963–1979), which ended when Park was assassinated by the then-director of the KCIA; allegations of involvement in lobbying efforts in the United States, to bribe members of Congress (the so-called Koreagate scandal, 1976); and kidnapping dissident South Koreans living abroad. In December 2011, the NIS was criticized for not knowing for two days that North Korean leader Kim Jong Il had died, until it was announced on North Korean media, raising questions about the quality of South Korean intelligence in watching its major threat.

More recently, the NIS was accused of trying to sway public opinion in the December 2012 presidential election in favor of the governing party candidate, Park Geun-hye. She won by a substantial margin, but the NIS activity clearly raised issues. Ironically, Park Geun-hye is the daughter of Park Chung-hee. (In 2016, President Park was impeached in an influence peddling case and subsequently sentenced to twenty-four years in prison.) The NIS director at the time of the election, Won Sei-hoon, was later indicted for bribery in separate charges. After serving that sentence, he was convicted in the election case in 2014. In that same year, two NIS counterintelligence officers were convicted of fabricating documents to build a spy case against a North Korean refugee. In 2017, three former NIS chiefs were arrested for bribery; all three were convicted in 2018. One of them, Nam Jae-joon, was sentenced to prison for abuse of power for blocking probes into NIS operations under President Park. This constant turmoil in NIS suggests that the agency has never been brought under complete political control and that there is a lack of oversight.

After years of talks and several postponements, South Korea and Japan signed an agreement to share intelligence about North Korean nuclear and missile weapons programs via the United States in 2016. This new arms-length agreement, using the United States as a conduit, makes it more politically palatable for South Korea, which still faces domestic opposition because of Japan's harsh colonial rule from 1905 to 1945.

Finally, some observations about smaller intelligence services on a regional basis.

Africa. Intelligence in Africa is of growing importance for several reasons. The main one is the possibility that terrorists will locate in and operate out of African states, especially those with little central control. Several African nations are also transshipping points for narcotics bound for Europe and North America. Finally, Africa has become the locus of economic competition between powers, such as China and India, for access to an array of raw materials. There is a continent-wide Committee of Intelligence and Security Services of Africa (CISSA) that meets annually. In 2018,

CISSA agreed to develop a plan to combat illegal migration and to dismantle human trafficking networks.

The quality of many of the intelligence services in Africa is highly questionable. They tend to have little experience, and many have been involved with periods of repression in their respective countries. This makes intelligence sharing with them difficult. For example, despite agreement on the need to contain and defeat the extremist group Boko Haram in northeastern Nigeria, the United States was reluctant to share intelligence with the Nigerian services or military, although this reluctance was overcome. However, as the incidence of terrorism in Africa grows—in Kenya and Mali, for example—there may be little choice but to expand intelligence relations.

The most important service is that of South Africa, which has several agencies. The National Intelligence Agency (NIA) is responsible for domestic intelligence and counterintelligence. The director general of the NIA is appointed by the president. The South African Secret Service (SASS) is responsible for nonmilitary foreign intelligence and for its own internal counterintelligence. Intelligence coordination is achieved via the National Intelligence Co-ordinating Committee (NICOC), which includes NIA, SASS, and military and criminal intelligence. Finally, there is the State Security Agency (SSA), a civilian intelligence agency created in 2009, bringing together five formerly separate intelligence agencies. SSA reports to the minister of state security.

One of the biggest problems for South African intelligence has been the integration of the "former watchers and watched"—that is, the former white South African operatives and the African nationalists who were their targets. There have also been repeated press stories about mismanagement in South African intelligence and concerns about foreign penetrations. SSA appears to have been caught in some of the internal African National Congress (ANC) jockeying for power. In 2015, the South African Revenue Service disbanded a secret intelligence unit that had no statutory authority to collect intelligence.

East Asia. Japan's intelligence service, like its military, had been severely limited since World War II. Shinzo Abe's government has made a number of changes, but the overall structure remains confusing and not overly capable. The Abe government created a National Security Council. The military and the Ministry of Foreign Affairs have organic intelligence units, as would be expected, but beyond that, intelligence is treated primarily as a police function. Japan is dependent to some degree on U.S. intelligence. The Cabinet Intelligence Research Office (CIRO) briefs the prime minister and collects open-source and geospatial intelligence. It has not really succeeded in its intended role as an intelligence coordinator. Defense Intelligence Headquarters (DIH) integrates intelligence collected by the Self-Defense Forces and collects communications and electronic intelligence. According to press accounts, the Defense Ministry controls a Directorate for Signals Intelligence that monitors telephone calls and emails passing through communications satellites, focusing on North Korea and other regional powers and possible cyberattacks. The Public Security Intelligence Agency (PSIA) oversees domestic subversion, counterintelligence, and counterterrorism functions. It is part of the Ministry of Justice. PSIA has no power to make arrests. Intelligence units in the Ministry of Foreign Affairs and National Police Agency are counted as part of Japan's intelligence structure.

The Cabinet Satellite Intelligence Center controls Japan's imagery satellites and SIGINT stations, most of which focus on China. Press accounts state that Japan will expand the number of intelligence satellites from four to eight, beginning in 2023. Japan is also investing $372 billion over the next ten years to expand its indigenous UAV capability. In 2018, Japan successfully launched an all-weather radar satellite. This satellite operates in tandem with an electro-optical satellite, which has better resolution but requires good weather over the target, which the radar satellite does not. There are also press reports that Japan wants to create a HUMINT intelligence service.

According to press accounts, Japan has increased its intelligence cooperation with the Five Eyes, with specific attention to China's military and information gathering, North Korean smuggling, and cyber and telecommunications issues.

As noted, Japan has signed an intelligence-sharing agreement with South Korea. The Shinzo Abe government in Japan succeeded in reforming the law governing the use of the military in September 2015. The law had limited the military to self-defense only. Abe's reforms—which seem very limited to an outsider but which were very controversial in Japan—allow Japanese forces to defend allies and friends under attack, including overseas. This is generally seen as a response to growing Chinese power, especially in the East China Sea, but terrorism is also an issue. Several Japanese citizens have been victims in terrorist incidents. In late 2015, the Foreign Ministry advertised for "temporary" analysts to work on al Qaeda, the Islamic State, and other terrorist groups in Southeast Asia and Africa.

Concerns about terrorism have led to a series of changes. Within the Ministry of Foreign Affairs, an International Terrorism Intelligence-Gathering Unit has been established. Four monitoring groups have been established to monitor extremists, gather intelligence, and cooperate with foreign intelligence agencies. The four groups are designated North Africa, the Middle East, Southeast Asia, and South Asia. Some politicians have suggested creating a Japanese CIA or MI6, but this might prove politically difficult under current conditions.

The Abe government also passed a new secrecy law in 2013 that mandates jail sentences of up to ten years (previously the sentence was one year) for officials who leak "specially designated secrets" in the areas of defense, diplomacy, and terrorism. Authority to classify such secrets has been broadened from the Defense Ministry to all departments. Critics argue that the secrecy law gives too much power to the government and has insufficient oversight provisions. Some have also complained about the record time in which the Diet (legislature) passed the law.

Japanese leaders were among those reportedly monitored by NSA. The Japanese reaction was low key, terming the reports "deeply regrettable." The Japanese government refused to comment on later press reports stating that Japan cooperated with NSA and had been given a "mass surveillance tool" to monitor communications.

Little is known publicly and authoritatively about North Korea's intelligence apparatus. There is even disagreement about its name, the two prevalent choices being Ministry of State Security or State Security Department. State Security is modeled on the Soviet KGB. Working in an authoritarian state, State Security's main concern is internal dissent and opposition, as well as counterintelligence. There is also the

Reconnaissance Bureau of the General Staff (RBG), which provides intelligence to the military. State Security has conducted various operations overseas, including infiltrations of South Korea; kidnapping; covert action and assassination—as in the case of Kim Jong Un's brother, Kim Jong Nam, in Kuala Lumpur; and the 1983 attempt on the life of South Korean president Chun Doo Hwan in Rangoon (now Yangon), in which twenty-one people died.

North Korea has an active cyber capability. The 2014 hack into Sony Pictures, apparently to punish Sony for the film *The Interview*, which dealt with an assassination attempt against Kim, captured a great deal of attention, largely because it was clearly a cyberattack by a nation state. Unit 180 of State Security has been identified as North Korea's cyber unit. North Korea is also thought to have conducted the "Wanna Cry" ransomware attack in 2017, which affected more than 200,000 computers in some 150 nations. Various steps were taken to defeat the attack, which still gained North Korea just over $130,000 paid in Bitcoin cryptocurrency.

Taiwan's intelligence service has two major interests. The primary one is China, which views Taiwan as a rebellious province. China is both a military threat and an espionage threat for both national security and economic targets. Spying on Taiwan also gives China additional access to U.S. military equipment. Arrests of Taiwanese for spying on behalf of China occur on a continuing basis. Secondarily, Taiwan must worry about U.S. support, although much of the intelligence on U.S. policy, but not all, can be collected through open source.

Europe. As noted, Europe remains an important center for espionage activity by Russia, which is seen as a growing threat, and by non-European states, such as Iran. The United States has reportedly collected intelligence in Europe through its NSA programs and through other means. Much of Europe is in NATO, which has broadened areas of interest for Russian intelligence, but non-NATO nations are also targets. Sweden is a prime example. Sweden is in the EU but not in NATO and has a sophisticated military and economy. Sweden has reported Russia, China, and Iran as its major espionage threats and Russia, China, and India as economic espionage threats. NATO announced that it was creating a Counter Intelligence Centre of Excellence to "identify and counter intelligence threats from the east and the south"—meaning Russia and the Middle East. Several countries—Norway, Sweden, Netherlands, Estonia, and Austria—have all noted an increase in Russian intelligence and cyber activity.

China is also a concern. In December 2018, the EU investigated a cyber hack of its diplomatic communications, allegedly by Chinese hackers. In January 2019, Poland arrested two Huawei employees, one Polish and one Chinese, and charged them with spying for Beijing.

Turkey, which is the only Muslim member of NATO and is also on the front line of the Syrian civil war, passed a law in 2014 that increases the power of the National Intelligence Organization. (MIT is the acronym in Turkish.) MIT now has access to information collected in public and private institutions without a court order and an expanded ability to carry out covert operations. Turkey's security challenges notwithstanding, this move was also seen as another bid by Recep Erdoğan, then prime minister and now president, to expand his power. The Erdogan government appears to be more aggressive about overseas espionage. Germany launched investigations into Turkey spying on followers of Fethullah Gülen, whom Erdogan says was behind the attempted 2016 coup against him. In 2016, the United States arrested three Turks (two were U.S. citizens) for smuggling military secrets out of the country.

Certain European states are still dealing with the effects of cooperating with early counterterrorism activities. Italy indicted and convicted in absentia several Americans for a terrorist-related rendition and in 2013 sentenced the former head of military intelligence to a ten-year sentence in this case; this sentence was later vacated. The former head of Poland's intelligence service was charged with assisting the CIA to set up a secret prison (one of the so-called black sites) to hold suspected al Qaeda members. The European Court of Human Rights censured Poland over this activity. At the same time, European intelligence services are also reacting to the need to do better in stopping terrorist attacks. Denmark has created a prison intelligence service; Belgium has stepped up efforts to collect intelligence from social media. Several European states have created a counterterrorism intelligence database where they can share intelligence more easily.

In 2016, NATO created the position of assistant secretary general for intelligence and security, its first intelligence position. This slot will focus on intelligence sharing on Russia's military buildup, as well as duplication in civilian and military intelligence. It is likely to address intelligence sharing on counterterrorism as well.

The EU itself continues to struggle to create community-wide levers of power, including military forces (which bring it into conflict with NATO responsibilities for most members) and intelligence assets. As noted in chapter 5, there has been a European consortium to create a satellite capability. The EU is also considering an independent collection array of satellites, drones, and surveillance aircraft. The idea had the support of Lady Catherine Ashton, the first EU foreign minister, as well as France, Germany, Italy, Spain, and Poland. Britain opposed the plan and had a veto, but this will not matter after Brexit if the other EU states are still interested. In May 2015, Jean-Claude Juncker, president of the European Commission, again called for an EU secret service. In January 2016, the EU opened the European Counter Terrorism Centre, a law enforcement center focusing on violent extremism, to share intelligence on foreign fighters, illegal finance, and firearms and to assist EU states in counterterrorism investigations. In the aftermath of the November 2015 attacks in Paris and the March 2016 attacks in Brussels, there has been increased intelligence sharing, but the national obstacles to an EU service remain. As noted, Germany is opposed to the concept. There is too great a disparity between the French services and everyone else, as well as concerns about security from service to service, many of which, such as the Belgian service, are seen as being extremely weak. In November 2018, EU members agreed to create a Joint EU Intelligence School, to be led by Greece and located in Cyprus. The choice of these two nations has raised counterintelligence concerns as they are among the EU states with warmest relations with Russia.

Several European governments protested reports about U.S. surveillance programs, although it was later revealed that many of them have programs of their own and also cooperate with the United States. Advocates of a stronger EU intelligence effort have argued that the EU needs a stronger intelligence capability to serve as a more effective "counterweight" to the United States. January 2014 press reports stated that intelligence officers from Britain, France, Germany, and Spain had met with officials from the regime of Syrian president Bashar al-Assad to share information on European extremists operating in Syria in its civil war. Interestingly, even though many European states reacted strongly to the Snowden revelations and have enacted stronger privacy laws, in the aftermath of the November 2015 Paris attacks, the EU is now asking U.S. technology firms to provide backdoors to their systems to assist in counterterrorism intelligence—a position similar to the directors of the CIA and FBI for the same reasons.

Switzerland's intelligence service tends to get little attention because it is neutral, although it is a member of Schengen free travel zone. The Swiss also recognize that they are a major site for foreign intelligence services to meet, given their neutral status. In 2016, Swiss voters approved a referendum to enhance the powers of the Federal Intelligence Service (FIS), including telephone taps, email and internet surveillance, and clandestine monitoring. Among the areas of interest are terrorism, economic espionage, and foreign intelligence activities. The FIS is overseen by the cabinet, the defense ministry, and parliamentary committees. The new law adds an independent watchdog.

Latin America. Intelligence activities are problematic in several Latin American countries that have had either military or civilian dictatorships in the past, during which the intelligence services took part, including violations of human rights. In many Latin American countries, there is also no strict division between foreign and domestic intelligence. It is generally assumed that Cuba is influential in the intelligence apparatuses of Nicaragua and Venezuela.

A major issue for many Latin American nations is narcotics, an issue that crosses foreign-domestic intelligence boundaries. The United States seeks to cooperate with these services in order to stop the flow of narcotics into this country. As noted, the large amounts of money associated with the narcotics trade makes it too easy to bribe officials at all levels, making any liaison relationship difficult.

Mexico is of special concern, given its long border with the United States. For years, Mexico has struggled with the violence associated with the drug trade, the corruption it spreads, and the best way to organize intelligence. Mexican intelligence has had several stops and starts. In January 2013, the interior minister announced the creation of a National Intelligence Center (CNI is its acronym in Spanish), analogous to the CIA. CNI is part of the Interior Ministry and is responsible for bringing together information generated by intelligence and police agencies at the federal and state levels. Within the Interior Ministry, CNI reports to the Center for Investigation and National Security (CISEN), which is a civilian agency responsible for generating intelligence. Mexican intelligence efforts benefited from U.S. funding under the Mérida antinarcotics initiative, which began in 2007, but it was not clear how this initiative would fare under the Trump administration given the increased strains in the relationship.

President Dilma Rousseff of Brazil was among those cited as a target of NSA collection. Rousseff's reaction was on par with Angela Merkel, canceling a state visit and raising the issue in her 2013 speech before the UN General Assembly. In 2014, Brazil announced an agreement with the European Union to lay an undersea communications cable between Europe and Brazil to reduce Brazil's reliance on the United States.

In Argentina, the mysterious death of prosecutor Alberto Nisman, who was investigating the 1994 bombing of a Jewish center, led President Cristina Kirchner to reform the Argentine intelligence service. The murky Nisman case includes allegations that the Kirchner government was colluding with Iran—which is widely suspected to have carried out the attack—to ensure that the investigation did not blame Iran. The Kirchner government was moving toward an agreement to conduct a joint inquiry into the bombing with Iran. Nisman's information apparently included recorded conversations, which prompted Kirchner to dissolve the Secretariat of Intelligence (SI) with a new Federal Intelligence Agency (AFI). AFI appears to have an economic intelligence emphasis. Authority for wiretapping was transferred to the attorney general. In 2016, the new government of President Mauricio Macri announced that Argentina would work with the U.S. FBI to help create a network of Intelligence Fusion Centers to detect and disrupt terrorism and organized crime.

Middle East. Other than Israel, the most important intelligence service in the Middle East is, arguably, that of Iran. The main role of Ministry of Intelligence and Security (MOIS; also referred to as VEVAK) is to protect the Islamic revolution. Therefore, it has a strong internal function to locate and suppress dissent. All other government agencies must share information with MOIS. The head of MOIS must be a cleric. MOIS has a Department of Disinformation to wage psychological warfare against enemies of Iran. MOIS conducts covert operations and oversees all Iranian covert operations, some of which are carried out by the Quds Force of the Iranian Revolutionary Guard Corps. The primary area of Iranian intelligence interest and operations is the Middle East, but it also has a significant presence in Latin America and Europe. Iranian intelligence has conducted many assassinations of regime opponents and was the likely perpetrator of the bombing of an Israeli-Argentine community center in Buenos Aires in 1994. Iran also works through allies, such as Syria, and surrogates, primarily Hezbollah.

Cyber analysts see Iran as a second-tier power but one whose sophistication is growing. Having been victimized in cyberspace by Stuxnet, Iran struck back at the Saudi oil facilities and at Western banks. An Iranian cyber espionage effort that some analysts called Operation Cleaver targeted some sixteen countries, including the United States, Israel, Saudi Arabia, and several in Europe. There have also been reports of an increase in Iranian cyber activity since the signing of the JCPOA.

There have been occasional press articles about attempts by Iran to steal U.S. defense technology, working through members of the U.S.-Iranian community.

The nuclear agreement between Iran and the permanent members of the UN Security Council plus Germany (P5+1) may raise Iranian concerns about counterintelligence as inspectors go in and out of Iran. At the same time, these may also represent collection opportunities.

Iran was reportedly shaken by Saudi Arabia's intervention in Yemen, which was not foreseen. Press reports said that Minister of Intelligence Mahmood Alawi might be sacked, but he kept his job. However, the intervention has turned into a quagmire for Saudi Arabia, to Iran's benefit.

All Arab states have an intelligence service of some sort (*al-Mukhabarat*, meaning intelligence) for their respective militaries as well as for domestic and foreign issues. There are several shared concerns: Israel and the Palestinian question, the activities of Iran, and Muslim radicals and terrorism. One concern must be the possibility of their service being penetrated by radical or terrorist groups.

The Arab Spring likely was a surprise for these services, whether there was unrest in their country or not, just as it was for Israel and for other intelligence services worldwide. Events like the Arab Spring (or the failed coup in the Soviet Union in 1991) call into question the ability of indigenous services in nations where dissent is a major concern to be able to gauge and report accurately the depth of that dissent. This issue places domestic services in a bind, as their main goal is to identify and help suppress dissent. They may find themselves torn in two directions. On the one hand, they do not want to dismiss dissent out of hand, as this can easily undercut budgets and manpower if the threat is diminishing. On the other hand, if they report it as a growing threat, their political masters may call into question the effectiveness of the service.

The Saudi intelligence service came under international scrutiny after the murder of Jamal Khashoggi in the Saudi consulate in Istanbul in October 2018. Khashoggi was a Saudi dissident and a journalist working in the United States. The Saudi government eventually admitted to the murder and had a series of different stories as to how and why it happened. The head of Saudi intelligence was sacked, and King Salman announced an effort to reform and modernize Saudi intelligence. This task was given to his son, Crown Prince Mohammed bin Salman, who is seen by many as the individual behind Khashoggi's murder. In November 2018, press reports said that the CIA had concluded that Crown Prince Mohammed was behind the murder, but President Trump publicly disregarded this conclusion.

CONCLUSION

When assessing different intelligence services, keep in mind that most have liaison relationships with other services, thus increasing their capabilities. The degree to which these relationships complement or overlap one another is important.

As should now be evident, comparing intelligence services with one another is an inexact and somewhat pointless endeavor. Each service is—or should be—structured to address the unique intelligence requirements of its national policy makers. Although the intelligence process discussed throughout this book is somewhat generic to any particular intelligence service, the specifics of key issues—such as internal versus external security functions, the relative safety of the state, the extent and nature of international relationships and interests—shape how the intelligence service functions and what its relationship is to policy makers. Some structures also reflect each nation's distinctive national and political development. Skills and capabilities also vary from service to service. The key issue in assessing any intelligence service is the one that has pervaded this book: Does it provide timely, useful intelligence to the policy process?

FURTHER READINGS

Literature on foreign intelligence services is uneven at best. The works cited below emphasize the current status of these organizations, instead of offering historical treatments, although some of these resources have been cited as well.

Compendia

Blancke, Stephen. *East Asian Intelligence and Organized Crime: China, Japan, North Korea, South Korea, Mongolia.* Berlin, Germany: Verlag Dr. Koster, 2015.

Brunatti, Andrew D. "The Architecture of Community Intelligence Management in Australia, Canada and New Zealand." *Public Policy and Administration* 28 (April 2013): 119–143.

Davies, Philip H. J., and Kristian C. Gustafson. *Intelligence Elsewhere: Spies and Espionage Outside the Anglosphere.* Washington, D.C.: Georgetown University Press, 2013.

De Graff, Bob, and James M. Nyce. *The Handbook of European Intelligence Cultures.* London: Rowman and Littlefield Publishes, 2016.

Gruszczak, Artur. *Intelligence Security in the European Union: Building a Strategic Intelligence Community.* London: Palgrave Macmillian, 2016.

Africa

Publications

Cline, Lawrence E. "African Regional Intelligence Cooperation: Problems and Prospects." *International Journal of Intelligence and Counterintelligence* 29 (fall 2016): 447–449.

Shaffer, Ryan. "Following in Footsteps: The History of Kenya's Post-Colonial Intelligence Services," *Studies in Intelligence* 63, no. 1 (2019): 23–40.

Website

https://cissaau.org/ (Committee of Intelligence & Security Services of Africa)

Australia

Publications

Barnett, Harvey. *Tale of the Scorpion.* Sydney, Australia: Allen and Unwin, 1988.

Blaxland, John. *The Protest Years: The Official History of ASIO, 1963–1975.* Sydney, Australia: Allen and Unwin, 2015.

Cain, Frank. "Australia." In *Routledge Companion to Intelligence Studies.* Ed. Robert Dover et al. New York: Routledge, 2014.

Commonwealth of Australia. Department of the Prime Minister and Cabinet. *2017 Independent Intelligence Review.* Canberra: Commonwealth of Australia, 2017. (Available at https://www.pmc .gov.au/sites/default/files/publications/2017-Independent-Intelligence-Review.pdf.)

Horner, David. *The Spy Catchers: The Official History of ASIO, 1949–1963.* Sydney, Australia: Allen and Unwin, 2014.

Toohey, Brian, and William Pinwill. *Oyster: The Story of the Australian Secret Intelligence Service.* Port Melbourne: Heinemann Australia, 1989.

Websites

www.asd.gov.au (Australian Signals Directorate)

www.asio.gov.au (Australian Security Intelligence Organisation)

www.austlii.edu.au/au/legis/cth/consol_act/isa2001216 (The Intelligence Services Act of 2001)

www.defence.gov.au/ago (Australian Geospatial-Intelligence Organisation)

www.defence.gov.au/dio/index.html (Defence Intelligence Organisation)

www.dpmc.gov.au/publications/intelligence_inquiry/index.htm (Report of the Inquiry Into Australian Intelligence Agencies—The Flood Report)

www.naa.gov.au/collection/explore/security/royal-commisson/#section3 (Royal Commission on Intelligence and Security)

www.ona.gov.au/about-ona/overview/oni (Office of National Intelligence)

Britain

Publications

Aldrich, Richard. *GCHQ: The Uncensored Story of Britain's Most Secret Intelligence Agency*. London: Harper Press, 2010.

Aldrich, Richard J., et al. *Spying on the World: The Declassified Documents of the Joint Intelligence Committee, 1936–2013*. Edinburgh, U.K.: Edinburgh University Press, 2014.

Andrew, Christopher. *Defence of the Realm: The Authorized History of MI5*. London: Allen Lane, 2009.

"Cats' Eyes in the Dark." *The Economist* (March 19–25, 2005): 32–34.

Cradock, Percy. *Know Your Enemy: How the Joint Intelligence Committee Saw the World*. London: John Murray, 2002.

Davies, Philip H. J. *Intelligence and Government in Britain and the United States: A Comparative Perspective*. 2 vols. (Vol. 1: Evolution of the U.S. Intelligence Community; Vol. 2: Evolution of the U.K. Intelligence Community). Santa Barbara, Calif.: Praeger, 2012.

———. "Spin Versus Substance: Intelligence Reform in Britain after Iraq." *Welt Trends* (summer 2006): 25–35.

———. "Twilight of Britain's Joint Intelligence Committee?" *International Journal of Intelligence and Counterintelligence* 24 (fall 2011): 427–446.

Dover, Robert, and Michael S. Goodman, eds. *Learning From the Secret Past: Case in British Intelligence History*. Washington, D.C.: Georgetown University Press, 2011.

Dylan, Huw. *Defence Intelligence and the Cold War: Britain's Joint Intelligence Bureau, 1945–1964*. Oxford, U.K.: Oxford University Press, 2014.

Dylan, Huw, and Michael S. Goodman. "Guide to the Study of British Intelligence." *The Intelligencer* 21 (spring/summer 2015): 35–40.

Falkland Islands Review. *Report of a Committee of Privy Counsellors* [Franks Report]. London: Her Majesty's Stationery Office, 1983. (Parliamentary paper Cmnd. 8787.)

Glees, Anthony, and Philip H. J. Davies. "Intelligence, Iraq and the Limits of Legislative Accountability During Political Crisis." *Intelligence and National Security* (October 2006): 848–883.

————. *Spinning the Spies: Intelligence, Open Government and the Hutton Inquiry*. London: Social Affairs Unit, 2004.

Glees, Anthony, Philip H. J. Davies, and John N. L. Morrison. *The Open Side of Secrecy: Britain's Intelligence and Security Committee*. London: Social Affairs Unit, 2006.

Goodman, Michael S. "The United Kingdom." In *Routledge Companion to Intelligence Studies*. Ed. Robert Dover et al. New York: Routledge, 2014.

————. *The Official History of the Joint Intelligence Committee, Vol. I: From the Approach of the Second World War to the Suez Crisis*. London: Routledge, 2014.

Herman, Michael. "Intelligence and the Iraqi Threat: British Joint Intelligence After Butler." *RUSI (Royal United Services Institute) Journal* (August 2004): 18–24.

Intelligence and Security Committee. *Report Into the London Terrorist Attacks on 7 July 2005*. May 2006. (Available at https://www.gov.uk/government/publications/report-into-the-london-terrorist-attacks-on-7-july-2005.)

The Iraq Inquiry. Executive Summary. A Report of a Committee of Privy Counsellors. [Chilcot Report]. London: Her Majesty's Stationery Office, 2016.

Jeffrey, Keith. *The Secret History of MI6*. London: Penguin, 2010.

Masse, Todd. *Domestic Intelligence in the United Kingdom: Applicability of the MI-5 Model to the United States*. Washington, D.C.: Congressional Research Service, May 19, 2003.

National Intelligence Machinery. London: Stationery Office, 2010. (Available at www.cabinetoffice.gov.uk/sites/default/files/nim-november2010.pdf.)

Omand, David. *Securing the State*. New York: Columbia University Press, 2010.

Review of Intelligence on Weapons of Mass Destruction: Report of a Committee Privy Counsellors [Butler Report]. London: Her Majesty's Stationery Office, July 14, 2004.

Smith, Michael. *New Cloak, Old Dagger: How Britain's Spies Came in From the Cold*. London: Gollancz, 1996.

————. *The Spying Game: The Secret History of British Espionage*. London: Politicos, 2003.

West, Nigel. "The UK's Not Quite So Secret Service." *International Journal of Intelligence and Counterintelligence* 18 (spring 2005): 23–30.

Websites

www.gchq.gov.uk (Government Communications Headquarters website)

www.gov.uk/government/organisations/cabinet-office (British Cabinet Office website)

www.gov.uk/government/organisations/interception-of-communications-commissioner (Investigatory Commissioner's Office)

www.gov.uk/government/organisations/national-security (National Security Secretariat website)

www.ipco.org.uk (Investigatory Powers Commissioner)

www.mi5.gov.uk (MI5 website)

www.mi6.gov.uk or www.sis.gov.uk (MI6 website)

www.ncsc.gov.uk (National Cyber Security Centre)

Canada

Publications

Brunatti, Andrew. "Canada." In *Routledge Companion to Intelligence Studies*. Ed. Robert Dover et al. New York: Routledge, 2014.

Forcese, Craig. "Spies Without Borders: International Law and Intelligence Collection." *Journal of National Security Law and Policy* 5 (June 2011): 179–201.

Hamilton, Dwight. *Inside Canadian Intelligence: Exposing the New Realities of Espionage and International Terrorism*. Toronto, Canada: Dundurn Press, 2006.

Lefebvre, Stephane. "Canada's Legal Framework for Intelligence." *International Journal of Intelligence and Counterintelligence* 23 (summer 2010): 247–295.

Websites

www.cse-cst.gc.ca (Communications Security Establishment)

www.canada.ca/en/privy-council.html (Privy Council Office)

www.canada.ca/en/security-intelligence-service.html (Canadian Security Intelligence Service)

www.sirc-csars.gc.ca (Security Intelligence Review Committee)

China

Publications

Cheng, Dean. *Cyber Dragon: Inside China's Information Warfare and Cyber Operations*. Santa Barbara, CA: Praeger Publishers, 2016.

Eftimiades, Nicholas. *Chinese Intelligence Operations*. Annapolis, Md.: Naval Institute Press, 1994.

———. "China." In *Routledge Companion to Intelligence Studies*. Ed. Robert Dover et al. New York: Routledge, 2014.

———. "Uncovering Chinese Espionage in the US," *The Diplomat*, November 29, 2018. (Available at https://thediplomat.com/2018/11/uncovering-chinese-espionage-in-the-us/.)

Lindsay, Jon R., Tai Ming Cheung, and Derek S. Reveron. *China and Cybersecurity: Espionage, Strategy, and Politics in the Digital Age*. New York: Oxford University Press, 2015.

Mattis, Peter. "A Framework for Understanding Chinese Intelligence." *Studies in Intelligence* 56 (September 2012): 47–57.

Stokes, Mark A., Jenny Lin, and L. C. Russell Hsiao. *The Chinese People's Liberation Army Signals Intelligence and Cyber Reconnaissance Infrastructure*. Arlington, Va.: Project 2049 Institute, November 11, 2011. (Available at http://project2049.net/documents/pla_third_department_sigint_cyber_stokes_lin_hsiao.pdf.)

Wise, David. *Tiger Trap: America's Spy War With China*. Boston: Houghton Mifflin Harcourt, 2011.

U.S.-China Economic Security Review Commission. *2007 Report to Congress*. Washington, D.C., June 1, 2007. (Available at http://www.uscc.gov/Annual_Reports/2007-annual-report-congress.)

U.S. House Select Committee on U.S. National Security and Military/Commercial Concerns with the People's Republic of China [Cox Committee]. 3 vols. 105th Cong., 2d sess., 1999.

Cuba

Publications

Ginter, Kevin. "Truth and Mirage: The Cuba-Venezuela Security and Intelligence Alliance." *International Journal of Intelligence and Counterintelligence* 26 (summer 2013): 215–240.

Latell, Brian. *Castro's Secrets: The CIA and Cuba's Intelligence Machine*. New York: Palgrave Macmillan, 2012.

Egypt

Publication

Sirrs, Owen L. *A History of the Egyptian Intelligence Service: A History of the Mukhabarat, 1910–2009*. London: Routledge, 2010.

France

Publications

Bajolet, Bernard. "La DGSE: Modele Francais d'Integration." June 2014. (Available at http://www.defense.gouv.fr/dgse/tout-le-site/la-dgse-modele-francais-d-integration-l-ena-hors-les-murs-juin-2014.)

Boring, Nicholas. "France," in *Foreign Intelligence Gathering Laws*. Washington, D.C.: Law Library of Congress, June 2016, 8–14. (Available at https://www.loc.gov/law/help/intelligence-activities/intelligence-gathering.pdf.)

Hayez, Philippe. "'*Renseignement*': The New French Intelligence Policy." *International Journal of Intelligence and Counterintelligence* 23 (fall 2010): 474–486.

Hayez, Philippe, and Hedwige Regnault de Maulmin. "Guide to the Study of French Intelligence." *The Intelligencer* 21 (spring/summer 2015): 47–53.

Lethier, Pierre. "France." In *Routledge Companion to Intelligence Studies*. Ed. Robert Dover et al. New York: Routledge, 2014.

Porch, Douglas. "French Intelligence Culture: A Historical and Political Perspective." *Intelligence and National Security* 10 (July 1995): 486–511.

Websites

www.defense.gouv.fr/dgse (*Direction Générale de la Sécurité Extérieure*)

www.interieur.gouv.fr/Le-ministere/DGSI (*Direction Générale de la Sécurité Intérieure*)

Germany

Publications

Daun, Anna. "Germany." In *Routledge Companion to Intelligence Studies*. Ed. Robert Dover et al. New York: Routledge, 2014.

Krieger, Wolfgang. "The German Bundesnachrichten Dienst (BND): Evolution and Current Issues." In *The Oxford Handbook of National Security Intelligence*. Ed. Loch K. Johnson. New York: Oxford University Press, 2010.

Websites

www.bnd.de/EN (*Bundesnachrichtendienst*)

www.verfassungsschutz.de (*Bundesamt fur Verfassungsschutz*)

India

Publications

Chaudhuri, Rudra. "India." In *Routledge Companion to Intelligence Studies*. Ed. Robert Dover et al. New York: Routledge, 2014.

Dhar, Maloy Krishna. *Open Secrets: India's Intelligence Unveiled*. New Delhi, India: Manas, 2007.

Mahadevan, Prem. *The Politics of Counterterrorism in India*. London: I. B. Tauris, 2012.

Shaffer, Ryan. "Centralizing India's Intelligence: The National Intelligence Grid's Purpose, Status, and Problems." *International Journal of Intelligence and Counterintelligence* 31 (spring 2018): 159–168.

_____. "Significant Distrust and Drastic Cuts: The Indian Government's Uneasy Relationship with Intelligence," *International Journal of Intelligence and Counterintelligence* 30 (fall 2017): 522–531.

_____. "Unraveling India's Foreign Intelligence: The Origins and Evolution of the Research and Analysis Wing." *International Journal of Intelligence and Counterintelligence* 28 (summer 2015): 252–289.

_____. "Centralizing India's Intelligence: The National Intelligence Grid's Purpose, Status and Problems," *International Journal of Intelligence and Counterintelligence* 31, no. 1 (2018): 159–168.

_____. "Indian Spies inside Pakistan: South Asian Human Intelligence Across Borders," *Intelligence and National Security* 34, no. 5 (2019): 727–742.

_____. "Significant Distrust and Drastic Cuts: The Indian Government's Uneasy Relationship with Intelligence," *International Journal of Intelligence and Counterintelligence* 30, no. 3 (2017): 522–531.

Shrivastava, Manof. *Re-Energizing Indian Intelligence*. New Delhi, India: Centre for Land Warfare Studies, 2013.

Singh, V. K. *India's External Intelligence: Secrets of Research and Analysis Wing (RAW)*. New Delhi, India: Manas, 2007.

Sood, Vikram. *The Unending Game: A Former R&AW Chief s Insights into Espionage*. New York: Penguin Viking, 2018.

Yadav, R. K. *Mission R&AW*. New Delhi, India: Manas, 2014.

Website

www.cfr.org/backgrounder/raw-indias-external-intelligence-agency (Research and Analysis Wing)

Iran

Publications

Modell, Scott, and David Asher. *Pushback: Countering the Iran Action Network*. Washington, D.C.: Center for a New American Security, 2013. (Available at http://www.cnas.org/files/documents/publications/CNAS_Pushback_ModellAsher_0.pdf.)

U.S. Library of Congress. *Iran's Ministry of Intelligence and Security: A Profile*. Federal Research Division, Washington, D.C., December 2012. (Available at www.fas.org/irp/world/iran/mois-loc .pdf.)

Wege, Carl. "Guide to the Study of Iran's Intelligence Establishment." *The Intelligencer* 21 (spring/ summer 2015): 63–67.

Israel

Publications

Bar-Joseph, Uri. "Strategic Surprise or Fundamental Flaws? The Source of Israel's Military Defeat at the Beginning of the 1973 War." *Journal of Military History* 72 (April 2008): 509–530.

———. "Israel." In *Routledge Companion to Intelligence Studies*. Ed. Robert Dover et al. New York: Routledge, 2014.

Bar-Zohar, Michael, and Nissin Mihal. *Mossad: The Greatest Missions of the Israeli Secret Service*. New York, Ecco Press, 2012.

Bergman, Ronen. *Rise and Kill First: The Secret History of Israel's Targeted Assassinations*. New York: Random House, 2018.

Black, Ian, and Benny Morris. *Israel's Secret Wars: A History of Israel's Intelligence Services*. New York: Grove Weidenfeld, 1991.

Gilboa, Amos, and Ephraim Lipid, eds. *Israel's Silent Defender: An Inside Look at Sixty Years of Israeli Intelligence*. Jerusalem, Israel: Green Publishing House, 2012.

Halevy, Efraim. *Man in the Shadows: Inside the Middle East Crisis With a Man Who Led the Mossad*. London: St. Martin's Press, 2007.

Kahana, Ephraim. *Historical Dictionary of Israeli Intelligence*. Lanham, Md.: Scarecrow Press, 2006.

Katz, Samuel M. *Soldier Spies: Israeli Military Intelligence*. Novato, Calif.: Presidio Press, 1992.

Pascovich, Eyal. "Military Intelligence and Controversial Political Issues: The Unique Case of the Israeli Military Intelligence." *Intelligence and National Security* 29 (April 2014): 227–261.

Raviv, Dan, and Yossi Melman. *Every Spy a Prince: The Complete History of Israel's Intelligence Community*. Boston: Houghton-Mifflin, 1990.

———. *Spies Against Armageddon: Inside Israel's Secret Wars*. Sea Cliff, N.Y.: Levant Books, 2012.

Thomas, Gordon. *Gideon's Spies: Mossad's Secret Warriors*. New York: St. Martin's, 1999.

Websites

www.mossad.gov.il/eng/Pages/default.aspx (Mossad site)

www.gov.il/en/Departments/israel_national_cyber_directorate (National Cyber Directorate0

Japan

Kobayashi, Yoshiki. "Assessing Reform of the Japanese Intelligence Community." *International Journal of Intelligence and Counterintelligence* 28 (winter 2015–2016): 717–733.

Kotani, Ken. "Japan." In *Routledge Companion to Intelligence Studies*. Ed. Robert Dover et al. New York: Routledge, 2014.

Latin America

Cepik, Marco. "Bosses and Gatekeepers: A Network Analysis of South America's Intelligence Systems," *International Journal of Intelligence and Counterintelligence* 30 (winter 2017–2018): 701–722.

New Zealand
Publication

Hunt, Graeme. *Spies and Revolutionaries: A History of New Zealand Subversion*. Auckland, New Zealand: Reed, 2007

Websites

www.dpmc.govt.nz (Department of the Prime Minister and Cabinet—DPMC)

www.dpmc.govt.nz/our-business-units/national-security-group (DPMC Security Intelligence Group)

www.gcsb.govt.nz (Government Communications Security Bureau)

www.nzsis.govt.nz (Security Intelligence Service)

Pakistan

Dulat, A.S., Aditya Sinha, and Asad Durrani. *The Spy Chronicles: RAW, ISI and the Illusion of Peace*. New York: HarperCollins, 2018.

Kiessling, Hein G. *Faith, Unity, Discipline: The Inter-Services Intelligence of Pakistan*. London: Hurst and Company, 2016.

Sirrs, Owen L. *Pakistan's Inter-Services Intelligence Directorate: Covert Action and Internal Operations*. London: Routledge, 2016.

Russia
Publications

Albats, Yevgenia. *The State Within a State: The KGB and Its Hold on Russia—Past, Present, and Future*. Trans. Catherine A. Fitzpatrick. New York: Farrar, Strauss, and Giroux, 1994.

Albini, Joseph L., and Julie Anderson. "Whatever Happened to the KGB?" *International Journal of Intelligence and Counterintelligence* 11 (spring 1998): 26–56.

Andrew, Christopher, and Oleg Gordievsky. *KGB: The Inside Story of Its Foreign Operations From Lenin to Gorbachev*. New York: HarperCollins, 1991.

Galeotti, Mark. *Putin's Hydra: Inside Russia's Intelligence Services*. London: European Council on Foreign Relations, May 2016. (Available at https://www.ecfr.eu/publications/summary/putins_hydra_inside_russias_intelligence_services.)

Garthoff, Raymond L. *Soviet Leaders and Intelligence: Assessing the American During the Cold War*. Washington, D.C.: Georgetown University Press, 2015.

Haslam, Jonathan. *Near and Distant Neighbors: A New History of Soviet Intelligence*. New York: Farrar, Strauss and Giroux, 2014.

Knight, Amy. *Spies Without Cloaks: The KGB's Successors.* Princeton, N.J.: Princeton University Press, 1996.

Meakins, Joss I. "Squabbling *Siloviki*: Factionalism Within Russia's Security Services," *International Journal of Intelligence and Counterintelligence* 31 (summer 2018): 235–270.

"Putin's People." *The Economist* (August 25–31, 2007): 25–28.

Shane, Scott, and Mark Mazzetti. "The Plot to Subvert an Election: Unraveling the Russia Story So Far." *New York Times*, September 20, 2018. (Available at https://www.nytimes.com/interactive/2018/09/20/us/politics/russia-interference-election-trump-clinton.html.)

Soldatov, Andrei, and Irina Borogin. *The New Nobility: The Restoration of Russia's Security State and the Enduring Legacy of the KGB.* New York: PublicAffairs, 2010.

Waller, J. Michael. *Secret Empire: The KGB in Russia Today.* Boulder, Colo.: Westview Press, 1994.

Websites

http://svr.gov.ru (SVR website)

www.fsb.ru (FSB website)

South Africa

Barnard, Niel. *Secret Revolution: Memoirs of a Spy Boss.* Cape Town, South Africa: Tafelberg, 2015.

South Korea

Publications

Seo, Hyesoo. "Intelligence Politicization in the Republic of Korea: Implications for Reform." *International Journal of Intelligence and Counterintelligence* 31 (fall 2018): 451–478.

Website

http://eng.nis.go.kr (National Intelligence Service)

APPENDIX 1
Additional Bibliographic Citations and Websites

This bibliography, arranged topically, contains readings that are in addition to those listed at the end of each chapter. It is not a comprehensive bibliography of intelligence literature. Instead, the works have been chosen based on their relevance to and amplification of the themes developed in the book. Some works, although older, remain highly useful.

The list of websites was originally compiled by John Macartney, who passed away in 2001. Macartney was a career intelligence officer (U.S. Air Force) and a longtime scholar and teacher of intelligence.

REFERENCE

Lowenthal, Mark M. *The U.S. Intelligence Community: An Annotated Bibliography*. New York: Garland, 1994.

U.S. Congress. House Permanent Select Committee on Intelligence. Compilation of Intelligence Laws and Related Laws and Executive Orders of Interest to the National Intelligence Community, as Amended through January 3, 1998. 105th Cong., 2d sess., 1998.

Watson, Bruce W., Susan M. Watson, and Bruce Gerald W. Hopple, eds. *United States Intelligence: An Encyclopedia*. New York: Garland, 1990.

GENERAL WORKS

Dearth, Douglas H., and R. Thomas Goodden, eds. *Strategic Intelligence: Theory and Approach*. 2d ed. Washington, D.C.: Defense Intelligence Agency, Joint Military Intelligence Training Center, 1995.

Dover, Robert, et al. *Routledge Companion to Intelligence Studies*. New York: Routledge, 2014.

George, Roger Z., and Robert D. Kline. *Intelligence and the National Security Strategist: Enduring Issues and Challenges*. Washington, D.C.: National Defense University Press, 2004.

Hilsman, Roger. *Strategic Intelligence and National Decisions*. Glencoe, Ill.: Greenwood, 1956.

Johnson, Loch K., and James J. Wirtz. *Intelligence: The Secret World of Spies*. New York: Oxford University Press, 2015.

Kent, Sherman. *Strategic Intelligence for American World Policy*. Princeton, N.J.: Princeton University Press, 1949.

Krizan, Lisa. *Intelligence Essentials for Everyone*. Washington, D.C.: Joint Military Intelligence College, 1999.

Laqueur, Walter. *A World of Secrets*. New York: Basic Books, 1985.

HISTORIES

Andrew, Christopher. *For the President's Eyes Only.* New York: Harper Perennial Library, 1995.

Montague, Ludwell Lee. *General Walter Bedell Smith as Director of Central Intelligence: October 1950–February 1953.* University Park: Pennsylvania State University Press, 1992.

Ranelagh, John. *The Agency: The Rise and Decline of the CIA.* New York: Simon and Schuster, 1987.

Troy, Thomas F. *Donovan and the CIA: A History of the Establishment of the Central Intelligence Agency.* Frederick, Md.: Greenwood, 1981.

ANALYSIS—HISTORICAL

McAuliffe, Mary S., ed. *CIA Documents on the Cuban Missile Crisis 1962.* Washington, D.C.: CIA, Historical Staff, 1992.

Price, Victoria S. *The DCI's Role in Producing Strategic Intelligence Estimates.* Newport, R.I.: U.S. Naval War College, 1980.

COVERT ACTION—HISTORICAL

Aguilar, Luis. *Operation Zapata.* Frederick, Md.: University Publications of America, 1981.

Bissell, Richard M., with Jonathan E. Lewis and Frances T. Pudlo. *Reflections of a Cold Warrior.* New Haven, Conn.: Yale University Press, 1996.

Blight, James G., and Peter Kornbluh, eds. *Politics of Illusion: The Bay of Pigs Invasion Reexamined.* Boulder, Colo.: Lynne Rienner, 1998.

Draper, Theodore. *A Very Thin Line: The Iran–Contra Affairs.* New York: Hill and Wang, 1991.

Persico, Joseph. *Casey: From the OSS to CIA.* New York: Viking, 1990.

Thomas, Ronald C., Jr. "Influences on Decisionmaking at the Bay of Pigs." *International Journal of Intelligence and Counterintelligence* 3 (winter 1989): 537–548.

U.S. Senate Select Committee to Study Governmental Operations with Respect to Intelligence Activities [Church Committee]. *Alleged Assassination Plots Involving Foreign Leaders.* 94th Cong., 1st sess., 1975.

Wyden, Peter. *The Bay of Pigs: The Untold Story.* New York: Simon and Schuster, 1979.

INTELLIGENCE WEBSITES

Searchable Databases

- intellit.muskingum.edu/maintoc.html (J. Ransom Clark, *The Literature of Intelligence: A Bibliography of Materials, With Essays, Reviews, and Comments,* 2002)

Armed Forces Journal

- www.afji.com

Central Intelligence Agency

- www.cia.gov

Director of National Intelligence

- www.odni.gov

National Security Archive

- https://nsarchive.gwu.edu/ (declassified documents)

Congressional Oversight Committees

- intelligence.house.gov
- www.intelligence.senate.gov

Geoint Intelligence

- https://www.nga.mil/Pages/Default.aspx (National Geospatial-Intelligence Agency)

Measurement and Signatures Intelligence

- www.fas.org/irp/congress/1996_rpt/ic21/ic21007.htm (Federation of American Scientists)

Open-Source Intelligence

- www.fas.org/irp/eprint/oss980501.htm (Federation of American Scientists)

Signals Intelligence

- www.nsa.gov (National Security Agency)

Counterintelligence

- www.dss.mil (Defense Security Service)
- http://evergreen.loyola.edu/khula/www/strategic-intelligence/intel/hitzrept.html ("Abstract of Report of Investigation, The Aldrich H. Ames Case: An Assessment of CIA's Role in Identifying Ames as an Intelligence Penetration of the Agency," October 21, 1994)
- www.dni.gov/index.php/ncsc-home (National Counterintelligence and Security Center)
- www.fbi.gov/investigate/counterintelligence (Federal Bureau of Investigation)

Covert Action

- https://archive.nytimes.com/www.nytimes.com/library/national/cia-invismain.html (*New York Times*)

Intelligence Reform of 1996

- https://www.govinfo.gov/app/details/GPO-INTELLIGENCE (Report of the Aspin-Brown Commission: *Preparing for the 21st Century: An Appraisal of U.S. Intelligence: Report of the Commission on the Roles and Capabilities of the United States Intelligence Community*)

Business (Competitive) Intelligence

- www.opsecsociety.org (Operations Security Professionals Society)

- www.scip.org (Society of Competitive Intelligence Professionals)

- www.stratfor.com (Stratfor)

Special Reports

- https://www.carnegie.org/media/filer_public/33/6e/336e40fd-5176-42c2-bb9d-afd7b3b6550a/ccny_report_1997_warning.pdf (*The Warning-Response Problem and Missed Opportunities in Preventive Diplomacy*, New York: Carnegie Commission on Preventing Deadly Conflict, 1997)

- www.fas.org/irp/cia/product/cocaine2/index.html (CIA inspector general report: *Report of Investigation: Allegations of Connections between CIA and the Contras in Cocaine Trafficking to the United States*)

- www.fas.org/irp/cia/product/jeremiah.html (Comments of Adm. David Jeremiah on his investigation into actions taken by the intelligence community leading up to the Indian nuclear test of 1998)

- www.fas.org/irp/congress/1998_cr/s980731-rumsfeld.htm (U.S. Senate, "The Rumsfeld Commission Report," *Congressional Record*, daily ed., 105th Cong., 2d sess., July 31, 1998)

- https://nsarchive2.gwu.edu//NSAEBB/NSAEBB341/IGrpt1.pdf ("Inspector General's Survey of the Cuban Operation and Associated Documents," CIA report on the Bay of Pigs)

Private Organizations

- www.afcea.org/site/ (Armed Forces Communications and Electronics Association)

- www.afio.com (Association of Former Intelligence Officers)

- www.crows.org (Association of Old Crows)

- www.iafie.org (International Association for Intelligence Education)

- http://intelligence-history.org/ (International Intelligence History Association)

- https://nmia.site-ym.com/login.aspx (National Military Intelligence Association)

- www.opsecsociety.org (Operations Security Professionals Society)

APPENDIX 2
Major Intelligence Reviews or Proposals

This appendix, which lists some of the most important reviews or proposals for change in the intelligence community, is based on a 1996 Congressional Research Service report, *Proposals for Intelligence Reorganization, 1949–1996*, by Richard A. Best Jr. The synopses offer insight into the major concepts that have been put forth over the years. However, they do not capture the many proposals made by individuals.

Eberstadt Report, 1945. Laid the basic groundwork for what became the National Security Act of 1947, creating the National Security Council (NSC), a *de jure* director of central intelligence (DCI), and the Central Intelligence Agency (CIA). Also created a unified defense structure, as opposed to separate War and Navy Departments.

First Hoover Commission, 1949. Raised concerns about the lack of coordination among the CIA, the military, and the State Department, resulting in duplication and some biased estimates. Urged a more central role for the CIA in national intelligence.

Dulles-Jackson-Correa Report, 1949. Recommended that the DCI concentrate on community-wide issues, with a subordinate running day-to-day CIA operations.

Doolittle Report, 1954. Urged more effective espionage, counterespionage, and covert action to deal with the Soviet threat and noted the need for technical intelligence to overcome impediments to human intelligence (HUMINT) in the Soviet bloc.

Taylor Commission, 1961. Offered an assessment of the Bay of Pigs invasion that criticized all agencies involved, the planning and concept of the operation, and the plausibility of deniability. Made recommendations regarding future planning and coordination for covert action.

Kirkpatrick Report, 1961. Was an internal CIA review of the Bay of Pigs, which also criticized the operation's planners.

Schlesinger Report, 1971. Questioned the increased size and cost of the intelligence community in contrast with little apparent improvement in analysis; the cost of duplicative collection systems; and insufficient planning for future resource allocations. Recommended strengthening the role of the DCI in these areas.

Murphy Commission (Commission on the Organization of the Government for the Conduct of Foreign Policy), 1975. Raised the issue of the DCI's responsibility versus authority but did not recommend increasing the DCI's line authority to agencies beyond the CIA. Argued for the DCI to spend more time on community-wide issues, delegating CIA's management to a deputy.

Rockefeller Commission (Commission on CIA Activities Within the United States), 1975. Formed in the wake of revelations about improper or illegal CIA activities (the "family jewels" report). Focused largely on proposals to prevent a recurrence and to direct CIA attention solely on foreign intelligence activities.

Church Committee (Senate Select Committee to Study Governmental Operations With Respect to Intelligence Activities), 1976. Prompted by the "family jewels" revelations. Recommended legislative charters for all intelligence agencies, spelling out roles and prohibited activities. Also recommended statutory recognition of the DCI's role as principal foreign intelligence adviser, with authority to establish national intelligence requirements, the intelligence budget, and guidance for intelligence operations. Recommended that the national intelligence budget be appropriated to the DCI, not to agency directors. Recommended banning assassinations.

Pike Committee (House Select Committee on Intelligence), 1976. Was House counterpart to the Church Committee. Presented recommendations not in a final approved release but as leaked to the *Village Voice* newspaper. Recommended separating the DCI from the CIA to focus on community-wide issues; a ban on assassinations in peacetime; greater congressional oversight of covert action; charter legislation for the National Security Agency; publication of the overall intelligence budget figure; and abolition of the Defense Intelligence Agency, with its functions divided between the Defense Department and CIA.

Tower Commission (*Report of the President's Special Review Board*), 1987. Formed after initial revelations about the Iran-contra affair. Recommended improvements in the structure and functioning of the NSC staff, more precise procedures for the restricted consideration of covert action, and a Joint Intelligence Committee in Congress. Raised concerns about the influence of policy makers on the intelligence process.

Boren-McCurdy, 1993. Presented recommendations of the chairs of the Senate and House Intelligence Committees (David L. Boren, D-OK, and Dave McCurdy, D-OK, respectively), including creation of a director of national intelligence (DNI), with budgetary programming authority across the intelligence community; two deputy DNIs, one for analysis and estimates and one for intelligence community issues; a separate director of the CIA, subordinate to the DNI; and consolidation of analytical elements under a deputy DNI.

Aspin-Brown Commission (Commission on the Roles and Capabilities of the U.S. Intelligence Community), 1996. Studied the future of the intelligence community after the cold war. Said the intelligence community needed to function more as a true community, overcoming agency barriers. Recommended a closer tie between intelligence and policy to improve the direction of roles, collection, and analysis; a second deputy DCI for the intelligence community; a fixed six-year term for the deputy DCI responsible for the CIA; realignment of the intelligence budget under discipline managers reporting to the DCI; and transfer of Defense HUMINT Service's clandestine recruitment role to the CIA Directorate of Operations.

IC21: The Intelligence Community in the Twenty-first Century, **1996.** Study by the staff of the House Permanent Select Committee on Intelligence, contemporaneous with Aspin-Brown. Sought to create a more corporate intelligence community, with the DCI acting as a chief executive officer. Recommendations included DCI concurrence in the secretary of defense's appointments of National Foreign Intelligence Program (NFIP) defense agencies; increased DCI programmatic control over NFIP agency budgets and personnel; creation of a second deputy DCI for community management; consolidation and rationalization of certain management and infrastructure functions across the intelligence community; creation of a Technical Collection Agency to manage signals intelligence, imagery intelligence, and measurement and signatures intelligence; and creation of an intelligence community reserve.

Council on Foreign Relations Independent Task Force (Making Intelligence Smarter: The Future of U.S. Intelligence), 1996. Recommended improvements in the requirements and priorities process; less emphasis on long-term estimates on familiar topics and broad trends; greater use of open sources; increased influence of the DCI over intelligence components; and creation of an intelligence reserve.

Hart-Rudman Commission (U.S. Commission on National Security, Twenty-first Century), 2001. Recommended, in Phase II of the study, that the National Intelligence Council devote resources to the issues of homeland security and asymmetric threats; the NSC should establish a strategic planning staff, one of the roles of which would be to establish national intelligence priorities; the DCI should emphasize recruitment of HUMINT sources on terrorism; and the intelligence community should place new emphasis on collection and analysis of economic and scientific and technologic security concerns and should make greater use of open-source intelligence, with budget increases for these activities.

9/11 Commission (National Commission on Terrorist Attacks Upon the United States), 2004. Some recommendations were enacted into law in 2004, primarily the supplanting of the DCI with a DNI not tied to any agency and the creation of a National Counterterrorism Center, which President George W. Bush already had under way. Also recommended that all analytic efforts be organized by topical centers and that the Defense Department be responsible for all paramilitary operations.

WMD Commission (Commission on the Intelligence Capabilities of the United States Regarding Weapons of Mass Destruction), 2005. Formed to investigate intelligence performance on Iraqi weapons of mass destruction (WMDs) and other issues. Recommended that the DNI create mission managers to be responsible for all aspects of intelligence on high-priority issues; a more integrated collection enterprise; a National Counterproliferation Center to coordinate collection and analysis for counterproliferation; an Open Source Directorate at the CIA; and a new national security service within the Federal Bureau of Investigation that would include counterintelligence, counterterrorism, and intelligence activities. In June 2005, President George W. Bush accepted seventy of the seventy-four recommendations.

AUTHOR INDEX

Kotani, Ken, 506
Kovacs, Amos, 275
Krieger, Wolfgang, 482, 504
Kringen, John A., 81
Krizan, Lisa, 81, 509

Lahneman, William J., 439
Lange, Rebecca S., 317
Laqueur, Walter, 10, 509
Latell, Brian, 491, 504
Latimer, Thomas K., 317
Lauren, Paul Gordon, 415
Leetaru, Kalev, 148
Lee, William T., 341
Lefebvre, Stephane, 503
Lethier, Pierre, 504
Levinson, Sanford, 415
Lewis, Jonathan E., 510
Library of Congress, 227, 506
Lieberthal, Kenneth, 164, 199
Light, Paul C., 317, 318
Lindgren, David T., 148
Lindsay, Jon R., 391, 503
Lin, Jenny, 503
Lipid, Ephraim, 506
Lockwood, Jonathan S., 199
Long, Letitia, 148
Lord, Jonathan, 147
Lowenthal, Mark M., 35, 66, 146, 149, 199,
    275, 341, 392, 439, 509
Lucas, Nathan J., 146

MacEachin, Douglas J., 199, 341
Mahadevan, Prem, 505
Mandiant, 354, 391
Marks, Ronald A., 199, 393, 394, 439
Marrin, Stephen, 199, 276
Martinez, Damien, 341
Masse, Todd, 394, 502
Masterman, J. C., 227
Masters, Barrie P., 415
Mastny, Vojtech, 34
Mattis, Peter, 503
May, Ernest R., 187, 232, 252
Mayer-Schoenberger, Viktor, 159, 198
Mazzetti, Mark, 252, 508
McAuliffe, Mary S., 510
McConnell, Mike, 66
McDonald, J. Kenneth, 34
McNulty, Timothy J., 227, 416

Meakins, Joss I., 508
Melman, Yossi, 506
Melton, H. Keith, 147
Mercado, Stephen C., 149
Mihal, Nissin, 506
Miles, Anne Daugherty, 317, 318
Miller, Carl, 149
Miller, Paul D., 276
Mitchell, William L., 226
Modell, Scott, 505
Montague, Ludwell Lee, 35, 510
Montefiore, Simon, 163
Moran, Matthew, 148
Morris, Benny, 506
Morrison, John N. L., 502
Moynihan, Daniel Patrick, 35, 149, 341

National Academies of Science (NAS), 149
National Air and Space Intelligence Center
    (NASIC), 149
National Commission for the Review of the
    National Reconnaissance Office, 149
National Commission on Terrorist Attacks
    Upon the United States (2004),
    66, 243, 439
National Counterintelligence and Security
    Center (NCSC), 392
National Counterintelligence Executive, 392
National Geospatial-Intelligence Agency
    (NGA), 148
National Insider Threat Task Force, 217, 227
National Intelligence Council (NIC),
    342, 390, 392, 393
National Intelligence Machinery, 502
National Security Agency (NSA), 150
Neary, Patrick C., 439
Neustadt, Richard E., 232, 252
Nikitin, Mary Beth, 393
9/11 Commission (2004), 66, 243,
    427–428, 439
Nolan, Cynthia M., 318
Nolan, James, 226
Nolte, William, 391
Nyce, James M., 500
Nye, Joseph S., 136–137, 199

O'Connell, Kevin, 147
Office of the Director of National Intelligence
    (ODNI), 66, 149, 200, 227, 228, 252, 276,
    318, 342, 391, 392, 394, 439

Sorel, Albert, 416
SPOT Image Corporation, 148
Stack, Kevin P., 199
Steiner, James E., 276, 394
Steury, Donald P., 199, 341
Stiefler, Todd, 252
Stokes, Mark A., 391, 503
Sulick, Michael J., 227

Tai Ming Cheung, 391, 503
Taubman, Philip, 148, 149
Tenet, George, 35
Theohary, Catherine A., 391
Thomas, Gordon, 506
Thomas, Ronald C., Jr., 510
Thomas, Stafford T., 276
Thompson, Clive, 149
Thompson, Richard M., II, 148
Thompson, Terence, 227
Tomkins, Shirley, 318
Toohey, Brian, 500
Treverton, Gregory F., 66, 252, 317, 390, 394, 439
Troy, Thomas F., 10, 35, 510
Turner, Michael A., 35, 199

United Nations Human Rights Council, 406, 416
U.S.-China Economic and Security Review Commission, 503
U.S. Computer Readiness Team, 391
U.S. Department of Justice, 35, 252
U.S. Information Security Oversight Office, 227
U.S. National Counterintelligence Executive, 392
U.S. National Insider Threat Task Force, 227

U.S. Office of the Director of National Intelligence
see Office of the Director of National Intelligence (ODNI)
U.S. Senate, 35

Wallace, Robert, 147
Wall, Andru E., 252
Walsh, James Igoe, 147
Walton, Timothy, 200
Waltz, Edward, 146
Warner, Michael, 10, 35, 150, 226
Watson, Bruce W., 509
Watson, Susan M., 509
Wege, Carl, 506
Weiser, Benjamin, 147
Weiss, Charles, 200
West, Nigel, 502
Wiebes, Cees, 150
Wilder, Dennis, 276
Williamson, Ray A., 147
Wippl, Joseph W., 147
Wirtz, James J., 146, 147, 200, 276, 509
Wise, David, 503
WMD Commission (2005), 65, 170, 425, 426, 427–428, 438
Wohlstetter, Roberta, 35, 87–88, 146
Wolfe, Thomas, 341
Woolsey, R. James, 392
Wyden, Peter, 35, 510

Yadav, R. K., 505

Zarate, Juan C., 392
Zeckhauser, Richard, 198
Zelikow, Philip, 390, 392
Zenko, Micah, 149
Zuehlke, Arthur A., 228

SUBJECT INDEX

Alien and Sedition Acts (1798), 12, 311
Ali, Muhammad Sayyid Saber, 464
Allende, Salvador, 235, 236, 240, 250, 397,
   411, 491
Allied intelligence services, 129, 202*b*
Allies, 6, 202*b*, 401, 484
All-source analysts, 48, 73, 132, 156, 255
All-source intelligence
   Australian intelligence services, 476
   Bureau of Intelligence and Research (INR),
      46, 56, 168, 430
   Central Intelligence Agency (CIA), 46, 48,
      50, 138, 156, 168, 184, 421, 430
   collection synergy, 86–87
   competitive analysis, 184
   cyberspace, 47, 171
   Defense Intelligence Agency (DIA),
      46, 168, 430
   functional perspective, 44*f*
   human intelligence (HUMINT) collection,
      132, 133
   mission centers, 428
   multi-int versus all-source intelligence,
      186, 430
   overlapping functions, 14–15, 46–47, 430
   stovepipes problem, 168
al Qaeda
   British intelligence services, 448
   captured combatant issues, 407
   CIA operations, 363
   covert arms assistance, 234
   cruise missile attacks, 247*b*
   drone strikes, 247
   French intelligence services, 457
   intelligence collection operations, 28, 173,
      371, 427
   interrogation tapes destruction
      incident, 304
   Japanese intelligence services, 494
   narcotics trafficking, 153
   paid informants, 480
   paramilitary operations, 363
   proliferation activities, 369
   recruitment operations, 248
   refuge in Afghanistan, 105, 250, 335,
      405, 490
   relations with Pakistan, 376, 490
   relations with the Taliban, 250, 405
   retaliatory attacks, 58
   Saudi Arabian oil fields, 381

   secret prisons, 496
   surprise attacks, 27
   threat assessments, 268, 359, 361, 362,
      363–364
   war on terrorism, 397
   World Trade Center terrorist attacks, 357
   see also September 11, 2001, terrorist
      attacks
Alternative analysis, 179–181
Alternative competing hypotheses (ACH), 181
Alternative for Germany (AfD), 484
al-Wuhayshi, Nasser, 364
al-Zawahiri, Ayman, 364
Aman, 460, 465
Amazon, 159, 380
Amazon Web Services Secret Region, 185
Ambassadors, 52
American Israel Public Affairs Committee
      (AIPAC), 218
American Psychological Association
      (APA), 239
Ames, Aldrich
   as carryover asset, 468
   damage assessments, 215, 468
   espionage activities, 26, 27, 202*b*, 225,
      304, 330
   espionage detection and discovery,
      213, 215, 279, 330
   motivational factors, 205*b*
   personal finances, 204
   polygraph tests, 203
   questionable behaviors, 26, 213
   as walk-in, 129, 134, 468
Amici curiae, 314
Amnesty International, 221
Analysis and production
   accountability and credibility, 165–166
   accuracy, 162, 190, 195–196
   agency restructuring and reform, 426–430
   alternative analysis, 179–181
   analysis-collection-covert action
      relationship, 16–17, 52–53, 164–169
   analyst fungibility/agility, 159–161, 429
   analyst training, 75
   analytical standards, 189–191, 191*b*,
      426–430
   British intelligence services, 445
   Canadian intelligence services, 480
   capabilities versus intentions debate,
      323–326, 331–332

clientism, 163–164

competitive versus collaborative analysis, 169–172, 184–185, 324–325

computer software, 180–181

consensus views, 167–168

content analysis, 116

crisis-driven requirements, 157–158

current vs long-term intelligence, 74–75, 154–155

data versus knowledge issue, 158–159

definition, 67–68

differences of opinion, 408–410, 410b

dissemination decisions, 68

estimative language, 176–177

French intelligence services, 456

functional analytical intelligence centers, 169–171

functional perspective, 42–43, 43f

German intelligence services, 482

global coverage considerations, 160

goals and objectives, 194–197

hierarchical perspective, 44–47, 44f

importance, 151

Indian intelligence services, 486

indications and warnings (I&W), 177–178, 352

intelligence briefings, 16, 18, 76, 155–157

intelligence sharing, 185, 189, 206, 347–348

Iraqi weapons of mass destruction (WMDs), 28–29, 159, 164, 168, 179–180, 183, 281, 324, 371, 427

lapses and failures, 326–330, 436–437

layering, 164

lessons learned capacity, 364–369, 430, 436–437

limited information situations, 173–175

linear thinking, 164, 339–340

management strategies, 162–163

metaphorical descriptions, 172b, 175

mirror imaging, 163, 325, 332, 363, 375b

moral and ethical considerations, 408–410

moral considerations, 408–410

multi-int versus all-source intelligence, 186, 430

national intelligence estimates (NIEs), 166, 167–169, 181–184

nation-state issues, 330–340, 429

negotiation and compromise, 408–410

New Zealand intelligence services, 488

normal versus clandestine operations, 319–320

objectivity, 280

on-the-ground knowledge and experience, 164–166

opportunity analysis, 178–179

organizational structure, 40f

overlapping functions, 14–15, 429–430

Pakistani intelligence services, 489

policy maker–intelligence relationship, 265–269, 408–410

politicized intelligence, 173, 180, 186–189, 195

recruitment process and policies, 160

requirements and priorities, 75, 152–154

reserve experts, 429

retention rates, 192, 193

secure communications networks, 185

South Korean intelligence services, 492

stovepipes problem, 168–169, 170

surge capacity, 429

training programs, 161–162

truthfulness, 408

uncertainties and ambiguities, 175–177, 266, 267b, 362, 363

wheat versus chaff problem, 158

workforce considerations, 191–193, 429, 430

see also All-source intelligence; Soviet Union

Analyst agility, 160, 429

Analyst bias, 161–162, 187, 245

Analyst fungibility, 159–161, 429

Analytical flaws, 8

Analytically driven collection, 75

Analytical standards, 189–191, 191b

Analytical workforce, 191–192

Analytic ombudsman, 190

Analytic penetration, 173

Analytic stovepipes, 168–169, 170

Anarchist assassinations, 357

Angleton, James, 213

Anonymous, 466

Anthrax scare, 376, 384

Antiballistic missile (ABM) treaty, 24, 98

Anti-satellite weapons (ASATs), 98–100, 452–453

Anti-status quo states, 337

Anti-Terrorism Act (2015), 480

Apple, 119, 123, 348, 380, 466

Baseball analogy, 191*b*
Bates, John D., 313
Battle damage assessment (BDA), 351–352
Bay of Pigs invasion, 17, 23, 24, 237, 241, 269, 414
Bean counting, 323
Bejucal, Cuba, 491
Belgium
    foreign espionage threats, 485
    satellite-based collection systems, 114
    social media intelligence (SOCMINT), 496
    terrorist attacks, 362, 458–459, 496
Bellingcat (website), 449, 474
Ben Ali, Zine El Abidine, 153
Benghazi, Libya, attack, 272–273
Bennett, Robert S., 304
Berber people, 361
Beria, Lavrenti, 451
Berra, Yogi, 164, 181
Bias, analyst, 161–162, 187, 245
Big CI (counterintelligence), 214–215
Big data, 142, 158–159, 388, 433, 434, 466
Bigot lists, 216
Bilateral relationships, 327
Bill of Rights, 32, 297, 442
Bin Laden, Osama
    assassination plots, 247*b*
    intelligence collection and analysis operations, 28, 433
    intelligence-military cooperation, 57, 230, 243
    operational tactics, 358
    raid and death, 87, 131, 231–232, 363–364, 376, 397, 405, 490
    refuge in Afghanistan and Pakistan, 131, 335, 361, 405, 490
    special operations forces, 230, 243
    surprise attacks, 3*b*, 27
bin Salman, Mohammed, 31, 499
Biological weapons, 369, 376
Biometric passports, 128
Bioterrorism, 384
Bitcoin cryptocurrency, 382, 470, 495
Blackmail, 401, 468
Black September, 357
Black sites, 496
Blair, Dennis
    on cyber threats, 347
    on drone strikes, 247
    foreign liaison relationships, 459

interagency relationships and rivalries, 38–39, 40, 49, 50, 52, 234, 260, 279, 280, 421
    oversight responsibilities, 279, 422
    professional qualifications, 274
    resignation, 30, 50
    stovepipes problem, 130
    technical collection systems, 84
Blair, Tony, 188, 442, 447
Blake, George, 205*b*, 447, 468
Blimps, 112
Blogs, 434, 469, 471, 485
Blowback, 241, 404
Boeing Company, 84, 85, 86
Boko Haram, 107, 130, 335, 359, 361–362, 493
Boland, Edward P., 288
Bolton, John, 4–5, 255, 268
Bonaparte, Napoleon, 194
Bond, James, 126
Border Patrol, 111, 254
Boren, David, 265
Boren-McCurdy (1993), 514
Bosnia, 92, 386, 410*b*
Boston Marathon bombing, 140, 141, 364, 419, 471
Botnets, 139
Bo Xilai affair, 333
Brandt, Willy, 134, 483
Brazil
    NSA metadata collection target, 497–498
    nuclear weapons programs, 374
    satellite-based collection systems, 114
    slavery, 399
Brennan, John
    agency restructuring and reform, 17, 75, 95, 132, 135, 169, 351, 425, 428, 433
    congressional nomination hearings, 289
    on drone strikes, 314
    hacking capabilities, 292
    interrogation programs, 239, 289
    presidential access, 50
    professional qualifications, 49, 261
    resignation, 50
    security clearance removal, 211
    on state-sponsored terrorism, 361
    targeted strike policy, 248, 249, 314
    telecommunication encryption, 123, 348
    workforce considerations, 193
Brent Scowcroft security adviser model, 255
Brexit, 442, 450, 496

intelligence oversight authority, 280–281
intelligence policy, 18, 27, 37, 70, 107, 113, 119, 244, 259, 301
intelligence requirements and priorities review, 264
interagency relationships and rivalries, 261–262
national intelligence estimates (NIEs), 263
national security advisers, 255, 279
opportunity analysis, 179
partisan politics, 274, 293
relationship with DNI, 48, 49, 260, 274, 423
terrorism policy, 27, 29, 58, 397
torture policy, 239, 368
wiretap policy, 120
Business sector, 378–382
  see also Economics
Butler Report (Britain), 176, 188, 281, 445, 447

Cabinet Intelligence Research Office (CIRO, Japan), 493
Cambodia, 398
Cambone, Stephen, 53
Cameron, David, 246, 444, 447, 448
Campbell, Kevin, 453
Cam Ranh Bay, Vietnam, 473
Canada
  Chinese intelligence threats, 453
  classified information leaks prosecutions, 216
  cyber capability and activity, 480, 481
  foreign economic espionage, 479
  foreign espionage threats, 474, 479, 480, 481
  foreign liaison relationships, 480
  intelligence services, 479–481
  intelligence-sharing agreements, 11, 92, 130, 202b, 481
  lone-wolf attacks, 480–481
  telecommunication encryption, 348
  see also Five Eyes
Canadian Security Intelligence Service (CSIS), 480–481
Capabilities, 322, 323–326, 354
Capabilities versus intentions debate, 323–326, 331–332
Carbonite-2 satellite, 446
Carlos the Jackal
  see Ramirez Sánchez, Ilich

Carlucci, Frank, 399
Carney, Jay, 272
Carnot, Sadi, 357
Carter, Jimmy
  congressional nomination hearings, 289
  foreign policy, 229, 327
  intelligence policy, 18, 167, 266b, 301
  partisan politics, 273, 274
  as presidential candidate, 337
  relationship with DNI, 50
  strategic arms limitation treaties, 187
Cartwright, James, 219–220
Casey, William J., 49, 54, 233, 261, 273, 303, 307
Castro, Fidel, 23, 212, 245, 336, 399
Catherine the Great (1762–1796), 322
Cellebrite, 466
Center for Investigation and National Security (CISEN), 497
Center on Climate Change and National Security, 385
Central Command (CENTCOM), 188, 243
Central Directorate of Internal Intelligence (DCRI), 456
Central Intelligence Agency (CIA)
  agency restructuring and reform, 17, 33, 47, 95, 132, 135, 169–170, 280, 351, 428
  all-source intelligence, 46, 48, 50, 138, 156, 168, 184, 421, 430
  analysis-collection-covert action relationship, 16, 24, 52–53
  assassination plots, 245
  Benghazi, Libya, attack, 272
  bin Laden raid, 232
  budget process and programs, 61, 63f
  climate change research, 385
  congressional investigations and reports, 292–293
  congressional jurisdiction, 307, 308
  counterintelligence and counterespionage functions, 47, 213, 216
  cover arrangements, 127–128
  covert operations, 23, 234, 241, 411, 414
  cyberspace activity, 351
  detention and interrogation program, 292, 293
  drone strikes, 248, 249–250, 288, 406
  espionage scandals, 25, 26–27, 129, 134, 213, 452

intelligence services, 450–455
intelligence-sharing agreements,
    373–374, 454
internal stability, 332–334, 339, 382,
    383, 455
Ministry of State Security bureaus,
    450–451
nationalist sentiment, 333
national security policies, 451
natural resources competition, 381, 386
nuclear proliferation agreements, 369
permissive environments, 111
politicized intelligence, 187
regional disputes, 331–332
relations with India, 486, 487, 491
relations with Pakistan, 491
satellite-based collection systems, 84, 96,
    98, 114, 118, 452–453
satellite export controls, 97, 112
unmanned aerial vehicles (UAVs), 111,
    112, 453
U.S.-Chinese relationship, 454–455
Chinese Communist Party, 331, 333
Chin, Larry Wu-tai, 26, 203, 205*b*, 452
Christmas Day attempted on-board airliner
    bombing, 363, 365, 422, 424, 433
Chun Doo Hwan, 495
Church Committee (1976), 514
Church, Frank, 245
Circular reporting, 137
Civilian casualties, 247–249, 250, 314–315,
    405–406, 435
Civil Liberties Protection Board
    see Privacy and Civil Liberties Oversight
        Board (PCLOB)
Civil War, 13, 18, 398
Civil wars, 237, 250, 262, 334, 335, 338,
    498–499
    see also Paramilitary operations
Clandestine service operations, 126–129, 143*f*,
    261, 372, 384, 476, 497
    see also Defense Clandestine Service (DCS);
        Foreign intelligence services; Human
        intelligence (HUMINT) collection
Clapper, James
    agency restructuring and reform, 42–43, 59
    on agency success, 424
    arms control monitoring and verification
        programs, 373
    on attribution, 353

bin Laden raid, 87
budget process and programs,
    286, 287, 299
on Chinese cyber espionage, 454
clandestine human intelligence
    collections, 59
classified information leaks, 221, 411–412
commercial imagery, 105
on confidence levels, 177
congressional oversight responsibilities,
    284–285
on cyber espionage, 139, 354, 355
on cyber threats, 346, 352
as DNI, 4, 30, 38, 39, 52
domestic intelligence collection, 57
espionage policy, 132
executive branch relationships, 262
GAO access issues, 297
intelligence collection policy, 71, 75, 87, 90
intelligence integration and opacity, 20, 39,
    42–43, 95, 423, 432, 435
on intelligence interests and priorities, 319
on intelligence reform, 418, 423
intelligence transparency principles,
    19, 435
interagency relationships, 75
on Internet of things (IOT), 356–357
job applicant checks, 203
on legacy computer systems, 432
national security policies, 217, 366
nomination confirmation, 296
on NSA intelligence collection, 303, 314,
    411–412
polygraph policy, 204
professional qualifications, 261
relationship with DOD, 53
relationship with USDI, 55
resignation, 30, 50
responsibilities and authorities, 422–423
threat assessments, 18, 345, 346, 352,
    354, 386
wiretap policy, 122
Classified information
    classification systems, 90–92, 91*b*, 205,
        220–221
    compartmented information, 205–206
    congressional legislation, 32
    counterintelligence concerns, 216–223
    cyber espionage, 354–355
    dissemination decisions, 295

social media intelligence (SOCMINT), 139–141, 143f, 192, 434, 496
stovepipes problem, 94, 130, 424–426
strengths and weaknesses, 101
technological reliance, 18–19
war on terrorism, 27–28
see also Geospatial intelligence (GEOINT) collection; Human intelligence (HUMINT) collection; Open-source intelligence (OSINT); Signals intelligence (SIGINT) collection; Technical intelligence (TECHINT)
Collection, intelligence
agency restructuring and reform, 417–437
analysis-collection-covert action relationship, 16–17, 52–53, 164–169
artificial intelligence (AI), 88–89, 110, 158, 235, 346, 357, 388, 434
Australian intelligence services, 475–479
British intelligence services, 442
budget process and programs, 83–85, 88, 144–145, 192, 264–265
bulk collection, 445
Canadian intelligence services, 479–481
capabilities versus intentions debate, 323–326, 331–332
chatter, 359
Chinese intelligence services, 451, 452–453, 479
classification systems, 90–92
classified information leaks, 30–31, 120–123, 132, 202b, 206, 216–223
collection synergy, 86–87, 115
commercial imagery, 96–97, 105, 106–108, 136, 272
comparison to journalism, 419
competing priorities, 89
competitive versus collaborative analysis, 169–172, 184–185, 324–325
content analysis, 116
crisis-driven requirements, 157–158
Cuban intelligence services, 491
definition, 67
demographic trends, 382–383
denial and deception (D&D), 95–96
dominant battlefield awareness (DBA), 387–388
European intelligence services, 495–497
failed states, 335–336
foreign economic espionage, 223, 379–380

French intelligence services, 456, 457–458
functional analytical intelligence centers, 169–171
functional perspective, 42–43, 43f
German intelligence services, 115, 400, 468, 481–485
health and environmental issues, 383–387
hierarchical perspective, 44–47, 44f
hostile intercepts, 211–215
importance, 73, 74, 83
Indian intelligence services, 486–487
indications and warnings (I&W), 116, 352, 359
information integration, 20, 94–95, 423, 432, 435
information technologies (IT), 431–434
intelligence-business collaboration, 378–379
intelligence transparency, 19, 294–295, 297, 396, 434–435
international peacekeeping operations, 386–387
Iranian intelligence services, 266b, 322, 498–499
Israeli intelligence services, 460–462, 464, 466
Japanese intelligence services, 493–494
Latin America, 497–498
legal considerations, 119–124, 367–368
liberty vs security considerations, 12, 19, 100–101, 121–124, 311–312
limited information situations, 173–175
market-based proposal, 435–436
metaphorical descriptions, 172b, 175, 189, 196
Mexico, 497
moral and ethical considerations, 133, 360, 367–368, 395–407
narcotics trafficking, 377–378
nation-state issues, 322, 358
New Zealand intelligence services, 478, 487–489
organizational structure, 40f
overarching themes, 83–101
overlapping functions, 14–15, 424–426, 429–430
Pakistani intelligence services, 244–245
policy maker–intelligence relationship, 264–265, 266b

assassination plots, 212, 245–247, 246*b*,
    247*b*, 473
bin Laden raid, 87, 131, 231–232, 243, 397
Chinese intelligence services, 451
controversial issues, 239–250
coups, 22, 236, 236*f*, 240, 250
covert arms assistance to Syrian rebels,
    234, 244, 294
criticisms, 17–18, 189
decision-making practices, 230–234
definition and characteristics, 229
economic destabilization, 235, 236*f*, 240
election interference, 399
executive oversight, 279
German intelligence services, 483
intelligence interests and priorities,
    319–320
interagency relationships and rivalries,
    57, 58, 234, 242–245
Iran-contra affair, 26, 233–234
Iranian intelligence operations, 498
Israeli intelligence services, 460, 464, 466
legal considerations, 232, 243–244, 247*b*,
    248–249
legislative reactions, 232
moral and ethical considerations, 231–232,
    250, 403–405
North Korean intelligence services, 495
objectivity, 280
operational management and outcome,
    241–242
operational support structure, 230
overlapping functions, 14–15
Pakistani intelligence services, 490
paramilitary operations, 236*f*, 237,
    241–243, 269–270, 279, 363, 404
plausible deniability, 236*f*, 238, 240–242,
    279, 294
policy maker–intelligence relationship,
    269–270
political activity, 235, 236*f*
prior notice requirements, 293–294
propaganda, 234–235, 236*f*, 241, 404
range of activities, 234–239, 236*f*
rationale and relevance, 229–230
risks and benefits, 230–231
sabotage, 235–236, 236*f*, 355–356, 370,
    380, 466, 498
success assessments, 250
unintended consequences, 128, 250

wartime versus peacetime norms,
    396–397, 404
weapons proliferation intelligence targets,
    369–374
Cox, Christopher, 214
Cox Committee, 213–214, 225, 452
Crack cocaine, 378
    see also Narco-traffickers
Crateology, 104–105
Crimea, 85, 331, 338
Criminal activity
    British intelligence services, 442
    failed states, 335
    intelligence interests and priorities, 319
    narcotics trafficking, 378
    transnational issues, 96, 153
Crosswalks, intelligence budget, 62
Cruel and unusual punishment, 302, 406
Cruise missile attacks, 247*b*, 457
Crypto-currencies, 382, 470, 495
Cryptographers/cryptography, 116, 117, 118,
    348, 469, 486
Cuba
    economic destabilization, 235, 240
    espionage activities, 203, 205*b*, 225, 491
    intelligence collection challenges, 322
    intelligence services, 491, 497
    missile crisis, 23–24, 87, 106*b*, 266*b*
    power leverage, 337
    Russian intelligence operations, 473, 491
    satellite export controls, 97
    signals intelligence, 491
    U.S. invasion, 17, 23, 24, 237, 241, 269, 414
    U.S. national security policies, 343
CubeSat, 113
Cumming, Sir Mansfield, 447
Current vs long-term intelligence, 74–75,
    154–155
CURVE BALL (secret agent), 17, 189, 437
Customs and Border Protection, 54, 109,
    111, 114
Cyber Command (USCYBERCOM),
    236, 350, 351
Cyber espionage
    Chinese intelligence operations, 112,
        354–355, 448, 451–454, 479
    collection disciplines, 139
    French intelligence services, 460
    German intelligence services, 485
    Iranian intelligence operations, 356, 498

responsibilities and authorities, 20, 21,
37–42, 46, 51–52, 68–72, 86–87, 279,
420–424
sources and methods protection, 411
staff turnover, 3–4, 29–30
technical collection systems, 84
terms of office, 49–50
Directors of central intelligence (DCIs)
budget process and programs, 41, 421–422
congressional jurisdiction, 307
congressional legislation, 32, 33, 37
congressional oversight
responsibilities, 289
covert operations, 234
functional role, 255, 420–424
human intelligence (HUMINT) collection,
134–135
intelligence briefings, 296
interagency relationships and rivalries,
57–58, 260, 261–262, 279
interrogation programs, 407
military influence, 38
organizational structure, 40–41, 40f
origins, 32
partisan politics, 273–274, 296
presidential access, 16, 48, 49–50, 156, 260
professional qualifications, 261
responsibilities and authorities, 19–20, 22,
37, 279, 411, 420–424
see also Central Intelligence Agency (CIA)
Disaggregated satellites, 99
Discontinuity scenarios, 339–340
Disease epidemics, 384
Disinformation, 140, 202, 235, 241, 467, 498
see also Propaganda
Dissemination decisions
classified information, 295
intelligence process, 68
product lines, 75–77
responsibilities and authorities, 76–77
Dissent channels, 184
Distance theory of intelligence, 15, 16–17
Divine intelligence (DIVINT), 137b
DJI (Dà-Jiang Innovations), 109
Doctors Without Borders, 221
Domestic intelligence
British intelligence services, 442
Canadian intelligence services, 480
CIA-NYPD liaison, 135
congressional legislation, 33, 37

French intelligence services, 458
German intelligence services, 468, 483, 485
Indian intelligence services, 487
interagency rivalries, 57
Japanese intelligence services, 493
Latin America, 497
as a law enforcement issue, 7, 27
liberty vs security considerations, 100–101,
311–312
narcotics trafficking, 377–378
National Geospatial-Intelligence Agency
(NGA), 113–114
South African intelligence services, 493
as subset of national intelligence, 5, 37,
39, 45
Domestic security, 5
Dominant battlefield awareness (DBA),
387–388
Donovan, William, 20, 21
Doolittle Report (1954), 513
Double agents, 212, 215
Double Cross system, 212
Douhet, Giulio, 347
Downstream activities, 74
Downward-flowing politicized
intelligence, 187
Drake, Thomas, 218–219
Drones
advantages/disadvantages, 108–110, 111
autonomous flight, 110
British intelligence services,
446, 447–448, 449
Chinese intelligence services, 453
civilian casualties, 247–249, 250,
405–406, 435
collection capabilities, 110
commercial use, 111–112
congressional oversight, 249, 250, 288
controversial issues, 246–250, 405–406
cost decisions, 84
covert actions, 18
European Union (EU), 496
geospatial imagery, 101, 106, 108, 363
hacking opportunities, 109, 111
importance, 46
intelligence collection, 88, 89,
108–110, 368
intelligence transparency, 295, 434–435
interagency relationships and rivalries, 248,
249–250, 288

Israeli intelligence services, 111, 464
Japanese intelligence services, 494
military applications, 109–110
moral and ethical considerations, 405–406
offensive operations, 363
overseas support, 112
permissive environments, 111
prior notice requirements, 294
processing and exploitation, 110
surveillance operations, 101
targeted strikes, 248, 301, 314, 315,
 405–406
as weapons platforms, 28, 89, 110–111, 239,
 246–247, 368, 405–406
see also UAVs (unmanned aerial vehicles)
Drucker, Peter, 159
Drug Enforcement Administration (DEA)
 agency restructuring and reform, 425
 functional perspective, 44, 44*f*
 human intelligence (HUMINT)
  collection, 126
 Inspectors General (IGs) investigations, 283
 organizational structure, 40*f*, 378
Drug trafficking, 377–378
 see also Narco-traffickers
Dubai, 245, 464
Duelfer, Charles A., 281–282
Dulat, A.S., 491
Dulles, Allen, 22, 23, 49, 52, 230, 261
Dulles-Jackson-Correa Report (1949), 513
Dulles, John Foster, 52
Dummies, 95, 105, 106
Durrani, Asad, 491
Duty-to-warn issue, 178

Eagan, Claire, 123, 314
Earmarks, 286
East China Sea, 494
East Germany
 see Germany
Eavesdropping, 402
 see also Wiretaps
Eberstadt Report (1945), 513
Ebola virus outbreak, 107, 384, 386
ECHELON, 379, 458
Echo reporting, 137, 380
Economics
 African nations, 492
 British intelligence services, 442
 Chinese tariffs, 331

competitive relationships, 378–379, 381
counterintelligence and counterespionage
 operations, 458
demographic trends, 383
destabilization operations, 235, 236*f*, 240
economic espionage, 202*b*, 223, 354–355,
 379–380, 449, 453, 457–458, 481, 495
financial intelligence (FININT), 382
foreign economic espionage, 223, 378,
 379–380, 457–458, 479, 495
French intelligence services, 457–458
key issues, 378–379
natural resources competition, 381
oil and natural gas supplies, 381–382
Swiss intelligence service, 497
transnational issues, 378–382
trends and shifts forecasting, 380–381
Eden, Anthony, 410*b*
Egypt
 Arab Spring revolt, 140, 153, 465
 democratic reforms, 338
 extremist exploitation, 364
 indications and warnings (I&W), 178, 465
 internal stability, 465
 Israeli intelligence operations, 461, 464
 leadership analysis, 336
Eichmann, Adolf, 464
Eighth Amendment (U.S. Constitution),
 302, 406
Eisenhower, Dwight D.
 covert operations, 230, 240, 241, 269, 273
 intelligence policy, 22, 23, 92, 259
 oversight responsibilities, 278
Eitan, Rafi, 461
Election interference
 Australia, 479
 ends versus means controversy, 397
 Nicaragua, 399
 Portugal, 399
 South Korean intelligence services, 492
 Western Europe, 397, 470
 see also Russian election interference
Electromagnetic spectrum, 125, 143*f*
Electronic intelligence (ELINT), 115, 117,
 118, 124, 143*f*
Electronic news media, 274
Electronic warfare, 451
Electro-optical (EO) imagery, 97, 104, 124, 143*f*
 see also Commercial imagery;
  Satellite-based collection systems

Elisabeth (Empress of the Austria-Hungary Empire), 357
Elizabeth I (Queen), 12
Ellsberg, Daniel, 289
el-Sisi, Abdel Fattah, 465
Email services, 469
Embassies
    accidental bombings, 455
    chatter, 359, 364
    closures, 364
    cover arrangements, 127
    espionage scandals, 461
    intelligence collection, 45, 46, 52, 137*b*, 151, 486
    interagency rivalries, 57
    surveillance operations, 460
    terrorist attacks, 3*b*, 247*b*
    unmanned aerial vehicles (UAVs), 112
Embedi (cybersecurity firm), 467
Emergency wiretaps, 120, 122
Encapsulated communications, 117
Encrypted communications, 116, 117, 118–119, 123, 348, 466, 477
Ends versus means controversies
    information technologies (IT), 431–432
    interrogation programs, 407
    moral and ethical considerations, 397–398
Enemies, 6
Energy supply, 381–382
Enhanced Cybersecurity Services, 101
Enhanced interrogation techniques (EITs), 238–239, 295–296, 368, 401
Environmental threats, 384–386
Erdogan, Recep, 495–496
Espionage
    British intelligence services, 442
    Canadian intelligence services, 479, 480, 481
    damage assessments, 215
    detection and discovery, 213–215, 278–279, 330, 467–468
    economic espionage, 202*b*, 223, 354–355, 449, 453, 457–458
    executive oversight, 279
    foreign economic espionage, 223, 378, 379–380, 457–458, 479
    French intelligence services, 457–458
    friendly powers, 202*b*, 225, 401
    German intelligence services, 482
    Israeli intelligence operations, 461–464

lapses and failures, 304
    liberty vs security considerations, 215
    moral and ethical considerations, 400
    motivational factors, 205*b*
    national security letters (NSLs), 122, 213, 223–224
    New Zealand intelligence services, 488
    Pakistani intelligence services, 490
    points of presence (PoPs), 454
    post-Cold War, 224–225, 330, 400
    recruitment process and policies, 126, 133, 134, 401–402, 443, 452, 468
    Russian intelligence operations, 225, 447, 448–449, 481
    sleeper agents, 129, 210, 211, 449, 474–475
    stovepipes problem, 94
    Swiss intelligence service, 497
    technological reliance, 18–19
    unmanned aerial vehicles (UAVs), 112
    wartime versus peacetime norms, 396–397
    World War II, 21
    see also Ames, Aldrich; Collection, intelligence; Counterintelligence (CI); Cyber espionage; Hanssen, Robert; Human intelligence (HUMINT) collection; Information leaks; Manning, Bradley; Snowden, Edward
Espionage Act (1917), 12, 30, 32, 218, 219, 223, 414
Espionage scandals
    Britain, 205*b*, 213, 447
    Central Intelligence Agency (CIA), 25, 26–27, 129, 134, 213, 452
    Department of Energy (DOE), 213–214, 278–279
    Federal Bureau of Investigation (FBI), 26, 27, 214
    France, 202*b*
    Germany, 134, 483
    Israel, 134, 202*b*, 461–464
    polygraph tests, 203–204
    see also Ames, Aldrich; Hanssen, Robert; Snowden, Edward; Walk-ins
Estimates
    see National intelligence estimates (NIEs)
Estimative language, 176–177
Estonia, 352, 356, 470, 474, 495

Ethics Committee
  see House Committee on Standards of
    Official Conduct
European Commission (EC), 496
European Convention on Human Rights, 442
European Counter Terrorism Centre, 496
European Court of Human Rights, 496
European Union (EU)
  Brexit, 442, 450, 496
  British intelligence services, 446
  communications wiretaps, 123
  competitive relationships, 6
  counterterrorism activities, 496
  cyber attacks, 498
  cyber espionage, 495
  encrypted communications, 348
  espionage scandals, 202*b*
  intelligence services, 495–497
  intelligence-sharing agreements, 458, 485,
    496, 497
  regional stability, 339, 382
  Russian espionage threats, 495
  satellite-based collection systems, 496
  social media intelligence (SOCMINT), 140
  terrorist attacks, 496
  U.S. surveillance operations, 458, 495
Evanina, William, 355
Evans, Jonathan, 448, 449, 468
Executive branch
  covert operations approval, 232–233
  executive orders, 280, 301
  goals and objectives, 258
  hostage-taking bargaining tactics, 293
  Inspectors General (IGs), 282–283
  intelligence briefings, 16, 18, 76, 155–157
  intelligence leaks, 220, 296
  intelligence oversight responsibilities,
    278–283
  intelligence requirements and priorities
    review, 264
  intelligence understandings and
    expectations, 308–310
  interagency relationships and rivalries,
    261–262
  national intelligence estimates (NIEs), 262
  national security policy, 253, 254
  partisan politics, 273–274
  relationship with DNI, 48, 49, 52–53, 260,
    261, 262, 274
  reporting requirements, 290–291

security clearances, 295
see also Congressional oversight
    responsibilities
Executive Committee (EXCOM), 45, 55, 278
Executive Highlights, 76
Executive Order 12333, 33, 201, 301, 420
Executive Order 13526, 33, 91*b*
Executive Order 13549, 207
Executive Order 13556, 91*b*
Executive Order 13587, 217
Executive Order 13691, 347
Executive Order 13732, 247–248
Executive orders, 280, 301
Export controls
  cyberspace, 349
  satellite-based collection systems, 97, 112

Facebook, 139, 140, 159, 235, 460, 470
Facial recognition software, 128, 140, 449
Fadden, Richard, 480
Failed states, 153, 334–336, 345, 386–387
Falklands War (1982), 448
False communication
  counterespionage, 202
  counterintelligence, 201
  cryptography, 116
  cyber espionage, 139
  data intelligence (data-int), 142
  denial and deception (D&D), 95
  disinformation, 140, 202
  foreign agents, 212
  human intelligence (HUMINT) collection,
    131, 135, 144*f*
  open-source intelligence (OSINT), 136
  propaganda, 234–235
  social media intelligence (SOCMINT),
    139, 140
False hostages, 167
Fast lightweight autonomy (FLA), 110
Fattah el-Sisi, Abdel, 465
Federal Agency for Government
    Communications and Information
    (FAPSI), 469
Federal Aviation Administration (FAA)
    Modernization and Reform
    Act (2012), 111
Federal Bureau of Investigation (FBI)
  agency restructuring and reform, 425
  budget process and programs, 61, 63*f*
  on Chinese intelligence operations, 452

Germany, 481–485
India, 486–487
Israel, 460–467
Japan, 493–494
New Zealand, 487–489
North Korea, 494–495
Pakistan, 244–245, 361, 489–491
research sources and reliability, 441
Russia, 467–475
South Korea, 492
Taiwan, 495
Foreign Intelligence Surveillance Act (1978), 32, 119, 120, 122, 215, 312, 315, 396, 449
Foreign Intelligence Surveillance Court (FISC)
    foreign intelligence collection, 119, 121–123, 215, 402
    functional role, 281, 312–315
    intelligence transparency, 435
    origins, 32
Foreign Intelligence Surveillance Court of Review, 312, 314
Foreign intelligence wiretaps, 119–124
Foreign language capabilities, 118, 141, 160–161
Foreign leaders, 336–337
Foreign liaison relationships
    Australian intelligence services, 476, 478
    British intelligence services, 444–445, 450
    Canadian intelligence services, 480
    Central Intelligence Agency (CIA), 52, 130
    Director of national intelligence (DNI), 50
    French intelligence services, 459
    German intelligence services, 482
    hostile nations, 130
    human intelligence (HUMINT) collection, 129–131, 225, 244–245
    importance, 499
    Indian intelligence services, 486
    intelligence-sharing agreements, 222, 225, 244–245
    Israeli intelligence services, 460, 462
    Latin America, 497
    leadership analysis, 336
    Pakistani intelligence services, 490
    Russian intelligence services, 474
    stovepipes problem, 130
    terrorism intelligence resources, 360–361

third party rule, 130, 220, 462
weapons of mass destruction (WMDs), 310
    see also Five Eyes
Foreign passports, 464, 481, 489
Foreign Service, 257
Foreign Service officers, 254
Fort Hood, Texas, shootings, 248, 362
Fragile states, 334, 335, 345
    see also Failed states
France
    anarchist assassinations, 357
    communications wiretaps, 123
    cyber capabilities, 354
    cyber espionage threats, 460
    drone operations, 111–112
    espionage activities, 225, 401, 447, 457–458
    espionage scandals, 202b
    intelligence briefings, 370
    intelligence services, 455–460
    intelligence-sharing agreements, 130, 459, 497
    leadership analysis, 336–337
    nuclear proliferation agreements, 369
    satellite-based collection systems, 114, 457
    terrorist attacks, 123, 348, 362, 447, 456–457, 458, 459, 496
Franklin, Lawrence, 218
Franks, Oliver Shewell, 448
Freedom of Information Act, 297
Freedom of speech, 297
Freedom of the press, 297, 413–414
Freeh, Louis J., 50
Friendly intelligence services, 129, 202b
Friendly powers, 6, 202b, 225, 401, 484
FSB
    see Federalnaya Sluzhba Bezopasnosti (FSB)
Fuchs, Klaus, 211
Fuerzas Armadas Revolucionarias de Colombia (FARC), 361
Fukuyama, Francis, 344
Full motion video (FMV), 110
Functional analytical intelligence centers, 169–171, 428
Fund for Peace, 334, 335
Fusion centers, 365–366
Fusion intelligence
    see All-source intelligence
Future Imagery Architecture (FIA), 84, 288

Gag orders, 224
Gandhi, Rajiv, 486
Gang of 4, 295, 296
Gang of 8, 295, 296, 297
Gates, Robert M.
  Cold War intelligence collection, 14, 343
  congressional nomination hearings, 289
  Executive Committee (EXCOM), 45
  on foreign economic espionage, 379
  human intelligence (HUMINT)
      collection, 59
  intelligence budget process and programs,
      14, 53
  intelligence-sharing, 338
  mission centers, 169
  partisan politics, 274
  politicized intelligence, 188
  professional qualifications, 49, 53, 261
  technical collection systems, 84
Gaza Strip, 338
Gehlen Organization, 482
Gehlen, Reinhard, 482
General Accounting Office (GAO)
  see Government Accountability Office
      (GAO)
General Data Protection Regulations
      (GDPR), 140
General Defense Intelligence Program
      (GDIP), 61
General Directorate for External Security
      (DGSE), 455–456, 457, 460
General Directorate for Internal Security
      (DGSI), 456
General Intelligence (RG), 456
Geneva Convention rights, 407
Geng Huichang, 453
Geocell, 115
GeoEye, 97
Geofence, 109
GEOINT Pathfinder project, 108
Geophysical phenomena, 124, 136, 143f
Geopolitical Forecasting Challenge, 159
Georgia (nation-state), 353, 470
Geospatial intelligence (GEOINT) collection
  advantages/disadvantages, 105, 143f
  alternative displays, 107b
  Australian intelligence services, 477
  battle damage assessment (BDA), 351–352
  bin Laden raid, 87, 363
  commercial imagery, 97, 105, 106–108, 363

definition and characteristics, 104
denial and deception (D&D), 105, 106
discipline relationships, 143f
experimental systems, 113
foreign liaison relationships, 130
functional perspective, 43f, 46
image resolution, 102–103f, 104–105, 108
Indian intelligence services, 486
intelligence-sharing agreements, 130
Japanese intelligence services, 493
photo interpretation, 105–106, 106b
shutter control, 107–108
social media, 140
stovepipes problem, 94, 424–426
terrorist-related intelligence, 360
Geospatial metadata analysis, 116
Geosynchronous orbit (GEO), 93
Geosynchronous Space Situational Awareness
      Program, 100
Germany
  anti-immigrant sentiments, 483–484
  communications wiretaps, 123
  cyber capability and activity, 485
  demographic trends, 383
  espionage scandals, 134, 483
  foreign espionage threats, 468, 474, 483,
      484–485, 496
  foreign liaison relationships, 482
  hacking capabilities, 346
  intelligence operations, 400, 484–485
  intelligence services, 468, 481–485
  intelligence-sharing agreements, 446, 452,
      484–485, 497
  Jewish concentration camps, 403
  Muslim unrest, 483
  nuclear proliferation agreements, 369
  political and industrial espionage, 447
  refugee crisis, 335
  satellite-based collection systems, 114, 482
  signals intelligence, 115, 482
  terrorist groups, 357, 464, 483
Glavnoye Razvedyvatelnoye Upravlenie
      (GRU), 449, 467
Glavnoye Upravlenie (GU), 467, 469, 474
Global climate change, 385–386
Global coverage, 160
Global Engagement Center, 241
Global findings, 279
Global food security, 386
Global Hawk, 109, 112, 115

Global recession, 380
Global warming, 310
Global water security, 386
Glomar Explorer, 414
Gmail, 469
Goldwater, Barry, 303, 307
Goldwater-Nichols Act (1986), 170
Google, 113, 123, 159, 185, 235, 348, 460, 470
Gorbachev, Mikhail S., 328–329, 330, 332, 336, 467
Gordievsky, Oleg, 448
Gore, Al, 188
Goss, Porter J., 16, 30, 41, 134–135, 239, 261, 425
Government Accountability Office (GAO), 297, 366
Government Communications Headquarters (GCHQ), 442, 443–444, 445, 448, 449
Government Communications Security Bureau (GCSB), 488–489
Government coups, 22, 236, 240, 250
Grant, Ulysses S., 387
Graymail, 32, 215
Graymail Law (1980), 32, 215
Greece, 496
Greenhouse gas emissions, 385
Greenpeace organization, 457
Greenwald, Glenn, 446
Grieve, Dominic, 446
GRIZZLY STEPPE, 350
Ground-launched cruise missile (GLCM), 374
Groupthink, 15, 29, 75, 168, 180, 371
GRU
    see Glavnoye Razvedyvatelnoye Upravlenie (GRU)
Guaranteed freedoms, 297
Guardian newspaper, 446
Guatemala
    government coups, 22, 236
    human rights violations, 133, 412–413
Guillaume, Gunter, 134, 483
Gülen, Fethullah, 496
Guzmán, Jacobo Arbenz, 22

Habeas corpus, suspension of, 12, 311, 398
Hacking capabilities and opportunities
    Chinese intelligence services, 208, 221, 451, 452–454, 495
    classified information leaks, 221

government computers, 119, 292, 346, 466–467
    hack backs/counterhacks, 348–349
    Israeli intelligence services, 466–467
    Russian intelligence services, 466–467, 470–472, 485
    security clearances, 208
    unmanned aerial vehicles (UAVs), 109, 111
Haiti, 335
Hale, Nathan, 126
Halperin, Morton H., 293
Hamas, 463, 465
Handheld cameras, 101
Hannigan, Robert, 444
Hanssen, Robert
    as carryover asset, 468
    damage assessments, 215, 304, 468
    espionage activities, 27, 202*b*, 225, 330
    espionage detection and discovery, 211, 213, 215, 330
    motivational factors, 205*b*
    personal finances, 204
    polygraph tests, 203
    questionable behaviors, 212, 213
    as walk-in, 129, 134, 468
Hariri, Rafik, 405
Harkat, Mohamed, 480
Harman, Jane, 305
Hart-Rudman Commission (2001), 515
Hasan, Nidal, 248, 362, 364, 368
Haspel, Gina
    on interrogation programs, 239
    interrogation tapes destruction incident, 304
    nation-state issues, 320, 330–331, 345
    on North Korean nuclear weapons and missile programs, 332
    professional qualifications, 49, 261
    threat assessments, 259
    workforce considerations, 193, 345, 429
Hastings, Alcee, 305–306
Hayden, Michael
    as DNI, 38
    Inspectors General (IGs) investigations, 283
    on intelligence publishing, 419, 432
    on interrogation programs, 238, 239, 401
    Iraqi weapons of mass destruction (WMDs), 281
    on noncombatant deaths, 249

Russian election interference investigation, 31, 307, 315, 353
targeted strike policy, 249, 301
technical collection systems, 84, 85
term limits, 306
House Select Committee on Intelligence (1976), 514
House Select Committee on U.S. National Security and Military/Commercial Concerns With the People's Republic of China

see Cox Committee

Housing market collapse, 380
Howard, Edward, 214
Huawei, 355, 444, 479, 489, 495
Hughes Aircraft Company, 457
Hughes, Thomas, 172*b*
Hu Jintao, 450, 455
Human-enabled cyber attacks, 355
Human intelligence (HUMINT) collection
advantages/disadvantages, 131–134, 144*f*
agency restructuring and reform, 424–425
analytic workforce, 191–192
attrition rates, 134–135
bin Laden raid, 87, 131, 231–232
British intelligence services, 443, 446
Chinese intelligence services, 451, 452
compartmented information, 206
computer-based surveillance and intelligence, 101
counterespionage, 213
cover arrangements, 127–129
cyber espionage, 139
definition and characteristics, 125–127
denial and deception (D&D), 131, 132
discipline relationships, 143*f*
dominant battlefield awareness (DBA), 387
financial intelligence (FININT), 382
foreign liaison relationships, 129–131, 225, 244–245
French intelligence services, 456
friendly services, 129
functional perspective, 43*f*, 46
German intelligence services, 482
historical perspective, 125–126
hostile intercepts, 212
human intelligence (HUMINT) collection, 421
intelligence briefings, 155

interagency relationships, 50, 52, 58, 133, 421
Israeli intelligence services, 460, 461, 464
Japanese intelligence services, 494
moral and ethical considerations, 133, 360, 400, 401–402
nation-state issues, 322
Pakistani intelligence services, 489, 491
recruitment process and policies, 126, 133, 134, 401–402
Russian intelligence services, 467–468
sleeper agents, 129, 449, 474–475
stovepipes problem, 94, 130, 424–426
suicide attacks, 132
technological reliance, 18–19
terrorist-related intelligence, 130–131, 133, 244–245, 359–360
training considerations, 191–192
walk-ins, 129, 134, 360, 401, 461, 467–468
war on terrorism, 27

see also Counterintelligence (CI)

Human Rights Act (1998), 442
Human rights organizations, 107, 496
Human rights violations, 133, 399–400, 412–413, 497
Human trafficking, 153, 335, 493
Humorous intelligence collection, 137*b*
Hunter, Duncan, 308
Hurricane Katrina, 267*b*
Hussein, Saddam, 179, 180, 282, 352, 405, 433, 478
Hyperspectral imagery (HSI), 104, 124

IC21: The Intelligence Community in the Twenty-first Century (1996), 515
ICITE (Intelligence Community Information Technology Enterprise), 185, 432
Idealism, 397
IKONOS imagery system, 96, 106–107
Illegal drug trafficking, 377–378

see also Narco-traffickers

Imagery intelligence (IMINT), 46, 387, 446, 457, 467, 482

see also Geospatial intelligence (GEOINT) collection

Imagery satellite systems
Australian intelligence services, 477
British intelligence services, 446
budget process and programs, 83–85, 88, 288, 309

Chinese intelligence services, 452–453
developmental lead times, 85–86
French intelligence services, 114, 456, 457
geospatial intelligence, 101
German intelligence services, 114, 482
hostage-taking bargaining tactics, 293
Israeli intelligence services, 114, 464
Japanese intelligence services, 494
limitations, 93–94
processing and exploitation, 73–74,
    87–89, 113
Immigration and Customs Enforcement
    (ICE), 54
Immigration and Naturalization
    Department, 254
India
    anti-satellite weapons (ASATs), 98
    classified information leaks
        prosecutions, 216
    cyber capability and activity, 354, 487
    espionage activities, 225, 495
    foreign liaison relationships, 486
    intelligence services, 486–487
    intelligence-sharing agreements, 487
    natural resources competition, 381
    nuclear weapons testing, 89–90, 369
    regional disputes, 486
    relations with China, 486, 487, 491
    relations with Pakistan, 486, 487
    satellite-based collection systems,
        114, 464
    terrorist attacks, 486, 490
Indian Police Service (IPS), 486
Indications and warnings (I&W),
    116, 177–178, 352, 359, 465
Indonesia, 380
Industrial espionage, 378
Infectious disease epidemics, 384
Information leaks
    classified information, xiv, 411–413
    counterintelligence concerns, 216–223
    damage assessments, 132, 207,
        350, 414, 458
    DNC documents, 470
    European reactions, 497
    information sharing practices, 347–348,
        365, 432–433, 434
    insider threats, 217
    leak prosecutions, 216–220
    sources and methods protection, 92–93

State Department documents,
    206, 412–413, 414
see also NSA metadata collection programs
Information operations, 346
Information Security Oversight Office
    (ISOO), 206, 207
Information sharing
    African intelligence services, 493
    classified information leaks, 347–348, 365,
        432–433, 434
    foreign liaison relationships, 222, 225,
        244–245
    Israeli intelligence services, 462–463
    law enforcement, 365–366
    lessons learned, 436–437
    policy maker–intelligence relationship, 11,
        129–131, 185, 189, 206, 222, 364–367,
        378–379
    proliferation, 373–374
    security safeguards, 207, 217
    social media, 348, 434
    sources and methods protection, 92–93
    weapons of mass destruction (WMDs), 92
    see also Five Eyes; Foreign intelligence
        services; specific country
Information technologies (IT), 431–434
Infrared (IR) imagery, 104
Infrastructure attacks, 346, 354, 367
Inglis, Chris, 351
Insider Threat Program, 217
Insider threats, 217, 222, 434
Inspectors General (IGs), 282–283
Inspire (jihadist magazine), 351
Intellectual dishonesty, 166
Intelligence
    accuracy, 195–196
    agency restructuring and reform, 417–437
    basic concepts, 1, 5–9
    clarity, 195
    confidence levels, 195
    congressional understandings and
        expectations, 308–310
    co-option issues, 302–303, 305
    foreign passport access, 464, 481, 489
    functional role, 2–5, 344
    GAO access issues, 297
    global scope, 14
    goals and objectives, 194–197, 258–263,
        265–269
    historical perspective, 12–14, 20–31

limitations, 8–9
moral and ethical considerations, 133, 360,
    367–368, 395–415
negotiation and compromise,
    408–410, 410*b*
normal versus clandestine operations,
    319–320
objectivity, 195
outside commissions investigations, 281
sources and methods protection, 90–93,
    132, 271, 273, 403, 411
specificity, 194–195
succinctness, 195
timeliness, 194
working concept, 9*b*
Intelligence Advanced Research Projects
    Agency (IARPA), 112, 159
Intelligence agencies, 2–5, 7
    see also U.S. intelligence community
Intelligence agenda
nation-states, 319–340
post-Cold War era, 343–345
Soviet Union, 320–330
transnational issues, 343–389
Intelligence analysis
    see Analysis and production
Intelligence and Security Committee (Britain),
    443, 445–446, 448
Intelligence Authorization Act (2010), 279
Intelligence Bureau (India), 486
Intelligence Center (EU), 458
Intelligence collection
    see Collection disciplines; Collection,
        intelligence
Intelligence community
    see U.S. intelligence community
Intelligence Community Directives (ICDs),
    33, 174, 190, 221, 222, 284, 430
Intelligence Community Information
    Technology Enterprise (ICITE),
    185, 432
Intelligence Community Whistleblower
    Protection Act (1998), 222, 413
Intelligence Directorate, 215–216
Intelligence Fusion Centers, 498
Intelligence Identities Protection Act (1982),
    32, 217
Intelligence integration, 20, 39, 42–43, 94–95,
    423, 432, 435
Intelligence Oversight Act (1980), 32, 284

Intelligence process
agency restructuring and reform, 17, 33,
    47, 95, 132, 135, 169–170, 280, 351,
    417–437
circular model, 78, 79*f*
dissemination decisions, 68
information integration, 20, 39, 42–43,
    94–95, 423, 432, 435
intelligence transparency, 19, 294–295, 297,
    396, 434–435
key elements, 67–68
multilayered model, 78, 80, 80*f*
national security policy, 3–4
open-to-secret information ratio, 6, 97
overlapping functions, 14–15, 424–426,
    429–430
partisan politics, 18, 189
policy maker–intelligence relationship,
    68–72, 263–274
policy-making support and influence, 4–5,
    5*b*, 258–259
requirements and priorities, 67, 94–95, 426
schematic model, 78, 79*f*
see also Analysis and production; Collection,
    intelligence; Congressional oversight
    responsibilities; Moral and ethical
    considerations; Oversight; Processing
    and exploitation
Intelligence reform
administrative reforms, 434
analytical standards, 426–430
challenges, 437
collection disciplines, 424–426
comparisons of DNI and DCI functions,
    420–424
information technologies (IT), 431–434
intelligence process, 435
key issues, 420–437
lessons learned, 436–437
market-based proposal, 435–436
purpose, 417–419
reserve experts, 429
stovepipes problem, 424–426
workforce considerations, 434
Intelligence Reform and Terrorism Prevention
    Act (2004)
agency restructuring and reform, 37, 39,
    45, 47
alternative analysis, 179–180
analytical standards, 189–190

technical collection systems, 84, 96, 114
unmanned aerial vehicles (UAVs), 111
weapons of mass destruction (WMDs),
465–466
Iranian Revolutionary Guard Corps, 466, 498
Iraq
analytical standards, 427
congressional investigations and
reports, 292
cyber attack operations, 352
drone operations, 109, 112
intelligence collection and analysis, 28–29,
49, 324
intelligence-sharing agreements, 129
intervention versus nonintervention
debate, 312
Kuwait invasion, 263, 405
limited information situations, 173, 174
mirror imaging, 375b
national intelligence estimates (NIEs), 183,
262, 309–310
nuclear weapons programs, 374, 375b
outside commissions investigations,
281–282
paramilitary operations, 242
power leverage, 371
use of force policy, 254
see also Weapons of mass destruction
(WMDs)
Iraq Inquiry (Chilcot Report), 447
Iraq Liberation Act (1998), 240, 399
Iraq Survey Group (ISG), 281
Ireland
foreign espionage threats, 469
terrorist groups, 361, 442, 447
Irish Republican Army (IRA), 361, 442, 447
Iron ore, 381
Irrational behaviors, 8
Irvine, David, 476
ISIS
see Islamic State (ISIL)
Islamic Jihad, 109
Islamic State (ISIL)
Australian intelligence services, 478
British intelligence services, 447–448
capabilities versus intentions, 358–359
drone strikes, 246
French intelligence services, 457, 458
intelligence collection operations, 28
intelligence-sharing agreements, 459

international status quo challenges, 13–14
Japanese intelligence services, 494
lone wolves, 364, 458
multinational air campaign, 92
operations analysis, 367
politicized intelligence, 188
quasi-state status, 13–14, 337–338, 358
recruitment practices, 337–338, 362
Russian airliner attack, 471
state-sponsored terrorism, 361
terrorist attacks, 363
unmanned aerial vehicles (UAVs), 111
war on terrorism, 397
Israel
assassination plots, 245, 464–465, 466, 483
covert operations, 460, 464, 466
cyber attacks, 498
cyber capabilities, 354, 460, 466
espionage activities, 225, 401
espionage scandals, 134, 202b, 461–464
fake passport use, 464, 481, 489
hacking capabilities and operations,
466–467
indications and warnings (I&W), 178, 465
intelligence failures, 465
intelligence services, 460–467
intelligence-sharing agreements, 130, 222,
462–463
Iran-contra affair, 233
nuclear weapons programs, 462
satellite-based collection systems,
114, 464
surprise attacks, 178, 464, 465
unmanned aerial vehicles (UAVs), 111, 464
Visa Waiver Program, 462
Israel Defense Forces (IDF), 460, 466
ISR (intelligence, surveillance, and
reconnaissance), 83
Italo-Turkish War (1911–1912), 347
Italy
air warfare development, 347
demographic trends, 383
intelligence services, 496
renditions, 238
satellite-based collection systems, 114
terrorist groups, 357
Ivan the Terrible, 12

Jacoby, Lowell, 268
Jammu, 490

McChrystal, Stanley, 247
McCone, John, 23, 48
McConnell, Mike
  as DNI, 38
  Executive Committee (EXCOM), 45, 55
  intelligence briefings, 16
  on intelligence reform, 423
  intelligence sharing, 185, 206
  Iraqi weapons of mass destruction
    (WMDs), 29
  joint duty assignments, 170
  national intelligence estimates (NIEs),
    29, 166, 183, 262–263, 310
  on open-source intelligence (OSINT),
    137, 138
  oversight responsibilities, 278, 422
  policy dynamics, 258
  professional qualifications, 261
  resignation, 30, 50, 274
  security clearance process, 118, 210
  technical collection systems, 86
  wiretap policy, 120
McKinley, William, 357
McLaughlin, John, 262, 358, 421
McMaster, H. R., 449
McNamara, Robert S., 23
Measurement and signatures intelligence
  (MASINT)
  advantages/disadvantages, 144*f*
  collection disciplines, 124–125
  definition, 104
  discipline relationships, 143*f*
  functional perspective, 43*f*
  open-source intelligence, 136
  stovepipes problem, 94, 424–426
  terrorist-related intelligence, 360
MEDEA (Measurements of Earth Data for
  Environmental Analysis), 385
Media sources
  blowback, 241, 404
  classified information leaks,
    218–220, 223
  comparison to intelligence collection, 419
  First Amendment rights, 297, 413–414
  German intelligence operations, 482–483
  moral and ethical considerations, 413–414
  open-source intelligence (OSINT),
    136–138, 143*f*
  policy maker–intelligence relationship,
    274, 310–311

terrorist-related intelligence, 360
  twenty-four-hour news sources, 419
Medium earth orbit (MEO), 93
Medium-range missiles, 87
Memo of notification (MON), 233
Merkel, Angela, 335, 484, 485
Methamphetamines, 377
  see also Narco-traffickers
Mexico
  economic crisis, 380
  intelligence services, 497
  internal stability, 339
  narcotics trafficking, 377–378, 497
Meyers, Richard, 308
MI5
  see British Security Service (MI5)
MI6
  see British Security Service (MI6)
Micius communications satellite, 118
Microdrones, 113
Microsatellites, 113, 114–115, 472
Microsoft, 460
Middle East
  covert operations policies, 233, 250
  cyber attack operations, 352, 356
  demographic trends, 383
  as espionage threat, 494, 495
  food security, 386
  intelligence requirements and priorities,
    152, 263
  intelligence services, 498–499
  Japanese intelligence operations, 494
  Pakistani intelligence operations, 490
  refugee crisis, 483
  regional disputes, 499
  regional stability, 332, 338, 339, 340,
    373, 482
  Russian intelligence policy, 68
  terrorist groups, 357, 483
  terror suspect renditions, 238
  unmanned aerial vehicles (UAVs), 112
  see also Arab Spring revolt
Milan rendition, 238
Military espionage, 354
Military information, 6
Military intelligence
  Arab intelligence services, 499
  Australian intelligence services, 477
  Canadian intelligence services, 481
  congressional jurisdiction, 59

Morison, Samuel L., 218
Morocco, 362
Morrell, Michael, 49, 272
Morsi, Mohamed, 465
"Mosaic pieces" metaphor, 172*b*
Mossad, 460, 463, 464, 465, 466, 467
Mossadegh, Mohammad, 22, 250
Moynihan, Daniel Patrick, 303, 307
Mubarak, Hosni, 140, 153, 464
Mueller, Robert, 31, 50, 224, 259, 353, 469, 470
Mullen, Mike, 195
Multi-int, 430
Multinational peacekeeping operations, 386–387
Multi-satellite constellations, 113, 115
Multi-source intelligence (multi-int), 87, 186, 430
Multispectral imagery (MSI), 104, 124
Mumbai terrorist attacks, 486, 490
Munich Olympics (1972), 464, 483
Murphy Commission (1975), 514
Musudan missile program, 370
Mutual assured destruction (MAD) doctrine, 325
Myers, Gwendolyn, 491
Myers, Kendall, 205*b*, 491
Mysteries versus puzzles analogy, 270

Nakasone, Paul, 350
Nam Jae-joon, 492
Nanosatellites, 113, 114
Narco-traffickers
 African nations, 492
 British intelligence services, 442
 crop eradication and substitution, 377–378
 failed states, 335
 financial intelligence (FININT), 382
 hacking capabilities, 109
 human intelligence (HUMINT) collection, 133, 402
 intelligence interests and priorities, 319
 Latin America, 497
 requirements and priorities, 153
 threat assessments, 345
 transnational issues, 96, 153, 169, 345, 377–378
Nasser, Gamal Abdel, 464
National Air and Space Intelligence Center (NASIC), 47, 98
National Archives, 206

National Assessments Bureau (NAB), 488
National Background Investigations Bureau, 209
National Center for Counter Terrorism (France), 456–457
National Center for Medical Intelligence, 47
National Clandestine Service, 38, 304, 425
National Climate Assessment, 385
National Commission for the Control of Intelligence Techniques (CNCTR), 459
National Commission on Terrorist Attacks Upon the United States (2004), 29, 37, 169, 243, 515
National Counterintelligence and Security Center (NCSC)
 CIA mission centers, 170
 counterintelligence and counterespionage functions, 216
 cyber espionage, 380
 DNI oversight, 38, 216
 hierarchical perspective, 44*f*
 national intelligence managers (NIMs), 423
 organizational structure, 40*f*
 security clearance safeguards, 209, 217
National counterintelligence officer (NCIO), 171
National Counterproliferation Center (NCPC), 38, 40*f*, 44*f*, 46–47, 169, 170, 423, 428–429
National Counter-Terrorism Authority (NACTA), 491
National Counterterrorism Center (NCTC)
 analysis and production, 421
 DNI oversight, 37, 38, 46, 52
 hierarchical perspective, 44*f*
 intelligence-sharing agreements, 365
 interagency relationships, 421
 interagency relationships and rivalries, 170
 national intelligence managers (NIMs), 423
 organizational structure, 40*f*
 origins, 169, 428
 responsibilities and authorities, 47
National Counterterrorism Program, 61
National Cyber Directorate, 467
National Cybersecurity and Communications Integration Center (NCCIC), 350
National Cyber Security Centre (NCSC), 443, 444, 489
National Cybersecurity Coordination Centre (NCCC), 487

National Declassification Center, 91*b*
National Defense Authorization Act
(2017), 256
National Defense University, 363, 387
National Directorate of Intelligence
and Customs Investigations
(DNRED), 458
National foreign intelligence, 37
National Foreign Intelligence Program
see National Intelligence Program (NIP)
National Geospatial-Intelligence Agency
(NGA)
budget process and programs, 62, 63*f*
as combat support agency, 388
commercial imagery, 97, 106–107
congressional jurisdiction, 308
domestic intelligence, 113–114
foreign liaison relationships, 130
functional perspective, 46
health and environmental issues, 386
hierarchical perspective, 44*f*
measurement and signatures intelligence
(MASINT), 125
NSC oversight, 278
organizational structure, 40*f*, 41, 94
polygraph tests, 217
presidential briefings, 76, 156
relationship with USDI, 55
satellite operations, 99
security clearance safeguards, 209
special projects, 108
National Geospatial-Intelligence
Program, 61
National Ground Intelligence Center, 47
National Imagery and Mapping Agency
(NIMA)
see National Geospatial-Intelligence
Agency (NGA)
National intelligence, 5–6, 12–15, 278
National Intelligence Agency (NIA), 493
National Intelligence Board, 182
National Intelligence Center (CNI,
Mexico), 497
National Intelligence Collection Management
Committee (NICMC), 478
National intelligence collection officer
(NICO), 171
National Intelligence Co-ordinating
Committee (NICOC, South
Africa), 493

National Intelligence Coordination
Committee (NICC, Australia),
477–478
National Intelligence Council (NIC)
DNI oversight, 38, 46
hierarchical perspective, 44*f*
national intelligence estimates (NIEs),
183, 309–310
organizational structure, 40*f*
presidential briefings, 76, 156
National Intelligence Daily, 76
National Intelligence Directorate (NID,
Pakistan), 491
National intelligence estimates (NIEs)
analysis and production, 166, 167–169,
181–184
capabilities versus intentions debate, 324
confidence levels, 176–177, 195
criticisms, 183–184
DNI oversight, 46
estimative language, 176
functional role, 181–184
global warming, 310
hostage-taking bargaining tactics, 293
importance, 427
intelligence briefings, 76
interagency relationships and rivalries,
181–182, 262, 266–267
on Iran's nuclear intentions, 166
missile threat report, 309
open-source intelligence (OSINT), 425
Soviet military capabilities, 325
terms of reference (TOR), 181
weapons of mass destruction (WMDs),
17, 28–29, 183, 218, 309–310, 371,
377, 425, 465–466
National Intelligence Grid (NATGRID), 487
National intelligence managers (NIMs), 43,
71, 95, 171, 423
National intelligence officers (NIOs), 46, 76,
171, 181, 421
National Intelligence Open Source
Committee, 478
National Intelligence Organization (MIT,
Turkey), 495
National Intelligence Priorities Framework
(NIPF), 42–43, 43*f*, 70–72, 75, 90,
264, 319
National Intelligence Priorities (NIPs,
Australia), 477

National Security Law (China), 451
National security letters (NSLs), 122, 213, 223–224, 368
National security policy
  analytical standards, 426–430
  bilateral relationships, 327
  China, 451
  climate change impacts, 385–386
  commercial imagery, 108
  failed states considerations, 335
  global food and water security, 386
  goals and objectives, 258–263
  historical perspective, 20–21
  influencing events, 20–31
  liberty vs security considerations, 12, 19, 100–101, 121–123, 398
  long-term intelligence expertise, 3–4
  New Zealand intelligence services, 488
  overall intelligence spending, 297–299, 298b
  partisan politics, 18, 189, 306–307
  policymaker role, 253–274
  post-Cold War era, 343–345, 388–389
  regional stability issues, 337–339
  requirements and priorities, 152–154
  secure communications networks, 185
  South Korean intelligence services, 492
  Soviet Union, 13, 14, 18, 68–69, 70, 320–322, 343
  structural characteristics, 253–254
  terrorism, 344, 357–369
  threat-based policies, 13–14
  unauthorized disclosures, 217
National Space Defense Center, 99
National technical means (NTM), 24–25, 98
National Technical Research Organization (NTRO), 486
National Threat Assessment Centre (NTAC), 476
Nation-states
  analysis and production, 330–340, 429
  capabilities versus intentions debate, 331–332
  current state of affairs, 330–340
  cyber capabilities, 354, 356
  denial and deception (D&D), 95–96
  failed states, 334–336
  intelligence collection approaches, 322, 358
  intelligence interests and priorities, 319–320

internal stability, 332–334, 339
leadership analysis, 336–337
linear thinking versus discontinuity scenarios, 339–340
military capabilities, 323–326
mirror imaging, 332, 375b
normal versus clandestine operations, 319–320
opportunity analysis, 331
permissive environments, 111
post-Cold War reconnaissance, 96–97
power leverage, 331–332, 340
proliferation activities, 369–377
regional stability, 337–339
surprise attacks, 352
technical collection systems, 84, 96, 322
threat-based national security policies, 13–14
warning analysis, 331
  see also Soviet Union; Transnational issues
Natural resources competition, 381, 386
Navy intelligence, 62, 63f
Near-failed states, 335
  see also Failed states
"Need to know" policy, 185, 205–206
Negation search, 105–106
Negative politicized intelligence, 187
Negotiation and compromise, 408–410
Negroponte, John
  agency restructuring and reform, 425
  intelligence briefings, 16
  interagency relationships, 38
  organizational challenges, 41
  professional qualifications, 50, 274
  relationship with DOD, 53
  resignation, 30
  responsibilities and authorities, 422
  technical collection systems, 84
Neo-Nazi groups, 483–484
Netanyahu, Benjamin, 461–462, 466, 467
Netherlands, 470, 474, 495
Neutral powers, 6
New Orleans, Louisiana, 267b
News media
  blowback, 241, 404
  classified information leaks, 218–220, 223
  comparison to intelligence collection, 419
  First Amendment rights, 297, 413–414
  German intelligence operations, 482–483
  moral and ethical considerations, 413–414

open-source intelligence (OSINT),
136–138, 143*f*
policy maker–intelligence relationship,
274, 310–311
twenty-four-hour news sources, 419
New York Police Department (NYPD), 135
New York Times, 412, 414
New Zealand
cyber capability and activity, 488–489
intelligence services, 478, 487–489
intelligence-sharing agreements, 11, 92,
130, 202*b*, 487
Israeli intelligence operations,
463–464, 489
telecommunication encryption, 348
Nicaragua
Corinto incident, 303, 307
covert operations, 233, 237
Cuban intelligence operations, 491, 497
election interference, 399
Iran-contra affair, 16–17, 26, 233–234, 241,
288, 329, 330
Russian intelligence operations, 473
Nicholson, Harold, 205*b*
Nielsen, Kirstjen, 470
Nigeria
commercial imagery, 107
failed state status, 335
intelligence-sharing agreements, 130, 493
satellite-based collection systems, 114
terrorist groups, 107, 130, 335, 359,
361–362, 493
9/11 Commission (2004), 29, 37, 169, 184, 243,
298, 308, 364–365, 427–428, 516
9/11 terrorist attacks
see September 11, 2001, terrorist attacks
Nisei, 12
Nisman, Alberto, 498
Nitze, Paul, 320
Nixon, Richard
covert operations, 411
intelligence policy, 259
liberty vs security considerations, 12
national security advisers, 255
national security policies, 24–25, 254
partisan politics, 273
U.S.-Chinese relationship, 454
Watergate scandal, 25, 273
"No fly" list, 365
Noise versus signals, 87–88

Noncombatant deaths, 247–249, 250, 314–315,
405–406, 435
Nonofficial cover (NOC) agents, 128, 458
Non-state actors
cyber attacks, 352, 353, 354, 356
intelligence collection targets, 96
intelligence interests and priorities, 6, 47,
71, 319
surprise attacks, 352
unmanned aerial vehicles (UAVs), 111
Normal versus clandestine operations,
319–320
North Atlantic Treaty Organization (NATO)
combat with the Taliban, 335
cyberspace agreements, 356
European military capability, 458
foreign espionage threats, 468–469, 495
indications and warnings (I&W), 178
intelligence services, 496
intelligence-sharing agreements, 92
international peacekeeping operations, 386
Libyan civil war, 262
opportunity analysis, 179
peacekeeping operations, 386
threat assessments, 338–339, 345
wartime versus peacetime norms, 397
Northern Alliance, 57, 58, 237
Northern Ireland, 358, 361, 442
North Korea
assassination plots, 495
cyber capability and activity, 353, 495
demilitarized zone (DMZ), 90
denial and deception (D&D), 96
espionage activities, 447
failed state status, 335
intelligence collection challenges, 322
intelligence services, 494–495
internal stability, 333
leadership analysis, 337
nuclear weapons and missile programs,
332, 369, 370–371, 374–375
permissive environments, 111
power leverage, 332, 337, 371–372
regional disputes, 331–332
sabotage operations, 236
satellite export controls, 97
South Korean intelligence services, 492
state-sponsored terrorism, 358
technical collection systems, 84, 96
uranium processing facilities, 370

North, Oliver L., 233
Norway, 470, 495
Novichok nerve gas incident, 127, 245, 449, 474
No-year appropriations, 287
NSA metadata collection programs
    congressional oversight responsibilities, 302–303, 314, 411–412
    damage assessments, 222, 417
    diplomatic impact, 123, 201, 202*b*, 355, 454, 489
    intelligence sharing considerations, 206
    judicial and legislative authorization, 121–123, 302, 314, 402
    legal considerations, 121–123
    outside commissions investigations, 281
    removable storage devices, 218
    safeguards and security, 30–31, 119, 123
    telephone calls and text message records, 120–121, 368
Nuccio, Richard, 413
Nuclear weapons, 87, 89–90, 125, 236, 325, 369, 462, 466
Nunes, Devin, 307, 449
Nye, Joseph S., 136–137

Obama, Barack
    arms control treaties, 290
    bin Laden raid, 87, 131, 231–232
    classified information requirements, 220–221
    climate change policy, 385
    covert arms assistance to Syrian rebels, 234, 244, 294
    cyber espionage agreement, 355, 379, 453
    cyber security responsibility, 350, 356
    information sharing practices, 347
    Inspectors General (IGs) investigations, 283
    intelligence briefings, 16, 51, 155, 296
    intelligence leaks, 218, 220
    intelligence oversight authority, 280–281
    intelligence policy, 18, 30–31, 41, 71, 114, 121–122, 171, 469
    intelligence requirements and priorities review, 264
    intelligence-sharing agreements, 207, 217
    Iranian nuclear programs, 466
    judicial advocates, 313
    leak prosecutions, 218, 219–220
    limited information situations, 175

narcotics trafficking policy, 378
national intelligence estimates (NIEs), 263
national security letters (NSLs), 224
national security policy, 256, 262, 281, 302, 311, 484
nuclear proliferation policy, 370
Pollard release, 461
as presidential candidate, 337
prior notice requirements, 294
relationship with DNI, 48, 280
Russian election interference, 353
security clearance safeguards, 208–209
targeted strike policy, 246–249, 314–315, 368–369, 406, 435
terrorism policy, 27, 58, 109, 110–111, 363, 389
torture policy, 239, 368
veto threats, 296, 297
Object-based production (OBP), 181
Offensive intelligence, 201
Office of Intelligence and Analysis (OIA), 44*f*, 45, 54, 192–193, 366–367, 382
Office of Intelligence Programs, 278
Office of Intelligence Support, 61
Office of Management and Budget (OMB), 283, 287, 453–454
Office of National Assessments (ONA), 476
Office of National Intelligence (ONI), 475–476
Office of National Security Intelligence, 378
Office of Personnel Management (OPM), 139, 208, 354
Office of Strategic Services (OSS), 12, 13, 20–21
Office of Terrorism and Financial Intelligence, 45
Office of the Director of National Intelligence (ODNI)
    analytical standards, 190, 430
    budget process and programs, 53, 63*f*
    classified information requirements, 221
    as combat support agency, 388
    finished intelligence, 86, 190
    information sharing practices, 432
    information technologies (IT), 432
    Inspectors General (IGs), 282–283
    intelligence briefings, 156
    intelligence transparency, 295, 396
    limited information situations, 174
    national security letters (NSLs), 224

noncombatant deaths, 247
open-source intelligence (OSINT), 425
polygraph policy, 204
responsibilities and authorities,
    37, 53, 278
Visa Waiver Program, 462
wiretap policy, 120
see also Director of national intelligence
    (DNI)
Office of the Director of National Intelligence
    (ODNI) Community Management
    Account (CMA), 61
Office of the Intelligence Community
    Inspector General (IC IG), 222
Office of the Secretary of Defense (OSD),
    53, 253, 257
Official cover, 127
Officials Committee for Domestic and
    External Security Coordination
    (ODESC), 488
Oil and natural gas supplies
    competitive relationships, 381–382
    power leverage, 331
    retaliatory cyberattacks, 356, 498
Omand, David, 139–140
Omar, Mullah, 490
Ombudsman, analytic, 190
OneWeb, 472
Online mapping, 97
    see also Commercial imagery;
        Satellite-based collection systems
On-the-ground knowledge and experience,
    164–166
Open Skies Treaty (1992), 473
Open Source Center, 138, 425
Open Source Directorate, 425
Open Source Enterprise, 425
Open-source intelligence (OSINT)
    advantages/disadvantages, 136–138, 144*f*
    agency restructuring and reform, 425
    commercial imagery, 96–97, 136, 272
    definition and characteristics, 135–136,
        425–426
    discipline relationships, 143*f*
    financial intelligence (FININT), 382
    functional perspective, 43*f*
    German intelligence services, 482, 483
    health and environmental issues, 384, 385
    Japanese intelligence services, 493
    processing and exploitation, 136, 271–272

stovepipes problem, 94
terrorist-related intelligence, 360
Open-to-secret information ratio, 6, 97
Operational Preparation of the Environment
    (OPE), 243
Operational tempo (OPTEMPO), 109
Operational tradecraft, 202, 214–215
Operation Cleaver, 356, 498
Operation Iraqi Freedom, 92
Opioids, 377
    see also Narco-traffickers
Opium production, 377, 378
Opportunity analysis, 178–179, 258, 331
ORCON (originator controlled)
    intelligence, 206
Organization of Petroleum Exporting
    Countries (OPEC), 331, 381
Organized crime, 442
Overseas contingency operations (OCOs),
    64, 287
Oversight
    accountability reviews, 279
    Australian intelligence services, 478
    British intelligence services, 445–446
    definitions, 277*b*
    executive branch responsibilities, 278–283
    French intelligence services, 459
    functional role, 277
    global findings, 279
    Government Accountability Office
        (GAO), 297
    Inspectors General (IGs) investigations,
        282–283
    Israeli intelligence services, 460–461, 465
    judicial system, 312–315
    moral and ethical considerations, 411–413
    New Zealand intelligence services,
        488, 489
    NSC responsibilities, 278
    Office of Management and Budget (OMB),
        283, 287
    outside commissions investigations,
        281–282
    propriety of intelligence activities, 280
    South Korean intelligence services, 492
    Swiss intelligence service, 497
    see also Congressional oversight
        responsibilities
Overt action and collection, 143*f*, 230
    see also Collection disciplines; Covert action

Photo interpretation, 105–106, 106*b*
Pico satellites, 113
Pike Committee (1976), 514
Pilotless drones, 108
Pine Gap, Australia, 477
Pinochet, Augusto, 250
Pitch (agent recruitment), 126–127
Pizza intelligence (PIZZINT), 137*b*
Plame, Valerie, 217
Planet, 113
Plausible deniability, 236*f*, 238, 240–242, 279, 294
Plumbing, 230
Points of presence (PoPs), 454
Poland, 400, 474, 496
Policy maker–intelligence relationship
  alternative analysis, 179–181
  analysis and production, 265–269, 408–410
  analysis-collection-covert action relationship, 16–17, 52–53, 164–169
  analyst bias, 161–162, 187, 245
  analytical standards, 189–191, 191*b*, 426–430
  arms control monitoring and verification programs, 372–373
  Benghazi, Libya, attack, 272–273
  bilateral relationships, 327
  budget process and programs, 264–265
  capabilities versus intentions debate, 323–326, 331–332
  commercial imagery, 108
  congressional hearings, 288–289
  consumer-producer relationship, 15–17, 68–78
  correct expectations, 268*b*
  cover arrangements, 128
  covert operations, 269–270
  crisis-driven requirements, 157–158
  current vs long-term intelligence, 74–75, 154–155
  cyberspace, 346–357
  demographic trends, 382–383
  differences of opinion, 408–410, 410*b*
  dominant battlefield awareness (DBA), 387–388
  economic issues, 378–382
  ends versus means controversy, 397–398
  failed states, 334–336
  goals and objectives, 194–197, 258–263, 265–269

health and environmental issues, 383–387
Hurricane Katrina, 267*b*
importance, 7–8
information technologies (IT), 431–434
intelligence briefings, 16, 18, 76, 155–157
intelligence collection, 263–265, 266*b*
intelligence process, 68–72, 263–274
intelligence processing and exploitation, 271–273
intelligence-sharing agreements, 11, 92, 129–131, 185, 189, 206, 222, 244–245, 364–367, 378–379, 432–433
interagency relationships and rivalries, 261–262, 266–267, 267*b*, 273
international peacekeeping operations, 386–387
leadership analysis, 336–337
lessons learned capacity, 364–369, 430, 436–437
liberty vs security considerations, 12, 19, 100–101, 121–123, 398
limited information situations, 173–175
long-term expertise, 3–4
market-based proposal, 435–436
mirror imaging, 8, 163, 325, 332, 363, 375*b*
narcotics trafficking, 133, 319, 345, 377–378
national intelligence estimates (NIEs), 166, 167–169, 266–267
national security policy process, 253–274
nation-states, 319–340
news media, 274, 310–311
outlook differences, 261–262
partisan politics, 18, 189, 273–274
policy-making support and influence, 4–5, 5*b*, 258–259
politicized intelligence, 4–5, 15–17, 162, 186–189, 262–263, 267–268, 270, 325, 409
post-Cold War era, 96–97, 344–345, 388–389
proliferation activities, 369–377
regional stability issues, 337–339
requirements and priorities, 152–154, 263–264
secrecy responsibilities, 5
status quo challenges, 13–17, 337, 339–340
surprise attacks, 2, 3*b*, 352
terminology differences, 263
terrorism, 357–369

Presidential Policy Directive 20 (PPD-20), 350, 356
Presidential Policy Directive 28 (PPD-28), 150, 281
President's Daily Brief (PDB), 51, 76, 156–157, 425
President's Foreign Intelligence Advisory Board (PFIAB), 278, 279, 324–325
President's Intelligence Advisory Board (PIAB), 278–279, 280
President's Intelligence Oversight Board (PIOB), 280
Prime, Geoffrey, 447, 468
Principals Committee, 51, 255
Printer cartridge bombs, 245
Priority creep, 71
PRISM, 121
Prisoner X espionage scandal, 463
Privacy and Civil Liberties Oversight Board (PCLOB), 280–281, 312, 314
Private-sector cooperation, 347–350
Privy Council Office (PCO), 479
Processing and exploitation
    artificial intelligence (AI), 88–89, 434
    budget process and programs, 84, 88
    challenges, 87–89
    congressional oversight, 85
    definition, 67
    electronic surveillance operations, 118
    intelligence collection, 67, 73–74, 84, 87–89, 110
    open-source intelligence (OSINT), 136, 271–272
    policy maker–intelligence relationship, 271–273
    requirements and priorities, 74
    technical collection systems, 73–74, 87–89, 113
    unmanned aerial vehicles (UAVs), 110
Professional head of intelligence analysis (PHIA), 445
Project Maven, 89, 185, 348
Proliferation
    Canadian intelligence services, 480
    chemical and biological weapons, 369, 376
    clandestine operations, 372
    development and program termination, 374–377
    financial intelligence (FININT), 382
    French intelligence services, 456

human-enabled cyber attacks, 355
    as intelligence collection target, 369–374
    intelligence-sharing agreements, 373–374
    Israeli intelligence operations, 465–466
    loose nukes, 376
    South Korean intelligence services, 492
    transnational issues, 169, 369–377
    weapons of mass destruction (WMDs), 369–377
Propaganda, 234–235, 236f, 241, 404, 467
Proprietary information, 396
Proximate reality, 7
Proximate theory of intelligence, 16–17
Psychological warfare, 498
Public Security Intelligence Agency (PSIA, Japan), 493
Purple Code, 115
Putin, Vladimir
    assassination plots, 245, 448, 473–474
    on collapse of Soviet Union, 468
    election interference, 31, 259, 353, 470
    on espionage activities, 468, 469, 471–472
    foreign policy, 160, 221, 338, 469
    INF treaty withdrawal, 374
    leadership analysis, 337
    political supremacy, 333
    power leverage, 331, 471–472
Puzzles versus mysteries analogy, 270

Qaddafi, Muammar, 130, 179, 262, 352, 377, 405
al Qaeda
    British intelligence services, 448, 468
    captured combatant issues, 407
    CIA operations, 363
    covert arms assistance, 234
    cruise missile attacks, 247b
    drone strikes, 247
    French intelligence services, 457
    intelligence collection operations, 28, 173, 371, 427
    interrogation tapes destruction incident, 304
    Japanese intelligence services, 494
    narcotics trafficking, 153
    paid informants, 480
    paramilitary operations, 363
    proliferation activities, 369
    recruitment operations, 248

refuge in Afghanistan, 105, 250, 335, 405, 490
relations with Pakistan, 376, 490
relations with the Taliban, 250, 405
retaliatory attacks, 58
Saudi Arabian oil fields, 381
secret prisons, 496
surprise attacks, 27
threat assessments, 268, 359, 361, 362, 363–364
war on terrorism, 397
World Trade Center terrorist attacks, 357
see also September 11, 2001, terrorist attacks
Qom, Iran, 370
Quantum cryptography, 118
Quantum satellites, 453
Quasi-states, 13–14, 337–338, 358
Quds Force, 466, 498
Questions for the record (QFRs), 288–289

Racial profiling, 100
Radar imagery, 97, 104, 114, 125, 143*f*
see also Commercial imagery; Geospatial intelligence (GEOINT) collection; Satellite-based collection systems
Radiation sensors, 125, 143*f*
Rainbow Warrior bombing, 457, 489
Raison d'état, 398, 403
Ramirez Sánchez, Ilich, 360, 402
RAND Corporation, 221
Rangoon (Yangon) diplomatic attack, 492, 495
Rare earth metals, 381
Rasmussen, Nick, 358, 359, 362
Rational actor model, 327
Reagan Doctrine, 329
Reagan, Ronald
assassination ban, 245
bilateral relationships, 327
defense spending, 343
intelligence policy, 18, 33, 188, 229, 301, 309, 420
Iran-contra affair, 16–17, 26, 233–234, 241, 288, 329, 330
leadership analysis, 336
national security advisers, 255
partisan politics, 273, 293
strategic arms limitation treaties, 187, 265, 267*b*, 290, 329

Realpolitik, 397
Reaper, 109, 112, 447
Recessions, 380
Reciprocity, 209
Reconnaissance, 83
Reconnaissance Bureau of the General Staff (North Korea), 495
Red Army Faction, 357, 483
Red Brigades, 357
Red cells/red teams, 180, 184
Redmond, Paul J., 202
Red Scare, 357
Refugee crisis, 334–335, 383, 483
Regional stability, 337–339
Religious terrorism, 358
Remote collection systems, 324
Render, 27
Renditions, 237–238, 289, 363, 367–368, 406–407, 446, 496
Reno, Janet, 50
Renseignements Généraux (RG), 456
Reporting requirements, 290–291
Report of the President's Special Review Board (1987), 514
Reprogramming requests, 286
Republican Party
intelligence policy, 18
intervention versus nonintervention debate, 312
partisan politics, 189, 306–307, 315
Russian election interference, 315
Requirements
assessment and prioritization strategies, 67, 68–72, 70*f*, 94–95, 319–320, 345–346
classified information, 220–221
competing collection priorities, 89
crisis-driven requirements, 157–158
definition, 67
geographic considerations, 153
intelligence collection, 72–73, 94–95, 104–105, 152–154, 263–265
intelligence process, 67–68, 426
policy maker–intelligence relationship, 263–264
potential threats, 345
see also Analysis and production; Transnational issues

Research and Analysis Wing (RAW, India), 486–487
Resolution, image, 102–103*f*, 104–105
Responsibility to provide standard, 206, 207
Retaliatory cyberattacks, 354, 356, 498
Revelation intelligence (REVINT), 137*b*
Review Group on Intelligence and Communications Technologies, 281
Revolution in military affairs (RMA), 387, 388
Reyes, Silvestre, 306
Rice, Susan, 124, 272
Richelieu, Cardinal de, 12
Ridge, Tom, 207, 366
Right-wing political groups, 484
Right-wing terrorism, 442
Risen, James, 220
Risk versus take, 117
Rivalries, 6, 57–58
Rizzo, John, 289
Roberts, John, 313
Robertson, James, 313, 314
Roberts, Pat, 59, 306, 308, 425
Rockefeller Commission (1975), 514
Rockefeller, John D., IV, 306
Rockefeller, Nelson A., 25
Rodriguez, Jose, 292, 304
Rogers, Mike, 75, 118, 307, 350, 354, 454
Roosevelt, Franklin D.
  on classified information leaks, 216
  health issues, 336
  intelligence policy, 20
Roscosmos, 472
Rosenberg, Julius, 205*b*, 211, 224, 396
Rosen, Steven J., 218
Rousseff, Dilma, 484, 497–498
Roving wiretaps, 33
Royal Canadian Mounted Police (RCMP), 480
Rumor intelligence (RUMINT), 137*b*
Rumsfeld, Donald
  competitive rivalries, 58, 243, 254, 257
  creation of USDI, 55
  military intelligence access, 308
  missile threat assessment, 309
  missile threat report, 309
  policy dynamics, 257
  as Secretary of Defense, 45, 53
  use of force policy, 254
Ruppersberger, Dutch, 307
Rusk, Dean, 266*b*

Russia
  anti-satellite weapons (ASATs), 98–99
  arms control treaties, 265, 267*b*, 290, 293, 328, 374
  assassination plots, 245, 448–449, 469, 473–474
  clandestine operations, 128–129
  commercial satellites, 85
  covert military activity, 237
  cyber capability and activity, 350, 352–353, 354, 469–472
  demographic trends, 383
  denial-of-service attacks, 352–353, 356
  economic espionage, 380, 495
  economic weakness, 331
  espionage activities, 225, 447, 448–449, 481, 483, 495
  foreign liaison relationships, 474
  hacking capabilities and operations, 466–467, 470–472
  INF treaty withdrawal, 374
  intelligence collection challenges, 322
  intelligence interests and priorities, 319
  intelligence services, 7, 330, 448, 467–475
  intelligence-sharing agreements, 129, 130, 373–374, 463, 471
  intelligence sources and methods protection, 92
  internal stability, 332–334, 339, 471
  leadership analysis, 337
  military capabilities, 331
  Muslim unrest, 471
  nuclear proliferation agreements, 369
  oil resources, 381, 382
  permissive environments, 111
  power leverage, 331
  sleeper agents, 129, 449, 474–475
  technical collection systems, 84, 96, 98, 114, 471–472
Russian election interference
  congressional investigations and reports, 55, 60, 292, 307, 310
  cyber exploitation, 470
  Director of national intelligence (DNI), 49
  disinformation campaigns, 235
  document declassification, 260, 315
  ends versus means controversy, 397
  goals and objectives, 31, 353, 470
  information leaks, 219, 221

Security classifications, 90–92, 91*b*
Security Clearance Oversight and Reform
 Enhancement Act (2014), 208
Security clearance process
 Canadian intelligence services, 480
 compartmented information, 205–206
 congressional legislation, 208
 congressional staff members, 295
 contract employees, 121, 208, 209,
  222, 434
 foreign language speakers, 118
 hacking opportunities, 208
 high-risk behavior indicators, 217
 homeland security issues, 207
 interagency reciprocity, 209
 mental health assistance, 204
 "need to know" policy, 205–206
 new-hire vetting process, 208–211
 politicization, 211
 purpose, 207
 reserve experts, 429
 risk-avoidance approach, 210
 security safeguards, 208–209, 434
Security Intelligence Review Committee
 (SIRC), 480
Security Intelligence Service (New Zealand),
 488, 489
Security Service Act (1989), 442
Security Service Act (1996), 442
Segev, Gonen, 463
Seismic sensors, 124–125
Selfies, 434
Self-revealing activities, 323
Self-revealing targets, 105
Senate Appropriations Committee, 285
Senate Armed Services Committee, 56, 59–60,
 285, 292, 307, 308, 411, 420
Senate Committee on Homeland Security &
 Governmental Affairs, 308
Senate Defense Appropriations subcommittee,
 60, 285–287, 422
Senate Finance Committee, 290
Senate Foreign Relations Committee, 60, 268,
 284, 411
Senate Governmental Affairs Committee
 (SGAC), 59, 308
Senate Intelligence Committee
 on analysis and production, 172
 Benghazi, Libya, attack, 273
 bipartisan cooperation, 306–307

congressional jurisdiction, 308
congressional relationships, 59–60
covert operations support, 233
groupthink issues, 29, 371
hearings, 288, 411–412
Inspectors General (IGs), 282–283
intelligence briefings, 295–296
intelligence budget reductions,
 299–300
intelligence sharing, 207
intelligence understandings and
 expectations, 309–310
interagency relationships, 54
interrogation policies, 239, 368
investigations and reports, 291–292, 301
Iraqi intelligence collection and analysis,
 29, 49, 371
judicial advocates, 313
lapses and failures, 303
layering accusations, 164
member selection criteria, 305–306
membership advantages/disadvantages,
 304–305
national intelligence estimates (NIEs),
 309–310
partisan politics, 306–307
politicized intelligence, 188
prior notice requirements, 294
Russian disinformation campaigns, 235
Russian election interference
 investigation, 353
satellite-based collection systems, 85
strategic arms limitation treaties, 265
tactical imagery support, 108–109
targeted strike policy, 249, 250, 301
term limits, 306
Senate Resolution 400 (1976), 32
Senate Select Committee on Intelligence, 32,
 260, 270, 285, 289, 290, 310, 412
Senate Select Committee to Study
 Governmental Operations With Respect
 to Intelligence Activities (1976), 514
Senior Executive Intelligence Brief, 76
Sensitive but unclassified (SBU)
 documents, 221
Sensitive compartmented information facilities
 (SCIFs), 207
Separation of powers, 290–291, 294, 315
 see also Congressional oversight
  responsibilities

September 11, 2001, terrorist attacks
al Qaeda involvement, 362
analytical standards, 427
lessons learned, 189, 364–365, 436–437
limited information situations, 173–174
outside commissions investigations, 281
surprise attacks, 2, 3b, 27
Serbia, 397
Serious Organized Crime Agency, 442
Severe acute respiratory syndrome (SARS), 384
Sex, 401
S files, 456
Shadow Brokers, 119, 221
Shared rationality, 8
Sharif, Nawaz, 491
Shedd, David, 337
Shelby, Richard, 207, 366
Sherman Kent School (CIA), 162
Sherman, William T., 387
Shevardnadze, Eduard A., 328, 329
Shevchenko, Arkady, 403
Shin Bet, 460, 461
Shinseki, Eric, 254, 257
Shultz, George P., 56, 186, 233
Shutter control, 107–108
Siemens, 355
Signals intelligence (SIGINT) collection
Australian intelligence services, 477
battle damage assessment (BDA), 351–352
bin Laden raid, 87
British intelligence services, 443–444, 446
Canadian intelligence services, 481
capabilities versus intentions debate, 324
Chinese intelligence services, 452–453
Cuban facility, 491
cyber espionage, 139
deception policy, 95
definition and characteristics, 115
discipline relationships, 143f
dominant battlefield awareness (DBA), 387
economic espionage, 379
encrypted communications, 466
espionage capabilities, 19
financial intelligence (FININT), 382
foreign language capabilities, 118
foreign liaison relationships, 130
French intelligence services, 456, 457
functional perspective, 43f, 46
German intelligence services, 115, 482
health and environmental issues, 384

Indian intelligence services, 486
intelligence briefings, 155
intelligence-sharing agreements, 130
interception capabilities, 115–116, 117,
118, 211
Israeli intelligence services, 460, 462, 466
Japanese intelligence services, 493, 494
legal considerations, 119–124
New Zealand intelligence services,
488–489
open-source intelligence, 136
Pakistani intelligence services, 490
risk versus take issues, 117
Russian intelligence services, 467, 469, 473
stovepipes problem, 94, 424–426
technological challenges, 118
terrorist-related intelligence, 360
unmasking policy, 124
vulnerabilities, 116–118, 144f
World War II, 21
see also Human intelligence (HUMINT)
collection
Signature strikes, 246, 248
Single Intelligence Account (SIA), 444
Single-source analyst, 73
Sinn Fein, 442
see also Irish Republican Army (IRA)
SIPRNET (Secret Internet Protocol Router
Network), 433
el-Sisi, Abdel Fattah, 465
Situation Centre (SitCen), 458
Skripal, Sergei, 129, 245, 449, 469, 474
Skybox, 113
Skype, 469
Slavery, 399
Sleeper agents, 129, 210, 211, 449, 474–475
Sleeper drones, 112
Sluzhba Vneshnei Razvedki (SVR), 468, 469,
472, 474–475
Smallpox, 384
Smith, Jeffrey, 283
Smith, Walter Bedell, 22
Snepp, Frank, 207
Snowden, Edward
asylum in Russia, 471
damage assessments, 122, 132, 207, 222,
350, 414, 458
European reactions, 446, 458, 459,
460, 497
information accessibility, 121, 208

information sharing practices, 365, 432, 434
insider threats, 217
intelligence transparency, 435
leak indictments, 219
questionable behaviors, 213
security clearance process, 208, 434
telecommunication encryption, 123, 348
as whistle-blower, 222, 413
see also NSA metadata collection programs
Social media
Chinese intelligence operations, 485
cover arrangements, 128–129
disinformation campaigns, 235, 241
geospatial imagery, 107*b*
German intelligence operations, 485
insider threats, 434
as intelligence collection tool, 136,
139–142, 143*f*, 192, 496
job applicants, 203
open-source intelligence (OSINT), 136
regional disputes, 332–333
Russian intelligence operations, 469, 470,
472–473
terrorist recruitment, 337, 358
Social norms and rules, 8
Society for Worldwide Interbank Financial
Telecommunications (SWIFT), 368, 382
Somalia, 248, 335, 368, 397
Sony Pictures, 353, 495
Sorensen, Theodore, 289
Source (agent recruitment), 126–127
Sources and methods protection, 90–93, 132,
271, 273, 403, 411
South Africa, 336, 374, 493
South African Secret Service (SASS), 493
South China Sea, 331, 332, 455
South Korea
assassination plots, 492
economic crisis, 380
intelligence services, 492
intelligence-sharing agreements, 492, 494
satellite-based collection systems, 114
South Sudan, 335
Soviet Union
Afghanistan invasion, 231, 250, 327
analytical judgments, 426–427
anti-satellite weapons (ASATs), 98
assassination plots, 245, 473
bilateral relationships, 327
capabilities versus intentions debate, 324

collapse and dissolution, 26, 326–330
containment policy, 320–321
covert military activity, 237
deception policy, 95, 322
defense spending issues, 167
espionage activities, 205*b*, 213, 224–225,
403, 447
as intelligence target challenge, 321–322
internal security, 7
military capabilities, 323–326
national intelligence estimates (NIEs), 182
sleeper agents, 129, 210, 211
statistical intelligence, 326–327
strategic missiles, 22–24, 87, 92, 189
technical collection systems, 84, 87, 322
U.S. national security policies, 13, 14, 18,
68–69, 70, 320–322, 343
wartime versus peacetime norms, 396–397
Space-based surveillance satellite (SBSS), 100
Space debris, 100
Space Imaging Company, 106
Space race, 22
Space Surveillance System, 100
Space X, 85
Spain
intelligence services, 474
intelligence-sharing agreements, 497
satellite-based collection systems, 114
Spanish-American War (1898), 13
Spearphishing, 139
Special access programs (SAPs), 297
Special Intelligence Oversight Panel
(SIOP), 286
Special national intelligence estimates
(SNIEs), 76
Special Operations Command (SOCOM),
58, 62, 63*f*, 141, 237, 243
Special operations forces, 237, 243–244, 476
Special political action (SPA), 229
Spicer, Sean, 449
Spies, 89–90
see also Collection, intelligence; Espionage;
Human intelligence (HUMINT)
collection
Spillover effect, 334–335
SPOT imagery system, 96, 107
Spying
see Espionage; Human intelligence
(HUMINT) collection
Sri Lanka, 486

Stalin, Josef, 163, 194, 246*b*, 473
Standards, analytical, 189–191, 191*b*
Standoff collection systems, 324
Stasi, 481–482, 484
State actors, 71
State Department
    Benghazi, Libya, attack, 272, 273
    classified information leaks,
        206, 412–413, 414
    congressional oversight, 60
    cyber attacks, 356
    disinformation campaigns, 241
    dissent channels, 184
    information sharing practices, 432–433
    intelligence briefings, 76
    intelligence collection, 46, 52–53, 56–57
    national intelligence agencies,
        14–15, 16, 40
    national intelligence estimates
        (NIEs), 182
    national security policy, 253, 254
    policy dynamics, 257
    politicized intelligence, 186
    polygraph tests, 203
    see also Bureau of Intelligence and Research
        (INR)
State Security Agency (SSA), 493
State Security Department (North Korea),
    494, 495
State-sponsored terrorism, 357–358,
    360–361, 381
Status quo challenges, 13–14, 337, 339–340
Steganography, 117
Sterling, Jeffrey, 220
Stevens, J. Christopher, 272
Stewart, Potter, 194
Stinger antiaircraft missiles, 231
Stovepipes problem, 94, 130, 168–169, 170,
    424–426
Strategic arms control agreements, 24–25, 98,
    265, 267*b*, 290, 325, 329, 374
Strategic arms limitation talks (SALT I/II),
    24–25, 98, 187
Strategic Arms Reduction Treaty (START), 98,
    265, 290
Strategic Defense Initiative (SDI), 329
Strategic intelligence, 28, 184
Strategic-range Soviet missiles, 22–24,
    87, 92, 189
Strategic Support Force (China), 451

Strategic surprise, 2, 3*b*, 7, 21, 27, 174, 178,
    352, 465
    see also Indications and warnings (I&W)
Strategic warnings, 157
Strauss-Kahn, Dominique, 336–337
Stuxnet virus, 236, 355–356, 466, 498
Sub-Interagency Policy Committees, 255, 256
Sub-Saharan Africa, 112
Sub-sources (agent recruitment), 127
Sudan
    failed state status, 335
    satellite export controls, 97
    slavery, 399
    state-sponsored terrorism, 361, 381
Sun-synchronous orbit, 93
Sun Tzu, 12
Supplemental appropriations bills, 64, 287–288
Supply chain targeting, 380
Support to military operations (SMO)
    see Military support
Sûreté de l'Etat (Safety of the State), 456
Surface-to-air missiles (SAMs), 108, 109
Surge capacity, 429
Surprise military attacks, 2, 3*b*, 6, 14, 21, 174,
    352, 465
    see also Indications and warnings (I&W)
Surrey Satellite Technology, 114
Surveillance
    bin Laden raid, 87, 131, 231–232, 363
    British intelligence services, 443
    definition, 83
    European Union (EU), 458, 495, 496–497
    French intelligence services, 459, 460
    German intelligence services, 482, 483, 484
    intelligence transparency, 295
    judicial oversight, 312, 313, 314
    liberty vs security considerations, 311–312
    lone wolf terrorists, 458
    moral and ethical considerations, 402–403
    New Zealand intelligence services, 489
    NSA programs, 402–403, 484–485
    Pakistani intelligence services, 490
    space-based surveillance satellite
        (SBSS), 100
    Swiss intelligence service, 497
    video surveillance, 101
    see also Geospatial intelligence (GEOINT)
        collection; Human intelligence
        (HUMINT) collection; Signals
        intelligence (SIGINT) collection

Suspension of *habeas corpus*, 12, 311, 398
Swarm ball phenomenon, 90, 94
Sweden, 374, 446, 468, 470, 474, 495
SWIFT (Society for Worldwide Interbank
    Financial Telecommunications), 368, 382
Switzerland, 399, 470, 485, 497
Symantec, 221
Symington, Stuart, 22, 411
Syria
    assassination plots, 405
    chemical weapons use, 29, 234, 376, 447
    civil war, 334, 335, 338
    covert arms assistance, 234, 244, 294, 396
    drone operations, 109, 112
    espionage activities, 447
    indications and warnings (I&W), 465
    intelligence collection challenges, 322
    intelligence-sharing agreements, 92, 129,
        130, 497
    Israeli intelligence operations,
        461, 463, 465
    nuclear reactors, 369, 374–375
    power leverage, 337
    refugees, 334–335
    Russian interventions, 471
    satellite export controls, 97
    war on terrorism, 397
    wartime versus peacetime norms, 396–397
Systems and Research Analyses (SRA)
        office, 42

Tactical intelligence, 28, 109, 189, 193
Tactical Intelligence and Related Activities
        (TIARA), 39, 40*f*, 60
Tactical nuclear weapons, 87
Tactical surprise, 2, 174
Tactical UAVs (TUAVs), 112
Taiwan
    espionage activities, 225
    intelligence services, 495
    nuclear weapons programs, 374
    regional disputes, 331–332
    satellite-based collection systems, 114
    U.S.-Chinese relationship, 455
Taliban
    CIA-Northern Alliance cooperation, 57,
        58, 237
    CIA operations, 363
    combat with NATO, 335
    drone operations, 248

drug trafficking, 153, 345
paid informants, 480
paramilitary operations, 237
recruitment practices, 359–360
relations with Pakistan, 131, 244–245,
    361, 490
rule of Afghanistan, 250, 404–405, 490
state-sponsored terrorism, 361
threat assessments, 345
Talking points, 271, 272–273
Tallinn Manual, 356
Targeted strike policy
    British intelligence services, 447–448
    congressional oversight
        responsibilities, 301
    intelligence transparency, 434–435
    legal considerations, 248–249, 314–315,
        368–369, 405–406
Task forces, 169
Tasking, processing, exploitation, and
        dissemination (TPED), 74, 85, 426
Taylor Commission (1961), 513
Taylor, Francis X., 54
Tearline, 108
Technical collection
    anti-satellite weapons (ASATs), 98–99
    British intelligence services, 446
    budget process and programs, 73, 83–85,
        88, 264–265, 288, 309
    Chinese intelligence services, 84, 96, 98,
        114, 118, 452–453
    commercial imagery, 96–97, 105, 106–108,
        136, 272
    Cuban Missile Crisis (1962), 87
    debris fields, 100
    deception policy, 95
    denial and deception (D&D), 105, 106
    developmental lead times, 85–86
    European Union (EU), 496
    export controls, 97, 112
    French intelligence services, 114, 457
    German intelligence services, 114, 482
    health and environmental issues, 385
    hostage-taking bargaining tactics, 293
    image resolution, 102–103*f*, 104–105, 108
    Israeli intelligence services, 114, 464
    Japanese intelligence services, 494
    limitations, 93–94
    nation-state issues, 322
    orbital patterns, 93–94

information technologies (IT), 433
intelligence interests and priorities, 319
intelligence policy, 18, 153
intelligence-sharing agreements, 130–131,
   244–245, 364–367
interagency rivalries, 57–59
intergroup relationships, 361–362
intervention versus nonintervention
   debate, 312
Israeli intelligence operations, 461, 463
Japanese intelligence services, 494
lessons learned, 364–369, 436–437
liberty vs security considerations, 311
limited information situations, 173–174
lone wolves, 364, 448, 458, 480–481
mirror imaging, 363
missed opportunities, 364–365
moral and ethical considerations,
   404–407
narcotics trafficking, 153, 345, 378
offensive operations, 362, 363
operational tactics, 358–360
operations analysis, 367–368
outside commissions investigations, 281
proliferation activities, 369–377
recruitment practices, 337, 358, 359–360
right-wing terrorism, 442
signals intelligence, 117, 119–121, 123–124
social media intelligence (SOCMINT), 140
South Korean intelligence services, 492
state-sponsored terrorism, 357–358,
   360–361, 381
status quo challenges, 13–14
surprise attacks, 2, 3*b*, 27, 123, 174
Swiss intelligence service, 497
targeted strike policy, 246–249, 314–315,
   368–369, 405–406, 434–435
technical collection systems, 84, 110
threat assessments, 345
transnational issues, 96, 153, 169, 344,
   357–369
U.S. intelligence community, 27–28,
   192–193
U.S. national security policies, 344,
   357–369
war on terrorism, 27, 57, 58, 193, 244,
   362–364, 389, 397
see also Bin Laden, Osama; Islamic State
   (ISIL); September 11, 2001, terrorist
   attacks

Terrorism Threat Integration Center, 169
Tet offensive, 24
Thailand
   economic crisis, 380
   satellite-based collection systems, 114
Thatcher, Margaret, 336, 448
Third offset strategy, 388
Third option, 229, 240
Third party rule, 130, 220, 462
Threat-based national security policies, 13–14
Tillerson, Rex, 260
Title 10 (U.S. Code), 244
Title 50 (U.S. Code), 244
TOP SECRET classification, 91*b*
Torricelli, Robert G., 412–413
Torture, 238–239, 302, 368, 406–407
Totalitarian states, 7
Tower Commission (1987), 514
TPED (tasking, processing, exploitation, and
   dissemination), 74, 85, 426
Tracfin, 458
Tradecraft, operational, 202, 214–215
Trade embargoes, 235
Traffic analysis, 116
Transnational issues
   Canadian intelligence services, 480
   CIA mission centers, 169, 170
   collection disciplines, 96
   criminal activity, 96, 153
   cyberspace, 346–357
   demographic trends, 382–383
   economics, 378–382
   failed states, 153, 334–336
   global findings, 279
   health and environment, 383–387
   intelligence interests and priorities, 319
   military support, 387–388
   narcotics trafficking, 96, 153, 169, 345,
      377–378
   national intelligence managers (NIMs), 171
   nonproliferation, 169
   peacekeeping operations, 386–387
   proliferation, 369–377
   terrorism, 96, 153, 169, 344, 357–369
   threat assessments, 345–346
   see also Nation-states
Transparency, intelligence, 19, 295–296, 297,
   396, 434–435
Transportation Security Administration (TSA),
   54, 254

whistle-blowers, 217, 222–223, 413
workforce considerations, 191–193, 270,
    344–345, 429, 430, 434
see also All-source intelligence; Analysis and
    production; Congressional oversight
    responsibilities; Counterintelligence
    (CI); Covert action; Cyberspace;
    Foreign liaison relationships; Human
    intelligence (HUMINT) collection;
    Information sharing; Intelligence
    process; Moral and ethical
    considerations; Soviet Union
USIS LLC, 208
U.S. Postal Service, 101
U.S. Special Operations Command
    (SOCOM)
    see Special Operations Command
        (SOCOM)
UUVs (unmanned underwater vehicles), 112

Vaccination programs, 128, 250
Vacuum cleaner problem, 87, 93
Vandenberg Air Force Base, 99
Vandenberg, Arthur, 284
Vanunu, Mordechai, 464
Vardo, Norway, 473
Venezuela, 337, 339, 381, 382, 491, 497
VENONA intercepts, 211, 224–225
Verification programs, 25, 290, 372–373
VEVAK
    see Ministry of Intelligence and Security
        (MOIS, Iran)
Vickers, Michael, 424
Video surveillance, 101, 108–111
Vietnam, 332, 473
Vietnam War, 12, 18, 24, 254, 312
Virtual currencies, 382
Visa Waiver Program, 462
Voice-over-Internet Protocol (VoIP)
    technology, 117
von Clausewitz, Karl, 387

Walesa, Lech, 400
Walker, John, and family, 26, 134, 205*b*
Walk-ins, 129, 134, 360, 401, 461, 467–468
Walton, Reggie, 313
"Wanna Cry" ransomware attack, 495
Warner, John W., 308
Warner, Mark, 60, 307
Warning analysis, 331, 338

War on terrorism, 27, 57, 58, 193, 244,
    362–364
Warrantless wiretap surveillance program,
    119–120
Warsaw Pact, 136, 178, 343, 386, 400
Wartime intelligence, 12, 21
Wartime versus peacetime norms, 396–397
Washington, George, 13, 301
Washington Post, 414
Waterboarding, 239, 296, 401
Watergate scandal, 25, 273
Water resources, 386
Watkins, Ali, 220
Weapons of mass destruction (WMDs)
    alternative analysis, 179–180
    analysis-collection-covert action
        relationship, 376–377
    analytical standards, 189, 427
    Australian intelligence services, 478
    British intelligence services, 442, 445, 447
    Canadian intelligence services, 480
    capabilities versus intentions debate, 324
    competitive analysis, 15
    congressional investigations and
        reports, 292
    denial and deception (D&D), 105
    espionage targets, 403
    failed states, 335
    false impressions, 159, 164, 168, 174, 189
    foreign liaison relationships, 310
    French intelligence services, 456, 458
    human-enabled cyber attacks, 355
    information reliability concerns, 132
    intelligence collection and analysis,
        15, 49
    intelligence interests and priorities, 319
    intelligence policy, 27, 153
    intelligence-sharing agreements, 92
    Iran, 465–466
    Israeli intelligence operations, 465–466
    lessons learned, 436–437
    measurement and signatures intelligence
        (MASINT), 125
    monitoring operations, 386–387
    national intelligence estimates (NIEs),
        17, 28–29, 183, 218, 309–310, 371,
        377, 425, 465–466
    opportunity analysis, 179
    outside commissions investigations,
        281–282

politicized intelligence, 29, 49, 188, 260, 377, 447, 478

proliferation activities, 369–377

threat assessments, 345

see also Iraq; North Korea

Weapon systems espionage, 354

Weasel words, 175

Webster, William H., 50, 129, 273

Weinberger, Caspar W., 233, 254

Weinstein, Warren, 247

Weissman, Keith, 218

Welch, Richard, 217

Wen Jiabao, 354

West Germany

see Germany

Wet affairs, 212, 245, 473–474

see also Assassination plots

WhatsApp, 117

Wheat versus chaff problem, 73, 87, 137, 158

"Where and when" phenomenon, 105–106

Whistleblower Protection Act (1989), 222

Whistle-blowers, 217, 222–223, 413

White-collar crime, 223

WikiLeaks

classified information leaks, 30, 93

DNC documents, 470

First Amendment protections, 219, 414

purpose, 221

State Department documents, 127, 206, 414

use of false identity, 135

Wilson, Edith, 336

Wilson, Woodrow

health issues, 336

liberty vs security considerations, 12

Winner, Reality, 219

Wiretaps

Argentine intelligence operations, 498

British intelligence services, 442

congressional investigations and reports, 293

congressional legislation, 33

constitutional violations, 311

false allegations, 449

Inspectors General (IGs) investigations, 283

legal considerations, 119–124, 215, 283

liberty vs security considerations, 311

metadata collection, 314

Swiss intelligence service, 497

Trump administration, 449

see also Surveillance; Telephone communications

Wise, David, 214

Witt, Monica, 135

WMD Commission (2005)

agency restructuring and reform, 30, 425, 427–428

analytical standards, 426

British intelligence services, 446

CIA mission centers, 170, 171

covert operations recommendations, 58

functional role, 516

interagency competition, 170

Iraqi weapons of mass destruction (WMDs) review, 188, 281

layering accusations, 164

politicized intelligence, 29, 188

Wolfe, James, 220, 296

Wolf, Markus, 400

Women's suffrage, 399

Won Sei-hoon, 492

Woolsey, R. James

congressional relationships, 54

on foreign economic espionage, 379, 458

partisan politics, 274

presidential access, 48, 260

Workforce, analytical, 191–192

World Trade Center terrorist attacks, 344, 357

WorldView-1 satellite, 97

World War I

air warfare development, 347

geospatial intelligence, 101

intervention versus nonintervention debate, 312

leak prosecutions, 218

liberty vs security considerations, 311

signals intelligence, 115

World War II

assassination plots, 246*b*

deception policy, 95

geospatial intelligence, 101

intelligence collection, 21, 403

intervention versus nonintervention debate, 312

liberty vs security considerations, 311

national intelligence, 12, 13, 20–21

Worldwide Intelligence Review (WIRe), 76

World Wide Web, 138, 140, 141, 143*f*, 192, 241, 360, 469

see also Cyberspace

Worst-case analysis, 324, 325

Wray, Christopher, 259

Wyden, Ron, 289, 303, 412
Wye River peace talks (1998), 461–462

X-37B (Orbital Test Vehicle-2), 112
XB-47 UCAS (unmanned combat air
    system), 112
Xi Jinping, 333–334, 355, 379, 450,
    453, 455
Xing Yunming, 451
xView Detection Challenge, 89

Yaalon, Moshe, 462
Yagoda, Genrikh, 451
Yang Jiechi, 454
Yanjun Xu, 452
Yeltsin, Boris N., 329
Yemen
    civil war, 334, 364, 498–499
    drone operations, 109, 248, 294, 368

internal security forces, 58
printer cartridge bombs, 245
war on terrorism, 397
Yeonpyeong Island shelling incident, 492
Yezhov, Nikolai, 451
Yom Kippur War (1973), 178, 464, 465
Yongbyon complex, North Korea, 370
Younger, Alex, 449
YouTube, 235
Yugoslavia, 358, 398

Zakayev, Akhmed, 448
Zaporozhsky, Alexander, 225
Zero-day vulnerabilities, 357, 444
Zhou Yongkang, 333–334, 451
Zika virus, 384
Zimmermann Telegram, 115
ZTE, 479
Zygier, Ben, 463